NORTH DAKOTA
STATE UNIVERSITY

APR 0 3 2008

SERIALS DEPT.
LIBRARY

Resources
for
American Literary Study

EDITORS
Jackson R. Bryer, *University of Maryland*
Richard Kopley, *The Pennsylvania State University, DuBois*

EDITORS EMERITI
Martha E. Cook, *Longwood College*
Maurice Duke, *Virginia Commonwealth University*
M. Thomas Inge, *Randolph-Macon College*
George C. Longest, *Virginia Commonwealth University*
Carla Mulford, *The Pennsylvania State University, University Park*
Robert Secor, *The Pennsylvania State University, University Park*

ASSOCIATE EDITOR
Ralph Bauer, *University of Maryland*

BOOK REVIEW EDITOR
Phyllis Cole, *The Pennsylvania State University, Delaware County*

EDITORIAL ADVISORY BOARD
Nina Baym, *University of Illinois*
Bernard W. Bell, *The Pennsylvania State University, University Park*
Alfred Bendixen, *California State University, Los Angeles*
John C. Broderick, *Potomac, MD*
Lawrence I. Buell, *Harvard University*
Jerome Klinkowitz, *University of Northern Iowa*
J. A. Leo Lemay, *University of Delaware*
Joel Myerson, *University of South Carolina*
James Nagel, *University of Georgia*
David S. Reynolds, *Baruch College, CUNY*
Robert Secor, *The Pennsylvania State University, University Park*
David S. Shields, *The Citadel*
G. Thomas Tanselle, *John Simon Guggenheim Memorial Foundation*
Linda Wagner-Martin, *University of North Carolina, Chapel Hill*

EDITORIAL ASSOCIATES
Christopher G. Hale, *University of Maryland*
Sarah E. Johnson, *University of Maryland*

EDITORIAL ASSISTANT
Donna Brantlinger Black

RESOURCES
for
AMERICAN LITERARY STUDY

Volume 29

Editors
Jackson R. Bryer
and
Richard Kopley

Associate Editor
Ralph Bauer

Book Review Editor
Phyllis Cole

AMS Press
New York

RESOURCES
for
AMERICAN LITERARY STUDY

Volume 29

Copyright © 2005 by AMS Press, Inc.
All rights reserved

ISSN: 0048-7384
SET ISBN: 0-404-64625-5
VOLUME 29: ISBN 0-404-64629-8

All AMS books are printed on acid-free paper that meets the guidelines for performance and durability of the Committee on Production Guidelines for Book Longevity of the Council on Library Resources.

AMS PRESS, INC.
Brooklyn Navy Yard, 63 Flushing Ave – Unit #221
Brooklyn, NY 11205-1005, USA

MANUFACTURED IN THE UNITED STATES OF AMERICA

RESOURCES FOR AMERICAN LITERARY STUDY

CONTENTS

VOLUME 29   2003–2004

Editors' Note   x

A Resource for "Resources"

Founding a Journal: *Resources for American Literary Study*   1
   M. THOMAS INGE

Prospects 13

Prospects for the Study of William Dean Howells   9
   SARAH B. DAUGHERTY

Articles

Promoting Pennsylvania: Penn, Pastorius, and the Creation of a
Transnational Community   25
   PATRICK M. ERBEN

Making the A-List: Reformation and Revolution in Crocker's
Observations on the real rights of women   67
   CONSTANCE J. POST

The James Family and the Boston Athenaeum: A Bibliography   89
   GLEN MACLEOD

Kate Field: A Primary Bibliography   141
   GARY F. SCHARNHORST

Willa Cather's Process of Composing   165
   CHARLES W. MIGNON

Fostering the Poet: An Unpublished Robert Frost Letter   185
   DAVID SANDERS

Tragic Stasis: Love, War, and the Composition of Hemingway's
"Big Two-Hearted River"   199
   HILARY K. JUSTICE

"Precipitation into Poetry": The Bishop-Lowell Letters and the
Boundaries of the Canon   217
   THOMAS TRAVISANO

Transformative Stages: Williams's *Vieux Carré* in New York
and London   235
   CRAIG CLINTON

"Wish I Were There": Ten Letters from William S. Burroughs
to Paul Bowles, 1972–79   253
COREY M. TAYLOR

Review-Essays

Parker's *Melville*: The Life Complete   275
SANFORD E. MAROVITZ

Asian American Literary Studies at Maturity   285
NOELLE BRADA-WILLIAMS

What Are We Doing in the Humanities Today?
Cather as Case Study   301
SUSAN J. ROSOWSKI

Jeffers Redux   317
STEPHEN GOULD AXELROD

Classics of Twentieth-Century American Theater   331
THOMAS P. ADLER

Book Reviews

Felicia Hardison Londré and Daniel J. Watermeier,
*The History of North American Theater. The United States, Canada,
and Mexico: From Pre-Columbian Times to the Present*   343
WILLIAM W. DEMASTES

Tom Quirk, *Nothing Abstract: Investigations in the American
Literary Imagination*   345
KENT P. LJUNGQUIST

Carla Mulford and David S. Shields, eds.,
Finding Colonial Americas: Essays Honoring J. A. Leo Lemay   348
JOANNA BROOKS

Sargent Bush Jr., ed., *The Correspondence of John Cotton*;
Michael P. Winship, *Making Heretics: Militant Protestantism
and Free Grace in Massachusetts, 1636–1641*   351
ALBERT J. VON FRANK

James Fenimore Cooper, *The Spy. A Tale of the Neutral Ground.
The Writings of James Fenimore Cooper,* historical introduction by
James P. Elliott; explanatory notes by James H. Pickering; text
established by James P. Elliott, Lance Schachterle, and
Jeffrey Walker   354
WAYNE FRANKLIN

M. Thomas Inge and Edward J. Piacentino, eds.,
The Humor of the Old South; David Rachels, ed., *Augustus Baldwin Longstreet's "Georgia Scenes" Completed: A Scholarly Text*   357
KATHRYN B. MCKEE

Grace Farrell, *Lillie Devereux Blake: Retracing a Life Erased*   361
NICOLE TONKOVICH

Ronald A. Bosco and Joel Myerson, eds., *The Later Lectures of Ralph Waldo Emerson, 1843–1871. Volume 1: 1843–1854; Volume 2: 1855–1871*   364
NANCY CRAIG SIMMONS

S. T. Joshi, ed., *The Collected Fables of Ambrose Bierce*   367
DONALD T. BLUME

Axel Nissen, *Bret Harte: Prince and Pauper*   371
DONNA M. CAMPBELL

Paula Bernat Bennett, ed., *Palace-Burner: The Selected Poetry of Sarah Piatt*   374
ANDREW C. HIGGINS

Susan E. Gunter, ed., *Dear Munificent Friends: Henry James's Letters to Four Women*; Susan E. Gunter and Steven H. Jobe, eds., *Dearly Beloved Friends: Henry James's Letters to Younger Men*   377
MICHAEL ANESKO

Jennifer S. Tuttle, ed., *The Crux: A Novel by Charlotte Perkins Gilman*   381
DENISE KNIGHT

June Howard, *Publishing the Family*; William Dean Howells et al., *The Whole Family: A Novel by Twelve Authors*   383
GIB PRETTYMAN

Eleanor Alexander, *Lyrics of Sunshine and Shadow: The Tragic Courtship and Marriage of Paul Laurence Dunbar and Alice Ruth Moore, a History of Love and Violence among the African American Elite*   387
JOANNE BRAXTON

Jesse S. Crisler, Robert C. Leitz III, and Joseph R. McElrath Jr., eds., *An Exemplary Citizen: Letters of Charles W. Chesnutt, 1906–1932*; Dean McWilliams, *Charles W. Chesnutt and the Fictions of Race*   390
KEITH WILLIAMS

Barbara Ozieblo, *Susan Glaspell: A Critical Biography* 394
CHERYL BLACK

Emily Bernard, ed., *Remember Me To Harlem:
The Letters of Langston Hughes and Carl Van Vechten*; Langston
Hughes, *The Political Plays of Langston Hughes*, with
introductions and analyses by Susan Duffy 396
DONNA AKIBA HARPER

Carla Kaplan, ed., *Zora Neale Hurston: A Life in Letters*;
Venetria K. Patton and Maureen Honey, eds., *Double-Take:
A Revisionist Harlem Renaissance Anthology* 399
ALICIA KENT

George Killough, ed., *Minnesota Diary 1942–46*, by Sinclair Lewis 403
SALLY E. PARRY

Anne Blythe Meriwether, ed., *Blood of My Blood*, by Marjorie Kinnan
Rawlings; Rodger L. Tarr, ed., *Max and Marjorie: The Correspondence
between Maxwell E. Perkins and Marjorie Kinnan Rawlings* 406
JILL C. JONES

Albert J. Devlin and Nancy M. Tischler, eds.,
The Selected Letters of Tennessee Williams: Volume 1, 1920–1945 409
RALPH F. VOSS

Robert J. DeMott, *Dave Smith: A Literary Archive* 413
JEROME KLINKOWITZ

Index

Index to Volumes 28 and 29 of *Resources for American
Literary Study* 415
HEATHER MCHALE

Grateful acknowledgment is made for permission to print and/or reprint the following:

G. Thomas Tanselle letter of 28 February 1974 by permission of G. Thomas Tanselle.

John C. Broderick's verse on RALS by permission of John C. Broderick.

Willa Cather papers courtesy of a private donor.

Robert Frost letter to Eugene Gay-Tifft, 16 December 1927, courtesy of and by permission of Peter S. Russ.

Photograph of Robert Frost taken circa 1921 at his residence in South Shaftsbury, VT, courtesy of Dartmouth College Library, Hanover, NH, and by permission of the Blackington Collection/Yankee Publishing Inc., Dublin, NH.

Photograph of Robert Frost writing in his notebook courtesy of and by permission of Dartmouth College Library, Hanover, NH.

Elizabeth Bishop letters to Robert Lowell, bMS Am 1905 (62)–(264), by permission of the Houghton Library, Harvard University, Cambridge, MA.

Robert Lowell letters to Elizabeth Bishop by permission of Special Collections, Vassar College Libraries, Poughkeepsie, NY.

Excerpts from the unpublished letters to Robert Lowell by Elizabeth Bishop copyright (c) 2004 by Alice Helen Methfessel. Reprinted by permission of Farrar, Straus and Giroux, LLC, on behalf of the Elizabeth Bishop Estate. Excerpts from unpublished letters to Elizabeth Bishop by Robert Lowell copyright (c) 2004 by Harriet Lowell and Sheridan Lowell. Reprinted by permission of Farrar, Straus and Giroux, LLC, on behalf of the Robert Lowell Estate. All rights reserved.

Citations from the "Vieux Carré" manuscript courtesy of Tennessee Williams Papers, Rare Books and Manuscripts Library, Columbia University, New York, NY.

Citations from *Vieux Carré* by permission of the Williams Estate, copyright by The University of the South. Reproduced by permission of The University of the South, Sewanee, TN.

William S. Burroughs letters to Paul Bowles, 28 April 1972, 13 April 1974, 15 February 1975, 8 November 1975 [stamped date], 24 December 1976, 6 March 1978, 13 May 1978, 26 February [1979], 4 June 1979, and 16 November 1979, courtesy of Paul Bowles Papers, Special Collections, University of Delaware Library, Newark, DE, and by permission of the William S. Burroughs Trust, Lawrence, KS.

Henry James letter to William Morton Fullerton (c. 1892), bMS Am 1094.1 (112), by permission of the Houghton Library, Harvard University, Cambridge, MA.

Editors' Note

The editors of *RALS* would like to thank, once again, the director of the AMS Press, Gabriel Hornstein, whose kind encouragement has been so important to the new life of the journal. We acknowledge, with gratitude, the excellent service on the Board of Editors of the late Sargent Bush Jr. We are pleased to thank Nina Baym, as well, whose contribution has been considerable and long-standing; she is stepping down from the Board after this volume. We are indebted to the excellent work of Phyllis Cole as Book Review Editor; she, too, will be stepping down with this volume. We welcome our new Book Review Editor, Beverly Peterson; books for review should be sent to her at Penn State Fayette—The Eberly College, One University Drive, P. O. Box 519, Route 119 North, Uniontown, PA 15401. Our editorial associate, Marc Singer, has moved on; we are happy to note his important contributions. We are thankful to Christopher G. Hale and Sarah E. Johnson for their work as Editorial Associates on this volume. Continuing with RALS are Associate Editor Ralph Bauer, the other members of our distinguished Editorial Board, and our invaluable editorial assistant, Donna Brantlinger Black. We are delighted to recognize the fine work of this volume's contributors. And we extend our deep appreciation to Diane M. Disney, Dean of the Commonwealth College of Penn State, and Charles Caramello, Chair of the Department of English at the University of Maryland, for their generous support of the journal.

As always, the editors welcome contributions involving archival study and bibliographical analysis.

Founding a Journal:
Resources for American Literary Study

M. THOMAS INGE
Randolph-Macon College

How a journal comes into being has as much to do with serendipity and coincidence as it has to do with intent. It is a falling together of interests, needs, and people rather than inevitability, although in retrospect it may seem that it was a natural product of the scheme of things. It could just as easily not have happened. Some journals serve their purpose and die a natural death while others become continual essential resources for criticism, scholarship, and the general advancement of our knowledge of things literary. *Resources for American Literary Study* is now thirty-four years old and seems destined to survive. This might be an appropriate time to reflect on how it all began.

Partly it had to do with my fascination, when I was a graduate student at Vanderbilt University, with such unusual scholarly journals as *American Notes and Queries, The Explicator,* and *Bulletin of Bibliography*. While material published in these journals often was ephemera—sources and definitions, brief close readings of texts, and checklists of publications by and about literary figures—I realized that these pieces were the beginning points, the building blocks for larger critical and cultural projects. It is commonplace to dismiss bibliographies as inconsequential scholarship since presumably anyone could assemble one. As I began compiling bibliographies of my own, I found that to be a great misjudgment. Creating truly comprehensive ones—and there is no point in doing any other kind—is demanding work that requires discipline, ingenuity, and often creativity in locating out-of-the-way or lost items. The value of a complete bibliography is immeasurable. With it, the scholar or critic can locate everything needed to begin work on a specific writer, find out what has already been done, and avoid the danger of simply repeating ideas and theories already expressed. A good deal of contemporary scholarship suggests that less repetition would occur if reliable bibliographies were available and young scholars would consult them rather than reinvent the wheel.

While I was serving as a Fulbright Lecturer in Spain during the 1967–68 academic year, I came across a book in a shop in Madrid, an

American publication, *The Critical Reputation of F. Scott Fitzgerald: A Bibliographical Study*, by one Jackson R. Bryer and issued by the Shoe String Press in 1967. I had seen earlier checklists by Bryer on Richard Wright, Eugene O'Neill, Wallace Stevens, John Barth, John Hawkes, Thornton Wilder, and John Steinbeck published between 1960 and 1965 in such journals as *Wisconsin Studies in Contemporary Literature, Modern Drama, Twentieth Century Literature, Critique,* and *Modern Fiction Studies*, and he seemed to be a one-man bibliography factory. But I was unprepared for the scope, comprehensiveness, and genuine usefulness of the Fitzgerald volume, which placed at the fingertips of the scholar over two thousand items, nearly all annotated, extending from contemporary reviews of Fitzgerald's books through critical essays, book-length studies, foreign criticism, and dissertations. This was what a bibliographic study should be, and it demonstrated how invaluable such work was. Strangely enough, it spawned no imitators, probably because few other scholars were willing to commit the same amount of time and energy to a single author as Bryer had done. And this was no dissertation simply moved into print since Bryer had written his doctoral thesis on Margaret Anderson and the *Little Review* at the University of Wisconsin in 1964.

In the fall of 1969, I moved from Michigan State University to the recently founded Virginia Commonwealth University in Richmond. Already in the English Department was Maurice Duke, who had been trained in textual scholarship at the University of Iowa and had recently completed as his dissertation a bibliographic study of James Branch Cabell's library. One way to help put a university on the map is to publish a journal building on existing strengths and interests. I thought about the fact that there was no one place in which to publish bibliographic checklists, essay-reviews of reference books, and unpublished documents—the resources for literary scholarship—so the basic idea for a journal seemed obvious. Maurice Duke was enthusiastic about the project, but our first impulse was to take all of English and American literature as our purview. In fact, my first idea for a title was simply "Literary Scholarship: A Guide to Research and Bibliography."

In December of 1969, I was one of many teachers assembled by the Educational Testing Service to read the College Board essays in a hotel near the bitterly cold beaches of Atlantic City—a hotel inexpensive presumably because of the usually barren city in the wintertime (before the arrival of the casinos). There were no distractions from the work at hand of reading and grading essays for eight hours a day, a sort of sadomasochistic exercise for English teachers that had a strangely cleansing effect. The readings were later moved to Princeton, and in the new environment the experience was somehow less invigorating. In any case, among the readers participating was Jackson R. Bryer of the University of Maryland. We met, talked, and I explained my idea for a new journal. Naturally, this was just the sort of thing that appealed to him, if he had not already considered such an idea, and we were happy to have him on board as another editor. It remained for us to sharpen our concept and approach our respective universities for support.

In the spring of 1970, we met in College Park at a coffee shop near the campus of the University of Maryland. Among the things decided at that initial editorial meeting was that we would focus on American literature rather than the entire body of literature written in English. The latter would have been impossible to manage anyway, and we were already specialists in American literature. Thus we sought another name for the journal and agreed finally on *Resources for American Literary Study* (my file contains a guest check borrowed from the waitress on which I wrote the title for the first time). We also agreed on specific kinds of material we wanted to publish and made a list of the following:

1. Fully annotated and evaluative checklists of critical and biographical scholarship on the significant works (prose, poetry, and drama) of major authors or the total work of minor authors.
2. Evaluative essay-reviews of modern scholarship on major authors, works, genres, trends, and periods. (Models are the essays contained in *Eight American Authors*, ed. Floyd Stovall, and *Fifteen Modern American Authors*, ed. Jackson R. Bryer.)
3. Informative accounts or catalogues of significant collections of research materials of literary and cultural interest available in archives and libraries. Special attention will be given to reports of recent acquisitions (e.g., the Fugitive Poet collections at Vanderbilt, the Faulkner collections at the University of Virginia, the Cabell collection at Virginia Commonwealth University, the Katherine Anne Porter collection at the University of Maryland).
4. Edited correspondence, personal papers, unpublished essays, and other documents of interest to literary scholars and cultural historians.

We made a list, as well, of some of the most prominent scholars and bibliographers in American literature at the time, and, after explaining our intentions to them, invited them to serve on our editorial advisory board: John C. Broderick, Matthew J. Bruccoli, John C. Gerber, Norman S. Grabo, C. Hugh Holman, Walter B. Rideout, Jack Salzman, Floyd Stovall, G. Thomas Tanselle, Arlin Turner, and James Woodress. To a person, they agreed to serve and lend their names to the project.

The English Department at the University of Maryland readily agreed to support the journal partially, but Virginia Commonwealth University remained to be convinced. After gathering the information we needed on probable costs and receiving bids from several printers, Maurice Duke and I wrote the following "Background Statement" to submit to the administration:

> The proposal to establish RESOURCES FOR AMERICAN LITERARY STUDY grew out of the recognition for the need of a journal which would direct scholars and advanced graduate students to the myriad resource materials in American literature available to them in this country. At present no publication speaks to this need.
>
> We have noticed over the past several years—in discussion with colleagues at other universities across the country and at various regional and national professional meetings—a growing concern over the lack of one central source which would inform scholars of the location and significance of major collections of manuscripts, letters, and documents in the field of American literature. In addition, scholars and students alike need to have available to them fully annotated checklists of scholarship on the works of major authors, and evaluative essay reviews centering on the trends in contemporary scholarship on American writers and their culture. RESOURCES FOR AMERICAN LITERARY STUDY will fill these needs.
>
> Of central significance is the fact that the three editors are all trained in the kinds of scholarship which will form the heart of the journal. Each is also a specialist in American literature. Professors Inge and Bryer have both published books in this area; Professor Duke has published several articles. Also, the Editorial Advisory Board is composed of the major national figures in the field. Each of them has major publications to his credit, and at least eight of the eleven have produced germinal studies in the field over the past twenty-five years.
>
> We have conversed with scholars from universities representing all parts of the United States, and not one of them has been less than enthusiastic over the possibility of RESOURCES FOR AMERICAN LITERARY STUDY. We feel that the interest of our colleagues is indicative of the need for the publication; it is also a good barometer by which to judge its future success.
>
> The administration at the University of Maryland, the institution at which Professor Bryer teaches, has expressed a keen interest in RESOURCES FOR AMERICAN LITERARY STUDY, and assures us that half of the operational expenses will be forthcoming. They have agreed to take care of subscriptions, mailing, and distribution. Thus we plan for circulation to be centered on the College Park campus and the editorial offices to be housed at Virginia Commonwealth

University. We need no additional space other than our faculty offices, however.

Finally, our operational budget, below, was arrived at by consultation with three Richmond printers, and is, we feel, quite realistic. We plan to use a city firm to insure maximum communication between editors and printer. It is our hope that after the two-year trial period, the journal will be self-supporting.

Operational Budget

For a two-year time period, two volumes to be issued, two issues per volume in the spring and fall.

Printing costs for 4 issues, 500 copies per issue	$7,000.00
Printing costs, advertising flyer	200.00
Stationery and mailing envelopes	300.00
Postage	200.00
Miscellaneous (phone calls, secretarial help, etc.)	300.00
	$8,000.00

If the publication costs are equally shared by Virginia Commonwealth University and the University of Maryland, each university will provide $4,000 for the two-year period, or $2,000 per year.

The statement worked, and the funds were forthcoming.

How do you fill the pages of the first issue of a journal that no one knows exists? We wanted to be sure, too, that all of the kinds of submissions we sought were represented. Knowing of the rich manuscript collections on Henry Miller at Randolph-Macon College and on the Fugitives/Agrarians at Vanderbilt University, we invited specialists at those schools (Edgar MacDonald in the first case and Martha E. Cook and Thomas Daniel Young in the second) to prepare surveys of those collections. Linda W. Wagner (before she became Linda Wagner-Martin) at Michigan State was writing extensively about American poetry, so we asked her to write a review of research and criticism on William Carlos Williams. Maurice Duke and I decided to provide two other types of articles ourselves to serve as models. I compiled an annotated checklist of criticism on William Faulkner's *Light in August*, and he prepared a bibliographic guide to the contents of the thirty-five issues of *The Reviewer*, a little magazine published in Richmond between 1921 and 1925. This was the only time we contributed to the journal, except for several years when I wrote an unsigned narrative of brief reviews of books that were not to be given full reviews at the end of each issue. Miraculously, G. Thomas Tanselle, then at the University of Wisconsin and long before he became Senior Vice President and

Secretary of the Guggenheim Foundation, agreed to write a general essay on "The State of Reference Bibliography in American Literature," which set exactly the tone we wanted in our lead article, laying out the territory of where we were and where we needed to go in bibliographic scholarship. It was one of those fortuitous circumstances that could not have been planned better. The other essay in the first issue was Edward C. Peple Jr.'s "The Background of the Hawthorne-Thoreau Relationship." Once the inaugural issue appeared and the word got out, the next three issues would include contributions by a series of now well-known scholars near the start of their academic careers: John M. Reilly, John E. Bassett, Everett Emerson, David E. E. Sloane, William J. Scheick, and Jerome Klinkowitz among them. We even received and published a letter from Henry Miller correcting some errors in the survey of his collections at Randolph-Macon.

One of the pleasures in the beginning of bringing *Resources* into being was the opportunity to work directly with the selected printer, Whittet and Shepperson, one of the most respected firms in Richmond. We wanted the journal to have a distinguished appearance from the start and thus chose Olde Style 60 pound paper for the interior, an antique tan paper for the cover, and Baskerville type for the text, basically following the style of the *Princeton University Library Chronicle* at that time. Even better was the fact that Whittet and Shepperson still operated a letterpress, a form of printing that was once considered irreplaceable in style and appearance. It was much more handsome than Linotype, Offset Lithography, or any other method of printing. There was an aesthetic pleasure in reading proof and seeing the journal through to completion that is no longer possible in contemporary printing. Finally, however, we had to yield to the pressures of cost and time and seek less expensive printers. Not long after we left our first printer, Whittet and Shepperson was forced to replace the letterpress with more cost-effective equipment. The cover design was selected from several designs submitted by students under the direction of prominent designer Phil Meggs, who taught at Virginia Commonwealth University.

Our original request for subvention had been based on the notion that we would be self-supporting through subscriptions in two years. That was a foolish assumption. Despite the fact that we had moved from two hundred and fifty subscribers to four hundred by the third volume, expenses still exceeded income. Publishing larger issues and paying legal fees associated with tax-exempt status didn't help, so back we went to the universities for additional support. To bolster our case, we asked for letters of evaluation from our distinguished editorial advisory board. Their response was overwhelmingly favorable. It might be more informative to publish one letter here in its entirety (this one from

G. Thomas Tanselle, dated 28 February 1974) rather than to select excerpts from several letters:

> I am happy to give you my candid appraisal of RESOURCES FOR AMERICAN LITERARY STUDY, for the journal seems to me to have established itself, during the three years of its existence, as one of the most important, useful, and respected of the scholarly journals devoted to the study of American literature.
> When the journal was first proposed, I thought the idea was an excellent one, because there was no other journal which concentrated on the kind of material which the editors had in mind—that is, there was no journal which set out exclusively to offer the student of American literature bibliographical articles and annotated checklists surveying the scholarship on various authors or works, descriptions of collections of source materials, and printings of the texts of previously unpublished documents. Such material naturally turns up from time to time in other journals, but no other journal specialized in it; obviously this kind of work is basic and of permanent usefulness, and the existence of a journal devoted to it ought to stimulate its production by providing an outlet for it. For these reasons I was happy to support the journal at its inception. Normally I am somewhat dubious about the starting of new scholarly journals, but what this journal proposed was clearly so useful and so much needed that I was all in favor of it.
> I am pleased to be able to report that after three years my opinion has not changed, for the journal has fully lived up to my hopes for it. It has published not only high-quality material of the kind mentioned above but also many excellent reviews of relevant books. I have long felt that there were not enough outlets for thorough, searching reviews of books in this field, and *RALS* is helping to alleviate that situation. Because the articles it publishes are basic to other work, the file of *RALS* becomes—more than is the case with many scholarly journals—an important reference work. I keep my own set on the shelf with my other frequently used reference books, and I find in conversation with my colleagues in American literature that they feel the same way about the journal. I know that some articles in it have been required reading in certain graduate seminars; and I know that graduate students frequently turn to it for guidance. As the years go by and it has an opportunity to cover still more authors, its usefulness as a reference work of this sort will of course be correspondingly enhanced.
> It is rare indeed for a journal to live up to its advance billing, and rarer still for a journal in three years to come to be regarded as established and basic. *RALS* has accomplished both these feats, and I look forward to following its future contributions. Let me take this opportunity to offer my

congratulations to you and the other editors on what you have achieved, and to wish you all the best for the volumes to follow.

John C. Broderick of the Library of Congress was even moved to include a bit of verse on a separate card that came with his letter:

> Poems written or chanted or spoken in halls,
> Freudian lapses and fortunate falls,
> Careful revisions and juvenile scrawls,
> How could they be studied if there were no *RALS?*

Somehow we raised the money and *Resources* continued, not just for a few more issues, but for over three decades now. Maurice Duke and I left for other tasks and opportunities eventually, but Bryer remained at the helm. Other editors have stepped in to help: Martha E. Cook (1979–84), George C. Longest (1979–80), Carla Mulford (1985–92), Robert Secor (1993–95), and presently Richard Kopley (1995–). All have made important contributions that have guaranteed the journal's survival and success. This essay reflects my memory of events, and both Bryer and Duke probably have different stories to tell. But I suspect that we would all agree that it is eminently satisfying to watch one's intellectual brainchild grow and mature into something with which one is proud to be associated. I hope it survives for decades to come.

Prospects for the Study of William Dean Howells

SARAH B. DAUGHERTY
Wichita State University

Despite his image as a Victorian gentleman in a straw hat, William Dean Howells presents a formidable challenge to scholars and analysts. "More than anything," observes Susan Goodman, "he believed in work" (17), to the point that even the *Selected Edition* of his writings is still an unfinished project. The primary venue for meetings of the William Dean Howells Society is the annual conference of the American Literature Association—an appropriate arrangement, given Howells's role in establishing the canon and anticipating our current interests. But because most Howellsians are active teachers with multiple duties, discussions are all too brief. And few of us can match the author's range as a critic of literature and culture.

Then again, Howells is an almost ideal subject for further study: he is a major writer whose potential has not yet been exhausted by academic professionals. Thanks to judicious editors, his most important writings are now in print, and many deserve closer reading, especially in the light of contemporary theory and of Howells's own turn from realism toward modernism. Scholars drawn to archival research will find a great deal of additional material worthy of publication as we reconstruct literary history and attempt to do justice to multiculturalism. Howells is likewise an instructive presence in the classroom. To quote George C. Carrington Jr., "[H]e knew the central modern American situation: the endlessly renewed attempt to plug along, with honor, in a chaotic world" (228).

Editions, Bibliography, and Collections

The starting point for researchers is the *Selected Edition*, now under the general editorship of David J. Nordloh. Twenty-five of thirty-two projected volumes are currently in print: six volumes of letters (Twayne), fourteen of fiction, two of memoirs and autobiography, and three of literary criticism (Indiana UP). The editors' introductions cite essential contextual material, including biographical and publication data, Howells's notes and comments, and letters and reviews by his contemporaries.

Other editions feature less-familiar texts inviting extended analysis. Thomas Wortham's collection *Early Prose Writings* (1990) provides a basis for a study of Howells's experimentation with many modes, including political satire ("The Independent Candidate" [1854]) and fictive melodrama ("Geoffrey Winter" [1861]), as well as journalistic sketches and criticism. (Howells's bemused reaction to the poetry of Whitman is of particular interest.) Another important anthology, *Selected Short Stories* (1997), includes thirteen representative tales with excellent notes and introductions by the editor, Ruth Bardon. Bardon's "annotated story list," with references to forty-six additional tales, may inspire more comprehensive editions. Recent critics have focused on the later psychic romances, which destabilize Howells's concept of realism following the death of his daughter Winifred (see Crowley, *Mask* 135–55; Knoper; and Rubin).

As a dramatist, Howells was also prolific, though his plays often expose his weakness for the melodrama satirized in his fiction. (He once proposed a stage version of *A Hazard of New Fortunes* [1890] that concludes with Margaret and Conrad happily announcing their engagement.) Walter J. Meserve's 1960 edition of *The Complete Plays* has been supplemented by George Arms, Mary Bess Whidden, and Gary Scharnhorst's *Staging Howells: Plays and Correspondence with Lawrence Barrett* (1994), which features the original text of *A Counterfeit Presentiment* (1877), a recently discovered translation (1878), and a fragment of another. The editors comment on Howells's willingness to "pander to the demands of the temperamental actor" (xix)—a willingness ironically represented in a neglected novel, *The Story of a Play* (1898). The author's more serious engagements with drama, including the plays of Henrik Ibsen, are recorded in his later reviews, which are collected by Brenda Murphy in her 1992 edition, *A Realist in the American Theatre: Selected Drama Criticism of William Dean Howells*. Still needed, however, is a more analytical study of the connections between Howells's dramatic efforts and his more subtle fiction. Like his colleague Henry James (whose novel *The Tragic Muse* [1890] was an influence), Howells modified his ethical conception of character in response to his theatrical experience. The text of *Hazard* supports Beaton's observation in the novel: "'There's the making of several characters in each of us; ... and sometimes this character has the lead in us, and sometimes that ... '" (486).

Several volumes document Howells's lengthy career as editor, critic, and colleague of other writers. While introducing their 1980 collection *John Hay–Howells Letters: The Correspondence of John Milton Hay and William Dean Howells*, George Monteiro and Brenda Murphy note Howells's "consistent attempts to secure Hay's literary talents for his magazines" (xix), as well as his gratitude for intelligent responses to his writing.

Henry Nash Smith and William M. Gibson's *Mark Twain–Howells Letters* (1960) is still the key source on the most important of Howells's literary relationships. But the material here is so rich that it now calls for fresh presentation. A model is Michael Anesko's *Letters, Fictions, Lives: Henry James and William Dean Howells* (1997), a chronological arrangement of the criticism of Howells and Henry James, along with their correspondence, which is enhanced by Anesko's perceptive commentary.

We should remember, however, that Howells developed his critical standards through his reading of minor authors as well as major ones. Especially useful is James W. Simpson's facsimile of the "Editor's Study" columns, *Editor's Study* (1983). When I devoted much of a sabbatical to reading these, I was impressed by Howells's huge workload and his ability to separate the wheat from the chaff. These columns provide an intellectual context for the fiction, with their many reviews of philosophical and historical works (e.g., those of John Fiske). Another facsimile edition, *Prefaces to Contemporaries, 1882–1920* (1957; rpt. 1978), records Howells's later efforts to promote both European and American writers while grappling with divergent definitions of realism (xi). A limited edition deserving wider circulation is Ulrich Halfmann's *Interviews with William Dean Howells* (1973), reprinted from the Fall 1973 issue of *American Literary Realism*; highlights include exchanges with Hamlin Garland, Stephen Crane, and Theodore Dreiser, as well as a previously unpublished interview with Laura Stedman (granddaughter of literary historian E. C. Stedman). But further editions, especially of Howells's neglected twentieth-century writings, would be welcome. In particular, the "Editor's Easy Chair" columns (1900–1919), with their conversational style and modern subjects, merit republication and discussion. As Howells lost confidence in the "conveniently providential view of American history" (Anesko 162), he balanced his literary preoccupations with larger political and cultural concerns, thus entering a stage of his career comparable to the "fourth phase" of Henry James. Howells's critiques of capitalism and imperialism, and his defenses of human rights, are more pointed and readable than James's late writings.

Edwin H. Cady's recent compilation *Pebbles, Monochromes, and Other Modern Poems, 1891–1916* (2000) should create interest in Howells's poetry, a genre in which the author's ambitions sometimes exceeded his accomplishments. Nonetheless, Cady presents a strong case for regarding the later Howells as a modernist who was influenced by Emily Dickinson and Crane and affiliated with Edwin Arlington Robinson and Robert Frost. Among the more interesting selections are "Father and Mother: A Mystery" (1900) and "Black Cross Farm" (1916), poems with religious themes problematized by dramatic and narrative strategies. Also noteworthy is "After the Wedding" (1906), another dialogue, in which a daughter's marriage precipitates a conflict between her parents. An edition of Howells's earlier poems, including the elegiac verses admired by Henry James, would supplement this collection. (According to Cady, a volume of complete poems was planned for the *Selected Edition* but failed to make the cut when federal funding was withdrawn.)

The indispensable guide for seekers of excluded texts remains William M. Gibson and George Arms's *A Bibliography of William Dean Howells*, originally published in 1948. However, as the editors acknowledged in a note to the 1971 reprint, the bibliography definitely needs updating since it omits many contributions (some unsigned) to newspapers and books. Even a selective expansion of the bibliography, with entries for such recently published pieces as "The Home-Towners" (composed in 1916 but not in print until 1998), would be a boon to scholarship.

We also need modern critical editions of novels often difficult to obtain but pivotal to Howells's development—and revealing in their unresolved conflicts. One of my selections would be *Private Theatricals* (1875–76), whose central character, the actress Belle Farrell, "generates psychic mayhem" (Prioleau 37) but projects Howells's rebellion against the cult of domesticity (Daugherty, "Ideology"). Another key novel is *Annie Kilburn* (1889), a searching critique of bourgeois charity and of the Christian alternative proposed by Leo Tolstoy (Boudreau 139–66; Daugherty, "Howells, Tolstoy"). *The World of Chance* (1893), a novel that influenced Crane (Sorrentino 51), deserves rereading in the context of T. J. Jackson Lears's fascinating cultural history *Something for Nothing: Luck in America* (2003). *The Landlord at Lion's Head* (1897) likewise challenges ethical assumptions and also affiliates the realist, reluctantly, with his naturalist successors. As John W. Crowley remarks, Howells appears "helpless to stop a cad's progress in a world where character seems to be worth no more than the paper a character is written on" ("Giving a Character" 53; cf. Haralson, "Romancing"). In contrast, *New Leaf Mills: A Chronicle* (1913) reflects the author's persistent, if skeptical, engagement with his father's Swedenborgianism (Crowley, *Mask* 193–213; Marovitz, "Imposing"). The image fostered by the *Selected Edition*—Howells the committed realist—becomes more dynamic when we consider Howells the seeker and experimenter.

As we discover interesting texts, we should share them with our students. Custom publishing may provide an alternative to cumbersome anthologies, which neglect Howells or represent him with selections too predictable to elicit discussion (see Crowley, "Howells in *The Heath*"). Moreover, now that literary criticism has merged with cultural studies, the political novels should be revived. In a recent conference paper, Frederick Wegener proposed a paperback edition of *The Son of Royal*

Langbrith (1904), a critique of imperialism and capitalism, as well as of patriarchal marriage. And two novels have been the subject of so many articles and book chapters that critical editions are warranted. One is *A Hazard of New Fortunes*; a number of analysts have explained how modern New York City tested not only Howells's social values but also his representational strategies (Kaplan 44–64, Parrish, Harmon, Bramen, Prettyman, Stretch, Rennick). The second is *An Imperative Duty* (1892), which would be an excellent choice for an edition highlighting interpretive conflicts in the manner recommended by Gerald Graff in *Professing Literature: An Institutional History* (1987). Affirmative readers share Joseph R. McElrath Jr.'s view that the narrative presents "a real personal problem solved in a commonsensical, humane, and believable way" (452; cf. Petrie) while skeptics argue that Howells appropriates blackness to explore abnormal psychology (Wonham) or to defuse anxieties concerning race, class, and national identity that the comedy fails to resolve (Clymer; Daugherty, "*An Imperative Duty*").

The Howells archives are rich in materials for larger projects on history and culture. Visitors to the Houghton Library at Harvard, the most extensive collection of Howells materials, should consult the accessions catalogs, as well as HOLLIS and OASIS (the electronic databases), since manuscripts are in the process of being received and classified. Unlike Henry James, Howells saved his correspondence, so the Houghton collection includes not only family documents, but also letters from other writers: Henry Adams, Stephen Crane, Charlotte Perkins Gilman, Thomas Hardy, William James, Sarah Orne Jewett, Henry Wadsworth Longfellow, James Russell Lowell, Edith Wharton, and many more. Of special interest is the collection of daughter Mildred Howells, who corresponded with modern academic critics (Oscar Cargill, Jay Hubbell, Fred Lewis Pattee, Arthur Hobson Quinn) as she prepared her still-valuable *Life in Letters of William Dean Howells* (1928). Each year the library solicits applications for the William Dean Howells Memorial Fellowship, which provides a stipend of twenty-five hundred dollars and access to all the Harvard collections. (The current fellow, Claudia Stokes, is working on a history of American literature as an academic discipline.)

The Houghton also oversees the Howells home at Kittery Point, Maine, the site of the author's personal library and of conferences scheduled every few years by the Memorial Committee. David Nordloh is in the process of preparing a catalog of realia and a new visitors' guide to this delightful Victorian dwelling. An inventory of Howells's books might reveal further sources of his fiction while affording a personal view of his intellectual life.

Other notable collections include the Howells/Fréchette papers at Alfred University (with correspondence between the author and his sister Annie) and the papers at the Massachusetts Historical Society (reflecting wife Elinor Mead Howells's interest in the genealogy of the Mead and Howells families). These collections have been described for *Resources for American Literary Study* by Ginette de B. Merrill (1981), who notes the closeness and occasional possessiveness of the various Howellses. The University of Southern California has another outstanding collection, comprising Howells's correspondence with Hamlin Garland, manuscripts of the "Easy Chair" columns for *Harper's*, and contemporary reviews of Howells's fiction. Columbia University owns microfilms of the *Harper's* contracts. The Huntington Library is also a good source of material, especially on Winifred Howells, James T. Fields and his wife, Annie Adams Fields, and writers connected with the *Atlantic Monthly*. Scholars doing research on the author's Ohio background may examine the holdings of Miami University, featured this year during a commemoration in Hamilton (the original Boy's Town). Miami's microfilms are available through interlibrary loan.

The best source of updated information on Howells is the William Dean Howells Society Web site maintained by Donna M. Campbell at <http://guweb2.gonzaga.edu/faculty/campbell/howells/indexa.html>. Particularly useful is "Current Critical Commentary on Howells," an annotated bibliography of recommended books and articles. The site also incorporates news of conferences and Howells Society activities, links to the Web sites of related authors, and a discussion list inviting queries.

Biography and Criticism

Edwin H. Cady's two-volume biography of Howells, *The Road to Realism: The Early Years 1837–1885 of William Dean Howells* (1956) and *The Realist at War: The Mature Years 1885–1920 of William Dean Howells* (1958), is a remarkably durable and well-researched narrative to which future scholars will remain indebted. As the titles imply, the account centers on Howells's efforts to promote nuances of characterization over sensational turns of plot and his opposition to such neoromantic bestsellers as *Trilby* and *The Prisoner of Zenda* (*Realist* 53). Cady links the writer's aesthetics to his politics and ethics, citing Howells's defense of the Chicago Anarchists at the risk of his own reputation. *The Light of Common Day: Realism in American Fiction* (1971), Cady's polemic in favor of responsible criticism and pedagogy, still rings with undeniable truth. But Cady's approach to Howells does have some limitations. The diligent professional dominates the ambivalent private man, and interpretations of the novels sometimes neglect the works' ambiguities. Then, too, the chapters on Howells's career after the realism war—"The Dean in the Easy

Chair" and "The Sunset Academician"—project a misleading image of complacency.

Other biographers explore the author's psychology in greater depth but focus more narrowly on the first decades of his life. Kenneth S. Lynn's *William Dean Howells: An American Life* (1971) includes appreciative close readings of the early novels and critical essays, with responses to H. L. Mencken, Van Wyck Brooks, and other modern detractors. But Lynn deplores Howells's failure to emulate Tolstoy, notably in *Annie Kilburn* and *A Hazard of New Fortunes*. (Not surprisingly, Lynn's exemplary American novelist is Dreiser.) Crowley's classic study *The Black Heart's Truth: The Early Career of W. D. Howells* (1985) invokes Freud to explicate the author's "psychological juggle" and his achievement in *A Modern Instance* (1882). Rodney D. Olsen's *Dancing in Chains: The Youth of William Dean Howells* (1991), which draws on the theories of Erik Erikson, illuminates Howells's struggle to reconcile his family loyalties with his literary ambitions.

A comprehensive biography, citing recently discovered sources, is obviously needed, and readers will be pleased to learn that Susan Goodman and Carl Dawson's *William Dean Howells: A Writer's Life* is forthcoming from the University of California Press. No doubt this project will provoke further discussions of the shape of the author's complex career.

The critical fortunes of Howells have waxed and waned. Despite the barbs of his antagonists, reviews of his novels were often favorable, and in 1891 no less an authority than Thomas Wentworth Higginson praised his "school" of realism as "the hope of American literature" (14). Nonetheless, Crowley's *The Dean of American Letters: The Late Career of William Dean Howells* (1999) describes the neglect of Howells's writing as he became a public figure—and subsequently a target for modernists who scorned "women, gentility, and three-barreled literary names" (56). The revival of Howells, initiated by academic critics of the 1950s, is outlined by Crowley in the opening pages of *The Mask of Fiction* (4–7). Some of the early monographs have not been superseded, notably James L. Woodress's *Howells and Italy* (1952), Everett Carter's *Howells and the Age of Realism* (1954), and George N. Bennett's two books on Howells's development as a novelist (*Howells* [1959], *Realism* [1973]). A useful retrospective is *On Howells: The Best from "American Literature"* (1993), edited by Cady and Louis J. Budd.

Rejoinders to these traditionalists were provided by Kermit Vanderbilt (*The Achievement of William Dean Howells* [1968]) and George C. Carrington Jr. (*The Immense Complex Drama* [1966]), whose interpretations underscore the personal, political, and philosophical uncertainties problematizing realism. In the 1980s, Elizabeth Stevens Prioleau (*The Circle of Eros* [1983]) and Crowley (*The Black Heart's Truth* [1985]) extended Freudian analysis to Howells's fiction, with chronological discussions charting patterns of psychic conflict and reintegration.

But if Freud helped to revive Howells, other theorists threatened to extinguish him. Poststructuralists had little interest in an author who championed "truth," at least in the statements best known to general readers. And by choosing texts to fit his argument, Michael Davitt Bell could claim that Howells's failure to become a theorist himself served to reinforce "cultural orthodoxy" (8). New Historians offered some provocative, if deflationary, rereadings. Contributors to *New Essays on "The Rise of Silas Lapham"* (1991), edited by Donald E. Pease, successfully challenged interpreters of the novel as a moral fable. But, inevitably, Howells was represented as a victim of the system he sought to critique, and even as an apologist for corporate capitalism (Corkin).

Yet Howells has proved more durable than the skeptics. Alfred Habegger's defense of Howells against James has been strengthened by Anesko's edition—and by Jamesians' frequent overestimates of the expatriate's political engagement. Elsa Nettels has analyzed Howells's meticulous use of dialect, even when his faithful renderings of American speech undermined his egalitarian theories. *Writing Realism: Howells, James, and Norris in the Mass Market*, Daniel H. Borus's influential 1989 study of the literary marketplace, reinforces the arguments of Cady as it describes Howells's attempts to educate—and respond to—the tastes of his multicultural audience. More recently, Susan Goodman in *Civil Wars: American Novelists and Manners, 1880–1940* (2003) has argued for the centrality of the novel of manners, portraying Howells as an American progenitor who wrested the genre from the upper class (17). The best evidence of the author's vitality may be the endorsements of two contemporary writers, novelist John Updike and literary journalist Adam Gopnik. By recommending Howells in the pages of *The New Yorker* while also addressing academic conferences, they have reenacted the crucial role of the man of letters.

Within the academy, interdisciplinary scholars have promoted Howells as a thinker whose virtue is flexibility. Drawing analogies with the "failed promise" of contract law, Brook Thomas returns to *The Rise of Silas Lapham* (1885) because it explores "the difficulty and necessity of assessing individual responsibility in an economy of the unaccountable" (16–17). Rigid determinists, notes Thomas, replicate Lapham's errors (124). In the realm of philosophy, Howells has profited from the revival of pragmatism initiated by Richard Rorty and furthered by Louis Menand in *The Metaphysical Club* (2001). (Significantly, William James preferred Howells's novels to those of Henry.) Sämi Ludwig's new book proposes a "cognitive paradigm" in which consistency yields to a pluralism of negotiated meanings. Here again Howells plays a central role as a practicing novelist rather than as a theorist.

How, then, can we contribute to the ongoing discussion? On this point, Henry James may offer useful advice when he invokes "the analytic and historic spirit" (Anesko 453) as the one required. That is, we should unite criticism and scholarship instead of regarding them as separate activities. Analysis without context is often abstruse or anachronistic, and history without analysis leads to the collection of trivia and to editions that gather dust on library shelves.

A number of projects invite those willing to synthesize research and close reading. An extended study might deal with Howells's ambivalence toward small-town Ohio and his equivocal relationship to the regionalist movement. As Campbell reminds us, Howells was known—and often belittled—for his advocacy of local color, culturally indexed as feminine (17); but he also encouraged authors who resisted regionalism, including Crane, Garland, and Frank Norris. The description of Dulldale in "Geoffrey Winter," notes Wortham, presages the modern "revolt from the village" (Howells, *Early Prose Writings* 236).

The publication of Matthew Pearl's novel *The Dante Club* (2003), for which Howells was a source (Pearl 370), may spark interest in *Literary Friends and Acquaintance* (1900). Howells's respect for the Brahmins, as well as for a new generation of women writers, eventually made him a target for Van Wyck Brooks, who detected a conspiracy against the masculine values epitomized by Mark Twain. The Cambridge men of letters—Lowell, Longfellow, and Oliver Wendell Holmes—welcomed the neophyte Howells, though the Concord Transcendentalists did not; and as Peter Gibian has suggested, the "culture of conversation" fostered cosmopolitan attitudes and dialogic techniques (1–11). We should review the Brahmins', and Howells's, roles in developing American literature as an academic field, despite the later valorization of the Romantics (Shumway 143). The Longfellow Institute at present-day Harvard extends a rich tradition of multilingual study to which Howells contributed.

Also worthy of review are Howells's attitudes toward race and gender, supported by close readings and attention to the dynamics of his career. Though Cady's *Young Howells and John Brown: Episodes in a Radical Education* (1985) describes Howells's "radical education," the aspiring poet and novelist cared more for literary success than for abolitionist politics. *Uncle Tom's Cabin* presented an obstacle because of its sentimental mode and its reliance on an eroding foundation of Christian belief. Yet, unlike many Northern liberals, Howells refused the false consolations of Reconstruction. The ambiguous comedy of *An Imperative Duty* is counterbalanced by the unfinished tragedy of "The Home-Towners," in which the protagonist, a failed writer, is overcome by the poverty of Southern blacks and the violence of a white lynch mob. Without assuming the mantle of William Faulkner, Howells signaled his own limitations.

In writing of gender roles, the novelist was more confident. But confidence has bred criticism, particularly from feminists who observe his adherence to the Victorian stereotypes he sometimes challenged (Crowley, *Mask* 83–114; Daugherty, "Ideology"; Henwood). Of more than historical importance, then, is the resistance he encountered from the women in his family. The letters of Elinor Mead Howells, collected in the volume *If Not Literature: Letters of Elinor Mead Howells* (1988), reveal her to have been an independent thinker with a keen sense of humor. (Her nickname for her new husband was "Pokey" [40].) Further, a major essay by Polly H. Howells, the author's great-granddaughter, describes the increasingly active role of Mildred following her sister Winifred's death and her mother's decline in health. Notwithstanding her devotion to her father, Mildred wrote poems and letters that express a rebelliousness that may have been responsible for her refusal to marry. Howells's later fiction probably encodes his perceptions of his wife's and daughters' constricted lives. The Father in his chapter for the collaborative novel *The Whole Family* (1908) advocates "coeducation as a preliminary to domestic happiness" (6)—and perhaps as an alternative to the outworn courtship plot. A comprehensive study might establish the causal connections between Howells's personal motives and his aesthetic ones. We need to know more about the role of his sisters in Ohio, who, says Polly H. Howells, "did not always appreciate their brother's idealization of their homebound service" (25).

A related topic deserving exploration is that of Howells and male bonding. Crowley's chapter "Howells, Stoddard, and Male Homosocial Attachment" (*Mask* 56–82) provides a good starting point, for Crowley is surely correct about the author's close friendships with other men, including avowed homosexuals, despite his distaste for "same-sex genitality" (72). (His sympathetic bond with Edmund Gosse is another case in point [*Mask* 197–98].) More evidence can be found in Howells's late writings on Henry James, including a reference to James's "oddity" in the draft of a late review (Anesko 471). The Howells-James correspondence as a whole documents a warm friendship crossing sexual boundaries. Most recently, critics have noted the ways in which androgyny complicates Howells's fiction. In *A Modern Instance*, argues Warren Hedges, Ben Halleck's "indeterminate relationship to heterosexuality" underlies his critique of "character" and of "the fetishism that supports it" (34); and in *Silas Lapham*, contends Graham Thompson, the "love story" of Silas and Tom Corey is far more passionate than the belated romance of Tom and Penelope (21–45). The time is right, then, for an extended study of Howells in the light of queer theory and of the pre-Freudian psychological models prevailing in the nineteenth century. Significantly, Eric Haralson, who has just published a book on James and queer modernity, proposed a complementary project on Howells during the 1996 Memorial Conference. At the least, remarked Haralson, Howells suggests "that genteel domesticity, with its mutually reinforcing ideologies of true womanhood and true manhood, exacts a considerable price" ("Representing" 3).

We could benefit from more detailed analyses of the novelist's relations with his publishers and his readers. The scholarship of Augusta Rohrbach, centered on photographs in the Houghton collection, underscores "the degree to which Howells sought the identifying marks of professionalization," his mustache being a signifier for "prestige and legitimacy" (91, 95). According to George Monteiro, material at Harvard and in the files of the various Houghton companies might document a full-scale study of "The Man of Letters as a Man of Business," especially during Howells's Boston years (Untitled 1–2). But the effect of his business experience on the fiction is more subtle than cultural materialists, including Rohrbach, might allow. Monteiro also observes that *A Modern Instance* alludes obliquely to Howells's giving *Dr. Breen's Practice* (1881), not to Houghton, but to a rival publisher, Osgood. The parallel dealings of Bartley, however, are represented as shady or even unethical (Untitled 5).

As for Howells's readers, future scholars should build on the work of Cady and Borus. The gibes against Howells in such middlebrow magazines as *Life* (Banta) may be indirect evidence of his popular success. And the topic of his literary influence still awaits development. Two exemplary studies are Sanford E. Marovitz's essay on Howells and the later Melville and Paul Sorrentino's article on Howells and Crane. Because (unlike James) Howells seldom recruited disciples, he encouraged other writers in finding their own subjects and voices.

More might be written of the skepticism that allied Howells with other writers of the nineteenth century yet resulted in his own distinctive voice. One of his last essays, "Eighty Years and After" (1919), begins with a startling confession, "All my life I have been afraid of death" (157), but ends with a qualified affirmation: "We know that somewhere there is love" (167). In the novels, however, the narrator's anxiety, generated by the remnants of Christian faith, destabilizes the pragmatic comedy. A comprehensive book might document the various influences on Howells (Emanuel Swedenborg, Tolstoy, William James) that left him unable either to accept faith or to reject it. Although usually described as an agnostic (Cady, *Road* 148–51), Howells lacked the assurance of the scientific materialists.

Finally, we need further studies of Howells's role as the most important critic of his generation. His central achievement was his promotion of two disparate geniuses, Henry James and Mark Twain. Not only did he distinguish them from a myriad of lesser talents, but also, especially in his later writings, he laid the groundwork for modern academic criticism. Perhaps, as Crowley has argued, his inadequate appreciation of Dreiser and Edith Wharton signaled the waning of his powers (*Dean* 73–82); yet his silences may have resulted both from philosophical disagreements with these writers and from disappointment at their relatively conventional styles. Toward authors with potential he was usually generous. Though he had reservations concerning the romantic excesses of Norris (Crisler) and the didacticism of Charlotte Perkins Gilman (Karpinski) and Charles W. Chesnutt (McElrath), he furthered the careers of these writers with appraisals endorsed by today's critics. At this writing, Jesse S. Crisler plans to anthologize the essays cited here, along with a number of others on Howells's literary relations. However, what is called for is a major work that would trace Howells's critical contributions while refining the definitions of realism and other key terms.

Large projects, of course, may be daunting for busy professionals, yet we can learn from the realists of earlier generations. In a recent issue of the *American Scholar*, Phyllis Rose makes the case for "Embedding Trollope" as a novelist who can "exercise our attention spans, . . . teach us the lesson of time and the virtue of perseverance, and . . . keep before our eyes the blessings of a democratic society" (6). Howells critic Glen A. Love has suggested that the process of "muddling through" might even have the adaptive value sought by evolutionary biologists (42). For our sake and our students', let us embed Howells.

ACKNOWLEDGMENTS

I wish to thank Jesse S. Crisler, for information on his anthology in progress; Susan Goodman, for invaluable advice on archival material, as well as notice of her forthcoming biography; Roger Stoddard and his assistant Denison Beach, for their hospitality at the Houghton; and the participants at the 2003 conference of the American Literature Association, particularly session chairs Sanford E. Marovitz and Elsa Nettels, for their collegiality and friendship.

WORKS CITED

Anesko, Michael, ed. *Letters, Fictions, Lives: Henry James and William Dean Howells*. New York: Oxford UP, 1997.

Banta, Martha. "The Vicissitudes of 'the Great Particularizer'; or, the Contemporary Case Against Howells." Working papers of the W. D. Howells Memorial Conference, "Howells Studies: Past, Passing, and to Come." Kittery Point, ME. 14 and 15 June 1996.

Bell, Michael Davitt. *The Problem of American Realism: Studies in the Cultural History of a Literary Idea*. Chicago: U of Chicago P, 1993.

Bennett, George N. *The Realism of William Dean Howells, 1889–1920*. Nashville: Vanderbilt UP, 1973.

———. *William Dean Howells: The Development of a Novelist*. Norman: U of Oklahoma P, 1959.

Borus, Daniel H. *Writing Realism: Howells, James, and Norris in the Mass Market*. Chapel Hill: U of North Carolina P, 1989.

Boudreau, Kristin. *Sympathy in American Literature: American Sentiments from Jefferson to the Jameses*. Gainesville: UP of Florida, 2002.

Bramen, Carrie Tirado. "William Dean Howells and the Failure of the Urban Picturesque." *New England Quarterly* 73 (2000): 82–99.
Brooks, Van Wyck. *The Ordeal of Mark Twain.* New York: Dutton, 1920.
Cady, Edwin H. *The Light of Common Day: Realism in American Fiction.* Bloomington: Indiana UP, 1971.
———. *The Realist at War: The Mature Years 1885–1920 of William Dean Howells.* Syracuse: Syracuse UP, 1958.
———. *The Road to Realism: The Early Years 1837–1885 of William Dean Howells.* Syracuse: Syracuse UP, 1956.
———. *Young Howells and John Brown: Episodes in a Radical Education.* Columbus: Ohio State UP, 1985.
Cady, Edwin H., and Louis J. Budd, eds. *On Howells: The Best from "American Literature."* Durham: Duke UP, 1993.
Campbell, Donna M. *Resisting Regionalism: Gender and Naturalism in American Fiction, 1885–1915.* Athens: Ohio UP, 1997.
Carrington, George C., Jr. *The Immense Complex Drama: The World and Art of the Howells Novel.* Columbus: Ohio State UP, 1966.
Carter, Everett. *Howells and the Age of Realism.* Philadelphia: Lippincott, 1954.
Clymer, Jeffory A. "Race and the Protocol of American Citizenship in William Dean Howells' *An Imperative Duty.*" *American Literary Realism* 30.3 (1998): 31–52.
Corkin, Stanley. *Realism and the Birth of the Modern United States: Cinema, Literature, and Culture.* Athens: U of Georgia P, 1996.
Crisler, Jesse S. "Howells and Norris: A Backward Glance." *Nineteenth-Century Literature* 52 (1997): 232–51.
Crowley, John W. *The Black Heart's Truth: The Early Career of W. D. Howells.* Chapel Hill: U of North Carolina P, 1985.
———. *The Dean of American Letters: The Late Career of William Dean Howells.* Amherst: U of Massachusetts P, 1999.
———. "Giving a Character: Howellsian Realism in *The Landlord at Lion's Head.*" *Harvard Library Bulletin* n.s. 5.1 (1994): 53–66.
———. "Howells in *The Heath.*" *New England Quarterly* 72 (1999): 89–101.
———. *The Mask of Fiction: Essays on W. D. Howells.* Amherst: U of Massachusetts P, 1989.
Daugherty, Sarah B. "Howells, Tolstoy, and the Limits of Realism: The Case of *Annie Kilburn.*" *American Literary Realism* 19.1 (1986): 21–41.
———. "The Ideology of Gender in Howells' Early Novels." *American Literary Realism* 25.1 (1992): 2–19.
———. "*An Imperative Duty:* Howells and White Male Anxiety." *American Literary Realism* 30.3 (1998): 53–64.
Gibian, Peter. *Oliver Wendell Holmes and the Culture of Conversation.* Cambridge, UK: Cambridge UP, 2001.
Gibson, William M., and George Arms. *A Bibliography of William Dean Howells.* 1948. New York: Arno P, 1971.
Goodman, Susan. *Civil Wars: American Novelists and Manners, 1880–1940.* Baltimore: Johns Hopkins UP, 2003.
Goodman, Susan, and Carl Dawson. *William Dean Howells: A Writer's Life.* Berkeley: U of California P, forthcoming [2005].
Gopnik, Adam. "A Hazard of No Fortune." *New Yorker* 21 and 28 Feb. 2000: 183–94.
Graff, Gerald. *Professing Literature: An Institutional History.* Chicago: U of Chicago P, 1987.
Habegger, Alfred. *Gender, Fantasy, and Realism in American Literature.* New York: Columbia UP, 1982.
Halfmann, Ulrich, ed. *Interviews with William Dean Howells.* Arlington, TX: *American Literary Realism,* 1973.

Haralson, Eric. *Henry James and Queer Modernity.* Cambridge, UK: Cambridge UP, 2003.

———. "Representing Howells: 'Gender, Sex, and All That Jazz.'" Working Papers of the W. D. Howells Memorial Conference, "Howells Studies: Past, Passing, and to Come." Kittery Point, ME. 14 and 15 June 1996.

———. "Romancing the Beast: Howells' *The Landlord at Lion's Head.*" *American Literary Realism* 25.3 (1993): 42–59.

Harmon, Charles. "*A Hazard of New Fortunes* and the Reproduction of Liberalism." *Studies in American Fiction* 25 (1997): 183–95.

Hedges, Warren. "Howells's 'Wretched Fetishes': Character, Realism, and Other Modern Instances." *Texas Studies in Literature and Language* 38 (1996): 26–50.

Henwood, Dawn. "Complications of Heroinism: Gender, Power, and the Romance of Self-Sacrifice in *The Rise of Silas Lapham.*" *American Literary Realism* 30.3 (1998): 14–30.

Higginson, Thomas Wentworth. *The New World and the New Book: An Address Delivered Before the Nineteenth Century Club of New York City, Jan. 15, 1891, with Kindred Essays.* Boston: Lee & Shepard, 1892.

Howells, Elinor Mead. *If Not Literature: Letters of Elinor Mead Howells.* Ed. Ginette de B. Merrill and George Arms. Columbus: Ohio State UP for Miami U, 1988.

Howells, Mildred, ed. *Life in Letters of William Dean Howells.* 2 vols. New York: Doubleday; London: Heinemann, 1928.

Howells, Polly H. "Mildred Howells as the Father's Daughter: Living within His Lines." *Harvard Library Bulletin* n.s. 5.1 (1994): 9–28.

Howells, William Dean. *Annie Kilburn.* New York: Harper, 1889.

———. *The Complete Plays of W. D. Howells.* Ed. Walter J. Meserve. New York: New York UP, 1960.

———. *Dr. Breen's Practice.* Boston: Osgood, 1881.

———. *The Early Prose Writings of William Dean Howells.* Ed. Thomas Wortham. Athens: Ohio UP, 1990.

———. *Editor's Study.* Ed. James W. Simpson. Troy, NY: Whitston, 1983.

———. "Eighty Years and After." 1919. *Selected Letters, Volume 6: 1912–1920.* Ed. William M. Gibson and Christoph K. Lohmann. Boston: Twayne, 1983. 157–67.

———. *A Hazard of New Fortunes.* 1890. Ed. David J. Nordloh et al. Bloomington: Indiana UP, 1976.

———. "The Home-Towners." *William Dean Howells in St. Augustine.* Ed. William McGuire. Spec. issue of *El Escribano: The St. Augustine Journal of History* 35 (1998): 77–102.

———. *An Imperative Duty.* New York: Harper, 1892.

———. *The Landlord at Lion's Head.* New York: Harper, 1897.

———. *Literary Friends and Acquaintance: A Personal Retrospect of American Authorship.* New York: Harper, 1900; 2nd ed. [including *My Mark Twain*] New York: Harper, 1911.

———. "The Man of Letters as a Man of Business." *Scribner's* 14 (1893): 429–45.

———. *A Modern Instance.* Boston: Osgood, 1882.

———. *New Leaf Mills: A Chronicle.* New York: Harper, 1913.

———. *Pebbles, Monochromes, and Other Modern Poems, 1891–1916.* Ed. Edwin H. Cady. Athens: Ohio UP, 2000.

———. *Prefaces to Contemporaries, 1882–1920.* Ed. George Arms, William M. Gibson, and Frederick C. Marston Jr. 1957. Delmar, NY: Scholars' Facsimiles & Reprints, 1978.

———. *Private Theatricals.* 1875–76. Republished as *Mrs. Farrell.* New York: Harper, 1921.

———. *A Realist in the American Theatre: Selected Drama Criticism of William Dean Howells.* Ed. Brenda Murphy. Athens: Ohio UP, 1992.

———. *The Rise of Silas Lapham.* Boston: Ticknor, 1885.

———. *A Selected Edition of W. D. Howells.* Ed. Edwin H. Cady, Ronald Gottesman, Don L. Cook, and David J. Nordloh. 25 vols. to date. Bloomington: Indiana UP, 1968– / Boston: Twayne, 1979–83.

———. *Selected Short Stories of William Dean Howells.* Ed. Ruth Bardon. Athens: Ohio UP, 1997.

———. *The Son of Royal Langbrith.* New York: Harper, 1904.

———. *Staging Howells: Plays and Correspondence with Lawrence Barrett.* Ed. George Arms, Mary Bess Whidden, and Gary Scharnhorst. Albuquerque: U of New Mexico P, 1994.
———. *The Story of a Play.* New York: Harper, 1898.
———. *The World of Chance.* New York: Harper, 1893.
Howells, William Dean, et al. *The Whole Family.* 1908. Durham: Duke UP, 2001.
James, Henry. *The Tragic Muse.* 2 vols. Boston: Houghton, 1890.
Kaplan, Amy. *The Social Construction of American Realism.* Chicago: U of Chicago P, 1988.
Karpinski, Joanne B. "When the Marriage of True Minds Admits Impediments: Charlotte Perkins Gilman and William Dean Howells." *Patrons and Protégées: Gender, Friendship, and Writing in Nineteenth-Century America.* Ed. Shirley Marchalonis. New Brunswick: Rutgers UP, 1988. 212–34.
Knoper, Randall. "American Literary Realism and Nervous 'Reflexion.'" *American Literature* 74 (2002): 715–45.
Lears, T. J. Jackson. *Something for Nothing: Luck in America.* New York: Viking, 2003.
Love, Glen A. "Slouching towards Altruria: Evolution, Ecology, and William Dean Howells." *Harvard Library Bulletin* n.s. 5.1 (1994): 29–44.
Ludwig, Sämi. *Pragmatist Realism: The Cognitive Paradigm in American Realist Texts.* Madison: U of Wisconsin P, 2002.
Lynn, Kenneth S. *William Dean Howells: An American Life.* New York: Harcourt, 1971.
Marovitz, Sanford E. "Imposing Memories of Ohio in Howells' Late Fiction." American Literature Association Convention. Cambridge, MA. 22 May 2003.
———. "Melville among the Realists: W. D. Howells and the Writing of *Billy Budd.*" *American Literary Realism* 34 (2001): 29–46.
McElrath, Joseph R., Jr. "W. D. Howells and Race: Charles W. Chesnutt's Disappointment of the Dean." *Nineteenth-Century Literature* 51 (1997): 474–99.
Menand, Louis. *The Metaphysical Club.* New York: Farrar, 2001.
Merrill, Ginette de B. "Two Howells Collections." *Resources for American Literary Study* 11 (1981): 81–90.
Monteiro, George. Untitled. Working papers of the W. D. Howells Memorial Conference, "Howells Studies: Past, Passing, and to Come." Kittery Point, ME. 14 and 15 June 1996.
Monteiro, George, and Brenda Murphy, eds. *John Hay–Howells Letters: The Correspondence of John Milton Hay and William Dean Howells.* Boston: Twayne, 1980.
Nettels, Elsa. *Language, Race, and Social Class in Howells's America.* Lexington: UP of Kentucky, 1988.
Olsen, Rodney D. *Dancing in Chains: The Youth of William Dean Howells.* New York: New York UP, 1991.
Parrish, Timothy L. "Howells Untethered: The Dean and 'Diversity.'" *Studies in American Fiction* 23 (1995): 101–17.
Pearl, Matthew. *The Dante Club.* New York: Random, 2003.
Pease, Donald E., ed. *New Essays on "The Rise of Silas Lapham."* Cambridge, UK: Cambridge UP, 1991.
Petrie, Paul R. "Racial Duties: W. D. Howells' *An Imperative Duty.*" American Literature Association Convention. Cambridge, MA. 24 May 2003.
Prettyman, Gib. "The Next Best Thing: Business and Commercial Inspiration in *A Hazard of New Fortunes.*" *American Literary Realism* 35 (2003): 95–119.
Prioleau, Elizabeth Stevens. *The Circle of Eros: Sexuality in the Work of William Dean Howells.* Durham: Duke UP, 1983.
Rennick, Andrew. "'A Good War Story': The Civil War, Substitution, and the Labor Crisis in Howells' *A Hazard of New Fortunes.*" *American Literary Realism* 35 (2003): 247–61.
Rohrbach, Augusta. *Truth Stranger Than Fiction: Race, Realism, and the U. S. Literary Marketplace.* New York: Palgrave, 2002.

Rose, Phyllis. "At Large and at Small: Embedding Trollope." *American Scholar* 72.3 (2003): 5–10.
Rubin, Lance. "The Ambivalence of Memory in (and about) Howells' Late Short Fiction." American Literature Association Convention. Cambridge, MA. 22 May 2003.
Shumway, David R. *Creating American Civilization: A Genealogy of American Literature as an Academic Discipline.* Minneapolis: U of Minnesota P, 1994.
Smith, Henry Nash, and William M. Gibson, eds. *Mark Twain–Howells Letters.* 2 vols. Cambridge, MA: Harvard UP, 1960.
Sorrentino, Paul. "A Re-Examination of the Relationship Between Stephen Crane and W. D. Howells." *American Literary Realism* 34 (2001): 47–65.
Stokes, Claudia. "Reading Howells into American Literary History." American Literature Association Convention. Cambridge, MA. 24 May 2003.
Stretch, Cynthia. "Illusions of a Public, Locations of Conflict: Feeling Like Populace in William Dean Howells' *A Hazard of New Fortunes.*" *American Literary Realism* 35 (2003): 233–46.
Thomas, Brook. *American Literary Realism and the Failed Promise of Contract.* Berkeley: U of California P, 1997.
Thompson, Graham. *Male Sexuality under Surveillance: The Office in American Literature.* Iowa City: U of Iowa P, 2003.
Updike, John. "A Critic at Large: Howells as Anti-Novelist." *New Yorker* 13 July 1987: 78–88.
Vanderbilt, Kermit. *The Achievement of William Dean Howells: A Reinterpretation.* Princeton: Princeton UP, 1968.
Wegener, Frederick. "Imperial Paternity in *The Son of Royal Langbrith.*" American Literature Association Convention. Cambridge, MA. 22 May 2003.
The William Dean Howells Society. Home page. 2 Feb. 2005. <http://guweb2.gonzaga.edu/faculty/campbell/howells/indexa.html>.
Wonham, Henry B. "Writing Realism, Policing Consciousness: Howells and the Black Body." *American Literature* 67 (1995): 701–24.
Woodress, James L., Jr. *Howells and Italy.* Durham: Duke UP, 1952.

Promoting Pennsylvania: Penn, Pastorius, and the Creation of a Transnational Community

PATRICK M. ERBEN
Omohundro Institute of Early American History and Culture and
University of West Georgia

On 7 March 1684, five months after the arrival of the first German settlers in Pennsylvania, Francis Daniel Pastorius (1651–1719) wrote to the Frankfurt Pietists who sponsored German immigration and had appointed him as their agent in America: "[T]wo hours from here [Philadelphia], lies our Germantown, where already forty-two people are living in twelve dwellings. . . . The way from here to Germantown they have now, by frequent going to and fro, trodden out into good shape" (Myers 399).[1] Pastorius's description of a well-trodden path encapsulates—for prospective immigrants in seventeenth- and eighteenth-century Europe, as well as readers today—the manifold exchanges and contacts between English and German immigrants in early Pennsylvania.[2]

Of course, it has become a both popular and scholarly commonplace that Penn's colony attracted a diversity of religious, cultural, and ethnic groups, resulting in a remarkably pluralistic society. Yet scholarship has largely ignored how the literature promoting immigration to Pennsylvania anticipated, theorized, and prepared structures of transnational communication and communal construction.[3] While assuming that "[p]romotional literature acquainted large numbers of people with settlement opportunities," historian Marianne S. Wokeck admits in her recent study of German immigration to colonial America that "[n]o systematic survey and analysis of the promotional literature in the Rhine lands in the eighteenth century exists" (*Trade* 26). If early accounts of Pennsylvania did indeed play a pivotal role in drawing immigrants to the new province (especially from areas along the Rhine), how did they anticipate or prepare immigrants for the cultural, ethnic, and linguistic diversity that scholars have described as the benchmark of community in Penn's province? How did these tracts allow German and English readers to envision the new society, specifically, their contact and interaction with members of a different culture and speakers of a different language?

With this essay, I do not presume to rewrite existing historical or sociological models for the formation of community in early Pennsylvania; I largely build on the extensive historical scholarship describing the settlement of the province and the interaction between English and German immigrants.[4] While scholars agree on the prominence of religious, ethnic, and cultural diversity in the province, they often stress either the acculturation and assimilation of German immigrants or their cultural and ethnic persistence.[5] My work intervenes in these debates by arguing that the promotional texts discussing the nature of community in Pennsylvania reveal how complex discourses and intellectual maps guided the communal encounter with cultural and linguistic difference. Instead of claiming new evidence for concrete communal interactions or an immediate impact of textuality on immigrant subjectivity, I suggest that the promotional literature on early Pennsylvania provided readers with the vocabulary and theoretical frameworks for grasping the possibilities and challenges inherent in forming a transnational, multilingual community. My approach thus focuses on the agency of various literacies in furnishing individuals and groups with multiple avenues for constructing communal identities. Specifically, I attempt through this essay to mend the neglect of the crucial role translation played in the textual negotiation of community—as a practical tool for facilitating translingual communication, as well as a theoretical trope for the encounter with and mediation of difference in general. Rather than tracing concrete evidence for the exchanges Pastorius described as a "frequent going to and fro" between Germantown and Philadelphia, I demonstrate how German and English promotional accounts directly responded to each other and to the prospects of communal difference, thus articulating the possibilities and problems of intercultural contact in early Pennsylvania.

A thoroughly intertextual and comparative reading of English and German promotional tracts—particularly those texts translated and adapted for readers different from the original target audience—reveals a preoccupation with questions of linguistic, cultural, and national difference along with the hope for a widely accepted communal ethics to make life more harmonious and ordered.[6] The literature describing and advertising early Pennsylvania thus prefigured textually the manifold problems and possibilities of communal formation in the new province. Before settlers began to interact with each other, the writers, editors, translators, and booksellers involved in the promotion of the province had paved a textual path of exchange that allowed immigrants to imagine not only their encounter with strange cultures, languages, and political systems but also the possibility for their own transcultural or translingual mobility.[7]

Accounts of early Pennsylvania written by William Penn (1644–1718), Francis Daniel Pastorius, and other authors passed through a process of translation, editorial amendment, and dissemination that adjusted the promotional discourse to culturally and linguistically specific sensibilities. In reading these tracts, prospective German and English immigrants encountered textual examples of cultural flexibility while coming to expect a degree of partisan confrontation. Since the new province was textually represented to various constituencies as a malleable space adapted to their interests, immigrants could feasibly hope to become involved in the future construction of the new community. The heterogeneous textual project of promotion, in other words, projected a participatory model of communal interaction relying on the ability of individuals to contribute to forms of literary negotiation.

This transnational adaptation of the promotional discourse on early Pennsylvania did not proceed in a single direction, from a monolithic English literature to a complex discourse reflecting a German minority position. Without trying to conceal obvious power imbalances in the province, I claim that a scholarly focus on English social and political dominance has unduly marginalized German influence on the structures and the representation of community. In fact, English promotional tracts acknowledged and praised German immigrant contributions to the settlement of early Pennsylvania, particularly the German immigrant's role in building a self-sufficient colonial economy. Textually, the translation and adaptation of the promotional discourse for a non-English readership abridged and dispersed Penn's authority over the construction of community.[8] Translators and editors continually enhanced clauses on religious freedom still weak or obscure in the English originals in order to cater to an audience of German sectarians. Through forms of linguistic and cultural translation, a colonial and promotional project that could have been geared purely toward English imperial expansion instead devolved power and textual authority to non-English promoters who appealed to diverse national and cultural, particularly religious, audiences.

The production and dissemination of German tracts relied on the intercession of local agents and interest groups, such as the Frankfurt Pietists, who were themselves considering settlement in Pennsylvania and distributed Penn's writings among other prospective immigrants. Along with the translation and editorial amendment of the original English accounts, manuscript circulation further decreased Penn's discursive authority and decentralized the power structure of English colonization. Personal letters from immigrants or colonial agents and handwritten copies of printed tracts evoked feelings of communal affect. In turn, promotional literature highlighted personal relationships among prominent German and English individuals involved in the settlement of Pennsylvania as the embodiment of community.

For German readers, in particular, the friendship between William Penn and Francis Daniel Pastorius metaphorically linked both segments of the population.[9] The representation of their relationship emphasized the key role of personal and spiritual congeniality—rather than national affiliation—in generating communal cohesion. This essay focuses primarily on tracts by Penn and Pastorius—as well as their translation or editorial amendment—because they exerted the greatest influence on the popular imagination of Pennsylvania in Europe through most of the late seventeenth and much of the eighteenth century. Readers relied on these texts, not only to learn about the geographic and social features of the province, but also to anticipate their position among the various national and linguistic groups of early Pennsylvania. The promotional writings by Penn and Pastorius eventually were combined in multiauthored publications and left a lasting impression of transnational cooperation among subsequent waves of immigrants.

A comparative reading of the English and German literature promoting immigration to early Pennsylvania urges us to leave behind the English-only landscape of American literary history.[10] This essay contributes to the type of scholarship Werner Sollors initiated with his pathbreaking collection *Multilingual America: Transnationalism, Ethnicity, and the Languages of American Literature*. Although Sollors's call for a "major reexamination of American literature and history in the light of multilingualism" (7) has been widely credited among scholars of American literature, in practice we have hardly begun to attend to his thesis. My work joins what Sollors calls "a large collaborative effort" to write "a comprehensive history of multilingual literature of the United States" (7) by "taking seriously the task of examining the history of discrete language groups and their literary productions, as well as by crossing language boundaries (in comparative work centering on shared themes or genres)" (9). In comparing the promotional literature on early Pennsylvania, we can witness both: the transfer of German and English national traditions to the American colonies and their interaction across cultural and linguistic borders.[11]

In particular, I follow closely the work of Lawrence Venuti by tracing the role of translators and translations in the construction of communities. In his essay "Translation, Community, Utopia," Venuti asserts that translation inscribes a foreign text with the "domestic intelligibilities and interests" (468) of the translating culture, erasing differences in the process. Conversely, translations can preserve idiosyncrasies of the source text and "build a community with foreign cultures, to share an understanding, going so far as to revise and develop domestic values and institutions" (469). Translators who rigorously attend to the communication of foreign values in the target language follow what Venuti terms an "ethical politics of difference" (469). The preservation of the otherness of the foreign text, accordingly, honors the accomplishment and distinctiveness of another culture while aiding the translating culture to develop its understanding through an encounter with difference. Significantly, translators and editors preparing English colonial treatments for publication and dissemination in Germany regularly inscribed these texts with the "domestic intelligibilities" of a German audience. These translators also preserved and highlighted the difference between English and German cultural systems for potential German immigrants in order to anticipate their later communal confrontation with a foreign social and linguistic system.

Strictly adhering to an "ethical politics of difference," these translators performed an additional function of translation Venuti may not have considered. Bilingual and bicultural agents such as Benjamin Furly (1636–1714) did not merely disclose cultural differences to a German audience in order to prepare them for life in a pluralistic society. Translators also deployed their hybrid competencies to inform the English promoters of German cultural subjectivities and practical needs, thus actively trying to rewrite the original discourse of promotionalism. The "ethical politics of difference," in other words, operates in two directions in these tracts—it preserves otherness for a target audience and it relates awareness of difference back to the original, dominant, culture. Translators facilitated the transnational imagination of community in Pennsylvania by rendering difference *mutually* recognizable and meaningful, for English promoters of immigration and for potential German immigrants.

Although Venuti's argument for the agency of translation in constructing communities between culturally and linguistically different groups applies specifically to the properties of print culture today, I consciously use his critical framework to describe the promotional literature on early Pennsylvania. I thus attempt to fill a gap in our knowledge of the roles translation played in the formation of communities during the early modern period. Indeed, I argue that the ability of translation to connect different cultures in a common project of textual signification was even more pronounced in the late seventeenth and early eighteenth century, before print culture had gained its status as the primary locus of public discourse. By describing the relevance of manuscript circulation and the distribution of promotional literature through localized networks of agents, promoters, and prospective immigrants, I call attention to the inchoate status of print culture as an agent in the production of the public sphere during the early modern period. Translation, as well as localized distribution, curbed the ability of a few individuals or institutions to gain control over the representation of community. Specifically, the translator's role as a powerful mediator between a single textual and political authority and various culturally diverse constituencies was instrumental in turning the promotional discourse on early Pennsylvania from a centrally controlled advertising campaign into a heterogeneous textual model for the future negotiation of community.

The Translator's Visibility

Soon after William Penn had gained proprietary rights over Pennsylvania in April 1681, he and a network of publishers, booksellers, and land agents embarked on the project of describing and promoting the province to prospective immigrants in Europe. The dissemination of English promotional tracts among non-English-speaking readers required the consideration of their cultural and religious sensibilities, which produced significant deviations from the repetition of conventional elements established by Penn's first accounts of the province. Penn's accounts were not merely translated; editors, publishers, and translators altered them to appeal to a non-English audience, especially by underlining the principles of religious freedom valued among religious dissenters in Germany and Holland. Crucially, editions aiming at prospective German or Dutch immigrants rarely obscured the role of the translator in preparing translingual and transcultural versions of English promotional tracts.[12] Instead of eclipsing the role of the translator—a problem Venuti describes in his study *The Translator's Invisibility: A History of Translation*—the editions of Penn's promotional texts that were distributed on the Continent explicitly signaled the intervention of a translator or editor. Far beyond highlighting their own work, these translators directed their readers' attention to the theoretical and practical implications of the translation process. A metatextual narrative surrounding these editions explained the nonequivalence inherent in any translation and foregrounded the specific cultural adjustments of the promotional discourse for a non-English readership. Prospective German immigrants, therefore, did not consume virtual equivalents of Penn's tracts in their language, but recognized that his agents and promoters made certain efforts to meet their expectations and needs. The highlighting of the translation process allowed readers to grapple with "incommensurabilities, different ways of comprehending and evaluating the translated text and indeed the world" (Venuti, *Translator's* 342). For readers of these translated texts, the negotiation of difference awaiting German and English immigrants in Pennsylvania became a communal and a textual issue.

Penn's first pamphlet, *Some Account of the Province of Pennsilvania in America* (1681), specifies as the target audience "those of our own, or other Nations, that are inclin'd to Transport themselves or Families beyond the Seas" (1). The targeting of those "other Nations" relied on a network of agents, printers, translators, and editors on the Continent. The agents who coordinated the promotion of Pennsylvania among Dutch and German dissenters, particularly the Dutch-English Quaker Benjamin Furly, tailored the structure and content of Penn's tracts to the specific sensibilities of their readers.[13] The German edition—*Eine Nachricht wegen der Landschaft Pennsilvania in America*—follows the general structure of Penn's *Some Account*; its departures or additions, however, address the shortcomings of the English original as a promotional tool for a German audience while highlighting the inherent pitfalls of the translation process.[14]

The German translation of *Some Account* parenthetically inserts English words and phrases—especially legal and historical terms—in the German text and provides a glossary of the most difficult and important concepts. The bilingual insertions and glossary fulfill the complementary tasks of preparing prospective German immigrants for the strangeness of their linguistic and cultural experience in Pennsylvania and assuring them that the promoters of the province recognize their peculiar position. The anonymous translator introduces this bilingual feature in a preface that foreshadows the linguistic and cultural incongruities German immigrants would encounter in America:

> How difficult, I dare not say impossible, it is to translate adequately and clearly the meanings of many expressions, particularly in the ancient laws and customs of a foreign country and its language, into the High-German, is sufficiently known to those who have dealt with this problem themselves. Therefore, I did not deem it inconvenient here to add both the English words in several instances as well as a short glossary of some of them in the end, hoping that the well-inclined reader will not be offended, but rather to receive it, as it is intended, favorably. (*Eine Nachricht* 2)[15]

This subtle and ambiguous preface on one level justifies the parenthetical insertions of English terms and the English glossary as a crutch or short-cut for overcoming the translator's self-avowed difficulties in transferring specific historical and legal terms from English to German. While presenting this bilingualism as a weakness in his own abilities and politely asking the readers for their forbearance, the translator obliquely yet cleverly instructs prospective immigrants that it would be in their own interest not to rely on seemingly straightforward translations but to learn the English terms and their various connotations themselves.

On a more fundamental level, then, the translator's preface prepares the readers—who are already thought of as immigrants—for the vagaries and uncertainties of a translingual *and* transcultural experience in the new province. In defamiliarizing the German translation through the insertion of English words, the account seems to oppose the primary task of any promotional tract, which was, after all, to familiarize readers in the Old World with unknown and faraway places in the New World. An exclusively German-language account would somewhat mitigate the strangeness of the subject matter, for at least the language would be completely familiar to the German readers. Of course, promotional accounts traditionally performed the seemingly paradoxical combination of describing exotic and utterly strange discoveries while at the same time comparing them to the familiar objects or features of one's one land. In other words, most promotional tracts attempted to familiarize the strange with the use of familiar language.

The translator of Penn's *Some Account* is faced with the dilemma of translating a dual strangeness for readers of the German edition. As a promotional treatment, Penn's account already attempts to "translate" the actual features of a foreign land in addition to the projected characteristics of his colonial vision to readers and prospective immigrants and purchasers in England. The German translator, then, has to transduce an account of a foreign land in a foreign tongue for the readers in Germany. Of course, the translator has no claim on the truthfulness of Penn's relation of the new province of Pennsylvania. Yet, as his concern primarily lies with the translation of Penn's account for German readers, his preface at least attempts to acquaint the readers with a dilemma sufficiently familiar to other translators but often eliminated for readers who are accustomed to consuming writing that is either written in or translated into their mother tongue. For those people who do not speak any foreign language, bilingual or multilingual competence implies a firm knowledge of the correspondences (i.e., the translations) between a mother tongue and a foreign tongue. The translator's preface, however, subtly introduces the problem that competence in a foreign language only increases an individual's awareness of the impossibility of understanding two languages as analog systems of signs denoting (and connoting) the very same concepts. By mentioning the difficulty of translating specific words from a historical or legal context, the preface addresses the awareness of the cultural complexity of language a translator or bilingual individual may have, but can hardly pack into the basic "translation" from one word to another.

Faced with this problem, the translator of *Some Account* chooses not to cover up the remoteness between signifier and signified but to reproduce among his readers his own awareness of the tenuous and vague correspondences between the English language and the German language and their respective systems of cultural and historical meanings. Thus, the German edition of Penn's *Some Account* acquaints German readers with the fact that immigration to Pennsylvania will entail confrontation with an unknown country and sets of foreign linguistic, legal, and social systems. The translator's preface hints at the limitations of any promotional treatment—particularly in translation—in anticipating the immigrant experience. At the same time, however, the partially bilingual structure of this account fulfills the seemingly opposite didactic purpose of preparing these immigrants for their experience by anticipating words and expressions that they will need to understand in order to master their business and comprehend their actions within a community that is culturally and linguistically English. On the one hand, therefore, the translator of the tract stresses difference, strangeness, and the importance of cultural knowledge for the understanding of a linguistic system. By providing in advance the linguistic correspondences that would ease the future understanding of cultural, social, or political circumstances in Pennsylvania, on the other hand, the translator renders difference comprehensible and eases the later acquisition of a situated linguistic and social competence.

The translator's combination of a monolingual German translation of Penn's *Some Account* with the English correspondences and a glossary of terms thus follows Venuti's notion of translation as a catalyst of community. Any German translation of Penn's tracts rendered the promotional enterprise intelligible by substituting meaningful German equivalents for complex social, historical, or legal terms in English, thus inscribing the original with "domestic intelligibilities and interests" (Venuti, "Translation" 468). The translator of *Some Account*, however, knew that this emphasis on domestic knowledge and sensibilities in replacing English terms severed the link between the original and its cultural context. By inserting English terms in parentheses and their explanations in the glossary, the translator performed a complementary task of translation described by Venuti, the creation of "foreign intelligibilities and interests, an understanding in common with another culture, another tradition" ("Translation" 477). Adhering to an "ethical politics of difference," the translator of *Some Account* does not obscure but, rather, highlights the encounter with cultural and linguistic otherness to render difference visible and comprehensible.

Apparently, the translator deemed the charter, or "Patent," granted to Penn by Charles II the most important and most difficult part of the entire tract for his German readers. Virtually all of the parenthetical insertions of English words or terms occur in this section. In the absence of a constitution or set of laws for Pennsylvania, the "Patent" was the closest to a legal text available for the new plantation. The "Patent" lays out the specific rights and obligations to which Penn as a proprietor was bound and ordains the establishment of English Common Law in the province. For most German readers, its legalistic language may have been the first encounter with the concepts and terms of this law. The inserted English terms, therefore, highlight the incongruity between the cultural, social, and political conditions of both countries. The translator realized that competence in the jargons and codes of official English would be crucial for the success of prospective German immigrants in Pennsylvania.[16]

The translator's glossary—titled "a short explanation of a number of English words which appear herein and are uncommon in several other languages and countries" (*Eine Nachricht* 29)[17]—completes the task of adopting the linguistic representation of Penn's account to the needs of prospective immigrants in German. Referring exclusively to words in the "Patent," the glossary explains in detail specific legal or social terms that are particularly difficult to translate because there may not be a German analogue or because the implied concept and historical background do not exist in German culture. In the example of the ancient English term "View of Franke-pledge," the glossary provides a lengthy entry describing not only the current meaning but also its heritage and former usage.[18] The cumbersome explanation of the term illuminates the interplay between familiarization and estrangement inherent in the project of translating English promotional texts for a German audience. An unambiguous monolingual translation would obscure the incongruity between English and German terms and thus erase the differences between the respective legal and cultural systems. By calling attention to this incongruity and adding a historical apparatus, the translator seemingly accomplishes a more complete translation from one system to another, thereby familiarizing German readers with the English system. Paradoxically, these explanations only heighten the perception among these readers of the discrepancy between their own and the respective foreign cultural system.

The adaptation of the promotional discourse across cultural and linguistic divisions was particularly pronounced with regard to the status of religion in the new province. Surprisingly, Penn's first promotional tract nowhere mentions religious toleration—the provision that attracted multitudes of English and German dissenters.[19] In *Some Account*, Penn promises the adoption of a constitution, but does not specify that freedom of conscience will be part of it: "[As] soon as any are ingaged with me, we shall begin a Scheam or Draught together, such as shall give ample Testimony of my sincere Inclinations to encourage Planters, and settle a free, just and industrious Colony there" (5). Sensing that this promise was not specific enough for German readers, the translator added the following clause to Penn's sentence: "and also there to institute the freedom of conscience for anyone to practice their faith and to worship publicly" (*Eine Nachricht* 10).[20]

In grafting the clause on religious liberty onto *Some Account*, the translator or editor was drawing from the precedent Penn had set with his extensive writings on religious freedom before his acquisition of Pennsylvania.[21] In order to bolster the emphasis on religious toleration, the German edition of *Some Account* included a letter arguing in favor of toleration for Quakers that Penn had sent to the magistrates of the cities of Emden and Danzig. The letter was published in English as *Christian Liberty . . . Desired in a Letter to Certain Foreign States* (1674) and in German as *Ein Send-Brieff An Die Bürgermeister und Rath der Stadt Danzig* (1675). In *Eine Nachricht*, Penn's letter is reproduced with a special emphasis on its original printing in "English, Latin, High- and Low-German" (22).[22] German and Dutch readers of the tract, therefore, perceived Penn's promotion of Pennsylvania in light of his earlier activism on behalf of religious liberty; the original printing of the letter in languages other than English also signaled to prospective immigrants that Penn's efforts in defense of religious freedom were not limited to a single national audience.

As promised in his first promotional account, Penn immediately began drafting a constitution for Pennsylvania. The first *Frame of Government of the Province of Pennsilvania in America*, published in May 1682, was the result of some intense political and textual wrangling over the specific rights of the proprietor and the new settlers. The drafting process produced at least twelve preliminary documents and involved Penn's collaboration with several other interested individuals.[23] Furly severely criticized the changes made between the initial draft, "The Fundamentall Constitutions of Pennsylvania," and the *Frame* of 1682. "Fundamentall Constitutions," the most liberal of all the drafts, opened with a proclamation of religious freedom, which had been absent from Penn's first promotional account in English.[24] In the *Frame* published in 1682, however, liberty of conscience was downgraded from the prominent status of a preamble to an almost insignificant position as item number 35. Through a letter to Penn, Furly expressed his indignation over the changes: "Who has turned you aside from these good beginnings, to [establish] things unsavory & unjust; as fundamental to wch all Generations to come should be bound?" (Penn, *Papers* 2: 235). Furly objected to the less prominent position of religious toleration, as well as to the absence of any regulation against excessive litigation. Thus, Furly attempted to communicate to Penn his insight into the interpenetration of the legal and religious sensibilities of German and Dutch immigrants: "Consider further that there are many Christians in holland [sic] & Germany that look upon it as unlawfull to sue any man at the Law, as to fight wth armes[.] These then having no other fence but their prudence in intrusting none but honst [sic] men" (Penn, *Papers* 2: 232). Furly claimed that inheritance laws and a xenophobic naturalization policy disadvantaged non-English immigrants.[25] The second *Frame* adopted in Pennsylvania in 1683 did not grant Furly's open naturalization policy, yet it conferred the "property and inheritance rights of citizens" (Soderlund 266) to all foreigners having purchased land in Pennsylvania. Furly, the promoter of Penn's enterprise in Germany and Holland, thus attended to the "ethical politics of difference" in relating the interests of his constituents to the proprietor and in attempting to change the original discourse through a confrontation with "foreign intelligibilities."

Admittedly, Furly's success in molding the laws of Pennsylvania to the advantage of German and Dutch immigrants was limited. Nevertheless, he was able to use his power as editor and translator of subsequent promotional pamphlets to highlight existing provisions that were profitable for his constituents in Germany and Holland yet had been discursively demoted in English laws and promotional tracts. After his arrival in Pennsylvania in 1682, Penn published his *Letter to the Free Society of Traders* (1683), which became a textual focal point for promoters in England, Holland, and Germany. In his preface to the German translation, titled *Beschreibung der in America neu-erfundenen Provinz Pensylvanien* (1684), Furly highlights, somewhat self-servingly, his disputes with Penn and elevates the qualities of the new province he deemed most attractive to potential German immigrants.[26] The preface relegates Penn's account to the background and assures German readers that their sensibilities influenced the construction and representation of community in the province.

Furly's extensive preface to *Beschreibung* assured prospective immigrants from Germany that specific measures were being taken to attract and integrate them in the settlement process. It adds much practical information regarding the purchase of land and the laws of the province—particularly religious toleration, which had been stipulated in the *Frame of Government* yet was again missing from Penn's latest promotional tract. Furly scathingly explains that his preface augments the shortcomings of Penn's tract: "Since not one word is being said therein about the manner and conditions according to which the governor sells his land and also nothing about the laws [of the province], I deemed [it] necessary to instruct you herein" (2).[27] Realizing that Penn's "promotional" tract omitted those qualities and aspects of the province that would have contributed most to its promotion among Germans, Furly virtually took it upon himself to place the most effective elements of the Pennsylvanian experiment in the very front of the tract.

While Furly's preface does not change or add anything to the laws and institutions already in place in Pennsylvania, it does summarize and highlight clauses that had been stipulated in the *Frame of Government* but *not* in the promotional tracts. The preface specifies at length what immigrants from different social positions—landowners, tenants, servants, and children—would have to expect in the province. Furly explains that those families who are able to pay for the passage but not for their land will receive fifty acres per person in hereditary tenancy for only a nominal amount (3). Both these tenants and their children and servants— once they had come of age or finished their term of service—would become freeholders who would obtain extensive political rights, including the right to vote "not only in elections for the authorities in the places where they live, but for the council and a general assembly, which constitute together with the governor the highest government and authority; and, moreover, the freeholders will themselves be elected into a number of offices if they are deemed fit to do so by the community where they live, all without discrimination with regard to the *nation* or *religion* to which they belong" (Penn, *Beschreibung* 4; emphasis added).[28] Familiar with the lack of political rights among the peasantry in the absolutist German principalities at the time, Furly highlighted the laws of the new province that would elevate these disenfranchised groups to the status of citizens with a political voice. He also underscored the crucial link between political and religious freedom by explicitly mentioning that discrimination against individuals based on religious affiliation would be eliminated in Pennsylvania. Immigration, in other words, would be able to mend the inequities plaguing society in Europe, particularly in the absolutist principalities of Germany.

In order to stress political enfranchisement more explicitly, Furly explained that the system of elections for government in Pennsylvania eliminated both fraud and reprisals through the implementation of secret ballots. A government determined through universal and secret ballot was unfamiliar to most German immigrants and required such special mention. Furly emphasized the reduction of lawsuits through the orderly recording of all immovable goods and estates, as well as large or long-term debts. As in his criticism of Penn's *Frame of Government,* Furly geared his preface to the specific aversion to civil litigation among his German constituents, particularly Protestant dissenters. Finally, Furly summarized or paraphrased the laws that most concerned prospective German immigrants. This section included the provisions stipulating freedom of conscience and ordinances for public morality. In order to separate the affairs of church and state, Furly explains, the laws of Pennsylvania stipulate that "no official church shall be introduced, and no one shall be threatened or forced to pay any contribution for any religious gathering or any preacher" (5).[29] In other words, the laws of Pennsylvania eliminated the tithes German citizens were forced to pay in support of a state-sponsored church. The separation of church and state was also to prevent the domination of certain government offices through members of specific denominations. Freedom of conscience not only granted individual liberty in matters of faith but also freed political culture from religious sectionalism.

While the axiom of religious freedom determined political culture, it also influenced the life and manners of the community in a more general sense. Furly knew that religious dissidents from Germany particularly welcomed freedom from religious oppression but would abhor the loss of social conventions that checked public indecency, crime, and any antisocial or amoral behavior.[30] Even though English Quakers shared similar expectations and anxieties about the new province, the original English text of Penn's *Frame of Government* obscured or relegated to less prevalent places the passages that addressed the balance between liberty and social restraint. In his preface, Furly highlighted the fact that the proper balance between freedoms and social controls would be instituted in the new province. On the one hand, the laws of Pennsylvania promised that "everyone may enjoy liberty of conscience, which all meek and peaceful people should have and are entitled to by nature, it has been determined that not only should nobody be forced to attend a certain public performance of worship, but further everyone should possess the full liberty to conduct their own public worship" (Penn, *Beschreibung* 5). On the other hand, rules were established to "prevent everything that could cause and provide occasion to bring people to vanity, frivolity, impudence and audacity, godlessness, and a dissolute life and tempt them to desecrate the name of the Lord." Specifically forbidden was a long list of vices, including "gambling," "comedies," "cursing," "incest," "haughty dress," "prostitution," "dueling," and "toasts and drunkenness." Furly explains his motivation to name this illustrious list of moral degeneracy, which "I considered necessary to mention here in order to encourage even more all good and pious people who are inclined to move there and to ensure that the others ought not to imagine that they might be free to live there in all their vices" (6).[31] This passage reflects both the hopes and the anxieties that German immigrants projected onto the political and social conditions in the province and explains why much of their writing in the new world balances seemingly contradictory notions of individual liberty and communal control.[32] Furly thus inscribed the English laws of the province thoroughly with German cultural interests and transformed Penn's *Letter to the Free Society of Traders* into an effective tool for the promotion of immigration among his German and Dutch constituents.

Building a Community of "Christian Friends"

With the crucial textual changes made by Furly and other translators or editors, the German versions of English promotional accounts of Pennsylvania specifically catered to the expectations of those German separatists whom Penn had visited during a missionary trip down the Rhine in 1677. A few years later, Penn's agents relied on such personal contacts in disseminating his promotional tracts in Germany and Holland. When a strong demand made printed volumes scarce, German promoters circulated handwritten transcriptions among their friends. Furly sent both personal letters and printed accounts to the Frankfurt Pietists whom Penn had visited in 1677 and to interested individuals such as the Lübeck pastor Jaspar Könneken (1629–1715).[33] In turn, these groups or individuals produced manuscript transcriptions of printed texts or personal letters. Könneken assembled an impressive manuscript collection of primary accounts from Pennsylvania, including letters or tracts by Penn, Pastorius, and other English, German, and Dutch writers. Passing through this network, the promotional discourse not only was adapted to the social and political predicaments of local audiences but also gained a deeply personal dimension. Penn's own presence in these accounts was paired with the social and spiritual bonds among local communities.

Manuscript circulation of promotional tracts on Pennsylvania throughout Germany may have rivaled the spread of printed material on this issue.[34] Since handwritten copies of printed promotional tracts could be produced informally and on demand, central participants in the promotional process could disseminate information without relying on the availability of printed tracts. Successive printed accounts responded explicitly to the demand for and the resulting dearth of promotional tracts on Pennsylvania. In the preface to the German translation of Penn's *Letter to the Free Society of Traders*, Furly acknowledged that "the former brief account of the province of Pennsylvania, printed in the year 1681, is not easily to be found now" (*Beschreibung* 2).[35] Manuscript transmission of printed texts or unpublished letters filled the gaps between successive printed tracts and increased the reach of the promotional project. Similar to printed accounts, manuscripts assumed the public function of informing a large audience about the settlement of Pennsylvania. Unlike printed tracts, however, manuscript copies of promotional texts created the semblance of private communication and thus generated an imagined bond of affection between author and reader.

An extant manuscript copy of Penn's *Letter to the Free Society of Traders* located in the Historical Society of Pennsylvania combines the formality and authority of printed accounts with the intimacy of manuscript communication.[36] The manuscript, "Ein Brief von William Penn Eigenthumbs Herrn und Befehlshabern in PENNSYLVANIA" ["A Letter from William Penn, Proprietor and Governor in Pennsylvania"], contains no introductory matter or title page, but immediately starts with the title and the address "Meine werthen freunde" ("My dear friends"). Without the title page specifying the Society of Traders in London as the original recipients of the letter, such an address seems to speak directly to the readers of the manuscript in Germany. Further, the manuscript produces no reference regarding transcription or translation and thus gives the impression of an original letter from Penn to his friends in Germany. Most important, the letter is written in the old script common in Germany until the early twentieth century. Reading a handwritten letter in German script not only enhanced the inscription of foreign texts with "domestic intelligibilities" but also added *personal* intelligibilities. The manuscript transmission of Penn's *Letter to the Free Society of Traders* created a sense of familiarity between the author and the recipient that would elude a printed edition. At the same time, the perfectly linear, clear, neat, and formal presentation of the transcription allows the assumption that this manuscript was not prepared for the personal use of the scribe or translator. Instead, this transcription most likely was produced with a number of copies for distribution to interested individuals and prospective immigrants. Manuscript transmission, in other words, rendered the promotional project personal and private even as it allowed a widespread public dissemination.

Manuscript circulation thus forged a discursive sphere of promotionalism that allowed its participants to imagine a personal connection between themselves and the proprietor and, by extension, between themselves and the province as a whole. At the same time, individual readers and prospective immigrants relied on a chain of interlocutors who translated, copied, and distributed such texts, diminishing Penn's textual authority over the representation of Pennsylvania. As opposed to printed accounts that could be shipped to booksellers in large cities after having been produced by a central printing house, manuscript transmission required the active participation of groups and individuals who shared a personal interest in furthering the colonial project. German immigrants to Pennsylvania perceived the discourse of promotion through the inflection of communal networks that mediated the delivery and reception of these texts.

Pastorius's experience of first learning about Penn's province from his Pietist friends in Frankfurt is modulated by different modes of transmission—oral, manuscript, and print—as well as a local community of affect that triggers his desire to immigrate. In a retrospective biographical account, Pastorius writes,

> I . . . was glad to enjoy the ancient familiarity of my . . . Acquaintances . . . especially of those Christian Friends who frequently assembled together in a house, called the Saalhof . . . who sometimes made mention of William Penn & of Pennsilvania, and moreover communicated unto me as well some private letters from Benjamin Furly, as also a printed Relation concerning the sd province, and finally the whole Secret could not be withholden from me, viz. that they purchased 15000. Acres of land in this remote part of the world, some of 'em entirely resolv'd to transport themselves, families & all; this begat such a desire in my Soul to continue in their Society, and with them to lead a quiet, godly & honest life in a howling wilderness. (*Bee-Hive* 221)[37]

Penn's printed tract is embedded within manifold other factors influencing Pastorius's decision to immigrate to Pennsylvania. What is perhaps most striking about Pastorius's account is the prominence he allots to the domestic community of the Pietists and the lure of continuing in their company.[38] Penn's publications thus gained their greatest efficacy, not as textual emblems of a centralized, national project of colonization, but as agents within a complex local network of personal and textual relationships. If the colonial project were to succeed through this transnational but locally adapted process of textual dissemination, the colonial community projected in these writings had to transcend English national or imperial interest as well.

In his most popular tract, the *Letter to the Free Society of Traders*, Penn defines Pennsylvania as such a community of affect between himself and members of different ethnicities and nations. His preface juxtaposes the disparagement he received in his own country with an image of multinational and multiethnic unity:[39] "But if I have been Unkindly used by some I left behind me, I found Love and Respect enough where I came; a universal kind Welcome, every sort in their way. For here are some of several Nations, as well as divers Judgments: Nor were the Natives wanting in this, for their Kings, Queens and Great Men both visited and presented me; to whom I made suitable Returns" (*Letter* 1).[40] While Penn had invited people from "other Nations" to immigrate to Pennsylvania in *Some Account*, now immigrants "of several Nations" awaited the governor upon his arrival. His detractors in England had to learn a lesson from foreigners and Indians in terms of tolerance and forbearance. Penn's gesture in turning from domestic squabbles to a "universal kind Welcome" in Pennsylvania synecdochically links the figure of the governor as a universally welcome person to the province as a universally welcoming community. Through this rhetorical maneuver, Penn promotes his province as a transnational community of mutual affection.

Pastorius's hopes to transplant to Pennsylvania the affection he had found within the Pietist community in Frankfurt were thwarted by the group's failure to follow their agent into this "howling wilderness." While retaining his official assignment to promote and administer a German settlement in the province, Pastorius found personal and spiritual affinity in relationships with many English immigrants, particularly William Penn. Pastorius's first letter to his Frankfurt friends—published as a promotional tract titled *Sichere Nachricht* (*Positive Information*) in Germany—ostensibly evaluates the chances of an exclusively German community, but his appraisal of Penn values intellectual and spiritual consanguinity over national affiliation in the construction of community in Pennsylvania.[41]

According to *Sichere Nachricht*, the affection between the two men relied strongly on common visions for the spiritual and social development of the province and on bonds of a common intellectual heritage, including the mastery of Latin and French.[42] Penn and Pastorius clearly enjoyed each other's company in spite of protracted negotiations over the land purchased by the Frankfurt investors. Pastorius reports that Penn "often invites me to his table and has me walk and ride in his always edifying company; and when I lately was absent from here a week . . . and he had not seen me for that space of time, he came himself to my little house and besought me that I should at least once or twice a week be his guest" (Myers 396).[43] Passing by the house Pastorius had built in Philadelphia, Penn read the Latin motto from Vergil's *Aeneid* above the door: "Parva domus sed amica bonis, procul este prophani" ["A little house, but a friend to the good; remain at a distance, ye profane"] (Myers 404; *Sichere* 5). Pastorius proudly reports that Penn was pleased by his inscription. Penn and Pastorius thus shared the cosmopolitan intellectual heritage of the late Renaissance, epitomized by their common knowledge of classical languages and literature. Elite members of the inchoate settlement were able to transfer existing bonds of European intellectualism to the new province and harness these initial ties for the construction of a transnational community in Pennsylvania.

If the congeniality provided by an elite European education was beyond the reach of most immigrants, a shared vision of spiritual renewal under Pennsylvania's motto of "brotherly love" could attract religious dissenters from any class or social standing. Pastorius's praise of Penn thus moves Christian fellowship and love to the center of communal bonding in the province:

> I, on the following day, delivered to William Penn the letters that I had, and was received by him with amiable friendliness; of that very worthy man and famous ruler I might properly . . . write many things; but my pen . . . is much too weak to express the high virtues of this Christian—for such he is indeed. . . . He heartily loves the [*Germans*],

and once said openly in my presence to his councillors and those who were about him, I love the [*Germans*] and desire that you also should love them. Yet in any other matter I have never heard such a command from him. . . . I can at present say no more than that William Penn is a man who honors God and is honored by Him, who loves what is good and is rightly beloved by all good men. I doubt not that some of them will come here and by their own experience learn, that my pen has in this case not written enough. (Myers 396–97; emphasis added)[44]

Pastorius's elaboration of Penn's welcome corresponds to Penn's description of his own reception in the province by members of various nations. Curiously, Pastorius here seems to espouse the notion of transnational unity crystallized in Penn as a symbolic figure while stressing the proprietor's bias in favor of the Germans in particular.

Yet Pastorius's apparent joy over Penn's favoritism toward one particular national group, the Germans, is, ironically, an error of interpretation readers today will inevitably make by relying on the only available translation, prepared by Gertrude Selwyn Kimball in the early twentieth century. The translator inserted the national group marker "Germans" in the blanks left in the original printed version of Pastorius's *Sichere Nachricht*. Kimball simply assumed that Pastorius represented all Germans and that Penn expressed his preference for all Germans. In fact, a comparison between the printed version of *Sichere Nachricht* and a handwritten transcription—possibly from Pastorius's original letter— in the Könneken manuscript yields "Ffr" or "Frankfurter" (356) as the text that was erased in the printed version.[45] Penn, in other words, praised the Frankfurt Pietists whom he had visited on his missionary trip in 1677 and who had subsequently purchased a tract of land in Pennsylvania. The Pietist sponsors who formed the "Frankfurt Land Company" to manage their estate in Pennsylvania may have omitted this specific reference in printing *Sichere Nachricht* as a promotional text because it was too specific for a tract disseminated throughout Germany. Another possible explanation is that the Frankfurt Pietists noticed the rhetorical goal Pastorius pursued in emphasizing Penn's preference for them.

In fact, Pastorius actually rebukes his Frankfurt sponsors because he already sensed that they hesitated—and would ultimately fail—to live up to their promise of transplanting their Christian community to America. Consequently, Pastorius begins to expose the economic rather than spiritual logic that binds him to the Frankfurt group. Sensing that their relationship was primarily one between investors and their agent— rather than between mutual friends—Pastorius refuses to turn his account into a standard promotional tract that exaggerates the features of the land in order to enhance the economic opportunities of a colony or settlement. From Columbus onward, explorers and settlers in the New World deployed their own inability to do justice to the marvels of their discoveries—such as monstrous animals or luscious landscapes—as a trope to increase their readers' sense of wonder and expectation of financial exploits.[46] Pastorius, in contrast, describes the character of a seemingly familiar person—Penn—in terms of discovery and wonder, ultimately resulting in the failure of representation itself. Only personal experience, according to Pastorius, can do justice to Penn's character. Yet, unlike the dangerous encounters with the unknown that had been presaged by other promotional accounts, a meeting with Penn would be completely benign and also promise great spiritual advancement. Thus, Pastorius subtly implicates the Pietists' reluctance to join him, for, assuming they count themselves among "all good men," they would find only love and affection in coming to Pennsylvania while their failure to immigrate would taint their very integrity and sincerity. In light of Penn's specific preference for the Frankfurt Pietists, their unwillingness to live up to the promise they made Pastorius before his immigration—to settle together in a howling wilderness—becomes even more inexcusable.

Pastorius's explicit invocation of biweekly dinner invitations from Penn, as well as joint walks or rides through the woods, exchanges the "ancient familiarity" he had formerly felt for his "Christian Friends" in Frankfurt for a similar affinity for the English proprietor. In *Sichere Nachricht*, therefore, Pastorius abandons the emphasis on economic opportunity common in traditional promotional tracts and focuses entirely on the question of spiritual community. *Sichere Nachricht* ends in a Christian allegory that deploys the language of natural abundance and fruitfulness at the heart of most promotional tracts to evaluate the spiritual progress of community:

> Ah, dear friends, I could well wish that with this eagle's quill I could express the love I bear you and could convince you indeed that it is not a mere lip-love but one that desires more good for you than for myself. My heart is bound to yours by the bonds of love. Then let us now grow up together as trees which the right hand of God has planted by streams of water, that we may bring forth not only leaves but fruit in good season: fruits of repentance, fruits of peace, fruits of righteousness. For what profits such a useless tree, though the gardener spares it yet for some years, digs about it with all diligence and cultivates it, yet finally, no improvement following, cuts it down and casts it into the oven? (Myers 410)[47]

Pastorius toys with the stock ingredients of the promotional genre while transferring its figures of speech to a spiritual agenda. He exhorts his friends not to seek wealth in a faraway land but to achieve spiritual and moral improvements. In Pastorius's *Sichere Nachricht*, the value of the land is determined by the purpose of the people who inhabit it. By reminding his friends of "the bonds of love" tying them together, he virtually disbands the legal, the economic, and even the national affiliations that obligated him to represent his sponsors in Pennsylvania and, ultimately, to write his report.[48]

Given Pastorius's implicit comparison of his "friends" with fruitless trees, one might expect that his Frankfurt sponsors would have suppressed his letter instead of publishing and distributing it as a promotional account. Yet they recognized that Pastorius's invocation of spiritual community in Pennsylvania and, particularly, his congeniality with Penn appealed to other potential immigrants who valued religious renewal above economic improvement. In fact, the Frankfurt Pietists deployed the Christian friendship between Penn and Pastorius as a promotional device in later publications. In the 1700 pamphlet *Umständige Geographische Beschreibung* (*Circumstantial Geographical Description*), the Frankfurt sponsors attached to a revised version of *Sichere Nachricht* a letter from Penn to Pastorius's father. Penn's appraisal of Pastorius perfectly mirrors Pastorius's own paean to the proprietor. Penn writes, "Your son was recently among the living and is even now in Philadelphia. This year he is justice of the peace, or was so very lately. Furthermore, he is called a man sober, upright, wise, and pious, of a reputation approved on all hands and unimpeached" (Myers 445).[49] Of course, this letter serves as an authenticating device to support the truthfulness of the foregoing account by Pastorius. On another level, Penn's appraisal of Pastorius allowed prospective immigrants from Germany to picture themselves—maybe vicariously—in a similar position. Since the integrity of Pastorius's character mattered most to the proprietor, their own virtue—rather than their national affiliation or prosperity—would allow them to gain access to a similar community of affect. Even though the Frankfurt Pietists had abandoned any thought of settling in Pennsylvania, they adjusted their promotional efforts to the sensibilities or "intelligibilities" of their audience.

Yet the publication of Pastorius's *Sichere Nachricht* by his spiritually fruitless and more materially inclined friends in Frankfurt testifies to the discursive flexibility and broad appeal of the promotional literature on Pennsylvania. Just as the editorial adjustment of English tracts allowed German readers to identify with and participate in the settlement of the province, the interpenetration of ostensibly competing discourses of religious renewal and economic improvement appealed to diverse constituencies in England and Germany. Transnational cooperation could be found not only in the token friendship between Penn and Pastorius, but also in the more mundane economic interactions of English and German settlers in Pennsylvania. The explicit mention of German immigrant contributions to a colonial economy in English promotional tracts fulfilled the dual purpose of making difference visible while familiarizing it through the inscription with "domestic intelligibilities." English readers, in other words, learned about the presence of "foreign" immigrants in Pennsylvania through an appraisal of their productivity and skill. For an English audience, these tracts rendered diversity acceptable or even desirable by inserting it into the context of a thriving colonial economy.

From Brotherly Love to a Reciprocal Economy

After evoking a transnational community of affect in the preface to his 1683 *Letter to the Free Society of Traders,* Penn resumed this theme in another promotional tract, *A Further Account of the Province of Pennsylvania and Its Improvements,* published in 1685.[50] While the scene at Penn's arrival projected that "Love and Respect" could provide cohesion to a nationally and ethnically diverse community, his description two years later emphasized that pluralism ensured economic and civic success: "The People are a Collection of divers Nations in Europe: As, French, Dutch, Germans, Sweeds, Danes, Finns, Scotch' Irish, and English; and of the last equal to all the rest: And which is admirable, not a Reflection on that Account. But as they are of one kind, and in one Place, and under One Allegiance, so they live like People of One County [sic]; which Civil Union has had a considerable influence towards the prosperity of that Place" (*Further* 3). Penn's version of *e pluribus unum* works because people from different European nations are united by a common civic purpose. The clause that the English are still "equal to all the rest" may be designed to dispel misgivings about cultural and linguistic diversity among Penn's English readers; however, what matters most to the proprietor is not a continued English dominance, but the unified agenda of the different immigrant groups. In Pennsylvania, civic unity replaces national or cultural homogeneity. Significantly, Penn's account does not merely describe a reality he meets with in Pennsylvania; it promotes a vision of transnational cooperation to his readers, particularly in England.

While translators, editors, and a network of individuals adapted the promotional discourse to attract German or Dutch immigrants to Pennsylvania, English texts, in turn, praised the diverse groups aggregating in the province. Most prominently, these accounts asserted that the transnational cooperation made good business sense. Writers recognized that specific immigrant groups, such as the German and Dutch settlers living at Germantown, possessed skills or qualities that contributed uniquely to the proper functioning of a colonial economy. Printed in Penn's *Further Account*, a letter by Robert Turner reports that "[t]he Manufacture of Linnen by the Germans goes on finely, and they make fine Linnen: Samuel Carpenter having been lately there, declares, they had gathered one Crop of Flax, and had sowed for the Second, and saw it come up well: And they say, might have had forwarder and better, had they had old seed, and not stayd so long for the Growth of the new seed to sow again. I may believe it, for large hath my experience been this Years, though in a small peece of Ground, to the admiration of many" (14). Turner's letter does not produce the detached reporting of an English settler about the separate activities of a different immigrant group. The writer himself follows the German progress and expertise in growing flax with great interest because he raises the same product and testifies to a similar experience as his German neighbors. The personal involvement of Samuel Carpenter, one of the richest and most influential English merchants in early Pennsylvania, confirms that German and English settlers had established active links worthy of admiration.

Just as Pastorius observed a beaten path of exchange between Germantown and Philadelphia, English writers discovered a web of economic relationships between English and German settlers. In the first promotional poem about Pennsylvania, Richard Frame (fl. 1692) describes the material and physical interconnectedness of both groups. Frame enumerates the various settlements in the province, but of all the towns he mentions, only Philadelphia and Germantown merit close attention:

> Philadelphia, that great Corporation,
> Was then, is now our choicest Habitation,
> Next unto that there stands the German-Town.
> (7)

The following section on the economic contributions of Germantown residents demonstrates that it is not merely geographic proximity that brings German and English settlers together. Frame describes the linen and paper industry in Germantown at length. The codependency of both trades becomes a metaphor for the close interactions between German producers and English consumers:

> The German-Town, of which I spoke before,
> Which is, at least, in length one Mile and More,
> Where lives High-German People, and Low-Dutch,
> Whose Trade in weaving Linnin Cloth is much,

> There grows the Flax, as also you may know,
> That from the same they do divide the Tow;
> Their Trade fits well within this Habitation,
> We find Convenience for their Occupation
> One Trade brings in imployment for another,
> So that we may suppose each Trade a Brother;
> From Linnin Rags good Paper doth derive,
> The first Trade keeps the second Trade alive:
> Without the first the second cannot be,
> Therefore since these two can so well agree,
> Convenience doth approve to place them nigh,
> One in the German-Town, 'tother hard by.
> A Paper Mill neare German-Town doth stand,
> So that the Flax, which first springs from the Land,
> First Flax, then Yarn, and then they must begin,
> To weave the same, which *they* took pains to spin.
> Also, when on *our* backs it is well worn,
> Some of the same remains Ragged and Torn;
> Then of those Rags *our* Paper it is made,
> Which in process of time doth waste and fade.
>
> (7; emphasis added)

The German manufacturing of linen and paper participates in an organic cycle of production and consumption in which one station depends on the other. By 1690, Germantown settlers had established a thriving textile industry and, as a joint venture between Samuel Carpenter (1650–1714) and William Rittenhouse (1644–1708), the community had established the first paper mill in North America.[51]

Though Frame does not specifically identify the consumers of the linen and paper, his use of pronouns reveals that all members of the community, including English residents such as himself, use and enjoy the Germantown productions. While "*they* took pains to spin" the yarn that makes the cloth, "on *our* backs it is well worn," and, once torn, "of those Rags *our* Paper it is made." Since Frame's poem is published in Philadelphia, the very paper on which it was printed came, by implication, from the German paper mills. According to Frame's promotional poem, therefore, German and English community life in early Pennsylvania was both literally and metaphorically interwoven. English consumers were aware of the central role of the German contribution to the economy of the province and, by implication, to its publishing and printing. The continuation of the textual promotion of Pennsylvania— through tracts or poems such as Frame's work—depended in part on the German immigrants' material productions.

In his 1698 tract *An Historical and Geographical Account of the Province and Country of Pensilvania,* the English immigrant Gabriel Thomas (dates unknown; resided in Pennsylvania from 1682 to 1697) elaborated and praised the same productions as Frame: "All sorts of good Paper are made in the German-Town; as also very fine German Linen, such as no Person of Quality need be asham'd to wear" (42). Thomas's emphasis on the adequacy of the German linen, I argue, does not split the community into a working-class minority responsible for production and an English elite endowed with the means and leisure to consume these goods. In the fledgling colonial economy of early Pennsylvania, the domestic production of clothes and paper significantly reduced importation from England and kept scarce currency in the local market. The vitality of the colonial project thus relied to a large degree on the manufactures produced by German immigrants. English promotional tracts readily acknowledged this vital contribution and predisposed potential English immigrants, as well as established Pennsylvanians, to view German settlers as crucial members of a viable and, evidently, transnational community.

The writers, translators, and publishers who promoted Pennsylvania among prospective German immigrants thus adjusted existing English materials for the sensibilities of their constituents. German readers and prospective immigrants perceived the province as a sphere they could mold through their participation in textual and material exchange. Pastorius's personal friendship with the proprietor allowed German readers and prospective settlers to anticipate the possibility of communal coherence and affection across national or linguistic boundaries. The proprietor, William Penn, and other English writers of the period recognized the integral role of German immigrants in the life of the province, particularly its economy. Just as Frame's poem described how German productions and English consumption of textiles and paper made "each Trade a Brother," the promotional literature on Pennsylvania proclaimed that the diverse people of early Pennsylvania might be that closely related as well. The textual promotion of Penn's experiment, therefore, anticipated a transnational model of interaction in the province. Among successive generations of German immigrants, the transnational element of the promotional discourse on Pennsylvania created the hope and desire to participate in the negotiation of community.

Coda: The Stories They Told

Rising European demand for any written descriptions of Penn's new province eventually led publishers and booksellers to issue compilations of various accounts about Pennsylvania and to exceed the market value of individual publications. Because these composite texts frequently included accounts by English and German writers such as Penn, Pastorius, and Thomas, they enhanced the transnational character of the promotional discourse. Pastorius's *Umständige Geographische Beschreibung*, published in 1700, was actually a composite of various reports and letters he had written over a span of about fifteen years printed alongside translations of an excerpt from Penn's *Letter to the Free Society of Traders* and Thomas Paskell's *An Abstract of a Letter*, both originally published in 1683. Again, editorial insertions in Pastorius's *Beschreibung* highlighted the transnational adaptation and translation of the English components. A note to the excerpt from Penn's *Letter to the Free Society of Traders* appended to Pastorius's *Beschreibung* explains that "the previous report was first written in the English language and then translated into the High-German and published by Heinrich Heusch in 1684" (37).[52] Successive editions of Pastorius's *Beschreibung* in 1702 and 1704 even increased the composite and transnational textual enterprise of promotion. For both editions, publisher Andreas Otto appended a translation of Gabriel Thomas's *Historical and Geographical Account* (1698) and, published for the first time, Daniel Falckner's *Curieuse Nachricht von Pensylvania in Norden-America* ("Curious News from Pennsylvania in North America").[53] As with earlier adaptations of Penn's tracts for a German audience, these composite editions of German and English promotional texts increased the impression among German readers that transnational discursive representation of Pennsylvania signified a similar negotiation of community in the province.[54]

One might argue, of course, that the transnational cooperation in the representation of early Pennsylvania was nothing but a textual chimera created by profit-oriented publishers and booksellers. After all, the promotional literature may have produced an ideal of cultural interaction unsubstantiated by actual communal practices. Yet I argue that textuality—even the promotional tracts published and consumed in Europe—can provide proof of intricate relationships between diverse immigrant groups in Pennsylvania. In conclusion, I would like to suggest that members of both groups early on came to tell each other, as well as readers in Europe, similar stories of their new American home. In fact, I argue that these stories are so similar in word and spirit that only a joint interest in and conversation about the nature of community can account for such correspondences.

Specifically, English and German accounts largely agreed in evaluating the manners and customs of Native American life in the province. Based on their experience with the Delaware or Lenni Lenape people, most writers—particularly Quakers—interpreted the apparent modesty, simplicity, and religious devotion of the native population as evidence of Pennsylvania's potential for spiritual renewal among European immigrants. By coupling accounts of a peaceful Native American population with stories of the peaceful and just nature of Penn's dealings with these people, promotional literature—both English and German—painted an image of harmonious or even utopian interaction between vastly different people. The exuberant confirmation of the success of Penn's "holy experiment" in embracing a people formerly branded as "savage," however, relied largely on their textual exclusion from a definition of community. Ultimately, this textual marginalization accompanied and theorized the physical removal of Native Americans from the province.

In his first major account, *Sichere Nachricht*, Pastorius aims at drawing an image of community that includes the English proprietor, Penn; an Indian chief; and himself, the leader of German immigration: "I was once dining with William Penn where one of their [Indian] kings sat at table with us. William Penn, who can speak their language fairly fluently, said to him that I was a German" (Myers 400).[55] To be sure, Pastorius is interested in placing himself at a table with the Pennsylvanian "nobility"—both Native American and European—as he wishes to include this "king" (who remains unnamed!) in his concept of community.

Similarly, the English Quaker writer Thomas Budd (1648–99) paints a picture of Native American compliance rather than interaction in his 1685 account, *Good Order Established*. Budd claims that the "Indians are but few in Number, and have been very serviceable to us by selling us Venison, Indian Corn, Pease and Beans, Fish and Fowl, Buck Skins, Beaver, Otter, and other Skins and Furs" (28). Fifteen years later, Pastorius relates in a letter to his father in Germany that the peaceful acquisition of land through the proprietor had largely terminated any contact, let alone "community," between white settlers and the Delaware or Lenni Lenape:

> We Christians in Germanton and Philadelphia have no longer the opportunity to associate with them, in view of the fact that their savage kings have accepted a sum of money from William Penn, and, together with their people, have withdrawn very far away from us, into the wild forest, where after their hereditary custom, they support themselves by the chase, shooting birds and game, and also catching fish, and dwell only in huts made of bushes and trees drawn together. (Myers 437–38)[56]

For both German and English immigrants, the complete cultural otherness of the Native American people of the Delaware valley precludes their inclusion in the project of community. After an initial period of usefulness for the fledgling settlement, their strange customs make their removal necessary. For Penn and Pastorius, of course, the Pennsylvanian mandate of peacefulness transforms cultural incompatibility and removal into voluntary withdrawal.

Yet my point here is not to reiterate the tragedy of European-Indian "contact" and its devastating results for Native American peoples and cultures, which has been articulated so well by historians such as James Axtell and Daniel Richter. Instead, the stunning agreement of German and English promotional writers on the question of Native American culture and (in-)compatibility with "Christian" community uncovers a strategy of building a transnational society through actual, as well as textual, exclusion. Thus, German and English writers alike found it useful to tell each other and their readers stories of Indian chiefs whose "dying words" imparted both spiritual and political authority to the newcomers. Encapsulating this spiritually symbolic and culturally accommodating image of Native Americans was a widely circulated account of the "dying words" of the Delaware chief "Ockanickon" (spellings vary widely). Much like the speech of the Mingo chief Logan in the 1770s and 1780s circulated along the eastern seaboard, the "dying words" of this Delaware chief became popular in Pennsylvania during the mid-1680s.

Budd claimed in *Good Order Established* to have personally witnessed the dying words of Ockanickon. In a speech Budd supposedly had written down directly "from his Mouth" (29), the chief blamed those settlers who had arrived before Penn's founding of Pennsylvania as a "holy experiment" for introducing liquor among his people and fraudulently taking away Native American land. Ockanickon, however, welcomed Penn's people and advised his own successor to accommodate them: "[B]ut now there is a People come to live amongst us, that have Eyes, they see [the sale of liquor] to be for our Hurt: They are willing to deny themselves the Profit of it for our good; these People have Eyes; we are glad such a People are come amongst us" (Budd 29). Notably, Budd's "first-hand" account simultaneously performs two acts of exclusion designed to define the nature of the "new" community arising in Pennsylvania: first, the "dying words" of the chief effectively hand over power to the settlers arriving under Penn and declare the Lenni Lenape a people who die with their chief; second, their own noble treatment of the Indians raises the new settlers above those who came before them, notably, the Dutch and Swedes. Pastorius reproduces the speech in a 1692 account entitled "Kurtze Geographische Beschreibung" ("Brief Geographical Description") that specifically emphasizes the spiritual compatibility of the Native American population. In the winter of 1685, Pastorius writes, the same chief—here spelled "Colkanicha"—"visited our governor and testified to a great inclination for the Christian religion and felt a great desire for the light of truth in his heart" ("Kurtze" 31).[57] Moreover, in his dying speech, the chief accordingly instructed his successor in a pseudo-Christian doctrine of following good and abstaining from all evil. In other words, the chief urges his people to adopt Christian values and European culture. Yet, as noted above, Pastorius ultimately felt that Native Americans remained too different and thus excluded *themselves* from further interaction with the Christian settlers. Like Budd, Pastorius simultaneously blames any Native American corruption on previous Christian immigrants and thus excludes them from the new community.[58]

The accounts by Budd and Pastorius, therefore, furthered the promotional agenda by telling English and German readers a similar story of the Native American people living in the province. Both writers contributed to the protomythical construction of the peaceful interaction between Native Americans and the white immigrant population of Pennsylvania. Native people ceded authority to the newly established "Christian" community through the symbolic last words of a dying chief, and they ceded land through supposedly benevolent treaties and purchases. German and English writers alike told each other and their readers at home a similar story about their interaction with Native Americans in early Pennsylvania so they could together believe in a just and spiritually profitable project of settlement. As a result, the project of creating a transnational community of English and German immigrants required the physical and textual expulsion of those who could never belong.

To be sure, the similar usage of the "dying words" spoken by Indian chiefs in German and English promotional tracts reveals the limited agency of literacy in overcoming certain types of difference. While English and German writers and readers devised creative textual means to imagine and describe their new home as tolerant of cultural and linguistic difference, they could not or did not attempt to extend the definition of community to their Native American neighbors. Clearly, a tradition of featuring or even exaggerating the racial or cultural otherness of Native Americans served to crystallize the comparative similarity and compatibility of English and German culture. Yet scholars of American history and culture have already produced much work describing the strategies of exclusion, othering, and demonization Europeans deployed in their encounter with Native Americans and African Americans. With this essay, in contrast, I argue that we have not sufficiently accounted for the manifold ways in which cultural or linguistic minorities—such as the Germans in Pennsylvania—gained access to negotiations of community.

ACKNOWLEDGMENTS

I would like to thank Cristine Levenduski, Michael Elliott, Reiner Smolinski, Julie Cary Nerad, and Mike Duvall for comments on earlier drafts of this essay. The essay also profited from the insightful suggestions of the two reviewers who read my submission to *Resources for American Literary Study* and the careful eye of editorial assistant Donna Brantlinger Black. Research for this article was supported by a Richard P. Morgan Fellowship in the History of the Book at the Library Company of Philadelphia and the Historical Society of Pennsylvania. I would like to thank the staff and librarians at both institutions for their support.

NOTES

1. For convenience, all quotations from non-English primary texts will be given in English translation. I will provide the original texts (except for Bible texts) in endnotes in order to make comparisons possible and to retain, as much as possible, a record of the linguistic diversity of the literary archive of colonial Pennsylvania. All translations are mine unless otherwise noted. For easier reading, I modernized and transcribed all slashes [/] in the original German as commas.

Translated from German by Gertrude Selwyn Kimball: "Unfern darvon, nemlich 2. Stund von allhier, ligt unser Germantown, allwo bereits 42. Menschen in 12. Haußhaltungen leben. . . . Den Weg nach besagten Germantown haben sie durch offtmaliges hin und her wandern, allschon tapffer gebahnt" (Pastorius, *Sichere* 3).

2. For autobiographical sketches, see Myers 2–7; Pastorius, *Res Propriæ* 5–12; and Pastorius, *Bee-Hive* 221–26. For exhaustive biographical works on Pastorius, see Learned, Toms, and Weaver. For brief biographical sketches, see Brophy, Rosenmeier, and Wokeck, "Francis Daniel Pastorius."

3. Schwartz draws extensively from promotional tracts to establish a record of the diverse society inhabiting Penn's colony, yet she doubts that immigrants reflected and wrote much about questions of pluralism: "In colonial Pennsylvania . . . divergent groups joined together to create a new type of society in the wilderness. Each contributed ideas, customs, and institutions that blended together, if uneasily at times, to form the provincial culture, one that contemporaries *knew* was pluralistic, but *rarely theorized about*" (9; emphasis added). Schwartz does not explain how she determined that Pennsylvanians "knew" their society "was pluralistic" if they did not reflect on this insight in writing.

4. On general questions of diversity and community in the province, I have particularly relied on Bonomi, Frost, Schwartz, Tolles, and Zuckerman. Historical scholarship on German immigration to Pennsylvania is extensive. For a concise and very readable overview, see Brandt. On Pennsylvania-German culture in the colonial period, see Faust. For a less recent but eminently important attempt to measure the influence of German culture on America, see Pochmann. Trommler and McVeigh survey historical, sociological, and literary issues. For other recent scholarship on German immigrants, see Moltmann; Lehmann, Wellenreuther, and Wilson; Roeber, "Origin," and Roeber, *Palatines*; and Tolzmann. Fogleman provides excellent insights into the motivations and conditions causing German immigration, as well as the impact of German communal structures on the social and political development of immigrant communities in Pennsylvania. For studies of English-German interaction in colonial Pennsylvania, see Rothermund, Tully, and Wellenreuther.

5. Roeber's *Palatines* tries to dispel the notion that German-speaking immigrants easily and quickly assimilated to English cultural norms. He argues that German concepts of freedom and property markedly differed from that of their English neighbors but had a crucial impact on the formation of these ideals in the Early Republic. Roeber thus contradicts Wolf, who finds that, soon after their arrival in the New World, German immigrants adopted new American identities and values while retaining merely a German "accent" or cultural flavor. Parsons argues that German immigrants in Pennsylvania retained an identity distinctly different from that of the dominant English culture.

6. In comparing English and German immigrant writings, I frequently refer to "national" differences and use the term *transnational* to describe a crossing or bridging of divisions between both groups. I consciously apply this vocabulary to describe communal positions and group relationships in a period before the emergence of "nationalism" and the modern nation state. Essentially, I follow contemporary, that is, late seventeenth- and

early eighteenth-century uses of the term *nation*. Writers and immigrants recognized "national" difference in the "ethno-symbolic" sense described by Smith. Accordingly, before the emergence of nationalism, the term *nation* evoked a host of cultural, mythographic, and ethnic signifiers—including language, geography, and consanguinity—that helped members of a specific group to identify themselves and others. Even though this definition of *nation* or *nationality* embraces our present use of the term *ethnicity*, I prefer to use the term *nation* because it was meaningful and widely used during the period I investigate.

Ultimately, shared linguistic systems became most useful as the qualities and traits that allowed Pennsylvanians to categorize and comprehend difference. While the regional heritage of German immigrants meant little to English settlers in Pennsylvania, linguistic difference structured their everyday interaction. Moreover, the promotional tracts transmitted to Germany by individuals such as Pastorius, Daniel Falckner (1666–1741), and Justus Falckner (1672–1723) made very little reference to regional differences among German immigrants. Instead, they focused on the national, linguistic, and, especially, denominational differences that reverberated in the context of early Pennsylvania. In 1701, the Lutheran pastor Justus Falckner reported to the church authorities in Germany that "there are a great number of *Germans* here, who, however, have crept in with other sects which have the English language, which is being learned immediately by all who come here. Many of them are Quakers, Anabaptists, and some of them Free Thinkers, who are not aligned with anybody and let their children grow up in the same spirit" (6; emphasis added). Here, Falckner can speak summarily of "Germans" because what matters most to him is the fact that they learned English and that many joined the Quakers. Thus, the linguistic contact and religious diversity of colonial Pennsylvania blurred or concealed regional differences that might have been significant in the home country.

7. I use the terms *translingual* and *transcultural* to describe the quality or subjectivity of individuals, groups, communal activities, and texts that results from the practice of translation, both in a linguistic sense and in a cultural sense. I prefer the prefix *trans-* to *inter-* in terms such as *transcultural* because it denotes a bridging of differences resulting to a certain degree in the *trans*formation of the individuals involved in the process. As I will argue throughout this essay, both English and German notions of community were affected by the translingual and transcultural promotion of Pennsylvania.

8. For a recent biography of Penn, see Geiter. For a useful collection of essays on Penn's intellectual background, see Dunn and Dunn.

9. For a filiopietistic view of the friendship between Penn and Pastorius, see Turner.

10. Schwartz acknowledges the multilingual and multicultural structures of colonial Pennsylvania, yet she pursues her study predominantly from an English-only perspective:

> In recognition of the pluralism of Pennsylvania, this study attempts to be inclusive, to analyze the attitudes and behavior of colonists of all backgrounds and beliefs living throughout the province. It has, however, been pursued largely from the perspective of the overarching English culture, partly from *necessity* and partly from choice. Because Pennsylvania was a part of the British Empire, to which William Penn intended to transplant many aspects of English culture, a focus on "English" responses to and perceptions of the evolving society and culture is essential. And since other British colonies did not develop similar patterns, one must analyze the ways Englishmen understood and participated in the evolution of this new society in order to comprehend the uniqueness of the province. Nevertheless, because all peoples were welcomed and joined together to create a distinctive society, the responses of German, Scotch-Irish, and other Pennsylvania residents to their experiences are considered insofar as possible. (9–10)

Schwartz's approach bespeaks the perfunctory acknowledgement of multiculturalism, but particularly of multilingualism, in historical and literary scholarship on early America. Though published in 1987, Schwartz's championing of English writings still represents the majority of studies today, with scholars shying away from thoroughly comparative readings. The "necessity" of focusing less on non-English texts and groups, according to Schwartz, arises from the fact that "the source materials for this part of the study are not available to as great an extent as they are for people of English origins" (10). It is true that many types of source materials disclosing the German immigrant experience in Pennsylvania—such as letters, commonplace books, and manuscript hymnals—"are awaiting discovery," not only "in European archives," but also in domestic repositories such as the Library Company of Philadelphia and the Historical Society of Pennsylvania. The archival seclusion of these materials, however, plays a much smaller role in their marginalization than the fact that they are not written in English.

11. Following Pastorius's vivid image of a "frequent going to and fro" between different immigrant groups in early Pennsylvania, my study of the textual adaptation and integration of the promotional discourse reveals the inadequacy of our most widely adopted models describing communal construction among the diverse immigrant societies of colonial North America. Particularly, through my reading of the textual representation of Pennsylvania, I object to the application of Benedict R O'G Anderson's widely acclaimed *Imagined Communities* to the study of early American communal formation. Anderson's excellent study has become something of a panacea for anyone trying to understand the intercession of textuality—particularly print culture—in the formation of modern communities. Anderson argues that "print-languages laid the bases for national consciousness." Readers "became capable of comprehending one another via print and paper. In the process, they gradually became aware of the hundreds of thousands, even millions, of people in their particular language-field, and at the same time that *only those* hundreds of thousands or millions, so belonged" (44). Anderson's emphasis on "*only those*" reveals the discrepancy between the linguistic and cultural homogeneity of the nationally imagined community, on the one hand, and the multilingual and transnational consciousness and capabilities of the people in early America, on the other. My work is an attempt to point out new methods for comprehending the agency of writing in the formation of early American communities and departs significantly from models that presume textuality—particularly print—as an instrument for building a linguistically and, eventually, culturally unified nation state. I hope to render comprehensible the delicate balance early Pennsylvanians attempted to strike between communal unity and diversity. Thus, I offer the literature promoting colonial Pennsylvania as an instructive example for the ways in which textuality mediated the problems of difference and coherence in the construction of one specific early American community.

12. My findings usually apply to both German and Dutch editions of Penn's texts. However, the present study focuses exclusively on comparing English and German tracts because of my limited knowledge of Dutch and space constraints. Similar work for Dutch and other non-English language tracts promoting immigration to Pennsylvania is necessary and timely.

13. Albert Cook Myers, editor of *Narratives of Early Pennsylvania, West New Jersey and Delaware*, provides a succinct biography of Benjamin Furly, "a leading shipping merchant of Rotterdam, an English Quaker and the chief agent of William Penn on the Continent for the sale of lands, the issuing of descriptive pamphlets, and the general promotion of the colonization of Pennsylvania. Beginning his career as a merchant in his native town of Colchester, England, by 1660 he had removed to Amsterdam, thence to Rotterdam. He was a prolific writer in English, German, Dutch, and French, and gathered a remarkable collection of manuscripts and rare books. As a patron of learning, his home became the rendezvous of Leclerc, Limborch, Algernon Sidney, and Locke. Quaker meetings were held at his house, Fox, Penn, Keith, and other leaders of the Society resorting there" (405). Furly's transcultural experience and elite, multilingual education, therefore, made him, not just the center of the economic promotion of Pennsylvania in Germany and Holland, but, more significantly, the nexus of the cross-cultural negotiation—of its discursive construction. A similarly translingual and transcultural individual, I argue, Pastorius continued Furly's task of mediating linguistic and cultural differences in the community of early Pennsylvania.

14. The best historical survey of Penn's influence on German immigration is Hull's *William Penn and the Dutch Quaker Migration to Pennsylvania*.

15. "Wie schwer, ich will nicht eben sagen, unmüglich es sey, die eigentliche Bedeutung etlicher Redens-arten, sonderlich in denen alten Gesetzen und Gebräuchen, eines frembden Landes und derselben Sprache in die Hoch-Teutsche behörlichen und deutlichen überzutragen, ist denen, so dergestalt darmit umbgangen, satsam wissend; Derohalben habe

ich alhier nicht vor unbequehm zu seyn erachtet, so wohl an etlichen örtern die Englische Wörter, als auch am Ende eine kurtze Auslegung über einige wenige derselben beyzufügen, der guten Hofnung, es werde der freundlich-gewillete Leser mir solches nicht allein nicht [sic] verargen, sondern vielmehr, gleichwie es von mir gemeinet, im besten aufnehmen."

In general, my translations retain the strongly hypotactic sentence structures of the original German. In the present example, these syntactic difficulties contribute to the bifurcated meaning of the passage. In the first sentence, the subject ("those who have dealt . . .") is delayed until the end, placing the emphasis on the difficulty of literal translation. In other words, the sentence technically says that other translators share with the present translator the problem of multiple and obscure meanings of certain phrases in another language and the difficulty of expressing these meanings in a single translation. Yet, in placing the syntactic emphasis on those difficulties (not on the subjects who have already experienced them), the sentence speaks primarily not to those other translators but to the prospective immigrants who will encounter such difficulties in the future.

16. Grammatically, the bilingual insertions focus on verbs describing legal processes and actions, as well as on nouns referring to categories such as property rights, government, civil and criminal codes, and settlement structure. Such legal tautologies as "we do give & grant" ("wir geben und stehen zu" [*Eine Nachricht* 15]), "to have and to hold" ("zu behalten und zu besitzen" [16]), and "to perdon and abolish Crimes and offences" ("übelthaten und Verbrechen zu vergeben und zu vernichtigen" [17]) allow the translingual speakers to connect and actively deploy the text's more numerous static or structural terms. Structurally, the "Patent" moves from the top to the bottom of the pyramid of social organization, that is, from the relationship between the crown and the proprietor, who will hold the province "in free and common soccage" ("zu einer freyen und gemeinen Lehn-Erkendnüß") to Penn's enactment of laws in accordance with the will of the "Freeholders" ("Frey-Leute oder Frey sassen" [16]); his right to appoint "Judges, Lieutenants, Justices, Magistrates and Officers" ("Richtere, Beambten, Obrigkeiten und andere dergleichen Bedienten" [17]), the division of the "Countrey" ("Landschaft") into administrative units such as "Counties" ("kleinere Bezirck oder Kreisse"), "towns" ("bemauerte Flecken oder kleinere Stätte"), "Burroughs" ("freye Bürgers-Stätte"), and "Cities" ("grossen Stätten" [18]); and, finally, Penn's power to distribute land under different conditions, as, for example, to "assign" lots ("so viel und solche Stücke und Theile anzuweisen") or to "grant demise" ("zu verpachten" [19]). In many cases, the translator found no precise correspondence between the German and English terms, which results in somewhat awkward circumlocutions, as in "bemauerte Flecken oder kleinere Stätte" for the English "towns."

17. "Eine kurtze Außlegung etlicher Englischen Wörter, so hierinnen vorkommen, und in einigen andern Oertern und Sprachen ungewöhnlich sind."

18. It is unclear whether the translator truly understood the term "views of frankpledge" himself. In spite of its length, the explanation does not seem to make the meaning of the term very clear. Dunn and Dunn provide a useful definition: "Views of frankpledge, or courts-leet, were yearly assemblies of freemen within a manor or lordship. Originally held to view the frankpledges, or freemen, who were all mutually pledged for good behavior of the others, they evolved into courts in which juries made presentments and petty misdemeanors were punished. A court-baron was an essential element of every manor. Though it existed primarily to settle property disputes within the manor, it also sought redress in small debt cases, misdemeanors, and trespass" (Penn, *Papers* 2: 76n68).

19. One reason for this striking omission may be sought in Penn's apparent lack of complete authority over the laws governing Pennsylvania and, by implication, over the textual construction of the new province. Originally, Penn had inserted a phrase granting liberty of conscience into the draft of the "Charter" he was to receive from Charles II in March 1681. In revising Penn's draft of the "Charter," however, William Blathwayt (ca. 1649–1717), Secretary of the Lords of Trade, struck the clause, and the "Charter" was signed by the king without any provision for religious liberty (Penn, *Papers* 2: 62). Taken almost verbatim from the 1663 Rhode Island Charter, the passage struck by Blathwayt follows: "And because it may happen that some of the People and Inhabitants of the said Province may not in their private opinions be able to conforme to the publick exercize of Religion according to the Liturgy Form'd & Ceremonies of the Church of England or take or subscribe the Oaths &

Articles made and Established in this Nation in that behalfe; And for that the same by reason of the remote distances of those places will (as Wee hope) be noe breach of the Unity and Uniformity Established in . . ." (*Papers* 2: 71) [missing folio page; continuing here is text in Rhode Island Charter] "this nation: Have therefore thought Fit, and doe hereby publish, graunt, ordeyne and declare, That our royall will and pleasure is, that noe person within the sayd colonye, at any tyme hereafter, shall bee any wise molested, punished, disquited, or called in question, for any differences in opinione in matters of religion, and doe not actually disturb the civill peace of our sayd colony; but that all and everye person and persons may . . . freelye and fullye have and enjoye his and theire owne judgments and consciences, in matters of religious concernments . . ." (*Papers* 2: 76n63).

20. The entire passage in German is [the added section in italics]: "So bald als sich einige mit mir eingelassen haben, so wollen wir zusammen einen Entwurff tuhn, welches ein völliges Zeugnüs meiner aufrichtigen Genegenheit geben soll, um die neu-anbauende aufzumuntern, und um eine freye, gerechte, und fleissige Erbauung (Colony) *auch die Gewissens-Freyheit eines jedwedern nach seinem Glauben und zu dessen öffentlichen übung des Gottesdienstes aldar* zu stifften" (*Eine Nachricht* 10; emphasis added).

21. Penn had begun his struggle for freedom of worship and a cessation of state-sanctioned oppression of Protestant dissenters—particularly the Society of Friends—in Restoration England. According to Bronner, Penn most actively lobbied for religious toleration in the 1670s and, throughout his life, he wrote about two dozen essays on the subject (36). Penn's travels to Holland and Germany in 1670 and 1677 impressed upon him the particular plight of Protestant dissenters—such as Mennonites, Pietists, and Quakers—on the Continent, and he began to issue tracts in favor of religious freedom, often directly addressed to rulers and authorities. The dissemination of Penn's tracts on religious liberty in Germany and Holland prepared the infrastructure for the later distribution of Penn's promotional accounts in western Europe.

For Penn's stance on religious freedom, see Bronner, Mary Maples Dunn, and Barbour. For Penn's original manuscript journal of his travels in 1677, "An Account of my Journey into Holland & Germany," see *Papers* 1: 425–507.

22. "Englisch, Lateinisch, Hoch-und Nieder-Teutsch."

23. In my appraisal of the process that led to the first and second *Frame of Government*, I am following the documents selected in *The Papers of William Penn*, vol. 2.

24. The draft's commitment to religious toleration is unequivocal, granting to any person residing in Pennsylvania "the Free Possession of his or her faith and exercise of worship towards God, in such way and manner As every Person shall in Conscience believe is most acceptable to God" (*Papers* 2: 140).

25. Furly demanded that lands purchased by foreigners who died before occupying their possessions in the province (by dying at sea, for example) should be passed on to their heirs instead of being forfeited and returned to the proprietor.

26. Furly translated Penn's *Letter* from English to Dutch. The translator of the German version is merely identified as "J.W."

27. "Denn weil darin nicht ein Wort gesaget wird, auf was Art und Condition der Gouverneur sein Land jetzund überläst, auch nichts von den Gesetzen, so habe ich für nothwendig erachtet, euch etwas Unterricht darvon zu geben."

28. "stimmen, nicht nur in Erwehlung der Obrigkeit, in denen Plätzen, wo sie wohnen, sondern auch in Erwehlung der Glieder des Landt Rahts, und eine allgemeine Versamblunge, die mit dem Gouverneur allda, die hohe Regierung und Herrschafft machen, ja was noch mehr ist, so sollen sie selbst zu einige Aembter erwehlet werden, worzu sie bey der Gemeine, wo sie wohnen, tüchtig befunden werden, und solches ohne einiges Absehen zunehmen, von was Nation und Religion die selbige auch sein mögen."

29. The entire section in German reads, "Umb zu hindern das keine Secte, ihr Haubt über die andere erhebe, ümb einige öffentliche Plätze und Besoldung, welches die eine über die andere möchte heben, auß dem Gelde der Gemeinen Einkünfften der Kammer, welches von allen Einwohnern, ohne Unterscheidt einkompt. So soll da keine Haubt-Kirche eingeführet werden, und wessen Versamblung oder Prediger, Niemand soll angestrenget oder gezwungen sein etwas zu geben" (5).

30. German religious experiments, such as Johann Kelpius's Hermits of the Wissahickon or Conrad Beissel's Ephrata cloister, demonstrate that sectarian groups from Germany welcomed the freedom to practice their own mode of worship but instituted systems of tight civic control over members of their community.
31. I here quote the entire German passage:

> 5. Und zu dem Ende, das ein jeder die Freyheit des Gewissens geniessen möge, welche alle Sanffmütige und Friedfertige Menschen haben solten, und von Natur gebühret. So ist fest beschlossen, nicht allein, das Niemand soll gezwungen werden, ümb einigen öffentlichen Ubungen des GOttes-Dienstes beyzuwohnen: sondern sie sollen selber volle Freyheit haben, ihren eigenen GOttes-Dienst öffentlich zu üben, ohne daß dieselbige einiger massen, über ihre übung, oder wegen ihren meinungen von dem Glauben, oder von der Religion, sollen verunruhiget oder beschädiget werden, wann dieselben nur bekennen und profession machen von dem Glauben, daß ein einiger Allmächtiger, Ewiger GOtt, welcher ein Schöpffer, Unterhalter, und Regierer der Welt sey. Und das sie wegen ihres Gewissens schüldig und verpflicht seyn, Friedsamlich in der Burgerlichen Gemeine zu wohnen.
> 6. Zum abwenden und verhüten, alles dessen, welches verursachen und analß geben möchte, ümb das Volck zur Eitelkeit, Leichtfertigkeit, Frech- und Kühnheit, Gottlosigkeit, und zu einem lästerlichen Leben zu bringen, und verleiten, zu entheiligung des Nahmens GOttes; So werden dabey gewisse Straffen (welche mit gestrengigkeit an denen Verbrechern sollen vollenzogen werden) verboten, alle Wette-Spielen, Comædien, Doppelen, Kartenspielen, vermummungen, alles Fluchen, Schweren und Liegen, oder falsch Gezeugnüß geben, (weil der Eyd da nicht erlaubet ist,) alles faule geschwätz und schändliche Reden, Blutschande, Sodomiterey, Hurerey, Verrätherey, Hoffart in Kleidern, Meuterey, Auffruhr, Mord, Duelliren, Dieberey, Gesundheiten und Vollsauffen, und dergleichen übel, anstehentlichen sitten mehr: als welche ich gut befunden habe alhier zu erkennen zu geben, zu dem Ende, daß alle gute und frommen Leute, die ihre Lust und zuneigung dar zu haben, destomehr sollen auffgemuntert werden, dahin zu ziehen, und daß die andern ihnen selbst nicht mögen einbilden, daß sie in allen denen Lasteren frey, daselbst Leben mögen. (5–6)

32. Certainly, Furly did not make up a list of public vices prohibited in Pennsylvania for a German audience alone; rather, he paraphrased article 37 of the "Laws agreed upon in England" (appended to the *Frame of Government*), which contained a similar enumeration. It is all the more telling, however, that Furly translated the section on public and moral decency from the *Frame* as part of his preface to Penn's promotional tract. Furly apparently meant to apply the idea of "promotion" to a certain group of "good and pious" people who would be attracted rather than repelled by this strict social code.
33. Jaspar Balthasar Könneken (or, Casper Balthasar Köhn), bookseller in the northern German city of Lübeck and later pastor in the town of Behlendorf, was one of the individuals who received the most recent reports from Pennsylvania through Benjamin Furly, copied the tracts or letters, and passed them on to interested individuals throughout Germany. Early twentieth-century scholar of German-American history and literature and German-American patriot Julius Friedrich Sachse describes the elaborate network of manuscript transmission of promotional tracts and letters about Pennsylvania in which Könneken participated (Introduction 14). Könneken's manuscript collection concerning Pennsylvania comprises thirteen different texts and is today located in the collection "Geistliches Ministerium" (Ecclesiastical Administration) in the "Archiv der Hansestadt Lübeck" (Archive of the Hanseatic City of Lübeck). Among the reports collected in the "Könneken Manuscript" are letters and reports by William Penn, Benjamin Furly, Francis Daniel Pastorius, Thomas Paschall (German spelling: Paskell), and Jacobus van der Walle. Significantly, the manuscript collection displays a mixture of German- and Dutch-language accounts. Pastorius's letters to his parents (*Copia*) and to the German Society in Frankfurt (*Sichere Nachricht*) are copied in the original German while Penn's *Letter to the Free Society of Traders* is copied from the Dutch translation as *Missive van William Penn . . . 1683*. We can fairly say that Könneken did not speak English, for all of the tracts by Englishmen are tran-

scribed from Dutch translations. Overall, the circles of manuscript transmission of promotional tracts on Pennsylvania represented by Könneken's collection reveal the cosmopolitan nature of the dissemination and promotion of the province in Europe.

34. Quantitative assessments comparing the circulation of promotional accounts in manuscript and print are extremely difficult and lie outside the limits of this study. Counts of extant copies in print and manuscript would allow only limited conclusions regarding the quantity of copies circulating in the late seventeenth century. Pastorius's first extensive letter to his sponsors in Frankfurt, published as *Sichere Nachricht*, survives only in two historical versions: one printed copy located today in the City Library of Zürich, Switzerland, and one manuscript copy as part of the "Könneken Manuscript" in the City Archives of Lübeck, Germany.

35. "Weil der vorige kurtze Begriff von der Provintz Pansylvania [sic], so im Jahr 1681. gedruckt worden, nicht wohl zu finden ist."

36. I am referring to a photostat copy of a manuscript transcription of Penn's *Letter*, located in the Learned Collection of the Historical Society of Pennsylvania. The manuscript does not reproduce the introductory matter added by Furly in the 1684 German translation published as *Beschreibung*. Since Furly's preface is extremely useful for a German audience, it seems plausible that the transcription was not prepared from the printed text of *Beschreibung*. Possibly, the model could have been either the English original or the Dutch translation of Penn's tracts. The German text of the manuscript copy may thus represent an original translation independent from the text presented in *Beschreibung*. The assumption that both texts are different translations is corroborated by the fact that the section of *Beschreibung* reproducing Penn's original letter is titled "Sende-Schreiben von William Penn, Eygenthümer und Gouverneur von Pensylvania" while the manuscript transcription translates the title of the letter as "Ein Brief von William Penn Eigenthumbs Herrn und Befehlshabern in PENNSYLVANIA."

37. The original is written in English. Pastorius dedicated his manuscript writings to his sons; because they were born and raised in Pennsylvania, he assumed their first language would be English, not German.

38. On Pietism in general, see Beyreuther, Stoeffler, and Wallmann. For the role of the Frankfurt Pietists and their Frankfurt Land Company in the German and Dutch immigration to Pennsylvania, see Hull (132–39) and Pennypacker (21–50).

39. Penn's letter specifically mentions rumors circulating in England that he had become a Jesuit. His support for the Catholic King James II incensed English resentments against the Quaker leader and linked them to general fears of a return to Catholicism in England.

40. Penn's reference to his unkind treatment in England hints at rumors that he was secretly Catholic or even a Jesuit. These rumors relied on widespread speculations about Penn's close relationship to the Stuart kings Charles II and James II.

41. All subsequent quotations from *Sichere Nachricht* are taken from the English translation, *Positive Information*, by Gertrude Selwyn Kimball in Myers, ed., *Narratives of Early Pennsylvania, West New Jersey and Delaware*.

42. In a poem written upon Penn's return to Pennsylvania in 1699, Pastorius claims that, upon his own arrival in the province in 1683, he could "talk with him [Penn] but in the Gallic Tongue" (*Bee-hive* 177).

43. "Er lässt mich zum öfftern an seine Taffel bitten, auch in seiner jederzeit erbaulichen Gesellschafft außwandelen und reiten; und da ich letzthin 8. Tag vor hier . . . aussen war, und Er mich solche Zeit über nicht gesehen, kam Er selbst in mein Häusgen, und begehrte, ich solle doch wochentlich ein paar mal bey ihme zu Gast kommen" (*Sichere* 2).

44. ". . . da ich deß folgenden Tags die mithabende Schreiben an W. Penn überlieferte, und von ihme mit Liebvoller Freundlichkeit empfangen wurde; von diesem sehr werthen Mann, und rumwürdigen Regenten, solte ich billich

"II. Ein und anders überschreiben; allein, meine Feder . . . ist viel zu schwach, die hohe Tugenden dieses Christen, dann solches ist Er in der That, zu exprimiren. . . . Er hat die [blank] hertzlich lieb, und sagte einst offentlich in meiner Gegenwart zu seinen Räthen und Umbstehenden: Die [blank] hab ich lieb, und wil, daß ihr sie auch lieben sollet; Wiewol ich übrigens niemalen dergleichen Befehlchswort von ihm gehöret habe;

"... Ich kan anjetzo mehr nicht sagen, als daß Will. Penn, ein Mann sey, welcher Gott ehret, und von Ihme wieder geehret wird: welcher das gute liebet, und von allen guten mit recht geliebet wird, &c. Ich zweiffle nicht, es werden noch einige selbsten anhero kommen, und im Werck erfahren, daß meine Feder hierinnfalls noch nicht genug geschrieben" (*Sichere* 2).

45. For the transcription of Pastorius's *Sichere Nachricht* in the Könneken manuscript, see Könneken 358.

46. I am essentially following Greenblatt's interpretation of promotional writings on colonial America in *Marvelous Possessions*.

47. "Ach, liebwerthe Freund, ich möchte wol wünschen, daß ich mit dieser Adlers-Feder, die zu euch tragende Lieb außdrucken könte; und in der That bezeugen, daß es nicht eine blosse Lippen-Liebe, sondern die Euch mehr gutes gönnet, als mir selbsten. Mein Hertz ist durch das Band der Liebe an das Eure geknüpffet, So lasst uns nun zusammen wachsen, als Bäume, welche die rechte Hand Gottes an Wasserbächen gepflantzt hat, damit wir nicht nur Blätter, sondern Frücht bringen, zur rechten Zeit; Früchte der Buß, Früchte des Friedens, Früchte der Gerechtigkeit! Dann was hillfts einen solchen unnützen Baum, obschon der Gärtner seiner noch etliche Jahr verschonet, denselben mit allem Fleiß umbgräbt, und bearbeitet, doch endlich auff nicht erfolgende Besserung außhauet, und in Ofen wirfft" (*Sichere* 7–8).

48. The reorganization of the Pietists' Pennsylvanian investments in 1686 confirmed Pastorius's suspicions. Renamed from the original "German Society" to "Frankfurt Land Company," the group now pursued an exclusively economic agenda in America. The printed text of their 1686 constitution abandons any reference to the establishment of a Christian community and charges Pastorius with the work of a business executive. Instead of reporting about the spiritual progress of the settlement, the representative of the company had to prepare a minute inventory or "Inventarium" (Pastorius, "Frankfurt Land Company Papers" 2), listing all assets in the province. Pastorius recognized that the transformation from a "Society" to a "Company" implied a shift from spiritual to economic goals. The change of designation from "German" to "Frankfurt" signaled the loss of any larger spiritual or national goals for the settlement and the pursuit of the investors' local interests. The document was printed and possibly distributed to people interested in purchasing land from the Frankfurt investors. The document is dated 12 November 1686; an original print is located in the Library Company of Philadelphia.

Pastorius's loss of a spiritual connection with the Frankfurt group resulted in rather infrequent communication and possibly in his neglect of the company's business transactions. In 1700, the company dismissed Pastorius and assigned Daniel Falckner as their executive. Falckner became involved in a scheme of real estate fraud that resulted in the loss of the company's holdings in Pennsylvania and its eventual dissolution.

All of Pastorius's manuscripts relating to the Frankfurt Land Company are located in the Pastorius Papers at the Historical Society of Pennsylvania. Wokeck provides a very brief account of the affair, in which Daniel Falckner, Pastorius's successor as executor of the Frankfurt Company, and the adventurer Johann Heinrich Sprögel (1679–1729), with the help of attorney David Lloyd (1656–1731), nearly evicted the original purchasers from their land ("Pastorius" 588). Sachse gives an account heavily biased against Pastorius's conduct while trying to re-establish Falckner's reputation (Sachse, *The German Pietists* 299–334). For an account in favor of Pastorius's role in the matter, see Pennypacker 21–50.

49. Penn's original letter to Pastorius's father is in Latin; *Umständige Geographische Beschreibung* provides a German translation. The English translation is by Gertrude Selwyn Kimball. "So viel mir wissend so ist dein Sohn noch im Leben, und hält sich anjetzo zu Philadelphia auff. Er ist dieses Jahr der Stadt Friedens-Richter, oder hat jüngst das Ampt abgelegt. Er ist sonst ein Mann mässig und nüchtern, fromm, verständig und gottesfürchtig, von deme ein gutes untadelhafftes Geruchte aller Orten erschallet . . ." (Pastorius, *Umständige* 97).

50. I have not been able to find a translation of Penn's *Further Account*.

51. On the Rittenhouse paper mill, see Green; for biographical information on Rittenhouse, see Rubincam and Brendle.

52. "Und ist obiger Berichts-Brieff erstlich in Englischer Sprache geschrieben, nachmals in die Hoch-teutsche übergesetzt und gedruckt worden durch J. W. zu Hamburg Bey Heinrich Heusch im Jahr 1684."

53. This compilation additionally complicates the diverse textual presentation of Pennsylvania in Germany. The English account by Thomas was wedged between two German accounts that appeared to assimilate the tract in the middle. This effect was enhanced by the title page to the translation of Thomas's account, which presented it as a continuation ("Continuatio") of Pastorius's *Beschreibung*. Further, the overtly spiritual agenda of Pastorius's and Falckner's descriptions overshadowed Thomas's goal to describe "the mighty Improvements, Additions, and Advantages that have been made lately" (v) in Pennsylvania.

54. Sachse appraised with great pathos the importance he allotted to the role of promotional tracts by Pastorius and Daniel Falckner, his successor as agent for the Frankfurt Company, in stimulating German immigration to Pennsylvania. In the introduction to his edition and translation of Falckner's account, *Curieuse Nachricht*, Sachse claims that the "successive editions of Pastorius and Falckner's accounts . . . called the attention of the sturdy yeomanry of the Fatherland to the advantages of Penn's colony, and started the great stream of emigration which at one time almost threatened to depopulate the Palatinate, brought thousands and thousands of Germans to our province and made Pennsylvania the great Commonwealth that it is to-day" (28). Though vastly inflated, Sachse's interpretation bears the important insight that German settlers in Pennsylvania throughout the eighteenth century had relied to a large degree on tracts such as Pastorius's *Description* and Falckner's *Curieuse Nachricht* in forming a conception of their future home and deciding in favor of immigration. Pastorius's account of Pennsylvania was revised and republished in Germany as late as 1792, then issued as *Geographisch-statistische Beschreibung der Provinz Pensylvanien, von Fr. Dan. Pastorius. Im Auszug mit Anmerkungen* by Andreas Seyler in Memmingen (Bavaria).

55. "Ich speiste einsten bey W. Penn, da einer von ihren Königen mit an der Tafel saß, diesem nun sagte W. Penn (welcher ihre Sprach ziemlich prompt reden kan) daß ich ein Teutscher, etc." (*Sichere* 4).

56. "Wir Christen zu Germanton and Philadelphia haben nun die Gelegenheit nicht mehr mit ihnen umzugehen, in Betrachtung, daß ihre wilden Könige vom William Penn ein Stück Geldes angenommen, und samt denen Ihrigen sehr weit von uns hinweg begeben haben, allwo sie ihrer angebohrnen Art nach sich mit jagen, Wild-und Vögel schiessen, auch Fischfangen ernehren, und nur in Hütten, von Büsch und Bäumen zusammen gezogen, wohnen" (*Umständige Geographische Beschreibung* 84–85).

57. Translation mine. "In dem Winter Anno 1685, besuchte der König Colkanicha unsern Gouverrneur, und bezeugte eine grosse Inclination zu der Christen Religion, und hatte eine grosse Begierde zu dem Liechte der Warheit in seinem Hertzen" (31).

58. In his 1700 *Umständige Geographische Beschreibung (Circumstantial Geographical Description)*, Pastorius claims that "the old Christians . . . have never had the upright intention to give these needy native creatures instruction in the true living Christianity, but instead they have sought only their own worldly interests, and have cheated the simple inhabitants in trade and intercourse, so that at length those savages who dealt with these Christians, proved themselves to be also for the most part crafty, lying, and deceitful, so that I can not say much that is creditable of either" (Myers 385–86; trans. Gertrude Selwyn Kimball). Original German: "[D]ie aus Europa angekommene alte Christen . . . haben niemahls die aufrichtige intention gehabt diesen eingebohrnen Hülffbedürfftigen Creaturen eine Unterweisung in dem lebendigen wahren Christenthum zu thun, sondern haben nur ihr propre Welt-Interesse gesuchet, und die einfältige Innwohner im Handel und Wandel betrogen, dahero endlichen die jenige Wilden so mit diesen Christen umgiengen, sich mehrentheils auch arglistig, lugenhafft, und betrüglich erwiesen, also daß ich von beeden nicht viel ruhmwürdiges melden kan" (*Umständige* 31).

WORKS CITED

Anderson, Benedict R O'G. *Imagined Communities: Reflections on the Origins and Spread of Nationalism*. Rev. and extended ed. London: Verso, 1991.

Barbour, Hugh S. "Penn's Arguments for Toleration." *William Penn on Religion and Ethics: The Emergence of Liberal Quakerism*. Ed. Hugh S. Barbour. Lewiston, NY: Mellen, 1991. 393–99.

Beyreuther, Erich. *Geschichte des Pietismus*. Stuttgart: Steinkopf, 1978.
Bonomi, Patricia. *Under the Cope of Heaven: Religion, Society, and Politics in Colonial America*. New York: Oxford UP, 1986.
Brandt, Armin M. *Bau deinen Altar auf fremder Erde: Die Deutschen in Amerika—300 Jahre Germantown*. Stuttgart: Seewald, 1983.
Bronner, Edwin B. "'Truth Exalted' Through the Printed Word." *William Penn's Published Writings, 1660-1726: An Interpretive Bibliography*. Ed. Edwin B. Bronner and David Fraser. *The Papers of William Penn*. Vol. 5. Philadelphia: U of Pennsylvania P, 1986. 24-45.
Brophy, Alfred L. "Francis Daniel Pastorius." *The Multilingual Anthology of American Literature: A Reader of Original Texts with English Translations*. Ed. Marc Shell and Werner Sollors. New York: New York UP, 2000. 12-15.
Budd, Thomas. *Good Order Established in Pennsylvania & New Jersey in America, Being a true Account of the Country*. [Philadelphia]: n.p., 1685.
Dunn, Mary Maples. *William Penn: Politics and Conscience*. Princeton: Princeton UP, 1967.
Dunn, Richard S., and Mary Maples Dunn, eds. *The World of William Penn*. Philadelphia: U of Pennsylvania P, 1986.
Falckner, Daniel. *Curieuse Nachricht von Pensylvania in Norden-America [. . .]*. Frankfurt and Leipzig: Andreas Otto, 1702.
Falckner, Justus. *Abdruck Eines Schreibens An Tit. Herrn D. Henr. Muhlen, Aus Germanton, in der Americanischen Province Pensylvania [. . .]*. Germantown [Germany?]: n.p., 1702.
Faust, Albert Bernhardt. *The German Element in the United States, with special reference to its political, moral, social and educational influence*. Boston: Houghton, 1909.
Fogleman, Aaron Spencer. *Hopeful Journeys: German Immigration, Settlement, and Political Culture in Colonial America, 1717-1775*. Philadelphia: U of Pennsylvania P, 1996
Frame, Richard. *A Short Description of Pennsilvania*. 1692. [Philadelphia]: Oakwood P, 1867.
Frost, J. William. "Religious Liberty in Early Pennsylvania." *Pennsylvania Magazine of History and Biography* 105 (1982): 419-52.
Geiter, Mary K. *William Penn*. New York: Longman, 2000.
Green, James N. *The Rittenhouse Mill and the Beginnings of Papermaking in America*. Philadelphia: Library Company, 1990.
Greenblatt, Stephen. *Marvelous Possessions: The Wonder of the New World*. Chicago: U of Chicago P, 1991.
Hull, William I. *William Penn and the Dutch Quaker Migration to Pennsylvania*. 1935. Baltimore: Genealogical, 1970.
Könneken, Jasper [Caspar Köhn]. "Könneken Manuscript" [Transcriptions of letters relating to the settlement of Pennsylvania]. MS. Fol. 356-72. "Geistliches Ministerium." Archiv der Hansestadt Lübeck, Lübeck, Germany.
Learned, Marion Dexter. *The Life of Francis Daniel Pastorius*. Philadelphia: Campbell, 1908.
Lehmann, Hartmut, Hermann Wellenreuther, and Renate Wilson. *In Search of Peace and Prosperity: New German Settlers in Eighteenth-Century Europe and America*. University Park: Pennsylvania State UP, 2000.
Moltmann, Günter, ed. *Germans to America: 300 Years of Immigration, 1683-1983*. Stuttgart: Institute for Foreign Cultural Relations, 1982.
Myers, Albert Cook, ed. *Narratives of Early Pennsylvania, West New Jersey and Delaware*. New York: Scribner's, 1912.
Parsons, William T. *The Pennsylvania Dutch: A Persistent Minority*. Boston: Twayne, 1976.
Paskell, Thomas. *An Abstract of a Letter From Thomas Paskell of Pennsilvania To his Friend J. J. Chippenham*. London: John Bringhurst, 1683.
Pastorius, Francis Daniel. *Bee-Hive*. Ms. Codex 726. Special Collections, Van Pelt Lib., U of Pennsylvania, Philadelphia.
———. "Frankfurt Land Company Papers." Folder in Ms. Pastorius Papers. Historical Society of Pennsylvania, Philadelphia.

———. *Geographisch-statistische Beschreibung der Provinz Pensylvanien, von Fr. Dan. Pastorius. Im Auszug mit Anmerkungen.* Memmingen: Andreas Seyler, 1792.

———. "Kurtze Geographische Beschreibung [. . .]." [Nürnberg, 1692]. *Kurtze Beschreibung der Reichs-stadt Windsheim.* By Melchior Adam Pastorius. Nürnberg: n.p., 1692.

———. *Res Propriæ.* Ms. Pastorius Papers. Historical Society of Pennsylvania, Philadelphia.

———. *Sichere Nachricht auß America, wegen der Landschafft Pennsylvania, von einem dorthin gereißten Teutschen, de dato Philadelphia, den 7. Martii 1684.* Photographic reproduction of the original in the City Lib. of Zürich. *The Life of Francis Daniel Pastorius.* Marion Dexter Learned. New York: Philadelphia: Campbell, 1908. 8 pp. following p. 128.

———. *Umständige Geographische Beschreibung Der zu allerletzt erfundenen Provintz Pensylvaniæ, In denen End-Gräntzen Americæ In der West-Welt gelegen.* Frankfurt and Leipzig: Andreas Otto, 1700. [Bound with Thomas, *Continuatio* (1702) and Daniel Falkner, *Curieuse Nachricht* (1702).]

Penn, William. *Beschreibung der in America neu-erfundenen Provinz Pensylvanien.* [Hamburg]: Henrich Heuss, 1684.

———. "Ein Brief von William Penn Eigenthumbs Herrn und Befehlshabern in PENNSYLVANIA." Signed "William Penn. Philadelphia den 1[2?]6 deß 6 Monaths genandt August, 1683." Photostat. Ms. Learned Collection. 1534–1776. Box 1. Historical Society of Pennsylvania, Philadelphia.

———. *Christian Liberty As it was Soberly Desired in a Letter, To Certain Forreign States, Upon Occasion of their late Severity to several of their Inhabitants, meerly for their Different Perswasion and Practice in Point of Faith and Worship towards God.* London: Andrew Sowle, 1674.

———. *A Further Account of the Province of Pennsylvania and Its Improvements.* London: n.p., 1685.

———. *A Letter from William Penn Proprietary and Governour of Pennsylvania in America: To the Committee of the Free Society of Traders of that Province, Residing in London [. . .].* London: Andrew Sowle, 1683.

———. *Eine Nachricht wegen der Landschaft Pennsilvania in America [. . .].* Amsterdam: Christoff Cunraden, 1681.

———. *The Papers of William Penn.* Ed. Richard S. Dunn and Mary Maples Dunn. Philadelphia: U of Pennsylvania P, 1982.

———. *Ein Send-Brieff An die Bürgermeister und Rath der Stadt Danzig, Von Wilhelm Penn, aus London neulich geschrieben, Und aus diesen Landen denen obgesetzten zugesandt [. . .].* Amsterdam: Christoff Cunraden, 1675.

———. *Some Account of the Province of Pennsilvania in America [. . .].* London: Benjamin Clark, 1681.

Pennypacker, Samuel Whitaker. *The Settlement of Germantown and the Beginning of German Emigration to North America.* 1899. New York: Blom, 1970.

Pochmann, Henry A. *German Culture in America: Philosophical and Literary Influences, 1600–1900.* Madison: U of Wisconsin P, 1957.

Roeber, Gregg A. "In German Ways? Problems and Potentials of Eighteenth-Century German Social and Emigration History." *William and Mary Quarterly* 44 (1987): 750–74.

———. "'The Origin of Whatever Is not English among Us': The Dutch-speaking and the German-speaking Peoples of Colonial British America." *Strangers within the Realm: Cultural Margins of the First British Empire.* Chapel Hill: U of North Carolina P and Institute of Early American History and Culture, 1991. 220–83.

———. *Palatines, Liberty, and Property: German Lutherans in Colonial British America.* Baltimore: Johns Hopkins UP, 1993.

Rosenmeier, Rosamund. "Francis Daniel Pastorius." *Dictionary of Literary Biography* 24.

Rothermund, Dietmar. "The German Problem of Colonial Pennsylvania." *Pennsylvania Magazine of History and Biography* 84 (1960): 3–21.

Rubincam, Milton, and Thomas R. Brendle. *William Rittenhouse and Moses Dissinger: Two Eminent Pennsylvania Germans.* Vol. 58. Publications of the Pennsylvania German Society. Scottdale, PA: Herald, 1959.

Sachse, Julius Friedrich. *The German Pietists of Provincial Pennsylvania, 1694–1708*. 1895. New York: AMS, 1970.

———. Introduction. *Curieuse Nachricht from Pennsylvania*. By Daniel Falckner. 1702. Lancaster: Pennsylvania-German Soc., 1905.

Schwartz, Sally. *"A Mixed Multitude": The Struggle for Toleration in Colonial Pennsylvania*. New York: New York UP, 1987.

Smith, Anthony D. *Myths and Memories of the Nation*. New York: Oxford UP, 1999.

Soderlund, Jean R., ed. *William Penn and the Founding of Pennsylvania, 1680–1684*. Philadelphia: U of Pennsylvania P, 1983.

Sollors, Werner, ed. *Multilingual America: Transnationalism, Ethnicity, and the Languages of American Literature*. New York: New York UP, 1998.

Stoeffler, F. Ernst. *The Rise of Evangelical Pietism*. Leiden: Brill, 1965.

Thomas, Gabriel. *Continuatio Der Beschreibung der Landschafft Pennsylvaniæ An den End-Grämtzen Americæ*. Frankfurt and Leipzig: Andreas Otto, 1702.

———. *An Historical and Geographical Account of the Province and Country of Pensilvania; and of West-New-Jersey in America [. . .]*. London: A. Baldwin, 1698.

Tolles, Frederick B. "The Culture of Early Pennsylvania." *Pennsylvania Magazine of History and Biography* 81 (1957): 119–37.

Tolzmann, Don Heinrich. *The German-American Experience*. Amherst, NY: Humanity Books, 2000.

Toms, DeElla Victoria. "The Intellectual and Literary Background of Francis Daniel Pastorius." Diss. Northwestern U, 1953.

Trommler, Frank, and Joseph McVeigh, eds. *America and the Germans: An Assessment of a Three-Hundred-Year History*. Philadelphia: U of Pennsylvania P, 1985.

Tully, Alan W. "Englishmen and Germans: National-Group Contact in Colonial Pennsylvania, 1700–1755." *Pennsylvania History* 45 (1978): 237–56.

Turner, Beatrice Pastorius. "William Penn and Pastorius." *Pennsylvania Magazine of History and Biography* 57 (1933): 66–90.

Venuti, Lawrence. "Translation, Community, Utopia." *The Translation Studies Reader*. Ed. Lawrence Venuti. London: Routledge, 2000. 468–88.

———. *The Translator's Invisibility: A History of Translation*. London: Routledge, 1995.

Wallmann, Johannes. *Der Pietismus. Die Kirche in ihrer Geschichte. Ein Handbuch*. Ed. Bernd Moeller. Vol. 4. Göttingen: Vandenhoeck & Ruprecht, 1990.

Weaver, John David. "Franz Daniel Pastorius (1651–ca. 1720): Early Life in Germany with Glimpses of his Removal to Pennsylvania." Diss. U of California, Davis. Ann Arbor: UMI, 1986.

Wellenreuther, Hermann. "Image and Counterimage, Tradition and Expectation: The German Immigrants in English Colonial Society in Pennsylvania, 1700–1765." *America and the Germans: An Assessment of a Three-Hundred-Year History*. Ed. Frank Trommler and Joseph McVeigh. Philadelphia: U of Pennsylvania P, 1985. 85–105.

Wokeck, Marianne S. "Francis Daniel Pastorius." *Lawmaking and Legislators in Pennsylvania: A Biographical Dictionary; Volume One, 1682–1709*. Ed. Craig Horle et al. Philadelphia: U of Pennsylvania P, 1991. 586–90.

———. *Trade in Strangers: The Beginning of Mass Migration to North America*. University Park: Pennsylvania State UP, 1999.

Wolf, Stephanie Grauman. *Urban Village: Population, Community, and Family Structure in Germantown, Pennsylvania. 1683–1800*. Princeton: Princeton UP, 1976.

Zuckerman, Michael, ed. *Friends and Neighbors: Group Life in America's First Plural Society*. Philadelphia: Temple UP, 1982.

Making the A-List: Reformation and Revolution in Crocker's *Observations on the real rights of women*

CONSTANCE J. POST
Iowa State University

In the last three decades, extraordinary efforts have been made to reclaim neglected or forgotten texts by and about women, and my work on Hannah Mather Crocker (1752–1829) is part of this reclamation project. The first female writer in the Mather family, Crocker wrote in several genres, including poetry, drama, and the essay. Much of this material remains unpublished; three texts, however, appeared in print in her lifetime: *A Series of Letters on Free Masonry* (1815), *The School of Reform, or Seaman's Safe Pilot to the Cape of Good Hope* (1816), and *Observations on the real rights of women, with their appropriate duties, agreeable to Scripture, reason, and common sense* (1818). Of the three, *Observations* merits special interest. Although Judith Sargent Murray's serialized essays had been reissued as a book in 1798 and Charles Brockden Brown's *Alcuin: A Dialogue* appeared the same year, Crocker's *Observations* marks the first sustained treatment of women's rights in America by a woman.[1]

Crocker situates these rights in a catalogue of outstanding women from antiquity to the present. To compile her list, Crocker relied on a variety of sources, including Valerius Maximus for women in antiquity, Henry Hunter for women of the Bible,[2] Mary Wollstonecraft for contemporary women, and Mercy Otis Warren for women who distinguished themselves in the American Revolution. Not all of the women who make her A-list appear in the lists of others, however.[3] Some are culled by Crocker from anecdotes, including one from John Hawkesworth's *Account of the Voyages* (1773) in which Captain Wallis records his arrival on Tahiti. Scurvy-ridden, he and his men were entertained by Queen Oberea, who presented them with lavish gifts before they returned to their boat. Seeing that Wallis remained in a weakened condition, the Queen instructed that he be carried by palace attendants even though Wallis showed a decided preference for walking. According to Wallis, "[S]he took me by the arm, and whenever we came to a plash of water or dirt, she lifted me over with as little trouble as it would have cost me to have lifted a child if I had been well" (Hawkesworth 1: 463–64). Crocker, however, does not use the anecdote to support a claim for equal physical strength, let alone a strong case for superior physical ability on the part of women that the example illustrates.[4]

In compiling a list of women, Crocker places herself within a tradition that stretches back as far as Plutarch's "Bravery of Women" in *Moralia* (n.d.); Giovanni Boccaccio's *Concerning Famous Women* (ca. 1365); Christine de Pizan's *The Book of the City of Ladies* (1405); Baldassare Castiglione's *The Book of the Courtier* (1528); Henricus Cornelius Agrippa's *Declamation on the Nobility and Preeminence of the Female Sex* (1529); and Gisbertus Voetius's "Concerning Women," part of his major work, *Politica Ecclesiastica* (1663–76), to mention only a few.[5] Crocker's text, however, appeared at a time of renewed interest in such compilations. A popular list circulating in Great Britain and the United States in the early nineteenth century was *Female Biography, or memoirs of illustrious and celebrated women, of all ages and countries. Alphabetically arranged* by Mary Hays (1803).[6] John Adams, following his term as second president of the United States, also contributed to this genre by writing *Sketches of the history, genius, disposition, accomplishments, employments, customs, virtues, and vices of the fair sex, in all parts of the world: interspersed with many singular and entertaining anecdotes* (1807).[7] As Ann Firor Scott notes, nineteenth-century compilers "borrowed freely from each other and did not always distinguish clearly between documented fact and legend" in their attempts to identify exemplary lives that might serve as role models for the young (113).

Like other lists of outstanding women, Crocker's catalogue reflects multiple borrowings and offers few surprises other than an occasional foray into territory seldom mined by compilers, as the reference to a Tahitian queen attests. More remarkable than the outstanding women selected by Crocker from the cameo biographies in the texts of Maximus, Hunter, Wollstonecraft, and Warren are the figures of Wollstonecraft and a host of others whom Crocker uses to construct her argument. Taken together, these sources suggest that Crocker's text on the *real rights of women* functions not only as a catalogue or commonplace book, but also as a site of cultural authority. The explanatory power of the sources cited by Crocker resides principally in the basis they provide for arguments about women's rights advanced by Crocker, especially the Protestant ideology that undergirds her *Observations*. A few of these sources have suffered little neglect, others have been recuperated within the last thirty years, and some have yet to receive much attention at all.

The writers examined in this essay share a distinctly Protestant ideology that Crocker does not openly identify but nevertheless relies on as she constructs her argument in *Observations on the real rights of women, with their appropriate duties, agreeable to Scripture, reason, and common sense.*

Making the A-list establishes for Crocker a list of authorities who have a significant bearing on one of the three bases on which she grounds her defense of women's rights—scripture, reason, and common sense—and often on all three. Those who make her A-list include Anna Maria van Schurman, who wrote *Dissertatio logica* and selected letters (in *Opuscula* 2nd ed., 1650);[8] François Poullain de La Barre, author of *The Equality of Both Sexes* (1673);[9] and Germaine de Staël whose essay *On Literature Considered in Its Relationship to Social Institutions* (1800) Crocker especially admired.[10] Each of these writers—Dutch, French, and Swiss—contributed to the transatlantic turn of ideas circulating about women's rights, and in Crocker's hand their ideas become a means of linking these rights with the Protestant Reformation and the American Revolution. A fourth writer, Hannah More, was so esteemed by Crocker that she dedicated *Observations* to More even though More's *Strictures on the Modern System of Female Education* (1799) is very much at odds with Crocker's ideas. The remainder of the essay will explore how Crocker complicates the history of women's rights represented by the figures of Hannah More and Mary Wollstonecraft.

Of the writers with deeply Protestant ideological roots whom Crocker cites, the first is Anna Maria van Schurman (1607–78), born in Cologne to Protestant parents who fled to Germany after Catholicism was forcibly reinstated in Antwerp. The family relocated to Franeker in the province of Friesland so that one of the sons, Johan Godschalk, could study medicine and the father could study theology with William Ames, who was appointed a professor at the University of Franeker in 1622. To Hannah Mather Crocker, who refers to herself as a direct descendant of the "four-fold line of Mathers" (*Observations* 84),[11] Anna Maria van Schurman's credentials were impeccable. A major reason is the association of Schurman's father with William Ames, cited by Cotton Mather in *Magnalia Christi Americana* (1702) as "[o]ne of the most eminent and judicious persons that ever lived in this world." Mather claims that Ames "was *intentionally* a New-England man, though not *eventually*" because of his untimely death. However, Providence "afterwards permitted his *widow*, his *children*, and his *library*, to be translated hither," notes Mather (1: 236).[12]

In compiling his list of learned women, including many from ancient Greece and Rome now relegated to obscure footnotes, Cotton Mather refers to the catalogues of illustrious women by Beverovicius [Jan van Beverwyck],[13] Johann Heinrich Hottinger, and Voetius and singles out "the writings of the most renowned Anna Maria Schurmian [sic]" for special praise (*Magnalia* 1: 135). In part, that praise was due to her mastery of nine languages, including ancient languages such as Greek, Hebrew, Ethiopian, Chaldean, Arabic, and Syriac.[14] Schurman's prodigious talent reflects a skill for which the Dutch, sometimes called the linguistic wizards of Europe, have long been recognized. The desire to study ancient languages, however, had its roots in the widely shared conviction among Reformation scholars that it is impossible to understand the Bible fully unless you can read it in the original languages.[15] Schurman acquired her learning largely but not exclusively by means of private tutors. Invited by Voetius to write poems on the occasion of the inauguration of the Academy of Utrecht (now the University of Utrecht), Schurman benefited from Voetius's willingness to arrange for her to attend lectures at the institution. These arrangements he managed by having Schurman placed in a special loge that concealed her from the gaze of male students.

Although Crocker lavishes praise on Schurman for her many accomplishments as "a painter, musician, engraver, sculptor, philosopher, and geometrician" (36), it was her scholarly achievements that made Schurman celebrated throughout Europe and sought out by royalty. Her 1638 dissertation in Latin on women's learning was reprinted in 1641, translated into French in 1646 and into English in 1659 as *The Learned Maid, Or, Whether a Maid May Be a Scholar*. This text and selected correspondence appear in her *Opuscula hebraea, graeca, latina, gallica, prosaica et metrica* (1650). By the time *Eukleria* appeared in print in 1673, Schurman had withdrawn from public life for more than two decades in her pursuit of an ideal religious community led by Jean de Labadie. The movement he inspired and the story of Schurman's life constitute the main parts of *Eukleria*, which was published five years before her death in 1678.

The praise of learning in Schurman's *Dissertatio logica* and selected letters (in *Opuscula* 2nd ed. [1650]) tackles the question of "Whether a Christian Woman Should be Educated." Of the fourteen theses Schurman summons to defend this idea, the first seven mainly respond to negative assumptions about women's capabilities; the final seven point out the moral and intellectual virtue of such learning. For her fourth argument, which addresses the matter of suitability for the study of letters, Schurman states, "Whoever longs greatly for a solid and enduring occupation" is most qualified to pursue such study (28). Moreover, says Schurman, those with the greatest amount of leisure have the greatest "need of a solid and enduring occupation," noting that it is wealthy women who have such leisure and hence can profit the most from such study (29).

Other arguments extend the reasons for study on the part of a Christian to men and women alike: argument six promotes the "diligent and serious mediation on the divine word, the knowledge of God, and the consideration of his most beautiful works," thereby claiming all of nature as its purview (29); argument ten urges the pursuit of right reason as a way to fortify oneself against heresies (31); and arguments twelve and thirteen assert the appropriateness of studying that which "leads to true greatness of soul" and "fills the human mind with exceptional and honest delight" (32). Schurman, who concludes by considering five objections to her arguments, later found that her mentor, Dr. André Rivet, had many more, which he revealed in a series of letters between them (39–56). His chief objection, however, was that Schurman constituted an exception to the rule about the suitability of education for women and hence should not be used as a reason to revise those views. Crocker, however, who praises Schurman's "extraordinary capacity in learning," situates Schurman within a long line of accomplished women who lend the force of example to her argument.

Another authoritative text cited by Crocker is *The Equality of the Sexes*, an essay by François Poullain de le Barre (1647–1723) that was published in Paris in 1673 and translated into English by A. L. four years later. Born in 1647, Poullain studied for the priesthood, which he entered in 1680 even though he already had grave doubts about his scholastic education, which he deemed worthless: "[N]othing I had learned was of any use in the world except to make a living in a profession which I did not wish to follow" (Poullain, *Equality* 3). Repudiating scholastic philosophy in favor of the philosophy of René Descartes, Poullain participated in the lively *querelle des femmes* by writing three books about it in as many years: *De l'Égalité des Deux Sexes* (*On the Equality of the Two Sexes*; 1673); *De l'Education des Dames pour la Conduite de l'Espirit dans les Sciences et dans les Moeurs* (*On the Education of Ladies*; 1674); and *De l'Éxcellence des Hommes, Contre l'Égalité des Sexes* (*On the Excellence of Men: Preface and Remarks*; 1675).[16] Although the title of the latter suggests that Poullain had retracted his earlier position, he actually had not. Surprised that no one opposed his views, he decided to present the other side, even though he said what prompted him to do so was not "to prove that [men] are superior to women since I am persuaded more than ever of the opposite" (*Equality* 4). A convert to Calvinism, Poullain left Paris after the revocation of the Edict of Nantes in 1685 and settled in Geneva where he wrote *La Doctrine des protestants sur la liberté de lire l'Ecriture Sainte* (*The Protestant Doctrine of Freedom to Read Holy Scripture*; 1720).[17]

The thread that ties together Poullain's *Equality of the Sexes* and *The Protestant Doctrine of Freedom to Read Holy Scripture* is his radical Cartesianism, which elevates reason above tradition.[18] According to Poullain, the subjection of women cannot be proved according to Scripture, and those who insist otherwise are guilty of eisigesis, that is, of reading into a text their own prejudices instead of recognizing the social conditions that produced the text in the first place. Earlier in *Equality*, Poullain argues against the habit of reading into nature a belief in the subjection of women. Those who make the laws are guilty of doing this, argues Poullain, since they "have attributed to nature a distinction which derives from custom" (82). Moreover, Poullain insists that the mind "has no sex" and that it "has the same nature in all human beings" (87). Any differences can be attributed solely to custom, says Poullain:

> The brain of women is exactly like ours. Sensory impressions are received in the brain and are combined in the same way; they are stored for the imagination and memory in the same way. Women hear by means of their ears, as we do; they see with their eyes and taste with their tongue; there is nothing unusual in the disposition of these organs in women except that they are usually more refined than in men, which is an advantage. Thus external objects affect them in the same way as they affect us, light through the eyes and sound through the ears. What would prevent them, therefore, from applying themselves to study their own selves . . . and engaging in the science called metaphysics? (88)

He answers resoundingly: "*nothing but custom*" (emphasis added).

Concluding that any faults that women have are either imagined or due to their education, Poullain ends the treatise with a scathing attack on many of the most eminent philosophers in the Western tradition (131–33): Plato, who thanked God he was not born a woman; Aristotle, who said women are monsters; the students of Philo, who argued that women are imperfect men—perhaps, says Poullain, because they lack a beard; Socrates, who compared women with a temple that "looks well but is built on a sewer," a remark, says Poullain, that "[o]ne could only laugh at . . . if it did not cause offence" (132); Diogenes, who likened two women talking together to two snakes exchanging their venom; and Cato, who asked the pardon of the gods should he ever disclose a secret to a woman.

Attacking ancient authorities is not Crocker's preferred mode; nevertheless, she makes similar assertions about women's rights. Her assertions, however, are grounded in Scripture rather than custom. According to Crocker, the equality of women, assured at creation, was lost at the time of the fall but has been restored through the redemptive act of Christ. The consequence of this redemptive act is that "[t]he offers of divine grace are equally tendered to both male and female; and all have equal right to accept the blessing" (*Observations* 14). The spiritual equality lauded by Crocker, however, is by no means restricted to the life hereafter. Like Schurman and Poullain, Crocker believed that here and now women should read the Bible in the vernacular on their own. As many historians have noted, promoting such reading practices led to high literacy rates among women in countries influenced by the Reformation. Unlike Schurman, however, few could read the Bible in any of the original languages with sufficient competency to engage in exegetical study. The horizon of expectations, then, was doubly raised for women during this period: from illiteracy to literacy, for most Protestant women, and literacy to superliteracy, for a very, very few such as Schurman.

Writing more than a hundred years after Schurman and Poullain, Germaine de Staël (1766–1817) serves Crocker as a major example of a woman writer who, building on the legacy of the Protestant Reformation, raised the bar yet again for what an educated woman could do. In chapter 4 of *Observations*, Crocker argues that contemporaneous women writers are equal to those of the past, especially "Madam de Staal [sic]," who "for strength of mind, true magnanimity, patriotism, and independence, as well as her literary talents and acquirements, shines unequalled" (44). Of particular relevance for Crocker was de Staël's book, *The Influence of Literature upon Society* (1800), also known by the title *On Literature Considered in Its Relationship to Social Institutions*. In the preface to the second edition, de Staël laments that readers have not bothered to respond to her theory but instead criticize her for daring to write at all. By way of summarizing those criticisms, she supplies her own translation of lines spoken by Arnolphe in act 1, scene 1, of Molière's 1662 play *The School for Wives*:

> I'll have nothing to do with an uplifted wit
> For a woman who writes is more knowing than fit.
> My own wife's understanding will not be sublime—
> She should never have even *heard* of a rhyme—
> And all my wife needs to be able to do
> Is, pray God, to love me, to spin flax, and sew.
> (qtd. in de Staël, *Extraordinary* 172)

Instead of challenging the criticism leveled at her, de Staël acknowledges that people may have multiple motives for attacking her, but takes the high road by assuming disbelief: "[T]o tell the Truth," she writes, "I am incapable of believing anybody really feels that way" (*Extraordinary* 172).

The section of her book "On Women Writers" (2.4) offers compelling evidence that de Staël recognized that there were plenty of people who felt that way, given that the structures of consciousness about women's equality in France had not yet undergone a fundamental change. In her vision of women's equality in France, de Staël writes that the "day will come when philosophical legislators will give serious attention to the education of women, to the laws protecting them, to the duties which should be imposed on them, to the happiness which can be guaranteed them. At present," argues de Staël, "most women belong neither to the natural nor to the social order" (201). Whether massive upheavals brought by the Reign of Terror may have brought about changes in the social order sooner than the social dislocations ushered in by the English Revolution is a matter that de Staël confronts twenty years later in her *Considerations on the Principal Events of the French Revolution* (1818).

Noting that religious quarrels started the English Revolution, de Staël acknowledges, "The Puritans were also affected by love of equality, the underground volcano of France, but the English were genuinely religious—and religious Protestants, which makes people more moderate as well as more austere" (*Extraordinary* 366). Given de Staël's Romantic view that cataclysmic change may disrupt yet be a part of a greater continuity, her attachment to the superiority of the French Revolution over that of the English would be understandable. Here, however, de Staël resists such an impulse, although elsewhere she unabashedly praises the literature produced in the colonies that once owed their allegiance to the British Crown as "the literature of an enlightened people, who have established liberty, political equality, and manners in harmony with such institutions. Right now," she declares, "the Americans are the only nation in the universe to which these reflections are applicable" (185).

Such a reflection was not likely to come from Hannah More (1745–1833), who took a very dim view of the American Revolution, judging by the frequency of her barbed comments about America and its citizens. By choosing More as the person to whom she dedicated her book and by using More as a site of cultural authority, Crocker richly complicates her *Observations*. At first glance, More seems an obvious choice. Like Schurman, Poullain, and de Staël, More expanded expectations for women's education from literacy to superliteracy. More's first play, *The Search after Happiness*, published in 1773 but written when she was sixteen, articulates her views about women who write and the hostility they evoke from both sexes:

> Tho' should we still the rhyming trade pursue,
> The men will shun us,—and the women, too;
> The men, poor souls! Of *scholars* are afraid,
> We shou'd not, did they *govern*, learn to read,
> At least in no abstruser volume look,
> Than the learn'd records—of a Cookery book;
> The ladies, too, in their well-meant censure give,
> 'What!- does she write? A slattern, as I live—
> 'I wish she'd leave her books, and mend her cloaths,
> I thank my stars I know not verse from prose.'[19]
> (qtd. in Clarke 157)

The theme of a needle or a ladle providing a better fit for a woman's hand than a pen is used by More to highlight the difference between literacy and superliteracy, a gain apparently not to be realized by all women.[20] In *Thoughts on the Importance of the Manners of the Great to General Society* (1788) and *An estimate of the religion of the fashionable world, by one of the laity* (1790), More enjoins middle- and upper-class women to abandon a life of dissipation in favor of one filled with purpose and meaning by exerting their influence to accomplish good in the world. To judge from many of the tracts More wrote, an especially suitable goal was to serve as an example for poor women whose own horizons were limited and should remain that way.

Extending the horizon of expectations from literacy to superliteracy clearly applied to herself. More received her earliest education from her schoolmaster father and later acquired facility in Latin, French, Italian, and Spanish at a school started by her eldest sister. The settlement of a lump sum in addition to a yearly payment of £200 following a broken engagement to William Turner gave More the freedom to pursue her own path. Initially she was drawn to the theater and enjoyed more than a modicum of success in 1777 with *Percy, A Tragedy*, a historical drama presented at Covent Garden by David Garrick from December 1777 to January 1778.[21] After Garrick's death, she turned from playwriting to writing poetry, essays, and a novel. These include her poem, "The Slave Trade" (1788); the essays in 1788 and 1790, already mentioned, directed to middle- and upper-class women; "Village Politics" (1792); a series of widely circulated *Cheap repository tracts*, including tales and ballads, that were published over a period of many years starting in 1795; and *Strictures on the Modern System of Female Education* (1799). The shift in genre signaled a corresponding shift in her social world. By 1785, both Garrick and Dr. Samuel Johnson had died, and More was no longer a member of the Garrick-Johnson-Reynolds circle or of the *Bas Bleu* set, epitomized by Lady Elizabeth Montagu. Instead, she turned her attention to the Anti Slave Trade Movement, led by William Wilberforce (More, *Selected Writings* xxvi).

Although a didactic element appears in several of More's plays, in her later writings the urge to reform became predominant and problematic. On the one hand, More inveighs against trafficking in human beings in "The Slave Trade," a poem credited by many with wielding considerable influence for the abolitionist cause. Dripping with disdain for those who argue against racial difference in mental powers, the lines of the poem cut no slack for the supporters of slavery:

> Perish th' illiberal thought which would debase
> The native genius of the sable race!

Perish the proud philosophy, which sought
To rob them of the pow'rs of equal thought

Does then th' immortal principle within
Change with the casual colour of a skin?
(*Works* 27)

In "The Sorrows of Yamba, or the Negro Woman's Lamentation," one of the many ballads she wrote in the series *Cheap repository tracts*, More unleashes her invective against the political system that created the conditions ripe for slavery, a system of government that directly contravenes the central tenets of Christianity on which she believed it to be based:

Cease, ye British Sons of murder!
Cease from forging's Afric's chain
Mock your Saviour's name no further,
Cease your savage lust of gain.

Ye that boast '*Ye rule the waves,*'
Bid No Slave Ship soil the sea,
Ye, that '*never will be slaves,*'
Bid poor Afric's land be free.
(*Selected Writings* 471)

On the other hand, "Village Politics, by Will Chip, a Country Carpenter," an essay widely known to have come from her pen, takes an ultra-counterrevolutionary position (*Works* 58–63). In it, More argues forcefully that the poor should reform themselves but in doing so should not expect to rise beyond their station in life as decreed by God. Despite the prosperity that had come to middle-class farmers as a result of improved agricultural methods, wage laborers were not encouraged during this period to believe that a rising tide would lift all boats. For factory workers, conditions were equally dismal (Hopkins 204–5).[22]

Reflecting the fear of the middle and upper classes that the French Revolution might take hold in Great Britain, "Village Politics" rails against liberty, equality, and the rights of man. When Jack Anvil, the blacksmith, sees the mason Tom Hod reading a book, he asks him what it is and why he looks so dejected. Tom replies, "Cause enough. I find here that I am very unhappy, and very miserable; which I should never have known if I had not had the good luck to meet with this book. Oh, 'tis a precious book!" (*Works* 1: 58). While reading the Bible was a desired outcome of gains in literacy for the poor, using their newly acquired skills to read Thomas Paine's *Rights of Man* (1791–92) or William Godwin's *Enquiry concerning political justice; and its influence on general virtue and happiness* (1793) was not what those who taught them to read had in mind (Hopkins 205). Later, when Jack interprets Tom's desire for a new constitution as a sign that he is ill, Tom counters, "I'm not sick; I want liberty and equality, and the rights of man." Jack responds, "What! Thou art a leveller and a republican, I warrant!" (*Works* 1: 58).

More makes no attempt to justify democratic ideas in her work (in fact, she consistently does the opposite); nevertheless, it is the rare instance of leveling rhetoric in her *Strictures on Female Education* that Crocker found especially appealing in mounting her own defense for women's equality. "My respected Miss H. More observes in her comparative view of the sexes," writes Crocker, that "whatever inferiority may be attached to women from the slighter frame of her body, or the more circumscribed powers of her mind, or from a less systematical education, or from the subordinate station she is called to fill in life, there is one leading circumstance, which raises her importance, and even establishes her equality. Christianity has exalted women to true and undisputed dignity in Christ Jesus" (*Observations* 23–24).[23] As proof, More borrows from Paul's Epistle to the Galatians (3.28), which Crocker also includes: "As there is neither rich nor poor, bond nor free, there is neither male nor female, in the view of that immortality which is brought to light by the gospel."[24] Earlier, in building her argument against female inferiority in *Observations on the real rights of women,* Crocker contrasted Muslim and Christian views of women, noting Lady Montagu's comment that, contrary to received opinion, Islam does affirm the belief that women have souls; however, according to Crocker, Montagu concedes that women's souls are judged by Muslims to be inferior to those of men (*Observations* 23).

To conclude this part of her argument, Crocker continues the long quotation from More's *Strictures,* the lengthiest in *Observations,* that "women make up one half of the human race, equally redeemed by the blood of Christ."[25] The two instances in which More uses some variant of the word *equal* (*equality* in the first example; *equally* in the second) stand out in stark contrast to the overall thrust of *Strictures,* which succeeds in isolating the spiritual equality More is willing to acknowledge—indeed, celebrate—from any notion of social or political equality. Although More may claim that Christianity has made women "heirs of a blessed immortality hereafter" and has raised them "to an eminence in the scale of beings unknown to the most polished ages of antiquity" (qtd. in Crocker, *Observations* 24), earthly matters in the here and now are given short shrift when it comes to equality. Nowhere is this more evident than in the rhetoric about rights in More's *Strictures.*[26]

Unlike Crocker, who highlights the real rights of women in the title and text of *Observations*, More claims in *Strictures* that "[i]t is her zeal for their true *interests* which leads her to oppose their imaginary *rights*" (2: 24). Using *rights* as a synonym for *equality*, More argues that, "among the innovations of this innovating period, the imposing term of *rights* has been produced to sanctify the claims of our female pretenders, with a view not only to rekindle in the minds of women a presumptuous vanity dishonourable to their sex, but produced with a view to excite in their hearts an impious discontent with the post which God has assigned them in this world" (*Strictures* 2: 21).[27] According to More, the assertion of rights by women would threaten to undo the series of interlocking pairs that subsumed individuals under God, citizens under the ruling monarch, communicants under the Archbishop of the Church of England, children under parents, wife under husband, and wage-laborer under farmer or factory manager. In short, Great Britain's orderly, well-regulated society would succumb to the anarchic forces unleashed by the French Revolution if women would refuse to be satisfied with their lot in life. By accepting their God-ordained position, women would find that the privileges they are denied have benefits that may have gone unrecognized, or so More would have her readers believe: if you do not attain an eminent position, then you will never suffer the shame of losing it; if you do not serve in an assembly, then you can avoid the duties that accompany such an honor, and so on. The final blow More delivers to women who aspire to the same rights as men is to accuse women of lacking Christian humility and the proper perspective; were they to have it, they would set their sights not on earthly rewards but on heavenly ones instead (*Strictures* 2: 38–39).

The Protestant ideology embraced by More brooked no dissent, or, rather, the dissent that it tolerated was exceedingly selective. Although she applauded the Church of England for its break with Catholicism in the sixteenth century, she evinced no sympathy for the Puritan Revolution a century later; or for the 1828 repeal of the Test and Corporation Acts in her own day that granted social and political freedom to Dissenters, albeit male; or for male Catholics who finally won their right to representation in 1829. The expectation that she would be sympathetic to these causes, and hence to women's rights, perhaps arises because of her link with the movement known as Evangelicalism. As Robert Hole notes, this is problematic because of the difficulty of defining the term in that period, especially given its Low Church associations. "More," says Hole, "disliked Methodists and Methodism, which she saw as a lower-class movement which weakened the alliance between church and state" (More, *Selected Writings* xli). He also cautions against the assumption that the concern Evangelicals harbored for the poor and for slaves represented an attempt to contravene the established order; however, he does so at the risk of overlooking the incipient equality contained in Paul's assertion that in Christ all differences are set aside. By bracketing spiritual equality, More left no room for a rhetoric of rights; for that, Crocker had to look elsewhere.

She needed to look no further than Mary Wollstonecraft (1759–97). In doing so, however, Crocker elides the differences between Wollstonecraft and More. Nowhere in *Observations* is there any acknowledgment that More's *Strictures on the Modern System of Female Education* was written as a rebuttal to Wollstonecraft's *A Vindication of the rights of woman* (1792); likewise, the clear political lines demarcated by More, who aligns herself with Edmund Burke and William Pitt against Wollstonecraft, Catherine Macaulay, and Thomas Paine, simply do not surface in Crocker's text. She concentrates, instead, on the ideas in *Vindication* that she finds congenial for the argument she pursues, in this instance, the desire to prove that women have produced writers who can hold their own with men and even surpass them. Of Wollstonecraft, Crocker writes that she "was a woman of great energy and a very independent mind; her Rights of Women are replete with fine sentiments." Crocker concedes, however, that "[Wollstonecraft's] theory is unfit for practice, though some of her sentiments and distinctions would do honour to the pen, even of a man" (Crocker, *Observations* 41).[28] Similarly, Crocker praises the writing ability of Macaulay, lamenting that she died without the recognition she richly deserved for "intellectual acquirements, supposed to be incompatible with the weakness of her sex." Judging her writing style, Crocker states approvingly that, "indeed no sex appears, for it is like the sense it conveys, strong and clear" (41).

The embrace of Wollstonecraft by Crocker extends further. The phrase, *rights of woman*, in the title of Wollstonecraft's text appears to have been borrowed by Crocker for her own use with slight modification: Crocker added *real* to *rights* and shifted from the singular to the plural form of *woman*. One could argue that Crocker demonstrates an attempt to balance the views of Wollstonecraft with those of More by adding to the title, *Observations on the real rights of women*, the phrase, *with their appropriate duties, agreeable to Scripture, reason, and common sense*, the remainder of her title. Substantively, Wollstonecraft also offered Crocker a firmer basis for the argument she advances than does More, who grants that in Christ men and women are equal, but shows no willingness to broaden an understanding of what such spiritual equality might mean. Wollstonecraft, in contrast, makes the leap immediately in *A Vindication of the rights of woman*:

> Gracious Creator of the whole human race! Hast Thou created such a being as woman, who can trace Thy wisdom in Thy works, and feel that Thou alone art by Thy nature exalted far above her, for no better

purpose? Can she believe that she was only made to submit to man, her equal—a being who, like her, was sent into the world to acquire virtue? Can she consent to be occupied merely to please him—merely to adorn the earth—when her soul is capable of rising to Thee? And can she rest supinely dependent on man for reason, when she ought to mount with him the arduous steeps of knowledge? (144)

Although Wollstonecraft rejected the Calvinistic doctrine of original sin in favor of Enlightenment values, the ideas she promotes in this passage situate her squarely within the Protestant tradition that emphasized the individual priesthood of the believer and hence gave rise to the idea of spiritual equality.[29]

This core belief lies at the root of western feminism, and Wollstonecraft's *Vindication* amply illustrates its tenacious hold even among those for whom the belief was no longer a matter of doctrinal adhesion. Certainly for Wollstonecraft it had ceased to be a matter of doctrine, even though she had attended church regularly for almost three decades.[30] She stopped, however, in 1787, the year *Thoughts on the education of Daughters* was published, despite the warnings she issues in that text about the perils of not being religious. Wollstonecraft's views on the subject, as Barbara Taylor notes, underwent more radical changes. In her *Letters Written during a short residence in Sweden, Norway, and Denmark* (1796), Wollstonecraft reserves high praise for those who dare to "deny the divinity of Jesus Christ, and . . . question the necessity or utility of the christian system" (qtd. in Taylor, *Mary Wollstonecraft* 95).[31] The many comments on religion in *Vindication*, published four years earlier, suggest that Wollstonecraft's views may have become secularized, but were not idiosyncratic.[32]

Of the dozens of passages in *Vindication* that employ religious themes,[33] the belief in the responsibility of the individual before God remains paramount, as the following suggests: "For if it be allowed that women were destined by Providence to acquire human virtues, and, by the exercise of their understandings, that stability of character which is the firmest ground to rest our future hopes upon, they must be permitted to turn to the foundation of light, and not forced to shape their course by the twinkling of a mere satellite" (88). Wollstonecraft's emphasis in *Vindication* on spiritual matters found a ready response in Crocker, unlike Ann Snitow who claims that Wollstonecraft's many "appeals to God and virtue are a dead letter to feminists now" (529). For Crocker, Wollstonecraft's treatment of religious themes had quite the opposite effect by lending vigor to her own argument, even though Crocker's stress on "vital piety, or heart religion" may not have been combined with an emphasis on reason to the exact degree that they were for Wollstonecraft.[34]

Common to Wollstonecraft, More, and Crocker is the emphasis on "mutuality," even though they register important differences in their understanding of it. For More, who stressed the relational distinctions between men and women, "mutuality" is occasionally invoked but the relation always remains hierarchical, except when it comes to spiritual matters. Wollstonecraft, always at the opposite end of the spectrum on the matter of hierarchy, tends to be nonrelational by emphasizing similarities between the sexes. Yet, even Wollstonecraft, as Margaret MacFadden notes in *Golden Cables of Sympathy: The Transatlantic Sources of Nineteenth-Century Feminism,* occasionally relies on the relationist language of republican motherhood in her conclusion to *A Vindication of the rights of woman* (134–35). The best example appears in her reflection that, to become "truly useful members of society," women must "acquire a rational affection for their country." For that to happen, Wollstonecraft argues, it is necessary to understand "that private duties are never properly fulfilled unless the understanding enlarges the heart; and that public virtue is only an aggregate of private" (291).

Occupying a place in the middle is Hannah Mather Crocker, whose arguments for women's rights are chiefly relational but not exclusively so. Although the appeal to republican motherhood figures much more significantly in Crocker than in Wollstonecraft, Crocker's relationist views do not reflect More's decidedly hierarchical bent. At the heart of Crocker's *Observations* lies a central contradiction that resists resolution because of a rhetorical strategy that elides difference from the start. On the page following the dedication of *Observations* to "Miss H. More," Crocker expresses in the "Author's Preface" the "hope, that the work will receive the candour and patronage of a free, enlightened, independent, federal nation" (iv). The strategy, pursued by Crocker throughout the text, appears in her observation about the rights of women in the penultimate chapter when she states, "Very little has been written on it in America" because "[i]t may naturally be supposed [that] the ideas of a free, independent people will be more liberal and expanded respecting the sexual rights" (65).

In constructing an argument for the equal rights of women by tracing its trajectory from the Protestant Reformation to the American Revolution, Crocker offers a genealogy whose blurred outlines are coming into sharper focus. The genealogy serves as a reminder that the points represented by Anna Maria van Schurman, François Poullain de La Barre, Germaine de Staël, Hannah More, and Mary Wollstonecraft in Crocker's text represents not a single path but the convergence of a variety of Protestant influences on the development of women's rights. Other trajectories employed by Crocker await the intrepid efforts of those engaged in the task of literary excavation.

NOTES

1. Crocker's *Observations* has received little scholarly attention. Barbara J. Berg's *The Remembered Gate: Origins of American Feminism* does not mention it at all, and Eleanor Flexner in *Century of Struggle: The Woman's Rights Movement in the United States* devotes only two pages to it (24–25) and a footnote (354n2). A notable exception is Robert Riegel's *American Feminists*, which acknowledges that Hannah Mather Crocker wrote "the first feministic book by an American woman" (7).

2. Hunter's *Sacred Biography of the History of the patriarchs, to which is added the history of Deborah, Ruth & Hannah being a course of lectures delivered at the Scots church* was also printed in London, New York, Philadelphia, Walpole (NH), and Burlington (VT). The text incorporates separate texts Hunter wrote earlier about the patriarchs and a history of Jesus. Hunter also translated the sermons of Joseph Saurin (1659–1737), whom Crocker cites in *Observations* as "the eloquent Saurin," in noting his observation concerning Adam and Eve that "reason is quickly deceived . . . when the senses have been seduced" (10).

3. Nor are women the only persons to make her A-list. In an apparent attempt to offer a balanced view of the sexes, Crocker includes a catalogue of illustrious men in the Appendix (75–89).

4. Focusing instead on equal mental abilities, Crocker aligns herself with other writers on the subject of women's rights. In listing outstanding women, Oberea seems to be Crocker's choice of a woman who exemplified Amazonian strength, a conclusion Hawkesworth's account invites. "A representation of the surrender of the island of Otaheite to Captain Wallis by the supposed Queen Oberea" (Cut No. 23, facing p. 27), however, suggests that the difference in physical strength is racial, given Hawkesworth's depiction of Tahitian men and women as a head or so taller than the Englishmen arriving on the island.

5. The most often cited text about women by Plutarch (46–120 BC) is "Bravery of Women." In *Concerning Famous Women* (ca. 1365), Giovanni Boccaccio (1313–75) wrote brief biographies of infamous women, although most of his are drawn from antiquity. Christine de Pizan (1365–1431) concentrates primarily on saintly women in *The Book of the City of Ladies* (1405). Baldassare Castiglione (1478–1529) wrote *The Book of the Courtier* (1528), which was first translated into English in 1561. In his *Declamation on the Nobility and Preeminence of the Female Sex* (1529), Henricus Cornelius Agrippa (1486[?]–1535) relied on both Plutarch and Boccaccio. Voetius's *Concerning Women* appears in book 1, treatise 4, of his major work, *Politica Ecclesiastica* (1663–76).

6. According to Ann Firor Scott, this compilation was followed by many more on both sides of the Atlantic. These biographies, which often started with Eve and ended with contemporary women, were based on a variety of sources, ancient (Biblical and classical) and modern. Samuel G. Goodrich (1793–1860) began his *Lives of celebrated women* (1844) by noting, "It may indeed be true that the *happiness* of women is generally to be found in the quiet of the domestic circle, but that all without distinction should be confined to it, and that whenever one of the sex departs from it she departs from her allotted sphere, is no more true than a similar proposition would be of men" (n.p.). Other compilations include *Noble Deeds of American women* (1851), for which the editor J. [Jesse] Clement (dates unknown) claimed that eight thousand copies had been sold in two years, and *Woman's Record; or, Sketches of all distinguished women, from "the beginning" till A. D. 1850* (1853) by Sarah Josepha Hale (1788–1879), which went through several editions.

7. Crocker does not mention Adams's catalogue as a source. Perhaps more surprising is her omission of any reference to Anne Bradstreet (c. 1612–72), a woman whose strong Protestant leanings take center stage in "A Dialogue between Old England and New; Concerning their Present Troubles, Anno, 1642" (*Tenth Muse* 180–90). Bradstreet's undated poem "In Honour of That High and Mighty Princess Queen Elizabeth of Happy Memory" does include a short catalogue of famous women, but Crocker does not appear to have used it as a source. Of those Bradstreet holds under scrutiny—Semiramis, Tomris, Cleopatra, and Zenobia—all pale in comparison with the great Elizabeth (*Tenth Muse* 199–20).

8. The section of Schurman's *Dissertatio logica* discussed in this paper is *Whether the Study of Letters Is Fitting for a Christian Woman* (*Whether a Christian Woman* 25–37). It is part of Schurman's *Opuscula*, which was Irwin's choice of text to translate in her 1998 edition of Schurman's writings. Nowhere in her book does Irwin mention why she did not choose to translate the first version of this *Dissertatio*, entitled *Amica Dissertatio* (1638).

9. Gerald M. MacLean's 1988 edition, which appears as *The Woman As Good As the Man, Or, Equality of Both Sexes*, relies on the English translation by "A. L." that Nathaniel Brooks published in 1677. The book was originally published in Paris as *De l'égalité des deux sexes* in 1673; *The Equality of the Sexes*, a translation from the original French with an introduction and notes by Desmond M. Clarke, was published in 1990.

10. Rpt. in de Staël, *An Extraordinary Women: Selected Writings of Germaine de Staël* 170–208. Born Anne-Louise Necker in Paris in 1766, she married Eric Staël von Holstein in 1786.

11. Richard Mather was her great great-grandfather; Increase Mather, her great-grandfather; Cotton Mather, her grandfather; and Samuel, Cotton Mather's sole surviving son, her father.

12. For Mather to mention that Ames's library was brought to New England, as well as his widow and children, is understandable, given the importance he attached to his own library, which had few rivals in sheer number of volumes. Mather also mentions Schurman in his *Diary* (2: 325).

13. Mather's reference is to Jan van Beverwyck's *Van de wtnementheyt des vrouwelicken geslacts* (1639).

14. In *Whether a Christian Woman Should be Educated and Other Writings from Her Intellectual Circle*, Joyce L. Irwin, editor and translator, notes that Schurman wrote an Ethiopian grammar (5).

15. Although Crocker mentions Madame De Gournay (1565–1645) right before her comments about Schurman (*Observations* 36), she says nothing about the criticism Gournay leveled at Schurman for spending so much time in the pursuit of the mastery of many languages. Schurman, however, acknowledges Gournay's criticism in her 8 December 1646 reply to De Gournay's letter (Schurman 70–71).

16. Translations of these three works appear in Poullain's *Three Cartesian Feminist Treatises*.

17. Noting that eighty persons a day were guillotined, Germaine de Staël comments that it was "as if the massacre of Saint Bartholomew's Day had begun again, drop by drop," a reference to the 1572 massacre of French Protestants ordered by Charles IX, son of Catherine de Medicis. The massacre started on the eve of a royal wedding, but the bloodbath did not end until the Edict of Nantes in 1598 (de Staël 368).

18. According to Desmond M. Clarke, Poullain makes it clear from the outset that he rejects ancient authorities in favor of reason (Poullain, *Equality* 22). In the preface to *Equality*, Poullain states that objections can "derive from the authority of famous men, and from Holy Scripture. As regards the first of these," says Poullain, "I think that I can answer them satisfactorily by saying that I recognise no authority apart from the authority of reason and of sound judgment" (44). On the issue of the authority of Scripture in the matter of the equality of the sexes, Poullain asserts that "objections which are derived from Scripture are only the fallacious arguments of prejudice, by which some passages are understood as if they applied to all women when they refer only to some individuals in particular, or something is attributed to nature which results only from education or custom or from what the sacred authors say about the customs of their own times" (44). Clarke asserts that Poullain's preface to *The Protestant Doctrine of Freedom* expresses a similar view by enjoining the reader "'not to take account of the age or novelty of beliefs, the number, titles, or wealth of those who defend them, except as supports which are common to truth and error and, at most, reasons for examining them'" (23).

19. Crocker expresses a similar sentiment in *Observations:* "There may be a few grovelling minds who think woman should not aspire to any further knowledge than to obtain enough of the cymical [sic] art to enable them to compound a good pudding, pie, or cake, for her lord and master to discompound. Others, of a still weaker class, may say it is enough for woman scientifically to arrange the spinning wheel and distaff, and exercise her extensive capacity in knitting and sewing, since the fall and restoration of woman these employments have been the appropriate duties of the female sex" (17).

20. Although sewing and cooking are both compared to writing by More and Crocker, Bradstreet invokes an analogy only with sewing. In the prologue to *The Tenth Muse*, Bradstreet declares, "I am obnoxious to each carping tongue, / Who sayes, my hand a needle better fits" (4).

21. Although this play was a box-office success, More's greatest admirers willingly admit that she had little in the way of dramatic talent. Other plays include *The Search after Happiness:*

A Pastoral Drama (1773); *The Inflexible Captive: A Tragedy* (1774), which she translated from *Attilio Regolo* by Pietro Metastasio (1698–1782); and *The Fatal Falsehood: A Tragedy* (1779).

22. Hopkins admits that More "acquiesced in the prevailing middle- and upper-class view that rigid social distinctions was God's own benevolent plan and that it was therefore wrong for the poor to try to raise themselves to higher economic or social levels by means of workers' unions or by efforts to change laws which bore harshly upon them" (203).

23. Crocker departs only slightly from More's original comment in *Strictures on Female Education:* "The practical use of female knowledge—Sketch of the female character,—A comparative view of the sexes" (2: 31–32).

24. Gal. 3.28 is rendered as follows: "There is neither Jew nor Greek, there is neither bond nor free, there is neither male nor female: for ye are all one in Christ Jesus" (KJV). Cf. Col. 3.11: "[W]here there is neither Greek nor Jew, circumcision nor uncircumcision, Barbarian, Scythian, bond nor free: but Christ is all and in all" (KJV). The allusion to Paul is not attributed by either More in *Strictures* or Crocker in *Observations* (24), perhaps because they could not imagine that their readers would be unable to identify the original source. More, however, places quotation marks around the phrases "rich nor poor," "bond nor free," and "male nor female" (2: 32).

25. More begins this quotation with the phrase, "To borrow the idea of an excellent prelate," but does not identify which one (*Strictures* 2: 32).

26. More complains in *Strictures* that "[t]he *rights of man* have been discussed, till we are somewhat wearied with the discussion. To these have been opposed, with more presumption than prudence, *the rights of woman*. It follows, according to the natural progression of human things, that the next stage of that irradiation which our enlighteners are pouring in upon us will produce grave descants on the *rights of children*" (1: 145).

27. More's conservative views about women's rights perhaps account for the absence of More in Moira Ferguson's *First Feminists: British Women Writers, 1578–1799* (1985), in which a frontispiece reproduction of Richard Samuel's 1799 painting "Nine Living Muses" depicts Hannah More, Elizabeth Montagu, Elizabeth Griffith, Catherine Macaulay, Elizabeth Carter, Anna Letitia Barbauld, Angelica Kauffman, Elizabeth Linley, and Charlotte Lenox. Of the nine women, More is one of only two whose writings are not excerpted in Ferguson's anthology.

28. Cathy N. Davidson comments that Wollstonecraft's *Vindication*, published in 1792 and reprinted in 1794, "was available from some 30 percent of the libraries in America" (131). An American printing of the text added to its popularity. As Davison notes, the publication of William Godwin's *Memoirs* in 1798 transformed the popularity into notoriety: "Reviewers did not praise Wollstonecraft's unconventional thought but condemned her unconventional life" (132). The result, says Davidson, is that "Wollstonecraftism (a word used to designate the equalitarian feminist movement) became a damning label for the loose feminine morals in which libertarian principles, ostensibly, necessarily ended" (133). Twenty years later, adds Davidson, Samuel Miller deemed it necessary to remind his parishioners of what "radical feminism had actually been" in his sermon "The Appropriate Duty and Ornament of the Female Sex" (*The Columbian Preacher; or, A collection of original sermons, from preachers of eminence in the United States, embracing the distinguishing doctrines of grace* [1808, 133; Davidson 295n68]). By the time Crocker's *Observations* was published in 1818, the passage of three decades had considerably softened critics of Wollstonecraft.

29. The belief in spiritual equality empowered a broad spectrum of Protestant women. On the one hand, it included such figures as Mary Astell, a High Anglican who asserted, "Whatever . . . Reasons Men may have for despising Women, and keeping them in Ignorance and Slavery, it can't be from their having learnt to do so in Holy Scripture. The Bible is for, and not against us, and cannot without great Violence done to it, be urged to our Prejudice" (84). On the other hand, it attracted women believers in various Protestant sects, including Elizabeth Ashbridge, a Quaker convert who records her steadfast search for truth despite her husband's fierce resistance in *Some Account of the Fore Part of the Life of Elizabeth Ashbridge* (1774).

30. See Taylor's discussion of Wollstonecraft's religious views in "For the Love of God" in *Mary Wollstonecraft and the Feminist Imagination*, 95–142.

31. Taylor points out that the remark refers to the Norwegians, whom Wollstonecraft considered to be "'the least oppressed people of Europe'" (273n4).

32. Godwin insisted that Wollstonecraft's religion "was almost entirely of her own creation" and was by no means systematic (*Memoirs of the Author* 215). Taylor, however, finds that Godwin's skepticism makes him an unreliable source in this matter of assessing Wollstonecraft's religious views (*Mary Wollstonecraft* 95–96).

33. By Taylor's count, there are at least fifty ("Religious Foundations" 104).

34. Although Flexner in *Mary Wollstonecraft: A Biography* claims that Wollstonecraft "rested her argument, not on appeals to justice, or logic—sheer reason itself—but on the basic principles of faith," she concedes that it was faith of a sort that aligns Wollstonecraft "with the ameliorists who believe that history moves in the direction of progress." Flexner maintains that Wollstonecraft "differs from the majority of them in her insistence that it is God who has put the power of regeneration in our hand, if only we will exert ourselves to that end" (161).

WORKS CITED

Adams, John. *Sketches of the history, genius, disposition, accomplishments, employments, customs, virtues, and vices of the fair sex, in all parts of the world: interspersed with many singular and entertaining anecdotes*. Boston: Joseph Bumstead, 1807.

Agrippa, Henricus Cornelius. *Declamation on the Nobility and Preeminence of the Female Sex*. 1529. Trans. Albert Rabil Jr. Chicago: U of Chicago P, 1993.

Ashbridge, Elizabeth. *Some Account of the Fore Part of the Life of Elizabeth Ashbridge*. 1774. Rpt. in *Journeys in New Worlds: Early American Women's Narratives*. Ed. William L. Andrews. Madison: U of Wisconsin P, 1990. 147–80.

Astell, Mary. *Reflections Upon Marriage* 3rd ed., *To Which is Added A Preface, in Answer to Some Objections*. 1706. Rpt. in *The First English Feminist: Reflections Upon Marriage and Other Writings by Mary Astell*. Ed. Bridget Hill. Aldershot, UK: Gower, 1986. 67–132.

Berg, Barbara J. *The Remembered Gate: Origins of American Feminism*. New York: Oxford UP, 1978.

Beverwyck [Beverwyck], Jan van. *Van de wtnementheyt des vrouwelicken geslacts*. Dordrecht: Printed by Hendrick van Esch for Jasper Gorissz, 1639.

Boccaccio, Giovanni. *Concerning Famous Women*. ca. 1365. Trans. Guido A. Guarino. New Brunswick: Rutgers UP, 1963.

Bradstreet, Anne. *The Tenth Muse, Lately sprung up in America*. 1650. *The Tenth Muse (1650) and, from the Manuscripts, Meditations Divine and Morall Together with Letters and Occasional Pieces by Anne Bradstreet*. Gainesville: Scholars' Facsimiles & Reprints, 1965.

Brown, Charles Brockden Brown. *Alcuin: A Dialogue*. 1798. Ed. Lee R. Edwards. New York: Grossman, 1971.

Castiglione, Baldassare. *The Book of the Courtier*. 1528. Trans. George Bull. New York: Penguin, 1967.

Clarke, Norma. *Dr. Johnson's Women*. London: Hambledon & London, 2000.

Clement, J[esse], ed. *Noble Deeds of American women*. Intro. L[ydia] H[oward] Sigourney. Boston: Lee & Shephard, 1851.

Crocker, Hannah Mather. *Observations on the real rights of women, with their appropriate duties, agreeable to Scripture, reason, and common sense*. Boston: Printed for the Author, 1818. Selections rpt. in *Women's Early American Historical Narratives*. Ed. Sharon M. Harris. New York: Penguin, 2003. 229–49.

———. *The School of Reform, or Seaman's Safe Pilot to the Cape of Good Hope*. Boston: John Eliot, 1816.

———. *A Series of Letters on Free Masonry*. Boston: John Eliot, 1815.

Davidson, Cathy N. *Revolution and the Word: The Rise of the Novel in America*. New York: Oxford UP, 1986.

Ferguson, Moira. *First Feminists: British Women Writers, 1578–1799*. Bloomington: Indiana UP, 1985.

Flexner, Eleanor. *Century of Struggle: The Woman's Rights Movement in the United States*. Cambridge, MA: Harvard UP, 1959.

———. *Mary Wollstonecraft: A Biography*. New York: Coward, McCann & Geoghegan, 1972.

Godwin, William. *Enquiry concerning political justice; and its influence on general virtue and happiness.* 1793. Rpt. 1798 ed. *Enquiry concerning political justice, and its influence on modern morals and happiness.* Harmondsworth: Penguin, 1976.

———. *Memoirs of the Author of "A Vindication of the Rights of Woman."* 1798. Harmondsworth: Penguin, 1987.

Goodrich, Samuel G. *Lives of celebrated women.* Boston: Bradbury, Soden, 1844.

Hale, Sarah Josepha. *Woman's Record; or, Sketches of all distinguished women, from "the beginning" till A. D. 1850.* New York: Harper, 1853.

Hawkesworth, John. *Account of the Voyages.* 3 vols. London: W. Strahan & T. Cadell, 1773.

Hays, Mary. *Female Biography, or memoirs of illustrious and celebrated women, of all ages and countries. Alphabetically arranged.* 6 vols. London: Printed by Thomas Davison for Richard Phillips, 1803.

Hopkins, Mary Alden. *Hannah More and Her Circle.* New York: Longmans, Green, 1947.

Hunter, Henry. *Sacred Biography of the History of the patriarchs, to which is added the history of Deborah, Ruth & Hannah being a course of lectures delivered at the Scots church.* 6 vols. Boston: J. White, Thomas & Andrews, 1794–95.

MacFadden, Margaret. *Golden Cables of Sympathy: The Transatlantic Sources of Nineteenth-Century Feminism.* Lexington: UP of Kentucky, 1999.

Mather, Cotton. *Diary.* 1911. 2 vols. New York: Frederick Ungar, 1957.

———. *Magnalia Christi Americana.* 1702. Rpt. 1853 ed. 2 vols. Carlisle, PA: Banner of Truth Trust, 1979.

Maximus, Valerius. *Memorable Doings and Sayings.* Trans. and ed. D. R. Shackleton Bailey. Cambridge, MA: Harvard UP, 2000.

Miller, Samuel. "The Appropriate Duty and Ornament of the Female Sex." *The Columbian Preacher; or, A collection of original sermons, from preachers of eminence in the United States, embracing the distinguishing doctrines of grace.* Comp. Nathan Elliot. Catskill, NY: Nathan Elliot, 1808. 249–64.

More, Hannah. *Cheap repository tracts, entertaining, moral and religious.* 3 vols. London: F. & C. Rivington, 1798.

———. *An estimate of the religion of the fashionable world, by one of the laity.* 1790. 3rd ed. London: n.p., 1791.

———. *The Fatal Falsehood: A Tragedy.* London: T. Cadell, 1779.

———. *The Inflexible Captive: A Tragedy.* Bristol: S. Farley, 1774.

———. *Percy, A Tragedy.* London: T. Cadell, 1784.

———. *The Search after Happiness: A Pastoral Drama.* Bristol: S. Farley, 1773.

———. *Selected Writings of Hannah More.* Ed. Robert Hole. London: William Pickering, 1996.

———. "The Slave Trade." *The Works of Hannah More.* 2 vols. New York: Harper, 1972. 1: 27.

———. "The Sorrows of Yamba, or the Negro Woman's Lamentation." 1795. *Selected Writings* 42–48.

———. *Strictures on the Modern System of Female Education.* 1799. Oxford: Woodstock Books, 1995.

———. *Thoughts on the Importance of the Manners of the Great to General Society.* London: T. Cadell, 1788.

———. "Village Politics." *The Works of Hannah More.* 2 vols. New York: Harper, 1972. 1: 58–63.

———. *The Works of Hannah More.* 2 vols. New York: Harper, 1872.

Murray, Judith Sargent. *Selected Writings of Judith Sargent Murray.* Ed. Sharon M. Harris. New York: Oxford UP, 1995.

Paine, Thomas. *Rights of Man.* 1791–92. Rpt. in *Common Sense, the Rights of Man and Other Essential Writings of Thomas Paine.* New York: Plume, 1984.

Pizan, Christine de. *The Book of the City of Ladies.* 1405. Trans. Earl Jeffrey Richards. New York: Persea, 1982.

Plutarch. "Bravery of Women." *Plutarch's Moralia.* n.d. Trans. and ed. Frank Cole Babbitt. Loeb Classical Lib. 14 vols. Cambridge, MA: Harvard UP, 1931. 3: 471–581.

Poulain[sic] de La Barre, François. *The Woman as Good as the Man, Or, Equality of Both Sexes.* 1673. Trans. Gerald M. MacLean. Detroit: Wayne State UP, 1988.

Poullain de La Barre, François. *Dialogues on the Education of Women.* 1674. Rpt. *On the Education of Ladies.* In *Three Cartesian Feminist Treatises* 139–251.

———. *La Doctrine des protestants sur la liberté de lire l'Ecriture Sainte, le Service divin en langue entendue, l'Invocation des Saints, le Sacrement de l'Eucharistie. Justifée par le Missel Romain et par des Réflexions sur chaque Point. Avec un Commentaire philosophique sur ces paroles de Jésus-Christ, Ceci est mon corps, Ceci est mon sang, Matth. Chap. XXVI, v. 26.* Geneva: n.p., 1720.

———. *The Equality of the Sexes.* 1673. Trans. Desmond M. Clarke. Manchester: Manchester UP, 1990.

———. *On the Superiority of Men, against the Equality of the Sexes.* 1675. Rpt. *On the Excellence of Men: Preface and Remarks.* In *Three Cartesian Feminist Treatises* 253–314.

———. *Three Cartesian Feminist Treatises. On the Equality of the Two Sexes* (*De l'Égalité des deux sexes* [Paris: Du Puis, 1673]), *On the Education of Ladies* (*De l'Education des dames pour la conduite de l'esprit dans les sciences et dans les moeurs* [Paris: Antoine Dezalier, 1679]), and *On the Excellence of Men: Preface and Remarks* (*De l'Éxcellence des homes, contre, l'égalité des sexes* [Paris: Du Puis, 1675]). Trans. Vivien Bosley. Chicago: U of Chicago P, 2002.

Riegel, Robert. *American Feminists.* Lawrence: U of Kansas P, 1963.

Schurman, Anna Maria van. *Amica Dissertatio inter Annam Mariam Schurmanniam et Andr. Rivetum de Capacitate ingenii muliebris ad scientias.* Paris: n.p., 1638. French trans. *Question Célèbre, s'il est nécessaire ou non que les filles soient scavantes?* Paris: n.p., 1646. English trans. *The Learned Maid, Or, Whether a Maid May Be a Scholar?* London: John Redmayne, 1659.

———. *Dissertatio logica* and selected letters. In *Opuscula* 28–95. Rpt. in *Whether a Christian Woman Should be Educated and Other Writings from Her Intellectual Circle* 25–71.

———. *Eukleria, seu melioris partis electio.* Pt. 1: Altona: Cornelius van der Meulen, 1673. Pt. 2: Amsterdam: n.p., 1685. Chaps. 1 and 2 of pt. 1 rpt. in *Whether a Christian Woman Should be Educated and Other Writings from Her Intellectual Circle* 73–94.

———. *Opuscula hebraea, graeca, latina, gallica, prosaica et metrica.* 1648. 2nd ed. Lugduni Batavorum [Leiden]: Ex officinâ Elseviriorum, 1650.

———. *Whether a Christian Woman Should be Educated and Other Writings from Her Intellectual Circle.* Trans. Joyce I. Irwin. Chicago: U of Chicago P, 1998.

Scott, Ann Firor. "Unfinished Business." *Journal of Women's History* 8.2 (1996): 111–20.

Snitow, Ann. "A Gender Diary." *Feminism and History.* Ed. Joan Wallach Scott. New York: Oxford UP, 1996. 505–46.

Staël, Germaine de. *Considerations on the Main Events of the French Revolution.* 1818. Rpt. in *An Extraordinary Woman* 359–73.

———. *Considerations on the Principal Events of the French Revolution.* New York: James Eastburn & Co., 1818.

———. *An Extraordinary Woman: Selected Writings of Germaine de Staël.* Trans. Vivian Folkenflik. New York: Columbia UP, 1987.

———. *The Influence of Literature upon Society.* 1800. Boston: W. Wells & T. B. Wait, 1813.

———. *On Literature Considered in Its Relationship to Social Institutions.* 1800. Rpt. in *An Extraordinary Woman* 170–208.

Taylor, Barbara. *Mary Wollstonecraft and the Feminist Imagination.* Cambridge, UK: Cambridge UP, 2003.

———. "The Religious Foundations of Mary Wollstonecraft's Feminism." *The Cambridge Companion to Mary Wollstonecraft.* Ed. Claudia L. Johnson. Cambridge, UK: Cambridge UP, 2002. 99–118.

Voetius, Gisbertus. "Concerning Women." In *Politica Ecclesiastica* 1:4. 1663–76. Rpt. in Anna Maria van Schurman, *Whether a Christian Woman Should be Educated and Other Writings from Her Intellectual Circle* 97–137.

Warren, Mercy Otis. *History of the rise, progress, and termination of the American Revolution: interspersed with biographical, political and moral observations.* 1805. Ed. Lester H. Cohen. 2 vols. Indianapolis: Liberty Classics, 1988.

Wollstonecraft, Mary. *Letters Written during a short residence in Sweden, Norway, and Denmark.* London: Printed for J. Johnson, 1796.

———. *Thoughts on the education of Daughters; with reflections on female conduct, in the more important duties of life.* London: Printed for J. Johnson, 1787.

———. *A Vindication of the rights of woman, with strictures on political and moral subjects.* 1792. Rpt. in *A Vindication of the Rights of Men with A Vindication of the Rights of Woman and Hints.* Ed. Sylvana Tomaselli. Cambridge, UK: Cambridge UP, 1995. 65–294.

The James Family and the Boston Athenaeum: A Bibliography[1]

GLEN MacLEOD
University of Connecticut, Waterbury

Early in 1864, the family of Henry James Sr. moved from Newport to Boston. The household consisted of the father; his wife, Mary; her sister, Aunt Kate; and the three "brilliant" children, William, Henry, and Alice. (Younger sons Wilky and Robertson were then serving in the Civil War and did not live with their parents afterward.) The house they rented, at 13 Ashburton Place on Beacon Hill, was just one block away from the Boston Athenaeum, at 10½ Beacon Street.

In June of that year, Henry Senior became a member of the Athenaeum. He renewed his membership annually, even after the family moved to Cambridge in 1866. Remarkably, the circulation records from this period still exist, making it possible to compile a complete list of the books taken out from the Athenaeum in Henry James Sr.'s name from 1864 through 1873 (when the records abruptly stop).[2] Many of these books were apparently borrowed for William, Henry, and Alice (see below), and perhaps for others in the household. What follows, then, is a bibliography of the James family's borrowings from the Athenaeum.

Part of the interest of this bibliography lies in guessing for whom each book was borrowed. Some cases are clear, as I will show below. Ultimately this listing is valuable because it is a detailed, factual record of books that were brought into the James household. Knowing the family bent for lively intellectual conversation, we can surmise that many of these books were not only read—perhaps by more than one person—but also discussed. They provide a partial register of the intellectual climate of the James household from 1864 to 1873. "We were the inhabitants of a distinct country,—the country of James," wrote William, referring to all the James children (qtd. in Freedman 2). Here is a rediscovered map to part of that legendary country.

The Boston Athenaeum was founded in 1807 as a private subscription library and a "repository" for the "fine and pleasing arts" that "shall provide for the improvement and emulation of artists and for the correction and refinement of taste in those, who aim to be connoisseurs, and able to bestow praise and censure with discrimination" (Quincy 174; qtd.

in Slautterback 13). The James family made the most of it. For young Henry, it was the premier cultural institution in Boston, as he recalled when he revisited the city in 1904: "To come up from School Street into Beacon was to approach the Athenaeum—exquisite institution, to fond memory, joy of the aspiring prime . . . this honoured haunt of all the most civilized—library, gallery, temple of culture, the place that was to Boston at large as Boston at large was to the rest of New England" (*American Scene* 172). The Athenaeum had a sculpture gallery on the first floor and a gallery of paintings on the third. The James children regularly attended exhibitions there—Henry reviewed one of them in 1874 ("The Duke")—so that the Athenaeum became for them the shared basis of their art education, a touchstone for future cultural explorations. When Henry was visiting the Vatican for the first time, he wrote to his sister, Alice: "There is at the Vatican a statue of Demosthenes—you may see a cast of it at the Athenaeum—a fine wise old man with his head bent and his hands dropped, holding a scroll—so perfect and noble and beautiful that it amply satisfies my desire for the ideal" (*Letters* 1: 165). And when William wanted to convey to Henry the quality of Venetian paintings he was viewing in Dresden, he drew his analogy from their common experience at the Athenaeum: "The 'blondness' of some Venetian things here!, as if the picture were breathed on the canvass. (That head 'Isaac of York' by Allston in the Boston Atheneum [sic] will give you an idea of the kind of thing I mean. . .)" (*Correspondence* 1: 41).

Since the exhibitions at the Athenaeum were open to the public, the chief advantage of membership was the use of its private library. The Athenaeum was (and still is) owned by shareholders, each of whom was entitled to invite two guests per year to join for a small fee: "Each Proprietor and Life-Subscriber [shareholders] shall be entitled to give tickets to members of his immediate family, and *two tickets to other persons,—for all of whom he shall be responsible,—permitting them to visit the Library and Reading-room, and take out books*, under the regulations, for a period not longer than one year" (*By Laws* 3–4; emphasis added).[3] Henry James Sr. became a member on the share of his banker and friend Samuel Gray Ward.[4] The record of books he borrowed for his own use has interest in itself, since he was a well-known figure in his time.[5] He had a reputation as a lively conversationalist—W. D. Howells called him "the best talker in America" (Habegger 452). This helped him to cultivate a broad circle of intellectual and social acquaintance—including his friends Ralph Waldo Emerson and Thomas Carlyle—on both sides of the Atlantic. He regularly published books and articles on philosophical, religious, and social issues. Using this bibliography, we can see him reading (or rereading) important books in those fields and keeping up with newly published ones. In this latter category are books he reviewed, such as Carlyle's *Frederick the Great* (see item 64) and Frances Cobbe's *Broken Lights* (item 68), both for *The Nation* in 1865; along with James Hutchinson Stirling's *The Secret of Hegel* (item 356) and Horace Bushnell's *Vicarious Sacrifice* (item 59), both for the *North American Review* in 1866.[6]

The father's borrowing privileges were, according to the official *By-Laws* quoted above, strictly for his own use. But this was really, in effect, a *family* membership.[7] Henry Sr. was famously devoted to the education of his children, so it would have been characteristic of him to use his Athenaeum membership for their benefit. The James children seem to have enjoyed privileges reserved for members. They regularly visited not only the Athenaeum galleries (which were open to the public) but also the reading room (open to members only). Here is William describing for Henry Jr. a routine day-trip into Boston on 13 February 1873: "I went to town, paid a bill of Randidge's, *looked into the Atheneum* [sic] *reading-room,* got one dozen raw oysters at Higgins's saloon in Court Street, came out again, thermometer having risen to near thawing point, dozed half an hour before the fire, and am now writing this to you" (*Correspondence* 1: 191; emphasis added). It is even possible that family members were permitted to check out books on their own. That, at least, is one implication of the following passage from a letter William wrote to a friend on 24 January 1869: "I have been trying to get 'Hilton on Rest and Pain,' which you recommended, from the Athenaeum, but, *more librorum,* when you want 'em, it keeps 'out'" (*Correspondence* 4: 362). (The Hilton book [item 172] was checked out on 29 January 1869.) It seems clear that the James children considered the Athenaeum *their* library as much as their father's—certainly William and Henry did so, and probably Alice did as well.

The large number of medical and scientific works borrowed are almost certainly William's, since he was living at home during this period (except when traveling abroad), studying medicine and teaching at Harvard. But he also found time to participate in the family's literary discussions. As the father wrote to Henry Jr. on 14 January 1873: "Willy is going on with his teaching. . . . He uses himself up now and then visiting and all the rest of it, such as debating about *Middlemarch* and other transient topics, but on the whole he gets on very well" (qtd. in Matthiessen 123). (It was evidently an inspiring debate: volumes of *Middlemarch* [item 99] were checked out of the Athenaeum a week or two later, on 22 and 28 January 1873.) On the topic of American literature, William wrote to Henry Jr. on 19 January 1870, "I enjoyed last week the great pleasure of reading *The House of Seven Gables.* I little expected so *great* a work. It's like a great symphony with no touch alterable without injury to the harmony. It made a deep impression on me and I thank heaven that Hawthorne was an American. It also tickled my national feeling not a little to note the resemblance of Hawthorne's style to yours" (*Correspondence* 1: 141). (This remark incited Henry to respond that he hoped "to write as good a novel one of these days [perhaps] as the House of the Seven Gables" [*Letters* 1: 205].) It is likely that the copy William read was the one borrowed from the Athenaeum on 10 January 1870 (item 163).

Alice, too, took advantage of her family's borrowing privileges at the Athenaeum. On 13 October 1867, she recommended (to William) Erckmann and Chatrain's *Madame Thérèse*, adding, "I read it the other day for the first time" (Yeazell 54). The book (item 108) had been borrowed from the Athenaeum two days before. Alice surely accounts for many of the entries for George Sand novels (items 309–34), too, since she read virtually all of them (Strouse 262). Yet, Henry Jr. was also a great admirer of Sand, and there were doubtless others in the house. The bibliography lists twenty-five books by Sand, some containing multiple novels; the circulation records show that some were taken out two or three times, sometimes at great intervals, suggesting that a number of family members were reading these novels.

Young Henry apparently used the Athenaeum when he was doing background research for book reviews during his early career. It was probably Henry who, preparing to review a new edition of Goethe's *Wilhelm Meister's Apprenticeship* in 1865, consulted a copy of an earlier edition (item 144; on 5 May) and Eckermann's *Conversations of Goethe* (item 95; on 15 May).[8] For an 1865 review of G. S. Trebutien's translation of *The Journal of Eugénie de Guérin*, he seems to have consulted the French original (item 152; on 3 Sept. 1864).[9] And, in order to compare a new translation of Epictetus with Elizabeth Carter's 1758 version (on which it was based), he seems to have borrowed the Athenaeum's copy of the Carter version (item 103; on 2 Dec. 1865).[10] With this concrete evidence in mind, scholars may now ask how many other books in this bibliography Henry might have read and discussed during these crucial, formative years of his writing career. It is interesting to note that about thirty-five of these titles also appear in the mature novelist's library (see Edel and Tintner). Without additional information, however, we may only speculate as to whether the son may first have read any of these thirty-five books with the use of his father's library card.

This detailed record of the reading habits of the Jameses over a ten-year period should be useful not only for the new factual data it makes available to scholars but also for the broadly suggestive range of interests it registers. I hope that it will contribute to our understanding of this fascinating American literary family and that it will encourage further research at that "exquisite institution," the Boston Athenaeum.

* * *

In the chronological list of circulation records that follows, the date the book was checked out precedes the entry; the date it was returned follows it. The list of books is not an exact transcription of the handwritten entries in the original folio volumes, as those entries are very idiosyncratic and sometimes illegible. The entries often omit the author's name or use the editor's name instead; misspell or oddly abbreviate titles; or use the title from the spine of the book, which may bear little or no relation to that on the title page. I have regularized the list so that each book can be looked up in the bibliography alphabetically by the author's last name. If no author is given, as with titles of periodicals, there is no entry in the bibliography for that item. An index of periodicals is included as an appendix.

Book titles in the circulation records are capitalized according to the standard rules for capitalization. Except for this standardized listing of authors and titles, all other information in the circulation records—dates, volume numbers, and references to particular editions—is reproduced exactly as it appears in the original record books. Volume numbers appear in the first column after the title.

In the bibliography, however, only the first word of the book title is capitalized (except for proper names and German-language capitals). This is the method used in the Boston Athenaeum's 1871 catalogue (see below), as well as in its present on-line catalogue.

In the bibliography, the date to the right of each numbered entry refers to the foregoing circulation records. If more than one edition or title is listed in a single entry, then it was not possible to determine exactly which book was used. In such cases, an asterisk (if there is one) indicates the most likely candidate.

Foreign-language titles are given in the original language. Because the vast majority of these titles are self-evident (e.g., *Histoire de la littérature Anglaise* and *Journals et Lettres*), it seems to me that adding English translations for all of them, simply in order to be consistent, would be a useless annoyance for the reader. Retaining these foreign titles is appropriate because it emphasizes the multilingual facility of the James family while clarifying that the edition used was the original-language version. This distinction is important because the Boston Athenaeum possessed English-language translations of many of the very titles that the Jameses chose to borrow in the original-language editions.

Given the dates covered by this bibliography (1864–73), my chief authority is the five-volume *Catalogue of the Library of the Boston Athenaeum, 1807–1871* (1874). This catalogue is an accurate record of books that were actually in the Athenaeum in 1871. Books not in that catalogue (either inadvertently omitted from it or acquired after 1871) have been traced through the old Shelf List (ca. 1850–70) and the old Cutter card catalogue at the Boston Athenaeum. A number of questions have been resolved by examining the books themselves, many of which are still in the Athenaeum's collection. A few titles (mainly 1872–73), which are not in the 1871 catalogue and are no longer in the Athenaeum's collection, have been verified with reasonable certainty through the catalogues of other research libraries and the National Union Catalogue.

Boston Athenaeum—Circulation Records
James, Henry, on share of S. G. Ward

1864

June	29	Wynter, *Subtle Brains*		June 30
	30	Alcock, *Capital of the Tycoon*	1, 2	July 12
	30	St. John, *Forests of the Far East*	1, 2	July 5
July	5	Virchow, *Cellular Pathology*		July 15
	5	Hamilton, *Gala Days*		July 12
	12	Senior, *Biographical Sketches*		July 19
	15	Huxley, *Man's Place in Nature*		July 18
	16	Kelly, *Indo-European Tradition*		July 18
	21	Taine, *Histoire de la Littérature Anglaise*	2	July 28
	22	Taine, *Histoire de la Littérature Anglaise*	1, 3	July 28
	29	Mouhot, *Travels in Indo-China*		Aug. 3
Aug.	1	Huxley, *Elements of Comparative Anatomy*		Aug. 8
	3	Newman, *Apologia Pro Vita Sua*		Aug. 5
	5	Jowett, *St. Paul, with Notes*	1, 2	Aug. 19
	8	Cobbe, *Broken Lights*		Aug. 10
	9	Arnold, *French Eton*		Aug. 10
	12	Carlyle, *Frederick the Great*		Aug. 13
	12	Sand, *Le Meunier d'Angibault*		Aug. 19
	13	Mill, *Dissertations and Discussions*	1	Aug. 22
	18	Freytag, *Soll und Haben*		Sept. 17
	19	Michelet, *La Sorcière*		Aug. 22
	19	Prévost-Paradol, *Essais de Politique*		Aug. 22
	22	Carlyle, *Life of Sterling*		Aug. 29
	22	Whately, *Miscellaneous Remains*		Aug. 23
	24	Huxley, *Elements of Comparative Anatomy*		Aug. 30
	25	*British and Foreign Medical Chirurgical Review*	22	Aug. 27
	27	*North American Review*	97	Aug. 27
	27	Sand, *Mauprat*		Aug. 30
	29	Kingsley, *Hypatia*	1, 2	Sept. 13
	30	Lamber, *Récits d'une Paysanne*		Sept. 3
	30	Sévigné, *Lettres de Madame de Sévigné*	1	Sept. 3

Sept.	3	Guérin, *Journal et Lettres*		Sept.	19
	3	Dumas, *Vingt Ans Après*		Sept.	7
	5	Dumas, *Vingt Ans Après*	2, 3	Sept.	9
	10	Sand, *Indiana*		Sept.	17
	13	Dumas, *La Comtesse de Charny*	1	Sept.	21
	17	Freytag, *Soll und Haben*		Oct.	3
	17	Dumas, *La Comtesse de Charny*	2	Oct.	23
	19	Thackeray, *Pendennis*		Oct.	10
	21	*Putnam's Magazine*	1	Oct.	23
	23	Dumas, *La Comtesse de Charny*	3	Oct.	24
	23	Prescott, *Conquest of Mexico*	1	Oct.	29
	24	Dumas, *La Comtesse de Charny*	4, 5, 6	Oct.	29
	29	Sand, *Valentine*		Oct.	3
	30	Damon, *Leucocythemia*		Oct.	3
Oct.	3	Prescott, *Conquest of Mexico*	1, 2	Oct.	24
	4	Browning, *Dramatis Personae*		Oct.	8
	10	United States, *Report on the Conduct of the War* (Pt. 3)		Error	
	10	Dwight, *Modern Philology*		Oct.	21
	12	Dumas, *Le Vicomte de Bragelonne*	1, 2, 3	Oct.	21
	22	*Revue Nationale*	15	Oct.	26
	22	Dumas, *Le Vicomte de Bragelonne*	4, 5, 6	Nov.	1
	24	Huxley, *Elements of Comparative Anatomy*		Oct.	31
	30	Reade, *Love Me Little, Love Me Long*		Oct.	31
Nov.	1	Lamb, *Works* (Talfourd)	1	Nov.	17
	1	Huxley, *Elements of Comparative Anatomy*		Nov.	8
	2	Frothingham, *Philosophy as Absolute Science*		Nov.	4
	4	Farrar, *The War and Its Causes*		Nov.	4
	8	Oliphant, *Life of Irving*	1, 2	Nov.	14
	10	Pichot, *Life of Sir Charles Bell*		Nov.	11
	11	Huxley, *Elements of Comparative Anatomy*		Nov.	16
	17	Beale, *Anatomy of the Liver*		Nov.	21
	17	Arnold, *On Translating Homer*		Nov.	19
	19	Sand, *André*		Dec.	5
	23	*British and Foreign Medical Chirurgical Review* 1853	12	Nov.	25
	29	Harford, *Recollections of Wilberforce*		Dec.	1
Dec.	5	Brown, *Lectures and Essays*	1, 2	Dec.	7
	7	Kingsley, *Roman and Teuton*		Dec.	13
	8	Hazlitt, *Miscellaneous Works*	2	Dec.	14
	9	Hazlitt, *Liber Amoris*		Dec.	13
	14	Scherer, *Mélanges d'Histoire Religieuse*		Dec.	17
	14	Forster, *Essays*	2	Dec.	17
	17	Lewes, *Aristotle*		Dec.	19

	17 Sand, *Marquis de Villemer*		Dec. 27
	19 Mueller, *Lectures on Language*, 2 ser.		Dec. 27
	20 Sainte-Beuve, *Causeries de Lundi*	6	Dec. 23
	23 Arnold, *On Translating Homer*		Dec. 28
	28 Sainte-Beuve, *Portraits Contemporains*	2	Jan. 5
	28 Bernard, *Le Gentilhomme Compagnard*	1	Jan. 6
	31 Jackson, *Memoir of J. Jackson*		Jan. 5

1865

Jan.	5 Taine, *Essai sur Tite Live*		Jan. 12
	6 Bernard, *Le Gentilhomme Compagnard*	2	Jan. 9
	9 Taine, *Histoire de la Littérature Anglaise*	1, 3	Jan. 23
	14 Bronte, *Jane Eyre*		Jan. 26
	19 Taine, *Histoire de la Littérature Anglaise*	4	Jan. 25
	19 Eliot, *Adam Bede*		Jan. 20
	20 Stendhal, *La Chartreuse de Parme*		Jan. 30
	21 Gaskell, *Cranford*		Jan. 25
	23 Stendhal, *Le Rouge et le Noir*		Jan. 25
	25 Taylor, *John Godfrey's Fortunes*		Jan. 30
	28 *Revue des Deux Mondes* 1843	1	Jan. 30
	28 Forster, *Life of Goldsmith*		Feb. 24
	30 Thierry, *Tableau de l'Empire Romain*		Feb. 20
Feb.	4 Merivale, *Conversion of Roman Empire*		Feb. 13
	4 Lyell, *Antiquity of Man* (Am. ed.)		Feb. 27
	14 Abbott, *Sight and Touch*		Feb. 21
	20 Sainte-Beuve, *Port-Royal*	1	Mar. 4
	23 Mill, *Dissertations and Discussions*	2	Feb. 27
	24 Alger, *Doctrine of Future Life*		Mar. 1
	27 Abbott, *Sight and Touch*		Mar. 1
Mar.	1 Lewes, *Life of Goethe* (New ed.)		Mar. 6
	7 Sand, *Horace*		Mar. 17
	11 Sand, *Indiana*		Mar. 31
	14 Bates, *Naturalist on the Amazon*	1	Mar. 15
	14 Maury, *Amazon and South America*		Mar. 25
	16 Bates, *Naturalist on the Amazon*	2	Mar. 22
	17 Sand, *Jacques*		Mar. 31
	18 Taine, *Histoire de la Littérature Anglaise*		Mar. 18
			Error
	22 Lyell, *Antiquity of Man* (Eng. ed)		Mar. 31
	31 Scherer, *Mélanges d'Histoire Religieuse*		Apr. 7
Apr.	5 Mignet, *Charles-Quint*		Apr. 7
	7 Mill, *Dissertations and Discussions* (Eng. ed.)	2	May 5
	7 Lewes, *Aristotle*		Apr. 12

	8	Laugel, *Problèmes de la Nature*		Apr.	11
	11	Prescott, *Ferdinand and Isabella* (Eng. ed.)	1, 2	May	3
	12	Laugel, *Problèmes de la Nature*		Apr.	27
May	2	*Edinburgh Review* Apr. 1865		May	3
	3	Augier, *Le Fils de Giboyer*		May	5
	5	Goethe, *Wilhelm Meister* (Carlyle)	1	May	15
	11	Prescott, *Ferdinand and Isabella* (Am. ed.)	3	May	27
	15	Eckermann, *Conversations of Goethe*	1	June	2
	20	Valmiki, *Le Ramayana*	1	May	27
	20	Tylor, *Early History of Mankind*		May	27
	27	Michelet, *Histoire de France*	8	June	6
	27	Joubert, *Pensées*		May	30
	30	Sand, *Jeanne*		June	2
June	2	Sand, *Péché de M. Antoine*	1, 2	June	7
	26	Sand, *L'Homme de Neige*	1	June	29
	26	Sainte-Beuve, *Causeries de Lundi*	9	July	5
	27	Kidder, *Brazil and the Brazilians*		July	8
	27	Bates, *Naturalist on the Amazon*	1	June	29
	29	Sand, *L'Homme de Neige*	2, 3	July	5
July	1	Lucretius, *De Rerum Natura* (tr. Munro)	1	July	8
	5	Browning, *Poems*	1, 2	July	29
	8	Oakeley, *Tractarian Movement*		July	14
	24	Sainte-Beuve, *Causeries de Lundi*	4, 5	Sept.	4
	24	Sand, *Valentine*		Sept.	4
	24	Sand, *Teverino*		Aug.	3
	24	Sand, *Lucrezia Floriani*		Sept.	4
Sept.	4	Grote, *Plato*	1	Sept.	9
	6	Trollope, *Three Clerks*		Sept.	11
	9	Arnold, *History of Rome*	1	Sept.	23
	16	Hallam, *Middle Ages*	1	Sept.	30
	19	Grote, *Plato*	2	Sept.	25
	23	Arnold, *History of Rome*	2	Oct.	4
	25	Matter, *Mysticisme en France*		Oct.	2
	25	Mérimée, *Chronique de Charles IX*		Sept.	27
	27	Prévost-Paradol, *Essais de Politique*		Sept.	30
	30	Eckermann, *Conversations of Goethe*	2	Oct.	12
Oct.	4	Matter, *Mysticisme en France*		Oct.	7
	6	*Macmillan's Magazine*	6	Oct.	9
	7	About, *Vacances de la Comtesse*		Oct.	9
	10	Stirling, *Secret of Hegel*	1, 2	Oct.	17
	12	Taine, *Philosophes Français*		Oct.	25
	17	Capefigue, *Mesdemoiselles de Nesle*		Oct.	21
	20	Yonge, *History of England*		Nov.	13

	21	Taine, *Histoire de la Littérature Anglaise*	4	Oct. 28
	31	Erckmann and Chatrain, *Histoire d'un Conscrit*		Nov. 1
	31	Stendhal, *Le Rouge et le Noir*		Nov. 13
Nov.	1	Erckmann and Chatrain, *Waterloo*		Nov. 2
	1	Saint-Hilaire, *Mahomet et le Coran*		Nov. 10
	13	Renan, *De l'Origine du Langage*		Nov. 22
	13	Sand, *André*		Nov. 15
	14	Macaulay, *History of England*	12* [?] 1	Nov. 20
	15	Sand, *Histoire de Ma Vie*	1	Nov. 17
	17	Rands, *Henry Holbeach*	2	Nov. 24
	20	Rands, *Henry Holbeach*	1	Nov. 24
	20	*Revue des Deux Mondes* July–Sept. 1854		Nov. 22
	22	Sainte-Beuve, *Port-Royal*	1	Dec. 6
Dec.	2	Guérin, *Journal*		Dec. 6
	2	Epictetus, *Works* (tr. Carter)		Dec. 8
	2	Merle d'Aubigné, *Reformation*	4	Dec. 18
	6	Renan, *Averroès et l'Averroïsme*		Dec. 8
	12	Berry, *Extracts of the Journals*	1	Dec. 18
	18	Lamb, *Eliana*		Jan. 1
	30	Maury, *La Magie et l'Astrologie*		Jan. 18
	30	Farrar, *Chapters on Language*		Jan. 6
	30	Ruffini, *Doctor Antonio*		Jan. 6

1866

Jan.	6	Scott, *Woodstock*	1, 2	Jan. 9
	11	Ruskin, *Sesame and Lilies* (Eng. ed.)		Jan. 16
	16	Michelet, *La Sorcière*		Jan. 20
	18	Andersen, *Sammtliche Märchen*		Jan. 20
	18	Asbjornsen, *Popular Tales from the Norse*		Jan. 25
	20	Andersen, *Sand-Hills of Jutland*		Jan. 29
	20	Cox, *Literature of the Sabbath*	1, 2	Jan. 25
	25	Marsh, *English Language and Early Literature*		Feb. 24
	29	Hugo, *Oeuvres Complètes*	2	Feb. 8
Feb.	1	Bushnell, *Vicarious Sacrifice*		Feb. 8
	8	Merivale, *Conversion of Northern Nations*		Feb. 16
	8	De Quincey, *Opium Eater*		Feb. 19
	12	Hazlitt, *Life of Napoleon*	1	Feb. 24
	16	Parkman, *Pioneers of France*		Feb. 24
	19	Thackeray, *English Humorists*		Feb. 24
Mar.	6	Martin and Aytoun, *Book of Ballads*		Mar. 8
	6	Browne, *Artemus Ward*	2	Mar. 8
	13	Prévost, *Manon Lescaut*		Mar. 22
	15	Rokitansky, *Pathological Anatomy*	1, 2	Mar. 31

	16	Ruskin, *Ethics of the Dust*		Mar.	23
	22	Sand, *Le Chateau des Désertes*		Apr.	13
Apr.	4	Sand, *Laura*		Apr.	6
	6	Le Clerc and Renan, *Histoire Littéraire de France*		Apr.	13
	6	Palfrey, *History of New England*	2	Apr.	16
	13	Palfrey, *History of New England*	3	Apr.	16
	14	Beranger, *Oeuvres Complètes*	1	Apr.	24
	16	Goethe, *Autobiography*	1	May	7
	23	Beaumont, *Beaumont and Fletcher*		May	7
	25	Sophocles, *Tragedies*	1	May	1
	27	Sophocles, *Tragedies*	2	May	1
May	2	Hardy, *Legends of the Buddhists*		May	7
	7	Scott, *Works (Life 1, 2, 3, 4)*	89, 90, 91, 92	May	18
	18	Scott, *Works (Life 2)*	90	June	1
	28	Aeschylus, *Agamemnon* [and Euripides, *Bacchanals*] (tr. Milman)		June	5
June	1	Scott, *Works (Life 3)*	91	June	5
	21	Humboldt, *Werke*	7	June	26
	26	Lucretius, *De Rerum Natura* (tr. Munro)		July	18
	28	Retz, *Cardinal de Retz*	1	July	18
	28	Scott, *Works (Life 4)*	92	Returned	
	28	Browning, *Prometheus*		July	9
July	19	Homer, *Odyssey* (tr. Worsley)	1	Aug.	3
Aug.	1	Eliot, *Mill on the Floss*		Aug.	17
	3	Sand, *Le Meunier d'Angibault*		Aug.	24
	3	Bryce, *Holy Roman Empire*		Aug.	17
	24	Retz, *Cardinal de Retz*	2	Aug.	31
	24	Smith, *Lectures on the Study of History*		Aug.	31
	31	Michelet, *Histoire Romaine*	1, 2	Sept.	13
Sept.	7	Fuller, *Memoirs of Margaret Fuller Ossoli*	1	Sept.	26
	13	Arnold, *History of the Roman Commonwealth*		Oct.	10
	15	Lucretius, *De Rerum Natura* (tr. Munro)	1	Oct.	10
	26	Fuller, *Memoirs of Margaret Fuller Ossoli*	2	Oct.	10
Oct.	15	Arnold, *History of the Roman Commonwealth*	2	Nov.	3
	20	Lucretius, *De Rerum Natura* (tr. Munro)	1	Nov.	2
	26	Doellinger, *First Age of the Church*	1, 2	Nov.	3
Nov.	2	Holmes, *System of Surgery*	2	Nov.	20
	3	Todd, *Clinical Lectures*		Nov.	20
	3	Erichsen, *Railway Injuries*		Nov.	12
	3	*Clinical Lectures and Reports*		Nov.	15
	20	Edwards, *Leçons sur la Physiologie*		Nov.	21
	26	Grote, *History of Greece*	3, 4	Dec.	17

	26	Aeschylus, *Agamemnon* [and Euripides, *Bachhanals*] (tr. Milman)		Dec. 3
Dec.	5	Edwards, *Leçons sur la Physiologie*	4	Dec. 13
	7	Grote, *History of Greece*	6	Dec. 19
	8	Figuier, *L'Année Scientifique 1865*		Dec. 13
	17	Grote, *History of Greece*	8	Jan. 14
	17	Rawlinson, *Five Great Monarchies*	1	Dec. 26
	19	Balzac, *Les Paysans*	3	Jan. 8
	26	Lecky, *Rise and Influence of Rationalism*	1, 2	Jan. 1
	26	Lessing, *Schriften*	19	Dec. 28

1867

Jan.	3	Whately, *Life of Archbishop Whately*	1	Jan. 5
	5	*Revue des Deux Mondes* Nov.–Dec. 1864		Jan. 14
	8	Bodichon, *De l'Humanité*	1	Jan. 12
	12	Flaubert, *Madame Bovary*		Jan. 18
	15	Odling, *Animal Chemistry*		Jan. 18
	18	Grote, *Exploratio Philosophica*		Jan. 26
	19	Grote, *History of Greece*	11	Feb. 1
	21	*North British Review*	40	Jan. 29
	24	Bain, *The Emotions and the Will*		Feb. 4
	25	Humboldt, *Travels* (B.S.L.)[?]	1	Jan. 29
Feb.	1	Dallas, *The Gay Science*	1	Feb. 7
	12	Browning, *Aurora Leigh*		Feb. 26
	22	Hannay, *Course of English Literature*		Feb. 26
Mar.	2	Sand, *L'Homme de Neige*	1, 2, 3	Mar. 9
	2	Lucretius, *De Rerum Natura* (tr. Munro)	1	Apr. 2
	9	Gordon, *Letters from Egypt, 1863–65*		Mar. 15
	13	Epinay, *Mémoires de Madame d'Epinay*	1, 2	Mar. 19
	19	Diderot, *Mémoires*	1, 2	Apr. 12
	22	*Fortnightly Review*	1	Apr. 5
Apr.	13	Bodichon, *De l'Humanité*	1, 2	Apr. 27
	13	Sand, *Le Secrétaire Intime*		Apr. 18
	13	Murger, *Vie de Jeunesse*	6	Apr. 15
	15	Murger, *Le Pays Latin*		Apr. 18
	20	About, *Tollá*		Apr. 27
	20	Vigny, *Servitude et Grandeur Militaires*		May 4
May	1	Moore, *Lord Byron*		May 27
	4	Gibbon, *Roman Empire* (ed. Smith)	1	May 15
	4	Alger, *Genius of Solitude*		May 9
	9	Froude, *Short Studies on Great Subjects*	2	May 11
	15	Vigny, *Stello*		June 4
	27	Froude, *History of England*	2	June 4

GLEN MACLEOD   101

June	25	Froude, *History of England*	5, 6	July 5
	25	Sand, *Lettres d'un Voyageur*		July 9
July	2	Motley, *Rise of the Dutch Republic*	1	July 27
	5	Mignet, *Revolution Française*	1, 2	July 11
	9	Pepys, *Sketches in Russia*	1, 2	July 11
	11	Froude, *Short Studies on Great Subjects*	1	July 13
	11	Richter, *Flower, Fruit and Thorn Pieces*		July 27
	11	Mignet, *Revolution Française*	2	Aug. 8
	13	Campbell, *Reign of Law*		July 27
	24	Motley, *Rise of the Dutch Republic*	2	Aug. 3
	27	Mill, *Dissertations and Discussions*	4	Aug. 3
Aug.	3	Keats, *Life and Letters* (ed. Milnes)		Aug. 12
	3	Bagehot, *The English Constitution*		Aug. 8
	12	Kingsley, *Lectures on the Ancient Regime*		Aug. 13
	12	Motley, *Rise of the Dutch Republic*	2	Sept. 7
	14	Hunt, *Autobiography of Leigh Hunt*	1, 2	Aug. 21
	15	Hogg, *Life of Shelley*	1, 2	Aug. 24
	17	Hazlitt, *Memoirs*	1	Aug. 27
	22	Arnold, *On the Study of Celtic Literature*		Aug. 28
	24	La Villemarqué, *Chants Populaires*	1, 2	Aug. 27
	27	Sand, *Valentine*		Aug. 28
	27	Sand, *Jacques*		Sept. 7
Sept.	7	Motley, *Rise of the Dutch Republic*	3	Oct. 12
	7	Lewes, *History of Philosophy*	1	Sept. 17
	7	Sand, *Jeanne*		Sept. 23
	17	Lewes, *History of Philosophy*	2	Sept. 25
	21	Cherbuliez, *Un Cheval de Phidias*		Sept. 23
	23	Sand, *Confession d'une Jeune Fille*	1, 2	Sept. 25
	25	Balzac, *Les Rivalités*	39	Oct. 9
	26	Parsons, *Deus Homo*		Oct. 7
	30	Shelley, *Memorials*		Oct. 7
Oct.	7	Upham, *Salem Witchcraft*	1	Oct. 8
	9	Dumas, *Théâtre*	3, 5	Oct. 11
	11	Erckmann and Chatrain, *Madame Thérèse*		Oct. 15
	11	Erckmann and Chatrain, *Le Fou Yégof*		Oct. 12
	12	About, *Le Marquis de Lanrose*		Oct. 15
	12	Flaubert, *Madame Bovary*		Oct. 15
	12	Michelet, *Mémoires d'une Enfant*		Oct. 19
	15	Dumas, *Les Trois Mousquetaires*	1	Oct. 28
	15	Vaughn, *Revolutions in English History*	1	Nov. 1
	19	Sidney, *Countess of Pembroke's Arcadia*		Oct. 23
	28	Dumas, *Les Trois Mousquetaires*	2	Nov. 4
	28	Clément, *Jacques Coeur*		Oct. 31

Nov.	2	Smith, *Three English Statesmen*		Nov.	8
	2	Sand, *Consuelo*	1	Nov.	4
	4	Sand, *Consuelo*	2	Nov.	26
	8	Boswell, *Life of Johnson*	1, 2	Nov.	12
	12	Boswell, *Life of Johnson*	3, 4	Dec.	9
Dec.	9	Kingsley, *Hypatia*	1	Dec.	11
	9	Boswell, *Life of Johnson*	3, 4	Jan.	13
	13	Ruffini, *Lorenzo Benoni*		Jan.	17
	21	Petitot, *Collection des Mémoires*	66	Jan.	2
	26	Ruffini, *Vicenzo*	1	Jan.	31
	31	Ruffini, *Vicenzo*	2, 3	Jan.	2

1868

Jan.	2	Boswell, *Life of Johnson*	5	Jan.	20
	2	Petitot, *Collection des Mémoires*	76–77	Jan.	13
	13	Boswell, *Life of Johnson*	6, 7	Jan.	23
	13	Davesiès de Pontès, *Social Reform in England*		Jan.	28
	20	Boswell, *Life of Johnson*	8	Feb.	13
	20	Sand, *Le Compagnon*		Feb.	4
	28	Carlyle, *Essays*	3, 4	Feb.	4
Feb.	4	Karr, *La Pénélope Normande*		Feb.	13
	4	Reybaud, *Espagnoles et Francaises*		Feb.	19
	13	Karr, *Geneviève*		Feb.	19
	13	Thierry, *Lettres sur l'Histoire de France*	1	Feb.	29
	13	Thierry, *Récits des Temps Mérovingiens*	3	Mar.	11
	19	Thierry, *Récits des Temps Mérovingiens*	2	Mar.	11
	29	Helps, *Life of Las Casas*		Mar.	4
Mar.	4	Hugo, *Oeuvres Complètes*	3	Mar.	9
	11	Grote, *Mill's Examination of Hamilton*	2	Mar.	17
	11	Thierry, *Récits des Temps Mérovingiens*	2, 3	Apr.	25
	11	Hugo, *Théâtre*	3	Apr.	17
	19	Sand, *Simon*		Apr.	23
	23	Mérimée, *Chronique de Charles IX*		Apr.	25
	28	Craven, *Récit d'une Soeur*	1	Apr.	31
	31	Lamber, *Récits d'une Paysanne*		Apr.	17
Apr.	10	Hawthorne, *Scarlet Letter*		May	12
	21	Trollope, *Lotta Schmidt*		Apr.	27
	25	*Revue des Deux Mondes* (1859, Sept.–Oct.) (1856, Nov.–Dec.)		Apr.	27
May	2	Ruffini, *Doctor Antonio*		May	12
	9	Reybaud, *Clémentine*		May	13
	12	Sand, *La Comtesse de Rudolstadt*	1	June	3
	13	Dickens, *Martin Chuzzlewit*	1	May	21

	13	Dickens, *Martin Chuzzlewit*	2	May	21
	21	Bunsen, *Memoirs of Baron Bunsen*	2	May	28
	30	Azeglio, *Recollections*	2	June	3
June	26	Azeglio, *Recollections*	1	July	3
	27	Roland de la Platière, *Mémoires de Mme. Roland*		July	3
July	3	Feuillet, *Histoire de Sybille*		July	8
Sept.	7	Guizot, *Histoire de France*	1	Sept.	19
	10	Guizot, *Histoire de France*	2	Oct.	10
	25	Dumas, *Les Frères Corses*		Oct.	10
Oct.	6	Guizot, *Histoire de France*	3	Oct.	17
	10	Guizot, *Histoire de France*	4	Oct.	27
	14	Scarron, *Oeuvres*	2	Oct.	27
	17	Dumas, *Les Trois Mousquetaires*	2	Oct.	31
	27	Guizot, *Histoire de France*	5	Nov.	6
	28	Balzac, *Oeuvres*	42	Oct.	31
	30	Fanshawe, *Memoirs of Lady Fanshawe*		Nov.	12
Nov.	2	Farrar, *Seekers after God*		Nov.	6
	2	Cowper, *Diary of Countess Cowper*		Nov.	12
	12	Mignet, *Histoire de Marie Stuart*	1	Nov.	25
	12	Evelyn, *Diary*	1	Dec.	3
	17	Mignet, *Histoire de Marie Stuart*	2	Nov.	25
	25	Evelyn, *Diary*	2	Dec.	11
Dec.	3	Schiller and Goethe		Dec.	29
	19	Lesley, *Man's Origin*		Dec.	29
	29	Wake, *Chapters on Man*		Jan.	2

1869

Jan.	4	Hawthorne, *Note-Books*	2	Jan.	6
	6	Hawthorne, *Note-Books*	1	Jan.	14
	12	*Putnam's Magazine* 1853	1	Jan.	25
	12	Freytag, *Pictures of German Life*	1	Jan.	28
	12	Dumas, *Le Capitaine Paul*		Jan.	14
	14	Dumas. *La Père la Ruine*		Jan.	21
	21	Goethe, *Faust* (tr. Hayward)		Feb.	6
	27	Freytag, *Pictures of German Life*	2	Feb.	4
	29	Hilton, *Lectures on Rest and Pain*		Feb.	12
Feb.	4	Helps, *Life of Columbus*		Feb.	8
	4	Freytag, *Pictures of German Life* (2 ser.)	1	Feb.	12
	8	Holden, *Human Osteology*		Feb.	26
	12	Freytag, *Pictures of German Life* (2 ser.)	2	Feb.	23
	23	Stirling, *Charles V*		Mar.	8
	24	Mignet, *Charles-Quint*		Feb.	26

	26	Edwards, *Influence des Agens Physique*		Mar.	8
	26	Prescott, *Conquest of Mexico*	1	Mar.	17
Mar.	11	Morley, *The King and the Commons*		Mar.	17
	24	Phelps, *Gates Ajar*		Apr.	1
Apr.	1	Bushnell, *Moral Uses of Dark Things*		Apr.	6
	6	Alford, *Poetical Works*		Apr.	10
	10	Forster, *Historical and Biographical Essays*	1, 2	May	11
	13	Humboldt, *Werke*	4	Apr.	14
	14	Shairp, *Studies in Poetry and Philosophy*		Apr.	21
	14	Cromwell, *Letters* (ed. Carlyle)	1	May	4
May	3	Zeller, *Socrates and the Socratic Schools*		May	4
	5	Cromwell, *Letters* (ed. Carlyle)	2	May	31
	5	Newman, *Verses on Various Occasions*		May	11
	19	Lewes, *Life of Robespierre*		May	31
	19	Humboldt, *Briefe*		May	31
June	19	Sand, *Les Mâitres Mosaïstes*		July	1
July	2	Maximilian, *Recollections*	1, 3	July	13
Aug.	31	Darwin, *Voyage of the Beagle*		Sept.	13
	31	Prendergast, *German*		Aug.	31
Sept.	13	Swinburne, *Atalanta in Calydon*		Sept.	24
	17	Lanfrey, *Napoléon I*	1	Sept.	24
	24	Lanfrey, *Napoléon I*	2	Oct.	2
Oct.	7	Lanfrey, *Napoléon I*	2	Oct.	14
	14	Lanfrey, *Napoléon I*	3	Oct.	21
	21	Garratt, *Medical Uses of Electricity*		Nov.	19
	21	Ruskin, *Modern Painters*	1, 2	Nov.	2
	23	Lanfrey, *Napoléon I*	3	Oct.	27
Nov.	19	Gilbert, *Lucrezia Borgia*	1	Nov.	20
	19	Mignet, *French Revolution*		Dec.	27
	29	Zeller, *Socrates and the Socratic Schools*		Dec.	13
Dec.	1	Sainte-Beuve, *Portraits Contemporains*	3	Dec.	15
	18	*Fortnightly Review*	10 or 11[?]	Dec.	24
	18	*Anthropological Review*	5	Dec.	24
	24	Schopenhauer, *Parerga und Paralipomena*	1, 2	Dec.	27
	30	Everett, *Science of Thought*		Jan.	4

1870

Jan.	4	Emerson, *Essays*, 2nd Ser.		Jan.	10
	7	*Fortnightly Review*	11	Jan.	15
	10	Hawthorne, *House of Seven Gables*		Jan.	15
	10	Lanfrey, *Napoléon I*	1	Jan.	28
	11	Emerson, *English Traits*		Jan.	20
	20	Thierry, *Lettres sur L'Histoire de France*		Feb.	7

GLEN MACLEOD   105

	28	Lanfrey, *Napoléon I*		Feb.	5
Feb.	7	Thierry, *Dix Ans d'Études Historiques*	2	Mar.	4
	20	Thierry, *Récits des Temps Mérovingiens*	1, 2	Mar.	22
Mar.	4	Auerbach, *Schriften*	3, 4	Mar.	22
	4	Erckmann and Chatrain, *Le Blocus*		Mar.	8
	8	Longman, *History of Edward III*	1	Mar.	18
	18	Longman, *History of Edward III*	2	Apr.	2
Apr.	2	Palgrave, *Central and Eastern Arabia*	1	Apr.	26
	13	Palgrave, *Central and Eastern Arabia*	2	May	5
	27	Lanfrey, *Napoléon I*	3	May	5
May	5	Wolzogen, *Schiller's Beziehungen etc.*		May	6
	5	Samuelson, *German Working Man*		May	12
	6	Tylor, *Early History of Mankind*		May	27
	25	Washburn, *Fair Harvard*		May	27
June	10	Newman, *Grammar of Assent*		June	21
	10	Auerbach, *Edelweiss*		June	21
	21	Forster, *Schriften*	1, 2	July	5
July	2	Sandeau, *Mademoiselle de la Seiglière*		July	7
	5	Forster, *Schriften*	7, 8	July	29
	29	Lockhart, *Life of Scott*	1, 2, 3	Aug.	21
	29	Forster, *Schriften*	9	Aug.	27
Aug.	27	Vauvenarges, *Oeuvres*	1, 2	Sept.	12
Sept.	12	White, *Life of Blanco White*	1, 2	Sept.	17
	17	White, *Life of Blanco White*	3	Sept.	19
	17	Eckardt, *Modern Russia*		Sept.	28
	28	[illegible]		Oct.	5
Oct.	5	Eastlake, *Household Taste*		Oct.	12
	11	Azeglio, *Recollections*	1, 2	Oct.	19
	12	Prescott, *Conquest of Mexico*	1, 2	Oct.	26
	19	Prescott, *Conquest of Mexico*	3	Nov.	14
	24	De Morgan, *From Matter to Spirit*		Nov.	14
	26	Hartt, *Geology of Brazil*		Nov.	3
Nov.	12	Mitford, *Life of Mary R. Mitford* (Am)	1	Nov.	14
	14	Mitford, *Life of Mary R. Mitford* (Am)	2	Nov.	21
	21	Mitford, *Life of Mary R. Mitford* (Eng)	1	Nov.	28
	29	Wordsworth, *British Poets*	2	Dec.	27
	29	Tennyson, *Idyls of the King*		Dec.	27

1871

Jan.	4	Sand, *Jacques*		Jan.	16
	10	Froude, *History of England*	2	Jan.	21
	10	Gautier, *Le Peau de Tigre*		Jan.	20
	10	Lowell, *The Biglow Papers*		Feb.	2
	20	Manning, *Ancient and Medieval India*	1	Jan.	27

	27 Lubbock, *Origin of Civilization*		Feb. 4
Feb.	13 Lever, *That Boy of Norcott's*		Feb. 16
	13 Goethe, *Werke*	3	Mar. 10
Mar.	10 Froude, *History of England*	10	Mar. 24[?]
	17 Trollope, *Decade of Italian Women*	1	Apr. 12
Apr.	12 Roscoe, *Vittoria Colonna*		Apr. 17
	15 Gilbert, *Lucrezia Borgia*	1	Apr. 28
	17 Oliphant, *Francis of Assisi*		Apr. 24
	28 Trollope, *Decade of Italian Women*	2	May 31
May	4 Trelawney, *Recollections of Shelley*		May 18
	12 Newman, *Europe*		May 16
	23 Forsyth, *Novels and Novelists*		May 31
June	27 Masson, *British Novelists*		July 19
July	3 Stephen, *Playground of Europe*		July 5
	25 Lecky, *European Morals*	1	Aug. 16
	25 Trollope, *Decade of Italian Women*	2	Aug. 16
Aug.	___ Balzac, *Contes Drolatiques*	12	Aug. 16
Sept.	1 Stephen, *Lectures on France*	1	Sept. 18
	13 Newman, *Apologia Pro Vita Sua*		Oct. 12
	18 Hutton, *Essays (Literary)*	2	Oct. 7
Oct.	4 Sardou, *Piccolino*		Oct. 18
	18 Vigée-LeBrun, *Souvenirs*	1	Oct. 24
	24 Vigée-LeBrun, *Souvenirs*	2	Nov. 6
	24 Berkeley, *Works*	1	Nov. 1
	24 Bailey, *Review of Berkeley*		Nov. 1
Nov.	1 Lathy, *Memoirs of Louis XIV*	1	Nov. 1
	1 Carlyle, *Autobiography of Alex. Carlyle*		Nov. 20
	1 Abbott, *Sight and Touch*		Nov. 7
	1 *North British Review* 1864	41	Nov. 7
	1 *Macmillan's Magazine* Nov.–Apr. 1866	13	Nov. 22
	6 Sardou, *Les Diables Noirs*		Nov. 21
	21 Goncourt, *La Femme*		Nov. 27
	28 *Quarterly Review*	262	Dec. 23
	28 *Fortnightly Review*	1	Dec. 5
Dec.	2 Venn, *Characteristics of Belief*		Dec 16
	8 Niebuhr, *Lectures on Roman History*	1	Dec. 11
	11 Merivale, *History of the Romans*	1	Dec. 19
	16 Merivale, *History of the Romans*	2	Jan. 2
	16 Brodie, *Works*	1	Jan. 19
	16 Brown, *Principles of Ecclesiastical Truth*		Jan. 19
	19 Merivale, *History of the Romans*	3	Jan. 26

	19	Bucknill and Tuke, *Psychological Medicine*		Jan. 29
	26	Merivale, *History of the Romans*	4	Jan. 19
	29	*Fortnightly Review* 1868		Jan. 1
	29	Mill, *Analysis of the Human Mind*		Jan. 6

1872

Jan.	1	*Fortnightly Review*	12	Jan. 9
	2	Merivale, *History of the Romans*	5	Jan. 4
	3	*Fortnightly Review*	8	Jan. 5
	5	Boner, *Memoirs*	1	Jan. 8
	9	*Fortnightly Review*	13	Jan. 29
	9	Parkman, *Book of Roses*		Jan. 12
	30	Merivale, *History of the Romans*	5	Feb. 14
Feb.	6	Grauvogl, *Physiologie*		Mar. 25
	14	Beattie, *Journal of Germany*	1	Mar. 15
	15	Jameson, *Social Life in Germany*		Mar. 15
	15	Martineau, *Visits and Sketches*	1, 2	Mar. 28
	15	Hutton, *Essays*	1	Mar. 28
	26	*Westminster Review* Jan. 1872		Mar. 28
	26	Newman, *Apologia Pro Vita Sua*		Mar. 14
	26	Gurney, *Chapters from French History*		Mar. 7
Mar.	5	*Dublin Review* July 1871		Mar. 7 Special
	7	*Dublin Review* Oct. 71		Mar. 9
	11	Burritt, *London to Land's End*		Apr. 15
	11	Burritt, *London to John O'Groats*		Apr. 15
Apr.	15	Jardine, *Christian Sacerdotalism*		Apr. 19
	25	Lewes, *History of Philosophy*	2	May 16
May	16	Wigan, *Duality of the Mind*		May 29
June	25	Coleridge, *Northern Worthies*	2	July 8
	25	Morley, *Edmund Burke*		July 8
July	8	Bayne, *Essays*	x	Aug. 7
	8	Auerbach, *Schriften*	1, 2	Aug. 7
Aug.	21	Palgrave, *Hermann Agha*		Aug. 29
Sept.	4	Sand, *Pierre Qui Roule*		Sept. 16
Oct.	2	Lewes, *History of Philosophy*	1, 2	Oct. 14
	12	Freytag, *Lost Manuscript*		Oct. 24
	12	Goethe, *Letters to Leipzig Friends*		Oct. 24
Nov.	9	Freytag, *Lost Manuscript*	1, 2	Nov. 15
	15	Williams, *Window Gardening*		Nov. 18
	18	Gaboriau, *Mystery of Orcivale*		Nov. 25

1873

Jan.	18	Harvey, *Works*		Mar.	19
	22	Eliot, *Middlemarch*	5	Mar.	28
	28	Eliot, *Middlemarch*	6, 7	Feb.	3
Feb.	14	Lytton, *Night and Morning*		Mar.	10
	21	Flint, *Relations of Urea to Exercise*		Mar.	10
Mar.	10	Hare, *Memorials of a Quiet Life*	2	Mar.	12
	12	Mayo, *Never Again*		Mar.	18
	18	About, *Trente et Quarante*		Apr.	4
	19	Richardson, *Songs from Old Dramatists*		Apr.	25
May	12	Ideville, *Journal d'un Diplomate*		May	30
	14	Aeby, *Der Bau des menschlichen Koerpers*		May	16
	14	Sand, *Le Beau Laurence*		May	19
	30	Stockman, *Memoirs of Baron Stockman*		June	6
	30	2nd cop. Cox and Jones, *Popular Romances of the Middle Ages*			

Bibliography

[Date(s) to the right of the item refer to date(s) in the foregoing circulation records.]

1. Abbott, Thomas Kingsmill   1865, 1871
   Sight and touch: an attempt to disprove the received (or Berkeleian) theory of vision
   London, 1864
2. About, Edmond   1867
   Le marquis de Lanrose [vol. 3 of *La vielle roche* (3 vols.)]
   Paris, 1865
3. About, Edmond   1867
   Tollá
   Paris, 1856
4. About, Edmond   1873
   Trente et quarante. Sans dot. Les parents de Bernard
   Paris, 1862
   Paris, 1868
5. About, Edmond   1865
   Les vacances de la comtesse [vol. 2 of *Le vielle roche* (3 vols.)]
   Paris, 1865
6. Adam, Juliette   1864, 1868
   Récits d'une paysanne par Juliette Lamber
   Paris, [1862]
7. Aeby, Christoph   1873
   Der Bau des menschlichen Koerpers
   Leipzig, 1868

8. Aeschylus 1866
     Agamemnon [and the *Bacchanals* of Euripides],
     trans. Henry Hart Milman
         London, 1865
 9. Alcock, Sir Rutherford 1864
     The capital of the tycoon: a narrative of a three years' residence in Japan
         London, 1863 (2 vols.)
10. Alford, Henry 1869
     The poetical works of Henry Alford
         Boston, 1853
11. Alger, William Rounseville 1865
     The critical history of the doctrine of a future life
         Philadelphia, 1864
12. Alger, William Rounseville 1867
     Solitudes of nature and of man, or the loneliness of human life
         Boston, 1867 [Alt. Title: *Genius of Solitude*]
13. Andersen, Hans Christian 1866
     Sammtliche Marchen
         Leipzig, [18--] (8e Auflage)
14. Andersen, Hans Christian 1866
     Sand-hills of Jutland
         Boston, 1860
15. Arnold, Matthew 1864
     French Eton, or middle-class education and the state
         London, 1864
16. Arnold, Matthew 1867
     On the study of Celtic literature
         London, 1867
17. Arnold, Matthew 1864
     On translating Homer: three lectures given at Oxford
         London, 1861
18. Arnold, Thomas 1866
     History of the later Roman commonwealth to the death of Caesar, and the reign of Augustus; with a life of Trajan
         London, 1849 (2 vols.)
19. Arnold, Thomas 1865
     History of Rome
         London, 1843–44 (3 vols.)
20. Asbjornsen, Peter Christen 1866
     Popular tales from the Norse: with an introductory essay on the origin and diffusion of popular tales by George Webbe Dasent
         New York, 1859
21. Auerbach, Berthold 1870
     Edelweiss
         Stuttgart, 1861

22. Auerbach, Berthold 1870, 1872
    Gesammelte Schriften
        Stuttgart, 1857–58 (20 vols.)
23. Augier, Guillaume Victor Emile 1865
    Le fils de Giboyer
        Paris, 1863
24. Azeglio, Massimo Taparelli 1868, 1870
    Recollections, trans. and with notes and introduction by
    Count Maffei
        London, 1868 (2 vols.)
25. Bagehot, Walter 1867
    The English constitution, from the *Fortnightly Review*
        London, 1867
26. Bailey, Samuel 1871
    Review of Berkeley's theory of vision
        London, 1842
27. Bain, Alexander 1867
    The emotions and the will
        London, 1859
28. Balzac, Honoré de 1871
    Contes drolatique (in *Oeuvres complètes*)
        Paris, 1865–66 (45 vols.) [?This is the only edition listed
        in the 1871 catalogue. Volume 12 of this edition does
        not contain *Contes drolatique*.]
29. Balzac, Honoré de 1868
    Oeuvres complètes
        Paris, 1865–66 (45 vols.)[?]
30. Balzac, Honoré de 1866
    Les paysans (*Oeuvres complètes*, vol. 3)
        Paris, 1865–66 (45 vols.) [?No separate edition of
        Les Paysans is listed, and it does not seem to be in
        volume 3 of these collected works.]
31. Balzac, Honoré de 1867
    Les rivalités (*Oeuvres complètes*, vol. 39)
        Paris, 1865–66 (45 vols.)[?]
32. Bates, Henry Walter 1865
    The naturalist on the Amazon
        London, 1863 (2 vols.)
33. Bayne, Peter 1872
    Essays in biography and criticism
        Boston, 1871
34. Beale, Lionel Smith 1864
    *On some points in the anatomy of the liver of man and vertebrate
    animals [. . .]*
        London, 1856

35. Beattie, William — 1872
    Journal of a residence in Germany
    London, 1831 (2 vols.)
36. Beaumont, Francis — 1866
    Beaumont and Fletcher, beauties selected by L[eigh]. Hunt
    London, 1855
37. Beranger, Pierre Jean de — 1866
    Oeuvres Complètes
    Paris, 1850 (2 vols.)
38. Berkeley, George — 1871
    Works of George Berkeley
    Oxford, 1871 (4 vols.)
39. Bernard, Charles de — 1864, 1865
    Le gentilhomme compagnard
    Paris, 1857 (2 vols.)
40. Berry, Mary — 1865
    Extracts of the journals and correspondence of Miss Berry, 1782–1852, ed. Lady T. Lewis
    London, 1865 (3 vols.)
41. Bodichon, Eugène — 1867
    De l'humanité
    Brussels, 1866 (2 vols.)
42. Boner, Charles — 1872
    Memoirs and letters of Charles Boner, ed. R. M. Kettle
    London, 1871 (2 vols.)
43. Boswell, James — 1867, 1868
    Life of Samuel Johnson
    London, 1848 (10 vols.)
44. Brodie, Sir Benjamin Collins — 1871
    Works
    London, 1864 (3 vols.)
45. Bronte, Charlotte — 1865
    Jane Eyre
    New York, 1848
46. Brown, James Baldwin — 1871
    First principles of ecclesiastical truth, on the church and society
    London, 1871
47. Brown, Samuel — 1864
    Lectures on the atomic theory, and essays scientific and literary
    Edinburgh, 1858 (2 vols.)
48. Browne, Charles Farrar — 1866
    Artemus Ward his book
    New York, 1865
    Artemus Ward his travels
    New York, 1865 [vol. 2 of *Comic Books by Artemus Ward*]

49. Browning, Elizabeth Barrett 1867
    Aurora Leigh
    Boston, 1857
50. Browning, Elizabeth Barrett 1865
    Poems
    New York, 1852 (2 vols.)
    New York, 1863 (4 vols.)
51. Browning, Elizabeth Barrett 1866
    Prometheus bound, etc. (*Prometheus of Aeschylus, Sonnets from the Portuguese, Casa Guidi windows*)
    New York, 1856
52. Browning, Robert 1864
    Dramatis personae
    London, 1864
    Boston, 1864
53. Bryce, James 1866
    The holy Roman empire
    Oxford, 1864
    London, 1866
54. Bucknill, John Charles, and D. H. Tuke 1871
    Manual of psychological medicine
    London, 1858
55. Bunsen, Frances Waddington, Baroness 1868
    Memoirs of Baron Bunsen
    London, 1868 (2 vols.)
56. Burritt, Elihu 1872
    A walk from London to John O'Groats
    London, 1864
57. Burritt, Elihu 1872
    A walk from London to Land's End and back
    London, 1868
58. Bushnell, Horace 1869
    Moral uses of dark things
    New York, 1868
59. Bushnell, Horace 1866
    The vicarious sacrifice grounded in principles of universal obligation
    New York, 1866
60. Campbell, George Douglass 1867
    The reign of law
    London, 1867
61. Capefigue, M. (Jean Baptiste Honoré Raymond) 1865
    Mesdemoiselles de Nesle et la jeunesse de Louis XV
    Paris, 1864

62. Carlyle, Alexander 1871
    Autobiography of Rev. Dr. Alexander Carlyle, minister of Inveresk
       Edinburgh, London, 1860
63. Carlyle, Thomas 1868
    Critical and miscellaneous essays
       Boston, 1860 (4 vols.)
64. Carlyle, Thomas 1864
    History of Friedrich II of Prussia, called Frederick the Great
       London, 1858–65 (6 vols.)
       New York, 1858–64 (4 vols.)
65. Carlyle, Thomas 1864
    The Life of John Sterling
       Boston, 1851
66. Cherbuliez, Victor 1867
    Un cheval de Phidias, causeries Athéniennes
       Paris, 1864 (2nd ed.)
67. Clément, Pierre 1867
    Jacques Coeur et Charles VII
       Paris, 1866
68. Cobbe, Frances Power 1864
    Broken lights, an inquiry into the present condition and future prospects of religious faith
       Boston, 1864
69. Coleridge, Hartley 1872
    Lives of Northern worthies
       London, 1852 (3 vols.)
70. Cowper, Mary Clevering, Countess 1868
    Diary of Countess Cowper, 1714–20
       London, 1864
71. Cox, George William, and Eustace Hinton Jones 1873
    Popular romances of the Middle Ages
       London, 1871
72. Cox, Robert 1866
    Literature of the Sabbath question
       Edinburgh, 1865 (2 vols.)
73. Craven, Augustus, Mme. 1868
    Récit d'une soeur, souvenirs de famille
       Paris, 1867 (2 vols.; 2nd ed.)
74. Cromwell, Oliver 1869
    The letters and speeches of Oliver Cromwell, with elucidations by Thomas Carlyle
       London, 1845 (2 vols.)
75. Dallas, E. S. 1867
    The gay science
       London, 1866 (2 vols.)

76. Damon, Howard Franklin 1864
    Leucocythemia, Boylston prize essay, 1863
       Boston, 1864
77. Darwin, Charles Robert 1869
    Zoology of the voyage of the Beagle under command of Fitzroy
       London, 1837–43 (3 vols.)
78. Davesiès de Pontès, Lucien 1868
    Social reform in England, trans. Mme. D.
       London, 1866
79. De Morgan, Sophia Elizabeth [Mrs. Augustus] 1870
    From matter to spirit, the result of ten years' experience in spirit manifestations
       London, 1863
80. De Quincey, Thomas 1866
    Confessions of an English opium eater
       Philadelphia, 1823
       Boston, 1851
    Notebook of an English opium eater
       Boston, 1855
81. Dickens, Charles 1868
    Martin Chuzzlewit, life and adventures of
       Leipzig, 1844 (2 vols.)
       London, 1858 (2 vols.)
82. Diderot, Denis 1867
    Mémoires, correspondance, et ouvrages inédits, 1759–80
       Paris, 1830–31 (4 vols.)
83. Doellinger, Johann Joseph Ignaz von 1866
    The first age of Christianity [and the church]
       London, 1866 (2 vols.)
84. Dumas, Alexandre 1869
    Le capitaine Paul
       Paris, 1862
85. Dumas, Alexandre 1864
    La comtesse de Charny
       Paris, 1860 (6 vols.)
86. Dumas, Alexandre 1868
    Les frères corses. Othon l'archer
       Paris, 1862
87. Dumas, Alexandre 1869
    Le père la ruine
       Paris, 1860
88. Dumas, Alexandre 1867
    Théâtre complet
       Paris, 1863–64 (14 vols.)

89. Dumas, Alexandre   1867, 1868
    Les trois mousquetaires
        Paris, 1853 (2 vols.)
90. Dumas, Alexandre   1864
    Le vicomte de Bragelonne
        Paris, 1853
        *Paris, 1860–61 (6 vols.)
91. Dumas, Alexandre   1864
    Vingt ans après, suite des trois mousquetaires
        Paris, 1853 (3 vols.)
        Paris, 1863
92. Dwight, Benjamin Woodbridge   1864
    Modern philology, its discoveries, history, and influence
        New York, 1864 (2 vols.)
93. Eastlake, Charles Lock [the younger]   1870
    Hints on household taste in furniture, upholstery, and other details
        London, 1868
94. Eckardt, Julius Wilhelm Albert von   1870
    Modern Russia
        London, 1870
95. Eckermann, Johann Peter   1865
    Conversations of Goethe with Eckermann and Soret, trans.
    J. Oxenford
        London, 1850 (2 vols.)
96. Edwards, Henri Milne   1866
    Leçons sur la physiologie et l'anatomie comparee de l'homme et des animaux
        Paris, 1857–65 (8 vols.)
97. Edwards, William Frederic   1869
    Influence des agens physiques sur la vie
        Paris, 1824
98. Eliot, George   1865
    Adam Bede
        New York, 1859
99. Eliot, George   1873
    Middlemarch, a study of provincial life
        [edition unidentified]
100. Eliot, George   1866
    The mill on the Floss
        [edition unidentified]
101. Emerson, Ralph Waldo   1870
    English traits
        Boston, 1856

102. Emerson, Ralph Waldo　　　　　　　　　　　　　　　1870
　　　Essays, second series
　　　　　Boston, 1844
103. Epictetus　　　　　　　　　　　　　　　　　　　　1865
　　　Works, trans. Elizabeth Carter
　　　　　London, 1758
104. Epinay, Louise Florence Pétronille Tardieu d'Esclevelles,
　　　Mme., marquise d'　　　　　　　　　　　　　　　1867
　　　Mémoires et correspondance
　　　　　Paris, 1818 (3 vols.)
105. Erckmann, Emile, and A. Chatrain　　　　　　　　　1870
　　　Le blocus, épisode de la fin de l'Empire
　　　　　Paris, 1868
106. Erckmann, Emile, and A. Chatrain　　　　　　　　　1865
　　　Histoire d'un conscrit de 1813 (11e ed.)
　　　　　Paris, n.d.
107. Erckmann, Emile, and A. Chatrain　　　　　　　　　1867
　　　L'invasion, ou le fou Yégof (7e ed.)
　　　　　Paris, n.d.
108. Erckmann, Emile, and A. Chatrain　　　　　　　　　1867
　　　Madame Thérèse (new ed.)
　　　　　Paris, n.d.
109. Erckmann, Emile, and A. Chatrain　　　　　　　　　1865
　　　Waterloo, suite de Conscrit de 1813 (8e ed.)
　　　　　Paris, n.d.
110. Erichsen, John Eric　　　　　　　　　　　　　　　1866
　　　Railway and other injuries of the nervous system
　　　　　London, 1866
111. Euripides　　　　　　　　　　　　　　　　　　　1866
　　　The Bacchanals [see Aeschylus]
112. Evelyn, John　　　　　　　　　　　　　　　　　　1868
　　　Memoirs, ed. W. Bray
　　　　　London, 1827 (5 vols.)
　　　Diaries and correspondence
　　　　　London, 1850–52 (4 vols.)
113. Everett, Charles Carroll　　　　　　　　　　　　　1869
　　　The science of thought, a system of logic
　　　　　Boston, 1869
114. Fanshawe, Anne (Harrison), Lady　　　　　　　　　1868
　　　Memoirs, by herself
　　　　　London, 1829
　　　　　London, 1830
115. Farrar, C. C. S.　　　　　　　　　　　　　　　　　1864
　　　The war, its causes and consequences
　　　　　Cairo, IL; Memphis, TN [etc.], 1864

116. Farrar, Frederick William 1865
    Chapters on language
    London, 1865
117. Farrar, Frederick William 1868
    Seekers after God
    London, 1868
118. Feuillet, Octave 1868
    Histoire de Sybille
    Paris, 1863
119. Figuier, L. 1866
    L'année scientifique et industrielle
    Paris, 1857–69 (14 vols.)
120. Flaubert, Gustave 1867
    Madame Bovary, moeurs de province
    Paris, 1862
121. Flint, Austin 1873
    On the physiological effects of severe and protracted muscular exercise: with special reference to its influence upon the excretion of nitrogen [Alt. title: *Relations of urea to exercise*]
    New York, 1871
122. Forster, Johann Georg Adam 1870
    Sammtliche Schriften
    Leipzig, 1843 (9 vols.)
123. Forster, John 1864, 1869
    Historical and biographical essays
    London, 1858 (2 vols.)
124. Forster, John 1865
    The life and times of Oliver Goldsmith
    London, 1848
125. Forsyth, William 1871
    Novels and novelists of the eighteenth century
    London, 1871
126. Freytag, Gustav 1872
    The lost manuscript, a novel, trans. Mrs. Malcolm
    London, 1865 (3 vols.)
127. Freytag, Gustav 1869
    Pictures of German life in the XVth, XVIth, and XVIIth centuries, trans. Mrs. Malcolm
    London, 1862–63 (2 series in 4 vols.)
128. Freytag, Gustav 1864
    Soll und Haben, Roman in sechs Buchern
    Leipzig, 1858 (2 vols.)
129. Frothingham, Ephraim Langdon 1864
    Philosophy as absolute science
    Boston, 1864

130. Froude, James Anthony   1867, 1871
    History of England from the fall of Wolsey to the death of Elizabeth
        London, 1856–70 (12 vols.)
        New York, 1870 (12 vols.)

131. Froude, James Anthony   1867
    Short studies on great subjects
        London, 1867–71 (2 series in 3 vols.)

132. Fuller, Margaret   1866
    Memoirs of Margaret Fuller Ossoli
        Boston, 1852 (2 vols.)

133. Gaboriau, Émile   1872
    The mystery of Orcivale, trans. Jules Guérin
        [edition unidentified]

134. Garratt, Alfred Charles   1869
    Electrophysiology and electrotherapeutics, showing the best methods
    for the medical uses of electricity
        Boston, 1860

135. Gaskell, Mrs. [Elizabeth Cleghorn]   1865
    Cranford
        New York, 1853

136. Gautier, Théophile   1871
    Le peau de tigre
        Paris, 1866

137. Gibbon, Edward   1867
    History of the decline and fall of the Roman empire, ed. W. Smith
        Boston, 1854–55 (8 vols.)

138. Gilbert, William   1869, 1871
    Lucrezia Borgia, duchess of Ferrara
        London, 1869 (2 vols.)

139. Goethe, Johann Wolfgang von   1866
    The autobiography of Goethe. Truth and poetry, from my life,
    ed. Parke Godwin
        New York, 1846–47 (2 vols.)

140. Goethe, Johann Wolfgang von   1868
    Correspondence between Schiller and Goethe [see Schiller]

141. Goethe, Johann Wolfgang von   1869
    Faust, trans. A. Hayward
        London, 1834

142. Goethe, Johann Wolfgang von   1872
    Goethe's letters to Leipzig friends, ed. Otto Jahn, trans. Robert Slater
        London, 1866

143. Goethe, Johann Wolfgang von   1871
    Werke
        Wien, 1816–21 (26 vols.)
        Stuttgart, 1854–55 (6 vols.)

144. Goethe, Johann Wolfgang von 1865
   Wilhelm Meister's apprenticeship and travels, trans. Thomas Carlyle
     Boston, 1828 (3 vols.)
     London, 1842 (3 vols.)
145. Goncourt, Edmond de, and Jules Goncourt 1871
   La femme au dix-huitième siècle
     Paris, 1862
146. Gordon, Lucy Austin, Lady Duff 1867
   Letters from Egypt, 1863–65
     London, 1865
147. Grauvogl, Dr. von 1872
   Die Grundgesetze der Physiologie, Pathologie, und homoeopathischen Therapie
     Nurenberg, 1860
148. Grote, George 1866, 1867
   A history of Greece
     London, 1846–56 (12 vols.)
149. Grote, George 1865
   Plato and other companions of Socrates
     London, 1865 (3 vols.)
150. Grote, George 1868
   Review of the work of Mr. John Stuart Mill entitled "Examination of Sir William Hamilton's philosophy"
     London, 1868 [The reference in the circulation records to a second volume is a mystery.]
151. Grote, John 1867
   Exploratio philosophica: notes on modern intellectual science, pt. 1
     Cambridge, 1865
152. Guérin, Eugénie de 1864, 1865
   Journal et letters
     Paris, 1862
   Journal of Eugénie de Guérin, ed. G. S. Trebutien
     London, 1865
153. Guizot, Francois Pierre Guillaume 1868
   Histoire de la civilization en France
     Paris, 1829–32 (5 vols.)
154. Gurney, John Hampden 1872
   Chapters from French history
     London, 1871
155. Hallam, Henry 1865
   View of the state of Europe during the Middle Ages
     Philadelphia, 1824 (2 vols.)
     Boston, 1861 (3 vols.) [In this edition are incorporated the supplemental notes, at first published separately.]

156. Hamilton, Gail [pseud.: Mary Abigail Dodge] 1864
     Gala Days
         Boston, 1863
157. Hannay, James 1867
     A course of English literature
         London, 1866
158. Hardy, Robert Spence 1866
     Legends and theories of the Buddhists
         London, 1866
159. Hare, Augustus John Cuthbert 1873
     Memorials of a quiet life
         New York, 1873
160. Harford, John S. 1864
     Recollections of William Wilberforce
         London, 1864
161. Hartt, Charles Frederick 1870
     Thayer expedition, geology and physical geography of Brazil
         Boston, 1870
     The geology of Brazil
         In *American Geographical and Statistical Society Journal*
         vol. 2, pt. 2, 1870
162. Harvey, William 1873
     Works, trans., with life, R. Willis
         London, 1847
163. Hawthorne, Nathaniel 1870
     The house of the seven gables, a romance
         Boston, 1851
164. Hawthorne, Nathaniel 1869
     Note-books
         In *Atlantic Monthly* 17–18 (1866)
     Passages from the American note-books of Nathaniel Hawthorne
         London, 1868 (2 vols.)
165. Hawthorne, Nathaniel 1868
     The scarlet letter, a romance
         Boston, 1850
166. Hazlitt, William 1864
     Liber amoris, or the new Pygmalion
         London, 1823
167. Hazlitt, William 1866
     Life of Napoleon
         London, 1828–30 (4 vols.)
168. Hazlitt, William 1867
     Memoirs of William Hazlitt
         London, 1867 (2 vols.)

169. Hazlitt, William 1864
Miscellaneous Works
New York, 1859 (5 vols.; vols. 1, 2: *Table Talk*)
170. Helps, Arthur, Sir 1869
The life of Columbus, the discoverer of America
London, 1869
171. Helps, Arthur, Sir 1868
The life of Las Casas, "the apostle of the Indies"
Philadelphia, 1868
172. Hilton, John 1869
Influence of rest in the treatment of surgical diseases, and diagnostic value of pain
London, 1863
173. Hogg, Thomas Jefferson 1867
Life of Shelley
London, 1858 (2 vols.)
174. Holden, Luther 1869
Human osteology
London, 1861
175. Holmes, Timothy 1866
System of surgery, in treatises by various authors
London, 1860–64 (4 vols.)
176. Homer 1866
Odyssey, trans. P. S. Worsley
Edinburgh, 1861–62 (2 vols.)
177. Hugo, Victor 1868
Oeuvres complètes
[edition unidentified]
178. Hugo, Victor 1868
Théâtre
Paris, 1858 (6 vols.)
179. Humboldt, Alexander von 1867
Personal narrative of travels to the equinoctial regions of the New Continent, 1799–1804 [. . .], trans. H. M. Williams
London, 1818–29 (7 vols.; vol. 1 is 3rd ed.)
Same, trans. and ed. T. Ross
London, 1852–53 (3 vols.)
180. Humboldt, Wilhelm, Freiherr von 1869
Briefe von Wilhelm von Humboldt an eine Freundin
Leipzig, 1860
181. Humboldt, Wilhelm, Freiherr von 1866, 1869
Gesammelte Werke
Berlin, 1841–52 (7 vols.)

182. Hunt, James Henry Leigh 1867
    Autobiography, with reminiscences of friends
        London, 1850 (3 vols.)
        New York, 1850 (2 vols.)
183. Hutton, Richard Holt 1871, 1872
    Essays theological and literary
        London, 1871 (2 vols.)
184. Huxley, Thomas Henry 1864
    Evidences as to man's place in nature
        London & Edinburgh, 1863
185. Huxley, Thomas Henry 1864
    Lectures on the elements of comparative anatomy
        London, 1864
186. Ideville, Henri Amédée le Lorgne, comte d' 1873
    Journal d'un diplomate en Italie [. . .] 1862–66
        Paris, 1873
187. Jackson, James 1864
    Memoir of J. Jackson, Jr., M.D., with extracts from his letters
        Boston, 1836
188. Jameson, Mrs. (Anna) 1872
    Social life in Germany
        London, 1840
189. Jameson, Mrs. (Anna) 1872
    Visits and sketches
        New York, 1834 (2 vols.)
    [The circulation record for 15 February 1872 lists the
    author as "Martineau" (q.v.), presumably Harriet Martineau,
    a contemporary and correspondent of Mrs. Jameson, who
    did not publish a book of this title. Since James took out this
    book together with another book by Mrs. Jameson on the
    same day, the attribution to Martineau may be a mistake.]
190. Jardine, John 1872
    Christian sacerdotalism
        London, 1871
191. Joubert, Joseph 1865
    Pensées
        Paris, 1864 (2 vols.)
192. Jowett, Benjamin 1864
    The epistles of St. Paul [. . .] with critical notes and dissertations
        London, 1855 (2 vols.)
    [The circulation record lists "Jowett, Commentaries."]
193. Karr, John Baptiste Alphonse 1868
    Geneviève
        Paris, 1857

194. Karr, John Baptiste Alphonse 1868
    La Pénélope Normande
        Paris, 1858
195. Keats, John 1867
    Life, letters, and literary remains, ed. R. M. Milnes
        New York, 1848
196. Kelly, Walter Keating 1864
    Curiosities of Indo-European tradition and folklore
        London, 1863
197. Kidder, Daniel P., and J. C. Fletcher 1865
    Brazil and the Brazilians
        Philadelphia, 1857
198. Kingsley, Charles 1864, 1867
    Hypatia, or new foes with an old face
        Boston, 1854 (2 vols.)
199. Kingsley, Charles 1864
    The Roman and the Teuton, a series of lectures delivered before the University of Cambridge
        London, 1864
200. Kingsley, Charles 1867
    Three lectures on the ancien regime, as it existed on the continent before the French Revolution
        London, 1867
201. Lamb, Charles 1865
    Eliana, the uncollected writings of Charles Lamb, ed. J. E. Babson
        Boston, 1864
202. Lamb, Charles 1864
    Works [. . . and a sketch of his life by T. H. Talfourd]
        New York, 1838 (2 vols.)
        Philadelphia, 1854–56 (5 vols.)
203. Lamber, Mme. Juliette [pseud.; see Adam, Juliette] 1864, 1868
204. Lanfrey, Pierre 1869, 1870
    Histoire de Napoléon I
        Paris, 1869–75 [5 vols.: vols.1–4, 4e ed.; vol. 5, 5e ed.]
205. Lathy, Thomas Pike 1871
    Memoirs of the court of Louis XIV
        London, 1819 (3 vols.)
206. Laugel, Auguste 1865
    Les problèmes de la nature
        Paris, 1864
207. La Villemarqué, Théodore Claude Henri Hersart, vicomte de 1867
    Barzoz-breiz, chants populaires de la Bretagne
        Paris, 1846 (2 vols.)

208. Lecky, William Edward 1871
 History of European morals from Augustus to Charlemagne
 London, 1869 (2 vols.)
209. Lecky, William Edward 1866
 History of the rise and influence of the spirit of rationalism in Europe
 London, 1865 (2 vols.)
210. Le Clerc, Joseph Victor, and Ernest Renan 1866
 Histoire littéraire de France, en XVI siècle
 Paris, 1865 (2 vols.)
211. Lesley, John Peter 1868
 Man's origin and destiny, lectures before the Lowell Institute
 Philadelphia, 1868
212. Lessing, Gotthold Ephraim 1866
 Sammtliche Schriften
 Berlin, 1784–1824 (30 vols.)
213. Lever, Charles James 1871
 That boy of Norcott's
 London, 1869
214. Lewes, George Henry 1864, 1865
 Aristotle, a chapter from the history of science
 London, 1864
215. Lewes, George Henry 1867, 1872
 History of philosophy from Thales to Comte
 London, 1867 (2 vols.)
216. Lewes, George Henry 1865
 The life and works of Goethe (2nd ed.)
 London, 1864
217. Lewes, George Henry 1869
 The life of Maximilian Robespierre
 Philadelphia, 1849
218. Lockhart, John Gibson [1866], 1870
 Memoirs of the life of Sir Walter Scott
 [see Scott, Walter, Sir, *Works*]
219. Longman, William 1870
 History of the life and times of Edward III
 London, 1869 (2 vols.)
220. Lowell, James Russell 1871
 The Biglow papers, 1st and 2nd series
 Boston, 1867
221. Lubbock, John, Sir 1871
 Origin of civilization and primitive condition of man
 London, 1870
222. Lucretius Carus, Titus 1865, 1866, 1867
 De rerum natura, trans. H. A. J. Munro
 London, 1864 (2 vols.)

223. Lyell, Charles, Sir — 1865
    The geological evidence of the antiquity of man (2nd ed.)
        Philadelphia, 1863 (2nd Am. ed.)
        London, 1863

224. Lytton, Edward Bulwer — 1873
    Night and morning
        New York, 1841
        Leipzig, 1843

225. Macaulay, Thomas Babington — 1865
    The history of England from the accession of James II
        London, 1849–61 (5 vols.)
        Boston, 1849–61 (5 vols.)

226. Manning, Mrs. C. (formerly Mrs. Spier) — 1871
    Ancient and medieval India
        London, 1869 (2 vols.)

227. Marsh, George Perkins — 1866
    Origin and history of the English language and of the early literature it embodies
        New York, 1862

228. Martin, Theodore, and W. E. Aytoun — 1866
    Book of ballads, ed. Bon Gaultier (pseud.)
        London, 1849
        New York, 1852

229. Martineau, [Harriet] [see Jameson, Mrs.] — 1872
    [Although Martineau did not publish a book titled *Visits and Sketches*, her *Biographical Sketches* (London, 1869), which the Athenaeum owned, includes a "literary" sketch of Mrs. Jameson. However, it is in only one volume.]

230. Masson, David — 1871
    British novelists and their styles
        Cambridge, 1859

231. Matter, Jacques — 1865
    Le mysticisme en France au temps de Fénelon
        Paris, 1865

232. Maury, Louis Ferdinand Alfred — 1865
    La magie et l'astrologie dans l'antiquité et au moyen âge
        Paris, 1864

233. Maury, Matthew Fontaine — 1865
    The Amazon, and the Atlantic slopes of South America
        Washington, 1853

234. Maximilian, Emperor of Mexico — 1869
    Recollections of my life
        London, 1868 (3 vols.)

235. Mayo, William Starbuck 1873
Never again
New York, 1873
236. Mérimée, Prosper 1865, 1868
Chronique de règne de Charles IX
Paris, 1856
237. Merivale, Charles 1866
The conversion of the Northern nations, Boyle lectures for 1865
London, 1866
238. Merivale, Charles 1865
The conversion of the Roman empire, Boyle lectures for 1864
London, 1864
239. Merivale, Charles 1871, 1872
History of the Romans under the empire
London, 1852–72 (7 vols.)
New York, 1863–65 (7 vols.)
240. Merle d'Aubigné, Jean Henri 1865
History of the reformation in the sixteenth century [. . .]
New York, 1843–56 (5 vols.)
History of the reformation in Europe in the time of Calvin
London, 1863–76 (7 vols.)
241. Michelet, Jules 1865
Histoire de France
Paris, 1833–66 (16 vols.)
242. Michelet, Jules 1866
Histoire Romaine, république
Paris, 1843 (2 vols.)
243. Michelet, Jules 1864, 1866
La sorcière
Paris, 1863
244. Michelet, Jules, Madame 1867
Mémoires d'une enfant
Paris, 1867
245. Mignet, François Auguste Alexis 1865, 1869
Charles-Quint, son abdication [. . .]
Paris, 1855
246. Mignet, François Auguste Alexis 1867
Histoire de la revolution Française, 1789–1814
Bruxelles, 1833 (2 vols.)
247. Mignet, François Auguste Alexis 1868
Histoire de Marie Stuart
Paris, 1851 (2 vols.)
248. Mignet, François Auguste Alexis 1869
History of the French revolution
New York, 1827

249. Mill, James 1871
   Analysis of the phenomena of the human mind
   London, 1829 (2 vols.)
   London, 1869 (2 vols.)
250. Mill, John Stuart 1864, 1865, 1867
   Dissertations and discussions, political, philosophical, and historical
   London, 1859–75 (4 vols.)
   Boston, 1865–67 (4 vols.) [contents of vols. 1 & 2 differ from London ed.]
251. Mitford, Mary Russell 1870
   The life of Mary Russell Mitford [. . .]
   London, 1870 (3 vols.)
   New York, 1870 (2 vols.)
252. Moore, Thomas 1867
   Life, letters, and journals of Lord Byron
   London, 1847
253. Morley, Henry 1869
   The king and the commons, cavalier and puritan song
   London, 1868
254. Morley, John 1872
   Edmund Burke, a historical study
   London, 1867
255. Motley, John Lothrop 1867
   The rise of the Dutch republic
   New York, 1856 (3 vols.)
256. Mouhot, Alexandre Henri 1864
   Travels in the central parts of Indo-China, Cambodia, and Laos, during the years 1858, 1859, and 1860
   London, 1864 (2 vols.)
257. Mueller, Friedrich Max 1864
   Lectures on the science of language
   London, 1861–64 (2nd series)
258. Murger, Henri 1867
   Le pays latin
   Paris, 1862
259. Murger, Henri 1867
   Scènes de la vie de jeunesse
   Paris, 1862 [1 vol.; the volume "6" of the circulation record is a mystery]
260. Newman, Francis William 1871
   Europe of the near future, with three letters on the Franco-German war
   London, 1871

261. Newman, John Henry 1864, 1871, 1872
    Apologia pro vita sua
        London, 1864
        New York, 1865
262. Newman, John Henry 1870
    Essay in aid of a grammar of assent
        London, 1870
263. Newman, John Henry 1869
    Verses on various occasions
        London, 1868
264. Niebuhr, Barthold 1871
    Lectures on the history of Rome, ed. L. Schmitz
        London, 1852, 1849 (3 vols.: vol. 1, 3rd ed.; vols. 2 & 3, 2nd ed.)
265. Oakeley, Frederick 1865
    Historical notes of the Tractarian movement, 1833–45
        London, 1865
266. Odling, William 1866
    Lectures on animal chemistry
        London, 1866
267. Oliphant, Mrs. Margaret 1871
    Francis of Assisi
        London, [1871]
268. Oliphant, Mrs. Margaret 1864
    The life of Edward Irving [minister of the National Scotch Church, London]
        London, 1862 (2 vols.)
269. Ossoli, Margaret Fuller [see Fuller, Margaret] 1866
270. Palfrey, John Gorham 1866
    History of New England
        Boston 1859–75 (4 vols.)
271. Palgrave, William Gifford 1872
    Hermann Agha, an Eastern narrative
        New York, 1872
272. Palgrave, William Gifford 1870
    Narrative of a year's journey through central and eastern Arabia
        London, 1866 (2 vols.)
273. Parkman, Francis 1872
    Book of roses
        Boston, 1866
274. Parkman, Francis 1866
    Pioneers of France in the new world [vol. 1 of *France and England in North America*]
        Boston, 1865–77 (5 vols.)

275. Parsons, Theophilus — 1867
    Deus homo, God-man
        Chicago, 1867
276. Pepys, Charlotte, Lady — 1867
    Domestic Sketches in Russia
        London, 1861 (2 vols.)
277. Petitot, Claude Bernard — 1867, 1868
    Collection des mémoires relatifs à l'histoire de France
        Paris, 1819–27 [1e ser.] (52 vols.)
        Paris, 1820–29 [2e ser.] (78 vols.)
278. Phelps, Elizabeth Stuart — 1869
    The gates ajar
        Boston, 1869
279. Pichot, Amédée — 1864
    The life and labours of Sir Charles Bell
        London, 1860
280. Prendergast, Thomas — 1869
    The mastery series: German
        New York, 1869
281. Prescott, William Hickling — 1864, 1869, 1870
    History of the conquest of Mexico
        New York, 1843 (3 vols.)
282. Prescott, William Hickling — 1865
    History of the reign of Ferdinand and Isabella the Catholic of Spain
        London, 1838 (2 vols.)
        Boston, 1838 (3 vols.)
283. Prévost, abbé — 1866
    Histoire de Manon Lescaut et du Chevalier des Grieux [. . .]
        Paris, 1860
284. Prévost-Paradol, Lucien Anatole — 1864, 1865
    Essais de politique et de littérature
        Paris, 1861
285. Rands, William Brighty — 1865
    Henry Holbeach, student in life and philosophy
        London, 1865 (2 vols.)
286. Rawlinson, George — 1866
    Five great monarchies of the ancient eastern world
        London, 1862 [1861]–67 (4 vols.)
287. Reade, Charles — 1864
    Love me little, love me long
        New York, 1859
        London, 1859
        Leipzig, 1859

288. Renan, Ernest 1865
    Averroès et l'averroïsme
    Paris, 1861
289. Renan, Ernest 1865
    De l'origine du langage
    Paris, 1859
290. Retz, Cardinal de 1866
    Memoirs of Cardinal de Retz, trans. T. Evans
    Philadelphia, 1817 (3 vols.)
    Cardinal de Retz; a literary curiosity
    London, 1844 (2 vols.)
    **Le cardinal de Retz et son temps*, par L. Curnier
    Paris, 1862–63 (2 vols.)
291. Reybaud, Henriette Etiennette Fanny, Mme. 1868
    Clémentine
    Paris, 1861
292. Reybaud, Henriette Etiennette Fanny, Mme. 1868
    Espagnoles et Françaises
    Paris, 1863
293. Richardson, Mrs. Abby (Sage) 1873
    Songs from old dramatists
    New York, 1873
294. Richter, Jean Paul Friedrich 1867
    Flower, fruit and thorn pieces, trans. E. H. Noel, with a memoir by Thomas Carlyle
    Boston, 1863
295. Rokitansky, Carl Joseph Wenzelaus Prokop, Freiherr von 1866
    Manual of pathological anatomy
    London, 1849–54 (4 vols.; vol. 1, 1854)
296. Roland de la Platière, Marie Jeanne Philipon, Mme. 1868
    Mémoires, avec des notes par C. A. Durban
    Paris, 1864
297. Roscoe, Mrs. Henry 1871
    Vittoria Colonna, her life and poems
    London, 1868
298. Ruffini, Giovanni 1865, 1868
    Doctor Antonio
    Leipzig, 1861
299. Ruffini, Giovanni 1867
    Lorenzo Benoni, or passages in the life of an Italian
    New York, 1853
300. Ruffini, Giovanni 1867
    Vicenzo, or sunken rocks
    London, 1863 (3 vols.)

301. Ruskin, John 1866
    Ethics of the dust
    London, 1866
302. Ruskin, John 1869
    Modern painters
    London, 1846–60 (5 vols.: vol. 1, 3rd ed.)
    New York, 1854 (2 vols.)
    New York, 1855–60 (5 vols.)
303. Ruskin, John 1866
    Sesame and lilies
    London, 1865
304. Sainte-Beuve, Charles Augustin 1864, 1865
    Causeries du lundi
    Paris, 1852–62 (15 vols.)
305. Sainte-Beuve, Charles Augustin 1864, 1869
    Portraits contemporains
    Paris, 1852 (3 vols.)
306. Sainte-Beuve, Charles Augustin 1865
    Port-royal
    Paris, 1860 (5 vols.)
307. Saint-Hilaire, J. Barthélemy 1865
    Mahomet et le Coran
    Paris, 1865
308. Samuelson, James 1870
    The German working man
    London, 1869
309. Sand, George 1864, 1865
    André
    Paris, 1857
310. Sand, George 1873
    Le beau Laurence
    Paris, 1870
311. Sand, George 1866
    Le chateau des désertes; Isidora
    Paris, 1854
312. Sand, George 1868
    Le compagnon du tour de France
    Paris, 1852
313. Sand, George 1868
    La comtesse de Rudolstadt
    Paris, 1857 (2 vols.)
314. Sand, George 1867
    La confession d'une jeune fille
    Paris, 1865 (2 vols.)

315. Sand, George 1867
 Consuelo
  Paris, 1861–64 (3 vols.)
 *Consuelo, trans. F. G. Shaw
  Boston, 1847 (2 vols.)
316. Sand, George 1865
 Histoire de ma vie
  Paris, 1856 (10 vols.)
  Berlin, 1855 (20 vols.)
317. Sand, George 1865, 1867
 L'homme de neige
  Paris, 1861 (3 vols.)
318. Sand, George 1865
 Horace
  Paris, 1857
319. Sand, George 1864, 1865
 Indiana. Melchior
  Paris, 1853
320. Sand, George 1865, 1867, 1871
 Jacques
  Paris, 1857
321. Sand, George 1865, 1867
 Jeanne
  Paris, 1858
322. Sand, George 1866
 Laura, voyages et impressions
  Paris, 1865
323. Sand, George 1867
 Lettres d'un voyageur
  Paris, 1857
324. Sand, George 1865
 Lucrezia Floriani. Lavinia
  Paris, 1857
325. Sand, George 1869
 Les maîtres Mosaïstes
  Paris, 1861
326. Sand, George 1864
 Marquis de Villemer
  Paris, 1864
327. Sand, George 1864
 Mauprat
  Paris, 1853
  Paris, 1858

328. Sand, George 1864, 1866
   Le meunier d'Angibault
      Paris, 1857
329. Sand, George 1865
   Le péché de M. Antoine
      Paris, 1857 (2 vols.)
330. Sand, George 1872
   Pierre qui roule
      In *Revue de Deux Mondes* May–Oct. 1869
   Pierre qui roule
      Paris, 1870
331. Sand, George 1867
   Le secrétaire intime
      Paris, 1837
   Le secrétaire intime. Mattéa. La vallée noire
      Paris, 1857
332. Sand, George 1868
   Simon. La Marquise. Monsieur Rousset. Mouny-Robin. Relation d'un voyage chez les sauvages de Paris
      Paris, 1857
333. Sand, George 1865
   Teverino. Leone Leoni
      Paris, 1856
334. Sand, George 1864, 1865, 1867
   Valentine
      Paris, 1856
335. Sandeau, Jules 1870
   Mademoiselle de la Seiglière, comédie en quatre actes et en prose
      Paris, 1869
336. Sardou, Victorien 1871
   Les diables noirs, drame en quatre actes
      Paris, 1864
337. Sardou, Victorien 1871
   Piccolino, comédie
      Paris, 1861
338. Scarron, Paul 1868
   Oeuvres
      Paris, 1786 (7 vols.)
339. Scherer, Edmond Henri Adolphe 1864, 1865
   Mélanges d'histoire religieuse
      Paris, 1864
340. Schiller, Friedrich 1868
   Correspondence between Schiller and Goethe, 1794–1805, trans. George H. Calvert
      New York, 1845

341. Schopenhauer, Arthur　　　　　　　　　　　　　　　　1869
   Parerga und paralipomena
      Berlin, 1851 (2 vols.)
342. Scott, Walter, Sir　　　　　　　　　　　　　　　　　　1866
   Woodstock, or the cavalier
      Philadelphia, 1826 (2 vols.)
343. Scott, Walter, Sir　　　　　　　　　　　　　　　1866, [1870]
   Works
      Edinburgh, 1829–39 (100 vols.)
      [vols. 89–98, Lockhart, J. G., *Memoirs of the Life of Sir Walter Scott*]
344. Senior, Nassau William　　　　　　　　　　　　　　　1864
   Biographical sketches
      London, 1863
345. Sévigné, Marie de Rabutin-Chantal, marquise de　　　　1864
   Lettres de Madame de Sévigné
      Paris, 1853 (6 vols.)
346. Shairp, John Campbell　　　　　　　　　　　　　　　1869
   Studies in Poetry and Philosophy
      Edinburgh, 1868 [The circulation record lists "Shairp, Essays."]
347. Shelley, Jane Gibson, Lady　　　　　　　　　　　　　1867
   Shelley memorials, from authentic sources
      Boston, 1859
348. Sidney, Philip, Sir　　　　　　　　　　　　　　　　　1867
   The Countess of Pembroke's Arcadia
      London, 1867
349. Smith, Goldwin　　　　　　　　　　　　　　　　　　1866
   Lectures on the study of history
      New York, 1866
350. Smith, Goldwin　　　　　　　　　　　　　　　　　　1867
   Three English statesmen, a course of lectures on the political history of England
      London, 1867
      London, 1867; Manchester, 1867
      New York, 1867
351. Sophocles　　　　　　　　　　　　　　　　　　　　1866
   Tragedies, trans. H. Plumptree
      London, 1865 (2 vols.)
352. Stendhal (Henri Beyle)　　　　　　　　　　　　　　　1865
   La chartreuse de Parme
      Paris, 1853
353. Stendhal (Henri Beyle)　　　　　　　　　　　　　　　1865
   Le rouge et le noir
      Paris, 1854

354. Stephen, James, Sir 1871
  Lectures on the history of France
    London, 1851 (2 vols.)
    London, 1857 (2 vols.)
355. Stephen, Leslie, Sir 1871
  The playground of Europe
    London, 1871
356. Stirling, James Hutchinson 1865
  The secret of Hegel
    London, 1865 (2 vols.)
357. Stirling, William, Sir 1869
  Cloister life of the emperor Charles V
    London, 1852
358. St. John, Spenser, Sir 1864
  Life in the forests of the far east
    London, 1863 (2 vols.)
359. Stockman, Ernst Alfred Christian, Freiherr von 1873
  Memoirs of Baron Stockman, by his son
    London, 1873
360. Swinburne, Algernon Charles 1869
  Atalanta in Calydon, a tragedy
    London, 1865
361. Taine, Hippolyte 1865
  Essai sur Tite Live
    Paris, 1856
362. Taine, Hippolyte 1864, 1865
  Histoire de la littérature Anglaise
    Paris, 1863–64 (4 vols.)
  [The circulation records for 1864 give the title in English. As far as I can tell, there was no English translation available until 1871.]
363. Taine, Hippolyte 1865
  Philosophes Français du 19e siècle
    Paris, 1857
364. Taylor, Bayard 1865
  John Godfrey's fortunes
    New York, 1865
365. Tennyson, Alfred, Lord 1870
  Idyls of the king
    Boston, 1860
366. Thackeray, William Makepeace 1866
  English humorists of the eighteenth century
    London, 1853

367. Thackeray, William Makepeace 1864
    History of Pendennis
        New York, 1850 (2 vols.)
        New York, 1863 (2 vols.)
368. Thierry, Amédée 1865
    Tableau de l'empire romain
        Paris, 1862
369. Thierry, Augustin 1870
    Dix ans d'études historiques
        Paris, 1851
    **Oeuvres de Augustin Thierry*, vol. 2 (*Dix ans d'études historiques*)
        Paris, 1866
370. Thierry, Augustin 1868, 1870
    Lettres sur l'histoire de France
        Paris, 1856
371. Thierry, Augustin 1868, 1870
    Récits des temps Mérovingiens
        Paris, 1856 (2 vols.)
    [The reference in the circulation record to a third volume is a mystery.]
372. Todd, Robert Bentley, M.D. 1866
    Clinical lectures on certain diseases of the urinary organs, and of dropsies
        Philadelphia, 1857
    Clinical lectures on paralysis and diseases of the brain
        London, 1856
373. Trelawny, Edward John 1871
    Recollections of the last days of Shelley and Byron
        London, 1858
374. Trollope, Anthony 1868
    Lotta Schmidt
        London, 1867
375. Trollope, Anthony 1865
    The three clerks
        New York, 1860
376. Trollope, Thomas Adolphus 1871
    A decade of Italian women
        London, 1859 (2 vols.)
377. Tylor, Edward Burnett, Sir 1865, 1870
    Researches into the early history of mankind and the development of civilization
        London, 1865
378. United States. Congress. House 1864
    Report on conduct of the war
        Washington, 1863 (8 vols.)
        [circulation records list "Error"]

379. Upham, Charles Wentworth 1867
    Salem witchcraft
        Boston, 1867 (2 vols.)
380. Valmiki 1865
    Le Ramayana, poème sanscrit, trans. Hippolyte Fauche
        Paris, 1864 (2 vols.)
381. Vaughn, Robert 1867
    Revolutions in English history
        London, 1859–63 (3 vols.)
382. Vauvenarges, Luc de Clapiers 1870
    Oeuvres complètes
        Paris, 1821 (3 vols.)
383. Venn, John 1871
    On some characteristics of belief, scientific and religious
        London, 1870
384. Vigée-Lebrun, Louise-Elisabeth 1871
    Souvenirs de Madame Vigée-LeBrun
        Paris, 1869 (2 vols.)
385. Vigny, Alfred de 1867
    Servitude et grandeur militaires
        Paris, 1864
386. Vigny, Alfred de 1867
    Stello, les consultations du docteur-noir
        Paris, 1865
387. Virchow, Rudolph Ludwig Karl 1864
    Cellular pathology as based upon physiological and pathological histology, trans. F. Chance
        London, 1860
388. Wake, C. Staniland 1868
    Chapters on man
        London, 1868
389. Washburn, William Tucker 1870
    Fair Harvard, a story of American college life
        New York, 1869
390. Whately, Elisabeth Jane 1867
    Life and correspondence of Richard Whately, D. D., late Archbishop of Dublin
        London, 1866 (2 vols.)
391. Whately, Richard 1864
    Miscellaneous remains from the commonplace book [. . .], ed. Miss E. J. Whately
        London, 1864
392. White, Joseph Blanco 1870
    The life of the Reverend Joseph Blanco White
        London, 1845 (3 vols.)

393. Wigan, Arthur Ladbroke 1872
The duality of the mind; structure, functions, and diseases of the brain
London, 1844
394. Williams, Henry T. 1872
Window gardening
New York, 1872
395. Wolzogen, Alfred, Freiherr von 1870
Schiller's Beziehungen zu Eltern, etc.
Stuttgart, 1859
396. Wordsworth, William 1870
British Poets
[unidentified; circulation record lists "Brit. Poets Wordsworth"]
397. Wynter, Andrew 1864
Subtle brains and lissome fingers, being some of the chisel-marks of our industrial and scientific progress
London, 1863
398. Yonge, Charles Duke 1865
History of England to the peace of Paris, 1856
London, 1857
399. Zeller, Eduard Gottlob 1869
Socrates and the Socratic schools, trans. A. J. Reichel
London, 1868

Appendix: Index of Periodicals

[Date(s) to the right of the item refer to date(s) in the foregoing circulation records, and not to the date(s) of the periodical itself.]

Anthropological Review	1869
British and Foreign Medical Chirurgical Review	1864
Clinical Lectures and Reports (London Hospital)	1866
Dublin Review	1872
Edinburgh Review	1865
Fortnightly Review	1867, 1869, 1870, 1871, 1872
Macmillan's Magazine	1865, 1871
North American Review	1864
North British Review	1867, 1871
Putnam's Magazine	1864, 1869
Quarterly Review	1871

Revue des Deux Mondes 1865, 1867, 1868
Revue Nationale 1864
Westminster Review 1872

NOTES
   1. Work on this bibliography was made possible by a Mary C. Mooney Fellowship at the Boston Athenaeum. Thanks to the library staff for their help with this project, especially Lisa Starzyk-Weldon, who called my attention to these circulation records and has been an invaluable source of information and advice, Stanley Cushing, Stephen Nonack, Catharina Slautterback, and Mary Warnement. I owe a special debt of gratitude to William Vance for first directing my attention to the Boston Athenaeum as a rare scholarly resource.
   2. The circulation records were kept in twenty-six folio volumes, dated 1827–72. After that time, apparently, either the library stopped keeping records this way or the records have been lost.
   3. I cite the 1865 edition of the *By-Laws* since it was adopted only a few months after Henry James Sr. joined the Athenaeum. The language of this edition was retained in later editions during his lifetime.
   4. Samuel Gray Ward (1817–1907) was a banker in Boston and New York. Like Henry James Sr., he was a friend of Emerson and other Transcendentalists. He also shared James's interest in Swedenborg. James's letters to Ward are in the Houghton Library, Harvard University. Gray was a Proprietor of the Boston Athenaeum from 1850 to 1878 (when he sold his two shares).
   5. For recent critical interest in Henry James Sr., see Habegger and Taylor.
   6. Bibliographies of Henry James Sr.'s published writings may be found in W. James, *Literary Remains* 469–71; Warren 261–65; and Young 321–25.
   7. It is not entirely clear to what extent membership privileges extended to the family. Thanks to Stephen Nonack and Lisa Starzyk-Weldon for many helpful discussions about this issue.
   8. Unsigned review, *North American Review* 101 (1865): 281–85; rpt. in H. James, *Literary Criticism: European* 944–49.
   9. Unsigned review, *The Nation* 1 (1865): 752–53; rpt. in H. James, *Literary Criticism: European* 429–33.
   10. Unsigned review, *North American Review* 102 (1866): 599–606; rpt. in H. James, *Literary Criticism: Essays* 5–14.

WORKS CITED

Boston Athenaeum. *Catalogue of the Library of the Boston Athenaeum, 1807–1871*. Boston, 1874–82. Boston: Hall, 1969.

By-Laws of the Proprietors of the Boston Athenaeum 9 Jan. 1865.

Edel, Leon, and Adeline R. Tintner, eds. *The Library of Henry James*. Ann Arbor: UMI Research P, 1987.

Freedman, Jonathan, ed. *The Cambridge Companion to Henry James*. Cambridge, UK: Cambridge UP, 1998.

Habegger, Alfred. *The Father: A Life of Henry James, Sr.* New York: Farrar, 1992.

James, Henry. *The American Scene*. 1907. New York: Penguin, 1994.

———. "The Duke of Montpensier's Pictures at the Boston Athenaeum." *Atlantic Monthly* 34 (1874): 633–37. Rpt. in Sweeney 79–87.

———. *Letters*. Ed. Leon Edel. 4 vols. Cambridge, MA: Harvard UP, 1974.

———. *Literary Criticism: Essays, American and English Writers*. Ed. Leon Edel. New York: Lib. of America, 1984.

———. *Literary Criticism: European Writers and the Prefaces*. Ed. Leon Edel. New York: Lib. of America, 1984.

James, William. *The Correspondence of William James*. Ed. Ignas K. Skrupskelis and Elizabeth M. Berkeley. 11 vols. Charlottesville: UP of Virginia, 1992.

———, ed. *The Literary Remains of Henry James*. 1884. Upper Saddle River, NJ: Gregg, 1970.
Lewis, R. W. B. *The Jameses: A Family Narrative*. New York: Farrar, 1991.
Matthiessen, F. O. *The James Family*. New York: Knopf, 1947.
Quincy, Josiah, Jr. *The History of the Boston Athenaeum, With Biographical Notices of the Deceased Founders*. Cambridge: Metcalf, 1851.
Slautterback, Catharina. *Designing the Boston Athenaeum: 10½ at 150*. Boston: Boston Athenaeum, 1999.
Strouse, Jean. *Alice James: A Biography*. New York: Knopf, 1980.
Sweeney, John L., ed. *The Painter's Eye: Notes and Essays on the Pictorial Arts by Henry James*. Cambridge, MA: Harvard UP, 1956.
Taylor, Andrew. *Henry James and the Father Question*. Cambridge, UK: Cambridge UP, 2000.
Warren, Austin. *The Elder Henry James*. New York: Macmillan, 1934.
Yeazell, Ruth Bernard, ed. *The Death and Letters of Alice James: Selected Correspondence*. Berkeley: U of California P, 1981.
Young, Frederic Harold. *The Philosophy of Henry James, Sr.* New York: Bookman, 1951.

Kate Field: A Primary Bibliography

GARY F. SCHARNHORST
University of New Mexico

The journalist, poet, playwright, actor, travel writer, lecturer, art and theater critic, dress reformer, and editor Mary Katherine (Kate) Field (1838–96) was "one of the best-known women in America" during the Gilded Age, according to her obituary in the *New York Tribune* ("Kate Field Dead"). Nevertheless, she is virtually unknown today. Although she was among the figures sketched over seventy years ago in the *Dictionary of American Biography*, Field has since been erased from most historical and literary accounts of nineteenth-century America. While living with her mother in the expatriate community in Florence from 1859 until 1861, she served as the Italian correspondent of the *Boston Courier*, the *Boston Transcript*, and the *New Orleans Picayune*. The travel writer Frances Power Cobbe claimed that during these months Field filed "some of the best letters ever sent to a newspaper" (397). Field included the Brownings, the Trollopes, Walter Savage Landor, Harriet Beecher Stowe, George Eliot, the artists Elihu Vedder and Harriet Hosmer, and the actor Charlotte Cushman among her circle of friends; she later reminisced about them in some of the earliest articles contributed by a woman to the *Atlantic Monthly*: "Elizabeth Barrett Browning" (1861), "English Authors in Florence" (1864), and "Last Days of Walter Savage Landor" (1866). She also contributed a lengthy obituary/memoir of Eliot to the *New York Tribune* in 1880. Field covered the American theatrical tour of Adelaide Ristori in 1866 for the *New York Tribune* and the *Boston Transcript* and subsequently wrote biographies of both Ristori (1867) and the actor Charles Albert Fechter (1882). She covered Charles Dickens's final American speaking tour for the *New York Tribune* and, as Mark Twain reminisced, she "made a wide, spasmodic notoriety in 1867" with the letters she telegraphed to the newspaper. "Kate Field became a celebrity at once" (1: 157).[1] She later revised these dispatches into a popular book, *Pen Photographs of Charles Dickens's Readings: Taken from Life* (1868; rev. ed., 1871). She covered the visit of the Shah of Persia to England in 1873 for the *New York Tribune*—besting her erstwhile rival Twain, who covered the visit for the déclassé *New York Herald*. Field worked at various times as the New York correspondent of the *Springfield*

Republican and the *Chicago Tribune*, Boston correspondent of the New York *Evening Mail*, Newport correspondent of the *Boston Post* and the *Boston Journal*, and London correspondent of the *Louisville Courier-Journal*, the St. Louis *Missouri Republican*, and the *New York Herald*. In all, as I have argued elsewhere ("James and Kate Field"), Field inspired, I believe, the character of Henrietta Stackpole—Henry James's version of an American feminist—in his novel *The Portrait of a Lady* (1881).

Unfortunately, Field wrote no formal autobiography, but her hundreds of travel essays and other creative nonfiction constitute a rather complete story of her life. Many of her most popular early travel essays were compiled in her bestseller *Hap-Hazard* (1873). As one of the first celebrity journalists, moreover, Field both reported the news and was the subject of news reports. She delivered her lecture on behalf of women's rights, "Woman in the Lyceum," dozens of times between March and December 1869 to public acclaim before publishing it as "Stray Sketches" in the *New York Tribune* in April 1870. She interviewed such figures as archeologist Heinrich Schliemann, playwright and theatrical impresario Dion Boucicault, explorer Henry Stanley, theatrical collaborators William S. Gilbert and Arthur S. Sullivan, pianist Arthur Rubenstein, musician Julius Benedict, and President Grover Cleveland, and in turn she often sat for interviews while on a play or lecture tour. In September 1873, the only journalist allowed to pass through military lines, Field covered the Spanish revolution and interviewed Emilio Castelar, the leader of the short-lived Spanish Republic, for the *New York Tribune* in 1874, an experience she reworked into her book *Ten Days in Spain* (1875). Field made her debut on the New York stage in November 1874 and acted in such plays as Mark Twain's *The Gilded Age* over the next four years. In 1878, she was hired by Alexander Graham Bell to publicize the telephone; in fact, she once demonstrated the invention by singing Irish folk songs to Queen Victoria over the wire. The following year, she helped to found the Shakespeare Memorial Theatre in Stratford. In the early 1880s, Field pioneered and managed the Co-operative Dress Association of New York City, and in a series of essays and lectures in the mid-1880s, she turned her attention to exposing Mormon patriarchy as a threat to women. Upon her death, the *Chicago Times-Herald* credited her, more than any other individual, with the "extirpation of American polygamy" ("Kate Field's Career"). As the editor and publisher of the weekly paper *Kate Field's Washington* (1890–95), moreover, she campaigned for the establishment of Yosemite National Park and helped to launch the career of Charlotte Perkins Gilman by publishing thirty of her earliest poems, stories, and essays. In 1893, Field covered the Columbian Exposition in Chicago for the *Chicago Herald*. Among her friends and acquaintances over the years were W. D. Howells, Bret Harte, Susan B. Anthony,

Elizabeth Cady Stanton, Lucy Stone, Louisa May Alcott, Wendell Phillips, Helen Hunt Jackson, P. T. Barnum, Julia Ward Howe, Clara Barton, Annie Adams Fields, Edwin Booth, Wilkie Collins, William Lloyd Garrison, Charles Warren Stoddard, Louise Chandler Moulton, and Oscar Wilde. At her death, she was traveling in Hawaii on assignment for the *Chicago Times-Herald* to campaign for U. S. annexation of the islands. Even then she did not altogether escape the buzz of notoriety: she was nursed in her final illness by Mabel Loomis Todd, best known today as one of Emily Dickinson's first editors.

The recovery of Field's life and career perforce requires a reconstruction of her oeuvre. (A selected, scholarly edition of her correspondence appeared in 1996 [*Kate Field: Selected Letters*].) The following primary bibliography lists over 800 articles, all of Field's known publications other than the pieces she wrote for *Kate Field's Washington*. In order to compile it, I have worked in the morgues of literally dozens of newspapers and magazines in the United States and England. These 800-plus articles, including juvenilia and a hundred or so items that appeared unsigned or under pseudonyms,[2] appeared in local newspapers and ephemeral journals as well as in such prominent periodicals as the *Atlantic Monthly, Lippincott's, Appleton's, Scribner's, Independent, Belgravia, Christian Union, Harper's New Monthly, Harper's Weekly, North American Review, Athenaeum,* and *Examiner*.[3]

"Boston Correspondence." *New Orleans Picayune* 3 Dec. 1855, afternoon ed., 3:1–2; rpt. 4 Dec. 1855, 2:4.
"Letter from Boston." *New Orleans Picayune* 30 Dec. 1855, 6:1–2.
"Letter from Boston." *New Orleans Picayune* 31 Jan. 1856, afternoon ed., 1:4–5; rpt. 1 Feb. 1856, 2:2–3.
"To Charlotte Cushman" [poem]. *Saturday Evening Gazette* [Boston] 12 June 1858, 2:6.
"Letter from Straws, Jr." *Boston Courier* 17 Mar. 1859, 1:6–7; 25 Mar. 1859, 1:6–7; 18 Apr. 1859, 1:5–6; 25 Apr. 1859, 1:5–6; 9 May 1859, 1:5–6; 30 May 1859, 1:5–7; 8 June 1859, 1:7; 10 June 1859, 1:5; 13 June 1859, 2:1–2; 18 June 1859, 1:5; 27 June 1859, 1:5–6; 4 July 1859, 1:5–6; 11 July 1859, 1:6; 28 July 1859, 1:5–6; 8 Aug. 1859, 1:6–7; 18 Aug. 1859, 1:6.5; 1 Sept. 1859, 1:6–7; 7 Sept. 1859, 1:6–7; 21 Sept. 1859, 1:6–7.
"Foreign Correspondence of the Transcript." *Boston Transcript* 13 Feb. 1860, 2:2; 20 Feb. 1860, 2:3; 24 Feb. 1860, 2:2; 14 Mar. 1860, 2:3; 17 Mar. 1860, 2:2; 27 Mar. 1860, 4:1–2; 2 Apr. 1860, 4:1–2; 10 Apr. 1860, 2:2; 13 Apr. 1860, 2:2–3; 16 Apr. 1860, 1:1–2; 23 Apr. 1860, 2:3; 26 Apr. 1860, 4:1; 7 May 1860, 1:2–3; 14 May 1860, 1:1–2; 25 May 1860, 1:1–2; 18 June 1860, 2:2; 30 June 1860, 1:1–2.

[Introduction to Elizabeth Barrett Browning's "A Tale of Villafranca"]. *New Orleans Picayune* 19 Feb. 1860, 3:1.

"Letter from Italy." *New Orleans Picayune* 19 Feb. 1860, 10:1–2; 26 Feb. 1860, 10:1–2; 4 Mar. 1860, 10:1–2; 25 Mar. 1860, 10:3; 8 Apr. 1860, 10:1–2; 28 Apr. 1860, 6:1–2.

"Victor Emmanuel in Tuscany." *Boston Transcript* 18 May 1860, 1:1–2.

"Ball at the Pitti." *Boston Transcript* 23 May 1860, 2:2.

"Our Country Disgraced by a Consul." *Boston Transcript* 31 May 1860, 4:1.

"An Italian Seago." *Boston Transcript* 6 June 1860, 1:2–3.

"A Chain of Personals." *Boston Transcript* 21 June 1860, 1:1–2.

"Modern Art in Florence." *Boston Transcript* 6 July 1860, 1:1–2.

"Letter from Florence." *New Orleans Picayune* 8 July 1860, 1:6–7; 12 July 1860, afternoon ed., 1:5–6; rpt. 13 July 1860, 5:2–3; 17 July 1860, afternoon ed., 1:6; rpt. 18 July 1860, 3:2–3; 18 July 1860, afternoon ed., 1:5–6; rpt. 19 July 1860, 5:3–4; 22 July 1860, 1:7–2:1; 5 Aug. 1860, 6:1–2.

"Letter from a Garibaldino." *Boston Transcript* 16 July 1860, 2:2.

"Miss Abby Fay's Debut in Florence." *Boston Transcript* 1 Aug. 1860, 2:2.

"Letter from Italy." *New Orleans Picayune* 8 Aug. 1860, afternoon ed., 1:6; rpt. 9 Aug. 1860, 5:4; 9 Aug. 1860, 1:6–7; 12 Aug. 1860, 6:2–4; 19 Aug. 1860, 6:1–2; 25 Aug. 1860, 1:6–7; 29 Aug. 1860, afternoon ed., 1:6; rpt. 30 Aug. 1860, 6:4; 7 Sept. 1860, afternoon ed., 1:6; rpt. 8 Sept. 1860, 6:3; 23 Sept. 1860, 7:1–2; 30 Sept. 1860, 3:1–2; 4 Oct. 1860, 1:6–7; 13 Oct. 1860, afternoon ed., 1:6–7; rpt. 14 Oct. 1860, 12:1–2; 17 Oct. 1860, afternoon ed., 1:5–6; rpt. 18 Oct. 1860, 3:2–3; 28 Oct. 1860, 3:1–2; 11 Nov. 1860, 8:1–2; 11 Nov. 1860, 10:1–2; 18 Nov. 1860, 12:1–2; 25 Nov. 1860, 3:1–2; 9 Dec. 1860, 10:1–2; 16 Dec. 1860, 9:4–5; 16 Dec. 1860, 12:1–2; 30 Dec. 1860, 7:1–2; 30 Dec. 1860, 11:2–3; 13 Jan. 1861, 9:1–3.

"Robert Hart's Bust of Theodore Parker." *Boston Transcript* 15 Jan. 1861, 2:2.

"A Bundle of Fagots from Rome." *New Orleans Picayune* 16 Feb. 1861, 12:1–2.

"Letter from Italy." *New Orleans Picayune* 28 Feb. 1861, 8:1–2; 10 Mar. 1861, 6:2–3; 5 Apr. 1861, 1:5–6; 6 Apr. 1861, afternoon ed., 1:6–7; rpt. 7 Apr. 1861, 3:3–4; 14 Apr. 1861, 2:2–3; 28 Apr. 1861, 1:7–2:1.

"Harmony at a Discount, Protests at a Premium." *New Orleans Picayune* 22 June 1861, afternoon ed., 1:6–7.

"Garibaldi." *Boston Courier* 1 July 1861, 2:3–4.

"Elizabeth Barrett Browning." *Atlantic Monthly* 8 (Sept. 1861): 368–76.

"Anthony Trollope on America." *Continental Monthly* 2 (Sept. 1862): 302–14.

"An Appeal in Behalf of the Discharged Soldiers' Home." *Boston Transcript* 26 Sept. 1862, 1:4–5.
"What Northern Women Ask of the Government." *Boston Commonwealth* 20 Dec. 1862, 1:5–6; 3 Jan. 1863, 1:7–2:1; 10 Jan. 1863, 1:7–2:1; 24 Jan. 1863, 1:7–2:1; 31 Jan. 1863, 1:7–2:1.
"To John Bright" [poem]. *Boston Commonwealth* 13 Mar. 1863, 1:1.
"Mrs. Browning's Essays on the Poets." *Christian Examiner* 75 (July 1863): 24–43.
"The Great Sanitary Fair." *Springfield Republican* 6 Apr. 1864, 1:5–6.
"The Metropolitan Fair." *Springfield Republican* 9 Apr. 1864, 1:3–4.
"The Great Sanitary Fair." *Boston Journal* 11 Apr. 1864, 4:4.
"The Metropolitan Fair." *Springfield Republican* 11 Apr. 1864, 2:2.
"Ramblings Through the Fair." *Springfield Republican* 16 Apr. 1864, 2:4–5.
"The Great Fair." *Boston Journal* ca. 17 Apr. 1864 [BPL scrapbook].
"The Great Fair." *Boston Journal Supplement* 20 Apr. 1864, 1:8.
"The Great Sanitary Fair." *Boston Journal Supplement* 21 Apr. 1864, 1:8.
"[James Jackson] Jarves's Collection of 'Old Masters.'" *Round Table* 23 Apr. 1864, 296–97.
"Sacrificial Offerings to the Fair." *Springfield Republican* 23 Apr. 1864, 1:2–3.
"The Great Fair." *Boston Journal* 26 Apr. 1864, 4:2.
"Pictures at the Great Fair." *Springfield Republican* 30 Apr. 1864, 2:4–5.
"Private Theatricals in New York." *Springfield Republican* 14 May 1864, 1:2–3.
"The New York Women in Council." *Springfield Republican* 21 May 1864, 2:4–5.
"From New York/The National Academy of Design." *Springfield Republican* 22 June 1864, 2:1–2.
"Class Day at Harvard." *Springfield Republican* 29 June 1864, 1:4–5.
"An Esthetic View of Boston's Fourth." *Springfield Republican* 9 July 1864, 1:3–4.
"The Season at Newport." *Springfield Republican* 13 Aug. 1864, 2:1–2.
"Life at Newport." *Boston Journal* 20 Aug. 1864, 4:3.
"Newport on Wheels." *Springfield Republican* 24 Aug. 1864, 2:1–2.
"The Season at Newport." *Boston Journal* 26 Aug. 1864, 4:3–4.
"The Season at Newport." *Boston Journal* 29 Aug. 1864, 4:4.
"The Season at Newport." *Boston Journal* ca. 30 Aug. 1864. [The only known copy of this column is located in a scrapbook in the Field Collection, Boston Public Lib.]
"The Season at Newport." *Boston Journal* 6 Sept. 1864, 4:2–3.
"Newport on Wheels." *Springfield Republican* 7 Sept. 1864, 2:3–4.
"The Season at Newport." *Boston Journal* 7 Sept. 1864, 4:6.
"The Newport Season." *Springfield Republican* 14 Sept. 1864, 1:4–5.

"Life at Newport." *Boston Journal* 20 Sept. 1864, 4:2.
"The Season at Newport." *Springfield Republican* 19 Oct. 1864, 1:4–6.
"From New York/Literature, Art and Politics." *Springfield Republican* 15 Nov. 1864, 2:4–5.
"From New York/Art Gossip—Gross Injustice to the Negroes." *Springfield Republican* 22 Nov. 1864, 2:4–5.
"English Authors in Florence." *Atlantic Monthly* 14 (Dec. 1864): 660–71.
"The Rival Editions of Enoch Arden." *Springfield Republican* 21 Dec. 1864, 2:1–2.
"From New York/Englishmen in America." *Springfield Republican* 28 Dec. 1864, 2:2–3.
"From New York/The Artists' Fund Exhibition of Pictures." *Springfield Republican* 7 Jan. 1865, 4:3–4.
"From New York/The Bryant Festival in Book Form." *Springfield Republican* 14 Jan. 1865, 1:1–3.
"From New York/Negroes and the Fine Arts." *Springfield Republican* 8 Feb. 1865, 2:2–3.
"What Some Good Bostonians Saw at the Bowery." *Boston Advertiser* 10 Feb. 1865, 2:3–4.
"From New York/The Carnival Season." *Springfield Republican* 25 Feb. 1865, 1:2–3.
"[Jean-Leon] Gerome's Pictures." *Boston Advertiser* 24 Mar. 1865, 2:2.
"From New York/Politics and the Drama." *Springfield Republican* 29 Mar. 1865, 1:4–5.
"Letter from New York/Musical and Theatrical Gossip." *Springfield Republican* 12 Apr. 1865, 2:2–3.
"Periodical Literature." *Boston Advertiser* 13 Apr. 1865, 1:2–3.
"The Lesson of the Hour." *Springfield Republican* 3 May 1865, 1:3–4.
"A Side View of Solemn Things." *Boston Advertiser* 9 May 1865, 2:3.
"From New York." *Springfield Republican* 11 May 1865, 2:4–5.
"From New York/Theatricals and Readings." *Springfield Republican* 13 May 1865, 1:2–3.
"The Keans in Hamlet." *Boston Advertiser* 19 May 1865, 2:3.
"Echoes from Europe." *Boston Advertiser* 29 May 1865, 2:2.
"From New York/The Steeple-Chase at the Patterson Race-Course." *Springfield Republican* 17 June 1865, 6:1–2.
"Not a Racy Letter." *Boston Advertiser* Supplement 22 June 1865, 1:3–4.
"From New York/Philanthropy and Art." *Springfield Republican* 28 June 1865, 1:5–6.
"From New York/More about the National Academy of Design." *Springfield Republican* 4 July 1865, 1:5–6.
"National Academy of Design." *Boston Advertiser* Supplement 4 July 1865, 1:1–2; *Boston Advertiser* 12 July 1865, 1:4–5; *Boston Advertiser* Supple-

ment 19 July 1865, 1:7–8; *Boston Advertiser* 26 July 1865, 2:4; *Boston Advertiser* 29 July 1865, 6:2–3; *Boston Advertiser* 4 Aug. 1865, 2:3–4.
"From New York." *Springfield Republican* 12 July 1865, 2:3–4.
"From New York/War and Literature." *Springfield Republican* 22 July 1865, 6:1–2.
"En Route to Newport." *Boston Post* 8 Aug. 1865, 4:1–2.
"From Newport." *Boston Post* 16 Aug. 1865, 1:7–8.
"The Summer Resorts." *Boston Post* 22 Aug. 1865, 4:1–2.
"Newport on Tip-Toe." *Boston Post* 25 Aug. 1865, 1:8–2:1.
"Going to a Watering Place." *Springfield Republican* 2 Sept. 1865, 6:1–2.
"The Watering Places." *Springfield Republican* 6 Sept. 1865, 1:3–4.
"The Season at Newport." *Springfield Republican* 27 Sept. 1865, 2:1–2.
"The Opera in New York." *Boston Advertiser* 25 Dec. 1865, 2:3–4.
"From New York/The Theaters and the Opera." *Springfield Republican* 25 Dec. 1865, 1:4–5.
"Art and Fashion in Paris." ca. Dec. 1865 or Jan. 1866. [Undated clipping in the scrapbook in the Field Collection, Boston Public Lib.]
"From New York/Across the Continent—Down South." *Springfield Republican* 3 Jan. 1866, 1:5–6.
"From New York/Radicalism Religious and Political." *Springfield Republican* 13 Jan. 1866, 1:1–3.
"From New York/Two Lectures and Two Lecturers." *Springfield Republican* 20 Jan. 1866, 1:3–4.
"Dr. Rimmer Before the National Academy of Design." *Boston Advertiser* 22 Jan. 1866, 2:2–3.
"From New York/An Art Reception and Its Accompaniments." *Springfield Republican* 27 Jan. 1866, 1:2–3.
"From New York/The Great Charity Ball." *Springfield Republican* 3 Feb. 1866, 1:2–3.
"From New York/Miss Bateman and Edwin Booth." *Springfield Republican* 28 Feb. 1866, 2:1–2.
"From New York/Washington Topics in the Metropolis." *Springfield Republican* 7 Mar. 1866, 2:1–2.
"From New York/The Experience of 'Straws, Jr.' at an Opera Matinee." *Springfield Republican* 17 Mar. 1866, 1:2–3.
"Miss Bateman in 'Leah.'" *Boston Advertiser* Supplement 24 Mar. 1866, 1:4–5.
"Last Days of Walter Savage Landor." *Atlantic Monthly* 17 (Apr. 1866): 385–95; 17 (May 1866): 540–51; 17 (June 1866): 684–705.
"From New York/Abstractions—Artistic and Otherwise." *Springfield Republican* 5 Apr. 1866, 1:4–5.
"From New York/Periodical Literature—Past and Present." *Springfield Republican* 12 May 1866, 1:1–2.

"From New York/The National Academy of Design." *Springfield Republican* 23 May 1866, 1:1–2.

"National Academy of Design." *Boston Advertiser* Supplement 26 May 1866, 2:1–2.

"From Rhode Island/A New Yorker in the Country before His Time." *Springfield Republican* 2 June 1866, 1:4–5.

"Roman Women of Fashion." *Galaxy* 15 June 1866, 332–38.

"From New York/More about the National Academy of Design." *Springfield Republican* 20 June 1866, 1:1–2.

"Letter from Newport." *Boston Advertiser* Supplement 18 Aug. 1866, 2:2–3.

"Letter from Newport." *Boston Advertiser* 27 Aug. 1866, 2:2–3.

"The Naval Academy and the Hurdle Races." *Boston Advertiser* 5 Sept. 1866, 2:2–3.

"Ristori." *New York Tribune* 20 Sept. 1866, 5:1.

"Ristori in Medea." *New York Tribune* 21 Sept. 1866, 4:6.

"Ristori's Second Appearance in Medea." *New York Tribune* 24 Sept. 1866, 4:6.

"Ristori in Maria Stuarda." *New York Tribune* 25 Sept. 1866, 4:6.

"Second Appearance of Ristori in Queen Elizabeth." *New York Tribune* 4 Oct. 1866, 4:6.

"Ristori's First Appearance in 'Phaedra.'" *New York Tribune* 15 Oct. 1866, 6:7.

"Ristori's First Appearance in Lady Macbeth." *New York Tribune* 20 Oct. 1866, 4:6.

"Ristori's Last Appearance in 'Elizabeth.'" *New York Tribune* 27 Oct. 1866, 8:2.

"Ristori's Plays." *Boston Transcript* 29 Oct. 1866, 2:3–4.

"Ristori's First Appearance in Boston—Medea." *Boston Transcript* 30 Oct. 1866, 2:2–3.

"Ristori in Mary Stuart." *Boston Transcript* 31 Oct. 1866, 2:2–3.

"Criticism and the Drama." *Beadle's Monthly* 2 (Nov. 1866): 441–44; rpt. in *Aldine Press* 3 (Feb. 1870): 20.

"Ristori in Giacommetti's Play of Elizabeth of England." *Boston Transcript* 2 Nov. 1866, 2:2–3.

"Ristori in Judith." *Boston Transcript* 3 Nov. 1866, 2:2.

"Phaedra—Rachel and Ristori." *Boston Transcript* 6 Nov. 1866, 2:2–3.

"Ristori in Lady Macbeth." *Boston Transcript* 7 Nov. 1866, 2:3–4.

"Adrienne Lecouvreur." *Boston Transcript* 9 Nov. 1866, 2:3.

"Pia de' Tdomei." *Boston Transcript* 10 Nov. 1866, 2:2.

"Ristori as Adrienne Lecouvreur." *New York Tribune* 15 Nov. 1866, 4:5–6.

"Ristori as Elizabeth." *New York Tribune* 20 Nov. 1866, 5:1–2.

"Ristori's Benefit." *New York Tribune* 24 Nov. 1866, 4:6.

Adelaide Ristori: A Biography. New York: J. A. Gray & Green, 1867.
"Ristori as Mary Stuart." *New York Tribune* 1 Jan. 1867, 2:2.
"From New York." *Chicago Tribune* 10 Feb. 1867, 2:7–8; rpt. 11 Feb. 1867, 2:6–7; 24 Feb. 1867, 2:4–5; 3 Mar. 1867, 2:4–5; 10 Mar. 1867, 2:4; 17 Mar. 1867, 2:4–5; 24 Mar. 1867, 2:4–5; 31 Mar. 1867, 2:4–5; 9 Apr. 1867, 2:7–8; 14 Apr. 1867, 2:8–9; 23 Apr. 1867, 2:4–5; 5 May 1867, 2:7; 12 May 1867, 2:6; 22 May 1867, 2:7; 26 May 1867, 2:5–6; rpt. 27 May 1867, 3:1–2; 2 June 1867, 2:5; rpt. 3 June 1867, 2:4; 14 June 1867, 2:6; 16 June 1867, 2:6–7; rpt. 17 June 1867, 2:6–7; 23 June 1867, 2:6–7; 30 June 1867, 2:6; 1 July 1867, 2:6; 7 July 1867, 2:4–5; 17 July 1867, 2:5–6.
"Adelaide Ristori." *Atlantic Monthly* 19 (Apr. 1867): 493–501.
"Ristori." *Harper's New Monthly* 34 (May 1867): 740–52.
"Newport Menagerie: A Photograph." *Beadle's Monthly* 3 (June 1867): 495–505.
"Summer Rambles Out of Town." *Chicago Tribune* 25 July 1867, 2:4–5.
"Up the Hudson." *Chicago Tribune* 28 July 1867, 2:6–7; rpt. 29 July 1867, 2:9–10.
"Racing Week at Saratoga." *Chicago Tribune* 21 Aug. 1867, 2:7–8.
"Saratoga." *Chicago Tribune* 1 Sept. 1867, 2:4–6.
"Lake George." *Chicago Tribune* 15 Sept. 1867, 2:8–9.
"Mount Desert." *Chicago Tribune* 28 Sept. 1867, 2:4.
"New York." *Chicago Tribune* 29 Sept. 1867, 2:4; 6 Oct. 1867, 2:4; 27 Oct. 1867, 2:8–9; 3 Nov. 1867, 2:7.
"From Our Windows." *Chicago Tribune* 17 Nov. 1867, 2:9; 24 Nov. 1867, 2:6–7.
"Charles Dickens/His First Reading in America." *New York Tribune* 3 Dec. 1867, 1:5–6.
"Dickens/His First Reading in New York." *New York Tribune* 10 Dec. 1867; rpt. *Chicago Tribune* 13 Dec. 1867, 2:8.
"Dickens/His Second Reading." *New York Tribune* 11 Dec. 1867, 4:6.
"Mr. Dickens's Third Reading." *New York Tribune* 13 Dec. 1867, 4:5–6.
"Charles Dickens's Fourth Reading." *New York Tribune* 14 Dec. 1867, 4:6.
"Dickens in New York." *Boston Transcript* 14 Dec. 1867, 4:4.
Mad on Purpose: A Comedy in Four Acts [play]. Translated from Italian by Field. New York: John A. Gray & Green, 1868.
Pen Photographs of Charles Dickens's Readings: Taken from Life. Boston: A. K. Loring, 1868.
Planchette's Diary. New York: J. S. Redfield, 1868.
"Love and War: A Story of 1865" [story]. *Public Spirit* 2 (Jan. 1868): 312–21; rpt. in *Springfield Republican* 13 Jan. 1868, 6:1–4.
"Authors, Newspapers, and Magazines in New York." *Press* [Philadelphia] 3 Jan. 1868, 4:5–6.
"Mr. Dickens as Dr. Marigold." *New York Tribune* 3 Jan. 1868, 4:6.

"Charles Dickens in New York." *Springfield Republican* 8 Jan. 1868, 2:5–6.
"Mr. Dickens in Philadelphia." *New York Tribune* 14 Jan. 1868, 1:5.
"Pike's New Opera House in New York—Adelaide Phillipps." *Press* [Philadelphia] 17 Jan. 1868, 2:4–5.
"Adelaide Phillips, the American Contralto." *New York Tribune* 27 Jan. 1868, 5:4–5.
"Obituary/Charles Kean." *New York Tribune* 27 Jan. 1868, 2:1.
"Theatricals in New York/Ristori in Norma—Oliver Twist at Wallack's." *Press* [Philadelphia] 27 Jan. 1868, 2:1–2.
"Ristori as Marie Antoinette." *Lippincott's* 1 (Feb. 1868): 175–85.
"The Wisdom of Masks." *Public Spirit* 2 (Feb. 1868): 393–96.
"A Conversation on the Stage." *Atlantic Monthly* 21 (Mar. 1868): 270–77.
"Charles Dickens." *New York Tribune* 9 Apr. 1868, 4:6.
"The Isle of Shoals." *Boston Transcript* 20 July 1868, 2:2–3.
"A Pre-Raphaelite at Saratoga." *Lippincott's* 2 (Sept. 1868): 256–61.
"The Isle of Shoals." *New York Tribune* 3 Sept. 1868, 2:1–2; 8 Sept. 1868, 2:1–2.
"The Perry Statue." *New York Tribune* 14 Oct. 1868, 2:1–2.
"A Moving Tale" [story]. *Harper's New Monthly* 37 (Nov. 1868): 814–21.
"From Boston/The Radical Club and Women." *Springfield Republican* 23 Nov. 1868, 2:1–2.
"The Boston Woman's Club." *Springfield Republican* 30 Nov. 1868, 2:2–4; rpt. *Boston Commonwealth* 19 Dec. 1868, 1:7–2:1.
"A New Old Firm." *Springfield Republican* 14 Dec. 1868, 2:1–5.
"The New England Woman's Club." *Woman's Advocate* 1 (Jan. 1869): 25–33.
"A Visit to a New-England Agricultural Fair." *Hearth and Home* 16 Jan. 1869, 61.
"Radicalism at 'The Hub.'" *Evening Mail* [New York] 22 Mar. 1869, 1:1–2.
"Our Boston Letter." *Evening Mail* [New York] 12 Apr. 1869, 1:1–2.
"Boston Gossip." *Evening Mail* [New York] 1 May 1869, 1:1–3.
"Hints to the Jockey Club." *New York Tribune* 12 June 1869, 4:4–5.
"The Peace Jubilee." *New York Tribune* 17 June 1869, 1:2–4.
"The Story of the Peace Jubilee." *New York Tribune* 18 June 1869, 1:3–4.
"End of the Peace Jubilee." *New York Tribune* 21 June 1869, 1:4–6.
"Odds and Ends of the Peace Jubilee." *New York Tribune* 23 June 1869, 2:1.
"The Great Peace Jubilee in Boston." *Hearth and Home* 3 July 1869, 444.
"Gentlemen of the Press." *Springfield Republican* 14 July 1869, 6:4.
"Among the Adirondacks." *New York Tribune* 12 Aug. 1869, 2:2–3.
"Saratoga Seen with the Naked Eye." *New York Tribune* 12 Aug. 1869, 1:6–2:1.
"New Publications/Walter Savage Landor." *New York Tribune* 17 Aug. 1869, 6:1–3.

"Notes from the Adirondacks." *New York Tribune* 3 Sept. 1869, 2:2–3.
"In and Out of the Woods." *Atlantic Almanac 1870*. Boston: Fields, Osgood, 1869. 48–52; excerpted in *Evening Bulletin* [San Francisco] 13 Nov. 1869, 3:4.
"Stray Sketches/Leaves from a Lecturer's Notebook." *New York Tribune* 2 Apr. 1870, 2:3–5.
"Mr. Fechter as Claude Melnotte." *Evening Mail* [New York] 28 Apr. 1870, 2:3.
"Charles Albert Fechter: A Biographical Sketch." *Atlantic Monthly* 26 (Sept. 1870): 285–307.
"Fechter in Boston." *New York Tribune* 13 Sept. 1870, 4:6–5:1.
"Thomas Hughes, M.P." *New York Tribune* 12 Oct. 1870, 4:6.
"Fechter as Hamlet." *Atlantic Monthly* 26 (Nov. 1870): 558–70.
"Town-Talk/Dramatizations." *Every Saturday* 24 Dec. 1870, 835.
Pen Photographs of Charles Dickens's Readings: Taken from Life. Rev. ed. Boston: James R. Osgood; London: Trübner, 1871.
"Literature/Criticisms of New Books." *New York Herald* 14 Feb. 1871, 4:3–4 [on *Woven of Many Threads*].
"The Drama/No Thoroughfare at the Boston Theatre." *New York Tribune* 30 Mar. 1871, 4:6–5:1.
"Literature/Criticisms of New Books." *New York Herald* 10 Apr. 1871, 7:3–4 [on Elizabeth Stuart Phelps's *A Silent Partner*].
"Literature/Criticisms of New Books." *New York Herald* 23 Apr. 1871, 7:5–6. [on *The History of the Boston Peace Jubilee*].
"Literature/Criticisms of New Books." *New York Herald* 1 May 1871, 8:1–3 [on E. P. Whipple's *Success and Its Conditions*].
"The Use of Theaters/Views of Robert Collyer." *New York Tribune* 2 May 1871, 2:3–4.
"Leaves from a Lecturer's Notebook." *Every Saturday* 20 May 1871, 466; 27 May 1871, 502; 3 June 1871, 526–27; 10 June 1871, 550; 24 June 1871, 598; 15 July 1871, 71.
"Tom Hughes on America." *Boston Advertiser* Supplement 29 June 1871, 1:8.
"English Republicanism." *New York Tribune* 19 July 1871, 1:1–2.
"Republicanism in England." *New York Tribune* 7 Dec. 1871, 1:4–5; 2:3–4.
"Justin McCarthy, on 'Chicago and the Prairie Fires.'" *Every Saturday* 16 Dec. 1871, 594–95.
"A Martyr to Free Speech." mid-Dec. 1871–Jan. 1872; rpt. in *Hap-Hazard*. Boston: Osgood, 1873. 101–4.
"The Divine Right of Kings." *New York Tribune* 27 Jan. 1872, 2:1–3.
"Co-operation in England." *New York Tribune* 12 Feb. 1872, 4:6.
"Opening of Parliament." *New York Tribune* 22 Feb. 1872, 1:6–2:1.
"Republicanism in England." *New York Tribune* 14 Mar. 1872, 2:3–4.

"The Thanksgiving Service." *New York Tribune* 15 Mar. 1872, 1:3–4.
"Second Thoughts about the Thanksgiving." Mar.–Apr. 1872; rpt. in *Hap-Hazard.* Boston: Osgood, 1873. 149–55.
"Republicanism in Parliament." *New York Tribune* 3 Apr. 1872, 2:1–2.
"Americans Abroad/Letters from an American Girl to her Cousin out West." *American Register* [Paris] 22 June 1872, 3:3–4; 29 June 1872, 3:3–4; 13 July 1872, 6:2–3; 20 July 1872, 3:3–4; 27 July 1872, 3:3–4; 3 Aug. 1872, 3:2–3; 14 Sept. 1872, 3:4–5; 28 Sept. 1872, 3:3–4; 5 Oct. 1872, 3:3–4; 12 Oct. 1872, 3:3–4.
"Opinions Abroad on American Politics." *New York Tribune* 30 Aug. 1872, 1:3–4.
"The Discoverer of Livingstone." *New York Tribune* 21 Sept. 1872, 4:6.
"Kate Field at Sea/Letters from an American Girl to a Friend in Europe." *American Register* [Paris] 19 Oct. 1872, 3:4–5; 9 Nov. 1872, 3:4–5; 23 Nov. 1872, 3:4–5; 14 Dec. 1872, 3:4–5.
"Shall Italian Opera Be a Fact or Remain a Fiction?" *New York Herald* 10 Nov. 1872, 7:2–3.
"Free Lance Has a Tilt with His Critics." *New York Herald* 24 Nov. 1872, 7:3–4.
"The Turf." *New York Tribune* 29 Nov. 1872, 3:3.
"The American Drama/A Shakespearian Panorama and a Tilt at a Parsee." *New York Herald* 2 Dec. 1872, 4:5–6.
"'As You Like It' and 'Mignon.'" *New York Herald* 8 Dec. 1872, 7:3.
"The Greeley Press Fund." *New York Herald* 8 Dec. 1872, 7:6.
"The Lady of Lyons." *New York Herald* 15 Dec. 1872, 6:2–3.
Hap-Hazard. Boston: James R. Osgood, 1873.
"To W[hitelaw] R[eid]" [poem]. *Springfield Republican* 2 Jan. 1873, 4:4.
"The Time of Hamlet." *New York Tribune* 8 Jan. 1873, 6:1.
"Free Lancing/Lectures and Lecturers/Colonel John Hay on 'The Heroic Age in Washington.'" *New York Herald* 19 Jan. 1873, 5:3.
"The Charity Ball." *New York Tribune* 5 Feb. 1873, 4:6–5:2.
"An Appeal from 'Free Lance'/Rare Albums for Sale in Behalf of a Noble Charity." *New York Herald* 9 Feb. 1873, 7:4.
"Free Lance Again/Concerning Private Theatricals." *New York Herald* 23 Feb. 1873, 6:5.
"A Masked Ball at Florence" [poem]. *New York Tribune* 27 Feb. 1873, 6:1.
"Free Lance." *New York Herald* 2 Mar. 1873, 7:4–5 [partly on David Garrick].
"Drawing-Room Philosophy." *New York Tribune* 6 Mar. 1873, 8:2–3.
"Free Lance/Critics Criticized—Italian and Ethiopian Opera." *New York Herald* 17 Mar. 1873, 5:3–4.
"Free Lance." *New York Herald* 25 Mar. 1873, 13:5–6 [on Victorien Sardou].

"Americans at Home/Letters from an American Girl to a Friend in Europe/Concerning the Presidential Inauguration." *American Register* [Paris] 29 Mar. 1873, 3:4–5.
"A Social Critique." *New York Tribune* 5 Apr. 1873, 2:4–5.
"An Amusement Critique." *New York Tribune* 29 Apr. 1873, 2:1–2.
"The Training School for Nurses." *New York Tribune* 30 Apr. 1873, 2:1.
"Daly's Grand Opera House/Fechter in Monte Cristo." *New York Herald* 4 May 1873, 5:3–4.
"Marie Taglioni." *New York Herald* 19 May 1873, 3:2–3.
"On the Ocean Wave." *New York Tribune* 28 June 1873, 3:1–3 [interview with Arthur Rubenstein].
"The Shah of Persia." *New York Tribune* 1 July 1873, 1:1–3.
"The Shah in England." *New York Tribune* 4 July 1873, 1:2–3.
"The Shah of Persia." *New York Tribune* 7 July 1873, 1:4–5.
"Receiving the Shah." *New York Tribune* 9 July 1873, 4:6–5:1.
"The Shah of Persia." *New York Tribune* 12 July 1873, 1:6.
"The Shah at Windsor." *New York Tribune* 14 July 1873, 1:1–3.
"Return to European Life." *American Register* [Paris] 26 July 1873, 5:3.
"London Gossip/Fourth of July and Shah Talk." *New York Tribune* 1 Aug. 1873, 2:1–3.
"Letters to Lina." *American Register* [Paris] 2 Aug. 1873, 5:3–4; 9 Aug. 1873, 5:3–4; 16 Aug. 1873, 5:3–4; 23 Aug. 1873, 3:1–3; 30 Aug. 1873, 3:1; 6 Sept. 1873, 9:1–2; 13 Sept. 1873, 3:1–3.
"Royal Betrothals." *New York Tribune* 6 Aug. 1873, 4:6–5:1.
"Charles Bradlaugh." *Cincinnati Commercial* 17 Nov. 1873, 1:6–2:2.
"Relief of the Sufferers/Appeals by Miss Kate Field and the Cuban League." *New York Tribune* 19 Nov. 1873, 5:3–4.
"Ten Days in Spain." *New York Tribune* 1 Jan. 1874, 2:1–3; 7 Jan. 1874, 3:1–4; 10 Jan. 1874, 3:1–3; 31 Jan. 1874, 3:1–3; 23 Feb. 1874, 3:1–3; 23 Mar. 1874, 3:1–3; 6 Apr. 1874, 3:1–2; 9 May 1874, 3:1–4; 8 June 1874, 3:3–5.
"The Training School for Nurses." *New York Tribune* 2 Jan. 1874, 8:4.
"Railway Traveling in England." *Springfield Republican* 7 Jan. 1874, 3:5.
"An Old English Country House." *Springfield Republican* 2 Feb. 1874, 8:1.
"Holly Tree Inns." *New York Tribune* 15 Apr. 1874, 2:3–4.
"Notes from the United States." *Athenaeum* 18 Apr. 1874, 527; 25 July 1874, 112–13; 12 Sept. 1874, 351–52; 28 Nov. 1874, 714–15; 9 Jan. 1875, 52–53.
"Discoveries of a German Physician." *New York Tribune* 8 July 1874, 6:2.
"'Our Mutual Friend' in Manuscript." *Scribner's* 8 (Aug. 1874): 472–75.
"Republican Notes on England." *Missouri Republican* [St. Louis Daily] 30 Aug. 1874, 6:3–5; 6 Sept. 1874, 6:3–4; 13 Sept. 1874, 2:6–7; 20 Sept. 1874, 8:3–4; 27 Sept. 1874, 4:1–2; 4 Oct. 1874, 11:4–5; 18 Oct. 1874, 12:1–3; 25 Oct. 1874, 12:1–3; 1 Nov. 1874, 2:1–2.

Ten Days in Spain. Boston: James R. Osgood, 1875.
"The Drama/Madame Ristori's Rentree in America." *New York Tribune* 3 Mar. 1875, 6:6.
"Church and Theatre." *New York Tribune* 29 Mar. 1875, 3:1–3.
"George Eliot." *Echo* 10 Apr. 1875, 1.
"Walter Savage Landor." *Echo* 13 Apr. 1875, 1.
"Landor's Preferences among Italian Poets." *Echo* 14 Apr. 1875, 2.
"Echoes of the Fair." *Echo* 16 Apr. 1875, 4.
"Dramatic Criticism." *Echo* 17 Apr. 1875, 1.
"The Hippopotamus at Bangtown." *Echo* 18 Apr. 1875, 1.
"He. She." *Echo* 20 Apr. 1875, 4.
"The Land of Dinners." *Echo* 21 Apr. 1875, 2.
"What Kate Field Thinks of the Festival." *Cincinnati Commercial* 12 May 1875, 1:5, 4:3.
"Kate Field's Opinion of Oratorios." *Cincinnati Commercial* 13 May 1875, 1:4–5.
"Kate Field's Talk about Bach and Beethoven." *Cincinnati Commercial* 14 May 1875, 1:4–5.
"Kate Field's Farewell Chat about the Festival." *Cincinnati Commercial* 15 May 1875, 2:3–4.
"A Short Journey West." *New York Tribune* 19 June 1875, 4:1–2.
"Kate Field in London." *Louisville Courier-Journal* 9 Aug. 1875, 3:2–4; 17 Aug. 1875, 3:2–3; 27 Aug. 1875, 3:2–3; 25 Sept. 1875, 3:2–3; 2 Oct. 1875, 2:4–5; 12 Oct. 1875, 3:2–3; 16 Oct. 1875, 2:5–6; 2 Nov. 1875, 2:5–6; 6 Nov. 1875, 2:4–5; 15 Nov. 1875, 3:3–4; 20 Nov. 1875, 3:2–3; 29 Nov. 1875, 1:6–7; 9 Dec. 1875, 3:2–3; 13 Dec. 1875, 3:3–4; 20 Dec. 1875, 2:6–7; 29 Dec. 1875, 2:5–6; 24 Jan. 1876, 1:4–5; 7 Feb. 1876, 2:4–5; 21 Feb. 1876, 3:2–3; 24 Feb. 1876, 3:2–3; 8 Mar. 1876, 3:3–4; 22 Mar. 1876, 3:2–3; 3 Apr. 1876, 3:1–3; 18 Apr. 1876, 3:2–4; 28 Apr. 1876, 3:3–4; 30 May 1876, 2:4–5; 23 June 1876, 3:3–4; 27 June 1876, 3:4.
"English Opera in London/Revival of the National Lyric Drama." *New York Herald* 25 Nov. 1875, 4:1–2.
"The London Stage." *New York Tribune* 10 Jan. 1876, 5:4–5.
"The Drama Abroad/Alexandre Dumas' New Play, 'L'Etrangere,' in Paris/Mr. [Henry] Irving's Appearance in London as Othello." *New York Herald* 5 Mar. 1876, 6:1–3.
"A Letter from Kate Field." *Daily Graphic* [New York] 8 Apr. 1876, 321.
"American Artists in London." *New York Herald* 10 Apr. 1876, 5:1–2 [partly on James McNeill Whistler].
"London Literary Gossip/Walt Whitman's Merits Discussed." *New York Herald* 17 Apr. 1876, 3:5–6.
"Kate Field among the Lords." *Daily Graphic* [New York] 21 Apr. 1876, 416.

"The London Academy." *New York Herald* 22 May 1876, 5:1–2.
"London Gossip." *New York Herald* 12 June 1876, 5:6 [partly on Christine Nilsson].
"Life in London." *New York Herald* 19 June 1876, 6:1–3 [partly on the American Centennial Exhibition].
"The Drama in London." *New York Herald* 22 June 1876, 7:4–5 [on Dumas's "L'Etrangere" and Sarah Bernhardt].
"The Drama and Fashion/Hermann Vezin and Genevieve Ward in 'Œdipus.'" *New York Herald* 3 July 1876, 8:1–2.
"London Gossip/Fourth of July Banquet at Westminster Palace Hotel/Mr. [Edwards] Pierrepont's Speech." *New York Herald* 17 July 1876, 5:4.
"London Gossip/Interesting Chat with Dion Boucicault." *New York Herald* 11 Aug. 1876, 6:5–6.
"Miss Emma Abbott." *Commercial* [Cincinnati] 23 Aug. 1876, 8:2.
"London's Dramatic Season/Two New Pieces at the Gaiety by Henry J. Byron." *New York Herald* 25 Sept. 1876, 10:1–2.
"Kate Field in Edinburgh." *Daily Graphic* [New York] 29 Sept. 1876, 616.
"Tenement-Life in Edinburgh." *Daily Graphic* [New York] 2 Oct. 1876, 635.
"Temple Bar." *New York Herald* 14 Oct. 1876, 5:3–4 [partly on Adelina Patti].
"English Opera Abroad/The Revival Instituted in London by Carl Rosa." *Daily Graphic* [New York] 23 Oct. 1876, 776.
"Wagner in English/Carl Rosa's Latest Triumph." *New York Herald* 23 Oct. 1876, 3:4–5.
"The London Stage/Lunch at Guildhall to the Actors and Actresses." *New York Herald* 6 Nov. 1876, 6:5–6.
"The London Stage." *New York Tribune* 20 Nov. 1876, 3:6.
"Kate Field and the Country Parson." *Daily Graphic* [New York] 5 Dec. 1876, 229.
"General [Luigi Palma di] Cesnola/His Discovery of Cypriote Antiquities." *New York Herald* 13 Dec. 1876, 5:4–5.
"Christmas and English Pantomime." *Daily Graphic* [New York] 25 Dec. 1876, 4.
"Four Parties and Their Leaders." *Independent* 28 Dec. 1876, 4–5.
Extremes Meet [play]. London: French, 1877; rpt. *New York Drama* 4.39 (1878): 91–96; rpt. as "Plato and Cupid: A Christmas Comedietta." *Kate Field's Washington* 1 Jan. 1890, 7–10.
"Drama." *Examiner* 13 Jan. 1877, 54–55.
"A Morning with Sir Julius Benedict." *Scribner's* 13 (Feb. 1877): 480–84.
"The Opening of Parliament." *Truth* 15 Feb. 1877, 214–16.
"Pantomimes." *Truth* 1 Mar. 1877, 277–78.

"Stage Stars in England." *Daily Graphic* [New York] 21 Mar. 1877, 138.
"The Battle of the Blues." *Truth* 29 Mar. 1877, 405–8.
"Kate Field on Art." *Daily Graphic* [New York] 16 Apr. 1877, 320.
"Current Topics in London." *Daily Graphic* [New York] 3 May 1877, 440; excerpted in "Miss Kate Field on Herself." *New York Tribune* 5 May 1877, 7:3.
"Private Views of People and Pictures." *Truth* 10 May 1877, 595–97; rpt. *World* [New York] 28 May 1877, 8:3.
"Our Twang." *Truth* 31 May 1877, 696–97.
"Forty to Twenty: A Drawing Room Drama" [poem]. *Appleton's* ns 2 (June 1877): 563–64; rpt. *Daily Graphic* [New York] 24 May 1877, 585; rpt. *Boston Traveller* 21 May 1885, 1:6.
"The Derby." *Truth* 7 June 1877, 725–27.
"General Grant." *New York Herald* 7 June 1877, 3:2–4.
"The Pierrepont and Badeau Receptions to General Grant." *Truth* 14 June 1877, 755–56.
"The Human Race at Ascot." *Truth* 21 June 1877, 788–90.
"Henry Schliemann." *New York Tribune* 30 June 1877, 7:1–5; rpt. *Belgravia* 33 (July 1877): 76–91.
"Feeding at Guildhall." *Truth* 5 July 1877, 19–20.
"The Glorious Fourth, and So Forth." *Truth* 12 July 1877, 52–53.
"Drama." *Examiner* 14 July 1877, 888.
"A Harrow-ing Game." *Truth* 19 July 1877, 84–86.
"Wimbledon Un-Common." *Truth* 26 July 1877, 117–19.
"London Lungs, Dress and Morals." *Truth* 2 Aug. 1877, 148–49.
"The American." *Examiner* 11 Aug. 1877, 1013–14.
"Intercepted Telegram." *Truth* 16 Aug. 1877, 220–21.
"A New Invention—The Age of Appreciation." *Truth* 23 Aug. 1877, 241–42.
"Barnum, Pongo, and Catastrophic Evolution." *Truth* 30 Aug. 1877, 271–72.
"Through the Looking Glass." *Whitehall Review* 1 Sept. 1877, 306; 22 Sept. 1877, 367; 3 Nov. 1877, 495–96; 10 Nov. 1877, 520; 17 Nov. 1877, 543; 8 Dec. 1877, 91.
"Crossing the Channel." *Truth* 27 Sept. 1877, 386–87.
"On the French Coast/Trouville a Paris by the Sea." *New York Herald* 28 Sept. 1877, 4:1–2.
"A French Seaport/Havre as a Watering Place." *New York Herald* 14 Oct. 1877, 9:4–5.
"A Leader of Fashion." *Truth* 1 Nov. 1877, 531–32.
"Drama." *Examiner* 3 Nov. 1877, 1400.
"The Telephone/Remarkable Experiments Near Liverpool." *Liverpool Daily Post* 6 Nov. 1877, 7:2–3.

"The Telephone." *Times* [London] 16 Nov. 1877, 3:6–4:1.
"Drama." *Examiner* 17 Nov. 1877, 1465.
"A Great Invention." *Times* [London] 19 Nov. 1877, 9:3–4. Rpt. in *The History of Bell's Telephone*. London: Bradbury, Agnew, 1878. 31–35.
"A Government Contract." *Times* [London]. Rpt. in *The History of Bell's Telephone*. London: Bradbury, Agnew, 1878. 35–36.
"The Telephone." *Times* [London] 29 Nov. 1877, 6:6.
"Mr. George Wilkes on Shakespeare." *Examiner* 1 Dec. 1877, 1521–22.
"The Telephone." *Manchester Guardian* 3 Dec. 1877, 8:4. Rpt. in *The History of Bell's Telephone*. London: Bradbury, Agnew, 1878. 56–57.
"The Parisian Whiteley." *Truth* 6 Dec. 1877, 684–86.
Interview with Miss Van Elsner. Excerpted in *New York Tribune* 10 Dec. 1877, 4:6. [Original source unlocated.]
"Americans in Europe." *Truth* 13 Dec. 1877, 715–17.
Interview with Frederick Worth. Excerpted in *Harper's Bazaar* 15 Dec. 1877, 787. [Original source unlocated.]
"London Gossip/Movements of Americans in London." *New York Herald* 16 Dec. 1877, 5:4–6.
"A Train of Thoughts." *Truth* 20 Dec. 1877, 747–48.
"The Telephone." *Examiner* 22 Dec. 1877, 1611–12.
"Very Private Theatricals" [play]. *Daily Graphic* [New York] 25 Dec. 1877, 5; rpt. *Argonaut* [San Francisco] 5 Jan. 1878, 3.
"Telephones in Barracks." *Pall Mall Gazette* 28 Dec. 1877. Rpt. in *The History of Bell's Telephone*. London: Bradbury, Agnew, 1878. 58.
"Literature/Thoreau." *Examiner* 29 Dec. 1877, 1646–48.
"The Telephone at the Crystal Palace." *Daily News* [London] 29 Dec. 1877. Rpt. in *The History of Bell's Telephone*. London: Bradbury, Agnew, 1878. 60.
"London Talk/Christmas and Its Cheer." *New York Herald* 31 Dec. 1877, 3:1–2.
"Interesting Experiments in Ireland." *Saunders's New Letter* [Dublin] 1 Jan. 1878. Rpt. in *The History of Bell's Telephone*. London: Bradbury, Agnew, 1878. 61–62.
"Whispering by Telephone." *East Anglican Daily Times* 2 Jan. 1878. Rpt. in *The History of Bell's Telephone*. London: Bradbury, Agnew, 1878. 62–63.
"A Concatenation According." *Truth* 3 Jan. 1878, 25–27.
"Concerning War, Cabmen, and Other Inflictions." *Truth* 10 Jan. 1878, 54–56.
"The Telephone at Court." *Times* [London] 16 Jan. 1878, 9:5. Rpt. in *The History of Bell's Telephone*. London: Bradbury, Agnew, 1878. 63–64.
"The Telephone at Osborne." *London Telegraph* 16 Jan. 1878, 3:7.
"London Streets and London Numbers." *Truth* 17 Jan. 1878, 89–91.

"A Scientific Wonder." *The Field* 19 Jan. 1878. Rpt. in *The History of Bell's Telephone.* London: Bradbury, Agnew, 1878. 65–67.

"The Telephone at the House of Commons." *Daily News* [London] 23 Jan. 1878, 5:3.

"The American Telephone." *New York Herald* 4 Feb. 1878, 2:4.

"Political Enthusiasts." *Truth* 7 Feb. 1878, 185–86.

"Cleopatra's Needle." *Truth* 21 Feb. 1878, 247–49.

"Stanley, the Explorer." *Daily Graphic* [New York] 21 Feb. 1878, 750; rpt. 22 Feb. 1878, 758.

"A Few Personal Remarks by Kate Field." *Daily Graphic* [New York] 22 Feb. 1878, 754.

"The 'Dear-Pen' in the House of Commons." *Truth* 28 Feb. 1878, 281–83; 14 Mar. 1878, 344–45; 21 Mar. 1878, 377–78.

"The Light Fantastic Toe." *Truth* 7 Mar. 1878, 313–14.

"London Gossip/A New Othello/Henry Irving as Louis XI." *New York Herald* 25 Mar. 1878, 4:1–3.

"After the Antique." *Truth* 28 Mar. 1878, 408–9.

"London Talk/England and the Paris Exhibition." *New York Herald* 1 Apr. 1878, 10:1–2.

"London Tattle/Picture Week in the West End Studios." *New York Herald* 8 Apr. 1878, 4:1–2.

"London Gossip." *Truth* 18 Apr. 1878, 502–3.

"Personal Points from London." *Daily Graphic* [New York] 18 Apr. 1878, 334.

"London Idols and Idylls/The Vicar of Wakefield on the Stage." *New York Herald* 22 Apr. 1878, 8:4–5.

"England in War Paint/The Peace Party Rebuked During the Easter Recess." *New York Herald* 29 Apr. 1878, 3:1–2.

"A Propos of the Divine William." *Truth* 2 May 1878, 569–70.

"The London Theatres/Easter Pieces and New Productions." *New York Herald* 13 May 1878, 4:1.

"Church and Theatre." *New York Tribune* 18 May 1878, 2:7.

"London Gossip/Public Reception of [Patrick Sarsfield] Gilmore at the Crystal Palace." *New York Herald* 3 June 1878, 4:3–4.

"A Side Show on Derby Day." *Truth* 13 June 1878, 760–61.

"A Woman's Hotel with a Vengeance." *Truth* 20 June 1878, 792–93.

"Cricket, and Other Little Games." *Truth* 27 June 1878, 823–24.

"The [Paris] Exhibition." *New York Tribune* 28 June 1878, 5:2.

"Sunday in Hyde Park." *Truth* 11 July 1878, 56–57.

"The Terrors of the Paris Exposition." *Truth* 18 July 1878, 85–86.

"The Last Panacea." *Theatre* ns 1 (Aug. 1878): 33–35.

"Mr. [William] Winter's New Poems." *Theatre* ns 1 (Aug. 1878): 91–92.

"Going to the Exposition with a Profile Perdu; or, Sitting for an Official Photograph." *Truth* 8 Aug. 1878, 169–70.

"The American Eagle at the Paris Exposition." *Truth* 15 Aug. 1878, 197–98.
"An Alpine Paradise." *Truth* 22 Aug. 1878, 226–28.
"Kate Field in Switzerland." *Daily Graphic* [New York] 31 Aug. 1878, 422.
"At St. Moritz." *Truth* 5 Sept. 1878, 279–81.
"Life in the Engadine." *Truth* 19 Sept. 1878, 338–40.
"A Tempest in a Teapot." *Truth* 3 Oct. 1878, 395–96.
"Tramping Over a Glacier with Louis Quinze Heels." *Truth* 10 Oct. 1878, 425–26.
"Sensational Scenery." *Truth* 17 Oct. 1878, 454–56.
"Mme. Macmahon's Great Fete." *Daily Graphic* [New York] 18 Nov. 1878, 115.
"Hotels, Cooks, Life and Lottery." *Truth* 21 Nov. 1878, 597–98.
"Forgery and Gossip." *Truth* 28 Nov. 1878, 633–34.
"A Tonsorial Tournament." *Truth* 2 Jan. 1879, 22–23.
"Making a Bonnet." *Truth* 9 Jan. 1879, 50–51.
"No. 527,127." *Truth* 23 Jan. 1879, 107–8.
"A Lottery of Great Expectations." *Truth* 6 Feb. 1879, 172–74.
"The Misery of Channel Tubs." *Truth* 13 Feb. 1879, 204–5.
"Lodging at the Screws." *Truth* 20 Feb. 1879, 237–39.
"The Shakespeare Memorial." *Daily Graphic* [New York] 20 Feb. 1879, 751.
"Mrs. Grundy's Manners and Morals." *Truth* 27 Feb. 1879, 268–69.
"House-Hunting." *Truth* 13 Mar. 1879, 332–33.
"Education in America." *New York Tribune* 15 Mar. 1879, 3:3–6.
"Our Cook." *Truth* 20 Mar. 1879, 365–66.
"Taking an Inventory." *Truth* 27 Mar. 1879, 395–97.
"Mrs. Jones on the Rampage." *Truth* 3 Apr. 1879, 428–29.
"What We Eat." *Truth* 10 Apr. 1879, 461–62.
"Cash and Credit." *Truth* 1 May 1879, 552–54.
"The Shakespeare Memorial." *Boston Advertiser* 12 May 1879, 2:3–4.
"A Registry Office." *Truth* 19 June 1879, 773–74.
"London Miseries and Joys." *Daily Graphic* [New York] 26 June 1879, 822.
"The Universal Provider." *Truth* 26 June 1879, 805–7.
"W. S. Gilbert." *Scribner's* 18 (Sept. 1879): 751–55.
"The Shakespeare Memorial." *New York Tribune* 20 Sept. 1879, 3:4.
"Arthur Sullivan." *Scribner's* 18 (Oct. 1879): 904–10.
"Life at a Water-Cure." *Truth* 23 Oct. 1879, 518–19.
"Grant in London." *Press* [Philadelphia] 23 Dec. 1879, 9:1–2.
"Co-operation in Dress." *New York Tribune* 1 Mar. 1880, 5:6.
"The Ladies' Cooperative Dress Association." *Boston Transcript* 10 Mar. 1880, 4:4.

"The Ladies' Dress Association." *New York Times* 12 Mar. 1880, 3:3.
"The Ladies' Dress Association." *New York Tribune* 30 May 1880, 5:6.
"Pictures of Travel/The Deer-Pen." *Christian Union* 7 July 1880, 5; rpt. in "Kate Field Visits Parliament." *Springfield Republican* 16 July 1880, 2:6.
"A Talk with [Charles] Bradlaugh." *New York Tribune* 25 July 1880, 2:3–4.
"London Stage Gossip." *Daily Graphic* [New York] 19 Aug. 1880, 361.
"An English War Correspondent." *Scribner's* 21 (Dec. 1880): 297–303.
"George Eliot Dead/Recollections by Kate Field." *New York Tribune* 24 Dec. 1880, 5:2–3.
"George Eliot." *New York Tribune* 28 Dec. 1880, 2:4.
"Cooperative Dress Reform." *New York Tribune* 12 Jan. 1881, 5:3.
"A Realistic View of the Passion Play at Ober-Ammergau." *Providence Journal* 19 Jan. 1881, 1:1–4.
"George Eliot and George Lewes." *New York Tribune* 14 Feb. 1881, 5:4–5.
"Forget-Me-Not." *Critic* 12 Mar. 1881, 67–68.
"The Cooperative Dress Association." *New York Tribune* 23 May 1881, 5:2.
"Two Quarrelsome Cousins" [play]. *Spirit of the Times* 24 Dec. 1881, 554–55.
Charles Albert Fechter. Boston: James R. Osgood, 1882.
"Art of Adornment/Shop Manners—A Realistic Study." *Our Continent* 15 Feb. 1882, 15.
"Art of Adornment/Gloves." *Our Continent* 22 Feb. 1882, 31.
"Art of Adornment/Knee-Breeches—Why Not?" *Our Continent* 1 Mar. 1882, 47; 8 Mar. 1882, 63.
"Art of Adornment/The Divinity of Beauty." *Our Continent* 15 Mar. 1882, 79.
"Art of Adornment/Do Women Dress Well?" *Our Continent* 22 Mar. 1882, 95.
"Art of Adornment/American Taste in Dress." *Our Continent* 29 Mar. 1882, 107.
"Art of Adornment/American Dress Goods." *Our Continent* 5 Apr. 1882, 127.
"Art of Adornment/Lady Habberton's 'National Gown.'" *Our Continent* 12 Apr. 1882, 142.
"Art of Adornment/Answers to Correspondents—That Three Dollar Bill." *Our Continent* 19 Apr. 1882, 158.
"Art of Adornment/New Goods—How to Make Them Up." *Our Continent* 19 Apr. 1882, 174.
"The Age of Appreciation." *Denver Tribune* 29 July 1883, 4:2–3.
"My Diary in the Engadine." *Manhattan* 2 (Aug. 1883): 144–50; 2 (Sept. 1883): 228–35.
"A Woman's Wrongs." *Boston Herald* 20 Jan. 1884, 16:1–3.

"Kate Field in Utah." *Boston Herald* 27 Jan. 1884, 13:1–2; 24 Feb. 1884, 14:1–2; 6 Apr. 1884, 20:3–4; 20 Apr. 1884, 14:1–6; 14 May 1884, 2:5–6.

"Music in Mormondom." *Boston Herald* 13 Apr. 1884, 13:1–2.

"Kate Field in Utah." *Boston Herald* Supplement 2 June 1884, 1:4–5.

"How to Treat Mormons." *Daily Graphic* [New York] 3 June 1884, 691.

"A Mormon Martyr." *Boston Herald* 8 June 1884, 12:7–8.

"A Polygamic Craze." *Boston Herald* 15 June 1884, 14:4–5.

"The Situation in Utah." *Daily Graphic* [New York] 21 June 1884, 844.

"The Graphic and the Mormons." *Daily Graphic* [New York] 8 July 1884, 47.

"More About the Mormons." *Daily Graphic* [New York] 19 July 1884, 134.

"My Diary in London." *Manhattan* 4 (Aug. 1884): 186–94; 4 (Sept. 1884): 333–40.

"Utah Politics and Morals." *New York Tribune* 7 Sept. 1884, 4:1.

"Kate Field—The Mormon Question." *Boston Traveller* 2 Oct. 1884, 5:5.

"Facsimile of a Letter from Kate Field." *Daily Graphic* [New York] 16 May 1885, 611 [on cremation].

"The Question of Cremation." *Daily Graphic* [New York] 24 May 1885, 6.

"Cleveland and the Mormons." *Daily Graphic* [New York] 7 June 1885, 7.

"Earnest Workers." *Daily Graphic* [New York] 14 June 1885, 7.

"How Shall Women Dress?" *Daily Graphic* [New York] 12 July 1885, 7; rpt. in "How Shall Women Dress? A Word to Sister Sinners." *Kate Field's Washington* 19 Aug. 1891, 117–19.

"Charles Fechter." *Actors and Actresses of Great Britain and the United States.* Ed. Brander Matthews and Laurence Hutton. New York: Cassel, 1886. 4: 207–28.

"Kate Field/Miss Field's Interview with President Cleveland." *Boston Traveller* 26 Feb. 1886, 2:4.

"The Presidency of the Mormon Church." *Harper's Weekly* 10 Apr. 1886, 235.

"Kate and the Mormons." *Chicago Tribune* 6 June 1886, 15:4–5.

"Mormon Blood Atonement." *North American Review* 143 (Sept. 1886): 262–67.

"Our Summer's Outing" [story]. *Harper's New Monthly* 75 (Oct. 1887): 651–66.

"North of the Golden Gate." *Picturesque California: Rocky Mountains and the Pacific Slope.* Ed. John Muir. New York and San Francisco: Dewing, 1888. 5: 219–33.

"Polygamy Unveiled." *Woman* 1 (Mar. 1888): 296–305.

"A Trip to Southeastern Alaska." *Harper's Weekly* 8 Sept. 1888, 681–84.

"San Rafael and the Golden Gate." *Harper's Weekly* 26 Jan. 1889, 70.

"Our Ignorance of Alaska." *North American Review* 149 (July 1889): 78–90.

"Kate Field on Prohibition." *New York Tribune* 26 July 1889, 7:4.

"Women as Politicians." *St. Louis Post-Dispatch* 3 Nov. 1889, 26:3–4.
"Kate Field's Beliefs." *New York Times* 1 Dec. 1889, 4:6.
"Kate Field to Graduates." *World* [New York] 28 June 1891, 25:1–2; rpt. *New York Tribune* 8 July 1891, 6:2; rpt. *New Orleans Picayune* 12 July 1891, 12:7.
"The Girl Who Thinks She Can Write." *Youth's Companion* 8 Sept. 1892, 447.
"All Depends on Our Women." American Press Association syndication, spring 1893. Rpt. in *Today Then: America's Best Minds Look 100 Years into the Future on the Occasion of the 1893 World's Columbian Exposition.* Helena: American & World Geographic, 1992. 108–9.
"A Talk" [31 May 1893]. *The Congress of Women.* Ed. Mary K. O. Eagle. Chicago: American Publishing, 1894. 77–79.
"Kate Field's Views." *Chicago Herald* 31 May 1893, 1:7.
"Hinges on the Rates." *Chicago Herald* 2 June 1893, 1:5.
"California as I Saw It." *San Francisco Examiner* spec. issue, 4 June 1893, 29.
"On to the Great Fair." *Chicago Herald* 4 June 1893, 1:5.
"What is the Matter?" *Chicago Herald* 6 June 1893, 9:3.
"Needs of the Fair." *Chicago Herald* 8 June 1893, 11:3.
"One Fare Round Trip." *Chicago Herald* 10 June 1893, 13:7.
"Congress of Cranks." *Chicago Herald* 11 June 1893, 10:5.
"Kate Field's Charge." *Chicago Herald* 13 June 1893, 13:7.
"Head Badly Needed." *Chicago Herald* 15 June 1893, 13:4.
"Irritate the Public." *Chicago Herald* 19 June 1893, 12:1.
"Is Glad He Was Born." *Chicago Herald* 20 June 1893, 9:7.
"More Seats Needed." *Chicago Herald* 22 June 1893, 9:3–4.
The Drama of Glass. Toledo: Libby Glass Co., 1894.
"Kate Field's Letter." *Chicago Times-Herald* 12 May 1895, 17:7; 18 May 1895, 8:7; 19 May 1895, 28:6; 22 May 1895, 6:6; 24 May 1895, 8:7; 28 May 1895, 6:6; 31 May 1895, 8:6; 3 June 1895, 6:6; 6 June 1895, 8:6; 9 June 1895, 28:6; 12 June 1895, 6:7; 14 June 1895, 6:7; 16 June 1895, 28:7; 19 June 1895, 6:7; 22 June 1895, 6:1–3; 24 June 1895, 6:6; 27 June 1895, 6:7; 30 June 1895, 22:6; 4 July 1895, 6:6; 7 July 1895, 20:7; 12 July 1895, 6:6; 17 July 1895, 6:7; 20 July 1895, 12:5–6; 22 July 1895, 6:5; 27 July 1895, 6:6; 28 July 1895, 20:5; 30 July 1895, 6:5; 1 Aug. 1895, 6:6; 3 Aug. 1895, 8:5; 5 Aug. 1895, 6:6; 7 Aug. 1895, 6:7; 9 Aug. 1895, 6:5; 11 Aug. 1895, 28:5; 13 Aug. 1895, 6:5; 15 Aug. 1895, 6:7; 17 Aug. 1895, 8:7; 19 Aug. 1895, 6:7; 21 Aug. 1895, 6:5; 31 Aug. 1895, 8:6; 6 Sept. 1895, 6:5; 9 Sept. 1895, 6:5; 12 Sept. 1895, 6:6; 14 Sept. 1895, 8:6; 18 Sept. 1895, 6:7; 19 Sept. 1895, 8:5; 21 Sept. 1895, 8:6; 22 Sept. 1895, 30:6; 24 Sept. 1895, 6:7; 25 Sept. 1895, 6:7; 27 Sept. 1895, 6:6; 1 Oct. 1895, 8:7; 3 Oct. 1895, 6:7; 5 Oct. 1895, 8:7; 7 Oct. 1895, 8:7; 9 Oct. 1895, 6:6; 10 Oct. 1895, 10:3–4; 13 Oct. 1895, 8:1–2; 14

Oct. 1895, 6:6; 18 Oct. 1895, 11:3; 19 Oct. 1895, 10:1–2; 23 Oct. 1895, 10:1–2; 26 Oct. 1895, 6:3–4; 27 Oct. 1895, 11:1; 28 Oct. 1895, 12:1–2; 30 Oct. 1895, 8:3–4; 2 Nov. 1895, 12:3–4; 3 Nov. 1895, 30:1–2; 5 Nov. 1895, 10:1; 9 Nov. 1895, 14:1–2; 10 Nov. 1895, 16:1–2; 16 Nov. 1895, 14:1–2; 17 Nov. 1895, 18:4–5; 18 Nov. 1895, 12:1–2; 23 Nov. 1895, 12:5–6.

"Kate Field's Appeal." *Harper's Ferry Sentinel* 24 Aug. 1895.

"Kate Field in Hawaii." *Chicago Times-Herald* 15 Dec. 1895, 36:7; 18 Dec. 1895, 6:6; 19 Dec. 1895, 6:6; 20 Dec. 1895, 6:7; 22 Dec. 1895, 26:6–7; 26 Dec. 1895, 9:3–4; 31 Dec. 1895, 6:6; 3 Jan. 1896, 6:6; 5 Jan. 1896, 14:7; 11 Jan. 1896, 14:1–2; 16 Jan. 1896, 6:6; 19 Jan. 1896, 24:1; 20 Jan. 1896, 9:7; 26 Jan. 1896, 35:4–5; 1 Feb. 1896, 14:1–2; 8 Feb. 1896, 10:5–6; 9 Feb. 1896, 24:1–3; 15 Feb. 1896, 6:3–4; 21 Feb. 1896, 6:7; 22 Feb. 1896, 10:1–2; 25 Feb. 1896, 6:6; 1 Mar. 1896, 15:1–3, 19:4; 2 Mar. 1896, 9:1–2; 9 Mar. 1896, 9:7; 14 Mar. 1896, 10:4–5; 15 Mar. 1896, 14:3–4; 16 Mar. 1896, 9:4–5; 21 Mar. 1896, 10:1–2; 22 Mar. 1896, 14:5–6; 30 Mar. 1896, 7:3–4; 6 Apr. 1896, 7:3–4; 11 Apr. 1896, 9:5–6; 12 Apr. 1896, 40:1–2.

NOTES

1. See also my "'He is Amusing but Not Inherently a Gentleman': The Vexed Relations of Kate Field and Samuel Clemens."

2. Field used a number of pseudonyms during her career, including St. Bernarde; Sempre Avanti; Fie; Straws, Jr.; Free Lance; and Puss.

3. For newspaper listings providing two numbers, the numbers indicate page and column numbers, respectively (e.g., 3:5–6 stands for p. 3, cols. 5–6). Otherwise, the number given is the page number.

WORKS CITED

Cobbe, Frances Power. *Italics: Brief Notes on Politics, People, and Places in Italy.* London: Trübner, 1864.

Field, Kate. *Kate Field: Selected Letters.* Ed. Carolyn J. Moss. Carbondale: Southern Illinois UP, 1996.

"Field, Mary Katherine Keemle." *Dictionary of American Biography.* New York: Scribner's, 1935. 6: 368.

James, Henry. *The Portrait of a Lady.* Boston: Houghton, 1881.

"Kate Field Dead." *New York Tribune* 31 May 1896, 7:5.

"Kate Field's Career." *Chicago Times-Herald* 1 June 1896, 6:2.

Scharnhorst, Gary. "'He is Amusing but Not Inherently a Gentleman': The Vexed Relations of Kate Field and Samuel Clemens." *Legacy* 18 (2002): 193–204.

———. "James and Kate Field." *Henry James Review* 22 (2001): 200–206.

Twain, Mark. *Mark Twain's Autobiography.* Ed. Albert Bigelow Paine. 3 vols. New York: Harper, 1924.

Willa Cather's Process of Composing

CHARLES W. MIGNON
University of Nebraska–Lincoln

In preparing volumes for the Cather Scholarly Edition, the editors necessarily gather up all materials appropriate to the task. Occasionally, new materials turn up. Such is the case with nine documents relating to *Sapphira and the Slave Girl* (1940), which are segments of Cather's story from book 4 ("Sapphira's Daughter") and book 8 ("The Dark Autumn"). They originate from more complete drafts that are lost, and they include part of a holograph draft and parts of eight typescripts. A tenth document from the Berg Collection is a complete set of corrected galleys for *Sapphira and the Slave Girl*. These ten documents together represent *all* the steps in Cather's own description of her composing process, and they also show some steps within steps that she did not mention.[1] Analyses of these documents with the Berg galleys, along with existing discoveries relating to other novels, will contribute to a more complete picture of Cather's overall process.

This essay will (1) review Cather's own accounts of her practices; (2) provide a contextual framework for discussing the *Sapphira* documents; (3) describe in more detail three points of conclusion drawn from an analysis of these documents (concerning overlapping texts, vertical revision, and the copyediting collaboration of Cather and Edith Lewis); and (4) add evidence from other novels that suggests additional refinements and presents a more complete picture of her writing process.

1

Cather's own description comes to us in an interview conducted by a reporter from the *Nebraska State Journal* on 2 November 1921:

> Miss Cather told of her method of working. Each morning she devotes two and a half hours to literary labor. Last winter these working hours were so interrupted by telephone calls that she had her telephone removed. The full plan of a story is distinct in her mind before beginning to write. The first draft is in long hand. She then rewrites by typewriter. This copy is again revised and retyped by Miss Cather, and again

revised before being turned over to a professional typist. The last copy is subject to many corrections and changes and is then ready for the printer. On the proof sheets much elimination and condensation takes place. (Bohlke 41)

Cather reveals, in addition to these five steps, further details in a letter to Alfred A. Knopf in the fall of 1933; she tells Knopf that she never writes a first draft of anything except by hand (Knopf, "Memoir, 1933"). A decade later, in a letter to Sinclair Lewis (22 Mar. 1944) responding to his request on behalf of a collector for manuscript material, she says she has no materials of that kind. She then goes on to explain that she copies her first draft on the machine mainly because it shows up her weaknesses, and that the professional typing shows up more stupidities. She notes that the original holograph copies of her works were usually lost or spoiled, and that she customarily asked Knopf to destroy the printer's copy (the final typescript).

Our textual research suggests that several details of the process as she described it may be questioned, namely, (1) that the full plan of a story was distinct in her mind before she began to write, (2) that she did not save her manuscripts and that holograph drafts were usually spoiled or lost, and (3) that she usually asked Knopf to destroy the printer's copy. However oversimple or misleading her claims may be, the main purpose of the following analysis of the *Sapphira* documents and of other similar discoveries is to reach a more complete description of her process.

2

To understand the place of the *Sapphira* documents in Cather's working practices, we must characterize the general process that these materials helped to form, and that process may be described as occurring in successive phases of generating, shaping, and polishing material. More particularly, in terms of intention and revision, the process may be explained by combining Michael Hancher's three separate elements of an author's intention (programmatic, active, and final)[2] with G. Thomas Tanselle's idea of vertical revision, which moves the work to another plane, and horizontal revision, which involves alterations on the same plane.[3] Most of the revisions in the *Sapphira* documents are horizontal, but there is some vertical revision, as I will show. In any case, the process is progressive and consequential: at the initial stage of the process, Cather's holograph drafting is programmatic, and such drafting is succeeded by several steps of progressively active copying and rewriting by typewriter, interrupted by small or large vertical revision at any stage, with final finishing in a series of polishing revisions.

More particularly, in determining how these purposes (design and revision) are progressively carried out, we must review the steps in more detail. In the holograph draft, Cather generates in a provisional way the raw material out of which a certain order and context would later be formed. In her first typing, she continues to compose, using the machine to do what she did in her holograph (canceling and supplying interlinear material by hand), which typing she would then go on to correct in hand. The characteristics of her first typing are typing errors, holograph and typeover cancellations, typed and holograph interlinear interpolations, the absence of five-em spacing between sentences, irregular key pressure, and the use of carbons as well as face sheets (top original typed sheets). In the second typing, Cather generates less new material and tries to produce cleaner copy for the next step. Her retyping may be distinguished from her first typing mainly by the substance in three ways: by the discrete changes she makes in word (most commonly name changes), phrase, and sentence; by the reshaping of material (combining earlier versions, as well as trimming back earlier versions); and by a cleaner presentation (the scarcity of interlinears and typeover cancellations). She and Edith Lewis (her editing partner and, later, her executor and trustee of her estate) then prepare a copyedited version of her material for her professional typist (Miss Bloom), whose work is characterized by the use of a fresh ribbon and the presence of five-em spacing between sentences, as well as by the absence of the typed interlinear interpolations characteristic of Cather's practice. Cather and her editing partner, Edith Lewis, then proof the typescript. Within this framing, nine of the newly discovered documents may be briefly described, with abbreviations given for ease of use in referring to them in succeeding discussions:

The holograph draft
HMS: fourteen pages of holographic material, with cancellations and corrections in Cather's hand, relating to parts of chapter 3 of book 8, "The Dark Autumn" (257–59 and 262–64 in the first edition)

The first typings
TS1: a four-page carbon typescript, typed by Cather, with strikeovers for cancellation and typed interlinear interpolations, corresponding to material in chapter 3 of book 8 (257–60 in the first edition)
TS2: a carbon of a typescript of ten pages, with Cather's typed and holographic interlinear interpolations and typed and holographic cancellations, accompanied by two pages of handwritten instructions, and corresponding to matter in chapter 1 of book 4, "Sapphira's Daughter" (115–128.12 in the first edition)

TS3: a face typescript (a top original) of six pages, with strikeovers, interlinears, typing errors, and irregular key touch (features of Cather's typing), with one correction in hand, corresponding to matter in chapter 1 in book 8 (243–49 in the first edition)

The retypings

TS4: a carbon typescript of five pages, with no holographic corrections, showing the marks of Cather's retyping, namely, a cleaner presentation and the presence of substantive alteration (earlier versions trimmed back), corresponding to material in the latter part of chapter 2 and the early pages of chapter 3 in book 8 (252–56 and 257–58 in the first edition)

TS5: two top face pages of typescript, very lightly corrected in type, with no holographic corrections, with the same signs of retyping as described above, corresponding to the first pages of chapter 2 in book 8 (250–52 in the first edition)

The professional typings

TS6: a top face typescript of six pages with some proofing, professionally typed (five-em spacing between sentences, new ribbon); material Cather removed from a late draft, which in more complete form may have found a place at the end of book 4 (around page 145 in the first edition)

TSX: a combination of professionally typed and Cather-typed material of some 150 pages, revised by Cather with about 850 words added in manuscript, and forming what the editors consider a consolidating and shaping typescript suitable for further revision and final professional typing

TS7: a top face typescript of fifteen pages, professionally typed as described above, with holographic corrections by Edith Lewis and Cather, corresponding to chapters 2 and 3 of book 8 (250–69 in the first edition).

From our study of these documents, five points stand out. First of all, the holograph (HMS) shows Cather at an initial stage of composing—what we might call programmatic or provisional casting. Second, the three carbon typescripts (TS1, TS2, and TS4) are the first confirmations that we have of Cather writing and rewriting her material by typewriter. Third, in one of the examples of a typescript prepared professionally (TS6), we have the only existing evidence of what Tanselle calls "vertical revision"—six pages of material that Cather removed from a late draft of *Sapphira*. Fourth, the final typescript, professionally prepared (TS7), provides us with an example of the copyediting collaboration of

Cather with Edith Lewis, her editing partner. And finally, four of these *Sapphira* documents cover the same material (HMS, TS1, TS4, TS7), a fact that allows us to compare these texts as to when they overlap, the resulting analysis giving us a running glimpse of the evolution of that part of the text.

3

In this section, I will describe in more detail three of the points just discussed: overlapping texts, vertical revision, and the Cather/Lewis copy-editing collaboration.

Comparison of Overlapping Texts

The three texts treated will be HMS, TS1, and TS7; the scene that these texts share appears in book 8, "The Dark Autumn" (page 259 in the first edition), and describes the moment when Fairhead, a friend of the family, observes Mary, the older of Sapphira's two granddaughters, who is sick with influenza and who nonetheless breaks the doctor's prohibition on eating by drinking a bowl of broth.

The text of the holograph (HMS) is unique in several ways. First, it contains *two* versions of the short scene just described. Their presence shows that Cather was giving herself choices, generating material for which focus and order would only later be found. Second, this material is so foreign to that of the standard of collation (first printing, first edition) that it could not be collated, a fact that demonstrates the uniquely provisional nature of the material.

In the holograph, Cather makes two casts of the scene in which Mary drinks the broth, one in each of the two sections (257–59 and 262–64 in the first edition), and both versions may be contrasted and then compared to similar material in TS1 and TS7.[4] The passage in the first section of the holograph is the longer of the two:

> I was coming out of the woodshed with a bucket of kindling for her morning fire when I saw a strange thing, I saw Mary, the older girl <who burst> came down the [2] back stairs in her nightgown. The <kitchen> stair door had been left open. She went straight to the table, sank down into the chair, and lifted the bowl up in her two hands and began to drink the soup. You see the smell of the broth had gone up the back stairs, and she had been starved for three days. I knew I ought to <drop my bucket get> go in there and take the bowl from her. But somehow I couldn't bring myself to do it. The stove hearth let out enough light so I could watch her. She drank slowly, resting her elbows

on the table. Put the bowl down, took a long breath, and then drank again. It <looked> seemed almost like a communion service.

The comparable passage in the second part of the holograph is shorter:

> Fairhead, splitting kindling outside the kitchen window, saw a white figure steal down the back stairs into the kitchen. It was Mary. She went directly to the kitchen table, lifted the bowl of broth in her two hands, and began to drink it. Her <hands trembled> arms wavered with the bowl at her lips, so she sat down <on> in the nearest chair, and resting her elbows on the table, slowly drank <the> at the bowl until it was empty. Fairhead knew he ought to go in and [end page]

The longer passage has more verbal parallels to the first edition than the shorter passage and may have been composed later than the shorter version. These passages illustrate the provisional nature of the material: in Hancher's words, we see the "author's intention to make something or other," and one for which there is an "open liability to miscarriage" (829–30). Cather is composing in a programmatic mode, generating ideas that will only later find more specific meanings. This holographic excerpt from a lost complete first draft is an excellent example of Cather's initial steps in the expressive stage of her creative process.

Now that we have seen two versions of the same scene in the holograph, we can review the succeeding typescripts that cover the same material. TS1 is a four-page carbon typescript, typed by Cather, corresponding to material in chapter 3 of book 8, "The Dark Autumn" (257–60 in the first edition). The TS1 typescript text begins to move toward the text of the first edition:

> She reached the table, sank down in a wooden chair, and lifted the bowl of broth in her two hands, resting her elbows on the table. She drank slowly, put the bowl down <and> for a moment and sat with her shoulders drooping forward. Streaks of firelight <flick> from the stove flickered over her and over the whitewashed walls. She took up the bowl again. Fairhead knew he ought to go in and snatch it from her. But he seemed unable to stir or make a sound. There was something solemn <if> in what he saw there in the kitchen, like a Communion service.

The later TS7 typescript is a face typescript of fifteen pages, professionally typed, corresponding to chapters 2 and 3 of book 8 (250–69 in the first edition). This typescript also contains the same scene; the part of the typescript that follows is actually two texts: (1) the professional typing of the passage and (2) the Cather/Lewis hand-corrected version that makes a *new* text (see fig. 4). The professional text, *unaltered*, and before it is corrected, shows some small differences from the earlier TS1, such as the order of some of the details, the split into two words of "white-washed," and the inclusion of a small *c* in the word "communion":

> She reached the table, sank down in a wooden chair and lifted the bowl of broth in her two hands. She drank slowly, resting her elbows on the table. She put the bowl down for a moment, and sat with her shoulders drooping forward. Streaks of firelight flickered over her and over the white washed walls and ceiling. When she toop [sic] up the bowl again Fairhead knew it was time for him to go in and snatch it from her. But he was unable to move or make a sound. There was something solemn in what he saw through the window like a communion service.

When we see the *corrected* version of this passage—with Cather's and Lewis's hands present—we can observe them canceling and adding new material that approaches the first edition text even more closely:

> She reached the table, sank down <in> on a wooden chair, and lifted the bowl of broth in her two hands. (She must have smelled the hot soup up in her bedroom; the stair door had been left open.) She drank slowly, resting her elbows on the table. <She put down the bowl for a moment, and sat with her shoulders drooping forward.> Streaks of firelight from the stove flickered over her and the whitewashed walls and ceilings. <When she took up the bowl again> Fairhead knew <it was time for him to> he ought to go in and <snatch it> take the soup from her. But he was unable to move or to make a sound. There was something solemn in what he saw through the window, like a Communion service.

What we see in these juxtapositions of overlapping texts is not only the evolution of a text, but also the sign of a ceaseless revising mind at work at each step of the way. The revising mind that simplifies was an idea Cather had put forth in an early interview. Responding to a question about what made some stories stand out above the mediocre, she identified the process of simplification as the difference: "Whether it is a pianist, or a singer, or a writer, art ought to simplify—that seems to me to be the whole process" (Slote 447). At this point in the process, Cather proceeds to shape a text toward her final intention.

Vertical Revisions in the Evolution of the Text

TS6 is a face typescript of six pages with some proofing, professionally typed; it is a scene that Cather removed from the novel, one that in more complete form may have found a place at the end of book 4 (around page 145 in the first edition). This scene involves Mrs. Blake's children (Sapphira's grandchildren), who are making plans for their summer holidays. They dress up and ask for a trip to see Grandfather at the mill. There, they enter their dream world of play that the miller promotes by showing them around the mill, serving them cakes and milk, and singing them songs. The focus is on the children's pleasure and on the sympathetic character of the miller.

This typescript is unique among materials related to Cather's published work in that it is the sole surviving example that we have of what Tanselle calls "a vertical revision"—although Cather did say she cut large sections from *The Song of the Lark* (1915) and *One of Ours* (1922). This typescript is as important as the "Casta Diva" section of *My Mortal Enemy* (1926), added late to that novel, as well as one book and two chapters of *Death Comes for the Archbishop* (1927), also added late to that novel. All of these are vertical changes to the original plans for those novels and represent major alterations, one by deletion and two by addition. The use of these "vertical revisions" marks the change from (in Hancher's words) "active" to "final" intentions on Cather's part.

The example of TS6 seems to contradict Cather's claim in the *Nebraska State Journal* interview that she had a full plan of a story distinct in mind before beginning to write, and several sources confirm that she did change her intentions about *Sapphira*. In an interview with Stephen Vincent Benét and Rosemary Benét, Cather reported that in writing *Sapphira*, she started it "as a complete history of the manners and customs of the valley" and then cut out all that background that was not essential to her story: "I weighed what I cut out—and it came to a good six pounds" (Bohlke 136). She repeats some of these details in a letter to Ferris Greenslet in which she explains that she had written many chapters of Virginia ways and manners for the relief and comfort of remembering them at a time of loss (see Woodress 480–81), but later cut what was too digressively reminiscent and rewrote the story along the lines of the design she set out in the first chapter. She then put the discarded material (deleted chapters and paragraphs) on the bathroom scales, found that they weighed six pounds, and was quite pleased (letter to Ferris Greenslet, 13 Dec. 1940).

The evidence makes clear that she may have begun with one intention, entering the sheltering world of reminiscences about her childhood, and, resting comfortably in this landscape, continued to write under this motive. TS6 is, obviously, only a small bit of this digressive material, but with this and other acts of cancellation, she demonstrated a change in what Hancher calls an "active intention"—she moved from one particular plan (a reminiscence of Virginia manners and customs) to another plan (Sapphira's story). As James Woodress points out, Cather mentioned to Bruce Rogers (the designer for the Houghton

Mifflin Autograph edition of 1938) a fear of diffuseness as a reason for these cuts (letter to Bruce Rogers, 25 Jan. 1941). Lewis confirms Cather's altered intentions: "She could have written two or three *Sapphiras* out of her material; and in fact she did write, in her first draft, twice as much as she used. She always said it was what she left out that counted" (183).

What Cather left out was what she described in her essay "The Novel Démeublé" (which appeared in the *New Republic* in 1922) as "tasteless amplitude."[5] This essay begins with the sentence, "The novel, for a long while, has been overfurnished," and in her last paragraph she completes the figure: "How wonderful it would be if we could throw all the furniture out of the window" (*Willa Cather on Writing* 35, 42). We can see in *Sapphira and the Slave Girl* her rejection of cluttering interior decoration that was her reaction against what she called Balzac's "presentation," and her agreement with Robert Louis Stevenson who wanted to blue-pencil a great deal of this "presentation" (*Willa Cather on Writing* 39). Cather's abandonment of material at such a late date suggests that she considered the children's mill party, in itself possibly interesting and pleasing, as superfluous to her final intentions.

The Copyediting Collaboration

TS7 is a face typescript of fifteen pages, professionally typed, corresponding to chapters 2 and 3 of book 8 (250–69 in the first edition). The distinctive features of this typing are the five-em spacing between sentences, the fresh ribbon, and the absence of interlinears and strikeovers. Strictly speaking, this typescript contains three texts: the initial professionally typed and uncorrected text, Cather's light holographic corrections to this text, and Lewis's more extensive holographic copyediting and corrections.

The collaboration of Lewis and Cather in the proofing of a final typescript is established by the changes that they both made, Lewis with fifty-nine cancellations, interlinears, and marginal corrections, and Cather with eight changes, including the added paragraph in her own hand pinned to page 163. That this was a Cather-Lewis collaboration with Cather having the final word can be established by comparing TS7 to the first edition with regard to the passage in which Cather explores Fairhead's state of mind following his sight of Mary drinking the broth. In TS7 one can see the uncorrected, as well as the corrected, text:

> He remembered that {sometimes} in dreams a <very> trivial thing <.climbing a tree or swimming in the mill dam, could give one a shudder of fright and foreboding out of all keeping with the dream itself.>

{became momentous in a way one could not explain} {took on a mysterious significance one could not explain}

The two multiple marginal additions in curled brackets above, in Lewis's hand, show Cather and Lewis in a programmatic mode even at this stage in the formation of the text. Cather accepts one of Lewis's two marginal alternatives and rejects the other, so that her condensed revision becomes, "He remembered how sometimes in dreams a trivial thing took on a mysterious significance one could not explain." This evidence confirms Cather's description of a late draft subject to many corrections and changes and also supports Lewis's claim that she read copy and proofs of all Cather's books from the time of *The Song of the Lark* onward (xvii–xviii). In fact, this occasion in TS7 where Cather makes a choice between two alternatives Lewis has proposed seems to indicate Lewis's incorporation of Cather's method of interlinear interpolation—of providing alternative readings for Cather's possible adoption into the text. We may thus come to see Lewis as Cather's copyediting alter ego.[6]

Although they represent only parts of the narrative, the nine *Sapphira* typescripts stand out, not just for their number and diversity, but more particularly because some of them represent phases in the process we have not so fully seen before, namely, retyping as shaping and reshaping by cancellation. Both of these practices show Cather grappling with competing points of focus as she shapes her material, and sometimes her programmatic (and even active) purposes were either more fully realized or aborted. In any case, when Cather did have a "full plan of a story distinct in her mind," most of her revisions are, to use Tanselle's terms, more horizontal than vertical; but, then, Cather was constantly making changes in her text throughout the process of bringing her ideas to particular effect.

4

These *Sapphira* documents do add to our understanding, for they show us that even Cather's own description does not completely capture the complexity of her revising process. In addition to these are materials connected to other Cather novels that confirm practices found in the already-discussed *Sapphira* documents. TS2 includes, pinned to one of its pages, a typed paragraph designed to replace one on page nine, thus combining new material with old. On a larger scale, Cather used an analogous practice to produce a complete draft in the retyped materials from *The Professor's House* (1925) and *Obscure Destinies* (1932). And there is additional evidence connected to other novels that shows us practices that we have not yet placed in a more complete description of her process of composition. After retyping her revisions and before handing over a revised typescript to Miss Bloom for a fresh typing, Cather sometimes produced a new text by *combining* versions she had already made from typescripts in original (face) and carbon forms, and by pasting or pinning new material (holograph or typed) to existing sheets, which she and Lewis then corrected by hand. And, of course, we have TSX, the long shaping typescript that combines professionally prepared material with typed drafts made by Cather and revised by her in anticipation of further revision and final professional typing. Still another method she used is represented by the corrected typescript of *My Mortal Enemy*, which shows the marks of a complete text typed by herself and then corrected in her hand. This complete-text version suggests a later phase of composition within the third step of her process: retyping her revisions of a complete manuscript with corrections in hand. Cather seems to have passed up opportunities to review her work only in the case of proofing her serial publications, for which we have only one example.

Another unique step that includes Cather's attention, but involves someone else's hand, is the complete corrected typescript of *Lucy Gayheart* (1935), which shows signs throughout of a Knopf copyeditor marking in red to prepare for publication. This typescript is professionally typed, with the characteristic five-em spacing between sentences. A step beyond this last example may be found in the complete corrected professional typescript of *Shadows on the Rock* (1931), which contains signs throughout, not only of a Knopf copyeditor marking in red, but also of a printer marking for two sets of galley numbers. This fact brings into question Cather's claim that Knopf was to have destroyed the printer's copy. Finally, an additional sign of her care for detail in a text was her request to Houghton Mifflin that her foreign words be checked, corrected when necessary, and italicized for the production of *Song of the Lark* (Willa Cather to R. Scaife, 12 May 1915).

At this point, we can turn to the steps Cather took *after* she submitted the final typescript to the press: she read galleys and page proofs, made corrections in texts after a book was published, and made changes in her texts for the Autograph Edition. We have the rare example of a corrected galley proof for three chapters of the *Forum* serial of *Death Comes for the Archbishop*—the only example we have of her proofreading a magazine printing of her work; and we have a set of uncorrected galleys for the first Knopf edition of this narrative. We also have a complete set of corrected page proofs of *Lucy Gayheart*, as well as corrected galleys for *Sapphira and the Slave Girl*. A brief description of some of the revisions she made in the galleys of *Sapphira* will confirm our claim that Cather constantly made changes in her text throughout the process of bringing her ideas to final form.

There are ninety-one galley sheets printed by the Plimpton Press on 28 August 1940 that contain altogether three hundred and eight changes in the text of *Sapphira*, changes both substantive and accidental. There were accidental changes (92), deletions of words, phrases, or sentences (40), additions (41), deletions accompanied by additions (117), and technical corrections of compositorial slips (18). (Collations show that in twelve instances Cather made changes in the galleys that were either not incorporated into the text by the compositor or later revised in the page proofs by her.) Three of Cather's *démeublé* cuts in these galleys focus on the condition of female slavery. In chapter 3 of book 2, "Old Jezebel," the first edition text (K1) describes the moment when "the fetters were taken off the female captives. They were not likely to make trouble" (K1.91.19). In the galleys, between "captives" and "They" Cather canceled the following sentence: "Flogging would take the place of irons if any disorder occurred." Soon after this in the narrative, Cather describes how "the women were turned out on the lower after deck without chains" (K1.92.15) and canceled the following sentence in the galleys after the word "chains": "The women seldom made any trouble except as they increased the stench." Finally, describing Jezebel (K1.93.28), Cather canceled the following sentence in the galleys: "She had none of the usual bodily characteristics of the African female; the hanging belly, heavy thighs, and over-developed breasts." While these changes produce the more restrained style of her late writing, the deletions seem designed to erase what one reader has called an overly racist attitude toward the African female.

In the evolution of the text before publication, the galleys are the penultimate point of polishing. Cather's attention to detail extends to accidentals—she makes new paragraphs; adds or subtracts punctuation and capitalization; and corrects spelling, as well as some of the compositor's entry errors. However, even then she was by no means through with her text, for the galleys do not contain the final personal note on Frederick County surnames (K1.295.7–20). She must have added this material at the page-proof stage.

5

The facts drawn from the ten *Sapphira* documents, combined with existing discoveries relating to other novels, lead us to a more complete picture of Cather's process of composition. I will refer in the following description, at each step, to the primary evidence in parentheses and to the secondary evidence in brackets. The steps are keyed to Cather's own description of her practices in the *Nebraska State Journal* interview.

(1) Cather begins with a handwritten draft, correcting it in hand as she writes (photo page one of the *Death Comes for the Archbishop* holograph found as a frontispiece in the Autograph Edition; *Sapphira and the Slave Girl* holograph segment HMS; see fig. 1) [Knopf, "Memoir, 1933"].

(2a) Having completed a corrected handwritten draft, Cather then writes her next draft by typewriter, composing anew as she types (*Sapphira* TS1; see fig. 2). She then (2b) corrects this first typescript by hand (*Sapphira* TS2; see fig. 3).

(3a) Cather retypes the previous draft with no holographic corrections (*Sapphira* TS4), or, lightly revising in type, makes one correction in hand (*Sapphira* TS3). (3b) There is a phase of reshaping: Cather brings together a whole manuscript by combining versions already made from carbons or face typescripts and pasting or pinning in new material ("Old Mrs. Harris" in *Obscure Destinies*), or she retypes a whole manuscript, correcting in type and by hand ("Two Friends" in *Obscure Destinies* and "My Mortal Enemy" Berg Collection complete corrected typescript). (3c) Cather adds material to a serial manuscript for book publication (the "Casa Diva" section in *My Mortal Enemy*, and one-quarter of *Death Comes for the Archbishop*) or revises a story for book publication (rewrites or restores the original version of "Coming, Eden Bower!" in *Smart Set* for "Coming, Aphrodite!" in *Youth and the Bright Medusa*).

(4a) Miss Bloom prepares material that is subsequently abandoned by Cather (*Sapphira* TS6) or that is prepared and proofed for periodical publication [*A Lost Lady*; Blanche Knopf to Willa Cather, 15 Dec. and 28 Dec. 1922], or, Cather uses a copy of a typescript used for periodical publication as the basis for a new or more complete version of a work to be published in book form [*A Lost Lady*; Willa Cather to Blanche Knopf, 16 Jan. 1923; *Death Comes for the Archbishop*; Willa Cather to Blanche Knopf, 7 Oct. 1926]. (4b) Cather gathers together typescript prepared by Miss Bloom and herself to form a nearly complete draft of *Sapphira and the Slave Girl* suitable for copyediting by herself and Miss Lewis prior to a final professional typing. Miss Bloom prepares a complete text, corrected by Cather and Lewis, with some copyediting by Lewis (*Sapphira* TS7; see fig. 4), or, same as above with Knopf copyediting "Two Friends" in *Obscure Destinies*, or, same with Knopf copyediting and printer's markings for galleys (*Shadows on the Rock*).

(5a) Cather reads the galleys (the only instance known) for magazine publication (*Death Comes for the Archbishop*), or, for book publication (*Sapphira and the Slave Girl*) [Willa Cather to Mary Virginia Auld, 19 Feb. 1927]. (5b) Cather reads page proofs of a book (*Lucy Gayheart*) [Alfred Knopf to Willa Cather, 24 Feb. and 3 Mar. 1923 concerning *A Lost Lady*] (5c) Cather asks Scaife at Houghton Mifflin to check her foreign

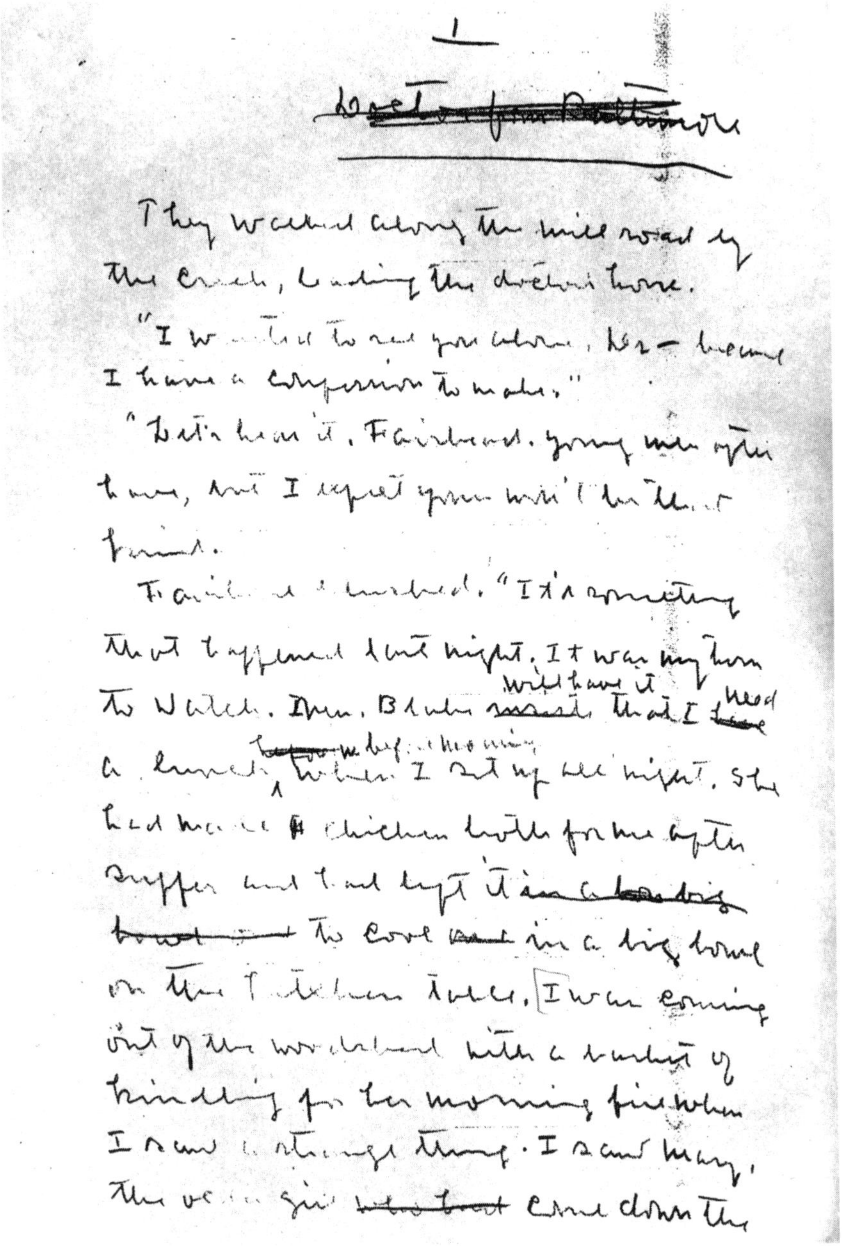

Fig. 1. Page 1 of an early holograph draft (HMS). Image derived from a digital scan (300 dpi, grayscale) of a photocopy.
Courtesy of a private donor

2

Fairhead went out into the yard and walked up and down under the great maples to watch the blue evening die into dusk and the silvery stars come out faintly over the pines on the hill.

He felt hopeless. He knew that Doctor W   Could do something. He was everything that Brush was not; intelligent, devoted to his profession--- and a gentleman. He had come to practise in Frederick County by accident. While he was training in a Baltimore hospital he met a Winchester girl who was visiting her aunt in the city and fell in love with her. When he found that she would never live anywhere but in her native town, he gave up the promise of a fine city practise and settled in Winchester. A foolish thing to do, but Worthington was like that,- so were his ancestors. His grandfather, while making the "Grand tour" as young bloods did in those days, married in Rome an Italian widow. The couple had lived happily and long on his estate near Alexandria. The sons and grandsons of that marriage had seemed to know what they most wanted had been a little "peculiar",- that is un
 married into the best families.

As Fairhead took the air under the maples (in the yard) he kept his eyes an eye on an upstairs window, the window of Mrs. Blake's own chamber. When the candlelight shown behind that window it was time for him to go up to his patients.. He circled the house, picked up some sticks from the woodpile and was about to go into the kitchen when he saw through the window something which startled him. A white figure emerged from the stairway
    the indoor duskiness .
and drifted through the duskiness of the room . It was Mary,

Fig. 2. Page 2 of a carbon draft (TS1) typed by Cather, with typed corrections. Image derived from a digital scan (300 dpi, grayscale) of a photocopy. Courtesy of a private donor

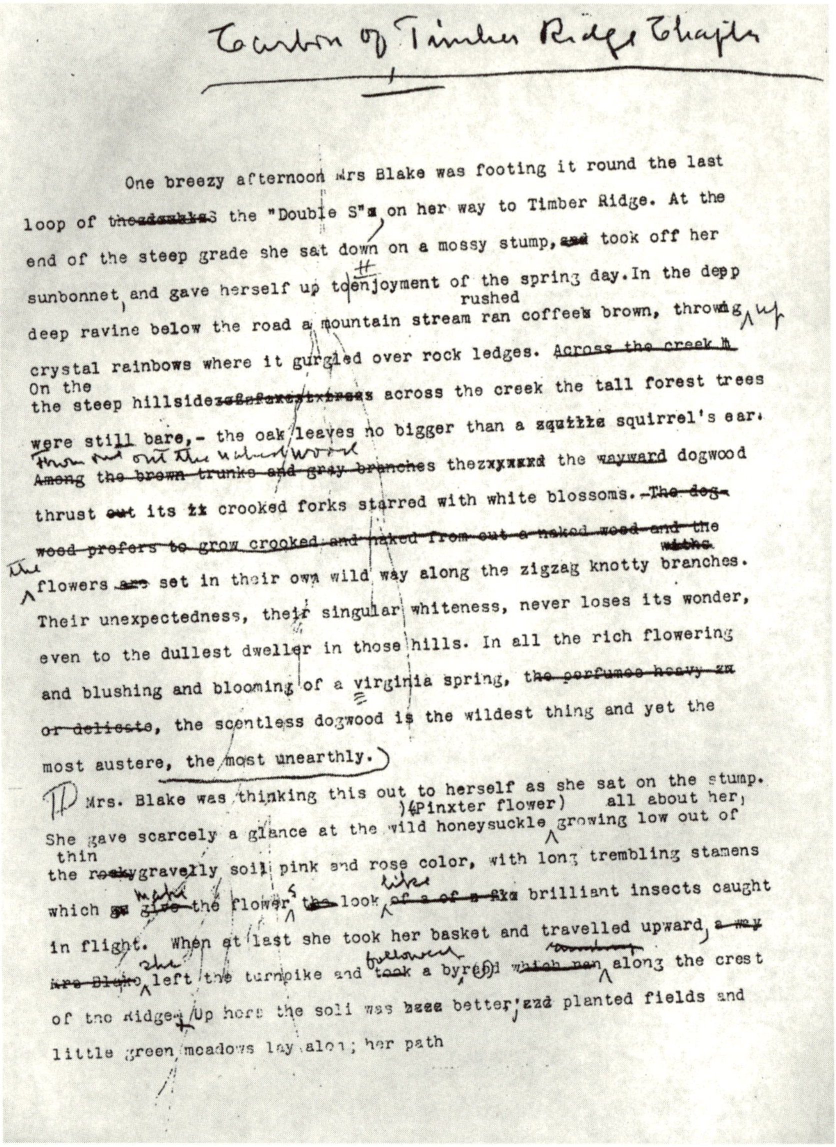

Carbon of Timber Ridge Chapter

One breezy afternoon Mrs Blake was footing it round the last loop of ~~theadoubles~~ the "Double S", on her way to Timber Ridge. At the end of the steep grade she sat down on a mossy stump, ~~and~~ took off her sunbonnet, and gave herself up to enjoyment of the spring day. In the depp deep ravine below the road a mountain stream rushed ran coffee brown, throwing up crystal rainbows where it gurgled over rock ledges. ~~Across the creek th~~ On the steep hillside ~~ofaforestxtrees~~ across the creek the tall forest trees were still bare, - the oak leaves no bigger than a ~~squirle~~ squirrel's ear. ~~Among the brown trunks and gray branches~~ thrown out over the naked wood the ~~zxxxxd~~ the wayward dogwood thrust ~~out~~ its ~~ix~~ crooked forks starred with white blossoms. ~~The dog-wood prefers to grow crooked and naked from out a naked wood and the withe.~~ The flowers ~~are~~ set in their own wild way along the zigzag knotty branches. Their unexpectedness, their singular whiteness, never loses its wonder, even to the dullest dweller in those hills. In all the rich flowering and blushing and blooming of a virginia spring, ~~the perfumes heavy or or delicate~~, the scentless dogwood is the wildest thing and yet the most austere, the most unearthly.

¶ Mrs. Blake was thinking this out to herself as she sat on the stump. She gave scarcely a glance at the wild honeysuckle (Pinxter flower) all about her, growing low out of the ~~rocky~~ thin gravelly soil, pink and rose color, with long trembling stamens which ~~gi~~ ~~give~~ make the flowers ~~the~~ look ~~of a of a fix~~ like brilliant insects caught in flight. When at last she took her basket and travelled upward, ~~a way~~ ~~Mrs Blake~~ she left the turnpike and ~~took~~ followed a byroad ~~which ran~~ wandering along the crest of the Ridge. Up here the soil was ~~base~~ better, and planted fields and little green meadows lay along her path

Fig. 3. Page 1 of a carbon draft (TS2) typed by Cather, with typed and handwritten corrections. Image derived from a digital scan (300 dpi, grayscale) of a photocopy. Courtesy of a private donor

168

was Mary, barefoot, in her nightgown, as if she were walking in her sleep, ~~or in delirium.~~ She reached the table, sank down ~~in~~ on a wooden chair, and lifted the bowl of broth in her two hands. She drank slowly, resting her elbows on the table. ~~She put the bowl down for a moment, and sat with her shoulders drooping forward.~~ Streaks of firelight flickered *from the stove* over her and over the whitewashed walls and ceiling. ~~When she took up the bowl again~~ Fairhead knew ~~it was time for him to~~ *he ought to take the soup* go in and ~~snatch it~~ from her. But he was unable to move or *to* make a sound. There was something solemn in what he saw through the window, like a *C*ommunion service~~.~~

After the girl had vanished ~~into~~ *up* the ~~closed~~ stairway, he still stood outside, looking into the empty room, wondering at himself. He remembered that in dreams a ~~very~~ *sometimes* trivial thing~~, climbing a tree or swimming in the mill-dam, could give one a shudder of fright and foreboding out of all keeping with the dream itself.~~ He might have thought he had been dreaming now, except that, when he at last went inside, he found his soup bowl empty.

Fairhead ~~He~~ climbed the stairs slowly and went to Betty's room. After he had washed out her throat with a clumsy thing called a swab, he got the last morsel of ice (wrapped in sacking on the window sill) and put it in her mouth. She looked up at him gratefully and tried to smile. He whispered that he would soon come back to her, took ~~her~~ *the* candle and crossed the hall to Mary's room. He did not know what he might find there. He listened at the crack of the door; dead silence. Shading the light with his hand, he went in softly and approached the bed. ~~She~~ *Mary* was lying on her side, fast asleep. ~~A clean swab and the sulphur mixture~~

[marginal notes: "She must have smelled the hot soup & the kitchen; the stove door had been left open."]
[marginal notes: "Shame nonetimes in a way no one could not explain. It is a mysterious significance one could not explain."]

Fig. 4. Page 168 of the professionally typed draft (TS7), with holograph corrections by Cather and Lewis. Image derived from a digital scan (300 dpi, grayscale) of a photocopy.
Courtesy of a private donor

languages carefully and to put them in italics for *The Song of the Lark* [Willa Cather to R. Scaife, 12 May {1915}].

Following publication, Cather made changes (mostly substantive) in novels requiring only minor adjustments to plates, but for *My Ántonia* she agreed to changes in the introduction to the 1926 revised edition (Ferris Greenslet to Willa Cather, 26 Jan. 1926; and Willa Cather to Ferris Greenslet, 15 Feb. 1926). For the collected Autograph Edition, she made marginal corrections in copies of novels, attaching a full list of changes on the endpapers of each volume (Willa Cather to Ferris Greenslet, 8 Sept. [1936]), particular examples of which have not survived.

Given the weight of these facts, we can see Cather's commitment to detail, not only in the composition, but also in the production of her works. Even though there are instances of vertical revision, her process of composition is dominated by the principle of horizontal revision—from the generation of material in the programmatic mode, through the shaping and reshaping of this material in an active mode, to the polishing of the material in a final mode even after the initial publication of her books.

We can understand Cather's feelings when she responded to Sinclair Lewis's request in 1944 for some of her manuscript material. She told him that she had bundled herself around to so many parts of the world that she simply had not the room to spare for storing old manuscripts and was glad to be rid of them. But the presence of such an assembly of prepublication holographs and typescripts cited above certainly places doubt on this claim. And the existence of so many final corrected typescripts also puts doubt on the statement that she asked Knopf to destroy the printer's copies (the final corrected typescripts). But, more positively, what all the materials cited do demonstrate is Cather's conviction that writing, typing, retyping, and proofreading gave her opportunities to detect weaknesses in her work. And detect and correct she did: she not only hated tasteless amplitude, but also sought higher and truer effects in her writing.

NOTES

1. My description of the process is based on two sources: (1) Cather's own comments on it in her letters, reviews, publications, and interviews; and (2) the textual work of the Scholarly Edition as it has produced collations and conflations of the texts of her novels in order to establish critical texts—in short, upon the textual revelations of a textual complexity unknown before this work. While the research on this topic of composing has issued from the ongoing work of the textual editors and is contained in their essays in the volumes of the project, the broader theme of Cather's creative process had already been treated well before the Scholarly Edition began by a number of scholars, but principally by Bernice Slote in *The Kingdom of Art*, Edward A. and Lillian D. Bloom in *Willa Cather's Gift of Sympathy*, and James Woodress in *Willa Cather: A Literary Life*. The composing process is in this essay conceived as the subfield of textual studies within the broader theme of the creative process. Working in this field with other textual editors, I frequently refer in this essay to our work together by using the word "we," but the work of this essay in summary is mine.

2. By programmatic intention, Hancher means the author's general plan to make something, one for which there is an open liability to miscarriage; by active intention, he means a more particular plan for which the author intends a certain kind of meaning; and by final intention, he means a particular plan to cause something to happen, namely, certain meanings that will have an effect on an audience or that will sell well and bring profit.

3. For Tanselle, a horizontal revision alters "the work in degree but not in kind" whereas a vertical revision reflects "an altered active intention in the work as a whole" (193). More particularly, a vertical revision "[a]ims at altering the purpose, direction, or character of a work, thus attempting to make a different sort of work out of it" (193) whereas a horizontal revision is one that intensifies, refines, or otherwise improves the work as then conceived.

4. In transcribing the holograph material, we use <pointed brackets> to enclose canceled matter, {curled brackets} to enclose interlinear interpolations, and [straight brackets] to indicate page numbers and editorial comment; in transcribing the typescript material, we use these signs, and <u>underlining</u> to mark added material.

5. Cather developed this idea in her 12 April 1922 article in the *New Republic*, "The Novel Démeublé," which was reprinted in *Not Under Forty* and *Willa Cather on Writing*.

6. It is important to know that Edith Lewis worked as a copyeditor at the advertising firm of J. Walter Thompson in Manhattan.

WORKS CITED

Bloom, Edward A., and Lillian D. Bloom. *Willa Cather's Gift of Sympathy.* 1962. Lincoln: U of Nebraska P, 1982.

Bohlke, L. Brent, ed. *Willa Cather in Person: Interviews, Speeches, and Letters.* Lincoln: U of Nebraska P, 1986.

Cather, Willa. "Coming, Eden Bower!" *Smart Set* 62.4 (1920): 3–25.

———. "Death Comes for the Archbishop." *Forum* 77.1–6 (Jan.–June 1927): 22–29, 130–37, 286–97, 450–61, 612–25, 770–84, 930–42.

———. *Death Comes for the Archbishop.* New York: Knopf, 1927.

———. Letter to Mary Virginia Auld. 19 Feb. 1927. Willa Cather Pioneer Memorial and Educational Foundation, Red Cloud, NE.

———. Letter to Ferris Greenslet. 26 Jan. 1926. Houghton Mifflin Collection. Houghton Lib., Harvard U, Cambridge, MA.

———. Letter to Ferris Greenslet. 15 Feb. 1926. Houghton Mifflin Collection. Houghton Lib., Harvard U, Cambridge, MA.

———. Letter to Ferris Greenslet. 8 Sept. 1936. Houghton Mifflin Collection. Houghton Lib., Harvard U, Cambridge, MA.

———. Letter to Ferris Greenslet. 13 Dec. 1940. Houghton Mifflin Collection. Houghton Lib., Harvard U, Cambridge, MA.

———. Letter to Alfred Knopf. Fall 1933. Knopf Collection. Harry Ransom Humanities Research Center, U of Texas at Austin.

———. Letter to Blanche Knopf. 16 Jan. 1923. Knopf Collection. Harry Ransom Humanities Research Center, U of Texas at Austin.

———. Letter to Blanche Knopf. 7 Oct. 1926. Knopf Collection. Harry Ransom Humanities Research Center, U of Texas at Austin.

———. Letter to Sinclair Lewis. 22 Mar. 1944. Willa Cather Pioneer Memorial and Educational Foundation, Red Cloud, NE.

———. Letter to Bruce Rogers. 25 Jan. 1941. Newberry Lib., Chicago, IL.

———. Letter to R. Scaife. 12 May 1915. Houghton Mifflin Collection. Houghton Lib., Harvard U, Cambridge, MA.

———. *A Lost Lady.* New York: Knopf, 1923.

———. *Lucy Gayheart.* New York: Knopf, 1935.

———. *My Ántonia.* Boston: Houghton, 1918.

———. "My Mortal Enemy." Complete corrected ts. Berg Collection. New York Public Lib., New York, NY.
———. *My Mortal Enemy.* New York: Knopf, 1926.
———. *Not Under Forty.* New York: Knopf, 1936.
———. *Obscure Destinies.* New York: Knopf. 1932.
———. *One of Ours.* New York: Knopf, 1922.
———. *The Professor's House.* New York: Knopf, 1925.
———. "Sapphira and the Slave Girl." First ed. book galleys (Plimpton Press). Berg Collection. New York Public Lib., New York, NY.
———. "Sapphira and the Slave Girl." HMS ms. Cather Editorial Offices. U of Nebraska, Lincoln, NE.
———. *Sapphira and the Slave Girl.* New York: Knopf, 1940.
———. "Sapphira and the Slave Girl." TS1 ts. Cather Editorial Offices. U of Nebraska, Lincoln, NE.
———. "Sapphira and the Slave Girl." TS2 ts. Cather Editorial Offices. U of Nebraska, Lincoln, NE.
———. "Sapphira and the Slave Girl." TS3 ts. Cather Editorial Offices. U of Nebraska, Lincoln, NE.
———. "Sapphira and the Slave Girl." TS4 ts. Cather Editorial Offices. U of Nebraska, Lincoln, NE.
———. "Sapphira and the Slave Girl." TS5 ts. Cather Editorial Offices. U of Nebraska, Lincoln, NE.
———. "Sapphira and the Slave Girl." TS6 ts. Cather Editorial Offices. U of Nebraska, Lincoln, NE.
———. "Sapphira and the Slave Girl." TS7 ts. Cather Editorial Offices. U of Nebraska, Lincoln, NE.
———. "Sapphira and the Slave Girl." TSX ts. Drew U Archive, Madison, NJ.
———. *Shadows on the Rock.* New York: Knopf, 1931.
———. *The Song of the Lark.* Boston: Houghton, 1915.
———. *Willa Cather on Writing: Critical Studies on Writing as an Art.* New York: Knopf, 1953.
———. *Youth and the Bright Medusa.* New York: Knopf, 1920.
Greenslet, Ferris. Letter to Willa Cather. 26 Jan. 1926. Houghton Mifflin Collection. Houghton Lib., Harvard U, Cambridge, MA.
Hancher, Michael. "Three Kinds of Intention." *Modern Language Notes* 87 (1972): 827–51.
Knopf, Alfred A. Letter to Willa Cather. 24 Feb. 1923. Knopf Collection. Harry Ransom Humanities Research Center, U of Texas at Austin.
———. Letter to Willa Cather. 3 Mar. 1923. Knopf Collection. Harry Ransom Humanities Research Center, U of Texas at Austin.
———. "Memoir, 1933." Knopf Collection. Harry Ransom Humanities Research Center, U of Texas at Austin.
Knopf, Blanche. Letter to Willa Cather. 15 Dec. 1922. Knopf Collection. Harry Ransom Humanities Research Center, U of Texas at Austin.
———. Letter to Willa Cather. 28 Dec. 1922. Knopf Collection. Harry Ransom Humanities Research Center, U of Texas at Austin.
Lewis, Edith. *Willa Cather Living: A Personal Record.* New York: Knopf, 1953.
Slote, Bernice, ed. *Kingdom of Art: Willa Cather's First Principles and Critical Statements, 1893–1896.* Lincoln: U of Nebraska P, 1966.
Tanselle, G. Thomas. "The Editorial Problem of Authorial Intention." *Studies in Bibliography* 29 (1976): 167–211.
Woodress, James. *Willa Cather: A Literary Life.* Lincoln: U of Nebraska P, 1987.

Fostering the Poet:
An Unpublished Robert Frost Letter

DAVID SANDERS
Saint John Fisher College

Background and Overview

On 16 December 1927, Robert Frost wrote a letter to a young man in Buffalo, New York, named Eugene Gay-Tifft.[1] Early in the previous month, on 9 November through 11 November, Frost had spent time at the University of Buffalo, where Gay-Tifft, a contributing editor of the *Buffalo Arts Journal* and himself a published poet, had attended Frost's public presentations and had interviewed him for the *Arts Journal*. When Gay-Tifft's article, "A Chat with Robert Frost," appeared, the young author sent Frost a copy along with one of his own poems; on 16 December, Frost, having returned to the "Stone Cottage" in South Shaftsbury, Vermont, responded with an expansiveness that seems to have surprised even Frost himself. Although Frost's letter makes a gesture toward further contact from Gay-Tifft, there is no evidence of any later communication between the two men.

Frost's letter, though written to no one of long-term importance in his life—no Louis Untermeyer or John Bartlett—is significant in a number of ways. Most generally, it shows how an apparently routine encounter can prompt an expression of one's enduring concerns and values, in this case Frost's convictions about the importance of poetry in both our private life and our public life, and thus in education. In all that it conveys to Gay-Tifft, whether as poet or as editor of the *Arts Journal*, the letter also exemplifies Frost's special sympathy for the young—something noted by one reporter for *The Bee*, the University of Buffalo newspaper, who mentions Frost's ability to anticipate the "questions and problems" of young people, as well as his "kindliness and constructive criticism of the poetry" that students brought to him ("Poetry Speaks"). Gay-Tifft's *Arts Journal* piece had acknowledged Frost's emphasis on the need to encourage young poets, and, when reading Frost's letter, one can sense his appreciation, even gratitude, for Gay-Tifft's way of understanding him. A touching expression of solicitude by one who himself has been touched, Frost's response to the younger poet completes an exchange that may seem to have sprung from their encounter five weeks earlier, but was rooted in a commitment to the arts that had already shaped the lives of both men.

Eugene Gay-Tifft

By the time he met Frost in 1927, Gay-Tifft had placed the arts at the center of his life.[2] Born in Buffalo in 1900, Gay-Tifft was educated at the Nichols School, Dartmouth College, and Harvard University. He was highly accomplished in music and languages and, upon returning to Buffalo in the 1920s, had become significantly involved in the cultural and civic life of the community. He had begun college with the intent of studying chemistry, but he quickly discovered his greater passion for literature. Although remaining interested in the sciences throughout his life, after Dartmouth Gay-Tifft spent a year at Harvard graduate school writing stories and poems and reading various works by writers from other countries. It was during this year that Gay-Tifft discovered the Norwegian novelist Knut Hamsun, winner of the 1920 Nobel Prize for Literature; and finding few of Hamsun's works translated into English, he set about reading him with the help of a Norwegian grammar and dictionary.

Through friendship with a native speaker, Ewald Hagen, and continued reading of Hamsun, Gay-Tifft perfected his command of Norwegian and, by 1929, after he and Hagen had opened a bookstore in the Buffalo Statler Hotel, Gay-Tifft secured his first contract to translate Hamsun with the Coward-McCann Company. Beginning with Hamsun's *Vagabonds* and *August,* published in 1930 and 1931, Gay-Tifft translated six of Hamsun's books. He later expanded his work into Danish and Swedish and then Polish, eventually translating fourteen books from European languages and reading many more as a literary scout for American publishers. By 1939, Gay-Tifft had made himself conversant in Japanese, French, German, and Spanish. His international interests were balanced by a strong sense of patriotism, and his 1982 obituary in the *Buffalo Evening News* quotes a nephew's report that "Uncle Gene always dressed for the Fourth of July and flew his flag out of real conviction" (Brady).

Gay-Tifft wrote poems and stories throughout his life, was often invited to speak about contemporary writers before local literary societies, and, by 1932, was considered one of the "Men You Ought to Know"—the title of an article in the *Buffalo Courier-Express* that profiled him along with two other local citizens (Smith). However, Gay-Tifft's interests extended beyond language and literature. His obituary mentions his editorial work for *Partners,* the magazine of a Chicago labor organization, and for a publication for railroad yardmasters—perhaps an outgrowth of his early fascination with the Buffalo trolley system. The 1932 article in the *Buffalo Courier-Express* cites his skill as a painter and his deeper interest in music. Proficient on the violin and cello, the piano and harmonium, Gay-Tifft had, while a student at Dartmouth, earned dinners at a local inn by organizing and performing in a classical trio. He later worked a year (during the early 1920s) as music critic for the *Boston Herald*, and throughout his life he remained active in the Buffalo music scene, playing for years in a string quartet and maintaining friendships with professional musicians around the world, many of whom were entertained by him and his wife when they came to Buffalo. A niece, Patricia Russ, reports his participation in a longtime chess circle, but stresses her uncle's modesty, describing him as "a private man" who "never talked about himself" and usually declined to perform for others on his Steinway grand piano. Although a member of a prominent Buffalo family that had amassed considerable wealth in the nineteenth century, Gay-Tifft lived modestly, Russ reports, and never seemed much interested in money. She adds that he and Lola Olzewska, whom he married in 1930, had a long and stable marriage but no children.

Robert Frost in 1927

The scope of Gay-Tifft's interests, his evident intelligence and sensitivities, and his responsiveness to Frost himself all suggest why Frost might have been charmed by the young man who interviewed and wrote about him in November of 1927. In any case, Frost was charmed enough to spend some of his treasured privacy in reaching out to someone who believed not only in him but also in so much of what he himself believed.

By December 1927, when he wrote the letter, Frost was well known and much in demand, having won a 1924 Pulitzer Prize for *New Hampshire*, his fourth book. Widely praised by reviewers, the volume boosted Frost's growing reputation and etched in the public imagination the shrewd and supposedly homespun farmer-poet who speaks in its title poem, "New Hampshire." The celebrity Frost enjoyed had resulted not simply from native genius, but from the development of that gift through years of work at writing, self-education, and self-promotion. And, if by 1927 Frost appeared to have left behind the unrecognized poet who, in 1912, had gone to England for a last try at literary success, this younger, unappreciated self resurfaces in his interview with Gay-Tifft and the letter he later writes to that young poet and scholar.

By 1927, Frost had, of course, made good use of the attention he had received on his return to America. Upon docking in New York City on

Fig. 1. Frost seated on a chair. This photograph of Frost was taken on the poet's South Shaftsbury farm by Alton Blackington. Its use by the *Boston Traveler* in 1921 suggests that the image of the farmer-poet was by then an established part of Frost's public identity.
Courtesy of the Blackington Collection/Yankee Publishing Inc., from the Dartmouth College Library

22 February 1915, Frost had bought a copy of the *New Republic* and discovered that *North of Boston*, issued that week by Henry Holt, had been enthusiastically reviewed by Amy Lowell, the *grande dame* of American verse. Later that year, Holt brought out an American edition of *A Boy's Will*, Frost's first London book, and followed, in 1916, with *Mountain*

Interval, Frost's third volume. As Frost's backlog of unpublished poems diminished, and as he capitalized on his celebrity in new ways, the rate of publication naturally slowed.

Meanwhile, responding to myriad requests for interviews, readings, and lectures, Frost began to develop the immensely successful public career that later prompted Allen Ginsberg to call him the "original entrepreneur of poetry" (qtd. in Parini 318). His effort at self-promotion was central to Frost's self-conception as a poet. As he had said in 1913, Frost wanted to be "a poet for all sorts and kinds." To "stand on my legs as a poet and nothing else," Frost had written to John Bartlett from England, "I must get . . . to the general reader who buys books in their thousands" (*Collected Poems, Prose, and Plays* 668).[3] Frost's motives, however, went beyond the economic. The poet who aimed to make "music out of . . . the sound of sense" (664)—to make poetry from the language of ordinary use—wanted to reach those who used that language. Having celebrated the realities of American life and labor, he wanted his poems to be for the people they were about.

At more than one moment, the letter to Gay-Tifft reflects a Robert Frost who does not want his poetry, or really any poetry, to find its audience mainly within the enclaves of privilege. At the same time, it reveals a Frost who by 1927 had given colleges and universities a central, if not a settled, place in his life and career. Having (as a student) left both Dartmouth and Harvard without a degree, and having abandoned a promising teaching career for England in 1912, Frost experienced a relationship to colleges and teaching that was anything but simple. In the decade following his return to America, the complication entered a new dimension. Almost inventing the poet-in-residence role, Frost accepted semester- and year-long contracts with Amherst College, then the University of Michigan, then with Amherst again, meanwhile making shorter visits to other campuses, which by 1927 included Queen's College in Ontario, Wesleyan University, Dartmouth, the newly established Breadloaf School of English, and, as we see from this letter, the University of Buffalo. Honorary degrees from Amherst, Middlebury, Yale, Bowdoin, and Michigan began a list that would eventually number twenty-six and include England's Oxford and Cambridge. Academic appointments and ceremonial occasions were interspersed with what Frost called his "barding around"—the extensive tours for talks and readings that allowed him to test and promote a verse exacting in craftsmanship and challenging in thought, yet vernacular in voice.

By the 1920s, Frost's speaking tours reached beyond New England and the upper Midwest to Louisiana, Texas, and Missouri. And while they paid good fees and increased Frost's audience and book sales, they also cost him dearly. Travel by train was slow, and Frost, who came to love the public platform, extended himself to audiences, often returning home exhausted and ill. Trying to cope with the stresses of his college and university involvements and the family problems that seemed to increase with the years, Frost struggled to find the peace of mind and the freedom from immediate demands that made poetry possible.

This general background should help us to understand and to appreciate much that Frost says in his letter to Gay-Tifft. Dated 16 December 1927, it followed by a month his three-day visit to Buffalo, where he gave two public lectures and met with various small groups at the University. It was at one of these smaller University gatherings that Gay-Tifft interviewed Frost and was clearly moved by his expression of concern for young poets like himself. Gay-Tifft's article for the *Buffalo Arts Journal* reproduced Frost's remarks on a number of his perennial concerns, such as poetry's need for intellectual substance and solid craftsmanship. But Gay-Tifft stressed, more than anything else, Frost's "loyalty to life," which included his effort to share the lessons he had taken directly from experience. "He had found a path through the woods," Gay-Tifft wrote, "and now he wanted to show others the way." Clearly responding to Frost's unpretentious manner, Gay-Tifft presented him as no "needle-nosed aesthete," but as a Johnny Appleseed of verse, who "wanders around the country from one college and university to another, and . . . tries to help young poets through the problems he understands so well." Judging from Gay-Tifft's article, Frost seems, in his Buffalo interview, to have treated Gay-Tifft as an ally in the cause of helping younger poets: "Give them an audience, write an article about them," he quoted Frost as saying, who was acknowledging Gay-Tifft's role as *Arts Journal* editor. "Help the youngsters out," Frost concluded in Gay-Tifft's piece. "Talk about them and publish their work. Never mind about me; I'm all right."

Along with portraying Frost as a seasoned and magnanimous survivor, Gay-Tifft's article registered the Yankee-bard persona that Frost had developed fully by 1927. The article opens with Gay-Tifft reflecting that he would rather "meet with Robert Frost . . . on a quiet hilltop in Vermont with low November clouds fumbling for the distant line of the Green Mountains" than have to interview him in "a stuffy steam-heated . . . university building, bells ringing some idiotic hour, . . . and a nervous time-keeper . . . standing by the window." In his letter to Gay-Tifft, Frost responded to these and other details of the sketch, making clear that he had read the young man's article, as well as a poem titled "Night-Freight" that Gay-Tifft also enclosed. Here, then, is the letter that Frost wrote:

Fig. 2. Frost writing. This photograph, taken by Blackington in the 1930s, shows Frost, as the photographer noted, with the "pad he always uses when writing a poem." Courtesy of the Dartmouth College Library

South Shaftsbury, Vermont
December 16, 1927

Dear Mr. Gay-Tifft:

Sometime you <u>must</u> meet him on a quiet hilltop in Vermont (this is an invitation), if only to repay you for taking so much trouble to reach and understand him in a schoolroom in Buffalo. By your description of November here, I judge you have been here before. When you come again, look in on me, spend some hours with me heedless of bells or whistles. I don't say this to many, because when I am away by myself I mean to be clear away; and I am clear away more months in the year than you might imagine. I dip into colleges for a few weeks a few times a year. (Thanks for ascribing to me so much generosity in dipping in). But nine months out of twelve I am so free from every duty and responsibility that I am often ashamed of myself.

And you mustn't be too hard on Buffalo University in your thoughts. You must make allowances for their just being started out there. The room where I was receiving was make-shift. And you have to remember, I was a new thing and quite a number wanted their chance at me. The conspiracy I'm in is to deformalize education all I can. I might hope that a city college would be a better subject for my schemes than any other for various reasons, but chiefly because it has less college life and so less disciplinary requirements and less social distraction. It might have real intellectual possibilities. It might, you know. You can help out there by breaking down the wall between college life and real life.* One of the things nearest my heart is to make college students expect as much of themselves as if they were not in college at all but out in a world of ideas and art and science. [Inserted in the margin next to this paragraph:] And I liked your poem. This is the main thing. Nothing else matters but our poetry.

This is more of a letter than I write to anyone. I may never write such another. I have to keep away from letters as well as schools most of the time.

Thanks and best wishes
Faithfully yours
Robert Frost

* Involve them in your magazine and art affairs. I'll be back that way sometime and see what you have done. RF

Whatever the hyperbole in his final comment—"This is more of a letter than I write to anyone. I may never write such another."—or in his opening sentence—"Sometime you <u>must</u> meet him on a quiet hilltop in Vermont (this is an invitation)"—Frost makes clear his wish to go beyond courtesy and extend a sense of welcome to one who has welcomed him in spirit. Frost's closing remark—"I have to keep away from letters as well as schools most of the time."—reminds us of what has tempted him beyond his usual limits, for Gay-Tifft had clearly echoed Frost's preference for the "wild free ways of wit and art" over the imaginative confinements of so many school curricula ("The Figure a Poem Makes," *CPPP* 777).[4] In fact, the main substance of Frost's letter lies in his self-confessed "conspiracy . . . to deformalize education," and we notice that early in his letter Frost is careful lest Gay-Tifft credit him with more involvement in college education than he wants to be credited with: "I dip into colleges for a few weeks a few times a year," Frost corrects.

But, if Frost's young admirer had exaggerated Frost's commitment to college education, the fault may be partly Frost's, for schools are a matter about which he remained ambivalent throughout his life, as we might expect from what he said to Sidney Cox in a letter of 17 July 1920 upon resigning from Amherst College in 1920. "I've kicked myself out

Fig. 3. Envelope: The envelope is addressed to Gay-Tifft in Frost's handwriting. The correction in Frost's own hand suggests that the materials Gay-Tifft sent Frost contained more than one address. The two U.S. postmarks indicate that the letter left South Shaftsbury, Vermont, one day after Frost dated it (16 Dec. 1927), and arrived in Buffalo, New York, on 19 December 1927.
Photoreproduction courtesy of Peter S. Russ

of Amherst and settled down to revising old poems when I am not making new ones," Frost wrote: "Teaching is all right, and I don't mean to speak of it with condescension. I shall have another go at it before the last employee is fired. I believe in teaching, but I don't believe in school. Every day I feel bound to save my consistency by advising my pupils to leave school. Then if they insist on coming to school, it is not my fault: I can teach them with a clear conscience" (qtd. in Parini 193).

In school or out, Frost considered the best means of teaching to be poetry, as he makes clear in "Education by Poetry," where he says, "Poetry begins in trivial metaphors . . . and goes on to the profoundest of thinking that we have" (*CPPP* 719). Poetry, Frost would say, teaches us about reality by exposing and revealing the essential form in one's material. In "Some Definitions" (1923), Frost describes his sort of realism not as the kind that renders the potato dirt and all but as the kind that brushes off the dirt to bring out the potato's contours (701). In "The Ax-Helve"—which was, Frost said, "as close as he liked to come 'to

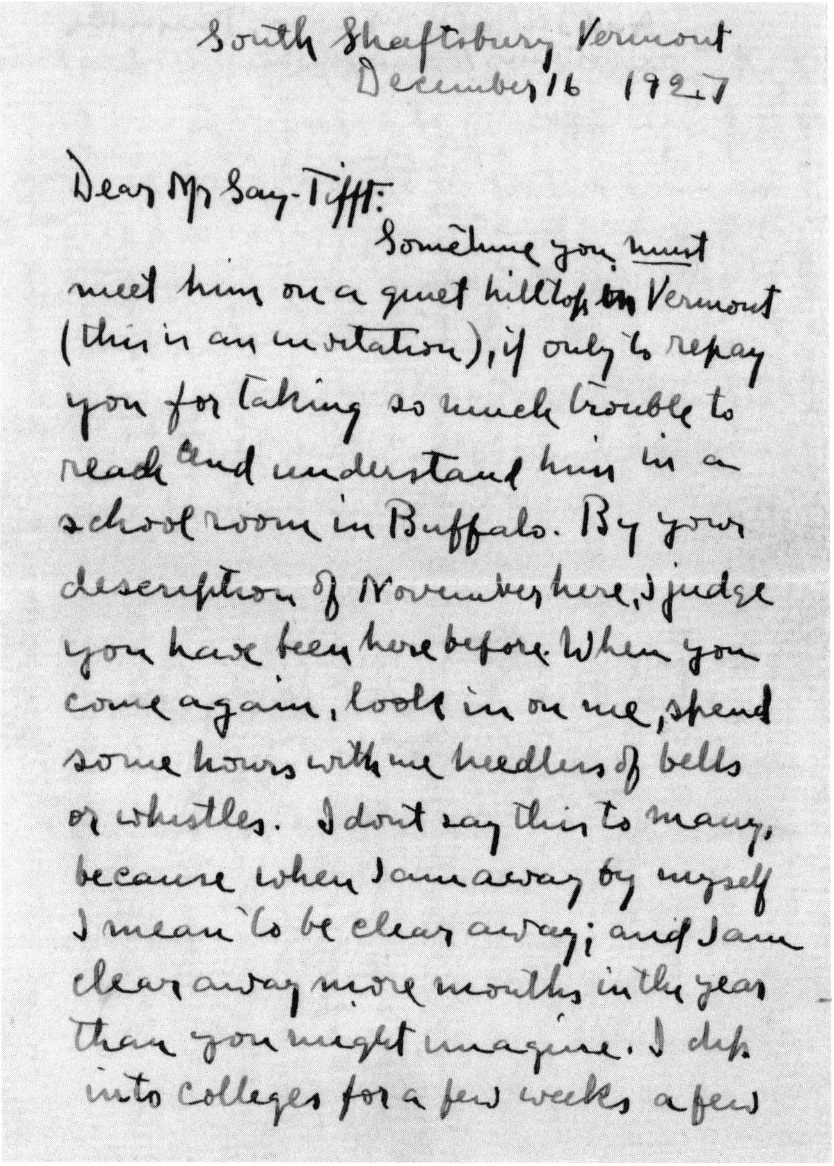

> South Shaftsbury Vermont
> December 16 1927
>
> Dear Mr Say-Tifft:
> Something you must meet him on a quiet hilltop in Vermont (this is an invitation), if only to repay you for taking so much trouble to read and understand him in a school room in Buffalo. By your description of November here, I judge you have been here before. When you come again, look in on me, spend some hours with me heedless of bells or whistles. I don't say this to many, because when I am away by myself I mean to be clear away; and I am clear away more months in the year than you might imagine. I dip into colleges for a few weeks, a few

Fig. 4. Letter, page 1: Frost's use of the full sheet to begin the letter indicates his customary practice. His shift to a folio arrangement as he turns the sheet suggests the realization that his letter was turning into more than the usual courtesy performance, as he acknowledges in his final paragraph: "This is more of a letter than I write to anyone."
Photoreproduction courtesy of Peter S. Russ

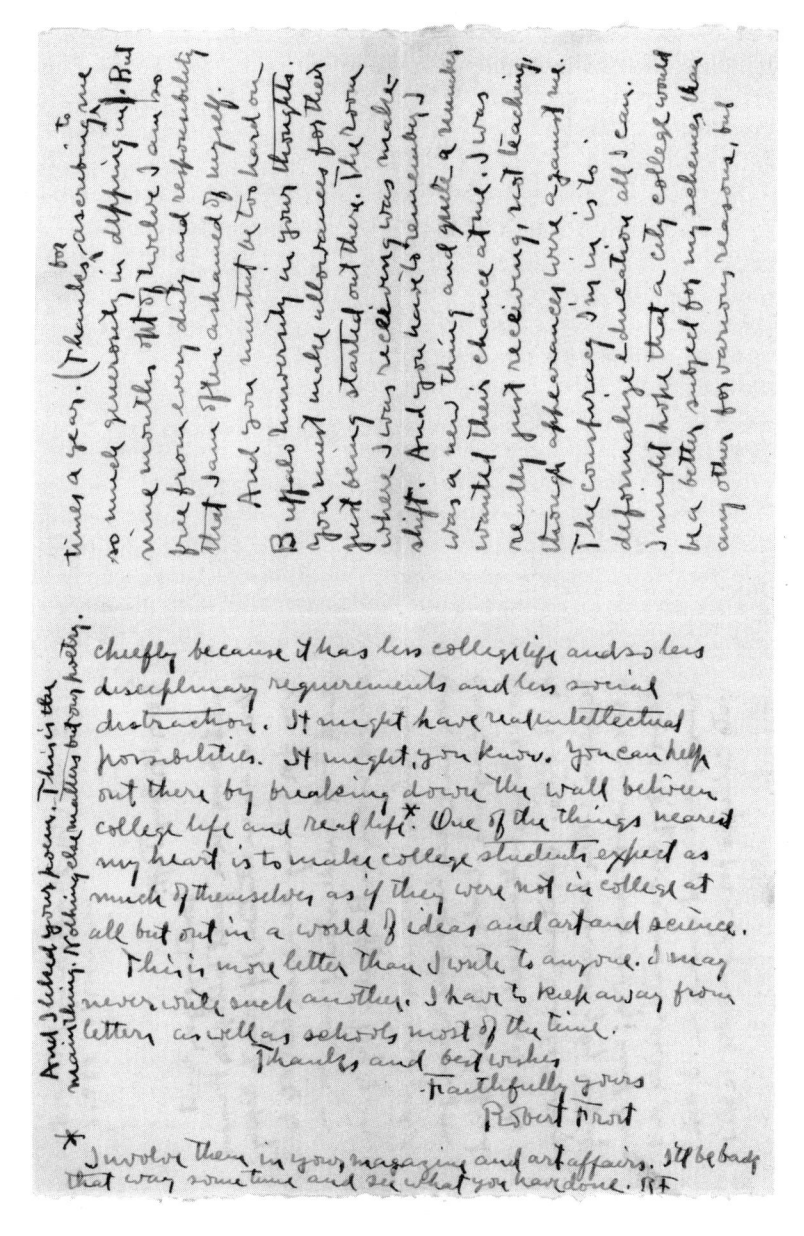

Fig. 5. Letter, pages 2 & 3: On side 2 of the sheet Frost instinctively scales his handwriting to the smaller frame, so that (excluding marginalia) all three pages have nearly identical word counts. Apparently determined not to extend his letter beyond page 3, but not wanting to omit his afterthoughts of advice and encouragement, Frost squeezes them into the side and bottom margins of the final page. Photoreproduction courtesy of Peter S. Russ

writing about art in a work of art . . .'" (Cramer 68)—the protagonist Baptiste reveals "the lines of a good helve" as "native to the grain before the knife / Expressed them, . . . its curves . . . no false curves / Put on it from without." In the poem, Frost deftly extends this principle from poetry to education. "[W]hat we talked about was knowledge," Frost's narrator says, "Baptiste on his defense about the children / He kept from school, or did his best to keep— / Whatever school and children and our doubts / Of laid-on education had to do / With the curves of his ax helves . . ." (*CPPP* 175–76). When the narrator wonders aloud "[What] . . . our doubts / Of laid-on education had to do / With the curves of his ax-helves," he calls our attention to Baptiste's rejection of the standardized form imposed on two of the things he cares about most: ax-helves and his children. To him, and to Frost, the uniform curve of machine-cut helves is like the education that the state would "lay on" every child as if it were mortar on a course of bricks. Each is suspect because each is an imposition in every sense of the word. The good educator, like the good woodcarver and the good poet, respects his material. To ignore the native grain, whether of a hickory branch or a student's mind, is to violate its nature. As if continuing the analogy to wood, Frost would later define "[t]he best educated person" as "the one who has been matured at just the proper rate. Seasoned but not kiln dried." ("Poetry and School," *CPPP* 807).

For Frost, "laid-on education" was part of the increasing standardization and conformity that, throughout his lifetime, he deplored in the country as a whole, especially in his beloved New England, where he knew the losses most intimately. "Originality and initiative are what I ask for in my country," he says in "The Figure a Poem Makes." There, again, he contrasts the artist's way of discovery—"as it happens in and out of books"—to that of the schoolboy, "who can tell you what he knows in the order in which he learned it" (*CPPP* 776)—on assignment, one assumes. That Frost does not blame the schoolboy he makes clear in his "Introduction" to a Dartmouth collection of student verse called *The Arts Anthology*: "The poet, as everyone knows, must strike his individual note sometime between the ages of fifteen and twenty-five. He may hold it a long time, or a short time, but it is then he must strike it or never. School and college have been conducted with the almost express purpose of keeping him busy with something else till the danger of his ever creating anything is past" (*CPPP* 710).

We can only guess whether Frost's casual style of teaching at Amherst and Michigan and, later, at Harvard, was arrived at more to benefit himself or to benefit his students. Frost would have felt that the question missed the point. Frost would assume that his approach—part reading and part rumination, part dialogue and largely monologue, part plan but mainly improvisation—would, by suiting the poet he was, encourage the poet in each of his students. In any case, by imposing few requirements and following his own bent, he left the students largely to theirs.

A casual style could not have been as much the case in Frost's first formal teaching appointment at Pinkerton Academy in 1907, which had to meet different demands to pay its bills. There Frost developed an ambitious curriculum for his students, including thirty to fifty "themes, written and oral," in each of the high-school years. Yet, even here we find Frost characteristically locating the final measure of learning inside his students. "The general aim of the course in English," the written document begins, "is twofold: to bring our students under the *influence* of the great books, and to teach them the *satisfaction* of superior speech." One can only speculate how such outcomes as "influence" and "satisfaction" would be received or defined in a climate of uniform standards and assessments. The question, it would seem, was of little concern to Frost. Even in Year IV of his Pinkerton curriculum, which lists "College requirements" first under "Reading," Frost writes, "Especially in this year a point is made of re-reading a great many selections remembered with pleasure from previous years" (*CPPP* 662–63). "Remembered with pleasure": the phrase is positively Wordsworthian. More than thirty years later, in "The Figure a Poem Makes," Frost would say that any poem written is "a trick poem and no poem at all" unless it "begins in delight and ends in wisdom" (*CPPP* 776). He seems to have thought that, to end in wisdom, even education must begin in pleasure.

Delight, discovery; knowledge "in and out of books." The "real intellectual possibilities," says Frost to Gay-Tifft, lie in "breaking down the wall between college life and real life," adding in the margin, "Nothing else matters but our poetry." This bit of hyperbole is just the overstatement needed to insist on the "originality and initiative" that Frost wants for his country. Poetry is what matters because metaphor, poetry's heart and backbone, demands both the imagination and the discrimination that is the aim of real education. "All metaphor," says Frost in "Education by Poetry," "breaks down somewhere. That's the beauty of it. It is touch and go with metaphor, and until you have lived with it long enough you don't know when it is going. You don't know how much you can get out of it and when it will cease to yield" (*CPPP* 723). Metaphor, Frost insists, is "enthusiasm taken through the prism of the intellect, . . . enthusiasm passed through an idea" (719), paralleling the combination of delight and wisdom that Frost associates both with real learning and with real poetry. In the same essay, he notes, "We still ask boys in college to think, as in the nineties, but we seldom tell them what thinking means; we seldom tell them it is just putting this and that together; it is just saying one thing in terms of another. To tell them this is to set their feet on the first rung of a ladder the top of which sticks through the sky" (722).

This metaphor of ascent conveys Frost's sense of the possibilities that education can open up if conducted poetically. "Education by Poetry"—a talk delivered in 1930—represents a moment of illumination in which Frost was able to capture the complex unity of his overlapping vocations as poet and teacher. Anticipating "Education by Poetry" by three years, the letter to Gay-Tifft expresses the same dual commitment while alluding to the conflicts and the balancing act that such a commitment requires. "I have to keep away from . . . schools most of the time," Frost confides. But not for too long, it seems, and never so far away that he couldn't return for another try at his own sort of education.

NOTES

1. The letter was made available by Gay-Tifft's grandnephew Peter S. Russ. Russ, thinking it might be of interest to scholars, had shown it to Richard Kopley, his former English professor and coeditor of *Resources for American Literary Study*, who invited me to introduce and comment on the document. I am grateful to Mr. Russ for permission to quote the letter and for providing photographs of the letter and envelope (see figs. 3–5).

My thanks also to the Blackington Collection/Yankee Publishing, Inc. and to Dartmouth College Library for permission to use the two photographs of Frost (see figs. 1 and 2); to the Rauner Special Collections at Dartmouth for supplying them; and especially to Joshua D. Shaw, for his generous and expert assistance in finding and transmitting these images.

2. Except for the information specifically attributed to a niece, Patricia Russ, the biographical facts about Gay-Tifft have been gathered from articles by H. Katherine Smith in the *Buffalo Evening News* and by Karen Brady in the *Buffalo Courier-Express*.

3. Whenever possible, quotations from Frost's verse or prose are taken from this volume. Subsequent references to it will be abbreviated as *CPPP*.

4. This short essay served as a preface for the 1939 and all later editions of Frost's *Collected Poems*.

WORKS CITED

Brady, Karen. "A Patriot Will Be Missing on the Fourth of July." *Buffalo Evening News* 30 June 1982: C2.

Cramer, Jeffrey. *Robert Frost among His Poems: A Literary Companion to the Poet's Own Biographical Contexts and Associations.* Jefferson, NC: McFarland, 1996.

Frost, Robert. *Collected Poems, Prose, and Plays.* Ed. Richard Poirier and Mark Richardson. New York: Lib. of America, 1995.

———. Letter to Eugene Gay-Tifft. 16 Dec. 1927. Private collection of Peter S. Russ.

Gay-Tifft, Eugene. "A Chat with Robert Frost." *Buffalo Arts Journal* 9 (1927): 562.

Parini, Jay. *Robert Frost; A Life.* New York: Holt, 1999.

"Poetry Speaks of the Mood Itself Says Robert Frost." *The Bee* 18 Nov. 1927: 1.

Russ, Patricia Telephone conversation with author. 2 Sept. 2003.

Smith, H. Katherine. "Men You Ought to Know." *Buffalo Courier-Express* 28 Feb. 1932, sec. 7: 12.

———. "Tifft Honors Family Prominent in Affairs of Buffalo." *Buffalo Courier-Express* 25 June 1939, sec. 2: 3.

Tragic Stasis:
Love, War, and the Composition of Hemingway's "Big Two-Hearted River"

HILARY K. JUSTICE
Illinois State University

> . . . when you are wounded
> or a little out of your head
> or in love with someone
> the surroundings are sometimes removed and they only come in at
> certain times
> —from the manuscript of *A Farewell to Arms*

Critics agree that Ernest Hemingway's "Big Two-Hearted River: Part I" and "Part II," first published in the Spring 1925 issue of *This Quarter* and collected in *In Our Time* (1925), is a well-crafted, compelling story. Most criticism foregrounds its protagonist, Nick Adams, by attempting to solve the mystery presumably posed by the story: What is causing Nick's unspecified internal preoccupation? The story's earliest critics usually identified Nick's behavior as shell shock, concluding that the story concerns "the war—and only the war" (Cowley, Young, et al., cited in Smith, *Reader's Guide* 88–99). In response to this critical uniformity, Smith asks, "But what if it was not that [the war], or not primarily that?" (*Reader's Guide* 98–99). Several psychoanalytic critics have since identified Nick's behavior as a response to "trauma" (Sempreora 19), and, accordingly, attempted to diagnose Nick by specifying the trauma (whether by locating it in Hemingway's own childhood [e.g., Sempreora 19, after Lynn 105] or in the psychological linking of his wounding at Fossalta with his confused partial recognition of "the onset of his fetishism and depression" [Eby 195]). An alternative methodological approach—the collation of the story's prepublished and published versions combined with inquiry into its context of composition—suggests recasting Smith's metacritical question: But what if the story does not pose a mystery?

Certainly, Nick's internal preoccupation drives Nick, and, equally certainly, Hemingway trusts his readers "to see more . . . than Nick himself realizes" (Phelan 66). However, what readers can see in the published story is not *what* Nick is avoiding, but *that* he is avoiding; readers see Nick enacting very consciously his desire not to realize—or to think, or to remember, or to write. Speculation regarding whatever it is that Nick is avoiding to think about is unavoidable; the story provokes a reader's curiosity. Nonetheless, whatever it may be that provokes Nick's thoughts, in the story the avoidance is all, for the thoughts themselves function as what Alfred Hitchcock called "a MacGuffin" (a device that drives the plot but, in the final analysis, is beside the point).[1]

The manner in which Hemingway constructed "Nick trying not to think" adds another possibility to the list of things Nick might not be thinking about because, in crafting the story, Hemingway drew upon his own memories of a similar fishing trip. On that trip, Hemingway was thinking (or trying not to think) about his broken heart—a matter of perhaps greater import than a war wound to the teenager he had been and to the writer he was (if not to the person he would eventually become). Nick's stated avoidance of "writing" suggests much about Hemingway's own creative process—not only how he transformed lived experience into writing, as Nick must avoid doing in the story, but also what kinds of things might trigger the beginnings of stories: those catalysts that the reader must perceive as triggers even as Nick consciously avoids realizing them as such. Finally, the crafting of key sections of the story suggests and confirms what Hemingway's artistic objectives were in writing it. At the time Hemingway chose to end *In Our Time*, his first book published in the United States, with "Big Two-Hearted River," the story represented his best effort to meet what would become a lifelong challenge: to capture and convey things that no writer had captured before, things that presented a technical challenge to him. Near the end of his career, Hemingway described this challenge by analogy: a painter is trying to capture the light in the water at the change of the tide (in chapter 3 of the unpublished "Garden of Eden" typescript [KL/EH 422.1/4]).[2] By capturing qualities of light in the water—a shadow, a flash of sunlight—he expresses the inexpressible: a human response to mourning.

While on the fishing trip that was to inspire the story a few years later, Hemingway was mourning—the loss of love, the loss of innocence, the loss of invulnerability, the loss of some transcendental surety rent from him simultaneously by love and war. In 1924, when he began writing the story, Hemingway was beginning to mourn analogous losses as the first blush receded from his first marriage. The deliberate stasis that characterized mourning for Hemingway is what he represented in the story; what caused it for Nick is impossible to determine from any of the story's versions.

Hemingway's notes on the binder that held his 1924 "Big Two-Hearted River" manuscripts indicate that he both did and did not follow his original plan for the story. The notes, written hurriedly,[3] appear on the cover, labeled "Black River Manuscript" and "Manuscripts—Big Two Hearted River—A Story":

> He thinks gets uncomfortable
> restless, tries to stop
> thinking, more uncomfortable
> and restless, the thinking
> goes on; speeds up, can't
> shake it—comes home to
> camp—hot before storm—
> storm—in morning creek
> flooded, shifts to the railroad. (KL/EH 281; original lineation preserved)

Although there is no literal storm in the story, a kind of storm organizes the story's earliest draft (a manuscript fragment, "They Got off the train at Seney" [KL/EH 279], and the first full manuscript draft [KL/EH 274]). Nick's internal preoccupation—whatever it is—probably provides the metaphoric tenor for which the storm was likely to be the vehicle in Hemingway's original vision.

How Hemingway crafted the presence of Nick's preoccupation reveals much about his own preoccupation at the time, a preoccupation that comprises the subtext of "Big Two-Hearted River." Several key passages in the manuscript, all concerning trout rising and the sun on the water, connect "Big Two-Hearted River" to three other works: "A Very Short Story" (1924), "Indian Camp" (1924), and *A Farewell to Arms* (1929). Considered together, this set of works reveals that, while Nick's preoccupation may remain unspecified, Hemingway's, in writing the story, was love.

What literal presence the war has in the story survives only symbolically, and only in the earliest fragment of what eventually became "Big Two-Hearted River: Part I" (KL/EH 279). In this manuscript fragment, a first-person account of a fishing trip that Hemingway took with two friends in the late summer of 1919, he located the war in a burnt-out hotel basement in Seney, Michigan:

> The fire had effaced the town. After a winter the snow melting and the rains of spring and summer the thirteen saloons had left not a trace. The stone foundations of the Mansion House Hotel were almost level with the ground. The lime stone chipped and split by the fire and was now washed smooth. They Al went over and looked into the basement filled pit where the hotel had been. There was twisted iron work, melted too hard to rust. In a heap beside Thrown together were four gun barrels, the ^pitted and twisted by the heat^ in one the cartridges had melted in the magazine and formed a swelling ^bulge^ of lead and copper. (KL/EH 279, 2–3; sigla added: deletions ^insertions^)

The description of the gun barrels provides an evocative image that reveals the connection in Hemingway's mind between the story and the war. Hemingway's leg wounds, from shrapnel, were healed by 1919, but for the rest of his life, shrapnel would occasionally work its way to his skin, forming subcutaneous swellings or bulges.

Even by the first full-length draft of the story (KL/EH 274), the shape-distorting cartridges, melted gun barrels, charred subterranean pit, and the characters' proximity to all three, were long gone, the fragment buried in Hemingway's papers as deeply as he buried the war in the narrative itself. The image would perhaps be unremarkable, even trivial, were it not for its return in *A Farewell to Arms* (and again, later, in "The Snows of Kilimanjaro" [1936; *Short Stories* 68]). The cartridges, again making their outer coverings "bulge," appear in the opening description of marching troops in *A Farewell to Arms* (4; also KL/EH 64.1.4):

> . . . their rifles were wet and under their capes the two leather cartridge boxes on the front of the belts, grey leather boxes heavy with the packs of clips of thin, long 6.5 mm. cartridges, bulged forward under the capes so that the men, passing on the road, marched as though they were six months gone with child.

The first manuscript draft of this passage shows that Hemingway revised very heavily around the "bulging" cartridges, but got the key word on the first try:

> . . . the two big leather cartridge boxes on the front of the belts, grey leather boxes ^heavy^ with the packs of clips of six ᐃlongᐃ t̶h̶i̶n̶ ̶l̶o̶n̶g̶ n̶o̶s̶e̶d̶ ̶s̶h̶e̶l̶l̶s̶ ^8 mm. shells^, bulged u̶n̶d̶e̶r̶ forward under the capes a̶s̶ t̶h̶o̶u̶g̶h̶ ᐃ^they^ᐃ t̶h̶e̶ ̶m̶e̶n̶ ̶w̶e̶r̶e̶ ̶g̶o̶i̶n̶g̶ ̶t̶o̶ ̶h̶a̶v̶e̶ ̶b̶a̶b̶i̶e̶s̶.̶ so t̶h̶e̶ ̶m̶e̶n̶ ^that the men^ ^passing on the road^ marched as though t̶h̶e̶y̶ ᐃheᐃ ^they^ were six months gone with child. (KL/EH 64.1.4–5; sigla added: d̶e̶l̶e̶t̶i̶o̶n̶s̶ ᐃdeleted insertionsᐃ ^insertions^)

The phrase "six months gone with child" quite obviously foreshadows Catherine's fatal pregnancy in the "love" side of this love-and-war novel. The origin of the passage in the "Big Two-Hearted River" fragment, which describes a male-bonding fishing trip in 1919, is the first of several indications of a similar love-war connection in the earlier story. In March of the fishing trip year, Hemingway had received the now-famous "Dear John" letter from Agnes von Kurowsky, the nurse of his World War I injuries, his first love, and the woman who would figure by name, "Ag," in the first appearances of "A Very Short Story" (in *In Our Time* [1925]) and as the primary model for Catherine Barkley in *A Farewell to Arms* in 1929. In 1924, when he first drafted both fragment and story of "Big Two-Hearted River,"[4] Hemingway had just spent a week away from his wife, Hadley, and their infant son,[5] trying to get the peace he needed in order to write. The lost days of his first love affair, about which he had just written, must have seemed peaceful by comparison, especially to the new father living in a cramped, noisy apartment over the sawmill at 113 rue Notre-Dame-des-Champs in Paris; certainly, he missed the peace of fishing with his relatively uncomplicated male friends, despite the broken heart he had been trying to heal during their 1919 trip.[6]

The first complete manuscript draft of "Big Two-Hearted River" (originally titled "Black River" despite the story's eventual setting on the Fox River near Seney) testifies that Hemingway reworked several key passages that combine to establish the energy Nick must expend to achieve a kind of emotional stasis, to avoid his "need for thinking, the need to write, other needs" (*Short Stories* 210). The most extensive revisions to the manuscript draft occur in the "trout at the bridge" passage,[7] near the beginning of the story.

The passage, as published, appears below:

> Nick . . . watched the trout keeping themselves steady in the current with wavering fins. As he watched them they changed their positions by quick angles, only to hold steady in the fast water again. Nick watched them a long time.
>
> He watched them holding themselves with their noses into the current, many trout in deep, fast moving water, slightly distorted as he watched far down through the glassy convex surface of the pool, its surface pushing and swelling smooth against the resistance of the log-driven piles of the bridge. At the bottom of the pool were the big trout. Nick did not see them at first. Then he saw them at the bottom of the pool, big trout looking to hold themselves on the gravel bottom in a varying mist of gravel and sand, raised in spurts by the current.
>
> Nick looked down into the pool from the bridge. It was a hot day. A kingfisher flew up the stream. It was a long time since Nick had looked into a stream and seen trout. They were very satisfactory. As the shadow of the kingfisher moved up the stream, a big trout shot upstream in a long angle, only his shadow marking the angle, then lost his shadow as he came through the surface of the water, caught the sun, and then, as he went back into the stream under the surface, his shadow seemed to float down the stream with the current, unresisting, to his post under the bridge where he tightened facing up into the current.
>
> Nick's heart tightened as the trout moved. He felt all the old feeling. (*Short Stories* 209–10)

The first draft is much shorter:

> Nick . . . watched the trout keeping themselves steady in the current with wavering fins. As he watched them they changed their positions by quick angles only to hold steady in the fast water again ~~their fins wavering~~ with ~~the~~ quick, vibrating fins. ~~motion.~~
> Nick watched them a long time. ^He watched them hold them hold themselves steady where the^ ^insert^ ~~It had been years since he had seen trout. As he watched a big trout shot upstream in a long angle burst through the surface of the water and~~ then ~~seemed to float dow back down stream with the current to its post under the bridge. Nick's heart tightened as the trout moved. He felt all the old thrill. This remained at any rate.~~ (KL/EH 247, 2–4; sigla added: ~~deletions~~ ~~deletions within larger deleted section~~ ^insertions^)

Hemingway crossed much of this out, and, marking an insertion point ("^insert^," above) after the stuttering "hold them hold themselves," substituted a three-page insertion (the only insertion of complete pages in the 100+-page manuscript):

> He watched them holding themselves ~~steady~~ with their noses ~~upstream~~ ^into the current^, many trout in ~~a pool of~~ ^deep,^ fast ~~flowing~~ moving water, slightly distorted as he watched far down through the glassy ~~top swell~~ ^convex surface^ to the ~~stream as it~~ ^pool, its surface^ pushing and swelling smooth against the resistance of the log driven piles of the bridge. At the bottom of the pool were the big trout. Nick did not see them at first. Then he saw them at the bottom of the pool, ~~dim in the water light~~ ^.^ Big trout looking to hold themselves ~~in~~ ^on^ the gravel bottom in a varying mist of gravel and sand raised in spurts by the current.
> Nick looked down into the pool from the bridge. It was a hot day. A Kingfisher flew up the stream. It was a long time since Nick had looked into a stream and seen trout. They were very satisfactory. As the shadow of the kingfisher moved up the stream a big trout shot up stream in a long angle, only his shadow marking the ~~shadow~~ angle, then lost his shadow as he came through the surface of the water, caught the sun, and then as he ~~re~~ went back into the ~~water~~ ^stream^ under the surface his shadow seemed to float ~~back~~ down the stream with the current, unresisting, to his post under the bridge where he tightened, facing, up stream.
> Nick's heart tightened as the trout moved. He felt all the old ~~thrill. This remained~~ feeling.
> He turned and looked down the stream. (KL/EH 274, insert to p. 3, 1–3; sigla added: ~~deletions~~ ^insertions^)

This insertion adds the kingfisher and the sun, as well as a "mist" that will figure later, to the "jumping trout" moment; the presence of a shadow that is "unresisting" emphasizes the energy the trout under the bridge must expend to maintain their stasis, soldier-like, at their "posts"[8] (an idea that may have occurred to him as he repeated "hold them hold themselves"). The interpretive significance of this moment is not immediately apparent. However, the "distorted" surface of the water and the trout breaching that surface for a brief, shining moment in which it "caught the sun" combine with several moments in the story to indicate that Nick, like the trout under the bridge, is expending a tremendous amount of energy to keep some thought (or memory, however distorted by time[9]) buried beneath the surface, beneath his consciousness.

After this early moment, Nick is "happy" (*Short Stories* 210); although no explanation is given for this (and the need for one is not obvious), later moments in the story indicate retrospectively that his happiness may derive from the fact that, even as his heart "tightened," he has managed not to interpret the moment, not to see in it significance beyond its visual beauty, not to "write" it in his head.

What he is not writing and not thinking about is, however, the subject that has inspired much if not all of the critical response to the story. Nick's visceral identification with the trout (in the writing, if—determinedly—not in his own mind) is underscored by the repetition of the word "tighten": his heart "tightens" as the trout "tightens" under the bridge. On one level, surely, it is a sublime moment; on another, darker level, his potential identification with the trout comes to symbolize the problem he must avoid. The trout is simultaneously both hunter (of the sun) and hunted (linguistically, if not literally, by the kingfisher; there is some irony at play here: kingfishers are small birds and thus can pose no physical threat to mature trout).[10] In Nick's successfully rejected memories, he, too, was both hunter and hunted—a complication Hemingway crafts deliberately in this passage and develops later in the story.

The sun in this passage is one clue to the fact that Nick's imminent memories may not exclusively concern having been wounded in battle, as critics have suggested, although the flashes of World War I artillery were, like the sun, blinding. In the first chapter of *A Farewell to Arms*, a comparison is drawn between artillery flashes and lightning, even though the narrative insists that "the nights were cool and there was not the feeling of a storm coming" (KL/EH 64.1, 2). The storm to which Hemingway alludes in his plan for "Big Two-Hearted River" may be the very storm that Frederic Henry does not sense in the opening of *A Farewell to Arms*: it breaks later in the novel, both literally—it rains frequently, during crucial moments—and figuratively, as Catherine and their baby die.[11]

Hemingway's shrapnel wounds were not his only battle scars. His first war and his first physical wounding coincided with his first love and his first heartbreak. If his brief love for Agnes—in which he, as a much younger man, was as much out of his element as the trout out of water—is figured here in fiction as "catching the sun," Hemingway's revisions to the "trout at the bridge" passage may provide at least a partial answer to Smith's question, "But what if it was not [the war], or not primarily that?" (*Reader's Guide* 98–99).

The connection of Agnes to the sun, especially were it more obvious, seems but a rehashing of a centuries-old metaphor (e.g., Romeo's lovestruck line "It is the east, and Juliet is the sun" [2.2.3][12]). However, Hemingway did figure his memories of Agnes thus, as is retrospectively apparent from the evolution of "A Very Short Story," begun in 1924 and finally revised to its current version for the second edition of *In Our Time* in 1930. In the first versions of the story, the unnamed protagonist's love for the character "Ag" (Hemingway's nickname for Agnes) provides the light in the literal darkness of the military hospital and in the figurative darkness of war; in the 1930 version of the story, Hemingway, by then aware of the legal consequences of using real people as bases for characters, changed "Ag" to "Luz," which is Spanish for "light."[13]

The jumping trout and the sun return in two later passages in the "Big Two-Hearted River" manuscript and published text (once in a later section of what became "Part I," and once early in what became "Part II"). After the "trout at the bridge" passage, Nick turns his back on the trout, the kingfisher, and the memories in whose current he has managed (for now) to hold himself steady, and, leaving the blasted landscape of what was once Seney behind, moves, "tired and very hot" (212), toward the woods, where the country is "alive again . . . [keeping] his direction by the sun" (*Short Stories* 212).

Between the "trout at the bridge" passage and Nick's nap in the shade, Hemingway emphasized the sun by inserting references to it in every other paragraph:

^leaving the burned town behind in the heat^ (KL/EH 274, 5)

^sweating in the sun^ (KL/EH 274, 7)

in the ^shimmering^ heat light over the ~~rolling~~ plain. If he looked too hard they were gone. But if he only half looked they were there, ~~the far off hills of the height of land~~ (KL/EH 274, 9) (sigla added: ~~deletions~~ ~~^deleted insertions^~~ ^insertions^)

The two original sun references are subtly emphasized by these additions. In the first, Nick, like the trout at the bridge, "catches" the sun: "Far off to the left ~~was the line of the river made a line of greener~~ was the line of the river. Nick followed it with his eye and caught glints of the water in the sun" (KL/EH 274, 8). The second also underscores the similarity of Nick's efforts to the trout's: Although Nick initially "knew where he was from the position of the river," like the trout in the current (KL/EH 9–10), he later "kept his direction by the sun," like the leaping trout, and the trout that will rise again later in the story (KL/EH 274, 13).

After his nap in an "island of pine trees" (*Short Stories* 213)[14] in the otherwise "shadeless pine plain" (212), Nick sleeps through sunset, awakening when "the sun [is] nearly down" (213) and,

> before he mounted to a piece of high ground to make camp, Nick looked down the river at the trout rising. They were rising to insects come from the swamp on the other side of the stream when the sun went down. The trout jumped out of water to take them. While Nick walked through the little stretch of meadow alongside the stream, trout had jumped high out of water. Now as he looked down the river, the insects must be settling on the surface, for the trout were feeding steadily all down the stream. As far down the long stretch as he could see, the trout were rising, making circles all down the surface of the water, as though it were starting to rain. (213–14)

Collation of the manuscript version of this "trout rising" passage against the proofs for the story's first publication (*This Quarter* [Spring 1925; Hanneman #C165, 144]) reveals an early, pre-proof-stage editorial intervention by someone other than Hemingway. There are two words and several deletion marks on the manuscript that match neither his handwriting nor the ink he used in drafting and in his own same-draft emendations.[15] In this brief but significant editorial revision, two phrases inviting overt comparison between Nick and the trout were altered to make that comparison depend less on signposting and more on the reader's perception of synchronicity:

> Nick looked down ~~the~~ the river at the trout rising. They were rising to insects ~~th The insects had settled on the settled on the surface of the water when the~~
>   ~~The insects had~~ come from the swamp on the other side of the stream when the sun went down. The trout ~~had~~ jumped out of water to take them. ~~Just as~~ ^While^ Nick ~~had been walking~~ walked through the little stretch of meadow alongside ~~the~~ the stream ~~the~~ trout had ~~been~~ jump~~ing~~ed high out of water. (KL/EH 274, 21–23; sigla added: ~~deletions~~ ^insertions^)

The deletion of the line "The insects had settled on the surface of the water when the The insects had" is not Hemingway; the effect is one of tightening, strengthening the connection of the rising trout to the swamp that will figure prominently later in the story (especially at the end of "Part II," when Nick muses that the fishing would be "tragic" [*Short Stories* 231] in the swamp, which also ends the story [232]). The substitution of "While" for "Just as" (and the verb tense change thus required) is likewise not Hemingway; the effect here is to render Nick's connection to the trout less imminent: "Just as Nick did X, the trout did Y" invites identification; "While Nick was X, the trout were Y" preserves this possibility but does not require it. Both emendations echo the effects of Hemingway's own emendations throughout the manuscript.

Whoever edited Hemingway's manuscript must have had access not only to the manuscript in the late spring of 1924 but also to the uncorrected proofs (which Hemingway received in December 1924): the handwriting on both documents matches. In all likelihood, this someone was his wife, Hadley, to whom Young and Mann (who first catalogued Hemingway's papers) attribute suggestions on the surviving *This Quarter* proofs (which were not used for setting copy). The suggestions on the proofs, as Paul Smith notes in *A Reader's Guide*, completely disregarded Hemingway's style; Hemingway ignored them—including the suggestion to change the word "noses" to "snouts," which would by proximity yield the unfortunate phrase "trout snouts" (KL/EH 280).[16] The emendations to the manuscript, in the same hand as the later proof suggestions, were as astute as the later suggestions were bizarre.

The cumulative effect of these editorial emendations and those made by Hemingway himself is to distance Nick from a too-conscious identification of his memories with the rising trout. These emendations achieve a very subtle effect: the reader must perceive what Nick resists perceiving. These "trout rising passage" emendations thus have the opposite effect of those in the "trout at the bridge" passage on Nick (who, in his relief at not interpreting the moment as one of identification, reveals his evasion of perception, not just as evasion, but as deliberate evasion). The "trout rising" emendations have, conversely, the same effect as the "trout at the bridge" emendations on the reader, who must perceive that identification for the story to work. In other words, the effect of the "trout rising" emendations is to bury the Nick/memory/trout identification just below the surface of his consciousness, where the identification remains visible to the reader, but is rendered invisible to Nick himself.

Later in the same passage, Hemingway himself revised the sentence in which the rising trout make circles on the water:

> . . . the trout were rising making circles ~~in the water~~ as ^all down the surface of the water as though^ though it were starting to rain, ~~except that the feeding deliberately and with tempo.~~ (KL/EH 274, 23–24; sigla

added: ~~deletions~~ ^^~~deleted insertions~~^^ ~~deletions within longer deleted sections~~ ^insertions^)

The published version reads: ". . . the trout were rising, making circles all down the surface of the water, as though it were starting to rain" (*Short Stories* 216). This version loses both the purpose of their rising and the adverbial phrase "deliberately and with tempo," further veiling the connection between Nick and the trout. It is obvious that Nick does everything in the story deliberately, carefully holding steady his internal tempo. The adverbial phrases are unnecessary; the visual image in the emended passage is strong enough to imply the same.

This passage contains several images that evoke the end of "Indian Camp," to which Hemingway would refer by name in the section of the "Big Two-Hearted River" manuscript that was separately (and only posthumously) published as "On Writing" (in *The Nick Adams Stories* [1972]). At the end of "Indian Camp," the first story in *In Our Time* ("Big Two-Hearted River" was the last), Nick and his father

> were seated in the boat, Nick in the stern, his father rowing. The sun was coming up over the hills. A bass jumped, making a circle in the water. Nick trailed his hand in the water. It felt warm in the sharp chill of the morning.
>
> In the early morning on the lake sitting in the stern of the boat with his father rowing, he felt quite sure that he would never die. (*Short Stories* 95)

At the end of this first story, Nick is anything but deliberate, anything but uncertain, anything but threatened. The sun on the water is sunrise; he is not hunting the bass; the water is warm and the air is chilly. In the last story in the collection, Nick is deliberate, uncertain, and threatened; the sunset on the water (which Hemingway will address overtly in "Part II") is "blinding," the water is "cold" in the heat of the day, and Nick has returned from the war conscious and certain of his mortality. "Indian Camp" ends with a father rowing his son in the morning sun; the climax of *A Farewell to Arms* begins with a father rowing his wife and unborn son at night, in the rain. Both are moments in which the protagonists know love. In between the writing of the two, Nick is alone and trying to resist feeling pain at love's loss.

The connections between "A Big Two-Hearted River" and *A Farewell to Arms* continue. In the next section of the manuscript, Hemingway emphasizes the mist rising in the swamp, drawing the reader's attention again to things "rising" and to the "swamp" (both of which are connected to Nick's memories and thoughts) by repetition. On page 36 of the manuscript, as Nick contemplates his dinner, "Across the river in the swamp, in the almost dark, he saw a mist rising."[17] Two paragraphs later, on page 39, Hemingway inserted another reference to the mist: "The other bank was in the white mist." The mist rises just before Nick's memories of his friend Hopkins surface, those of which he finally allows himself to make a story. The rising mist, which echoes the mist in which the trout held themselves in the inserted "trout at the bridge" material, will also figure prominently in the opening section of *A Farewell to Arms*, just after there is "not the feeling of a storm coming," in the same sentence in which the marching soldiers' cartridge boxes bulge under their capes (4). The swamp in "Big Two-Hearted River," in which Nick locates tragedy and which he delays exploring for other "days coming," begins to figure as a representation of Hemingway's memories of Agnes, which he would eventually revisit to write *A Farewell to Arms*.

The fact that Nick is avoiding perception in order to forestall his need to write is again made overt toward the end of "Part I," when he temporarily allows himself enough mental relaxation to free-associate between making coffee and remembering his friend Hopkins, and to laugh when he realizes that while free-associating he has subconsciously been crafting a well-formed story. Although he had been deliberately avoiding such memory triggers, such story catalysts, all day, Nick could laugh because he had made it to day's end. As Hemingway's emendations accumulate, they continue to underscore the similarity between the trout at the bridge expending energy to maintain stasis in the current and Nick expending energy to preserve his emotional equilibrium. In the manuscript draft of this moment, Nick's laughter concludes with the line "He had been happy all day" (KL/EH 274, 30). A same-draft (and probably same-sitting) emendation added a double negative, which contributes to the distancing of Nick from what he has been avoiding; Hemingway added "NOT" and "un-" to the line, resulting in the published version, "He had not been unhappy all day." Both versions continue, "But this was a different feeling." Neither his thoughts of Hopkins, triggered by the coffee and perhaps by the grasshoppers (called "hoppers")[18] that Nick examines earlier in the story, nor the mental writing of these thoughts as story threatens his emotional stasis. He is consciously avoiding something else, but knows he will soon lose consciousness in sleep.

There is, however, one impediment to his sleep: a mosquito. The following moment evokes the trout catching the sun, and prefigures the blinding sun on the water in "Part II":

> A mosquito hummed close to his ear. Nick sat up and lit a match. The mosquito ~~blinded by the light~~ was on the canvas over his head. Nick moved the match quickly up to it. The mosquito made a ~~tiny~~ ^satis-

factory^ hiss in the flame. ~~Nick blew~~ The match went out. (KL/EH 274, 46–47; sigla added: ~~deletions~~ ^insertions^).

The mosquito neatly dispatched, and the "blinded by the light" reference deleted for later use, in "Part II," Nick is able to sleep—and Hemingway is able to let him do so.

Early in "Part II," which takes place the next day, Hemingway again adds a reference to the sun to introduce Nick's musings on difficult fishing conditions, thereby reuniting the rising trout and the setting sun from the end of "Part I":

> In the afternoon ^after the sun had crossed toward the hills,^ the trout would be in the cool shadows on the other side of the stream. The very biggest ones would lie up close to the bank. ~~As the~~ You could always pick them up there on the Black. Bill and he had discovered it. ~~In~~ When the sun was down they all would out into the current. Just when the sun made the water blinding in the glare before it went down you were liable to strike a ^big^ trout anywhere in the current. It was almost impossible to fish then ~~for,~~ the surface of the river was blinding like a mirror shooting sun in your eyes. (KL/EH 274, 80–81; sigla added: ~~deletions~~ ^insertions^)

The published version of the story follows:

> In the afternoon, after the sun had crossed the hills, the trout would be in the cool shadows on the other side of the stream.
>
> The very biggest ones would like up close to the bank. You could always pick them up there on the Black. When the sun was down they all moved out into the current. Just when the sun made the water blinding in the glare before it went down, you were liable to strike a big trout anywhere in the current. It was almost impossible to fish then, the surface of the water was blinding as a mirror in the sun. (*Short Stories* 228–29)

Other than the reference to Hemingway's friend Bill, deleted in "Big Two-Hearted River" (but preserved by editor Philip Young in "On Writing" [*The Nick Adams Stories*], of which this passage comprises the second full paragraph), the changes between draft and published version are minimal: he altered the wording of the last line, from "the surface of the river was blinding like a mirror shooting sun in your eyes" (KL/EH 274, 81) to "the surface of the water was blinding as a mirror in the sun" (*Short Stories* 229). (Young followed the published version for "On Writing" [*Nick Adams* 233].) The original "shooting sun in your eyes" echoes the trout's "catching the sun" and connotes the artillery flashes discussed previously—in the original version, Nick in his mind has become the trout, aiming for the sun, but shot down by it, blinded like the mosquito he killed the night before.

For Hemingway, writing this passage breached the surface. In the manuscript version, the Nick Adams story essentially disappears immediately following this paragraph; it is displaced by an extremely personal Hemingway rant—about himself, about being married to Hadley (renamed "Helen" in "On Writing"), about remembering how he had been "married" to fishing, about how he had once had a "horror" of married people, about how marriage to Hadley had divorced him from fishing and from his fishing friends, and about how before his marriage "all the love went into fishing and the summer" (*Nick Adams* 235).

His rant continues with his bitterness at the loss of that love. He complains that he had those old feelings now only "in dreams. He would dream that the summer was nearly gone and he hadn't been fishing. It made him feel sick in the dream, as though he has been in jail" (*Nick Adams* 236). He continues with more memories of summers at Walloon Lake, his family's summer home, and, finally, the storm from the notes on the binder breaks (complete with the boat and umbrella that would reappear, coupled with impending fatherhood and loss, in *A Farewell to Arms*): "The hills at the foot of Walloon Lake, storms on the lake coming up in the motorboat, holding an umbrella over the engine to keep the waves that came in off the spark plug, pumping out, running the boat in big storms . . . climbing up, sliding down, the wave following behind, . . . too rough to land" (236). The stream-of-consciousness continues, via bullfighting, to writing, including the reference to "Indian Camp" (238), and to his definition of the sacred—which for him was the writing moment: "You had to do it from inside yourself. There wasn't any trick. Nobody had ever written about country like that. He felt almost holy about it. It was deadly serious. You could do it if you would fight it out. If you'd lived right with your eyes" (239). It was impossible to do when the sun shot into them—when emotion overcame clarity and memory was too fraught to provide material.

In the published story, the "blinding sun" passage is followed, not by a personal rant, but by the continuation of the fishing narrative, which moves Nick closer to, but not into, the swamp of memory that had derailed Hemingway for over a dozen pages. But the "blinding sun" passage prompted Hemingway to pierce the surface of his own thoughts. Just as the sun in the passage effaces what the trout have to do to stay alive (their need to eat) but reveals the source of Hemingway's wound—also the way the fire "effaced" the town of Seney but revealed the distorted gun barrels beneath the hotel—so, too, does the sun's glare on the water temporarily blind the fisherman the way the first flush of love can blind one to the practical reality of daily existence. Hemingway's

1919 attempt to pierce that blindness, his return home to get the job that he thought was the only impediment to his marriage to Agnes, was thwarted by her Dear John letter. At the end of their affair, Hemingway was, like the gun barrels in the story's earliest fragment, but a melted shell of a man; he concealed his emotional wound in a manner that revealed its source.

In writing and emending the manuscript for the story, Hemingway hides his autobiographical impulse (his nostalgia for Agnes, his continuing pain at her rejection, and his frustration with the impediment his wife and child had become to his writing) behind Nick's deliberate writer's block. Yet, Hemingway carefully worked certain passages that rise from beneath the surface of his prose to reveal the centrality of love and its loss to his writing. Love, for Hemingway, was nothing more— and nothing less—than the transcendental denial of mortality, young Nick's feeling in "Indian Camp" that he was "quite sure that he would never die" (*Short Stories* 95). This transcendental denial bore little similarity to the life of the frustrated writer living over a sawmill, or to the life of the new father married to a woman whose motherhood changed their relationship permanently. Ironically, the one substantive emendation Hadley Hemingway made to any of her husband's early stories was to the story in which Hemingway identified why he would, eventually, leave her: he refused to pierce beneath the surface of the blinding light of new love, to enter the misty, complicated world of real life, and to risk the loss of control—the control with which he might govern his vulnerability to the pain of mourning, but which precluded his openness to joy.

Simply stated, the irresolvable conflict between love and fear had become Hemingway's eternal dilemma. Having caught and lost the sun, in Agnes, and having given life to his first son, the son he would lose by leaving Hadley, in 1924 he chose not to choose. This was the tragic stasis that inspired Nick's affect in "Big Two-Hearted River." Whatever the cause of Nick Adams's affect, the love-fear dilemma would haunt Hemingway for the rest of his life, and would result in some of his subtlest and best writing.

NOTES

1. Hitchcock coined the term *MacGuffin* to describe the purpose of the actual Maltese falcon in *The Maltese Falcon*. The *OED* defines the term *McGuffin*, after Hitchcock, as "a particular event, object, factor, etc., initially presented as being of great significance to the story, but often having little actual importance for the plot as it develops." See Duguid.

2. KL/EH #.#/#–"# .#" denotes the file number, "/#" the folder number (when applicable), in the John F. Kennedy Library's Ernest Hemingway Collection.

3. The crossing of the *t*s in these notes occurs after the vertical; this pattern is unusual for Hemingway's handwriting of the period.

4. Part of the fragment (KL/EH 279) appears on the verso of page 10 of the first full draft (KL/EH 274); the paper used in the draft, which numbers 103 pages, is uniform.

5. John Hadley Nicanor Hemingway was born on 10 October 1923 and was six months old when Hemingway left Paris the following April to spend a week alone in Provence, just before writing "Big Two-Hearted River" (Reynolds, *Annotated Chronology* 34).

6. James Phelan's identification of an analogy "between mortar shells and wives" (64) in his consideration of "Now I Lay Me" is thus exceptionally insightful.

7. The "trout at the bridge" title for this passage is from Paul Smith's unpublished notes.

8. I am grateful to my student Kevin McKinnon for this interpretive insight. My thinking regarding this passage owes much to conversations with McKinnon and with Paul Smith.

9. The distortions wrought on memory by time eventually yielded Hemingway's insight that "Memory is never true" (*Death in the Afternoon* 100).

10. The kingfisher in the story may be read as an allusion to the sexual wounding of the Fisher King.

11. Hemingway's use of pregnancy as a metaphor for premarriage romance returns in his later story "Hills Like White Elephants" (Justice, "'Well, well, well'").

12. This was a line Hemingway knew full well, given that he structured most of a chapter of *Death in the Afternoon* around the first line of Romeo's balcony speech, "He jests at scars who never felt a wound" (*Rom.* 2.2.1; *Death in the Afternoon* 102; Justice, *The Necessary Danger* 69).

13. To an extent, Hemingway's choice of a new name for the "Ag" character was governed by printing technology—he needed a short name so that Scribner's would not have to cast a new set of plates for the story, as they did for "Mr. and Mrs. Elliot." There are many short women's names; his choice of "Luz," especially after emending the "Big Two-Hearted River" manuscript to include so many references to the sun, is particularly evocative. I am grateful to Robert Trogdon for his insights into Scribner's 1930 printing practices and to Rosa Salguera for confirming the translation.

14. The first break in the manuscript draft of the story occurs after Nick "shut his eyes again and went to sleep" (213). This line ends in the middle of page 14 of the manuscript; the rest of the page is blank. The text resumes, as "Nick woke stiff and cramped" (213), at the top of manuscript page 15 (KL/EH 274, 14–15).

15. Although both ink colors were probably originally black, the ink Hemingway used has now faded to dark green. The changes mentioned here have not faded; the ink is still nearly black, tending toward brown.

16. The handwriting disqualifies Gertrude Stein, a more likely editor. Other likely editors are also disqualified: Hemingway had yet to meet F. Scott Fitzgerald; Ford Madox Ford was out of the country (the composition of "Big Two Hearted River" was interrupted by Hemingway's having to edit the *Transatlantic Review* in his absence [Smith, *Reader's Guide* 85–86]); Ezra Pound was then living in Rapallo. The handwriting nearly matches Hadley's; it also bears an eerily close resemblance to Agnes's. Neither Michael Reynolds, in his biography of Hemingway (*The Paris Years*), nor James Nagel, in either his research into Hemingway's relationship with Agnes or his edition of their letters, gives any indication that Hemingway and Agnes met again after World War I. Although it is somehow tempting to speculate that, during Hemingway's solo trip to Provence in April 1924, he might have seen Agnes and shown her the manuscript, this is completely unverifiable. The likeliest candidate for having made the editorial marks is, therefore, Hadley Hemingway.

17. Nick's dinner also evokes Hemingway's Italian wartime experience. He mixes canned spaghetti, canned beans, and catsup, creating a portable Americanized version of the Italian dish *pasta fagiole*, which is comprised of pasta, beans, and marinara sauce. I am grateful to Robert Trogdon for this insight.

18. Again, I am grateful to Kevin McKinnon for noting this connection.

WORKS CITED

Duguid, Mark. "Hitchcock's Style." *Screenonline*. British Film Institute. 24 Jan. 2005 <http://www.screenonline.org.uk/tours/hitch/tour6.html>.

Eby, Carl P. *Hemingway's Fetishism: Psychoanalysis and the Mirror of Manhood*. Albany: State U of New York P, 1999.

Hanneman, Audre. *Ernest Hemingway: A Comprehensive Bibliography.* 2 vols. Princeton: Princeton UP, 1967.
Hemingway, Ernest. "Big Two-Hearted River—A Story." Ms. File 274. Ernest Hemingway Collection. John F. Kennedy Lib., Boston.
———. "Big Two-Hearted River." *In Our Time.* New York: Boni & Liveright, 1925. 179–214.
———. "Big Two-Hearted River." *This Quarter* 1.1 (1925): 110–28.
———. *Death in the Afternoon.* New York: Scribner's, 1932.
———. *A Farewell to Arms.* New York: Scribner's, 1929.
———. *A Farewell to Arms.* Ms. File 64.1. Ernest Hemingway Collection. John F. Kennedy Lib., Boston.
———. "The got off the train at Seney" [ms. fragment; became "Big Two-Hearted River"]. File 279. Ernest Hemingway Collection. John F. Kennedy Lib., Boston.
———. "Indian Camp." *In Our Time.* New York: Boni & Liveright, 1925. 15–21.
———. *The Nick Adams Stories.* Ed. Philip Young. New York: Scribner's, 1972.
———. Notes [became "Big Two-Hearted River"]. File 281. Ernest Hemingway Collection. John F. Kennedy Lib., Boston.
———. *The Short Stories of Ernest Hemingway.* New York: Scribner's, 1938.
———. Unpublished section of *The Garden of Eden.* Unpublished ts. File 422.1, folder #4. Ernest Hemingway Collection. John F. Kennedy Lib., Boston.
———. "A Very Short Story." *In Our Time.* New York: Boni & Liveright, 1925. 83–85.
———. "A Very Short Story." *In Our Time.* Rev. ed. New York: Scribner's, 1930. 83–85.
Justice, Hilary K. *The Necessary Danger: Hemingway and the Problem of Authorship.* Diss. U of Chicago, 2001. AAT 3006517.
———. "'Well, well, well': Cross-gendered Autobiography and the Manuscript of 'Hills Like White Elephants.'" *Hemingway Review* 18.1 (1998): 17–34.
Lynn, Kenneth S. *Hemingway.* New York: Simon, 1987.
McKinnon, Kevin. Conversations with the author. Fall 2002.
Phelan, James. "'Now I Lay Me': Nick's Strange Monologue, Hemingway's Powerful Lyric, and the Reader's Disconcerting Experience." *New Essays on Hemingway's Short Fiction.* Ed. Paul Smith. Cambridge, UK: Cambridge UP, 1998. 47–72.
Reynolds, Michael. *Hemingway: An Annotated Chronology.* Detroit: Omnigraphics, 1991.
———. *Hemingway: The Paris Years.* Oxford, UK: Blackwell, 1989.
Sempreora, Margot. "Nick at Night: Nocturnal Metafictions in Three Hemingway Short Stories." *Hemingway Review* 21.1 (2002): 19–33.
Shakespeare, William. *The Complete Works of Shakespeare.* 4th ed. Ed. David Bevington. New York: Longman, 1997.
Smith, Paul. *A Reader's Guide to the Short Fiction of Ernest Hemingway.* Boston: Hall, 1989.
———. "Trout at the bridge." Unpublished notes. Private collection, c. 1994.
Villard, Henry Seranno, and James Nagel. *Hemingway in Love and War: The Lost Diary of Agnes Von Kurowsky, Her Letters, and Correspondence of Ernest Hemingway.* Boston: Northeastern UP, 1989.
Young, Philip, and Charles W. Mann. *The Hemingway Manuscripts: An Inventory.* University Park: Pennsylvania State UP, 1969.

"Precipitation into Poetry": The Bishop-Lowell Letters and the Boundaries of the Canon

THOMAS TRAVISANO
Hartwick College

In the lead sentence of his incisive 1994 review of Elizabeth Bishop's *One Art: Letters* in the *Times Literary Supplement*, the poet Tom Paulin proclaimed, "The publication of Elizabeth Bishop's Selected Letters is a historic event, a bit like discovering a new planet or watching a bustling continent emerge, glossy and triumphant, from a blank ocean. Here is an immense cultural treasure being suddenly unveiled—and this hefty selection is only the beginning. Before the millennium is out, Bishop will be seen as one of this century's epistolary geniuses, like that modernist Victorian Gerard Manley Hopkins, whom she lovingly admired and learnt from" (3). Paulin hails not only the energy of Bishop's epistolary style but also the size of her epistolary achievement, and in the process he neatly echoes not just Keats's sonnet on Chapman's Homer as "a new planet swims into his ken," but Bishop's own "Crusoe in England," which describes how: "some ship saw an island being born: / at first a breath of steam, ten miles away; / and then a black fleck— basalt, probably— / rose in the mate's binoculars / and caught on the horizon like a fly" (*Complete Poems* 162). Paulin also slips in an echo of Bishop's "One Art" ("some realms I owned, two rivers, a continent"), while upping the ante from small island to large landmass. This expansion of scale seems appropriate, since Bishop's epistolary oeuvre is so vast, so multilayered, and so worthy of extensive exploration.

Elizabeth Bishop (1911–79), though comparatively neglected during her lifetime, has now been widely recognized as one of the great American poets of her midcentury generation. Robert Lowell (1917–77), another one of the great poets of that generation, was Bishop's friend and correspondent for three decades. Lowell foresaw the importance of Bishop's letters to her oeuvre when he observed, "When Elizabeth Bishop's letters are published (as they will be) she will be recognized as not only one of the best, but one of the most prolific writers of our century" (Bishop, *One Art* book jacket). Lowell, of course, knew whereof he spoke, since he had been the recipient of more than 250 of Bishop's most interesting and engaging letters. Significantly, Lowell saw Bishop's letters both as inevitably destined for publication and as an essential and extensive component of her ultimate published oeuvre. Yet the canonical status of a writer's letters remains ambiguous—are the letters merely ancillary to the writer's work in more established genres? Do they merely provide a commentary or amplification on more primary texts? Or should some writers' letters, as Paulin suggests, be "accorded aesthetic autonomy" (3)?

What follows is a report from another, and still only partially explored continent, one in which both Bishop and her friend Lowell hold a stake: I mean that literary realm encompassed by the complete letters between Elizabeth Bishop and Robert Lowell. I have the good fortune to be editing these letters as a volume for Farrar, Straus and Giroux. Publication is expected in fall 2006, following the June 2003 publication of Lowell's *Collected Poems* (edited by Frank Bidart, et al., and about which more later) and the forthcoming publication of Lowell's selected letters (edited by Saskia Hamilton and currently scheduled for June 2005). Here is a brief mapping of the Bishop-Lowell territory. The correspondence includes more than 470 letters, written between 1947 and 1977, including everything from postcards, telegrams, and brief handwritten notes to multipage, typed communications written over several days. All of the letters are contained in three libraries, the Rare Book and Manuscript Room at the Vassar College Library (Lowell to Bishop), the Houghton Library at Harvard University (Bishop to Lowell, 1947–69), and the Harry T. Ransom Center at the University of Texas, Austin (Bishop to Lowell, 1970–77). The complete letters total more than 320,000 words and will produce a book similar in size to Bishop's *One Art: Letters* (1994)—the 670-page selection, edited by Robert Giroux, that inspired Tom Paulin's acclaim. It is dangerous to discuss a book that is still in progress; yet, like Lowell, I cannot resist a prediction. And I predict that this will be a book to be reckoned with. For the correspondence is not merely vast, but vastly entertaining—peculiarly coherent yet full of the unexpected, in many ways historic yet teeming with everyday life—and in various ways prompting one to question the porous border between letters and more traditionally canonical genres.

Planning a seminar "on 'Letters!'" at Harvard, Bishop told friends that it would be about "just letters—as an art form or something" (qtd. in Paulin 3). Paulin's investigations of this "art form or something" lead him to ask, "And is there a poetics of the familiar letter?" Apparently finding none, he begins to supply the outlines of such a poetics, suggesting that letters, to qualify as literature, must paradoxically "construct themselves on an anti-aesthetic, a refusal of the literary." Speaking of a sentence in one of Bishop's early letters to Lowell, Paulin notes that "it leaps out as if she is an actor or a dancer, inspired by the intelligence and attention of her audience of one. For there is—it scarcely needs emphasizing—a keenly performative element in the epistolary art" (3). Yet this performative element, if the letter is to be of lasting interest, must aim—again paradoxically—"to flower once and once only in the recipient's reading and then disappear immediately. The merest suspicion that the writing is aiming beyond the addressee at posterity freezes a letter's immediacy and destroys its spirit" (3). It is the apparent absence of this interest in posterity on the part of two famous and obsessive craftsmen, their spontaneous attention to communication in the moment, that gives the Bishop-Lowell correspondence its lasting interest and appeal.

The focus on the performative moment emerges even in Lowell's first letter to Bishop, dated 23 May 1947 and written from his New York digs in response to one of Bishop's letters regretting missed connections due to illness. Opening "Dear Miss Bishop," it begins in a friendly but comparatively formal way: "Sorry to have missed dining with you yesterday, and the time before, and reading with you. I'm afraid that you have had a miserable winter. You are a marvelous writer, and your note was about the only one that meant anything to me."[1] Then the letter suddenly launches, without transition, into a paragraph of impromptu comic performance:

> Last night at three we had a fire. The man who started it fell asleep drunk and smoking. He ran back and forth from his room to the bathroom carrying a waste-basket with a thimble-full of water shouting at the top of his lungs; "Shush, shush no fire. Stop shouting you'll wake everyone up." Then the engines came out on the street. He kept saying: "An accident. Nobody injured," until a policeman shouted: "Nobody injured? Look at all the people you've gotten up." After it was over he went on talking: "I'm an American. I fought the fire. If it hadn't been for me you'd all be dead." Today my room smells like burnt tar-paper.

While much in the correspondence is in some sense historic, impromptu bits of detailed comic observation would continue to punctuate the letters from both sides for the next three decades, and even historic figures may be seen in casual, odd, domestic moments. Later in 1947, Lowell, then living in Washington, DC, would observe of two famous public figures and their families: "Sat in back of the Trumans at the Symphony. They never stirred. Next to them Admiral Nimitz and his daughters smiling, craning around, saying <u>this is it</u> (when the Tchaikovsky came on) then—having ignored each other thru the music and a long intermission—the Trumans and Nimitzes suddenly recognized and shook hands with unnecessary heartiness" (8 Dec. 1947). Neither correspondent felt the need of transitions between paragraphs—each could expect the other to follow each successive leap of thought. Thus, in an October 1948 letter in which Lowell notes his departure from his job as Poetry Consultant at the Library of Congress in Washington and his arrival at Yaddo, the artists' colony in Saratoga Springs, New York, Lowell writes in four successive paragraphs:

> An emotional last meeting with Pound: "Cal, god go with you, if you like the company."
> No use describing Yaddo—rundown rose gardens, rotting cantaloupes, fountains, a bust of Dante with a hole in the head, sets called <u>Gems of Ancient Literature,</u> <u>Masterpieces of the World</u>, cracking dried up sets of Shakespeare, Ruskin, Balzac, <u>Reminiscences of a Happy Life</u> (the title of two different books), pseudo Poussins, pseudo Titians, pseudo Reynolds, pseudo and real English wood, portraits of the patroness, her husband, her lover, her children lit with tubular lights, like a church, like a museum. . . .
> I'm delighted.
> Why don't you come?

And thus the letter ends, with an "Affectionately, Cal" (1 Oct. 1948).

Lowell's humor could also be self-deprecatory. Thus, a 24 January 1949 letter from Yaddo begins:

> Dearest Elizabeth:
>
> I was just making my bed (if you could call it "making") when I became aware of a dull burning smell. "God, I must have left my cigarette burning." I rush into my other room; no cigarette. Absent-mindedly I feel in my pocket. There, a lighted cigarette in holder consuming a damp piece of Kleenex. The pocket was also stuffed with kitchen matches. Oh my!

Bishop's subsequent letter begins with an amused yet practical rejoinder to Lowell's story:

> Dear Cal,
>
> I am mailing you a SAFE if not particularly esthetic ashtray—I got two of them a while ago. They're the only ones I've ever found that will really hold the cigarette while you write or scratch your head, and yet if you forget it, the cigarette automatically goes out . . . I was going to give one to Lloyd Frankenberg for Christmas, but they didn't come in time and now you're going to get it instead. (31 Jan. 1949)[2]

This dryly witty yet consistently supportive and sympathetic playing off of one another's anecdotes and observations is one of the joys of the correspondence. In a letter from the summer of 1948 in which Bishop has just described several lonely and depressing days in Maine, she writes:

> Well, things must improve I'm sure, and the place is beautiful there's no getting round that. I am working on Tobias and The Prodigal Son and I just started a story called 'Homesickness'—all very cheerful. I think almost the last straw here though is the hairdresser, a nice big hearty Maine girl who asks me questions I don't even know the answers to. She told me: 1, that my hair 'don't feel like hair at all.' 2, I was turning gray practically 'under her eyes.' And when I'd said yes, I was an orphan, she said 'Kind of awful, ain't it, ploughing through life alone.' So now I can't walk downstairs in the morning or upstairs at night without feeling I'm ploughing. There's no place like New England. (11 July 1948)

Lowell responds perfectly with a single line in a postscript to his next letter, "There's something haunting and nihilistic about your hairdresser" (14 July 1948).

Peter Taylor, Lowell's close friend for nearly forty years, noted more than once in interviews that Ian Hamilton's 1982 biography failed to capture two important aspects of Lowell: his capacity for friendship and his sense of humor. According to Taylor, "He was a wonderful friend; he could make you feel good about anything. One of the problems with Ian Hamilton's biography, although I thought it was good in many ways, was that it didn't give any impression of the other side of him. He had the most marvelous sense of humor; he was the gentlest person and the most loyal of friends" (McAlexander 62). Thus, Taylor felt, "with all the book's careful delineation of his madness, there is the danger of his being seen as an unrelieved grotesque. None of his friends saw him as that—not one of them" (McAlexander 39). By adding to the published record an extensive documentation of Lowell's capacity for spontaneous observation, his marvelous sense of humor, and his talent for friendship, the Bishop-Lowell letters promise to extend Lowell's published canon in an important way, not merely by offering valuable new perspectives for readers of his poetry, but by lending a degree both of availability and of permanence to many noteworthy passages of Lowell's epistolary art as it developed in interplay with Bishop's.

Lowell's recently published *Collected Poems*, adroitly edited by his friend, former student, and amanuensis Frank Bidart, attempts in significant ways to unsettle familiar views of Lowell. Responding to questions in a 17 August 2003 review-article of the *Collected Poems* for the *Boston Globe*, Bidart outlined the misconceptions he was trying to address: "People thought they knew Lowell's work, and that was part of the problem. There was something inert about people's relation to the poems they thought they knew. By surrounding the poems with textual stuff, stuff from the letters, stuff from what critics and other poets said that was illuminating, I wanted to put the poems in play again" (Polito). Bidart's edition achieves this effect by emphasizing Lowell's role as a tirelessly active and inventive creator. Bidart's introduction asserts that "Robert Lowell was above all an audacious maker" (*Collected Poems* vii), and Bidart amplified this in the *Globe* piece, "I genuinely believe the most central thing about Lowell is that he was a brilliant maker who was constantly thinking of ways to get the world and experience into a poem.... This was a life centered on the immense pleasures and satisfactions as well as the turmoil and fears about making" (Polito). Robert Polito, author of the *Globe* review-article, rightly concludes that, "By restoring Lowell as a consummate 'maker'—neither icon nor fossil—the 'Collected Poems' is a formidable and innovative bid for revival.... No edition familiar to me of a modern writer aims like the Lowell 'Collected' to pull a reader inside the tangles and mysteries of making a great poem—for Lowell, as for anyone, a transitory, multi-suggestive complex of circumstances, choices, false moves, crises, solaces, contradictions, dead ends, divergent vistas, and saving reconsiderations" (2).

Yet, in representing Lowell as maker, Bidart has emphasized, above all other qualities, Lowell's seriousness. Bidart describes Lowell as "not quite civilized" because he was so "unfashionably—even, at times, ruthlessly—serious," and Bidart further notes that Lowell once said to him, "'When I'm dead, I don't care what you write about me; all I ask is that it be serious'" (Fraser). Lowell's urge to present, in his poetry, a formidable armor of seriousness appears to derive, at least in part, from his schooling at the hands of such austere High Modernist masters as Allen Tate and T. S. Eliot. The *Publishers Weekly* notice of *Collected Poems* highlights this characteristic: "One can't help, reading through this massive, spellbinding volume, mourning some of what has been lost in American poetry since the 'Partisan Review' crowd was in the ascendant. Lowell's work evinces a contagious earnestness about writing (and rewriting) poetry in a bid for immortality, and an intellectual aggressiveness that is more ethical than metaphysical in nature" ("Robert Lowell: *Collected Poems*"). Yet, as Taylor's comments suggest, a portrait of Lowell that emphasizes his earnestness or his aggressiveness may omit other qualities needed to complete the picture, such as the qualities that Taylor identifies when he characterizes Lowell as a man with a "marvelous sense of humor" who was also "the gentlest person and the most loyal of friends." And, as we have seen, these qualities—humor, gentleness, loyalty, and friendship—are revealed in abundance in the Bishop-Lowell letters. If the Bishop-Lowell letters take their place as a part of Lowell's (as well as Bishop's) canon, they will provide a necessary supplement to the *Collected Poems*, helping to complete the self-portrait of Lowell as man and maker.

When Lowell felt free of the burden of his "bid for immortality," he was able to reveal aspects of himself that may appear only fleetingly in the poems. In fact, such qualities as gentleness and humor are most persistently present in the poems in his single most popular and influential work, *Life Studies* (1959)—a book that was deeply influenced by Bishop's example.[3] Bishop, no doubt, helped to draw those qualities out of Lowell in the letters, where one persistently sees Lowell's gentler, more vulnerable side. But since Bishop and Lowell were at once historic personages, ordinary people, and extraordinary observers equipped with deft senses of humor, it should surprise no one that everywhere in the letters one confronts a conjunction between the humorous and performatively descriptive on the one hand and the historical and literary-historical on the other—and often these elements are inextricably intertwined.

As Paulin has observed, "[E]ach letter occurs as a historic moment whose taut nowness can be immensely exciting" (3). There is so much dailiness in the letters that one sometimes feels surprised when one stumbles upon, not just historic events at the moment of their happening, but many famous poems—and books—receiving their first, or nearly their first, readings from a distinguished fellow craftsman. David Kalstone's justly famous *Becoming a Poet: Elizabeth Bishop with Marianne Moore and Robert Lowell* (1989) has already made this particular aspect of the correspondence familiar from Bishop's standpoint. However, in emphasizing the historical and developmental dimensions, Kalstone perhaps imparts a tone of high seriousness to the Bishop-Lowell correspondence that underplays its comic and performative elements and that may make it harder to see how dailiness and history so curiously intermingle as the letters unfold. And by rightly emphasizing Bishop's development, at a moment when Bishop's reputation still lagged behind Lowell's, Kalstone may have inadvertently made it harder to see that this correspondence is as exciting for its revelation of Lowell's process of becoming Robert Lowell as it is for Bishop's becoming Elizabeth Bishop.

Of course, such is the temporal and tonal complexity of the correspondence, so many are its attributes and layers, that it is difficult for any representation to do these letters full justice. Quoting any given sentence or paragraph out of its context removes it from the play of thought in a particular letter, and from the longer lines of interchange between the two poets. Nonetheless, one can derive some sense of this complex interplay by looking at the multiple layers of an "April Fools'

Day" letter of 1958, written by Bishop from Samambaia, Lota de Macedo Soares's house in the mountains above Petropolis, Brazil. The letter begins with a remarkable paragraph of performative description, rooted in the immediate moment:

Dearest Cal:

It's very cold and long swirling clouds of fog are blowing past the window and through the trees and re-coiling against the giant rocks above. It's just noon and two of Lota's "mens" have chosen to eat their lunch and heat their coffee on an alcohol lamp on the porch of my estudio. I went out once and one of them immediately sat on a small green apple he'd been munching, and I'm sure it was one of my eight Roman Beauties he'd stolen off the little tree, but I didn't like to go and count them right under his nose. Now he is singing a horrid monotonous ballad-like song, off tune, over and over, and making up the words, I think—the other man laughs at every refrain. Should I be a cranky old maid and go out and tell him to shut up and go away, or what? They're just trying to get out of the damp and wind, poor things, but heavens what a dreary song. We have three little apple trees, and they have already given enough apples to make a large pie on Lota's birthday (she insisted on apple-pie and ice-cream, American style, instead of a cake), and I have my eye on the rest of them; they grow at the same time as the oranges do! Oh—now it's twelve and the men have left. Peace and quiet. (Lunch hour's from 11–12 here.)

The second paragraph, leaving behind performative description, mixes the literary and the personal. Bishop's literary appreciation of a selection of Lowell's *Life Studies* poems, newly published in the *Partisan Review*, blends with her personal relief at Lowell's dawning recovery from a recent manic episode that had landed him in McLean Hospital, the Belmont, Massachusetts, sanatorium that provided a haven for mentally troubled members of the Boston elite, as well as such poets as Sylvia Plath and Anne Sexton. The paragraph interweaves praise for the poems, whose publication in book form would prove historic and triumphant, with pleasure at Lowell's recovery. And she strongly emphasizes her support of Lowell through his manic phase, offering reassurance about his prospects for recovery with a string of personal recollections—none of them performative, because here the focus is on Lowell himself, until the final flourish about the poet Jimenez:

PR with your poems in it and your letter came in the same mail, and I was pleased to see them both but extra-pleased, naturally, to have a letter from you again. You do sound well, Cal, and I hope and pray you are getting better every day. Maybe you're at home again now.

> McLean's is a good place, I think. I've been to see friends there and my mother stayed there once for a long time. I even have some snapshots of her in very chic clothes of around 1917, taking a walk by a pond there (?) However, I hope you don't have to stay very long—the people in such places are so fascinating I think one begins to find the usual world a bit dull by comparison. (I think I told you I was writing a hospital story, didn't I, but my characters aren't as lively as yours, I'm afraid. However, I think you may like it.) The poems in <u>PR</u> look very impressive, I think. Of course, I love the skunk one ["Skunk Hour"]. Actually I think the family group ["Memories of West Street and Lepke," "Man and Wife," "'To Speak of Woe That Is in Marriage'"] is the more brilliant, don't you? Now you say you've added to it, too. Where is that going to be published? Also I'd love to see the translation.[4] I like the "chocolate scented milk" and poor Mrs. Churchill—in fact that whole paragraph of your letter is almost on the point of precipitation into poetry as it is. You know there are several of our contemporary poets who always live in sanatoriums, feeling they're the only sensible place for a poet to live these days—& I've heard of one in Chile. And when [Juan Ramón] Jiménez was in Washington he went around from one to the other, with his poor wife, Zenobia. He finally got to one run by Moravians or some such sect—strictly vegetarian, sparsely furnished in golden oak, and with Bibles and hymn-singing (or so I heard)—a strange place for a Spanish poet. (1 Apr. 1958)

Lowell responds appreciatively, yet wryly, in his next letter, which begins:

> There's a saying that the true Bostonian has "a share in the Athenaeum, a lot in Mount Auburn and an uncle in McLean's." Well, "all roads lead to Rome," "God writes straight by crooked lines," etc. No matter what I do now, I shall end up as a true Bostonian.
> You make sanatoria sound like ports for poets; however, I am now well out. (20 Apr. 1958)

The acceptance and reassurance in Bishop's letter are emphasized in the third brief paragraph of her 1 April 1958 letter, dismissing Lowell's concerns about a previous letter, written during his manic episode: "You say you wanted to take back the letter you wrote before this last one. I don't see why—it's a perfectly nice letter! They've all been."

In its fourth paragraph, Bishop's letter modulates into a relaxed and cheerful dailiness, shifting from that into dazzling lyrical description, and then closing with a brisk series of sardonic and comic episodes:

> Remember me to Elizabeth and the baby. She must be starting to talk, by now. We are up to our necks in babies at the moment—all Lota's little "grandchildren" and their little mother are staying in a little

house down the road because there isn't any water in their little apartment in Rio . . . The youngest is 3 1/2 months, Lota's namesake, called "Lotinha." Yesterday, in the rain, we took everybody, including the cook and <u>her</u> child, <u>my</u> namesake, to market. It was quite an expedition. Everyone sooner or later had to be fed and either taken to some very squalid bathroom—through cafés full of truck-drivers—or in the case of Lotinha, breast-fed and <u>changed</u>. We all ate ice cream and got it all over us. There was a magnificent rainbow across one end of town, over the hideous new pink obelisk—they cut down all the Emperor's trees along the canals and put up this obelisk instead. On the way home we were hailed by a priest who wanted a lift and anti-clerical Lota shouted "Can't you see we're full of children?" There were nine souls in the Volkswagen bus. Lota is magnificent with child-problems. I suspect it's because she's had so much practice with me.

Bishop closes the paragraph on a comically self-deprecatory note perhaps designed to reassure Lowell about his own recent behavior. We are still only halfway through a letter that divagates in succession through the water and power problems of Rio; the writings of Robert Graves; the "silly old Institute" (the National Institute of Arts and Letters, which had again rejected Randall Jarrell for membership despite his nomination by Bishop and Lowell); Rio's latest Carnival; the death of Bishop's toucan; and James Agee's recently published *A Death in the Family* and modulates into plans for an Easter celebration: "I must change my clothes and put on a raincoat and go to town again. Easter guests are starting already. I've been having the poor cook blow eggs for several weeks now, for a dyeing party—one of my favorite indoor sports. I hope the Easter Rabbit is very nice to you."

The letter ends on a note of affirmation, reassurance, and eagerness for more writing from her fellow correspondent and poet: "With much love as always, Cal—for heavens sake don't worry about anything you did or wrote as far as I'm concerned: There's nothing to worry about in the slightest, and I wish I could write such good letters. Send me some poems!" As this letter makes clear, Bishop and Lowell were not only intimate friends, ready to share the dailiness of their lives with all its piquant and hilarious moments, but also eager readers—eager for the next letter, eager for the next poem. This letter from April 1958 is typical in the way it blends friendship and authorship, the dailiness of the poets' lives with their excited responses to one another's work as it emerged, poem by poem and (sometimes) draft by draft in an ongoing process of making. It is also typical in the way a historic event, the first publication of a substantial portion of *Life Studies* in the *Partisan Review*, is subsumed into a stream of everyday occurrences.

In an earlier book-length study titled *Elizabeth Bishop: Her Artistic Development* (1988), I divided Bishop's work into three major thematic periods: "Prison," "Travel," and "History." Yet, while I argued for the broad process of thematic evolution of Bishop's work, moving from psychic enclosures through travel to an ever-more-intricate involvement in public and private history, I had to acknowledge that each poem Bishop wrote is, stylistically, a fresh departure and finds a unique solution to its individual poetic problem. Lowell's work, however, just as clearly follows a book-by-book developmental pattern—a process that Lowell himself recognized and described cogently in his valedictory prose piece "After Enjoying Six or Seven Essays on Me" (1977; reprinted in *Collected Poems* 989–94). Each completed volume seems to mark the ending of a stylistic phase, and each new volume marks the discovery of fresh terrain, the opening of a new, and for the time, liberating stylistic venture.

The exciting thing about the Bishop-Lowell letters is that they catch both poets in 1947, at the moment of their youthful maturity—each had recently published a prize-winning first volume, Bishop's *North & South* (1946), which won the Houghton Mifflin Literary Fellowship Award, and Lowell's *Lord Weary's Castle* (1946), which won the Pulitzer Prize—and the correspondence carries through until the end of Lowell's career (he died in 1977) and until nearly the end of Bishop's (she died in 1979). In Lowell's case, this means that each volume he subsequently wrote, with the exclusion of his last one, *Day by Day* (1977), was sent to Bishop for her scrutiny and comment and became the subject of extended discussion—discussion that focused both on the individual poems and on the impact of the entire book. It would be hard to improve on this correspondence as a record of artistic development, of what Bidart terms "the immense pleasures and satisfactions as well as the turmoil and fears about making" (Polito).

Speaking of his early days of friendship with Lowell, Frank Bidart recalled, "I was a graduate student [at Harvard] and Lowell loved to show his work and talk about it, and I loved to look at it. I was a kind of sounding board. I would have been useless to him if I didn't tell him the truth. . . . He once said, quoting Auden, 'The best reader is someone who is crazy about your work but doesn't like all of it.' That describes me" (Dougherty). One aspect of the strength and endurance of the Bishop-Lowell friendship was that Bishop offered the same kind of sounding board for Lowell. She, too, was crazy about his work but didn't like all of it, and her unfolding reactions to the evolution of Lowell's work in both form and content—her outspoken praise when she was moved and impressed and her evident disquiet and genuine concern for Lowell and his reputation when she was less persuaded—are part of what make this particular record of artistic development so revealing.

For, though Bishop's fascination with Lowell's career was unflagging, her opinions of his individual books varied. Bishop praised "Falling Asleep over the Aeneid," but was politely lukewarm about much else in *The Mills of the Kavanaughs* (1953). She praised with genuine excitement Lowell's achievement in his three most outstanding middle-period books—*Life Studies, For the Union Dead* (1964), and *Near the Ocean* (1967). She raised detailed questions about two books that troubled her principles in different ways—*Imitations* (1961), because of its freely transformative treatment of the translation process, and *The Dolphin* (1973), because of Lowell's use and reshaping of private letters from his estranged wife, Elizabeth Hardwick. It is outside the scope of this discussion to review the entire history of Bishop's responses, book by book, to Lowell's work—fascinating as such a study might be. Such a book-by-book reading of Lowell's development will have to await the publication of the complete text of the Bishop-Lowell letters. Nonetheless, one may at least pause to observe the exchange emerging from Lowell's composition of one of his finest poems, "Waking Early Sunday Morning," which would serve as the cornerstone to *Near the Ocean* and to that volume's title sequence.

In protest over President Lyndon Johnson's escalationist policies in the Vietnam War, Lowell had recently withdrawn from a White House Festival of the Arts in an open letter, which was published on the front page of the *New York Times* on 3 June 1965. In this letter, addressed to President Johnson, Lowell acknowledged, "I am very enthusiastic about most of your domestic legislation," but continued, "I nevertheless can only follow our present foreign policy with the greatest dismay and distrust. . . . We are in danger of imperceptibly becoming an explosive and suddenly chauvinistic nation." He added, in apparent self-portraiture, "I know it is hard for the responsible man to act; it is also painful for the private and irresolute man to dare criticism." Still, Lowell concluded, "I feel I am serving you and our country best by not taking part in the White House Festival of the Arts" (*Collected Prose* 371). Lowell's stance stirred up a firestorm of support in artistic circles and prompted a titanic wave of Johnsonian ire from the White House. Yet Lowell's public position, which he handled with considerable acumen and grace, was nonetheless unsettling to the private individual and poet, who had already settled down to his usual summer of writing with his family in Castine, Maine.

The artistic result was the poem "Waking Early Sunday Morning," which Lowell sent to Bishop in a 16 July 1965 letter, noting, "I've finished nothing worth keeping for a year. But suddenly when I got up here with letters and long distance calls still swarming in about my White House business, I got going. I enclose the long poem I wrote. It sounds good, I think and is rather witty and tragic. I guess the only thing to do is to keep writing, but only publish what has a spark in it. I am old enough almost to wait." It is worth noting that Lowell refers to the poem's tone ("rather witty and tragic") as an artistic effect achieved after "I got going"—and not as a transparent reflection of his biography or mood. At the same time, the prolific Lowell alludes to his tendency to write—and sometimes publish—too much, as opposed to Bishop's tendency to write slowly and publish too little—at least in the view of her impatient readers. Lowell suggests that, despite his escalating fame—or notoriety—and Bishop's comparative obscurity, they still share what matters most, the problems of the lonely writer's life and the ongoing struggle with the writer's lonely decisions. Bishop's reply came some time later, in a 19 September 1965 letter from Ouro Preto that begins with a wry reflection on Lowell's growing public presence and continues with a drifting approach into the admired poem in question:

> Dearest Cal:
>
> (as I see you are called, according to TIME, August 27th)
> I have had this [enclosed] card for you for weeks now, and I did write you a letter in answer to yours of August 16th that Lota sent on—but it struck me as too dull to send. I left Rio in an awful hurry—had the chance of a ride all the way here—and have almost no books with me, and no poetry—so I was especially pleased to have some "modern poetry." The local bookshop had provided a complete Milton in paperback, and that was all, except for the Brazilian poets, & I seem to be quite sick of them. Now I find I can turn from that wonderful:
> For who loves that, must first be wise and good;
> But from that mark how far they roave we see
> For all this waste of wealth, and loss of blood. [Milton, "Sonnet XII"]
> to:
> Only man thinning out his kind
> sounds through the Sabbath noon, the blind
> swipe of the pruner and his knife
> busy about the tree of life . . . ["Waking Early Sunday Morning"]
> and feel the language hasn't deteriorated at all, even if the state of civilization stays the same, or just gets worse and worse.

Bishop goes on to comment specifically on the poem itself in some detail, focusing primarily, and rightly, on its extraordinary pace and tone:

> "Waking Early Sunday Morning" has many wonderful things in it—and not the least, I think, is the way it goes on in a leisurely way, like a Sunday morning—even if the meter is not leisurely, there seems to be

time,—to think—not like week-day thoughts. "In small war on the heels of small / war"—is marvelous—and now far truer than when you wrote it, I gather by the papers I see here.

Bishop refers to a further escalation of the Vietnam conflict that Johnson had recently ordered. She continues:

> I think you are a bit hard on yourself in stanza three. And I <u>love</u> the glass of water—a beautiful simple stanza—well, not simple,—simple like Chardin, maybe. I also like stanza 9 very much—since I feel that way myself so much of the time. "Wars flicker"—& "monotonous sublime" is a wonderful ending. I can't express it exactly—but sounds like Tennyson a hundred years later, <u>with</u> a sense of irony.[5]

While it is tempting to quote each eight-line stanza that Bishop singles out for praise, it is impossible not to quote the closing, which Bishop mentions early, then singles out for praise again, and which was also cited by many reviewers of *The Collected Poems* (June 2003) as a prescient anticipation of the present world situation:

> No weekends for the gods now. Wars
> flicker, earth licks its open sores,
> fresh breakage, fresh promotions, chance
> assassinations, no advance.
> Only man thinning out his kind
> sounds through the Sabbath noon, the blind
> swipe of the pruner and his knife
> busy about the tree of life. . . .
>
> Pity the planet, all joy gone,
> from this sweet volcanic cone;
> peace to our children when they fall
> in small war on the heels of small
> war—until the end of time
> to police the earth, a ghost
> orbiting forever lost
> in our monotonous sublime.
> (*Collected Poems* 320)

Lowell's next letter is so immersed in his response to Bishop's just-published *Questions of Travel* (1965) that he never quite gets back to Bishop's admiring comments on his own "Waking Early Sunday Morning." The letter's whole first paragraph is taken up with an impromptu commentary on Bishop's book. It is worth quoting at length:

> It was fun looking up echolalia (again), chromograph, gesso, and roadstead—they all meant pretty much what I thought. Oh and taboret, an object I've known all my life, but not the name. All the poems are good and the book reads with the steady excellence of some perfect short story, say my beloved "Coeur Simple" [Flaubert]. Santos gains a lot by being the opening door to the Brazilian section. My favorites are "Brazil[, January 1, 1502]"—how I envy the historical stretch at the end, so beautifully coming out of the vegetation—"Manuelzinho's" a dazzling masterpiece—"Armadillo"—how proud and swell-headed I am about the dedication, one of your absolutely top poems, your greatest quatrain poem, I mean it has a wonderful formal-informal grandeur—I see the bomb in it in a delicate way—"The Riverman," a sort of forsaken Merman, and a very powerful initiation poem that somehow echoes your own entrance in Santos—"Twelfth Morning" has lovely, strange touches—"The Burglar [of Babylon]" ballad is a special poem, and gives a huge sweep of Rio, and again, though a true narrative and ballad, tells a lot about your own judgments on your society, obliquely—"[First] Death in Nova Scotia" haunts me (It was weird this summer when I drove through New Brunswick and Nova Scotia on a short salmon fishing trip, to see everywhere the pale Maple Leaf Flag, more like (and pleasantly at last) a boy scout flag than a nation's—embittered anglophiles still fly the old Union Jack)—the poem is doubly provincial and remote, in time, the Prince of Wales and all, and in places, very sad and lovely—"Filling Station," just as good I think, one of your best "awful but cheerful" poems—Trollope ["From Trollope's Journal"], the more I read it the more I think he was right about Washington—at first I took the poem as a spoof at the superficial condescending Englishman—by the way your rhythm and riming are extraordinary, and of course unobtrusive—then Ezra ["Visits to St. Elizabeths"] is marvelous, you get bits of your old monument ["The Monument"] in it, nicely, and the whole is a success against every impossibility. . . . You were very right to put your story in ["In the Village"], it's one of your finest poems, and bridges the two sections. I rather wish you'd thrown <u>all</u>, or almost all, your stories in, even though it would have made jags in the book's pattern. (28 Oct. 1965)

In citing his favorites, Lowell has named nearly every poem in the book and shown his ongoing and intimate familiarity with Bishop's work.

What Paulin stresses in his impromptu "poetics of the familiar letter" is a quality of performative immediacy, and that is surely vital to these letters. Yet, as the Bishop-Lowell letters accumulated over three decades, they took on opposing qualities as well—in particular, the qualities of continuity and coherence. Read from beginning to end, or even in sustained, yearlong stretches, the letters establish not only an ongoing dialogical interchange between peers and equals, but also a compelling narrative line. They tell a story that is immersed in the quotidian, yet that constantly intersects with public and private history. And it emerges as a story of surprising coherence.

A poet's selected letters, however brilliant, must be of necessity partial and miscellaneous. A multivolume complete letters, though allinclusive, is, of necessity, both one-sided and diffuse. In contrast, the Bishop-Lowell letters, by combining spontaneous performance focused on the moment with narrative development and coherence, seem to me, at least, to take on much of the character of more traditionally canonical genres of art, which characteristically feature spontaneity and richness balanced by unity and coherence. Even though the literary scene may seem an arena of constant change, preconceptions about literary genres change very slowly. Yet, although predictions are dangerous, it seems just possible that the Bishop-Lowell correspondence will challenge preconceptions about letters as a secondary literary genre. Moreover, these letters will link the separate published canons of Bishop and Lowell in remarkable ways as we watch the parallel development of the two writers as poets, as people, and as epistolary stylists. Throughout their lives, both Bishop and Lowell were constantly exploring and questioning traditional artistic boundaries, so it seems fitting that we find them pushing those boundaries once again, posthumously, in the Bishop-Lowell letters.

NOTES

1. Excerpts from unpublished letters to Elizabeth Bishop from Robert Lowell copyright © 2004 by Harriet Lowell and Sheridan Lowell. Published by permission of Farrar, Straus and Giroux, LLC, on behalf of the Robert Lowell Estate.

2. Excerpts from unpublished letters to Robert Lowell from Elizabeth Bishop copyright © 2004 by Alice Helen Methfessel. Published by permission of Farrar, Straus and Giroux, LLC, on behalf of the Elizabeth Bishop Estate.

3. This and all other poetry volumes by Lowell referenced in the text are included in *Collected Poems*. All poetry volumes by Bishop referenced in the text are included in *Complete Poems*.

4. In his 15 March 1958 letter, Lowell told Bishop he had done "another family poem, a translation of Der Wilde Alexander's poem in the Penguin German anthology, and several Montale pieces from the Penguin Italian."

5. Bishop refers to the version of "Waking Early Sunday Morning" that appeared in the *New York Review of Books* (5 Aug. 1965). Stanzas three and nine from that version, which Bishop mentions, were both dropped from the poem as published in *Near the Ocean*, and the order of some other stanzas was changed. The *New York Review* text is reproduced in the "Magazine Versions" section of *Collected Poems* (933–36), and it is discussed in some detail in Bidart's introduction (ix–xiii).

WORKS CITED

Bishop, Elizabeth. *The Complete Poems*. New York: Farrar, 1983.

———. Letter to Robert Lowell. 11 July 1948. bMS AM 1905 (62)–(264). Houghton Lib., Harvard U, Cambridge, MA.

———. Letter to Robert Lowell. 14 July 1948. bMS AM 1905 (62)–(264). Houghton Lib., Harvard U, Cambridge, MA.
———. Letter to Robert Lowell. 31 Jan. 1949. bMS AM 1905 (62)–(264). Houghton Lib., Harvard U, Cambridge, MA.
———. Letter to Robert Lowell. 1 Apr. 1958. bMS AM 1905 (62)–(264). Houghton Lib., Harvard U, Cambridge, MA.
———. Letter to Robert Lowell. 19 Sept. 1965. bMS AM 1905 (62)–(264). Houghton Lib., Harvard U, Cambridge, MA.
———. *One Art: Letters.* Ed. Robert Giroux. New York: Farrar, 1994.
Bishop, Elizabeth, and Robert Lowell. *The Complete Letters between Elizabeth Bishop and Robert Lowell* [tentative title]. Ed. Thomas Travisano. New York: Farrar, forthcoming [2006].
Dougherty, Robin. "Weighing the Legacy of Robert Lowell." *Boston Globe* 10 Aug. 2003: H8.
Fraser, Caroline. "Madness and Scandal, Outlived by Art." *Los Angeles Times* 22 June 2003: R3.
Hamilton, Ian. *Robert Lowell: A Biography.* New York: Random, 1982.
Kalstone, David. *Becoming a Poet: Elizabeth Bishop with Marianne Moore and Robert Lowell.* New York: Farrar, 1989.
Lowell, Robert. *The Collected Poems.* Ed. Frank Bidart and David Gewanter. New York: Farrar, 2003.
———. *Collected Prose.* Ed. Robert Giroux. New York: Farrar, 1987.
———. *The Letters of Robert Lowell.* Ed. Saskia Hamilton. New York: Farrar, forthcoming [2005].
———. Letter to Elizabeth Bishop. 23 May 1947. Elizabeth Bishop Papers. Rare Books and Manuscripts, Vassar College Lib., Poughkeepsie, NY.
———. Letter to Elizabeth Bishop. 8 Dec. 1947. Elizabeth Bishop Papers. Rare Books and Manuscripts, Vassar College Lib., Poughkeepsie, NY.
———. Letter to Elizabeth Bishop. 14 July 1948. Elizabeth Bishop Papers. Rare Books and Manuscripts, Vassar College Lib., Poughkeepsie, NY.
———. Letter to Elizabeth Bishop. 1 Oct. 1948. Elizabeth Bishop Papers. Rare Books and Manuscripts, Vassar College Lib., Poughkeepsie, NY.
———. Letter to Elizabeth Bishop. 24 Jan. 1949. Elizabeth Bishop Papers. Rare Books and Manuscripts, Vassar College Lib., Poughkeepsie, NY.
———. Letter to Elizabeth Bishop. 15 Mar. 1958. Elizabeth Bishop Papers. Rare Books and Manuscripts, Vassar College Lib., Poughkeepsie, NY.
———. Letter to Elizabeth Bishop. 20 Apr. 1958. Elizabeth Bishop Papers. Rare Books and Manuscripts, Vassar College Lib., Poughkeepsie, NY.
———. Letter to Elizabeth Bishop. 16 July 1965. Elizabeth Bishop Papers. Rare Books and Manuscripts, Vassar College Lib., Poughkeepsie, NY.
———. Letter to Elizabeth Bishop. 28 Oct. 1968. Elizabeth Bishop Papers. Rare Books and Manuscripts, Vassar College Lib., Poughkeepsie, NY.
———. "Waking Early Sunday Morning." *New York Review of Books* 5 Aug. 1965: 3.
McAlexander, Hubert H., ed. *Conversations with Peter Taylor.* Jackson: UP of Mississippi, 1987.
Paulin, Tom. "Newness and Nowness: The Extraordinary Brilliance of Elizabeth Bishop's Letters." *Times Literary Supplement* 29 Apr. 1994: 3–5.
Polito, Robert. "The Return of the Native: A Monumental New Anthology Reveals the Making, and Remaking, of Robert Lowell's Poetry." *Boston Globe* 17 Aug. 2003: D2.
"Robert Lowell: *Collected Poems.*" *Publishers Weekly* 19 May 2003: 66.
Travisano, Thomas. *Elizabeth Bishop: Her Artistic Development.* Charlottesville: UP of Virginia, 1988.

Transformative Stages:
Williams's *Vieux Carré* in New York and London

CRAIG CLINTON
Reed College

The resounding failure of Tennessee Williams's autobiographical memory play *Vieux Carré*, which opened on Broadway in May 1977 and closed after only five performances, was offset when a revised version of the play was successfully produced in London fifteen months later. In New York, theater critics were unanimously of the opinion that Williams had been ill served by the production personnel. This view was succinctly expressed in the *New York Times* review by Walter Kerr, who described the Broadway production as "irresponsible" (30).

The text of *Vieux Carré* published in 1979 by New Directions (and, tellingly, dedicated by Williams to his British director, Keith Hack) is based on the London version of the play. For comparative purposes, there exists a manuscript once owned by Williams biographer Lyle Leverich, now in Columbia University's Tennessee Williams Collection, which Linda Dorff in her essay "'All Very (not!) Pirandello': Radical Theatrics in the Evolution of *Vieux Carré*" has identified as "very close to that of the Broadway production" (14).[1] Robert Bray, with his essay "*Vieux Carré*: Transferring 'A Story of Mood,'" has established Williams's clear preference for the revised London text, which the playwright thought "clarified and focused the play much beyond what it had been in New York" (151).

A comparison of the Columbia University (or New York) text with that of the published (or London) *Vieux Carré* reveals a number of significant changes and not only makes evident how revision achieved the clarity and focus that Williams desired but also provides an opportunity to reflect on the playwright's evolving vision regarding the self as subject.[2] The revisions take the form, in the published text, of interpolated new scenes, the addition of a crucial new character, and significant cutting. The clear intent of the majority of these revisions, as will be discussed below, was to intertwine the materials of a work that Williams had initially conceived as two autonomous one-acts.

The setting of *Vieux Carré* is a seedy New Orleans rooming house where Williams lived after leaving his family home in St. Louis in 1939, but, as Bruce Mann observes in "Memories and Muses," the true setting for *Vieux Carré* is "in the depths of Williams's mind, at the roots of his imagination where his self was originally formed, an underworld of muses and memories" (139). The play's characters—emotionally fragile, haunted, yet defiantly proud individuals—comprise a gallery of Williams archetypes. Robert Bray, in his introduction to the 2000 edition of *Vieux Carré*, reminds us of "the importance of these 1939 friendships and associations . . . because ineluctable elements of their personalities, 'fading but remembered,' resurface in Williams's *dramatis personae* elsewhere" (ix). The play's indebtedness to early works by Williams is readily observed. Indeed, the protagonist/narrator in act 1 of the New York text comments on "[m]aterial for a story now turned into a play" (Ms. 52), referring to a key source for that portion of the work, Williams's short story "The Angel in the Alcove" (1943). "The Lady of Larkspur Lotion" (1941), a Williams one-act, can be seen as source material for act 2.

In both the New York version and the London version, Williams participates as narrator in the present and as his recollected self as the past is conjured. At the play's outset, in a brief monologue spoken by Williams's mature surrogate—the Writer as Narrator—the play's characters are evoked. "Once this house was alive," he states: "[I]t was occupied once. In my recollection, it still is, but by shadowy occupants like ghosts. Now they enter the lighter areas of my memory" (5). The time frame shifts from present to past as the main characters are introduced; in the process, the Writer sheds his role as Narrator and merges into the action by becoming the play's male protagonist. Mrs. Wire, the deranged landlady in whose establishment the action unfolds, and her employee, Nursie, are the first to be introduced. Next is Jane, an unemployed fashion designer from New York, followed by Nightingale, a tubercular quick-sketch artist, and, finally, Tye, Jane's boyfriend who is a bouncer at a strip joint. Brief encounters with peripheral characters, chiefly two crones who share a perpetually darkened cubicle in the building's dank interior, complete the opening scene.

As it progresses, the play unfolds the Writer's evolving, sometimes intimate, relationships with the various denizens of the rooming house, as well as his determination, in an environment fraught with the emotional turbulence occasioned by these new associations, to define himself as a writer. Its action is essentially a rite of passage in the young Writer's life and concludes as he prepares to leave behind the rooming house and its inhabitants and head west to California and new opportunities.

The bifurcated nature of *Vieux Carré*, as it was performed in New York, was clearly evident to Keith Hack who, several months after the New York debacle he had witnessed in previews, met with Williams in London to discuss a new production. Hack regarded the play's two components as imperfectly linked; he would later remark, "I thought the play . . . had gone on before the writing was finished" (Clinton, "Reprise" 269). Hack's issues with the play—the bifurcated structure chief among them—were frankly discussed at the London meeting and resulted in Williams inviting the director to Key West to work on revisions. Throughout the revision process, Hack encouraged Williams to "interweave the sections even more, make it even more filmic" (Clinton, "Reprise" 271).

The play opened at the Nottingham Playhouse for a brief run and, on the strength of the reviews, transferred to London; it underwent further revisions before opening in London on 9 August 1978, approximately fifteen months after its New York debut. Although by no means universally celebrated, the London production elicited numerous enthusiastic notices. Anthony Curtis in *Drama* described the work as "a triumph" (51) while Sally Aire in *Plays and Players* observed, "In Tennessee Williams' latest play there is a sense of the writer reaching a new period of maturity, and a feeling of newly-found personal liberation. It is a very fine piece indeed" (20). Ned Chaillet of *The Times* declared, "Mr Williams is completely in control as a writer here, playing the stage like a musical instrument with rapid shifts of mood. He is served well by his company, and by his director." Under Hack's assured hand, the production received a sufficient number of positive reviews to enjoy an extended run, thus becoming, arguably, the professional high point in Williams's late career. Dotson Radar, in his memoir of the playwright, observes: "It was a happy time for Tennessee, to see received with enthusiasm a new play that, like so many others, had been damned in his homeland" (258).

While the transformation of *Vieux Carré* from its incarnation in New York to the production in London occurred over a relatively brief period of time, the play's gestation was, in fact, a protracted one. *Vieux Carré* manuscripts predating the Columbia University/New York text can be found in the Tennessee Williams papers at the Harvard Theatre Collection and in the Billy Rose Theatre Collection at the New York Public Library. The manuscripts are undated, but internal evidence suggests they were in circulation in the late 1960s. From these manuscripts it can be observed that, remarkably, the play's narrative thrust—its content and sequence of key events—was very much in place at the outset of the play's creation. In both the Harvard text and the New York Public Library text, Williams utilizes a framing or linking device—ostensibly a rehearsal-in-progress—to contain what are essentially the autonomous plays comprising the central core of *Vieux Carré*. And in both these early versions of the play, the one-acts are fundamentally the same in terms of character and event.

Act 1, titled "The Angel in the Alcove" in the Harvard and New York Public Library manuscripts, has as its protagonist a young Writer: "He is, of course, myself at twenty-eight," Williams notes in a stage direction in both manuscripts—a remark carried through to the text used in the New York production (Ms. 1). Act 1 develops the Writer's interactions with Mrs. Wire (the landlady of the boarding house) and the tubercular artist, Nightingale. Act 2, titled "I Never Get Dressed Till After Dark on Sundays," centers on a young down-at-heel fashion designer, Jane, who is ill with a blood disease, and her relationship with Tye, the stud bouncer at a strip club. The rehearsal-in-progress conceit is introduced early in both versions of the play. In the Harvard manuscript, the ostensible play being performed is interrupted by discord that erupts among the production personnel—director, actor, and playwright—while in the New York Public Library manuscript, the playwright and director are absent and the actor playing the role of Jane steps in to conduct a rehearsal of the play's two parts.

In each of these two early versions, Williams makes additional use of the rehearsal-in-progress construct to link the end of act 1 with the beginning of act 2. He reprises the device for the last time in shaping each text's concluding moments. As the one-acts are independent of one another (indeed, he refers to the work as a "framed" double bill in the New York Public Library manuscript), it seems likely that he conceived of his "rehearsal-in-progress" as a means of providing unity while potentially expanding, through the use of a metatheatrical lens, the artistic reach of the two works.[3]

Comparing these early *Vieux Carré* texts with the version ultimately published, Bray observes: "[W]hat began as a radical experiment evolved into a more 'acceptable' memory play that would eventually be compared unfavorably to his first success, *The Glass Menagerie* ("*Vieux Carré*" 147). Yet Williams's shift from what was essentially the marginal self-as-participant in these early versions of *Vieux Carré* to the centrality of the self-as-protagonist in the final version of the play reflects a circumstance central to Williams's career in the 1970s: his discovery of the marketable value of his own (gay) persona. Williams appeared in 1972 as an actor in his own *Small Craft Warnings*, successfully extending the play's off-Broadway run; three years later, he struck pay dirt with his sexually explicit *Memoirs*. The intertwining of past with present, of author with actor, and of the subjective self with the objective self had, through repetition, become both theme and technique—and the evolving versions of *Vieux Carré* reveal the author stepping forward, and "out," as he moves from the role of supporting player in earlier drafts of the play to that of a central player in the London version. The published version of the self-referential *Vieux Carré* marks the culmination of an enterprise—the self as subject—implicit in the work of many writers and made explicit by Williams in various endeavors in the 1970s.

When the play went into production in New York, the metatheatrical conceit of these earlier versions had been discarded and an attempt clearly had been made to provide narrative connection between the one-acts: crucially, by locating both plays in the same crumbling boarding house on Toulouse Street (as opposed to the independent locales of the earlier versions) and, significantly, by developing the Writer/Narrator as a character integral to each of the two parts. Also, the separate narratives that focus on the Writer, Nightingale, and Wire in act 1, and on Jane and Tye in act 2, are occasionally disrupted in the New York version, so that the characters from one play become, at least to a marginal degree, part of the fabric of the other. An example of this interlarding is found in the Columbia manuscript in the act 1 scene (revised but retained in the published text) involving the two destitute crones, Miss Carrie and Mrs. Wayne, who are lured into Mrs. Wire's kitchen by the smell of the gumbo she is cooking. The crones provide black-comic relief, the clear appeal of which, for their creator, is evidenced in their expansive role in the New York version of the play. In the London version, their presence is significantly reduced. The crones provide a suitable occasion for the author, through his alter ego, to comment on his dramas' stylistic essence. In the Columbia manuscript, the Writer, speaking as Narrator, observes: "Yes, here come the ladies, fast.—A pair of famished crones that keep themselves back of a locked door most of the time, creeping out barefooted to the bathroom with the stealth of thieves but charging forth like a pair of fire-horses in double-harness—oh, Christ, no description's necessary, you see them. . . . Now they enter the lighted area of my memory which is not—which is—not—realistic, as you must know by now" (Ms. 20).

Attempting to hide their interest in the gumbo, Miss Carrie chatters about the hats she makes and tells an outlandish joke ("Confucius say: 'rape is impossible because girl with skirts up can run faster than boy with pants down'"), and then the two of them sing a noisy duet together:

> DUET
> (with tottering steps)
> Goodbye m[y] lady love,
> Farewell my turtle dove,
> You were the idol, the darling of my heart.
> You will come back to [m]e
> And love me tenderly,
> So goodbye, my lady love, goodbye.

The song draws Jane, a key protagonist in act 2, into the room and promotes an exchange at the end of the duet:

JANE
Today was Tye's birthday and he promised he'd get a buddy of his to take over for him and he'd be back no later than twelve. It's—
  (SHE staggers. The WRITER catches her)
—Thanks, I'm getting so—light-headed . . .

MRS. WIRE
You <u>got</u> light-headed when you let him in here. Now git him out! O-U-T, out! Not just for tonight, but permanent, OUT!

JANE
  (Softly)
I—I love the boy . . .

MRS. WIRE
What was that she whispered?

WRITER
She said she loved the boy.

MRS. WIRE
Not possible! A strip-show barker?

WRITER
Yes—possible—very . . .

MISS CARRIE
Mrs. Wire, give her a cup of your wonderful French Market coffee, she's—

MRS. WAYNE
All broke up.

JANE
Thanks, no—I'm going to—demand an explanation at the show!
  (Starts to cross right)
I've earned more consideration! I've practically supported that boy and I will not be rewarded with—contempt! I'm going straight down there this minute and—

> MRS. WIRE
> Not in that kimona, not outa my house you won't!
>
> JANE
> No, I—have idiotic impulses . . .
>
> MRS. WAYNE
> (Wisely)
> Love.
>
> MISS CARRIE
> Infatuation: different: often seems stronger!
>
> MRS. WAYNE
> Yais, but doesn't last. . . .
>
> (Ms. 21–24)

The Writer helps Jane back to her room while the crones discuss a story about a mortician relative of one, widely known as "the Southern Planter," a tale retained in the published text, which leads to a corollary tale, not retained, involving Miss Dottie Reagan, whom Mrs. Wire regards as "the fattest woman I ever seen outside of a circus sideshow":

> MISS CARRIE
> She was about to enter Liggett's Drug store with that little ninety-pound fairy she runs around with, the one that carries a little beaded bag. They were about to step into Liggett's for ice cream sodas when Miss Dottie Reagan says to this ninety-pound fairy, "Oh, God, catch me, I'm going to fall!"
>
> MRS. WIRE
> Dottie ast God to catch her?
>
> (Ms. 27–28)

The sequence might be regarded as Williams indulging his particular brand of mordant humor which, although wickedly funny, in this instance results in a cul-de-sac in what is already a meandering narrative. He evidently acknowledged the peripheral nature of the pair in the action of the play overall and accordingly made cuts for the London production.

The clear intention to fuse the (essentially) separate stories of the two one-acts, evident throughout the Columbia manuscript as Williams involves the characters of one portion in the action of the other, is most fully realized in the concluding moments of the New York and London versions of the play. In the earlier, metatheatrical, versions of *Vieux Carré* (the Harvard text and the New York Public Library text), each one-act had a separate ending: the first involved the Writer, clutching a suitcase and his portable typewriter, and abandoning the house on Toulouse; the second involved Jane, her abandonment by Tye, and her confrontation with the certain knowledge of impending death. In the Columbia version of the play, however, the act break separating the earlier one-acts has been altered so that the Writer's story continues into act 2, and it is not until the play's conclusion that the Writer abandons the building, following a scene he shares with Jane. Thus, Williams achieves a union of sorts between the two narratives in the New York text, an interconnectedness that would be enhanced, through the interpolation of two new scenes, in the London production.

In the play's final moments in both the New York version and the London version, Williams focuses on Jane and the Writer in a two-person scene that provides closure for each character. However, in the New York version, the Writer stands outside the primary action and serves as commentator. Jane calls for her cat:

> JANE
> Beret, Beret . . .
>
> WRITER
> An animal is a comforting presence sometimes.
>
> JANE
> Beret . . .
>
> WRITER
> —And holds her close, closer, and looks up at the skylight with a question—eyes—dark as the skylight.
>
> JANE
> Dark as the skylight
>
> WRITER
> She said the word
>
> JANE
> Death.

(Ms. 90)

While this two-person scene will be significantly altered in the London version (although in both versions Jane is abandoned by Tye), an almost identical monologue from the Writer concludes both versions of the play. The New York version follows:

> They're disappearing—going. Such characters do disappear, the earth swallows them up, the walls absorb them like moisture. All that remains are echoes of echoes—echoes of no voices. Goodbye . . . (Picks up suitcase) This house is empty now. (Walks through door, exits)
>
> CURTAIN
>
> (Ms. 90)

It is evident that achieving a satisfactory ending was one of the most problematic aspects of the revision process. Both Jane and the Writer needed independent conclusions to their separate stories and yet, as the play's protagonists, the two needed to be linked in the final moments. Williams addressed this need for a shared resolution by establishing a bond between the Writer and Jane earlier in the play, a decision expanded upon in the London version by the interpolation of two new scenes into the first act. The first of these, scene 3, involves Jane's midmorning encounter with the Writer; she invites him into her apartment for coffee, where "Tye is in a seminarcotized state on the bed." Jane spars with Tye, claiming to be desperate for "a little society in a place where—frankly I am frantic with loneliness!" while Tye taunts the young Writer who, as he gazes with ill-concealed attraction at Tye, "appears to be hypnotized":

> JANE: I heard that you're a writer.
> WRITER: I, uh-write, but—
> JANE: What form of writing? I mean fiction or poetry or . . .
> TYE: Faggots, they all do something artistic, all of 'em.
>
> (31)

What is fascinating is that this scene from the published play existed in an embryonic state in the Columbia manuscript where it appeared in the form of narration in act 2. The Writer revealed to the audience: "Some mornings she would ask me in for coffee. I loved the skylight. And I admired her fashion sketches. But why I really came in—I'd try not to look right at him—but there he was . . ." (Ms. 60).

The Writer's transparent desire for Tye and, at the outset of the play, his seduction by the tubercular Nightingale establish the protagonist's homosexuality. Nonetheless, especially when regarded in the wake of the revelatory *Memoirs,* this autobiographical information is presented in *Vieux Carré* relatively matter-of-factly, as a "given" and not much more. Mann argues that the aging and diseased Nightingale "resembles the older Williams himself" (142) and thus provides a counterpoint to the youthful Writer, but such a fabrication on Williams's part seems unnecessary given the existence of the Writer's mature alter-ego, the Narrator. More compelling is David Savran's observation regarding the "complex association between homoeroticism and death" in Williams's work—the linking of desire and corruption that Savran regards as a "historically marked" (171) ambivalence engendered by the homophobic society in which Williams found himself situated, and which contextualized his creative endeavors.

The second interpolation occurs in scene 6, in which an emotional bond is established between the Writer and Jane. The scene establishes a relationship that progresses beyond the voyeuristic fixation of the initial meeting and points to the empathic emotional sharing that will culminate in the play's final moments. Both Jane and the Writer have received a letter in the mail: for the Writer it is a printed rejection slip for a short story with a handwritten addendum—a note of encouragement—for Jane it is a report informing her that her disease is no longer in remission. The Writer, aware that Jane's letter has come from a medical clinic, asks:

WRITER: Jane, what was the letter, wasn't it about you?
JANE: Let's just say it was a sort of a personal, signed rejection slip, too.
(54)

While Williams expands on the dynamics of Jane's and the Writer's relationship, it is significant to note the elimination of some of the self-conscious embroidery initially attached, without real purpose, to each of these characters. In the Columbia manuscript, Jane references Chekhov on two occasions, suggesting a background as an actor that, in the context of the overall play, leads nowhere:

JANE
All of the girls named Masha in Chekhov's plays wore black and—I played one of them once—I said "It's like a dream...."
(Ms. 65)

JANE
"Like a dream"—last line of first act of Chekhov's <u>Seagull</u>—Played Nina once—"I'm a seagull"—I must have fever—still talking to myself.
(Ms. 68)

In a similar vein, Williams strips from the Writer dialogue in which that character references the work of Paul Verlaine, Hart Crane, and Arthur Rimbaud, including the extended sequence that ends act 1. Here the writer mingles his own verse with lines from Crane's *My Grandmother's Love Letters*: "There are no stars tonight but those in my memory..." (Ms. 51). Clearly, Williams's use of the poem, infused with emotional connections to his own grandmother, incarnated in the play as the "Angel in the Alcove," is a deeply felt and matrixed homage, but its significance in the play as a form of emotional biography is opaque. Williams ends the act, in the published text, with a piercing scream from Mrs. Wire—a primal cry that speaks volumes for the frustration and isolation of all the play's characters.

Perhaps the most crucial of all the revisions distinguishing the London production from that in New York is the addition of a new character, the young musician, Sky. The introduction of Sky becomes a major component in the final shaping of the trajectory of *Vieux Carré* and provides the much-sought-after mechanism for uniting Jane and the Writer in the play's concluding moments. Williams refers to Sky in the opening moments of the published play and, at the same time, introduces a central thematic concern, the sense of impending "endings" which shadow all of the play's characters:

NURSIE: (*She stumbles on a heavy knapsack.*) Lawd! What that there?
MRS. WIRE: Some crazy young man come here wantin' a room. I told him I had no vacancies for Bourbon Street bums. He dropped that sack on the floor and said he'd pick it up tomorrow, which he won't unless he pays fifty cents for storage....
NURSIE: It's got something written on it that shines in the dark.
MRS. WIRE: "Sky"—say that's his name. Carry it on upstairs with you Nursie.
NURSIE: Mizz Wire, I cain't hardly get myself up them steps no more, you know that.
MRS. WIRE: Shoot.
NURSIE: Mizz Wire, I think I oughta inform you I'm thinkin' of retirin'.
(6–7)

One of life's inescapable realities is the fact that all things end—and Nursie's introduction of this subject can be seen as the initial spin on a topic that gathers momentum as the play progresses. The inevitability of change—of things coming to an end—eventually becomes the defining dynamic in the lives of all the characters.

Sky as a flesh and blood character doesn't appear until the beginning of the second act, but here he becomes that crucial structural element, the new agent appearing midway in the play's action, destined to steer the play to its conclusion. The groundwork for his function is provided in scene 8 of the published text—the first scene in the second act—in which the young musician and the Writer strike up a friendship as Sky makes a repair to the Writer's typewriter. Their interaction is interrupted by a major altercation between Mrs. Wire and Nightingale in which the landlady sets about evicting Nightingale from the boarding house. The Writer is stung by Mrs. Wire's cruelty and when Sky proposes they drive together to the West Coast, he seizes on the opportunity:

> WRITER: (with suppressed excitement): How would we live on the road?
> SKY: (rolling a cigarette with obvious practice): We'd have to exercise our wits. And our personal charm. And, well, if that don't suffice, I have a blanket in the car, and there's plenty of wide open spaces between here and the Coast. (He pauses for a beat.) Scared? Of the undertaking?
> WRITER: (smiling slowly): No—the Coast—starting when?
> SKY: Why not this evening? The landlady won't admit me to the house again, but I'll call you. Just keep your window open. I'll blow my clarinet in the courtyard. Let's say about six.
>
> (78)

Intriguingly, the trip to California from New Orleans, companioned by a young musician the Writer's age, was an event that sprang directly from Williams's own experience. Williams left New Orleans and traveled across country with a young musician, Jim Parrott, and roomed with him when they arrived in California. It is perplexing why Williams was so slow to incorporate this event in the context of a play defined by recollection. Perhaps it was the case that Sky, as a player in Williams's past, was primarily a catalyst while the figures in the boarding house proved, eventually, to have left deeply etched impressions in the author's psyche that would play out in his drama. Or, possibly, until he found the way through, Williams was loath to introduce what might be regarded as a "new beginning" in the midst of the death-haunted endings that dominate the play's atmosphere.

For the New York production, Williams had used a disembodied character as a device to move the Writer onward—an anonymous "sponsor" whom Mrs. Wire immediately fingers for what he is. As in the published version, the Writer announces his intention to leave for California following the blowout between Mrs. Wire and Nightingale. However, the circumstances in the New York version are vastly different:

WRITER
—Now Mrs. Wire that you have interrupted my work, I may as well tell you, Mrs. Wire, that I have found a sponsor, someone who believes in my work and has invited me to the West Coast as his companion while he—while he
(He is obviously a little embarrassed)
Of course I—will send you—

MRS. WIRE
You ain't leavin' here till you've worked off the back rent an' board you owe me, boy, I can prevent it by law if I have to. And as for your fallin' into the hands of some old fag—

WRITER
Nevertheless, be that as it may or may not be, Mrs. Wire—We are leaving for the West Coast where he has connections with agents who can get me published at least. And even if I hadn't providentially run into this—sponsor!—I doubt that I could have stayed on here any longer. Cruelty!—Your cruelty may be unconscious like a child's but I—can't take any more of it.

MRS. WIRE
So you go West to the Coast with some old man, rent and board paid for.

WRITER
Compromises are made for the sake of creative—

MRS. WIRE
Get your ass out on the street with them flyers.
(Ms. 57–58)

The introduction of Sky as an agent of change in the London version would seem to eliminate the darker aspects associated with the Writer's desire to get on in life through any means possible. The acceptance of "compromise"—the crassness and moral decadence underlying his careerism—disappears with the elimination of the "sponsor." Williams creates in Sky a highly nuanced character, and the role he will play in the Writer's life is ambiguous. Williams describes the young musician as "[a] lean, gangling young man, whose charming but irresponsible nature is apparent in his genial grin" (69). Sky reveals to the Writer that he had recently been married only to realize that he "wasn't ready to settle" (70). He abandoned his new bride with a cursory note and disappeared into the night, heading for a new life on the West Coast. It is soon apparent that, in addition to being self-centered, Sky is violence prone, inclined to petty theft, and cunningly in touch with the manipulative powers that stem from "personal charm." The musician's temperament is shown to be multifaceted, and not devoid of negative attributes. Yet, Williams must have seen in the jazz musician an Orpheus figure promising freedom—the artist as liberator—whose wanderlust represents a pilgrimage in search of meaning and self-understanding. Thus, while Sky's entrance into the Writer's life signals an end to things, this end is also a beginning. Even though the future is promising, there are deeply problematic elements in this rite of passage.

For the last two scenes of the London *Vieux Carré*, Williams expands his focus on the Writer and Jane while resolving their separate stories. In earlier versions of the play—the metatheatrical texts, as well as the text of the New York production—Jane reveals to Tye that her disease is no longer in remission and, with death impending, she is determined to go off with her own "sponsor," a wealthy Brazilian who will shortly be calling for her. The perplexing appearance of the Brazilian to collect Jane—always an extremely problematic moment in the play's early versions—is addressed with economy and finesse: Williams removes the encounter altogether and substitutes a moment more resonant with the play's major theme. In the published text, the commotion Jane takes for the Brazilian's arrival is in fact orderlies removing the deathly ill Nightingale on a stretcher. An awkward sequence has been eliminated, and a concept essential to the play's emotional arc has been reintroduced with shattering vividness. Tye tells Jane, "The Brazilian's out of the picture; those steps on the stairs were steps of hospital workers coming to take a—pick a dying fruit outa the place" (109).

The removal of Nightingale in the London version is a precursor to the additional "endings" that unfold in the final moments of the play, thus completing a pattern established at the play's beginning. At the outset, the aged Nursie announces her impending "retirement," and early in the first act, it is evident that the two crones are slowly starving to death. (Their duet, removed in the published text, also spoke of "endings.") In the second act, Nightingale is shown to be near death in his battle with tuberculosis; the liaison between Tye and Jane is at an end, as is her remission from illness; and Mrs. Wire is seen slipping into senility, confusing the Writer with a son long absent from her life. All of these bleak, death-haunted "endings," however, are challenged by the treatment accorded the Writer, whose "ending" in fact signals a beginning—a promise of things to come. Yet, the resolution combines both past and present. As Savran notes, at the play's conclusion, the protagonist steps "into a world swarming with . . . infinite promise and infinite disappointment" (172).

In the last scene of the published play, Williams brings Jane and the Writer together. The Writer tells Jane that he will shortly be leaving, heading West with a young musician, but the lateness of the hour suggests to Jane that the Writer has been left behind: "Each of us abandoned to the other," she says. "You know this is almost our first private conversation." As they prepare to play a game of chess, Jane relates her own fanciful travel plans, to which the Writer responds:

> WRITER: Jane, you don't have to make up stories, I heard your talk with Tye—all of it.
> JANE: Then you must have heard his leaving. How his steps picked up speed on the second flight down—started whistling . . .
> WRITER: He always whistles down stairs—it's habitual to him—you mustn't attach a special meaning to it.

Their conversation is interrupted by the sound of Sky's clarinet; "Your vagrant musician is late but you're not forgotten," Jane remarks. "Now go, quick. He might not wait, you'd regret it" (114–15).

As the Writer moves to exit the house, he speaks to the audience: "I stood by the door uncertainly for a moment or two. I must have been frightened of it. . . ." Drawing the door open, "*he is forced back a few steps by a cacophony of sound: the waiting storm of his future—mechanical racking cries of pain and pleasure, snatches of song. It fades out. Again there is the urgent call of the clarinet.*" He crosses to the open door and, exiting the house, turns to the audience, speaking the lines that crystallize for us the impact of the persons and events recorded in the play: "They're disappearing behind me . . . their voices are echoes, fading but remembered. (*The clarinet calls again. He turns for a moment at the door.*) This house is empty now" (116).

The house is empty, but the Writer carries with him the memory of its occupants; these personalities, we are aware, will assert themselves in the creation of his future—magisterial—dramas. The events recorded in *Vieux Carré*—autobiography as theater—reflect beginnings as well as endings: Williams, at a point near the end of his career, turns to his past to reimagine a crucial moment in his development as an artist. He situates himself at the play's center as protagonist and narrator—his own chronicler and judge. As Mann observes, "[N]ear the end of our lives, all of us must return in our minds to our muses, the forces that gave birth to our identity, so that they may teach us how (or how not) to grow old, to assess our lives, and to prepare for death" (142).

Late in his career, as Williams reflected on the evolving nature of his dramas, he offered a telling observation: "I used to write symphonies. Now I write chamber music, smaller plays. Everyone expects me to write another *Streetcar*. I don't want to, even if I could" (Rader 257). *Vieux Carré* was surely one of the most successful of these chamber works; indeed, when it was revived in a pocket theater production in 1983, Mel Gussow wrote in the *New York Times:* "[T]he play has a heartbeat. It is filtered through with limpid poetic imagery."

In the revisions to *Vieux Carré* leading up to the London production, Williams at last found a resolution that unified the threads of memory and imagination that constitute the play's textured fabric. The bifurcated nature of the New York version was eliminated; indeed, Williams titled the play's components "Part One" and "Part Two," indicating his perception of an interlocking design. He returned, in *Vieux Carré*, to a mythic motif deeply entwined in his drama—the figure of Orpheus, whom Williams associates with the redemptive capacity of art. For the playwright, art is a gift, a source of reconciliation that, in the words of Lord Byron in *Camino Real*, "translates *noise* into *music*, chaos into—*order* . . . —a *mysterious order!*" (77). Yet, paradoxically for the artist, the creation of the work of art represents conflict and disorder—a perpetual struggle associated with decoding and transforming the sources of the creative vision. For Williams, the odyssey of discovery and artistic expression is a dynamic comprised of light and shadow, pleasure and pain. *Vieux Carré* presents, through the study of its evolution, evidence of the type of struggle that Williams waged throughout his creative life, in his ascendancy and, surely with no less fervor, in his creative decline.[4]

NOTES

1. Dorff examines various drafts of *Vieux Carré* (and ancillary texts) with the object of "glimpsing the trajectory of Williams's evolving theatricalist poetics through the lens of a single play" (2). She is unequivocally of the opinion that the "multi-layered radical theatrics" of two early versions of *Vieux Carré*—those featuring the metatheatrical play-within-a-play design—display Williams's evolving postmodern sensibility, evinced in matters of form. Dorff states that this design is completely erased in the "milder published form" of the play (16). Chief among the excised formal innovations are examples of what Dorff terms "quotation theatrics"—essentially narration substituting for action—a practice that, in her view, "radically revises modernist constructions of character, plot and discourse" (11). Her interpretation seeks to validate what, from a less enthusiastic perspective, might be regarded as examples of problematic narrative technique.

2. In the citations that follow, page numbers referring to the Columbia University *Vieux Carré* manuscript are prefaced by "Ms." to distinguish them from page numbers referring to the published New Directions text.

3. For a full discussion of the two "metatheatrical" versions of *Vieux Carré*, see my "Tennessee Williams: Finding the Way to *Vieux Carré*."

4. I would like to thank the Williams estate for permission to quote from both texts of *Vieux Carré* (the Columbia University Manuscript and the New Directions text), copyright by The University of the South. Reproduced by permission of The University of the South, Sewanee, Tennessee. Citations from the *Vieux Carré* manuscript courtesy of Columbia University.

WORKS CITED

Aire, Sally. "Vieux Carré." *Plays and Players* 25.10 (1978): 20–21.
Bray, Robert. Introduction. *Vieux Carré*. By Tennessee Williams. 1979. New York: New Directions, 2002. vii–xii.
———. "*Vieux Carré*: Transferring 'A Story of Mood.'" *The Undiscovered Country*. Ed. Philip Kolin. New York: Peter Lang, 2002. 142–54.
Chaillet, Ned. "Vieux Carré." *Times* [London] 16 Aug. 1978: 16.
Clinton, Craig. "The Reprise of Tennessee Williams' *Vieux Carré*: An Interview with Director Keith Hack." *Studies in American Drama, 1945–Present* 7 (1992): 265–75.
———. "Tennessee Williams: Finding the Way to *Vieux Carré*." *Resources for American Literary Study* 26 (2000): 49–63.
Crane, Hart. *The Collected Poems of Hart Crane*. Ed. Waldo Frank. New York: Liveright, 1933.
Curtis, Anthony. "Plays in Performance." *Drama: The Quarterly Theatre Review* 127 (1978): 50–51.
Dorff, Linda. "'All Very (not!) Pirandello': Radical Theatrics in the Evolution of *Vieux Carré*." *Tennessee Williams Annual Review* 3 (2000): 1–23.
Gussow, Mel. "Theatre: 'Vieux Carré' by Tennessee Williams is Revived." *New York Times* 5 Apr. 1983: C13.
Kerr, Walter. "A Touch of the Poet Isn't Enough to Sustain Williams's Latest Play." *New York Times* 22 May 1977, sec. 2: 5, 30.
Mann, Bruce J. "Memories and Muses: *Vieux Carré* and *Something Cloudy, Something Clear*." *Tennessee Williams: A Casebook*. Ed. Robert F. Gross. New York: Routledge, 2002. 139–52.
Rader, Dotson. *Tennessee: Cry of the Heart*. New York: New American Lib., 1985.
Savran, David. *Communists, Cowboys, and Queers*. Minneapolis: U of Minnesota P, 1992.
Williams, Tennessee. "The Angel in the Alcove." *One Arm*. New York: New Directions, 1954. 137–49.
———. *Camino Real*. New York: New Directions, 1970.
———. "The Lady of Larkspur Lotion." *Twenty-seven Wagons Full of Cotton*. New York: New Directions, 1966. 63–72.
———. *Memoirs*. New York: Bantam, 1976.
———. *Small Craft Warnings*. New York: New Directions, 1972.
———. *Vieux Carré*. Ms. Billy Rose Theatre Collection. New York Public Lib., New York, NY.
———. *Vieux Carré*. Ms. Harvard Theatre Collection. Harvard U, Cambridge, MA.
———. *Vieux Carré*. Ms. Rare Books and Manuscripts Lib. Columbia U, New York, NY.
———. *Vieux Carré*. New York: New Directions, 1979.

"Wish I Were There":
Ten Letters from William S. Burroughs to Paul Bowles, 1972–79

COREY M. TAYLOR
University of Delaware

Introduction[1]

In his essay "The Name Is Burroughs," William Seward Burroughs (1914–97) writes, "As a young child I wanted to be a writer because writers were rich and famous. They lounged around Singapore and Rangoon smoking opium in a yellow pongee silk suit. They sniffed cocaine in Mayfair . . . and lived in the native quarter of Tangier smoking hashish and caressing a pet gazelle" (2). This reminiscence, although probably colored by hindsight, conveys features of Burroughs's personality that would define his adult lifestyle, his mode of writing, and, most important, the impact he would have on literary and popular culture in America and overseas. Not the least interesting feature of this brief passage is Burroughs's mention of Tangier, a port city in Morocco jointly controlled, for a time, by several different countries (not one of them being Morocco). While listed among other enticing and exotic locales in "The Name Is Burroughs," Tangier served as a fixture in both Burroughs's fiction and Burroughs's life. It was a place almost as diverse, paradoxical, and enigmatic as Burroughs himself, as evidenced by the ten letters reproduced below and housed in the Paul Bowles Papers of the Hugh M. Morris Library's Special Collections Department at the University of Delaware in Newark.

Tangier fascinated Burroughs several years before he ever visited or resided in the city. His interest in Moroccan peoples and culture first emerged during his undergraduate days at Harvard (1932–36), when he took an ethnology course taught by Carleton S. Coon, who had studied in Tangier for a number of years (Grauerholz, "Re: Letters"). Burroughs's fascination with Tangier later increased after he read *The Sheltering Sky* (1949) and *Let It Come Down* (1952), novels written by the American expatriate author Paul Frederick Bowles (1910–99). Prompted by Gertrude Stein (1874–1946) and Alice Toklas (1877–1967) to spend "some time away from Western culture . . . [to] discover his own style" (*Literature Resource Center*), Bowles heeded their advice and rented a flat in Tangier in 1931. Finding the change of scenery helpful, Bowles visited Tangier several times before permanently settling there in 1948. Several of Bowles's works, particularly *The Sheltering Sky* and *Let It Come Down*, deal with the unique culture of Tangier, a city that attracted a variety of people. Always seeking a new location in which to live and to write, Burroughs arrived in Tangier in early 1954 and remained there until late 1958 (when he moved to Paris), save for a brief visit to London in 1956—where he would later reside—to undergo John Yerbury Dent's heroin cure, which consisted of Burroughs taking apomorphine to normalize his drug-damaged metabolism (Caveney 84). While living in Paris and other locations abroad, Burroughs visited and lived in Tangier at various times between 1960 and 1964.

Post–World War I Tangier was literally an International Zone: created in 1923, it was governed jointly by the United States, the United Kingdom, France, Spain, and a host of other European countries until 1956, when it gained its independence along with Morocco (Grauerholz, Introduction xvii). Although newly free, Tangier maintained its international status in social climate if not in name. Many of Burroughs's contemporaries and acquaintances—Beat generation figures including Allen Ginsberg (1926–97), Jack Kerouac (1922–69), Gregory Corso (1930–2001), and Peter Orlovsky (b. 1933), along with other literati such as Tennessee Williams (1911–83), Alan Ansen (b. 1922), and Brion Gysin (1916–86)—found themselves drawn to Tangier for artistic and personal reasons, and with just cause. The Beats gravitated toward Tangier's unregulated and tax-free trade, relaxed social atmosphere, indifference toward the homosexual lifestyle, wide availability of sex, and easily obtainable drugs. In "International Zone," an article about Tangier originally intended for an American magazine but never published, Burroughs notes, "The special attraction of Tangier can be put into one word: exemption. Exemption from interference, legal or otherwise. Your private life is your own, to do exactly as you please. . . . Tangier is one of the few places left in the world . . . [that] is a sanctuary of noninterference" (59). Burroughs would fictionalize the lax laws and morals of Tangier society as Interzone—a pun on "International Zone"—the hallucinatory reality articulated in several of his novels, most prominently *Naked Lunch* (1962). In Interzone everything is permitted; there, one can see "a haze of opium, hashish, the resinous smoke of Yage, [and can] smell of the jungle and salt water and the rotting river and dried excrement and sweat and genitals" (Burroughs, *Naked Lunch* 98). Burroughs also describes Interzone as "[a] place where the unknown past and the emergent future meet in a vibrating soundless hum" (*Naked Lunch* 99). Tangier, then, was the perfect haven for a writer and human being such as Burroughs, a place that suited his idiosyncratic personal and artistic proclivities better than any previous locale, at least for a few years.

Burroughs became acquainted with Paul Bowles and his wife, Jane (1917–73), shortly after his arrival in Tangier in January 1954. Bowles had already established himself in Tangier's social and literary landscape, while Burroughs was a newcomer. Their first meeting was not altogether pleasant: "Burroughs seemed rather gray and insubstantial to [Bowles], as though flickering in and out of focus. . . . When Bowles made no effort to see him again, Burroughs felt snubbed" (Morgan 244). During a subsequent visit to Bowles's flat, Burroughs wrote that he had "sat around all day shooting junk and [then] dripped blood all over Paul Bowles'[s] first edition of *One Arm* by Tennessee Williams" ("The Name Is Burroughs" 11). Despite a shaky start, the two self-exiled authors eventually developed a strong friendship and warm, although sporadic, correspondence, both of which would last for nearly four decades. Bowles came to consider Burroughs "a true eccentric, thus very much worth knowing" (qtd. in Sawyer-Lauçanno 328), and Burroughs admired Bowles's work and central position in Tangier's social and artistic landscape. Burroughs met several members of Bowles's literary circle in Tangier—including Gysin, who would become one of Burroughs's closest friends and most important collaborators.

Thanks in part to Bowles's support, Burroughs experienced a healthy burst of productivity while in Tangier, writing material for four of his novels while there, including all of *Naked Lunch* and the bulk of *Nova Express* (1964), *The Soft Machine* (1966), and *The Ticket That Exploded* (1967). The increase in literary output probably resulted both from belonging to a circle of like-minded individuals and from the atmosphere of Tangier itself. However, the more time Burroughs spent in Tangier, the more severe his drug addictions became. In addition to smoking hashish, drinking alcohol, and shooting heroin, for several months Burroughs also "shot Eukodol [synthetic German morphine] every four hours, then he narrowed it down to two" (Morgan 247). Burroughs was often depressed and reluctant to work, a predicament that his heroin addiction did not help to alleviate. It took the combined forces of Ginsberg, Kerouac, and Ansen to pull Burroughs out of his heroin-induced haze to start typing, editing, and assembling the random notes that would become *Naked Lunch*. Paradoxically, the city that personally and artistically benefited Burroughs simultaneously worked to destroy his life and fiction.

In 1964, Burroughs grew uncomfortable in Tangier, due in large part to increased penalties for drug use and heightened anti-American sentiment. He went to New York City in late 1964 and stayed at the Hotel Chelsea until late 1965. Shortly thereafter, Burroughs settled at 8 Duke Street in London, living there more or less regularly until 1974. He visited Tangier in 1967, where he "rework[ed] *The Ticket That Exploded* . . . [and] started a first draft of *The Wild Boys* [1971]" (Burroughs, "The Name Is Burroughs" 14). After visiting New York City several times in the early 1970s, Burroughs eventually took up permanent residence there in 1974. Burroughs returned to Tangier only once after 1967, when he visited Bowles and met with film director David Cronenberg in 1985 to discuss the movie adaptation of *Naked Lunch*, which was released in 1992 (Grauerholz, "Re: Questions About"). Correspondence between Burroughs and Bowles, who remained mainly in Morocco until his death, was predictably irregular, given the frequency of Burroughs's movement from one country to another. The two authors met for the last time in 1995 when they, along with Ginsberg and poet John Giorno (b. 1936), lunched at a New York City hotel (Offman). It is possible that, although Burroughs left Tangier, Tangier never left Burroughs. For an author who, in "International Zone," fictionalized himself as Brinton, "a man without context, of no place and no time" (Burroughs, *Interzone* 50), Tangier represented the geographic equivalent to Burroughs's inner state and world-view. Tangier, like Burroughs's fiction and Burroughs himself, resisted solid definition. What country or countries could stake the most claim to Tangier prior to its gaining independence? What real-life features of Tangier did Burroughs transfer to Interzone without fictionalizing them? Was Burroughs a Beat Generation author, an early postmodernist, or something else entirely? There are perhaps no definite answers to these questions, but clearly the non-place of Tangier and the non-person of Burroughs complemented one another.

This brief chronology of Burroughs's relationship with Bowles and Tangier helps to contextualize the ten letters presented here, which illustrate the importance of this location to Burroughs's life and art, despite his feeling like "a man without context" (*Interzone* 50). Burroughs wrote these letters to Bowles at various times between 1972 and 1979 from his residences in New York City and Boulder, Colorado. While the Burroughs correspondence to Bowles in the Delaware collection consists of only a few short letters each year, the collection also contains five postcards and four Christmas cards to Bowles from Burroughs. One Christmas card from 1984 bears the inscription, "To the old Tangier hands." Letter 5, published here and dated Christmas Eve 1976, portrays a melancholy Burroughs wishing he were in Tangier: "I miss Tangier especially around Christmas and your letter about people who come and stay on and on reminded me"; he then gives his best wishes to those still in Morocco.

Through these letters and cards, we see the human side of a former junky, a counterculture icon, and a literary rebel who simply missed his friends on that particular Christmas Eve. Furthermore, the letters published here suggest new techniques for reading Burroughs's fiction, especially in terms of location. The letters indicate the importance of one specific place to Burroughs's work—which is characterized in part by not being grounded in one place (both fictionally and with respect to the author's life). In other words, these letters suggest that Tangier serves as a key to understanding Burroughs's fiction, just as Tangier serves as a key to understanding Burroughs himself.

Most of these letters contain a palpable sense of nostalgia for Tangier —stronger in some but always present, even if implied. This nostalgia often manifests itself when Burroughs simply mentions, as he often does, someone he and Bowles knew in Tangier, such as when Burroughs inquires after the health of Mohammed Mrabet (b. 1940; a Moroccan writer, artist, and Bowles's personal assistant), or in letters 6 and 7 when he writes, somewhat enviously, of Mohammed Hamri (dates unknown; a famous painter and musician, and Bowles's friend) returning to Morocco. Similarly, letter 7 includes Burroughs's description of his apartment complex in Boulder as "a sort of international house," complete with Moroccan boys and Arab music—two direct reminders of life in Tangier. These instances illustrate that even though Burroughs left Tangier in the mid-1960s, the city had a lasting effect both on his personal life and on his art. The more personal passages of these letters provide a clear glimpse into Burroughs's personality; they represent a decided contrast to the isolated and mysterious writer-self whom Burroughs portrayed in his works.

One can see Burroughs's unique personality and tastes come through in these letters: his attraction to young men (letter 7), his cynical political opinions, his unshakable Beatnik wanderlust (illustrated by the geographic variety of his addresses), his eccentricities (letter 7: "Whenever I take a walk in the country I carry a tear gas gun and heavy cane in case of a dog attack"), and his ultimate desire to settle in one place.[2] The people, places, and events Burroughs mentions in these letters appear as recurring themes and motifs in his novels: homosexual intercourse occurs in several of Burroughs's works, perhaps most graphically in *Naked Lunch*; William Lee, in *Junky* (1977; originally spelled *Junkie* [1953]) and *Queer* (1985), journeys from the Midwestern United States, to New York City, to Louisiana, to Texas, to Mexico City, and then to South America; and Burroughs mentions Tangier in works other than *Naked Lunch*, such as *The Western Lands* (1987).

In 1983, exactly thirty years after the publication of his first novel, *Junkie*—written under the pseudonym of William Lee—the American

Academy of Arts and Letters somewhat reluctantly admitted Burroughs into their ranks (Morgan 9). This was the first time the literary establishment recognized the validity of Burroughs's work. Although Burroughs has yet to be "officially" canonized, his influence on American literature and culture has subtly spread far and wide. His popularity and fame were more generally recognized in the 1970s—the time of the letters presented here. These letters mention some members of Burroughs's expansive circle of friends, which included well-known figures from literary, academic, entertainment, and political spheres. No longer merely the author of the notorious *Naked Lunch*, Burroughs emerged as a literary and cultural spokesman in the 1970s. Aside from calling musicians and authors such as Frank Zappa (1940–93), Mick Jagger (b. 1943), Keith Richards (b. 1943), John Ciardi (1946–86), and Norman Mailer (b. 1923) friends, Burroughs first coined and employed the term *heavy metal* in his "cut-up" trilogy of novels (*Nova Express, The Soft Machine,* and *The Ticket That Exploded*). *Heavy metal,* aside from appearing in other works by Burroughs, was eventually adopted as the definition of an entire genre of rock music that profoundly impacted popular culture, especially during the 1980s. The band Steely Dan took their name from a passage in *Naked Lunch* (83), and other prominent musicians such as the Rolling Stones, David Bowie (b. 1947), the Beatles, Pink Floyd, Patti Smith (b. 1946), the Ramones, and Debbie Harry (b. 1945) have utilized Burroughs's characters and literary techniques, particularly cut-ups, in their songs. In the mid-1970s, Burroughs contributed to the music magazine *Crawdaddy* by writing columns and conducting interviews with Led Zeppelin and other popular bands (Caveney 131–33).

Burroughs also influenced the punk and alternative rock countercultures in Britain and in America. Lou Reed (b. 1942), Iggy Pop (b. 1947), Tom Waits (b. 1949; Waits collaborated with Burroughs on *The Black Rider,* a Faustian opera first performed in 1990 and later released as an album in 1993 [Caveney 199–202]), and Kurt Cobain (1967–94; Cobain in 1993 set Burroughs's short story "The 'Priest,' They Called Him" to music while the author read the work [Caveney 198–99]) are only a few of the famous musicians directly impacted by Burroughs and his work.[3] Graham Caveney, in *Gentleman Junky: The Life and Legacy of William S. Burroughs,* attributes Burroughs's influence on the music world to his diverse lifestyle: "What Burroughs offers is a figure who embodies pop's repertoire of identities. Here is someone who pursued the hedonistic delights of appetite to their most rock-ish excesses. Burroughs's lifestyle puts the combined efforts of Keith Moon [1946–78; late drummer of the Who] and [Keith] Richards to shame" (191). Perhaps the most significant moment of public exposure for Burroughs occurred on 7 November 1981, when he gave a reading from *Naked Lunch* on *Saturday Night Live*. The host that evening, Lauren Hutton, introduced Burroughs as "America's greatest living writer" (qtd. in *Literary Resource Center*).[4]

In letters 9 and 10, below, Burroughs writes to Bowles of purchasing a house in either New Mexico or Florida and mentions lectures, readings, and talks he is scheduled to give in various faraway places. A nomad to the end of his life, Burroughs never grounded himself in one location, even when he settled down. Burroughs's experiences in Tangier during the 1950s and 1960s set the tone for his subsequent life experiences and literary works; the nostalgia for Tangier, evidenced by the longing tone of these letters, helps to acknowledge the validity of Burroughs's work and experiences during his stay there. Perhaps it is fitting that Burroughs achieved acceptance, if not fame, in Europe long before he did so in America, since he felt more comfortable, for the most part, in places other than America. Burroughs's fiction took on features of Tangier, the place that influenced him the most. Despite Burroughs's acceptance by a wider section of American popular, literary, and academic culture, some resistance to the study or even the reading of his works still persists. Perhaps this is due to the graphic representations of drug use, vivid depictions of homosexual and heterosexual intercourse, a false sense of inaccessibility, and a perceived lack of "literary value"—but these are ultimately superficial reasons for maligning his work. The letters printed below present a small yet insightful cross-section of William Burroughs's life and provide further evidence that he might be not only one of America's great literary and cultural figures, but also a fascinating individual with an inner life fittingly contrary to his outer life.

A Note on Editorial Principles

Burroughs was a meticulous and careful writer of fiction, but these letters portray a less thorough and more relaxed Burroughs at his typewriter. The letters are short, as if Burroughs wrote them in a hurry. I have attempted to preserve their idiosyncratic content without sacrificing their readability. The original layout, spacing, and paragraphing of Burroughs's letters remain intact, although the indentations have been regularized. I have also regularized the format of the return addresses, the salutations, and the placement of dates. Burroughs corrected a fair number of his typewritten mistakes in pen, and I have reproduced his words as corrected. In some cases, I add missing letters to words or add pertinent information to the letters, which I denote with square brackets. In the original typescript letters, there are obvious spelling errors, such as "San Francsico" (letter 3) and "graet" (letter 8), as well as clear mechanical errors (misplaced apostrophes in letter 7 and no spaces between words in several letters). I have silently corrected these mistakes, but have preserved instances where Burroughs misspelled names of persons and places, and where he omitted necessary punctuation. Therefore, all remaining spelling, grammatical, and mechanical errors are Burroughs's. Stray marks and cancelled words have not been reproduced. Because Burroughs often both signed and typed his name to his letters, I reproduce his signature in italics and his typed name in plain text.

At the head of each letter, I provide pertinent textual information and details about the letter. "TLS" stands for "typed letter signed," and I also note the stationery address headings when applicable. My endnotes attempt to explain Burroughs's whereabouts for each letter; to elucidate events he mentions; to describe objects and places he talks about; and to provide information about his extensive circle of literary, musical, and social acquaintances. I have tried to discuss the topical references to Tangier and to explain the spirit of Tangier that informs these letters, since these references are few. All letters are from William S. Burroughs to Paul Bowles, and are in series 1, box 1, folders 1–3 of the Paul Bowles Papers, housed in the Hugh M. Morris Library at the University of Delaware, Newark. I list the full catalogue information for these letters in my bibliography. See also the Paul Bowles Papers Web site, <http://www.lib.udel.edu/ud/spec/findaids/bowlespa.htm>.

1

TLS, 1 p.
April 28, 1972
5th Avenue Hotel
24 5th Avenue
NYC

Dear Paul

As you can see I have elected to visit the most exotic country of them all and have not been disappointed. New York has changed beyond recognition since I last saw it two years ago.[5] Any sex act can now be shown on the public screen with beautiful actors and that's a powerful sight. In fact not altogether to my advantage since when you can see it you are not so interested to read about it. Anything described in The Wild Boys can now be seen in color and close up.[6] And that means fewer sales. It seems I wasnt kidding when I said I was working to make myself obsolete. May make a sex flick myself after talking with a director in this genre. They have to be good or no one will go and see it.

Seems to be a lot going on here on all fronts. I saw Donald Richie[7] who sends you his best regards. He tells me that Japan is very strict on grass but loose in other matters.

I hear very destressing reports from Morocco of beatings, muggings and police suppression. What is your first hand impression?

Your book is in a window display in Brentano's.[8] I hope it is selling well. Barney Rossett[9] says the hard cover book is on the way out. Except of course for book of the month best sellers.

                    all the best
                    Bill B *Bill B.*

2

TLS, 1 p.   William Burroughs
                                                c/o Dick Seaver[10]
                                              333 Central Park West
                                                      NYC 10025

                                                      13 Apr [19]74

Dear Paul,

Mrabet asks me what I think about the Arab-Israeli situation.[11] Is not personal opinion. That is to say, since my personal opinion carries no weight or importance, I prefer not to express it. Or, in the words of Madame Porte, "Je ne pas un opinion."[12] He also asks how I would settle this question; I have not been called upon to do so. In conclusion he asks what I would do if I were President of the United States, and I can only reply I would never be President of the United States. Or, to put it another way, what I would do if I were somebody else? [P]robably act like somebody else.

I am, as you see, in New York, teaching a semester at New York City College.[13] Brion[14] is here on a visit; he now has a studio in Paris, but I know of no plans to open a gallery. New York is lively and interesting after London,[15] which now presents all the disadvantages of the Blitz with none of its togetherness.[16] Not enough bombs, you know—at least not yet. But I did hear one, which was right around the corner from me.

                    All the best from New York
                    to you in Tangiers, hasta luego—
                    Bill B.

3

TLS, 1 p.

William Burroughs
77 Franklin St.
New York City 10013

Box 842, Canal St. Station
New York City 10013[17]

Paul Bowles
P.O. Box 2117
Tanger Socco
Tangier, MOROCCO

15 Feb [19]75

Dear Paul,

After teaching a semester at New York City College, an experience which I would not care to repeat, I decided to settle in New York or at least somewhere in America, and have had no reason to regret it. I spent a week in San Francisco and Berkeley, giving readings and talks, which I found most instructive and enjoyable. After the dreary and irreversible decay of London, New York seems bright and lively.

I've been invited to have lunch with Moshe Dayan and the Egyptian ambassador somewhere in Alabama[18]—where else could such things happen?

John Hopkins[19] was anything but subdued the last time I saw him, at a party for the friends of the American School in the Dakota,[20] in the course of which he gave a speech. Brion has undergone major surgery in London and has been in a very bad way.[21] He is now apparently on the road to recovery and will return to Paris.

Did anything ever happen with the film based on <u>Let It Come Down</u>?[22] I think that an excellent film could be made from this book.

My best to Mrabet.

All the best for 1975,
William
William B.

WSB:jwg[23]

4

TLS, 1 p. (Stationery headed: William S. Burroughs / P.O. Box 842 / Canal Street Station / New York, N.Y. 10013)

NOV 8 1975
[stamped date]

Dear Paul:

Box number is indeed operative and I am settled in New York where no gendarmes [policemen] pound on one's door these days. I declined the invitation to dine with General Dyan and Governor Wallace since no funds for transport to and from were forthcoming.[24] After all I am a professional man.

At a recent reading in Ann Arbor Mich. I met a personable and well mannered young man named Dan Bente who had visited you in Tangier and asked to be remembered.[25] John Mitchell, who used to run The Black Cat on avenida Espana in Tangier[26] is now in New York planning to open a bar.

Brion has been very ill and has to visit the hospital in Paris several time[s] a week for an hour or so. He is naturally very depressed and I am sure he would like to hear from you.

Sorry to hear that Let It Come Down is not on the way. I think it would make a great film if properly handled.

Sanche and Nancy send their best. He has now changed his name to Ted Morgan.[27]

All the best
Bill
Bill B

P.S. Also met at a party here a rather formidable woman who knows you forget her name

5

TLS, 1 p.   December 24, 1976

Dear Paul:

Thanks for your letter. Despite my preference for America as a place of residence I miss Tangier especially around Christmas and your letter about people who come and stay on and on reminded me. Brion wrote and asked me about Benté but I couldnt tell him much. I do think that a biography of Brion would be an excellent idea unless Brion could be prevailed upon to write his own memoirs.

I keep very busy with articles, lectures, readings. One has the feeling being in the middle of something here I dont know just what. Why I was made an honorary citizen of Austin Texas by the Mayor himself.

Ahmed Jacoubi[28] lives just around the corner seemingly having decided that New York is real enough to live in.

My best to John and Joe and George Greeves[29] and Tangier and a to[a]st to Jay H[a]zelwood who dropped dead in the Parade Bar eleven years ago tom[o]rrow.[30]

And my best wishes for recovery to Mrabet. Only thing to do for hepetitis is lots of bottled water and rest.

Seasons Greetings
William
William B

6

TLS, 1 p. March 6, 1978
1155 Marine
Boulder, Colo.
USA[31]

Dear Paul:

A curious coincidence: I started to answer your letter yesterday to the effect that while it was cold here too the heating was quite adequate, and woke up this morning to find that the heating had failed completely. (Its back on now).

Boulder is bland and innocuous rather than exciting. It's a middle class town with no minorities and no slums at the same time a university town with a relaxed atmosphere, decriminalized pot, a mall and book stores and health food. Beautiful blond boys everywhere one looks but strictly decorative rather than functional. I have been working on a western and to get into the action have bought two pistols with which I practice on the public range.[32]

Sorry to hear that Mahrabet is paying the price of increased responsibility. I hope he is taking care of himself and drinking milk which is the thing for ulcers I understand.

Do you mean you cant leave Morocco because you would not be allowed to return? Hamri just phoned me from Los Angeles to say he has a letter from the king himself asking him to come back to Morocco.[33] I see Jacoubi in New York from time to time and he seems to be doing well.

I hear from Brion regularly. He seems to be keeping very busy. Please give my best regards to Mahrabet
>   Best Regards
>   *William B.*
>   William B

7

TLS, 1 p.   May 13, 1978

>   1155 Marine
>   #415
>   Boulder, Colo. 80302
>   USA

Dear Paul:
Stray dogs are a problem here too and there is a shoot on sight order. Good thing too. Whenever I take a walk in the country I carry a tear gas gun and a heavy cane in case of a dog attack.

Sorry to hear of Mrabet's health problems. Isn't the infection controlable with antibiotics? Please give him my wishes for recovery. My son had a liver transplant about a year ago and the incision still hasn't completely healed.[34] He is on a maintenance dose of morphine.[35]

Boulder is still clean. Summer weather here now and a parade of beautiful shirtless blond boys skateboard by my window. This apartment building is a sort of international house. Two Moroccan boys live opposite me and I hear Arab music all day. Some stores even have signs in Arabic.

Hamri is indeed on his way back to Morocco on personal invitation of the king. I just received a brochure put out by Air Maroc:[36]
>   Hamri
>   The Painter of Morocco
>   Presents
>   AN ARTISTS VIEW OF MOROCCO
>   Land of Blessing
>   and Beauty

I see Jacoubi from time to time he lives right around the corner from my N[e]w York loft. He seems to be doing well and doing some very good work.

Still doing a lot of reading and lectures. Will be going to New Castle [upon Tyne] in England in another month for a reading and panel. And giving some courses here later in the summer.
All the best
William
William B.

8

TLS, 1 p. (Stationery headed: William S. Burroughs / Box 213 / Canal St. Station / New York, N.Y. 10013)
February 26 [1979]

Dear Paul,
Looking foreward to longer prayer calls and higher gasolene prices? Not much different here. It wouldn't surprise me to hear prayer calls in Boulder.[37]
The Nova Convention was great fun but very strenuous.[38] There was a big party last night with an aluminium wash tub fill of Khool Aid and vodka just like Jonestown[39] and everybody agreed it was tasteful. Tim Leary[40] got pied at the party by Aaron Kay the professional pie thrower. He was searched at the door but sneaked into the kitchen some way and got a pie. He has covered Mayor Kock,[41] Anita Bryant, Andy Warhol and other luminaries.[42] One hasnt arrived until one has been pied.
I think the Dicken[s] comparison arose because like Dickens I am concerned primarily with characters.[43] It does seem to me that the resemblance ends there and I find Dickens very heavy going. When I think of Dickens I always remember the Evelyn Waugh book A Handful of Dust where the protagonist is forced by a madman in the South American jungle to read Dickens to him year after year.
Allen Ginsberg received a gold medal from the Arts Club[44] and read Cocksucker Blues.[45] The old ladies were upset but unable to stem the tides of change.
Please give my best to everyone in Tangier.
All the best
Bill
William Burroughs

9

TLS, 1 p.   June 4, 1979

222 Bowery
NYC 10012
USA[46]

Dear Paul:
Odd about the proofs. Does one surmise the woman killed her husband for the love of this Peter Bowles? Certainly you have an alibi. Seems most unlikely the proofs were interfered with in Santa Barbara.[47]
I dont believe I have had any direct dealings with Sylvia Pogorzalek of Bonn.[48] The deal must have gone through my agent and I dont remember the details.[49] I have never had any bad experience with German publishers.
I am leaving tomorrow for readings in Switzerland, Amsterdam and Rome. Inflation keeps one moving. I dream of buying a house
                all the best
                Bill B.

10

TLS, 1 p.   November 16, 1979

222 Bowery
NYC 10012
USA

Dear Paul,
Sorry to hear of your confused residence status.[50] Would it be any use to engage a lawyer? I know that Alan Ansen[51] had residence difficulties in Athens which were finally resolved by a Greek lawyer presumeably with connections. And I remember similar interventions in Mexico.
I have seen the collected stories. Looks like a very good edition.[52] What is the status of <u>Let It Come Down</u>? I have been a teacher of a course in "creative reading" at Naropa[53] and have this book on my list of neglected books but do not know where it can be obtained.
I dream of buying a house in the Tallahassee area of Florida which has a lot of trees and water, or perhaps in Northern New Mexico.[54]
                All best
                Bill
                William Burroughs

NOTES

1. I extend my thanks and appreciation to the several people who have helped me prepare this article: Professor Charles E. Robinson of the University of Delaware, for his invaluable editorial suggestions; James Grauerholz of William Burroughs Communications, for graciously allowing me to reproduce these heretofore unpublished letters and providing helpful information about Burroughs; L. Rebecca Johnson Melvin of the Special Collections Department of the Hugh M. Morris Library at the University of Delaware; Professor Susan Goodman, also of the University of Delaware, for being a willing and good-natured proofreader of the introduction; and Donna Brantlinger Black, for her superb copyediting of the piece.

2. Even after settling in America in 1974, Burroughs traveled extensively across the country and abroad, giving talks and lectures, which were his main sources of income. Burroughs gave approximately 150 readings and lectures around the world at about $500 each from 1974 to 1984, earning him $75,000 (*Literature Resource Center*). Bowles wrote to Ted Morgan on 19 December 1984 that he was "not in close touch with Burroughs, although occasionally I will get a postcard from him which I don't answer because I never know his address" (*In Touch* 522). Burroughs's nomadic impulse was not easily suppressed, even by old age.

3. In the 1980s and 1990s, Burroughs collaborated with several other musicians on their albums, including Laurie Anderson, Ministry (see below), Seven Souls, the Disposable Heroes of Hiphoprisy, and R.E.M. Burroughs also committed several of his own writings to tape, which include *The Elvis of Letters* (1985), *Dead City Radio* (1990), and a four-CD box set entitled *The Best of William Burroughs* (1998; Caveney 222). Burroughs featured prominently in the music video for Ministry's song "Just One Fix" from their album *Psalm 69* (1992). The song and the video both concern heroin addiction. In the video, Burroughs is seen (and heard) reading from his works, standing in front of tornado footage, and, most interestingly, firing a shotgun at plaques on which the words "history," "reality," "language," and "control" are written.

4. Fourteen years prior to his *Saturday Night Live* reading, Burroughs—along with a host of other literary, religious, and popular culture figures—appeared as a cardboard cut-out on the cover of the Beatles's album *Sgt. Pepper's Lonely Hearts Club Band* (1967). The real-life Burroughs landed many movie roles, including *Drugstore Cowboy* (1989), which starred Matt Dillon (b. 1964).

5. Burroughs visited New York City for two months in the summer of 1970 (Morgan 452). Save for brief stateside visits, Burroughs lived abroad for twenty-four years (1950–74) in Mexico City, Colombia, Tangier, Paris, and London. He returned to London after the visit mentioned in this letter, and then settled in New York City in 1974 to teach at City College of New York (see letters 2 and 3).

6. Burroughs's *The Wild Boys: A Book of the Dead* (1971) is the story of a group of time-traveling, violent, homosexual, drug-using cowboys who seek to establish a utopia where the traditional, controlling, and hierarchical standards of American society do not apply. Characters from the novel also appear in Burroughs's "Western trilogy" (see n. 32, below).

7. Donald Richie (b. 1924), American expatriate writer, spent most of his life in Japan. At the time of this letter, Richie worked as a film curator at New York's Museum of Modern Art.

8. Brentano's is an American bookstore chain that first opened in Paris in 1895. The Brentano's in New York City, to which Burroughs refers here, was located on 597 Fifth Avenue. Burroughs refers to *Without Stopping* (1972), Bowles's autobiography.

9. Barnet Lee Rossett Jr. (b. 1922) campaigned extensively against censorship and in 1951 founded Grove Press, the first American publisher of *Naked Lunch* (1962). *Naked Lunch* was deemed obscene by United States authorities as it was being serialized in the *Chicago Review* and then later in *Big Table*. The Massachusetts Supreme Court ruled against the obscenity charges on 7 July 1966 (Morgan 347), making Burroughs and Grove Press famous and "marking the end of (official) literary censorship in America" (Caveney 99). Grove Press published Burroughs's work until 1984 (see n. 10 and n. 49, below).

10. Dick Seaver (dates unknown) was Burroughs's editor at Grove Press for almost twenty years.

11. Mohammed Mrabet (Mohammed ben Chaib el Hajjam, b. 1940), Moroccan author, artist, and Paul Bowles's personal assistant for over two decades. After meeting Mrabet in the 1960s, Burroughs became one of Mrabet's important American supporters. A 1976 postcard promoting a New York exhibit of Mrabet's paintings features an endorsement from Burroughs: "The art of Mohammed Mrabet cannot be called primitive, for the draftsmanship is quite sophisticated. . . . [T]here is a fresh and original style which is uniquely Mrabet's own." Burroughs also refers to the still-unresolved struggle for land in the Middle East.

12. The correct French would be "Je na'i pas d'une opinion," which means "I have no opinion." Madame Porte (Janine Porte, b. 1933) said this when Jane Bowles asked her to sign a petition for the conservation of trees in the Gran Socco (Great Market) of Tangier (Morgan 588). I am grateful to James Grauerholz for the proper French spelling of this statement.

13. Burroughs was paid $7,000 to teach creative writing at the college, but the experience was less than profitable (Morgan 463, 472; see letter 3).

14. Brion Gysin (1916–86), English painter, photographer, and author who heavily influenced Burroughs. Gysin created the "cut-up" technique of writing, which involved taking randomly selected sections of text from newspapers, magazines, novels, and other media and arranging them in different ways. By cutting up texts, new meanings arose from the new combinations, and authors and artists could effectively eschew the controlling nature of language—one of Burroughs's greatest artistic and personal concerns. Burroughs believed that language was a "virus" and assaulted language in his cut-up fiction and in nonfictional pieces such as "Word" (*Interzone* 135–94). Burroughs employed cut-ups in *Naked Lunch*, *Nova Express*, *The Soft Machine*, and *The Ticket That Exploded*. Gysin and Burroughs collaborated on seven books: *Minutes to Go* (1960), *Exterminator!* (1960), *Brion Gysin Let the Mice In* (1973), *Colloque de Tanger* (Vol. 1; 1976), *The Third Mind* (1978), *Colloque de Tanger* (Vol. 2; 1979), and *The Cat Inside* (1986), several of which involved cut-ups.

15. Burroughs had lived at 8 Duke Street, St. James's, London, from 1966 through 1974.

16. The *blitzkrieg*, Nazi air raids on London during World War II that forced civilians into air raid shelters and Underground stations.

17. Burroughs's mailing address, which appears as the return address on many of his New York envelopes. 77 Franklin Street, in Soho, was his street address, where he moved in May 1974 (Morgan 481).

18. Moshe Dayan (1915–81), prominent Israeli militarist, statesman, and author. The meeting never occurred (see n. 24, below); Burroughs likely refers humorously to his conversation with Mrabet (see letter 2).

19. John Hopkins (b. 1938), Princeton-educated American expatriate writer, lived for nearly two decades in Tangier. His books include *Tangier Buzzless Flies* (1972) and *The Tangier Diaries 1962–1979* (1998). Hopkins also served as headmaster of the American School in Tangier, which Burroughs's son attended for a time (see n. 34, below).

20. The Dakota is a famous New York City hotel located at 72nd Street and Central Park West.

21. In December 1974, doctors diagnosed Gysin with colon cancer, for which he had three more surgeries in February 1975 (Morgan 482).

22. Bowles's novel *Let It Come Down*, first published in America in 1952 by Random House, tells the story of Nelson Dyar, an American banker who falls prey to the darker allures of Tangier (Caponi 157–61). A film of the novel was never made, but a biographical film about Bowles of the same name, directed by Jennifer Baichwal, was released in 1999 (*Let It Come Down*). Burroughs refers to this again in letter 4.

23. James W. Grauerholz (b. 1952), Burroughs's longtime secretary and personal assistant. After moving to New York City in 1974, Grauerholz helped Burroughs edit *Cities of the Red Night* (1981) and would go on to edit *Interzone* (1989), a collection of previously unpublished Burroughs writings, and coedit *Word Virus: A William Burroughs Reader* (1999) with Ira Silverberg. In addition, Grauerholz helped organize the Nova Convention in 1978 (see n. 38, below), currently runs William Burroughs Communications in Lawrence, Kansas—Burroughs's final residence (see n. 54, below)—and is the executor of Burroughs's estate. He is now working on a new, major biography of Burroughs (Grauerholz, "Re: Questions About").

24. That is, Moshe Dayan (see n. 18, above) and Alabama governor George C. Wallace (1919–98), an advocate for racial segregation who lost runs for the Presidency in 1968, 1972,

and 1976. Wallace was shot and paralyzed by Arthur Bremer (b. 1950) in 1972 (*Wallace Speeches*).

25. Dan Bente (dates unknown) taught at the American School in Tangier (Dillon 5).

26. The Black Cat was a popular bar frequented by the Beats and other Tangier denizens.

27. Sanche de Gramont (b. 1932) was Ted Morgan's original name, and Nancy was his wife. Morgan, a journalist, novelist, biographer, and friend of Burroughs, hailed from an aristocratic French family. He is the author of *Literary Outlaw: The Life and Times of William S. Burroughs* (1988).

28. Ahmed ben Driss el-Yacoubi (1931–85), Moroccan artist and author, was one of Bowles's closest friends until their falling out in the late 1960s. Yacoubi was "just the companion for whom Bowles had been searching" (Sawyer-Lauçanno 294), in that they shared similar artistic interests and were naturally compatible friends, although many believed them to be lovers—a claim that has never been proven. Whatever the exact nature of their relationship, Yacoubi's paintings, drawings, and stories earned wide praise thanks in large part to Bowles's patronage (Caponi 172).

29. John Hopkins (see n. 19, above), Joe McMasters, and George Greeves (two obscure references) were Tangier acquaintances of Burroughs and Bowles.

30. Jay Haselwood (19??–65), American expatriate from Kentucky, owned the Parade Bar, a Tangier hotspot, and died there of a heart attack at 2 p.m. on Christmas Day, 1965. Haselwood was "a fixture of the city, friend and confidant to all" (Caponi 148), and was particularly close with Jane Bowles (*In Touch* 378).

31. In a postcard (with envelope) to Bowles postmarked 23 December 1977, Burroughs said he was a resident of Colorado, even though he traveled from Boulder to New York City and back again several times during the year. Burroughs lived at this address until 1979 (when the cost of living became too high [Bockris 136]) while teaching at the Naropa Institute (see n. 53, below) so that he could visit his son Billy, who was often checked into local hospitals and clinics (see n. 34, below).

32. Burroughs wrote several books that featured Western characters and motifs, but three books in particular make up his "Western trilogy": *Cities of the Red Night* (1981), *The Place of Dead Roads* (1983), and *The Western Lands* (1987). The mention of pistols is ironic—Burroughs was an avid marksman and continued practicing even after he accidentally shot and killed his second wife, Joan Vollmer (b. 1924), in Mexico City on 6 September 1951.

33. Mohammed Hamri (dates unknown), "the Painter of Morocco," a friend of Bowles and a preeminent member of Tangier's cultural scene. An accomplished painter, Hamri also wrote novels and founded the Master Musicians of Jajouka (or Joujouka). In the late 1950s, Burroughs, Bowles, and Gysin (see n. 14, above) met Hamri and his band—which consisted of singers, traditional pipers, and other musicians—and recorded them, submitting the tape to the Library of Congress. Wider recognition came for the group when the Rolling Stones introduced them to the Western world in 1969 (see Kettlewell). The King of Morocco at the time was Moulay al-Hassan Ben Mohammed al-Alaoui Hassan II (1929–99), or Hassan II, who ruled from 1961 until his death.

34. William S. "Billy" Burroughs Jr. (1947–81) suffered severe mental and physical ailments throughout his life due to alcohol and drug addictions that began during his teenage years. His mother, Joan Vollmer (see n. 32, above), was addicted to Benzedrine while pregnant with Billy (Steinbeck 168). Four years old at the time of his mother's death, Billy went to live with his grandparents in St. Louis and Palm Beach, Florida, rarely seeing his father except for a visit to Tangier in 1963 (Burroughs, "The Name Is Burroughs" 13) and Boulder, Colorado (see n. 31, above). Burroughs Jr.'s first novel, *Speed* (1970), is a fictionalized account of his arrest in New York City for drug possession (Skerl vi–vii). Haunted for most of his adult life by his absent father's fame, Billy died of cirrhosis of the liver without ever connecting fully with Burroughs senior. *Kentucky Ham*, Billy's other novel, was published in 1973. For more on Billy, see David Ohle's *Cursed from Birth: The Short, Unhappy Life of William S. Burroughs, Jr.*

35. Ironically, a drug Burroughs himself was addicted to for most of his adult life. When he was fourteen, according to Morgan (34), Burroughs almost lost his left hand in an accidental chemical explosion. He recounted, "By the time I got to the hospital the doctors had to give me a morphine injection which they said was 'almost an adult dose.' . . . I've been

addicted ever since" (qtd. in Bockris 108–9). See the appendix to the Grove Press edition of *Naked Lunch*, "Letter from a Master Addict to Dangerous Drugs" (215–32), for a compendium of the drugs Burroughs used, their effects, and the possible health problems associated with their use.

36. Royal Air Maroc, an airline providing service to Morocco and elsewhere.

37. Burroughs probably alludes simultaneously to the gas shortage in the United States, the rise of Islamic radicals preaching in Tangier mosques, and the heavy population of Arabs in Boulder (see letters 6 and 7). Bowles wrote to Burroughs of the Tangier situation on 31 November 1978, talking of rising gas prices and of "loudspeakers at the tops of the minarets so that the calls will be sure to awaken everyone sleeping within two miles; the call used to last two minutes or so. Now it lasts twenty-five minutes" (*In Touch* 485).

38. The Nova Convention was a three-day (30 Nov.–2 Dec. 1978) seminar held in New York City in honor of Burroughs's life and works. Organized by Grauerholz (see n. 23, above), Sylvere Lotringer (currently professor of French at Columbia University), and poet John Giorno (b. 1936), Nova Convention attendees included "academics, publishers, writers, artists, punk rockers, [and] counterculture groupies" (Morgan 548). Frank Zappa and Patti Smith also gave performances, reading from *Naked Lunch* and other works by Burroughs (Morgan 549–60).

39. A sarcastic reference to the People's Temple (a doomsday cult), whose members committed mass suicide in Jonestown, Guyana, South America, on 18 November 1978. Led by Reverend Jim Jones, 913 men, women, and children were ordered by Jones to drink Kool Aid spiked with cyanide so that they could "move to another planet for a life of bliss" (*People's Temple*).

40. Timothy Francis Leary (1920–96), psychologist, author, and former Harvard professor infamous for his experiments with mescaline, psychedelic mushrooms, and LSD (d-lysergic acid diethylamide). A staunch advocate for the use of hallucinogens as consciousness expanders, Leary coined the phrase "Tune in, turn on, drop out," which embodied a great deal of the counterculture's philosophy and influenced its resulting music and literature.

41. Ed Koch (b. 1924), mayor of New York City at the time.

42. Anita Bryant (b. 1940), recording artist and anti-homosexual crusader, ran the "Save Our Children" movement in Florida and served as spokeswoman for the Florida Orange Industry. Andy Warhol (1928–87), avant-garde filmmaker, photographer, and artist. Warhol was a friend of Burroughs; Bryant was not.

43. Anne Waldman (b. 1945), a colleague of Burroughs (see n. 53, below), compared him to Charles Dickens in a *New York Times* article (1 Dec. 1978). Bowles failed to see the relationship: "Dickens? With all his stuffy sentimentality? She [Waldman] says your readings remind her of his reading. How many times did she hear Dickens read, I wonder? I don't imagine you argued with her about it" (*In Touch* 485). Burroughs was slightly more sympathetic to Waldman's view.

44. The Gramercy National Arts Club hesitated for years to admit Beat generation poets and authors to their ranks. Allen Ginsberg (1926–97) is perhaps the most immediately recognizable of the Beat poets and the author of the controversial and influential *Howl* (1956) and *Kaddish* (1961). Ginsberg and Burroughs were lovers for a brief time in the early 1950s and maintained close personal and business relationships throughout their lives. They collaborated on *The Yage Letters* (1963), a collection of correspondence between the two authors while Burroughs was searching for yage, a sacred drug that supposedly grants its users telepathic powers, in South America during the early 1950s.

45. "Cocksucker Blues" is a poem by Ginsberg; it is also the title of a song by the Rolling Stones and an infamous documentary by Robert Frank (b. 1924) about the band (filmed in 1972 but unreleased). Burroughs and the Rolling Stones, especially Mick Jagger and Keith Richards, were well acquainted.

46. This address in New York was known as "The Bunker," an old YMCA locker room where Burroughs lived sporadically from 1975 until 1981 (the address does not appear in any of his previous letters to Bowles in the University of Delaware Collection). Barry Miles describes the Bunker as "a large concrete space, lacking windows but with a fridge and air conditioning that buzzed and hummed, amplified by the bare walls and floor, giving the room peculiar acoustics. The bathroom still had its rows of urinals and lavatory stalls . . . [t]he room was artificially lit and . . . Burroughs [had] to open the metal gates which

guarded the front door. Three more locked doors had to be negotiated in order to reach his rooms" (181). Burroughs hosted several parties for his friends (and himself) at the Bunker, which became a counterculture headquarters/outpost. One of Burroughs's favorite rallying cries was, "We must hold the Bunker at all costs." John Giorno (see n. 38, above) lived upstairs from Burroughs at the time and now owns the Bunker.

47. In a letter dated 11 April 1979, Bowles wrote to Burroughs of an incident at his American publishers, Black Sparrow Press: "Then the editor of Black Sparrow wrote me, 'unnerved,' 'stunned' by a visit from two detectives looking for me.... A woman in Santa Barbara had got rid of her husband by putting eight bullets into him; among her papers was an unmailed letter to Peter Bowles, Black Sparrow, etc. The detectives decided that Peter must be Paul, but refused to give the woman's name or suggest what might be in the letter. Could it be that the proofs were interfered with in Santa Barbara?" (*In Touch* 488). Bowles refers to the books *Tennessee Williams in Tangier* by Mohamed Choukri (trans. Bowles) and *The Collected Stories of Paul Bowles 1939–1976*, both published that year by Black Sparrow with no legal repercussions.

48. Sylvia Pogorzalek (dates unknown) worked for Expanded Media, Burroughs's German publishers. Expanded Media published Burroughs's *Naked Scientology / Ali's Smile* (1978) and *The Four Horsemen of the Apocalypse* (1984).

49. Peter Matson (dates unknown) was Burroughs's literary agent from 1965 until 1984, when Burroughs left Grove Press and Matson for Viking and Andrew Wylie (dates unknown), his new publisher and agent (Morgan 596–97).

50. The Tangier of the 1950s and 1960s was a distant memory by 1979. Bowles "could not leave Tangier, having been arrested as a spy the last time he traveled to another city ... [and] was afraid to leave Morocco, as he had been told he would not be readmitted.... It was like a form of house arrest" (Morgan 544). To make matters worse, Bowles's tax and residence status came under scrutiny by Moroccan and American authorities.

51. Alan Ansen (b. 1922), Harvard-educated classics scholar, expatriate author, professor of Greek Literature, and former secretary for W. H. Auden. While visiting Tangier in 1956, Ansen helped edit, organize, and type Burroughs's scattered notes and writings, which became *Naked Lunch* (Morgan 265). He published *William Burroughs: An Essay* in 1986.

52. *The Collected Stories of Paul Bowles 1939–1976.*

53. The Naropa Institute, now Naropa University, was founded in Boulder, Colorado, in 1974. It was the first accredited Buddhist institute of higher education in the United States. That same year, Ginsberg (see n. 44, above) and fellow poet Waldman founded the Jack Kerouac School for Disembodied Poetics at the institute, which still exists and offers bachelors and masters degrees in poetics and writing. Burroughs taught at Naropa from 1975 until the early 1980s, mostly in the summers. The experience was much more enjoyable than his brief tenure at New York City College (see n. 13, above).

54. Burroughs never settled in either of these places, but chose to live in Lawrence, Kansas, from 1981 until his death in 1997.

WORKS CITED

American National Biography. American Council of Learned Societies and Oxford UP, 2001. 7 Dec. 2001 <http://www.anb.org/articles/index.html>.

"Avant-Garde Unites Over Burroughs." *New York Times* 1 Dec. 1978: C11.

The Beatles. *Sgt. Pepper's Lonely Hearts Club Band.* Perf. George Harrison, John Lennon, Paul McCartney, and Ringo Starr. EMI, 1967.

Biography Resource Center. Gale Research Group, 2001. 5 Dec. 2001 <http://www.galenet.com/servlet/BioRC>.

Bockris, Victor. *With William Burroughs: A Report from the Bunker.* New York: Seaver, 1981.

Bowles, Paul. *The Collected Stories of Paul Bowles 1939–1976.* Santa Barbara, CA: Black Sparrow, 1979.

——. *In Touch: The Letters of Paul Bowles.* Ed. Jeffrey Miller. New York: Farrar, 1994.

——. *Let It Come Down.* New York: Random, 1952.

——. *The Sheltering Sky.* New York: New Directions, 1949.

Brentano's. Corp. Web site. 5 Dec. 2001 <http://www.brentanos.fr>.

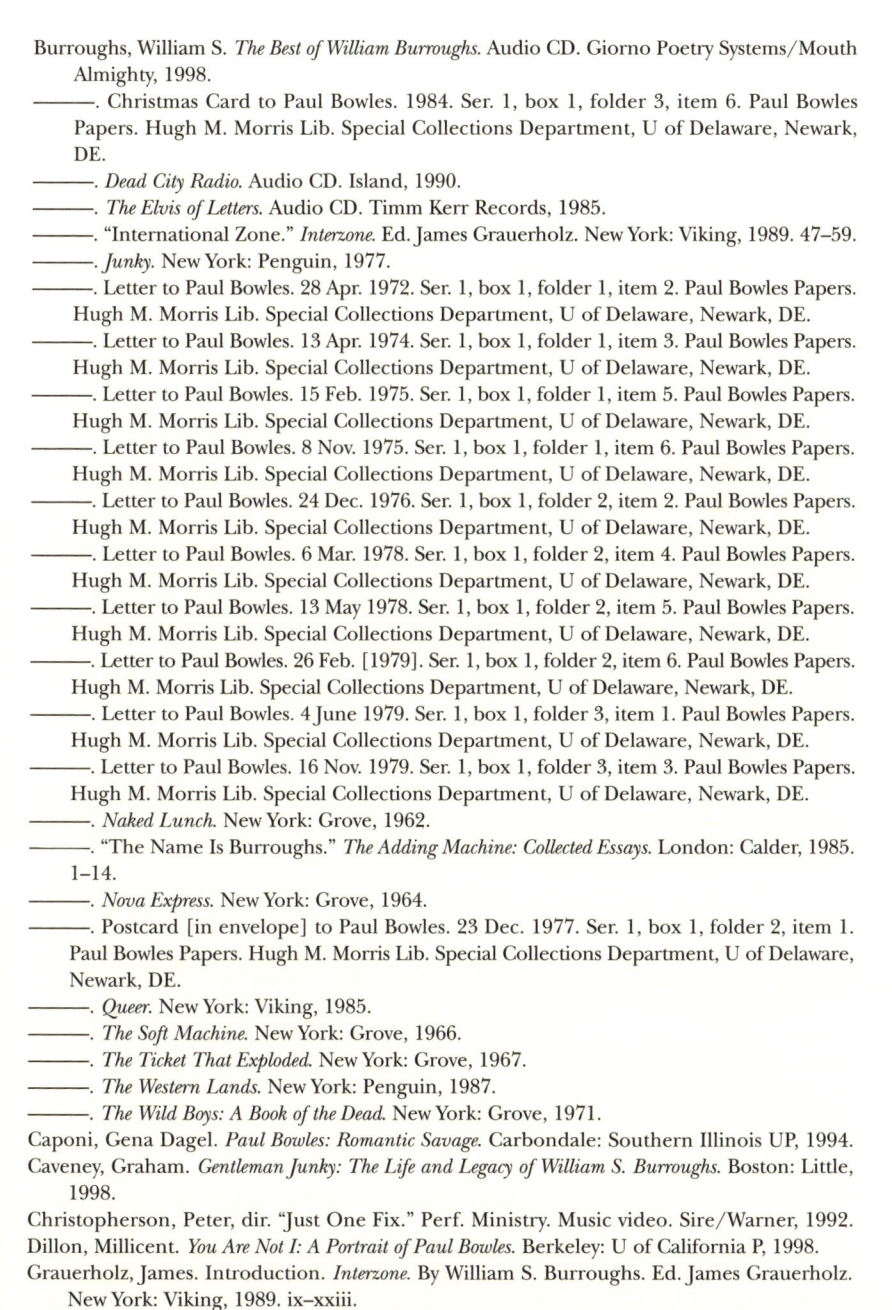

Burroughs, William S. *The Best of William Burroughs.* Audio CD. Giorno Poetry Systems/Mouth Almighty, 1998.
———. Christmas Card to Paul Bowles. 1984. Ser. 1, box 1, folder 3, item 6. Paul Bowles Papers. Hugh M. Morris Lib. Special Collections Department, U of Delaware, Newark, DE.
———. *Dead City Radio.* Audio CD. Island, 1990.
———. *The Elvis of Letters.* Audio CD. Timm Kerr Records, 1985.
———. "International Zone." *Interzone.* Ed. James Grauerholz. New York: Viking, 1989. 47–59.
———. *Junky.* New York: Penguin, 1977.
———. Letter to Paul Bowles. 28 Apr. 1972. Ser. 1, box 1, folder 1, item 2. Paul Bowles Papers. Hugh M. Morris Lib. Special Collections Department, U of Delaware, Newark, DE.
———. Letter to Paul Bowles. 13 Apr. 1974. Ser. 1, box 1, folder 1, item 3. Paul Bowles Papers. Hugh M. Morris Lib. Special Collections Department, U of Delaware, Newark, DE.
———. Letter to Paul Bowles. 15 Feb. 1975. Ser. 1, box 1, folder 1, item 5. Paul Bowles Papers. Hugh M. Morris Lib. Special Collections Department, U of Delaware, Newark, DE.
———. Letter to Paul Bowles. 8 Nov. 1975. Ser. 1, box 1, folder 1, item 6. Paul Bowles Papers. Hugh M. Morris Lib. Special Collections Department, U of Delaware, Newark, DE.
———. Letter to Paul Bowles. 24 Dec. 1976. Ser. 1, box 1, folder 2, item 2. Paul Bowles Papers. Hugh M. Morris Lib. Special Collections Department, U of Delaware, Newark, DE.
———. Letter to Paul Bowles. 6 Mar. 1978. Ser. 1, box 1, folder 2, item 4. Paul Bowles Papers. Hugh M. Morris Lib. Special Collections Department, U of Delaware, Newark, DE.
———. Letter to Paul Bowles. 13 May 1978. Ser. 1, box 1, folder 2, item 5. Paul Bowles Papers. Hugh M. Morris Lib. Special Collections Department, U of Delaware, Newark, DE.
———. Letter to Paul Bowles. 26 Feb. [1979]. Ser. 1, box 1, folder 2, item 6. Paul Bowles Papers. Hugh M. Morris Lib. Special Collections Department, U of Delaware, Newark, DE.
———. Letter to Paul Bowles. 4 June 1979. Ser. 1, box 1, folder 3, item 1. Paul Bowles Papers. Hugh M. Morris Lib. Special Collections Department, U of Delaware, Newark, DE.
———. Letter to Paul Bowles. 16 Nov. 1979. Ser. 1, box 1, folder 3, item 3. Paul Bowles Papers. Hugh M. Morris Lib. Special Collections Department, U of Delaware, Newark, DE.
———. *Naked Lunch.* New York: Grove, 1962.
———. "The Name Is Burroughs." *The Adding Machine: Collected Essays.* London: Calder, 1985. 1–14.
———. *Nova Express.* New York: Grove, 1964.
———. Postcard [in envelope] to Paul Bowles. 23 Dec. 1977. Ser. 1, box 1, folder 2, item 1. Paul Bowles Papers. Hugh M. Morris Lib. Special Collections Department, U of Delaware, Newark, DE.
———. *Queer.* New York: Viking, 1985.
———. *The Soft Machine.* New York: Grove, 1966.
———. *The Ticket That Exploded.* New York: Grove, 1967.
———. *The Western Lands.* New York: Penguin, 1987.
———. *The Wild Boys: A Book of the Dead.* New York: Grove, 1971.
Caponi, Gena Dagel. *Paul Bowles: Romantic Savage.* Carbondale: Southern Illinois UP, 1994.
Caveney, Graham. *Gentleman Junky: The Life and Legacy of William S. Burroughs.* Boston: Little, 1998.
Christopherson, Peter, dir. "Just One Fix." Perf. Ministry. Music video. Sire/Warner, 1992.
Dillon, Millicent. *You Are Not I: A Portrait of Paul Bowles.* Berkeley: U of California P, 1998.
Grauerholz, James. Introduction. *Interzone.* By William S. Burroughs. Ed. James Grauerholz. New York: Viking, 1989. ix–xxiii.
———. "Re: Letters." E-mail to the author. 9 Apr. 2003.
———. "Re: Question about Unpublished Letters." E-mail to the author. 1 Mar. 2003.
Kettlewell, Ben. "The Master Musicians of Jajouka." *Alternate Music Press: The Multimedia Journal of New Music* 7 Dec. 2001 <http://www.alternatemusicpress.com/features/jajouka.html>.

Let It Come Down: The Life of Paul Bowles. Zeitgeist Films Web site. 7 Dec. 2001 <http://www.zeitgeistfilms.com/current/letitcomedown/letitcomedown.html>.
Literature Resource Center. Gale Research Group, 2001. 28 Nov. 2001 <http://www.galenet.com/servlet/LitRC>.
Miles, Barry. *William Burroughs: El Hombre Invisible.* London: Virgin, 1992.
Ministry. "Just One Fix." *Psalm 69.* Perf. Al Jourgensen et al. Sire/Warner, 1992.
Morgan, Ted. *Literary Outlaw: The Life and Times of William S. Burroughs.* New York: Holt, 1988.
Offman, Craig. "The Beats Order Lunch." *Salon.com.* 14 Mar. 2003 <http://www.salon.com/books/log/1999/05/04/beats/>.
Ohle, David. *Cursed From Birth: The Short, Unhappy Life of William S. Burroughs, Jr.* New York: Grove, 2001.
Paul Bowles Papers: 1960–1985. U of Delaware Lib. Special Collections Department Web site. 2 Nov. 2001 <http://www.lib.udel.edu/ud/spec/findaids/bowlespa.htm>.
The People's Temple, Led by James Warren ("Jim") Jones. Web site. 7 Dec. 2001 <http://www.religioustolerance.org/dc_jones.htm>.
Sawyer-Lauçanno, Christopher. *An Invisible Spectator: A Biography of Paul Bowles.* New York: Weidenfeld & Nicolson, 1989.
Skerl, Jennie. Introduction. *Speed.* By William S. Burroughs Jr. Woodstock, NY: Overlook, 1984. v–ix.
Steinbeck, John, Jr. Afterword. *Speed.* By William S. Burroughs Jr. Woodstock, NY: Overlook, 1984. 165–70.
Van Sant, Gus, dir. *Drugstore Cowboy.* Perf. Matt Dillon, Kelly Lynch, and Heather Graham et al. 1989. Artisan Home Entertainment, 1999.
Wallace (George C.) Speeches. U of Southern Mississippi McCain Lib. Archives and Manuscript Collection Web site. 5 Dec. 2001 <http://www.lib.usm.edu/~archives/m308.htm>.

Parker's *Melville*: The Life Complete

SANFORD E. MAROVITZ
Kent State University

HERMAN MELVILLE: A BIOGRAPHY. VOLUME 2, 1851–1891. By Hershel Parker. Baltimore: Johns Hopkins UP, 2002. xx + 997 pp. $45.

At last the other shoe has dropped. Six years after the first half of Hershel Parker's long-awaited biography of Herman Melville appeared in 1996, the second and concluding volume was published in 2002. It was worth the wait, not only for the obvious reason that it completes the life, but also because, simply put, it is a better book from which we may gain deeper insight into Melville. The first volume gives disproportionate attention to his older brother, Gansevoort, and to the reviews of Melville's first five romances (the reviews of *Moby-Dick* are discussed in *Volume 2*). In contrast, the second volume provides a more sensitive and realistic representation of the author as both a family man and an isolated figure akin to the great folio whales that Ishmael describes so lovingly. In *Volume 2*, also, the numerous members of Melville's extended family—the Gansevoorts, Shaws, and Melvilles themselves—are portrayed more distinctively as individuals with readily identifiable personal characteristics; the same is true of Melville's closest friends and associates, from such early intimate acquaintances as Sarah Morewood and the Duyckinck brothers to the Stedmans, father and son, who met and befriended Melville late in his life.

To re-create an authentic, convincing life, the biographer must rely chiefly on documentable facts. Unfortunately, however, the facts do not always dovetail precisely; gaps occur that the biographer must bridge in order to explain a *what*, a *how*, or a *why*; and to bridge these gaps when additional data are unavailable, the biographer is left to his or her own resources. Parker, who surely knows more facts about Herman Melville and his family than anyone else on earth, has indeed written a full and extraordinarily detailed account of Melville's seventy-two years of life in eighty chapters and nearly two thousand pages. Nonetheless, he had to bridge many gaps, those deadly spaces between the facts that must be accounted for in order to anticipate with plausible answers questions from readers that missing links are likely to evoke. He has accomplished this in his own way, through a discreet use of his imagination. When reviewing *Volume 1* for this journal six years ago, I pointed out that, in an article of 1995, "Biography and Responsible Uses of the Imagination," Parker explains that in writing a biography, he employs a method similar to the one he uses as a textual editor, meaning that he emends as necessary to construct a coherent text. Hence, to make the life coherent where documentable facts are missing, Parker takes all relevant data into consideration and, "*by putting [him]self . . .* in Melville's place," determines on the basis of those data what Melville might naturally have done under the circumstances; then Parker has Melville act accordingly (Marovitz 113; emphasis in original). Although not all researchers would agree that this kind of hypothesizing falls within the bounds of accurate scholarship, Parker's use of it has enabled him to create a narrative that is coherent, engaging, authentic, and persuasive, with a strong ring of truth throughout.

The first volume portrays Melville from his birth on 1 August 1819, through early November 1851, immediately after the first copies of *Moby-Dick* were off the press in the United States. (The British edition, titled *The Whale*, had been published the preceding month.) The closing scene in that volume depicts Melville presenting Hawthorne—to whom *Moby-Dick* was dedicated—with one of the earliest copies of his new romance as they sit together in the dining room of a Lenox (MA) hotel, the two authors isolated from all others in the room. Although the basis of this dramatic episode—that the two men dined together at the hotel, perhaps on 14 November—has been documented, most of Parker's scenario is assumptive and imaginative, one of the best examples in *Volume 1* of his "*putting [him]self* in Melville's place," on what Parker believes was "the happiest day in Melville's life" (1: 883).

Volume 2 begins at that point and ends shortly after Melville's death on 28 September 1891. Early in the second volume, Parker delineates another example of interpersonal blending, but in this case it ostensibly involves only those about whom he is writing and not himself. The incident he describes occurred in May 1849 at New York Harbor when Melville boarded the ship on which his younger brother Tom was soon to depart as a member of the crew. Tom resembled Melville ten years earlier, when he was ready to sail for Liverpool on his first sea voyage, his brother Gansevoort having arranged it for him: "In Melville's mind . . . [the] two New York wharf scenes fused, and the bewilderingly similar pairs of brothers fused in his mind, Gansevoort merging into Herman even as he himself merged into Tom, and Tom into him" (2: 9). Parker persuasively supports this theoretical blending with reference to Albert Rothenberg's idea of "homospatial thinking" in his *The Emerging Goddess* (1979), "in which two disparate images become superimposed and fused, 'a conception leading to the articulation of new identities'" (2: 10). Such blending is further complicated by what I believe has become unavoidable for Parker, that is, the persistent merging of his own image with his subject's, and like Melville, he seems to be highly conscious of it, so much so that he often envisions himself in Melville's place and acts as he *knows* Melville himself would. Clearly, as Parker would not deny, there is a component of psychological autobiography in this intricate exploration and account of Melville's life, although it is more subtly incorporated in this second volume than in the first.

Beyond his aim to provide a closely examined and detailed life of Melville with ample attention to the writings as well, Parker has intentions in the two volumes that are not identical. In his preface to the first, he explains that he intends "to see Herman Melville as a human being living in nineteenth-century America; . . . as a member of his family and . . . literary circles" (1: xv). Although he certainly does not diverge from this major purpose in *Volume 2,* he also makes it clear that particularly in "*this* book" he has provided "a new portrait of Melville, drawn from the original manuscripts, rigorously condensed into a mere thousand pages[!]—forty years of human life, forty chapters" (2: xiv; emphasis added).

This "new portrait" is more than anything else a revelation of Melville's expanding yet deepening intellect and imagination. With all Melville's comings and goings tracked by family, friends, publishers, and other associates, Parker focuses on the growth of Melville's mind, especially as revealed in the transformation and continuous development of his art. From writing full-length narratives of adventure with embedded social criticism, Melville turned within a few months to publishing short fiction darkened with a tone of ironic restraint. Parker demonstrates, however, that, even before the first stories appeared in late 1853, Melville had completed and submitted for publication another full-length work titled "The Isle of the Cross," which evidently had been rejected and was consequently lost. That narrative was probably based on a story that Melville had heard in 1852 while visiting Nantucket with his father-in-law, Judge Lemuel Shaw, Chief Justice of the Supreme Court of Massachusetts; it was the account of a woman, one Agatha Hatch, betrayed by her sailor husband who remarried while away from home and left her loyally awaiting his return for years. Parker suggests that Melville was so affected by this woeful tale of loyalty and courage that he not only employed it as the basis of "The Isle of the Cross," but also identified with Agatha's alienation and steadfastness to the extent that the nature and tone of his fiction drastically and permanently changed.

Through the mid-1850s, Melville's ironic stories were brought out in two monthlies, *Harper's* and the newly established *Putnam's*. Then, late in the same decade, from a popular storyteller—as nearly all his readers then insisted on tagging him—he became a poet, expecting but failing soon afterward to publish a collection of his poems as early as 1860. Thoroughly dedicated to his new art, Melville as poet was all but disregarded by the public and literati alike until long after his death. Parker's account of Melville's shift from prose artist to poet is brilliant partly because Parker appears to have read everything that Melville himself did in order to comment on Melville's sources both knowledgeably and perceptively. He examines Melville's reading; refers abundantly and tellingly to poets and critics contemporary with Melville, as well as those whose works are part of the fabric of literary history; and exhibits the way in which the developing poet improved his own art through an ever-growing familiarity with theirs.

The early pages of chapter 18 constitute simultaneously a luminous display of the biographer's own erudition and a superb account of Melville's developing aesthetic as he strove in these years to become a poet, a *great* poet, *the* poet for whom America had been waiting, a poet to rank with Chaucer, Shakespeare, and Milton, whose works Melville devoured. A little over a decade earlier, when reviewing Hawthorne's *Mosses from an Old Manse*, Melville had written that "Shakespeares are this day being born on the banks of the Ohio," and "if Shakespeare has not been equalled, he is sure to be surpassed, . . . and surpassed by an American" (*Piazza Tales* 245, 246). Parker makes a strong case that Melville aimed to become not the American Shakespeare but *the* great poet of America in his and its own right. He grounds this assumption, first, on Melville's recognition that the majestic poem rather than the romance was the apex of literary achievement in the public eye to and through his own day and, second, on Melville's assiduous study of the art of poetry soon after returning from the Mediterranean and failing to garner more than a mediocre response to his lectures, about which he was reluctant from the start. His limited eyesight notwithstanding, he pored over collections of poems old and new, in the early 1860s and after, and he supplemented his intense reading of poetry by giving equal attention to criticism, poetic theory, and prosody. He aimed to formulate an aesthetic of his own in order to realize its possibilities in an epic poem grand enough to bring the United States such literary distinction that the still-young nation might emerge at last from the heavy shadow of British literature and perhaps even rise above it.

The initial result of this effort was his collection of Civil War poems, *Battle-Pieces and Aspects of the War* (1866), and exactly a decade later came *Clarel, A Poem and Pilgrimage in the Holy Land*, his contribution to the

American Centennial, a lofty poem in four books and almost 18,000 rough iambic-tetrameter lines. Written day by day over a period of some ten years, invested with the author's infinite hope and self-confidence, *Clarel* nevertheless received little attention on publication and marked the end of Melville's career as a writer for the public. In *Volume 2* of the biography, in four of the five chapters between 31 and 35 inclusive, Parker gives especial attention to *Clarel* with a deeply perceptive reading that emphasizes Hawthorne as the main source for Vine, one of its principal characters. Where it was not neglected on publication, it was misunderstood; the purblind response by the public led Melville from 1876 on to write only for those few among his small circle of family and friends who appreciated his work, and for himself.

Approximately five years prior to his death, Melville turned again to writing prose. The result was the nearly completed manuscript of *Billy Budd (Sailor): An Inside Story*, left unpublished until edited and added to the first collected edition of Melville's writings over thirty years later (1924), and brought out, ironically, in England. Parker's commentary on *Billy Budd* in the biography is limited because he has published significantly on that work in the past, particularly his book *Reading "Billy Budd"* (1990), but readers unfamiliar with his earlier criticism can gain enough from his analysis here to achieve a reasonable understanding of that short novel's thematic and textual complexities. Also in this volume, Parker is more specific on Melville's deteriorating health as he aged; whereas in the first volume he was vague on Melville's rheumatism and other ailments, here he describes the author's symptoms more precisely. This is especially true of the "crick" in Melville's back and his sciatica, both of which struck him simultaneously, creating a painful ordeal that occasionally left him bedridden and virtually helpless (2: 374; also see 261, 381).

In December 1866, Melville finally succeeded in acquiring a steady job with regular pay—a daily pittance of $4 (reduced temporarily to $3.50)—as an inspector for the New York Custom House. Having vainly depended on his pen to provide a living for his wife, Elizabeth, and their four children, as well as his mother and sisters, who lived with them for years, Melville had resorted to borrowing money from relatives and others; he desperately needed a job, and this was the first steady wage-paying position he had held since his return from the Pacific late in 1844. Parker meticulously details the author's fiscal liabilities, showing that sometimes Melville's arrangements for both borrowing and repaying crossed the line from unethical to illegal, and only the assistance of his maternal Gansevoort family and his sympathetic father-in-law enabled him to avoid severe penalties.

That Melville had financial problems for most of his life has long been well known, but in this volume Parker goes further than his predecessors to expose the serious economic difficulties Melville faced, including the support of ever-changing cooks and maids—mostly newly arrived, inexperienced Irish immigrants—without whom the family was virtually at a loss, as Parker explains. The financial distress was exacerbated by Melville's almost compelling desire to purchase books old and new; the latter he obtained directly from his publisher by having them charged to his account, but their cost was rarely covered by the sale of his own publications. Only in his final years were the financial problems relieved, when Lizzie received a substantial inheritance in 1888 that would have enabled her to live with her husband in the kind of luxury to which she had been accustomed before her marriage, but by then she was past sixty-five and too settled in her ways to make drastic changes in her lifestyle.

As is to be expected in a biography, Parker rarely loses sight of Melville himself while describing the activities of his family, which by and large are presented in contrast to the often-hermitic behavior of the focal subject. The contrast is mutually revealing. Primarily, it exhibits the family members as complementary to the strangely alienated man in the center who spends most of each day alone as a Customs examiner only to return home for a quiet meal before retreating to his room for long hours of reading and writing in solitude. Of course, Melville is never completely alone with books and pen in this biography because Parker is always with him, specifying by author, title, and text the subject of his author's concentrated efforts first to read and remember, then—often long afterward—to incorporate something from what he has read into his own writing. Here again is where the biographer and biographee seem to merge into one another as Parker reveals what Melville must have been thinking as he read these words of Shakespeare or those of Milton and adapted them, probably unconsciously, to suit his own needs in drafting his poems.

Additionally, however, the contrast enables readers to visualize the members of Melville's immediate and extended family with surprising distinction because their individual idiosyncrasies and eccentricities are best recognized in relation to the aging author as an almost neutral figure among them, so preoccupied is he with his own interests. In this respect, Parker seems to be employing a literary method described in chapter 44 of *The Confidence-Man*, where the narrator explains that truly original characters such as Hamlet, Don Quixote, and Milton's Satan rarely exist in literature because they must be part of the life, not merely the imagination, of the author. An original character is the illuminating center of the work: "[E]verything is lit by it, everything starts up to it," as with Hamlet and the others named (239). So it is in this biography with Melville, "[q]uite an original," as phrased in *The Confidence-Man* (238). It is by virtue of Melville himself that the other figures become distinctive portraits identifiable at once not simply by name (there are at least five Kates in Melville's family), but by their reflection of Melville's central light.

Parker's characterization of these figures is at times quite explicit, as if he viewed them through Melville's eyes but assessed them as he himself sees them. Jane, the second wife of Melville's younger brother, Allan, is depicted as an epitome of haughty egocentricity with enormous wealth; Allan himself is seen as basically good but too much an operator and social climber. The youngest brother, Tom, is described as everyone's darling; although little schooled, he worked his way up as an officer on cargo vessels to become captain of a fine clipper ship and ultimately governor of Sailors' Snug Harbor, a home for aged mariners on Staten Island. Melville's mother and wife are portrayed sympathetically but not uncritically; Parker finds no convincing evidence to support recent charges that Melville was violently abusive to Lizzie or their children. His youngest daughter, Frances, complained that he was difficult to live with, but when she married and had her own small family, Melville retained cordial relations with them. The two oldest of his four sisters, Helen and Augusta, especially the latter, appear here almost worthy of sainthood by virtue of their deep concern over the difficulties of others and their efforts to ease the lives of those around them. The two genealogical charts included near the end of both volumes are invaluable in helping readers keep track of the individual family members to whom Parker refers throughout, especially in their mutual references in letters and their continuous cycle of visits to each other's homes. An isolato of sorts during the last half of his life, Melville nevertheless belonged to a very large and sociable family.

And Parker considers another isolato. Despite Hawthorne's "gorgeousness" (2: 729, 787), as Parker refers to his appearance in his mid-to-late forties (about the time that Melville knew him in the early 1850s), the biographer assumes that Melville perceived the late romancer some two decades later as a Philistine decidedly limited in aesthetic sensitivity. Parker bases his assumption on the shortcomings of Hawthorne's posthumously published incomplete romances and serialized segments of his Italian notebooks, which Melville almost certainly read; beyond this, Parker is unduly hypercritical of Hawthorne throughout this volume, as if personally resentful that Melville's literary reputation sank as that of the Salem author ascended even after his death in 1864. Surprisingly, too, Parker includes no mention of Melville's "Monody," a short poem probably memorializing but not naming Hawthorne; ultimately, Melville included the poem in *Timoleon* (1891), a small collection published the year of his own death. Both the poem and its publication testify to the enduring sense of loss that Melville felt over his estrangement from Hawthorne long before. Once again, it is difficult to distinguish between Melville's response to someone or something and Parker's own.

One incidental lesson that readers will learn from this biography is that other families, historically significant or not, are often less different from their own than they might expect. Although each family has its peculiarities and eccentrics, seen as a whole the problems faced by a family then and now over love and money or the lack of either, antipathies, hostilities, devotion, obligation, and so forth are not unique among one's own relatives after all. In this respect, among others, the Melville family portrait can be an awakening.

As in the first volume, the shortage of documentation in *Volume 2* is disturbing at times. With regard to Melville's intensive reading of poetry in the 1860s, Parker identifies Whittier's *Snow-Bound* (1866) as "crucial in Melville's decision" to use the iambic-tetrameter line as the prosodic foundation for constructing *Clarel* as he prepared to draft his epic-length poem, but no source is cited for verification (2: 686). Parker is apparently viewing and assessing Whittier's narrative from Melville's perspective as he imagines it, but his attribution should have some kind of documentary support, even as little as an endnote to confirm that Melville had actually read *Snow-Bound* at that early stage of *Clarel*'s composition or any other time (no reference to that poem exists in Merton M. Sealts's *Melville's Reading* [1966; rev. ed., 1988]). A section for documentation precedes the index in this volume as in the first, and within it is a subsection that includes chapter-by-chapter references, but these citations are highly selective; far more are omitted than included. It is likely that Parker had assumed that his new edition of *The Melville Log* (1951; 2nd ed., 1969) would be published either in hard copy or electronically by the time *Volume 2* was available and that the *Log* would provide thorough documentation for both volumes. Meanwhile, however, questions regarding sources and confirmation will remain open until the *Log* is finally published, and even then readers of the biography will have to depend on an external reference for answers to them.

Nevertheless, this limitation should not receive more attention than it warrants in so massive and enlightening a study as this biography of Melville. Parker has fulfilled his expressed aims by portraying his subject in full dimensions, leaving no doubt of Melville's intensity as a reader, thinker, and artist, while also exposing the darker side of his existence as an alienated, often embittered man whose creative demon retained its hold over his mind and imagination to the end. During the last three decades of his life, Melville was known in his own country only as a writer of the past, the author of *Typee* and a few other early "adventure" stories. Disgusted over the reputation he had gained for the wrong reasons and his inability to reach the appreciative audience he sought, struggling to acquire the dollars that damned him through most of his writing career, and increasingly ailing physically as the years passed, Melville never gave in to the despair that persistently weighed heavily upon him. Determined to write the masterworks that would bring literary distinction to America as well as to himself, he pressed on, and only in his final years could he see, with the recognition coming to him chiefly from abroad, that he was indeed acquiring the kind of critical attention, even admiration, that he was always certain he deserved.

Parker makes all of this clear, even as he portrays in great detail Melville's idiosyncratic family and friends, drawing from their diaries and letters to track their visits, to expose their expectations and irritations, and to reveal their influential roles in the life of their sometimes notorious kinsman. All told, Parker's biography should appeal to every reader who admires Melville himself and gives his writing the kind of attention he sought. It is a majestic contribution to Melville scholarship that fills many gaps in the life and casts such new light on both the author and his writings that no serious reader of Melville can afford to disregard it. Still, maybe like the unknowable living whale that Ishmael feels helpless to describe, the inscrutable Bartleby, the endless sailor's knot in "Benito Cereno," the elusive identity of the Confidence-Man, and the enigmatic Captain Starry Vere, the essential truth of Herman Melville cannot be fathomed; but no one yet has come closer than Hershel Parker in this biography, "a great book" with "a mighty theme," never likely to be superseded.

WORKS CITED

Marovitz, Sanford E. "'Truth Hath No Confines': Two New Melville Lives." *Resources for American Literary Study* 24 (1998): 109–19.

Melville, Herman. *The Confidence-Man: His Masquerade. The Writings of Herman Melville.* Vol. 10. Ed. Harrison Hayford, Hershel Parker, and G. Thomas Tanselle. Evanston: Northwestern UP, 1984.

———. *The Piazza Tales and Other Short Pieces, 1839–1860. The Writings of Herman Melville.* Vol. 9. Ed. Harrison Hayford, Hershel Parker, and G. Thomas Tanselle. Evanston: Northwestern UP, 1987.

Parker, Hershel. *Herman Melville: A Biography, Volume 1, 1819–1851.* Baltimore: Johns Hopkins UP, 1996.

Asian American Literary Studies at Maturity

NOELLE BRADA-WILLIAMS
San Jose State University

ASIAN AMERICAN NOVELISTS: A BIO-BIBLIOGRAPHICAL CRITICAL SOURCEBOOK. Edited by Emmanuel S. Nelson. Westport, CT: Greenwood P, 2000. xi + 422 pp. $99.95.

BOLD WORDS: A CENTURY OF ASIAN AMERICAN WRITING. Edited by Rajini Srikanth and Esther Iwanaga. New Brunswick, NJ: Rutgers UP, 2001. xxiv + 442 pp. Hardbound, $59; paperback, $25.

A RESOURCE GUIDE TO ASIAN AMERICAN LITERATURE. Edited by Sau-ling Cynthia Wong and Stephen H. Sumida. New York: MLA, 2001. vi + 345 pp. Hardbound, $40; paperback $22.

WORDS MATTER: CONVERSATIONS WITH ASIAN AMERICAN WRITERS. Edited by King-Kok Cheung. Honolulu: U of Hawaii P/UCLA Asian American Studies Center, 2000. 402 pp. $25.95.

To understand where Asian American literary studies is now, one will find it helpful to examine where the field started. *Asian American* is an identification used to define Americans with ancestors from a variety of nations from the largest and most populous continent in the world and with a variety of histories and cultures that often vary greatly from (or have even been antagonistic toward) one another. Originally, it was used to replace the term *Oriental* and marked a specific political consciousness of one's racial identity. As shown in Cheung's *Words Matter: Conversations with Asian American Writers*, individuals vary greatly as to whether this label is more or less accurate than simply the national label of *American* or distinct ethnic identities such as *Chinese American, South Asian,* or *Indian American*. American laws, policies, and society do not always treat the various Asian ethnic communities in America consistently, and Asians in America are not uniform in their experiences or expression of American identity. However, there are enough commonalities in the various experiences of many Americans of Asian heritage to make the term a viable category for both political affiliation and scholarly analysis, including the shared histories of exclusionary immigration, anti-miscegenation, or alien land laws; mainstream suspicions of Asians as inherently unassimilable or un-American; domestic forms of Orientalism; the process of immigration and assimilation; and values, social norms, and forms of spirituality that span the boundaries defined by single ethnicities.

As the title of Rajini Srikanth and Esther Iwanaga's new anthology, *Bold Words: A Century of Asian American Writing*, makes clear, texts fitting within the category of Asian American literature have been written for over a century. However, just thirty-five years ago, American classrooms omitted virtually all aspects of what now might be called Asian America: its history, its culture, its literature. In the preface to his *Asian American Literature: A Brief Introduction and Anthology*, Shawn Wong states, "At no time in my undergraduate English and American literature studies or in my entire public school education had any teacher ever used or even mentioned a work of fiction or poetry by an Asian American writer" (xv). In *A Different Mirror: A History of Multicultural America*, one of his several important histories of multicultural America, Ronald Takaki describes the desire for a broader and thus more accurate study of American culture by citing Adrienne Rich: "What happens . . . 'when someone with the authority of a teacher' describes our society, and 'you are not in it'? Such an experience can be disorienting—'a moment of psychic disequilibrium, as if you looked into a mirror and saw nothing'" (16).[1]

Beginning in the late 1960s, students, artists, and community activists worked to construct an image in that mirror and created the concept of Asian American identity. The Third World Student Strike that took place at San Francisco State University in 1968–69 is a good event to use to mark the birth of this field as an academic discipline. Partially in response to the U.S. presence in Vietnam and inspired by the success of African Americans during the Civil Rights era, students demanded that the college curriculum reflect the real diversity of America rather than a narrowly defined American culture based solely on Euro-American literature and history. Student activism led directly to the founding of Ethnic Studies programs on the campuses of San Francisco State, the University of California at Berkeley, and other colleges and universities across the United States.

While students were demanding access to the study of Asian American literature and culture, Asian American community activists were directly connecting art and political concerns. In 1972, the Kearny Street Workshop was founded in San Francisco's Chinatown/Manilatown area, specifically at 854 Kearny Street in the International Hotel, the building that would become a symbol of grassroots Asian American community activism. Still bearing the title of "the oldest multidisciplinary Asian Pacific American arts organization in the country" (http://www.kearny street.org/about_ksw/history/index.html), Kearny Street is involved both in the training of artists and in the exhibiting, disseminating, and even publication of Asian American art in a variety of forms, including literature. Its mission statement exemplifies the direct connection members make between community politics and art: "The mission of Kearny Street Workshop is to produce and present art that enriches and empowers Asian Pacific American communities. Our vision is to achieve a more just society by connecting Asian Pacific American (APA) artists with community members to give voice to our cultural, historical, and contemporary issues" (http://www.kearnystreet.org/about_ksw/index.html).

The Asian American Theater Company (AATC) of San Francisco has also passed its thirtieth birthday. Founded in 1973, the AATC joined companies such as the East West Players of Los Angeles (founded in 1965) and the Asian American Theater Lab of the Mark Taper Forum (founded in 1967) in developing a community-based theater that explores Asian American themes and provides an outlet for Asian American artists. These early pioneers have been aided in the last three decades by a variety of other theaters in places as diverse as New York, Minneapolis, and San Diego. Roberta Uno's essay in *Bold Words* provides an excellent overview of the various theater companies working in this area and notes the dates of their foundings.

Bamboo Ridge Press in Hawaii, which focuses on the local literature of Hawaii, has been responsible for publishing a wide range of authors who fit under the rubric of Asian American writers, while the University of Washington Press has brought a large number of pre-movement Asian American texts back into print, including classics such as Carlos Bulosan's 1946 *America Is in the Heart* and even lesser-known texts such as Winnifred Eaton's 1903 *The Heart of Hyacinth*. Temple University Press is notable for its early commitment to publishing important scholarship on Asian American literary and cultural studies. Since 1991, the Asian American Writer's Workshop in New York has produced a great deal of important Asian American literary works via its workshops, journal, and small press. As a distinct field, Asian American literary studies has clearly reached maturity. Although the field is well established, the struggle to define and redefine it continues.

One marker of the established nature of Asian American literature and its study has been its overdue but inevitable recognition by cultural institutions not specializing in Pacific Rim or Asian American community issues and artists. Maxine Hong Kingston's critical success with *Woman Warrior* (1977) and Amy Tan's phenomenal commercial success with *The Joy Luck Club* (1989) have registered on the catalogs of large publishing firms and within the curriculum of literature and composition programs across the country. In Eileen Tabios's essay, which opens the section on poetry in *Bold Words*, "Introduction: Absorbing and Being Absorbed by Poetry," she notes Harold Bloom's explanation for why he could find nothing in the 1996 volume of *Best American Poetry*, edited by Adrienne Rich, for his *The Best of the Best American Poetry* (1988–97): "'That 1996 anthology . . . seems to me to be a monumental representation for the enemies of the aesthetic who are in the act of overwhelming us.' *Us?* Bloom continues, 'It is of a badness not to be believed, because it follows the criteria now operative: what matters most are race, gender, sexual orientation, ethnic origin, and political purpose of the would-be poet'" (Srikanth and Iwanaga 72; emphasis in original). And yet this defender of the faith of aesthetics against the "badness" of gender, ethnic origin, and the political affixed his name as editor to volumes of collected criticism titled *Asian-American Women Writers* (1997; in the Women Writers of English and Their Works series), *Asian-American Writers* (1999), *Amy Tan* (2000), and *Amy Tan's "The Joy Luck Club"* (2002; in the Modern Critical Views series). Amy Tan has indeed sold a great many books. Mining the scholarly and commercial possibilities of a previously untapped—or under-published—field of analysis is hard for anyone to resist. Yet readers should be aware that individuals who know the field or even appreciate the values inherent in its founding are not the only ones who are now taking it upon themselves to shape its discourse.[2] Anyone new to this area of study should remain conscious of the various political positions from which scholarship is written. Even the aesthetics-over-politics position that Bloom takes is itself a political position.

Fortunately, the process of coming of age as a field has generally fostered not only quantity, but also quality in both Asian American artists and the scholars studying Asian American literature. After over thirty years of production of self-identified Asian American literature, it seems only right that scholarship on Asian American literature and culture should also be a firmly established part of American literary studies. Just over ten years ago, I recall hearing Elaine Kim's *Asian American Literature: An Introduction to the Writings and Their Social Context* (1982) referred to as "the book," in deference both to its pivotal impact and to the fact that there was very little in-depth critical analysis of Asian American Literature available at that time. Since then we have had Shirley Geok-lin Lim and Amy Ling's *Reading the Literatures of Asian America* (1992), King-Kok Cheung's *An Interethnic Companion to Asian American Literature* (1996), as well as monographs by Stephen H. Sumida (1991), Sau-ling Cynthia Wong (1993), Cheung (1993), Lisa Lowe

(1996), Rachel C. Lee (1999), and Viet Thanh Nguyen (2002), among others. Today these are joined by a range of primary texts, reference works, and various forms of criticism.

With the advent of journals such as *Pedagogy* and the growing recognition across the literary disciplines that a major portion of what we as researchers do is teach, more and more areas of research have somewhat sheepishly begun to focus on the interconnection of research and teaching. The role of pedagogy in Ethnic American literature and Asian American literature in particular can never be forgotten, since the needs of students are what launched this field. Two of the four works that are the primary focus of this review-essay are explicitly useful in terms of the classroom, *Bold Words* for its use as an assigned text for students and *A Resource Guide to Asian American Literature* for its help in preparing teachers for the classroom, especially in its section "Pedagogical Issues and Suggestions."

It seems fitting to start by reviewing the anthology of primary texts, not only because the primary text is where literary scholarship begins, but also because anthologies are a primary way through which Asian American literature has constituted itself. Since the early movement-era anthologies made up largely of student work—such as *Roots: An Asian American Reader* (1971), edited by Tachiki, Wong, Odo, and Wong, or the first *Aiiieeeee!* (1974), edited by Chin, Chan, Inada, and Wong—in a conscious effort to define a literary tradition, anthologies have been key both to developing the pan-ethnic nature of Asian American identity and to getting otherwise overlooked or forgotten artists into print.

Srikanth and Iwanaga's anthology, *Bold Words*, begins with an introduction by Srikanth that explicitly describes the overall organization of the volume and the rationale behind it: "We organized *Bold Words* by genre to underscore the literary value of the writings. We wanted to work against the prevailing tendency to read works by ethnic writers as documents to be mined for the 'authentic' ethnic experience. Thus, we also stayed away from organization by ethnic groups. Similarly, we eschewed a thematic organization, so as to avoid having to frame and suggest limits to the experiences of Asian Americans around identifiable or defined themes" (xvii). The organization of the texts into four sections labeled "Memoir," "Poetry," "Fiction," and "Drama" does indeed put the focus on the texts as literature as opposed to documents of purely sociological or historical interest. This anthology would be a good choice for upper-division and graduate courses in Asian American or multiethnic American literature. The absence of thematic or ethnic categorization—except for the appendices of alternative lists of contents by "Themes and Topics" and "Ethnicity of Authors"—and any pedagogical framework, such as suggested discussion or writing topics, allows more flexibility to teachers with greater familiarity in the field and with more advanced students who can be counted on to create their own topics and support their ideas with their own research into the cultural and historical contexts of the pieces. A minimalist approach to background information gives this text the potential to straddle the line between the popular and scholarly as it is unencumbered by the pedagogical apparatus attached to many anthologies. It is one book that I would consider giving to non-academics interested in the field, as well as to people looking for models for their own writing. When all four parts of the collection are considered, the reader will find that the mix of contemporary and canonical provides a brief but solid overview of the field.

For teachers not familiar enough with the field (or without the time and resources) to provide information on the historical and cultural context of various pieces in their lectures, I suggest using Lim's *Asian American Literature: An Anthology* (2000). This text is at the other end of the spectrum from Srikanth and Iwanaga's work since it is set up thematically and provides headnotes on each piece, in addition to copious discussion and writing questions that would work well for advanced high school students, as well as composition, and other introductory-level college classrooms. The teacher's edition even goes so far as to provide answers to the discussion questions for those teachers who are themselves just learning about the field. For those looking for a greater depth of specifically contemporary models for their own poetry, I suggest tracking down a copy of Walter K. Lew's *Premonitions: The Kaya Anthology of New Asian North American Poetry* (1995). Despite the passage of the better part of a decade since its appearance, Lew's anthology still maintains its avant-garde edge, and individual selections such as Amitava Kumar's "Iraqi Restaurants" are eerily appropriate today. Unfortunately, its large size and the fact that only the more expensive hardcover edition remains in print today make it a difficult text to use in a classroom, especially a multiethnic literature or composition classroom requiring many additional texts as well. *Premonitions* is perhaps the most visually stunning literary anthology in Asian American—or perhaps American—literature today and explores not only the poetry of its title but also the experimental genre crossings between poetry and performance art or experimental prose narrative forms, such as those of Theresa Cha's *Dictée* (1982).

Three sections of *Bold Words* begin with an overview by a practitioner in the field—Gary Pak on fiction, Eileen Tabios on poetry, and Roberta Uno on drama. The other section, on memoir, begins with an interview of Mina Alexander, the writer of poetry, novels, and nonfiction who is best known for her memoir *Fault Lines* (1992). In their interview, the two editors ask Alexander about changes in the use of narrative by Asian American authors, including some of the authors included in the anthology, as well as the complexity of writing about an identity that may be splintered by geographical or cultural differences and the potential for agency that both writing and the experience of cultural dissonance might provide.

Some of the readers of *Bold Words*, especially popular or student readers, will be especially appreciative of the choice of practitioners, rather than strictly critics of the genre in question, to introduce each section. Uno's "Introduction: Asian American Theater Awake at the Millennium" offers an extremely informative overview of Asian American performance and its origins. Even a scholar knowledgeable about Asian American literature and its history will gain insight into an art form that tends toward the ephemeral and the highly local in its dissemination. Pak and Tabios both begin with more autobiographical focuses, but also provide brief overviews of the texts that follow in full or in excerpt.

Like Lim's text, *Bold Words* spans a broad historical period. Srikanth notes further in her introduction, "Within each genre, the materials are chronologically organized so as to give to readers a historical picture of the deployment of the genre among Asian American writers. We hope that readers will notice both the changes in and persistence of issues within each genre" (xvii). This organizing principle is especially useful in the first two sections on memoir and fiction. After the interview, the memoir section begins with Carlos Bulosan's "How My Stories Were Written"; however, Bulosan is the only pre-movement or pre-Asian American Studies author included in the memoir section. "Fiction" begins with Sui Sin Far's "In The Land of the Free" (1912), and includes the works of Bulosan, John Okada, Hisaye Yamamoto, and Toshio Mori, which collectively span from the 1930s to the 1950s. "Fiction" is the best section for examining both the founding ancestors and the cutting edge of Asian American writing. On the strength of the first five entries alone, the misconception that Asian American literature did not exist prior to the founding of Asian American literary studies is destroyed. This section truly lives up to the subtitle, *A Century of Asian American Writing*. However, to understand the strength of Asian American literature prior to its entry into academia, a reader must both remember the editor's introductory statement about the chronological structure and do his or her own research as to the chronological context of the various pieces, as neither dates of publication nor headnotes are provided (headnotes would be especially helpful with pieces such as the excerpt from Karen Tei Yamashita's *Through the Arc of the Rainforest* [1990], which is an extremely difficult text to excerpt given its vast assortment of characters and unusual narrative perspective). A curious reader can use the permissions pages to find dates by which to contextualize the more recent texts, but dates for the older works are unreliable as these works are either in the public domain or have had their copyright renewed sometime after their original publication. Thus, the strength of the chronological organization may be lost to readers not already familiar with Asian American literary history.

The section of *Bold Words* on poetry collects works that seem to come solely from the last third of the century, but even for this relatively short time a reader can see the great changes that have come about in Asian American poetry, particularly in its changing focus and subject matter. The section that concludes the book, "Drama," drops the historical look backward altogether in favor of a survey of currently active playwrights and performance artists. Readers hoping to find a broader historical spectrum, including the work of Wakako Yamauchi and Frank Chin or that of more commercially successful playwrights such as Philip Kan Gotanda or David Henry Hwang, may be disappointed. The editors have chosen pieces by six playwrights or performance artists who are relatively little known outside the locales where their work is produced. As Uno notes, the written text of contemporary performance art "can only partially convey [its] full intent and effect" (328). Nevertheless, this section may be the most informative for readers who are already familiar with Asian American literature, since it presents some exciting new artists whose work would otherwise be inaccessible in either print or video. Although the nature of an anthology regrettably requires that most of the drama and many of the works of fiction and memoir are excerpts rather than complete works, *Bold Words* provides a healthy sampling of some of the early grandfathers and grandmothers of contemporary Asian American literature, as well as a taste of the great diversity of present-day Asian American literary production in terms of genre, style, subject matter, ethnicity, and region.

Unlike *Bold Words*, King-Kok Cheung's *Words Matter: Conversations with Asian American Writers* is not likely to become widely used as a teaching text, except perhaps in some creative writing classrooms. However, both *Bold Words* and *Words Matter* are very appropriate for either a popular or a scholarly audience. In fact, it is difficult to read very far into *Words Matter* and not imagine a young writer who could benefit from the insights abundant in these interviews with twenty Asian American writers from a variety of ethnic backgrounds, engaged in various forms of writing, and from several generations. Actually, since several of the interviewers are creative writers as well as scholars, the book provides insight into the methods, motivations, and influences of more than twenty authors—for example, in poet Emily Porcincula Lawsin's brief description of her childhood experience with Jessica Hagedorn's writing before her interview with Hagedorn. This is icing on the cake for those of us who will devour this text the way some do interviews of their favorite movie stars in fan magazines.

Beyond the pure pleasure of peeking into the private lives of celebrities and personal idols lies a great deal of material for the researcher or teacher engaged in the major debates surrounding the study of Asian American literature today. Cheung's introduction puts the interviews in context by noting, "At a time when literature is largely defined by the marketplace, the popular media, academe, and various ethnic communities, *Words Matter* invites twenty authors to comment on how they would like their work to be read" (2). She describes the interview process, which was centered around seven sample questions, including "How comfortable are you with the label *Asian American writer?*" "Do you feel a sense of social purpose in your work?" "Does gender, class, or sexuality shape your writing?" and "Which writers do you admire?" (4). These basic questions, modified and combined in a variety of ways and eliciting an amazing range of responses, manage to give a sense of continuity to the volume without being repetitive.

The interviews are roughly organized into four sections, with each section taking a phrase from one of the interviews as a common theme for the section. The first section deals largely with immigrant authors and the complexity of the definition of "home." The interviews in the second section highlight the theme of community engagement and political activism that many authors see as a necessity in their work. Section three emphasizes the limitations that labels place on artists. The final section collects together the interviews of authors who have engaged in a variety of political issues and agendas in their writing, from Burma to Poston, Arizona. Unfortunately, many readers will consult the text for an interview with a particular author on whom they are currently working and miss out on some enlightening discussions by not reading beyond the most canonical or most commonly discussed authors. Even specialists may learn from the interviews with lesser-known authors such as Paul Stephen Lim and S. P. Somtow. When read together, the various interviews create an interethnic, cross-genre, cross-generational dialogue that reveals the complexity of Asian American literary production in a more concrete way than a single critical analysis could provide, no matter how insightful. In fact, researchers and teachers might use some of the points raised in these interviews about topics such as the role of labels, the political in art, the nature of the drive to create, identity formation, and methods of literary composition as starting points for discussion, debate, and further analysis.

The only weakness of *Words Matter* seems to be one common to most academic texts: there is an unfortunate lag in time between the beginning of the project and publication of the book. Based on references within the interviews, I would say that some are based on single interviews that occurred in the early to mid-1990s. However, all of the bibliographies have been updated for the 2000 publication, and some of the interviews have had additional updating. The early date of the start of this project means that many of the writers who have made the biggest impact in recent years—such as Jhumpa Lahiri or many Southeast Asian American writers—are necessarily left out.

The strongest interviews are those that were apparently part of an ongoing conversation that occurred over a series of meetings or communications. An exception is the interview that closes the volume, King-Kok Cheung's joint interview of old friends Hisaye Yamamoto and Wakako Yamauchi.[3] With the interplay not only between the interviewer and subject, but also between the subjects (individuals who have known each other for most of their lives yet still seem to be learning more about each other), this interview vividly captures a moment in time and allows its readers to participate vicariously in a lively and intimate conversation between old friends.

Greenwood Press has been very active in filling the void of reference materials for the study of ethnic literature. Emmanuel S. Nelson's *Asian American Novelists: A Bio-Bibliographical Critical Sourcebook* is part of a quartet of bio-bibliographical critical sourcebooks recently published by Greenwood Press on Asian American literature, including volumes focusing on autobiographers (Huang, *Autobiographers*), poets (Huang, *Poets*), and playwrights (Liu). Although I cannot claim familiarity with this series beyond Nelson's volume on Asian American novelists, I can say that the idea of bringing together information on a variety of writers working within the same discipline and coming from various parts of the large, polymorphous community known as Asian America is a highly useful concept. From my familiarity with Nelson's text, first as a researcher looking for resources on a single author and second as a reviewer attempting a thorough analysis, I would say that every library should have it. That being said, I wish some kind of disclaimer could be attached to the spine of the book, such as "Do not take this as comprehensive or as representative of a canon of Asian American literature."

To his credit, Nelson notes in his introduction, "My purpose in editing this volume is not to help define an Asian American literary canon. I am however, acutely conscious of the fact that a reference work such as this inevitably, even if unintentionally, will be implicated in the process of canon formation. The central objective of this volume is, in fact, to offer reliable, thorough, and up-to-date biographical, bibliographical, and critical information on a range of Asian American novelists" (xi). He goes on to describe the diversity of backgrounds of the various novelists, making a final point, "However, all of them, on some level, explore the personal and political implications of being Asian in America. In that process they redefine the very idea of America and who, precisely, is an American" (xi). Although making a very good point in general, the statement is awkward given that Nelson has lumped together American and Canadian authors in this volume, and the latter are *not* involved in the same *national* redefinition as their colleagues to the south. Nelson remarks that "the historical and current experiences of Asians in Canada and the United States are substantially similar" (x), yet in his brief but helpful historical overview, detailing events such as the "Immigration Reform Act of 1965" and the emergence of Asian American Studies "on campuses on the West Coast" (ix), he takes the United States as the unnamed generic and provides no details of Canadian history. The inclusion of major authors such as Joy Kogawa and Michael Ondaatje in a text on Asian American authors can be seen as a convenient extra, and there is indeed a great deal of border-crossing between Canada and the United States by authors such as Bharati Mukherjee or Winnifred Eaton. Yet the editor's preface and choice of authors may give the impression that Canada does not possess its own unique history, or that there are not enough Asian American novelists to fill the book's objectives. Simply titling the text "Selected Asian North American Novelists" would have described this volume more accurately. Nelson is right to note how a volume such as his will be read as defining the canon regardless of his intentions. Many instructors resist the rigidity of canonization, a process that originally denied ethnic literature entry into academia, by having students research texts beyond the necessarily limited number on the course syllabus. A reference work such as this is exactly where many students will go to begin their search. Nelson could have remedied this problem, at least for those who read prefaces, by clarifying that his volume is not in any way comprehensive.

Asian American literature has indeed grown beyond the point when all of the writers, even all of those working in a single genre, can be catalogued in one volume. Yet except for the passages cited above, no clear rationale is offered for how the subjects were chosen. Why were these seventy authors selected and why were other authors omitted from the collection? The level of productivity does not seem to have been the deciding factor, since the prolific children's or young adult author Lawrence Yep is left out while Himani Bannerji, the author of one adolescent novel, *Coloured Pictures* (1991), is given five pages and retains a place among many authors of single novels. Despite its inherent importance in literary studies, language does not seem to have been a factor, since sixty-nine of the authors discussed write predominantly in English while one, Susham Bedi, is introduced as "a leading Indian author, writing in Hindi and living in the United States" (13). The frequency of the novelist's works appearing in critical debates or the classroom does not seem to have been a criterion, since novelists such as Nora Okja Keller, R. Zamora Linmark, Sigrid Nunez, Peter Bacho, Ruth Ozeki, and Gish Jen have been omitted. Even ability is not asserted as a defining element in the selection of authors, since Wentong Ma's entry on novelist Evelyn Chao notes that her work "is not widely publicized and has received no scholarly attention beyond some favorable reviews that are not accessible" (47) and goes on to attack Chao's work apparently for not adopting a Marxist conception of China's history.

The question of selection is a difficult process for the entire field. In "The Fiction of Asian American Literature," Susan Koshy asserts, "The latest Asian American anthologies (even more so than the earlier ones) cannot even assume the existence of common ethnic roots, since they work to include the writings of as many of their different constituent groups as possible" (469). Koshy criticizes the way that many anthologies using the "additive" strategies of inclusion (in the context of her essay, of primary texts) have not ventured to analyze the way in which the additions of texts by new immigrant communities reshape the paradigm of *Asian American* or cogently theorize the differences that that term now encompasses. As Koshy notes, Asian Indians were able to change their U.S. census category from "other white" to "Asian American" only in 1980 (469). With the term *Asian American* now encompassing peoples of not only Hindu but also Islamic culture and belief, Asian American studies and, indeed, the Asian American community as a whole has a range of questions *that have yet to be answered*: Should the expansion of Asian American Studies from its traditional foundations in Far Eastern, largely Confucian-based cultures to South Asian Americans stop arbitrarily at the Pakistani border? In the wake of the destruction of the World Trade Center, the U.S. wars in the Southwestern Asian nations of Afghanistan and Iraq, and the tensions and hate crimes these events have evoked within America, should Asian Americans create ties of kinship or political affiliation with Islamic and/or Arab Americans?[4] What are the political responsibilities of Asian American activists, leaders, scholars, and artists in tensions between the United States and Islamic peoples?

Nelson's inclusion of twenty-six authors of Chinese ethnicity, ten with Japanese ancestors, seven Korean, five Filipino/a, and nineteen from the South Asian diaspora (with origins in what are now the nations of Pakistan, India, and Sri Lanka) is reflective of the demographics that have shaped and reshaped Asian America. His choice to place an Iranian American author such as Nahid Rachlin in his sourcebook could arguably be seen as reflective of the newly emerging discourse of

Iranian American literature and the potential for that discourse to become a part of the umbrella term *Asian American literature*. However, Nelson seems to leap beyond all ties of cultural or political affiliation when he includes William Peter Blatty, the Lebanese American who gained fame with *The Exorcist* (1971), and Vance Bourjaily, whose father was Lebanese. Yes, Lebanon is technically on the continent of Asia, but its culture seems to be as much defined as a part of Western, Mediterranean culture as it is as a part of Asia. At the same time, Nelson's text wholly ignores the presence of Southeast Asian American novelists such as the frequently taught and discussed Lan Cao or Wendy Law-Yone. My point is not that some writers are somehow less deserving of inclusion in a reference text such as this than other authors, but that the selection process needs to be logically and clearly mapped out so that the user understands what to expect of this particular *selection* of Asian (north) American novelists. I would also argue that academic terms and categories need to remain connected to the real-world communities, experiences, and historical and political dynamics from which they originate or they will lose their meaning.

Like *Words Matter, Asian American Novelists* collects works from contributors with varying levels of skill. Yet while Cheung's text evokes an overall sense of continuity and a guiding hand, Nelson's displays not only a haphazard selection process but also a lack of overall quality control. Nonetheless, this text can be helpful for researchers looking for an introduction to individual authors. If aware of its shortcomings, both professional and student researchers can find a fruitful introduction to individual authors, although not an end to their research or an overview of the field.

Sau-ling Cynthia Wong and Stephen H. Sumida's volume, *A Resource Guide to Asian American Literature*, is strikingly different from Nelson's in the way it directly reflects the issues and authors being discussed in classrooms and scholarship on Asian American literature. *A Resource Guide* is specifically useful for teachers as it brings together twenty-one essays on frequently taught individual novels and plays, with four survey essays on other forms of Asian American literature: two on poetry and one each on anthologies and short fiction. With their introduction, Sumida and Wong describe the organization of their volume and the contents of each entry, which contains the following: "Publication . . . [or] . . . Production Information, Overview, Reception, Author's Biographical Background, Historical Context for the Narratives . . . [and/or] . . . the Writing of the Text . . . , Major Themes, Critical Issues, Pedagogical Issues and Suggestions, Intertextual Linkages (indicating texts both Asian American and other than Asian American with which a given title can be compared), Bibliographic Resources, Other Resources (e.g. film and videos and, in one case, Web sites), and Bibliography (of works consulted in the writing of the unit)" (1). The exhaustive nature of this list typifies the encyclopedic quality of the thorough and systematic coverage provided. The fact that all of this fits within a text of less than 350 pages tells you that the segments of each essay—indeed, each unit—are more a sprint than a leisurely walk through the materials. The pieces on individual prose narratives and drama are more akin to Cliffs Notes than your standard scholarly article, so those expecting a nuanced argument from the authors' own perspectives will be better served by the texts cited in the bibliographies. Yet for many first-time teachers of Asian American literature or students trying to gain information about a text, the individual essays provide an amazing amount of information on a given text in less reading time than is available in the average lunch break. This collection is a godsend for the many high school and college composition teachers across the nation who are being encouraged to use ethnic American texts in their classrooms and yet have little or no training in the teaching or study of that discourse. Through the suggestions for intertextual linkages, this collection gives advice, not only on how one might teach particular works, but also on how to structure a reading list for a whole term. The only thing the text does not give advice on is what anthologies to order, since Wong's essay on anthologies is an overview of the entire field and not a direct report on what volume contains the largest number of texts, either in whole or in excerpt, that are discussed in the rest of the volume.

Many teachers at high schools and colleges with little or no experience with Asian American literature are now being asked to teach texts that reflect diverse student populations. Wong and Sumida's *Resource Guide* (and perhaps a text such as Cheung's *Interethnic Companion* or Lim and Ling's *Reading the Literatures* for a bit more insight into the context of distinct ethnic communities' cultural contexts and literary histories) supplies enough information for even the novice teacher's successful inclusion of Asian American literature into his or her curriculum. More experienced teachers and researchers will find this text useful for the way it collects a great deal of information in a compact form. The bibliographies are separate for each essay (whether focused on an individual text or a whole genre). The distinct bibliographies are ideal for individuals who just need to know about a particular text that they are teaching or researching and thus do not want to wade through irrelevant sources. However, if these individual "Works Cited" sections were combined into a single bibliography, one would have a relatively comprehensive list of what a specialist in the field should hope to know. More experienced teachers may have very different pedagogical practices in mind for various texts, but they will be hard pressed to deny the value in the information and methods described in this volume.

Sumida and Wong directly define their selection process and thus the way their text came to reflect the field in their introduction:

> Over the course of ten years we have constructed, and the contributors have filled, a manageable table of contents through a difficult questioning and juggling of the following criteria (which, we emphasize, are *not* listed in order of rank and are *not* applicable in all cases): aesthetic interest; commercial availability; current usage among college instructors; gender and ethnic subgroup variations; historical interest; role in the development of Asian American literature; "track record" of responses by readers, critics, and teachers; potential for generating intertextual linkages and encouraging comparative study; productivity in raising certain critical issues commonly debated in Asian American scholarship; and an elusive quality we call "teachability," the reality of which we can attest to only by anecdotes. (2)

If one is interested in learning about the "canon" of Asian American literature, I would argue that the editors have found the best way to define such a concept—through the dynamic forces and desires at work in the process of teaching and researching literature. Like *Words Matter, A Resource Guide* has been in the works for quite some time and is thus unable to reflect on (or be reflective of) the texts that have had the most recent impact on the field, particularly literature by the many new Southeast Asian American writers. Yet when the individual units are taken collectively, *A Resource Guide* presents an accurate overview of the field at the beginning of this century.

NOTES

1. Takaki is citing Rich's essay, "Invisibility in Academe" (1984), which focuses on lesbians in academia, but has pertinent points applicable to many marginalized groups vis-à-vis institutions of scholarship.

2. The mismatch in values is painfully obvious when Bloom uses the introduction to his collection *Amy Tan's "Joy Luck Club,"* not to discuss the volume, but to decry the fact that one of the essayists claims that Tan has a different take on issues raised by Emerson and Whitman. For Bloom, these great authors have already said everything worth saying, and women's and minority voices are merely (at best "charming") restatements of the masters.

3. This single interview no doubt benefited from the fact that Cheung has interviewed Yamamoto before, as seen in the written interchange included in Cheung's edition of Yamamoto's *Seventeen Syllables* for Rutgers' Women Writers Texts and Contexts Series.

4. These crimes have included murder, assault, arson, and other forms of vandalism. The most famous example of these crimes would be the murder of Balbir Singh Sodhi, a Sikh, in Arizona on 15 September 2001. The fact that Sodhi was not even a Muslim emphasizes just how difficult it is to determine and identify hate crimes when even the perpetrators of such crimes themselves misidentify their targets.

WORKS CITED

Alexander, Meena. *Fault Lines: A Memoir.* New York: Feminist, 1993.
Bloom, Harold, ed. *Amy Tan.* Philadelphia: Chelsea House, 2000.

———. *Amy Tan's "The Joy Luck Club."* Philadelphia: Chelsea House, 2002.
———. *Asian-American Women Writers.* Philadelphia: Chelsea House, 1997.
———. *Asian-American Writers.* Philadelphia: Chelsea House, 1999.
Bulosan, Carlos. *America Is in the Heart.* 1946. Seattle: U of Washington P, 1973.
Cha, Theresa Hak Kyung. *Dictée.* New York: Tanam, 1982.
Cheung, King-Kok. *Articulate Silences: Hisaye Yamamoto, Maxine Hong Kingston, Joy Kogawa.* Ithaca: Cornell UP, 1993.
———. *An Interethnic Companion to Asian American Literature.* New York: Cambridge UP, 1996.
Chin, Frank, Jeffrey Paul Chan, Lawson Inada, and Shawn Wong, eds. *Aiiieeeee! An Anthology of Asian American Writers.* Washington, DC: Howard UP, 1974.
Eaton, Winnifred. *The Heart of Hyacinth.* 1903. Seattle: U of Washington P, 2000.
Huang, Guiyou, ed. *Asian American Autobiographers: A Bio-Bibliographical Critical Sourcebook.* Westport, CT: Greenwood, 2001.
———, ed. *Asian American Poets: A Bio-Bibliographical Critical Sourcebook.* Westport, CT: Greenwood, 2002.
Kearny Street Workshop. 1 Mar. 2003 <http://www.kearnystreet.org/about_ksw/history/index.html>.
Kim, Elaine. *Asian American Literature: An Introduction to the Writings and Their Social Context.* Philadelphia: Temple UP, 1982.
Koshy, Susan. "The Fiction of Asian American Literature." *Asian American Studies: A Reader.* Ed. Jean Yu-Wen Shen Wu and Min Song. New Brunswick: Rutgers UP, 2000. 467–95.
Lee, Rachel C. *The Americas of Asian American Literature: Gendered Fictions of Nation and Transnation.* Princeton: Princeton UP, 1999.
Lew, Walter K., ed. *Premonitions: The Kaya Anthology of New Asian North American Poetry.* New York: Kaya, 1995.
Lim, Shirley Geok-lin, ed. *Asian American Literature: An Anthology.* Lincolnwood, IL: NTC, 2000.
Lim, Shirley Geok-lin, and Amy Ling, eds. *Reading the Literatures of Asian America.* Philadelphia: Temple UP, 1992.
Liu, Miles Xian, ed. *Asian American Playwrights: A Bio-Bibliographical Critical Sourcebook.* Westport, CT: Greenwood, 2002.
Lowe, Lisa. *Immigrant Acts: On Asian American Cultural Politics.* Durham: Duke UP, 1996.
Nguyen, Viet Thanh. *Race and Resistance: Literature and Politics in Asian America.* New York: Oxford UP, 2002.
Rich, Adrienne. "Invisibility in Academe." *Blood, Bread, and Poetry: Selected Prose 1979–1985.* New York: Norton, 1986. 198–201.
Sumida, Stephen H. *And the View from the Shore: Literary Traditions of Hawaii.* Seattle: U of Washington P, 1991.
Tachiki, Amy, Eddie Wong, Franklin Odo, and Buck Wong, eds. *Roots: An Asian American Reader.* Los Angeles: UCLA Asian American Studies Center, 1971.
Takaki, Ronald. *A Different Mirror: A History of Multicultural America.* Boston: Little, 1993.
Wong, Sau-ling Cynthia. *Reading Asian American Literature: From Necessity to Extravagance.* Princeton: Princeton UP, 1993.
Wong, Shawn, ed. *Asian American Literature: A Brief Introduction and Anthology.* New York: Harper, 1996.
Yamamoto, Hisaye. *Seventeen Syllables.* Ed. King-Kok Cheung. New Brunswick: Rutgers UP, 1994.
Yamashita, Karen Tei. *Through the Arc of the Rain Forest.* Minneapolis: Coffee House, 1990.

What Are We Doing in the Humanities Today? Cather as Case Study

SUSAN J. ROSOWSKI
University of Nebraska–Lincoln

A CALENDAR OF THE LETTERS OF WILLA CATHER. Edited by Janis P. Stout. Lincoln: U of Nebraska P, 2002. xix + 334 pp. $65.

WILLA CATHER REMEMBERED. Compiled by L. Brent Bohlke and Sharon Hoover. Edited by Sharon Hoover. Lincoln: U of Nebraska P, 2002. xxiii + 217 pp. Hardbound, $45; paperback, $19.95.

WILLA CATHER: THE CONTEMPORARY REVIEWS. Edited by Margaret Anne O'Connor. Cambridge, UK: Cambridge UP, 2001. xxv + 549 pp. $130.

WILLA CATHER AND THE POLITICS OF CRITICISM. By Joan Acocella. Lincoln: U of Nebraska P, 2000. 127 pp. $25.

WILLA CATHER: QUEERING AMERICA. By Marilee Lindemann. New York: Columbia UP, 1999. xvi + 185 pp. Hardbound, $45; paperback, $16.50.

WILLA CATHER AND OTHERS. By Jonathan Goldberg. Durham: Duke UP, 2001. xv + 228 pp. Hardbound, $54.95; paperback, $18.95.

WILLA CATHER'S SEXUAL AESTHETICS AND THE MALE HOMOSEXUAL LITERARY TRADITION. By John P. Anders. Lincoln: U of Nebraska P, 1999. xiv + 187 pp. Hardbound, $50; paperback, $18.95.

MEMORIAL FICTIONS: WILLA CATHER AND THE FIRST WORLD WAR. By Steven Trout. Lincoln: U of Nebraska P, 2002. ix + 225 pp. $40.

Having burst upon the academic scene as canonical, Cather ended the last millennium as the subject of scholarly and critical books that form (I imagine) concentric circles. At the core is a guide to Cather's letters, then a book of reminiscences and a volume of contemporary reviews, followed by critical studies confirming Cather's importance as a forum for ideas and issues of our time.

So I begin at the center, with Janis P. Stout's superb *A Calendar of the Letters of Willa Cather*. Because Cather's testamentary restrictions prohibit publication of her correspondence, direct access has been limited to those who have the means to travel to repositories throughout the United States and abroad while published references to her letters have consisted of paraphrases of passages taken out of context and tailored to fit the argument at hand. Not surprisingly, it is a situation that is rife with abuse. With *A Calendar of Letters*, Stout provides the corrective: a chronological listing of all correspondence—letters, notes, cards, and telegrams. Clear and accurate paraphrases reveal content and context, as well as often suggesting Cather's style. A biographical directory provides helpful identifications; indexes of names and titles facilitate cross-references. Stout sometimes provides explanatory materials inserted in brackets, as well as notes on Cather's handwriting. The pen provides nuance to words on the page, as anyone actually reading Cather's letters knows full well; the challenge, to read the letters in the original, is one that Stout reinforces with occasional annotations: "several words blotted out" (#1101), "signature illegible" (#1114).

A Calendar of the Letters is an essential resource for anyone working on Cather and a useful one for anyone aspiring to a writing life. It is a remarkably full record that reveals the day-by-day pattern of Cather's "double life" in terms reminiscent of her essay, "Katherine Mansfield" (1936). Half the time Cather is trying to protect her writing (real) life by securing conditions to write; the other half she is seeking the human relationships that circumstances and her own affections have woven about her. Correspondence with publishers, editors, reviewers, and others reveal the professional writer at work; woven through this correspondence (often in the same letters) is evidence of friendships, many of exceptional longevity. Her friend Carrie Miner has gone to college, fifteen-year-old Willa writes from Red Cloud in the first letter cited by Stout; a telegram, Christmas card, and letter from Cather to Carrie Miner Sherwood in Red Cloud are among Stout's final listings. "I measure high buildings by the Moonstone standpipe," Thea Kronborg says toward the end of *The Song of the Lark* (1915); "There are standards we can't get away from" (457).

Whereas the calendar of letters represents Cather's overtures to others, *Willa Cather Remembered* reverses the mirror by presenting others' impressions of her. It complements *Willa Cather in Person: Interviews, Speeches, and Letters* (1986), in which editor L. Brent Bohlke documents Cather's public appearances. Compiled by L. Brent Bohlke and Sharon Hoover, and edited by Sharon Hoover, *Willa Cather Remembered* "collect(s) in one place a selection of less accessible reminiscences and articles that reflects more on Cather as a person than as a writer, although the two are often inextricably mixed" (xxi). Sensibly rejecting the "helter-skelter scenario" of a simple chronological order, Hoover organizes the reminiscences in three groupings: (1) journalists, who were the first to write about Cather, and who continued to write about her as her reputation grew; (2) literary people writing "personality profiles"; and (3) people who knew her informally (xxii). Hoover's introductions summarize Cather's life relevant to each grouping; headnotes identify authors and provide contexts. Many reminiscences, by detailing the circumstances of encounters with Cather, provide glimpses into the world she inhabited; photographs throughout represent periods of her life.

Together the contents of *Willa Cather Remembered* present the dynamics of reputation, friendship, and celebrity. If the literary interview is "a distinctive genre of literary performance," as John Rodden has proposed in *Performing the Literary Interview: How Writers Craft Their Public Selves* (1), reminiscences similarly participate in rhetorical acts of crafting public selves. By writing about Cather as a person, her friends, family, and acquaintances responded to readers' desires to know the woman behind the writer; the rhetorical and linguistic terms of their essays provide case studies on literary reputation. Fanny Butcher (the reviewer for the *Chicago Tribune*) reflected that Cather, more than any other person she knew, succeeded in having "what she wanted of life . . . and that was to write" (98), whereas Witter Bynner (poet and critic) describes his pity for Cather's having sacrificed her life to art. Eleanor Shattuck writes as an observer of Cather as a guest at her family's inn in Jaffrey, New Hampshire, whereas Truman Capote occupies center stage in recreating his meeting with her in New York City. What are their (and others') rhetorical strategies and autobiographical implications? What parts do they play in the reception of Cather and her writing?

While *Willa Cather Remembered* focuses upon how the person was received, *Willa Cather: The Contemporary Reviews* documents how her *writing* was received. Throughout her introduction, editor Margaret Anne O'Connor recalls Cather's experience as a reviewer, summarizes the history of reviews of her books, and provides an extended discussion of cases for and against Cather in the twenties. For the most part, O'Connor reprints reviews in their entirety. Full citations enable readers to retrieve the reviews within the context of their original publication, and a list of "Additional Reviews" expands the field. O'Connor's editorial principle was to present "a representative sampling of the response to Willa Cather's work in the local, regional, national, and international English-language press" (xi). By traveling to libraries housing Cather materials throughout the country, O'Connor unearthed unindexed reviews from regions Cather wrote about, many responding to reviews in New York papers. The result is a volume especially responsive to questions of new regionalism: What is the role of place in reading, reception, and reputation? How do the provinces engage in conversation with New York City, and how does New York view the provinces?

"To those of us who read books for a living the knowledge that [Cather] has done another novel is as much hay to old Dobbin as a Dempsey-Tunney bout is to the sport editors," Fanny Butcher wrote (309). *The Contemporary Reviews* is a case study of the literary marketplace as reviewers take on the issue of what to "do" with Cather, how to categorize and "fix" her. Is she internationalist or regionalist? Does she keep up with the moderns, or slip into the past? Is she modern or genteel? Forward- or backward-looking? Does she rank above or below X? Beyond the sport of it all, reviewers were making their case for literature's role in their culture in terms that remain relevant today.

Cather's resiliency as a forum for issues, ideas, and values was amply confirmed at the close of the twentieth century. "What have the academics done to Willa Cather? Joan Acocella on a one-woman case study in the history of America's lit-crit wars," was the headline emblazoned on newsstand copies of the 27 November 1995 *New Yorker* magazine. Acocella's essay provoked a minor firestorm, including an overflow session at the year's meeting of the Society for the Study of American Women Writers. The essay was expanded by Acocella and published as a book by an academic press, then reissued as a trade paperback, *Willa Cather and the Politics of Criticism*. The volume elicited scores of reviews spanning the literary spectrum: literary superstars writing for newspapers and magazines, academics for professional journals, and locals for hometown papers.

Acocella uses Cather as a forum for challenging contemporary literary studies—and, implicitly, the humanities—in America's universities and colleges. She sets the stage by reviewing the history of Cather criticism: Cather was praised by H. L. Mencken and others in the 1910s; patronized by the sophisticates in the 1920s; attacked by the Left in the 1930s; claimed by the Right in the 1940s; ignored by the New Critics of the 1950s and 1960s; then, beginning in the 1970s, taken up by the women's movement, feminism, then lesbian and gay rights movements.

Acocella adapts the manner of Swiftian satire for her scourge of criticism's folly. That is, she presents a critic's argument through summary and quotation, and then goes to the primary sources upon which it draws to assess its validity. It is, needless to say, a particularly effective interrogation of the academy (where research is presumed to provide the underpinning of theory) in that Acocella employs scholarship to argue against criticism run amuck. Sharon O'Brien's argument, "widely accepted as the proof of Cather's lesbianism" (qtd. in Acocella 50), serves as her major exemplum. According to Acocella, O'Brien (1) defines lesbianism narrowly, so a woman must not only have close ties with other women, but also must be "self-identified" as lesbian; (2) proves Cather's lesbianism by paraphrasing a sentence from an 1892 letter that Cather wrote to Louise Pound; and (3) posits homosexuality as the "emotional source of [Cather's] fiction" by hearing words from Oscar Wilde's trial, "the Love that dared not speak its name," behind Cather's phrase—"the thing not named"—to describe the important quality of literature. By going to the actual letter (which cannot be quoted because of restrictions in Cather's will), Acocella charges that O'Brien's paraphrase is the exact opposite of what Cather said, and by citing Mallarmé and others, she recalls that, rather than being a "startling phrase," "the thing not named" was "a commonplace of *fin-de-siècle* aesthetics" (Acocella 49–51).

Here as elsewhere, Acocella's argument is not about homosexuality or feminism or Cather's sexual orientation (which she presumes was homosexual), but rather about the politics of reputation. In her final chapter, Acocella reads Cather as a Platonist who subordinates the emotion to the idea, the individual to the art. She writes, "Nature was the inspirer of Cather's irony, and of her tragic vision. Nature showed her that the world might be beautiful, and loud with life, yet wholly indifferent to the happiness of its creatures. . . . Such a view does not accord with any program of political reform" (89). The interpretation is not new; *commonsense* is the word sympathetic reviewers characteristically used in describing Acocella's reading of Cather.

But, of course, the "case" today is not for or against Cather, any more than it was in the 1920s. Whereas in the 1920s the issue was *her* relevance, at the turn of the millennium it is the relevance of literary studies (and hence the humanities) within American universities and colleges. "The current crisis of the University in the West proceeds from a fundamental shift in its social role and internal systems, one which means that the centrality of the traditional humanistic disciplines to the life of the University is no longer assured," writes Bill Readings in *The University in Ruins* (3).[1] Responses to *Willa Cather and the Politics of Criticism* demonstrate the point. *The Economist*'s reviewer describes "this sane and sometimes very funny critique of the critics" "as saying more about the state of criticism than about Willa Cather" ("The Presence of the Past"). Robert Leiter responds to this "devastating critique of academic criticism—and by extension, the fate of literary studies in the university during the last thirty years" (666). Acocella's brief book "shines with exemplary good sense," A. S. Byatt writes: "It is possibly because I am living through it that I feel that the fanciful partisan misdescriptions of the 1970s and 1980s are more dangerous to real literature, more dangerous to accurate and careful—even to meaningful—thought, than the errors of Cather's immediate contemporaries, or those of the 1930s, 1940s, and 1950s" (51). Joyce Carol Oates weighs in, dismissive of Cather (equating her reticence with prudery), but critical of the critics' "avid prurience" (4). Academics (who mainly reviewed Acocella's book in specialized professional journals) were represented in the public discourse by Terry Castle's lengthy review in the *London Review of Books*. After acknowledging the satiric charm and force with which Acocella "unfurl[s] a modern lampoon on academic folly" (15), Castle turns the tables to lampoon Acocella as "a good cop on the beat," before whose "steely-eyed moral authority" one goes "all weak and wobbly and compliant" (19). So far as I know, no one in Cather studies has engaged seriously with the issues that Acocella and her reviewers raise concerning the relationship of scholarship to criticism, of literature to culture, and of English departments to literature. When Castle writes of academic criticism as "an ongoing negotiation between truth and error, and sometimes, by an irritating yet ultimately productive dialectic, error is for a while in the ascendant" (20), what are the criteria of truth and error?

By way of answering, we might first remember that Cather was writing from a radically different premise from that of the Modernist project, which stems from an impulse toward the self-transparency of a self creating a world in perceiving it. Granted, Cather's premise of untranslatability and unknowability suggests her acute sensitivity to the conditions out of which modernism springs. A father is "absolutely unable to touch upon the vast body of experience he wished to communicate" to the youth who will (disastrously) marry his daughter (*One of Ours* 150). "The heart of another is a dark forest, always, no matter how close it has been to one's own," a husband thinks of his wife (*The Professor's House* 93). Cather writes, "There was no way in which [a French Catholic priest] could transfer his own memories of European civilization into the Indian mind, and he was quite willing to believe that behind [his Indian guide] there was a long tradition, a story of experience, which no language could translate to him. A chill came with the darkness" (*Death Comes for the Archbishop* 97). But unlike the modernist, Cather stresses the age-old and universal quality of such feelings (untranslatable though they are) seeking form in art: "what was any art but an effort to make a sheath, a mould in which to imprison for a moment the shining, elusive element which is life itself" (*The Song of the Lark*

304). And rather than presenting discontinuities and diversities as irreducible, Cather believed that literature models analogical thinking that affirms continuities between us and them, the present and the past, here and there. Reaching these continuities has to do with a belief that "something complete and beautiful" lies beneath differences. I am quoting here from the final passage (61) of "Neighbour Rosicky" (1932), but the sentiment appears throughout Cather's writing.

In the 1990s, instability is the premise for many, as radical epistemological skepticism yields poststructuralist rhetoric in which the reader becomes audience to the critic's performance—Here's my story; now where's yours? Jim Burden asks in delivering his manuscript to his creator in the original introduction to *My Ántonia* (my paraphrase; see xiii). The invitation is at the root of some of the most provocative recent work in Cather studies.

With *Willa Cather: Queering America*, Marilee Lindemann dedicates her "happily perverse" (30) reading to the cause of gay rights. Part 1 tracks the queer in Cather's writings (private and public) "with particular emphasis on the Pound letters and her first five novels" (12). Part 2 looks at Cather in cultural and literary politics of the 1920s as she sought to "subvert, problematize, and radically reconfigure the notion of the 'classic' that was shaping the canon and the new field of American literary study" (13) by changing publishers, editing *The Best Stories of Sarah Orne Jewett*, and writing *The Professor's House* and *Death Comes for the Archbishop*. The linchpin to Lindemann's argument is the term *queer* as Cather used it in her letters about herself, and as it is used today. Lindemann looks, for her springboard, to Cather's 1892 letter to Louise Pound, where she notes that the word *queer* occurs, and where she interprets rhetorical shifts and twists as revealing the energies and anxieties of lesbian love. From this letter, Lindemann generalizes, "Beyond these private, terrified acts of self-naming and -unnaming, the word 'queer' resonates throughout Cather's fiction with the snap, crackle, and pop of acute anxiety and ideological work." As Lindemann explains, *Queering America* attends to that continuous, extraordinary repetition as it echoes throughout Cather's career and presses into our own moment (12).

There is, Lindemann acknowledges, the risk of making too much of the scant epistolary record in which Cather writes about Pound. To the contrary, I wish for far more of this record, including research into the linguistic history of *queer* beyond an endnote quoting the OED definition, and including its uses in Lincoln and Red Cloud during the early 1890s, as well as Cather's use of it throughout her life. Such a history would remind us that by the late nineteenth century, the term was a standard literary device to signal blurring boundaries, as Cather would have known full well from two of her favorite authors. Mark Twain prefaces *The Adventures of Tom Sawyer* (1876) with his hope "to try to pleasantly remind adults . . . what queer enterprises they sometimes engaged in"; and Robert Louis Stevenson opens *The Strange Case of Dr. Jekyll and Mr. Hyde* (1886) with the resolve, "the more it looks like Queer Street, the less I ask." The fact that the *Red Cloud Chief* featured "Some of the Queer Words of Our Queer Language" (1900) among its stories makes me wish for more, as does skimming a few of Cather's stories and essays, where one finds that her characters act "queerly" in "An Affair at Grover Station" (1900; *Collected Short Fiction* 342); "Queer world, this," she writes in 1895 of responses to the Intermezzo (Slote 184); "It's queer, but the very arrival of Bernhardt brings about a sort of quickening of the spirit in matters dramatic. It reminds one that the drama is not all rot after all, that it's really an art" (Slote 120); and "one of the queer things about Chicago is that no one is really a native," she writes in "The Count of Crow's Nest" (1896; *Collected Short Fiction* 462). Decades later, Anton Rosicky looks up at Doctor Burleigh "with a gleam of amusement in his queer triangular-shaped eyes" ("Neighbour Rosicky" 7). Far from crackling with tensions and anxieties, *queer* appears quite comfortably throughout Cather's writing.

"It is queer what work the philosophers and critics make of artists anyway," Cather reflected in 1895 (Slote 255). So, what is "queer work" almost a century later? On the one hand, Lindemann acknowledges the multiplicity and fluidity of *queer* as it appears in Cather's oeuvre; on the other, she applies meaning retroactively from "our own moment," with *queer* signifying lesbian sexuality. Again, Cather's letter provides the springboard: "the force that 'drives' the passage in the letter is the joyous/ dangerous release of an energy that is palpably sexual—as sexual, say, as a pack of Lawrentian horses—and Cather seems intoxicated by the risks and the recklessness of such a release" (29). Remember, the historical scholar in me cautions, that rhetorical intoxication was Cather's way in the 1890s when she was writing about art as a "Bacchic orgy" (Slote 119) of feverish passion, great emotion, primitive energy, flaming love, glittering temptation, yearning desire, and barbarian force. Yet even while yearning for context, I acknowledge that *Willa Cather: Queering America* derives its strength from Lindemann's commitment to transparency in positioning herself within the field(s) of lesbian/ gay/queer studies, in naming herself within that field as lesbian (rather than queer), and in describing her motive as political activism and her goal as experimental ("i.e., to test the efficacy of queer critique as an interpretive procedure" [140]).

The result is, as one would expect, a decentered method. Rather than attempting to map a trajectory of Cather or her career, Lindemann sets out to "examine a few nodal points" (6) in which the queer erupts and inscribes in Cather's texts, and in their interrogations of national discourses. The prairie is queer as a space where anxieties over America's identity are played out; Thea Kronborg is triumphantly queer in subverting the system; Cather queered American literary study by rewriting its history to include Sarah Orne Jewett and herself with Nathaniel Hawthorne and Mark Twain; and so on. When fault lines appear, they serve Lindemann's experimental goal of testing the efficacy of queer critique. Her method, with its discursive multiplicity, is at odds with the binary logic of her argument, by which the "queerness" of "oppositionality" challenges "white heteronormativity" (6); and this fault line invited inquiry into how gay and lesbian studies meets queer theory.

Whereas Lindemann comes to Cather through gay activism, Jonathan Goldberg applies queer theory to Cather as a postscript to his *Queering the Renaissance* (1994). Goldberg's guiding suppositions for *Willa Cather and Others* are "that the secret in *Alexander's Bridge*—its open secret, indeed—is Cather's sexuality" and "that the difference between one first novel and the next has everything to do with how Cather's sexuality is implicated in her writing" (5). In an introductory romp through psychology, philosophy, biography, history, criticism, and theory, Goldberg posits desire as a motive force, reviews connections between Cather's two first novels, recalls Cather's allusions to the intuition of Henri Bergson's organic vitalism, and then concludes, "If this is Cather's position, it is no stretch to call it queer in its refusal of boundaries" (8). As did Lindemann, Goldberg makes *queer* the encompassing term. But whereas Lindemann traces how Cather queered America, Goldberg queers Cather. He does so by taking hold of two phrases in Cather studies: "the thing not named" and the "double life."

Goldberg launches *Willa Cather and Others* by extracting "the thing not named" from "The Novel Démeublé" (1936; collected in *Willa Cather on Writing*), maintains it by reiterating the phrase with mind-numbing frequency, then concludes by asserting, "It is because of such understatement that so little can mean so much in Cather" (177). In *Willa Cather and Others*, this means that understatement gives the critic free rein. The word *others* in his title signals, Goldberg explains, "at the highest level of generality, an alterity that I take to accompany all and any identity" (xiii). The book's cover illustration of Cather holding a dog's face to the camera presumably illustrates his point. Chapters present clusters of verbal, visual, and musical texts that Goldberg treats as "dense transfer points and occlusions" (119), each including a Cather novel. A chapter titled "Cather Diva" joins *The Song of the Lark* with Mary Watkins Cushing's memoir of Fremstad's life (1954), Marcia Davenport's version of Fremstad in the popular novel *Of Lena Geyer* (1936),

Cather's essay "Three American Singers" (1913), and Edith Lewis's 1953 memoir of Cather. Another chapter, "War Requiems," joins *One of Ours* with Pat Barker's 1990s World War I trilogy and with Siegfried Sassoon, Wilfred Owens, Stephen Tennant, and (again) Edith Lewis. With a chapter titled "Strange Brothers," Goldberg "weaves" around *The Professor's House* Blair Niles's 1931 novel of male homosexuality and the photographs of Laura Gilpin to pursue a "cross-cutting" reading of representation, all of which "has pertinence to the depiction of family in *The Professor's House*, to the aching of male-male desire and its locus in the ruins of Anasazi civilization" (xv).

Whereas Goldberg takes his method from "the thing not named," he takes his interpretive narrative from the "double life" that Cather writes about in her essay on Katherine Mansfield: "[H]uman relationships are the tragic necessity of human life; . . . they can never be wholly unsatisfactory, . . . every ego is half the time greedily seeking them, and half the time pulling away from them" (qtd. in Goldberg 9). From this quotation, Goldberg generalizes that "[h]uman psychology is necessarily ambivalent, founded in 'secret accords and antipathies which lie hidden under our everyday behaviour,' at its most extreme a battle of love and hate. Cather fights it over and again. . . . If Cather makes it difficult for the reader to exactly name the thing not named, it is in part because such struggles underlie her work. The thing not named does not simply translate something that can be said, and this is in part because of the deep ambivalences of the tug of war that Cather describes in her essay on Mansfield" (9). For Goldberg, the result is a reading of identifications and disidentifications, possessions, dispossessions, repudiations, and sacrifices. Complex identity entanglements of antipathy and desire play out in the "diva madness" of Cather and Fremstad, Lewis and Cather, Watkins Cushing and Fremstad and Cather; Cather revised *The Song of the Lark* to "diminish" Fremstad (52); she identified with Claude Wheeler by a "loving sadism" (87); and so on. What Cather writes of as "erasure of personality" Goldberg approaches as "disidentification" (50); what Cather opens as imaginative space for release from ego, Goldberg uses for an assertion of himself. For example, Gilpin's image "Navaho Shepherd Boy" in *The Enduring Navaho* sets in motion Goldberg's speculations about the "triangulated" (166) relationships among Gilpin, Elizabeth Warham Forster, and the Navaho, then the associations of the phrase, "unstated knowledge," that Gilpin describes as illuminating the image. "What knowledge is this? It need not be exclusively lesbian, but it is certainly about personal relationships," Goldberg writes, and then meditates upon sublimated relationships (176).

Here, as throughout *Willa Cather and Others*, Goldberg exhibits an extreme anthropomorphism in his lack of curiosity about the time, culture, place, and people he writes about. In his "cross-cutting" readings, Goldberg resists "a reductive contextualization . . . to allow for the resonance of alterities in the places of reading that Cather invites" (xv). In explaining these places of reading, Goldberg recalls that he first read "Tom Outland's Story" as science fiction in an unimaginable place (in high school he knew nothing of the ruins at Mesa Verde), then reflects: "I could not imagine it as being real. It was the place of reading. It was where I was. It is still—amazingly—where I often find myself reading Cather" (x). The result is the myopia and solipsism of criticism breezily independent of the world, with its real places and actual histories. It is a stance particularly startling when applied to Cather, for whom desire begins in engagement with the particulars of life as it is lived, then awakens in yearning to connect those particulars to an idea. *The Enduring Navaho* may be about people (as Gilpin's *The Rio Grande* [1949] is about landscapes), but Gilpin conceived of people and land as inextricably joined; and Blair Niles began writing as Mary Blair Beebe, often collaboratively with her husband, renowned naturalist C. William Beebe. *Willa Cather and Others* makes me want to open a window and let in fresh air by reading (for example) Audrey Goodman's discussion of Cather's first trip to the Southwest as a recapitulation of "the Southwest's history and its appeal to armchair as well as actual tourists" (149) in *Translating Southwestern Landscapes: The Making of an Anglo Literary Region* (2002).

Two recent critical studies demonstrate alternate approaches to "the thing not named," the seemingly ubiquitous phrase in Cather criticism these days. John P. Anders opens *Willa Cather's Sexual Aesthetics and the Male Homosexual Literary Tradition* with a reflection on two statements— "only the feeling matters," and "the thing not named"—that, together, "clarify Cather's artistic philosophy, her belief in literature as an intensely subjective experience dually created by the writer and reader" (1). By Anders's reading, friendship, particularly male friendship, shaped Cather's imagination and appears in her writing as homosexual feelings fundamental to her sexual aesthetics. In this reading, Anders writes from the "juncture of gender studies and gay studies" (5); and far from assuming that Cather retreated to a closet, he argues that her allusions to homosexual writing are as present as those to the classics, music, the visual arts, the Bible, and the like.

Anders lays the groundwork for his study by recovering forgotten texts and rereading familiar ones in the gay literary heritage available to Cather—classical, medieval, and Renaissance, American, British, and French writers. Placing Cather within this tradition, Anders reads the "intimations of homosexuality" in her narrative landscape as "an allusive density swelling into metaphor" (62). Cather "recreates homosexuality's most inspiring legend"—the Greek ideal embodied in the Sacred Band of Thebes (72)—by concentrating on male friendship in novels she wrote in the 1920s. Using homosexuality as her "most potent metaphor for [a] redemptive quest" seeking an original identity, Cather adopted a classical ideal of friendship in *One of Ours*; expanded her redemptive models and incorporated structural analogies in *The Professor's House*; and depicted idealized, spiritual friendship in *Death Comes for the Archbishop* (1927). In his concluding chapter, "Naming the Unnameable" (135–40), Anders states that Cather's treatment of homosexuality suggests the potential of Cather's art for social commentary and for evocation of readers' sympathy; Cather's sexual aesthetics distinguishes her artistic achievement as an allusive literary style associated with homosexuality, a sensitivity to variation, and a gift of sympathy.

Anders's *Willa Cather's Sexual Aesthetics* is a quiet, reflective book. It *suggests* (Anders's characteristic verb) rather than asserts; it builds its case through meticulous scholarship and discerning criticism. In specifying that his subject is Cather's art, not "the nature of homosexuality" (139), Anders trusts that Cather's art will yield homosexuality among the feelings "dually created by the writer and reader" (1). And through this trust in art, he dedicates himself to advocacy. With his preface, Anders proposes *Willa Cather's Sexual Aesthetics* as "a dialogue of sorts—a bridge, perhaps, between Cather studies and gay studies" (xii). In the end, he returns to "the fundamental realities of life and art" (139) that steady Cather's humanism, reiterates the case for a gay reading as an interpretive strategy and a social critique, and then concludes, "It is on another level, however, that Cather's gay fiction makes its deepest and most lasting impressions. . . . Because her humanism steadies her focus on the fundamental realities of life and art, homosexuality enters Cather's canon less as a fact than as a feeling. Indeed, homosexuality . . . becomes an integral aspect of Cather's immense design, *another glimpse of individuals caught in the complex behavior of living, and one of the few human stories repeating itself through history*" (139–40; emphasis added).

Last, for the purposes of this review-essay, "the thing not named" figures prominently in *Memorial Fictions: Willa Cather and the First World War*, in which Steven Trout brings historical scholarship to bear upon questions of national culture and identity, disproving yet again the old charge of Cather as escapist. As Anders recovered a homosexual tradition behind Cather's fiction, Trout recovers traditions of the Great War as among the "forgotten contexts" (8) for her war novels. Trout interprets "the iconography of remembrance" surrounding World War I as it was embodied in postcards, photographs, military awards, citations, and war memorials. He then places *One of Ours* within this context to argue that "Claude Wheeler's progress from miserable Nebraskan to exuberant *American*" reveals Cather's awareness of an emerging homog-

enized American world view made possible by "the military melting pot
... by technological advances in media (such as cinema), ubiquitous
consumerism, and the new science of public relations as practiced in
both the government and private sector" (9). In recovering the
accounts, legends, popular folklore, and situations of the war, Trout
argues that Cather represented soldiers' day-to-day experiences accurately, both reflecting and examining history and cultural myths promulgated to understand it.[2] By casting her protagonist as "one of ours,"
Cather uses Claude Wheeler's story "to explore the cultural constructs
through which Americans 'made sense' of the First World War" (148);
Trout sees *One of Ours* as "a disturbingly inconclusive study of American
martial idealism (especially its origins and ambiguities)" (149).

Whereas a strength of *Memorial Fictions* is Trout's research into popular
culture as a context for his reading of *One of Ours*, its surprise lies with his
reading of *The Professor's House* as a war novel. The war is "the thing not
named" in *The Professor's House*, Trout argues, haunting the novel by its
phantom presence. Trout's springboard is an extended reading of "the
thing not named" within the context of "The Novel Démeublé" and
Cather's literary aesthetics. Rather than assuming that "the inexplicable
presence of the thing not named" signifies an encoded sexuality, Trout
defines it simply as a "critical dictum" that invites readers to respond "with
a kind of double vision, focusing simultaneously on what the narrative
names and leaves unnamed. In other words, she encourages us to consider how the text's silence—or, to shift metaphors, its negative space—
contributes to its overall significance" (151). For Cather's university
professor of history, that interplay between text and context involves "the
turbulent academic background against which St. Peter's individual crisis unfolds" (158). The Great War offered American historians "the bitter spectacle of historical writing transmogrified into propaganda" and
also "the queasy sense of global madness—of a new dark ages—that so
haunted European intellectuals" (157).

Trout reviews the intellectual fissures that threatened the very
premises of the entire discipline of history, creating "the mood of
unease and soul-searching" from which few historians escaped in the
postwar years (157). The epistemological crisis of objectivity versus relativism was intensified by propagandistic work done by American historians in the 1920s, all resulting in skepticism about meaning in
history, about finding patterns and order. Trout returns to *The Professor's
House* to read key scenes with the assumption that the Great War as "the
thing not named" points to its very significance: St. Peter's encounter
with his longtime adversary, Professor Langtry, reveals St. Peter's dismay
over the rise of historical relativism; his "terse characterization of the
First World War as the 'great catastrophe' [is] a climactic passage that

openly addresses several war-related themes established almost invisibly elsewhere" (161); and his lecture on "'science as a phase of human development'" assumes an urgency "against the backdrop of a war that saw so many horrific technological 'advances'" (163).

Trout argues that the "daunting international theme" that Cather addressed in *The Professor's House* was "the impact of the Great War, with its unprecedented scale and destructiveness, on the intellectual foundations of Western Civilization" (150). Slightly more than seventy-five years later, we face another version of this theme, now cast as globalization, the war against terrorism, and preemptive strikes. Literature professors today, very much like Cather's history professor in her 1925 novel, are well situated to address what happens when an increasingly transnational global economy marginalizes the nation-state and (with it) the modern notion of culture. As Bill Readings writes, "This shift has major implications for the University, which has historically been the primary institution of national culture in the modern nation-state" (12). Without a legitimating metanarrative, "a major shift in the role and function of the intellectual is occurring" (192). It is, according to Reading, the relevance of belief that is at stake: "The problem that students and teachers face is . . . not so much the problem of what to believe as the problem of what kind of analysis of institutions will allow any belief to count for anything at all" (192).

As the books reviewed here (only a sampling of recent work in the field) demonstrate, Cather offers an exceptionally productive forum for exploring these issues: What is literature's role in our individual and collective lives? English departments' role within universities? Universities' role within our culture? And how does each relate to the "problem" of belief? By way of responding, I suggest that Cather unsettles the very idea of a "legitimating metanarrative," in the process interrogating religious and political dogma; *at the same time*, she affirms the deep meaning of "belief" as a habit of mind that involves placing trust or confidence in another,[3] and she looks to literature as a way of exploring what that means. That is, Cather believed in the capacity of literature to give aesthetic form to human feelings and, thus, to offer consolation and joy. I am thinking, as an example, of Cather's reflection in her first Nebraska novel, in which Alexandra Bergson and Carl Linstrum realize that "the old story has begun to write itself over"—of youth and age, life and death: "Isn't it queer: there are only two or three human stories, and they go on repeating themselves as fiercely as if they had never happened before; like the larks in this country, that have been singing the same five notes over for thousands of years" (*O Pioneers!* 110).

NOTES
 1. It is relevant to recall that Acocella, far from being hostile to Cather as a lesbian, addresses the question at some length and concludes, "What the evidence suggests is that Cather was homosexual in her feelings and celibate in her actions" (48). And it is relevant that Readings situates himself as a liberal (9) who is "personally in sympathy" with "left-wing criticism" (13).
 2. Trout's argument here provides a long-overdue *substantive* response to Hemingway's disparagement of Cather's war scenes and should be read alongside volume editor Richard Harris's superb historical essay and explanatory notes for *One of Ours*, in the Willa Cather Scholarly Edition.
 3. Here I am drawing upon the basic definitions provided by a standard desk dictionary, *The American Heritage College Dictionary* (3rd ed., 1993).

WORKS CITED
Byatt, A. S. "Justice for Willa Cather." *New York Review of Books* 30 Nov. 2000: 51–53.
Castle, Terry. "The Willa Cather Wars." *London Review of Books* 14 Dec. 2000: 15–20.
Cather, Willa. *Cather's Collected Short Fiction: 1892–1912*. Ed. Virginia Faulkner. Lincoln: U of Nebraska P, 1965.
———. *Death Comes for the Archbishop*. 1927. Lincoln: U of Nebraska P, 1999.
———. "Katherine Mansfield." *Willa Cather on Writing*. New York: Knopf, 1949. 105–20.
———. *My Ántonia*. 1918. Lincoln: U of Nebraska P, 1998.
———. "Neighbour Rosicky." *Obscure Destinies*. 1932. Lincoln: U of Nebraska P, 1998. 6–61.
———. *One of Ours*. New York: Knopf, 1922.
———. *O Pioneers!* 1913. Lincoln: U of Nebraska P, 1992.
———. *The Professor's House*. 1925. Lincoln: U of Nebraska P, 2002.
———. "Some of the Queer Words of Our Queer Language." *Red Cloud Chief* 21 Dec. 1900: 2.
———. *The Song of the Lark*. 1915. Lincoln: U of Nebraska P, 1978.
———. *Willa Cather in Person: Interviews, Speeches, and Letters*. Ed. L. Brent Bohlke. Lincoln: U of Nebraska P, 1986.
———. *Willa Cather on Writing*. New York: Knopf, 1949.
Goodman, Audrey. *Translating Southwestern Landscapes: The Making of an Anglo Literary Region*. Tucson: U of Arizona P, 2002.
Leiter, Robert. "Willa Cather's Critics." *Partisan Review* 68 (2001): 666–68.
Oates, Joyce Carol. "Female in America." *TLS-The Times Literary Supplement* 25 May 2001: 3–4.
"The Presence of the Past." *The Economist* 24 Feb. 2001: 88.
Readings, Bill. *The University in Ruins*. Cambridge, MA: Harvard UP, 1996.
Rodden, John. *Performing the Literary Interview: How Writers Craft Their Public Selves*. Lincoln: U of Nebraska P, 2001.
Slote, Bernice, ed. *The Kingdom of Art: Willa Cather's First Principles and Critical Statements, 1893–1896*. Lincoln: U of Nebraska P, 1967.
Stevenson, Robert Louis. *The Strange Case of Dr. Jekyll and Mr. Hyde*. 1886. Bartleby.com: Great Books Online. 2002. 30 Aug. 2003 <http://www.bartleby.com/1015/1.html>.
Twain, Mark. *The Adventures of Tom Sawyer*. 1876. The Literature Network. 30 Aug. 2003 <http://www.literatureproject.com/tom-sawyer/tom-sawyer_1.htm>.

Jeffers Redux

STEPHEN GOULD AXELROD
University of California, Riverside

THE COLLECTED POETRY OF ROBINSON JEFFERS. VOLUME 1: 1920–1928. Edited by Tim Hunt. Stanford, CA: Stanford UP, 1988. xxviii + 521 pp. $75.

THE COLLECTED POETRY OF ROBINSON JEFFERS. VOLUME 2: 1928–1938. Edited by Tim Hunt. Stanford, CA: Stanford UP, 1989. xv + 610 pp. $75.

THE COLLECTED POETRY OF ROBINSON JEFFERS. VOLUME 3: 1939–1962. Edited by Tim Hunt. Stanford, CA: Stanford UP, 1991. xix + 485 pp. $75.

THE COLLECTED POETRY OF ROBINSON JEFFERS. VOLUME 4: POETRY 1903–1920, PROSE, AND UNPUBLISHED WRITINGS. Edited by Tim Hunt. Stanford, CA: Stanford UP, 2000. xxiv + 561 pp. $75.

THE COLLECTED POETRY OF ROBINSON JEFFERS. VOLUME 5: TEXTUAL EVIDENCE AND COMMENTARY. Edited by Tim Hunt. Stanford, CA: Stanford UP, 2001. xiii + 1128 pp. $75.

THE SELECTED POETRY OF ROBINSON JEFFERS. Edited by Tim Hunt. Stanford, CA: Stanford UP, 2001. 758 pp. $24.95.

STONES OF THE SUR: POETRY BY ROBINSON JEFFERS. Photographs by Morley Baer. Edited by James Karman. Stanford, CA: Stanford UP, 2001. viii + 164 pp. $60.

One might have thought that Robinson Jeffers's literary reputation lay under a permanent cloud. An archetypal dead white male poet, Jeffers (1887–1962) exhibited minimal sympathetic interest in the viewpoints of his contemporaries. He thought of himself as a Cassandra, staunchly refuting modernism, which he equated with being "tricky" (C 3: 464; S 698). He did not inhabit the prestigious Boston–New York corridor, nor did he escape to London or Paris. Instead, he lived a reclusive life with his wife and sons in Tor House, a stone structure that he built by hand on the rugged Carmel coastline of central California. His poems are self-certain, humorless, and flintily libertarian. They resist the spirit of formal experimentation that animates the texts of H. D., T. S. Eliot, Marianne Moore, Ezra Pound, Gertrude Stein, and William Carlos Williams. If "form is meaning," as Marjorie Perloff has said (75), then Jeffers's poems might be said to have derivative meanings. A skeptic might say that his narrative poems aim for Greek tragedy yet only manage to foretell Douglas Sirk while his descriptive poems seem to have been written by a Walt Whitman who hated people. Nevertheless, in their passionate ecological awareness, their incomparable observational qualities, their meditative profundity, and their amazing verbal vibrancy, Jeffers's poems transcend such cavils as they survive time's decay.

Here is Jeffers as we have never seen him, in a massive, exquisitely produced, and meticulously edited five-volume *Collected Poetry* that puts all other editions of twentieth-century American poets to shame. It is complemented by a well-chosen *Selected Poetry* and a sampler of Jeffers's poems illustrated with glorious photographs of the scenes he described. No other twentieth-century American poet has received such an impressive display—not Williams, Wallace Stevens, Langston Hughes, or Robert Lowell, as impressive as their *Collected Poems* all are. Why has Jeffers received such star treatment? And why now?

The volumes themselves suggest some answers to these questions. I confess that the depth and the intensity of Jeffers's best poems came as a surprise to me. I have spent the last weeks reading them, as if in a fever dream. The sites and weathers of the central California coastline that Jeffers evokes so vividly have seemed more real to me than my own less dramatic surroundings somewhere in the Southern California metroplex. I first read Jeffers's poems many years ago, in a now-outdated and rather parsimonious edition of selected poems. I was in my mid-twenties and studying for my Ph.D. exams. The poems seemed to have nothing to do with the exciting innovations that I had learned to admire in the work of the modernist masters. Moreover, I was repelled by the poems' imagery of rocks, lichens, hawks, pounding surf, and lonely cliff sides at dawn or sundown. Happily married, with a baby boy, nice parents and friends, and a promising career ahead of me, I saw little in these solitary poems to identify with or care about. Now, past the middle of the journey, I find I like them better. These are poems—

especially the ones from his early career and then again from his last years—that one grows into. More than "Prufrock," Jeffers's poems reflect an old spirit. They suggest the emotional and perceptual life of a person who is essentially alone, a person with deep but not wide attachments. Sad to say, I get them now.

Jeffers composed two distinct kinds of poetry. He wrote intense narrative poems located on some border separating poetry from drama and fiction. These long poems typically tell of families with ingrown and brooding passions, and they end in pain and violence—a death by childbirth, a self-blinding of the patriarch, a burning of the ancestral house. Utterly engrossing if often lurid, these poems have been mostly neglected in the years following the sensation of their original publication. They are too long for anthologies, too old-fashioned for modernist chic, and frankly too extreme for comfort. Jeffers also wrote the shorter observational and meditative lyrics for which he is better known today. These poems are less stunning yet also less unsettling. They fit easily into anthologies, just as they fit into our notions of the romantic lyric tradition. Without people, providing only their articulate speaker for company, these lyrics at their best open our hearts to the unexpected beauty of both nature and language. They console us with things larger than ourselves, impersonal things—things, it must be said, that were abundant in Jeffers's time but increasingly despoiled in our own. So for the contemporary reader, these poems evoke anxiety as well as solace. They point to a ravishing and lonely world that is now in the process of being lost, probably forever.

Jeffers's career may be said to have three stages, though this characterization may just reflect our magical way of organizing oeuvres that we think of as important. The first stage—Jeffers in his prime—runs through the 1920s. This stage includes such narrative poems as *Tamar, Roan Stallion, Cawdor,* and *The Loving Shepherdess* and such lyrics as "To the Stone-Cutters," "Birds," "Boats in a Fog," "Apology for Bad Dreams," "Hurt Hawks," and "Bixby's Landing." The second stage—unfortunate from my perspective—runs through the 1930s and 1940s. These poems are frequently abstract, angry, and political. (Jeffers opposed FDR and World War II with a vengeance.) During these years, Jeffers seemed to have undertaken a vendetta against the human race, which he repeatedly described as blind, foolish, and insect-like. Unlike the earlier poems, these of the second stage seem dated and nearly lifeless today. Jeffers's third and last stage begins in 1950 and continues to his death in 1962. Stunned by the death of his beloved wife, Una, and obsessed by aging and death, Jeffers wrote gentler poems about loss and endurance. In poems such as "The Ocean's Tribute" and "It nearly cancels my fear of death," he returned to the lyric mode of his prime while discovering new qualities of reflection and resignation, an interest in the way things waste away.

Throughout these phases, Jeffers set his poems in a remarkably small number of locales. The first locale is the household, the site of his early narrative poems about dysfunctional families and of his later, mellow poems recalling his own wife and children. The second locale is the landscape and seascape of the Carmel–Big Sur region, the wild world that surrounds the domestic sphere and that serves as the principal focus of Jeffers's lyrics. The third locale is the space of the philosophic mind, wherein Jeffers struggled with the intellectual, spiritual, and aesthetic issues that organized and tormented his conceptual life. A fourth locale is the public arena of urban confusion, governmental cupidity, and battlefield stupidity—a peripheral, allusive space that became central during his middle phase. And finally, some poems are set in the lands and seas of Scotland, Ireland, and England, ancestral places that Jeffers and his wife visited on several occasions. That is a surprisingly circumscribed set of locations for one of the most prolific poets in our literature. The narrowness suggests both a basic lack of curiosity about the worlds available to him and an ability to mine deeply the few worlds about which he really cared. I will examine the way Jeffers explores such locales in the poems of his first and major phase. I will then skim over the productions of his middle and later years. I will conclude by giving some impression of the thoroughness and care with which Tim Hunt has approached his editorial task and by speculating about how Jeffers might have reacted to our contemporary material culture.

Of all of Jeffers's narrative poems, *Roan Stallion* (first published in 1925) is the best known and most respected. Tim Hunt tells us that when he asked his thirty advisors which poems to include in *Selected Poetry*, *Roan Stallion* was one of only two poems "on every list," along with "Boats in a Fog" (S 9). *Roan Stallion* has become the representative Jeffers narrative in part because of its concision and focus. Analogous to a short story rather than a novel, it has three key scenes, a driving pace, and a modernist laconic quality. For once, Jeffers's narrator and his characters do not feel compelled to overexplain. So there is both a pragmatic and an aesthetic reason for this poem's prominence. It is short enough to read in one sitting and to be anthologized. And it is powerful and mysterious enough to bear comparison to the best work of William Faulkner, Ernest Hemingway, and D. H. Lawrence.

The protagonist of *Roan Stallion* is a twenty-one-year-old wife and mother named California. Just as in *The Loving Shepherdess*, in which the compulsively ambulatory protagonist is named Clare Walker, this lead character's name comes weighted with allegory. Half Scottish and half "Spanish and Indian" (C 1: 179; S 115), she suggests Jeffers's sense of

California demographics—dominated by his own Anglo-Celtic ethnicity but complemented by dashes of Mediterranean and Native American cultures, or to put it another way, by Mexicans. California's husband, a gambler and drunkard named Johnny, traces his ancestry back to the Netherlands, and is thus outside this ethnic circle. Johnny, "shriveled with bad living" (C 1: 180; S 116), initiates a sexual encounter with his wife of such stunning badness that it is no that wonder both she and the reader detest him. He

> Felt the cool curve and firmness of her flank, and half rising caught her by the long wet hair.
> She endured, and to hasten the act she feigned desire; she had not for long except in dream, felt it.
> Yesterday's drunkenness made him sluggish and exacting. . . .
> At length she was permitted to put on her clothes.
> (C 1: 182; S 118)

Beyond his failures as a husband, Johnny is a washout as a father and regards their sickly daughter Christine with a mixture of indifference and "malice" (C 1: 188; S 124). California simmers in unhappiness. A solitary buggy ride to Monterey to buy Christmas gifts for Christine brings her turmoil to a boil, and it provides Jeffers with an opportunity to write the sort of nature description guaranteed to knock your socks off:

> All morning the clouds were racing northward like a river.
> At noon they thickened.
> When California faced the southwind home from Monterey it was heavy with level rain-fall.
> She looked seaward from the foot of the valley; red rays cried sunset from a trumpet of streaming
> Cloud over Lobos, the southwest occident of the solstice.
> (C 1: 182–83; S 118–19)

Soon it is night. California must ford a turbulent stream in the dark, and after a long struggle, she prays to Jesus for light. Miraculously, "light streamed: rose, gold, rich purple" (C 1: 185; S 121). The visionary radiance guides her and her mare to safety. California now senses that she possesses a supernatural awareness, which she connects to her cathected feelings toward her husband's red-roan stallion. When she tells Christine the story of her miraculous prayer to Jesus, she makes a Freudian slip, explaining that God was Jesus's father and Mary "the stallion's wife—what did I say—God's wife" (C 1: 187; S 123). If the stallion is God, he is also a phallus, as Johnny implies through double entendre:

"I show her how the red fellow act, the big fellow" (C 1: 88; S 124). The sensually and emotionally frustrated California slips from the house one April night, rides the stallion to a bare hill, and has a mystical sexual experience with the horse: "A woman covered by a huge beast in whose mane the stars were netted, sun and moon were his eyeballs, / Smiled under the unendurable violation" (C 1: 194; S 130). If we sense that no good can come of this, we are right. The next evening, when a drunken Johnny becomes sexually insistent, California runs to the corral, followed by her husband and daughter. Although handed a rifle by Christine, she does not use it as the stallion tramples Johnny to death, tearing at his body parts with his teeth. Only afterward does she shoot the stallion and then display for her little daughter "the mask of a woman / Who has killed God" (C 1: 198; S 134).

This enigmatic parable may equate the killing of the stallion with the crucifixion of Christ, or it may contrast those two deaths. California may have been driven mad by her mixed bloodline, her visionary capacity, or her abusive husband. Christine may have facilitated the catastrophe by bringing her mother the rifle, or she may be the story's central victim, a gentle being who must forever bear the burden of what she has witnessed. The ending, saturated in motifs from the New Testament and Greek tragedy, evokes pity, fear, and a sense of mystery more ancient than modern. Johnny, out of touch with his deeper self and the grandeur of the natural world, has unknowingly precipitated his own death, his wife's madness, and his daughter's suffering. Although Jeffers is the most patriarchal of writers, his best poems critique patriarchy from the inside, as does *Roan Stallion*. California, as transgressed and transgressive as Medea, has crossed boundaries in a way that brings disaster yet inspires awe. The poem attempts to say something profound about flawed human wishes that can bring down a social order while simultaneously giving it meaning: "Wild loves that leap over the walls of nature . . . / These break, these pierce, these deify" (C 1: 189; S 125).

Roan Stallion is spare and powerful, but I find some of the longer, more digressive narratives equally absorbing. These poems read as though they were written by Faulkner on Viagra, Robert Frost on acid, Eugene O'Neill on speed. The pity or fear that you feel as you read them is tinged with camp. *Tamar*, for example, is a great train wreck of a poem. You cannot take your eyes off of it. Although its Gothic excesses may provoke disbelief, it worms its way into the soul, telling us things about our obsessions that we both want to know and do not want to know. If we laugh, there is nervousness in our laughter. Enjoyable and unsettling, this poem is waiting to be rediscovered by contemporary psychoanalytic and cultural critics.

Inspired by the story of Amnon's rape of his sister Tamar and their brother Absalom's revenge (2 Sam. 13), *Tamar* tells the tale of the Cauldwell family, cooped up in a dilapidated mansion on the Carmel shore, coming undone under the pressure of inner demons and "unescapable fate" (C 1: 33; S 41). The patriarch, David, once had an incestuous affair with his sister Helen, and now his son Lee and daughter Tamar wish to have such an affair themselves. Unlike Faulkner's Caddy and Quentin, they act on their desire; unlike their biblical precursors, they both do so willingly. Their lovemaking has the glamour that sex between Johnny and California notably lacked. When Lee resists joining a naked Tamar in a woodland pond, she slips her face into the water as if to drown. Her

> auburn hair trailed forward
> Darkened like weeds, the double arc of the shoulders
> Floated, and when he had dragged her to the bank
>   both arms
> Clung to him, the white body in a sobbing spasm
> Clutched him, he could not disentangle the white desire,
> So they were joined (like drowning folk brought back
> By force to bitter life) painfully, without joy.
>   (C 1: 26; S 34)

When Tamar subsequently makes love to a suitor named Will, she finds that her desire pales in comparison to her passion for Lee. Soon the old mansion is awash in incest: Tamar and Lee, Tamar and her father, her father and the ghost of Helen. It is also awash in retribution. After various confrontations, Lee kills Will, and Tamar kills Lee, her father, her aunt, and herself. One has to wonder what is meant by all this "doubling and incest, repetition and revenge," as John T. Irwin calls it (17–20).[1] Do these activities point to the narcissism of the family's interior life? Do they imply homosexual desire? (Lee and Tamar seem androgynous, down to their names.) Do the incestuous and violent wishes reflect Jeffers's agon with the poetic discourses he loves best—those of Greek tragedy and the romantic and Victorian lyric? Do they evoke his sense of the uncanny way in which his texts mirror his inner life? Or do his characters' botched desires symbolize a larger human egotism that must be abolished if nature is to resume its rightful reign?

Writing before Faulkner and Allen Tate, Jeffers seems to forecast their imagery and themes, though in a mood of high melodrama and without the burden of Southern history behind him. Tamar seduces and rejects her father, first by positioning "her own bright throat and shoulder" in a mirror and then by showing her father his own image in it instead, his "hairy and horrible lips" and his "drizzling," hungry eyes (C 1: 64; S 72). After a succession of such over-the-top scenes, an idiot aunt starts a fire that burns down the house, an event that looks backward to *Jane Eyre* and forward to *Absalom, Absalom!* A now-dominant Tamar prevents anyone from leaving the house, proclaiming, "None of them will go out, / How can I help being happy?" (C 1: 89; S 97). Neither rounded nor complex, Jeffers's characters are driven by obsessive desire down a forkless path to destruction. Contemplating her family and their "withered house," Tamar exclaims, "No wonder if we go mad" (C 1: 24; S 32). This poem, both fascinating and risible, is Jeffers's greatest thrill ride.

The lyric poems, in contrast, are somber and subdued. Instead of exposing dramas of ingrown desire, they meditate Tor and distances, rocks and trees, creatures of the air and sea, and men watched warily from afar. Whereas the narratives plunge into locked rooms of desire, the lyrics inhabit an open-air realm of freedom. If the speaker of the long poems seems overwrought and mesmerized, like a medium at a séance, the speaker of the lyrics seems calm, his dour nature brightened by the glorious panoramas before him and by his matching powers of observation and language.

Consider the opening sentence of "Birds":

> The fierce musical cries of a couple of sparrowhawks hunting on the headland,
> Hovering and darting, their heads northwestward,
> Prick like silver arrows shot through a curtain the noise of the ocean
> Trampling its granite; their red backs gleam
> Under my window around the stone corners; nothing gracefuller, nothing
> Nimbler in the wind.
>
> (C 1: 108; S 103)

The kernel of the first segment of this three-part sentence is relatively unremarkable: the bird cries prick the ocean's noise. Perhaps one might note the auditory imagery of "cries" and "noise" and the masculinist aura of the verb that holds it all together, "prick." But the great power and richness of the description inheres not in the kernel but in the subordinate clauses. The sparrow hawks are "hunting on the headland, / Hovering and darting, their heads northwestward." In this set of embedded clauses (two participial phrases followed by an absolute), the syntax forces us to dwell on the movements of the hawks—what they are doing and how they look while doing it—even as we, in our habitual abstraction, may wish to get on with it. This series of particulars is then succeeded by two additional subordinate clauses, placed after the sentence predicate and separated from each other by the sentence object. The cries penetrate the noise "like silver arrows shot through a curtain," while the ocean is "trampling its granite." In these clauses, we move from observation to trope. The simile invites us to see an entirely different, mildly violent scene of arrows and a curtain, and to understand juxtaposed sounds (bird cries and ocean noise) in terms of the visualized movement of one set of objects through another (arrows piercing a curtain). The metaphor tropes the sea as a giant who tramples the granite (a kinesthetic as well as auditory image), even as he remains vulnerable to the smallest of pricks (bird's beaks as well as the cries that emanate from them). The scene is alive with verbal energy, expressed in a lovely series of participles: "hunting," "hovering," "darting," "trampling." At the same time, consonance conveys a sense of harmony underlying all the activity: "musi*c*al *c*ries of a *c*ouple of sparrowhaw*k*s," "sparrow*h*awks *h*unting on the *h*eadland, / *H*overing," and "*d*ar*t*ing, their hea*d*s northwes*t*war*d*." The second, brief sentence segment focuses attention on the bird's gleaming "red" color, now visible because the bird is directly below the speaker rather than high and far away, and in sharp contrast to the stolid gray "stone corners" of the building. The final segment brings a sense of closure by replacing participles with a rhyming pair of comparatives, somehow more eloquent for their hints of awkwardness: "nothing gracefuller, nothing / Nimbler in the wind."

What seems most powerful about this three-part sentence is its syntax: its elegant clauses, its oscillating movement from perception through figuration to moral judgment, and its interior echoes within a varied rhythm rich in trochees and dactyls and spun around the molossus (three stressed syllables) of "red backs gleam." In effect, the sentence moves cinematically from a distance shot (birds more audible than visible) to a closeup (their gleaming red backs)—and then to a fade that recursively recalls both the birds' beautiful flight lines and the sentence's beautiful sounds. The repeated noun "nothing" echoes the earlier participles as well as itself; the comparatives "gracefuller" and "nimbler" rhyme with each other; and "wind" culminates a flow of *w, n,* and *d* combinations ("headland," "northwestward," "window"), while its hard-stressed monosyllable brings closure after the soft-stressed syllables ending the previous sentence segments ("granite," "corners"). This descriptive passage, like so many in Jeffers's lyrics, is a triumph of the eye and the ear.

At times, Jeffers's magical syntax emphasizes a harmony between human beings and nature, as in this famous passage from "Boats in a Fog":

> A sudden fog-drift muffled the ocean,
> A throbbing of engines moved in it,
> At length, a stone's throw out, between the rocks and the vapor,
> One by one moved shadows
> Out of the mystery, shadows, fishing-boats, trailing each other
> Following the cliff for guidance,
> Holding a difficult path between the peril of the sea-fog
> And the foam on the shore granite.
>
> (C 1: 110; S 105)

Yet such a passage, lovely as it is, remains something of an anomaly in Jeffers. Although he wishes to make poetry of motorboats or airplanes, like Thoreau he does not really approve of machines. He eagerly awaits a future time when "the steel" will be "rusted," when the land and sea resume their original forms (C 1: 204; S 138). Jeffers typically evokes the "heart-breaking beauty" of the inhuman world (C 1: 239; S 147). Reading through Jeffers, for example, you feel transformed by his sunsets. First, you may ask yourself, Why don't I live where sunsets are this spectacular? Then, Even if I did, would I see them this intensely? And, finally, What does it matter? I have these to experience. Here is an example: "Figures of fire on the walls of to-night's storm, / Foam of gold in gorges of fire" (C 1: 206; S 139). Here is another: "[T]he fountain / And furnace of incredible light flowing up from the sunk sun" (C 1: 208; S 141). And here is a quieter instance: "Through rifts in the screen of the world pale gold gleams and the evening / Star suddenly glides like a flying torch" (C 2: 4; S 298). It is impossible in a brief compass to communicate the range of moods and visions that the early Jeffers constructs—the sea life, the redwoods, the birds, the storms, the dawns, the rocks—all transformed in his vivid and eloquent language, all pulsing with his love of the nonhuman world and his deep engagement with the one human production he adored, the English language.

When Jeffers looks closely at the human world, though, problems arise. For one thing, his portrayals often encompass a subtle racism. Anglo-Celts are the reasoning mind whereas darker-skinned people are something other—often sympathetic but also subordinate, loony, or a vanished trace. A not-so-subtle sexism also appears. Whatever else they are, Jeffers's women are objects of the male gaze. Their clothes tend to come off, revealing gleaming white flesh. They yearn for men's loins, going mad with desire. Even the most forceful woman needs "a man like a hawk to cover her" (C 3: 464; S 698). In Jeffers's world, it is hard to imagine a woman who is not sexually obsessed with men—or a man who is. At least, this is so on the surface; the deeper layers suggest more complexity.[2] Beyond Jeffers's lapses of social imagination, there is a simmering misanthropy evident in even the earliest of poems. "Shine, Perishing Republic" reminds us that the love of mankind is a "trap" to be avoided (C 1: 15; S 23). The speaker of "People and a Heron" finds a bird "dearer" than "many people" (C 1: 113; S 106). At his best, Jeffers can construct a moving interior dialogue around such feelings. In "Meditation on Saviors," the speaker balances his desire "not to be a fugitive" from people against his conviction that "one must not love" them (C 1: 398; S 174). However, by 1930 the misanthropy had begun to dominate.

In the 1930s and 1940s, Jeffers's poetry becomes didactic. Denouncing human civilization as "a transient sickness," the poet hopes for an apocalyptic event that "gathers multitude like game to be hunted," leaving "the cities gone down, the people fewer and the hawks more numerous" (C 2: 158, 282, 159; S 380, 397, 381). This poetry, at least from my perspective, seems thin, monotonous, and unforgiving. Its speaker seems convinced that he alone knows the difference between "truth" and "lies" (C 3: 3; S 553). Eventually, Jeffers's certitudes congeal into fury at World War II. Although he fantasized Hitler and Roosevelt hanging from the same tree (C 3: 109), the truth is that he had a soft spot in his heart for the German dictator:

> This morning Hitler spoke in Danzig, we heard his voice.
> A man of genius: that is, of amazing
> Ability, courage, devotion, cored on a sick child's soul. . . .
> (C 3: 16; S 562)

Equating Hitler with King Lear, Jeffers consistently portrayed World War II as "needless" (C 3: 365; 113). In "Pearl Harbor," he complains that "the men who conspired and labored / To embroil this republic in the wreck of Europe have got their bargain" (C 3: 115; S 577). In "Historical Choice," he denounces "our public fools and a loved leader's ambition" (C 3: 122; S 580). In "Invasion," he calls the American soldiers "fools and unconscious criminals" (C 3: 131; S 583). Even after the revelation of Nazi death camps, Jeffers held firm, arguing that although America's intervention in World War I had been bad, "it will be clear a few years from now that our intervention in the war of 1939 has been even terribly worse in effect" (C 4: 418). I readily admit that I am not the right audience for this line of argument. If Jeffers had been attended to, the United States would have stayed neutral in the war, Nazi Germany would have won, Germany would have installed an American regime submissive to its policy goals, and we would be living under that regime's inheritors today. Not a lovely prospect. Moreover, Jeffers's staunch antiwar principles faded surprisingly quickly after World War II. Although he had raged against Americans fighting Northern European fascists, he was relatively unruffled by Americans fighting Asian communists. His pacifism, therefore, seems a fraud that he perpetrated on his readers and himself. For two decades he mostly wasted his gift.

By 1950, Jeffers had had the stuffing knocked out of him. His war against antifascism had failed; his beloved wife, Una, had just died of cancer; and he himself was aging, alone, and in precarious health. As sad as the latter developments were, they were all good for his poetry. Abandoning his denunciatory voice, he returned to the lyric of nature. In "The Beauty of Things," he proposed that "natural beauty" is the sole business of poetry (C 3: 369; S 652). Soon he was going even further, arguing in "The Ocean's Tribute" that "we are fools / To turn from the superhuman beauty of the world and dredge our own minds" (C 3: 439; S 694)—this passage almost begs to be read as a regretful commentary on his poems of the preceding decades. He was, in several senses, in search of lost time. He wrote simply about the natural scene, the poetic quest, his failing body, his memories of Una, and his anticipation of death. In "Hand," written at the very end of his life, the speaker pleads, "Poor hand a little longer / Write, and see what comes forth from a dead hand" (C 3: 469; S 701).

Tim Hunt's five-volume edition of Jeffers's *Collected Poetry* allows us unprecedented access to Jeffers's oeuvre as it developed, poem by poem. Hunt aptly describes his edition as "a cottage industry" rather than a corporate endeavor (C 1: xii). Aided by many advisors, he made all the decisions and did most of the work himself. The effort has paid off handsomely. He has produced an edition that will remain definitive for as far as the eye can see. Volumes 1 through 3 contain Jeffers's canonical poems—the ones he published or intended to publish in his lifetime. Hunt made a risky editorial decision in these volumes. He has presented the poems in their order of composition rather than their order of publication or their arrangement in Jeffers's books. Hunt explains that he adopted this procedure to highlight "the actual shape of Jeffers' career" and to "disrupt our tendency to see the poems as emerging from some dramatically coherent, aesthetically autonomous realm" (C 1: ix; C 5: 11). He admits that his approach—like any approach—involves pluses and minuses. I believe that his method has succeeded overall. The poems do take on a fresh appearance in their new order, and readers who wish to study them in their earlier arrangements can do so by consulting the original collections' tables of contents at the end of the edition.

Volume 4 contains a broad selection of Jeffers's introductions and miscellaneous prose, as well as most of his early and unpublished poems and his poetic fragments. These materials shed considerable light on Jeffers's project—and on the poet himself, as an Emersonian "man thinking" and as a vulnerable and flawed person intent on building a poetic career. Volume 5 includes a detailed chronology and commentary. I would have liked the commentary to be even more exhaustive than it is. For example, Hunt prints Jeffers's notes identifying his characters in *Tamar* with their biblical predecessors, but he does not comment on the differences between the two stories. Still, this is a small quibble about a magnificent edition. It totals 3,304 large-format pages, exquisitely designed by Adrian Wilson of San Francisco and Wilsted & Taylor of Oakland, and nurtured to completion by Stanford University Press in an act of public beneficence both rare and welcome. Clearly a labor of love by all involved, this welcome edition brings Jeffers's words alive for a new century.

All research libraries and Jeffers scholars will want to own the *Collected Poetry*. Any lover of poetry would enjoy perusing the *Selected Poetry*, which contains the radiant gist of Jeffers's oeuvre. And aficionados will also want to have *Stones of the Sur* on their coffee tables. By placing the camera just so, Morley Baer (who died in 1995) produced gorgeous photographs that make Big Sur look as untraveled and untrammeled as it was in Jeffers's day. Introduced by an informative essay by James Karman, the photos and the selections from Jeffers's poetry engage in an eloquent dialogue with each other.

Reading Jeffers's early poems as they unfold in the *Collected Poetry*, I was struck by the breathtaking beauty of both the natural world he evoked and the language he used to evoke it. But I was equally overwhelmed by a poignant and anxious sense of change. Most of us now see the environment as fragile and endangered rather than mighty. Jeffers's lonely Carmel landscapes have an altered look today. The area has become a suburban and vacation haven, replete with B & Bs and country clubs, restaurants and craft stores, Shell stations and Safeway markets, Clint Eastwood's tavern and Doris Day's hotel, overpriced houses on every viewpoint and gridlock on every thoroughfare. Toward the end of his life, Jeffers saw what was coming. In "Carmel Point," he exclaimed: "This beautiful place defaced with a crop of suburban houses— / . . . / Now the spoiler has come" (C 3: 399; S 676). But I do not think he could have imagined the extent of the change—the utter annihilation of everything he held dear, except Tor House itself, maintained today as a tourist site. Even Big Sur, now a state park, is a nexus of campsites, lodges, and the bourgeoisie on holiday. If Robinson Jeffers could see what has happened to the spot of earth that he loved so well, he would surely weep bitter tears.

NOTES
1. Irwin suggests that Tamar and Lee's incestuous encounter in a pond like a "dark mirror" has clear narcissistic implications and that their repetition of their father's incest is yet another doubling. From *Tamar*, Irwin concludes, "the line of descent runs directly to Faulkner" (20).
2. Indeed, an early, previously unpublished lyric called "Aesthetics" suggests that homoeroticism was not unknown to Jeffers:

> I have seen a youth's broad shoulder brown with the sun
> Tug on the broad sweep of a bending oar;
> And that was beauty; while his close-curled head
> Drew forward on the strong columnar neck.
> (C 4: 433)

WORKS CITED
Irwin, John T. *Doubling and Incest/Repetition and Revenge: A Speculative Reading of Faulkner.* Expanded Ed. Baltimore: Johns Hopkins UP, 1996.
Perloff, Marjorie. *Twenty-First-Century Modernism: The "New" Poetics.* Oxford, UK: Blackwell, 2002.

Classics of Twentieth-Century American Theater

THOMAS P. ADLER
Purdue University

ALBEE: "WHO'S AFRAID OF VIRGINIA WOOLF?" By Stephen J. Bottoms. Cambridge, UK: Cambridge UP, 2000. xiv + 204 pp. Hardbound, $54.95; paperback, $19.95.

MILLER: "DEATH OF A SALESMAN." By Brenda Murphy. Cambridge, UK: Cambridge UP, 1995. xviii + 246 pp. Hardbound, $49.95; paperback, $16.95.

O'NEILL: "LONG DAY'S JOURNEY INTO NIGHT." By Brenda Murphy. Cambridge, UK: Cambridge UP, 2001. xvi + 250 pp. Hardbound, $59.95; paperback, $21.95.

WILLIAMS: "A STREETCAR NAMED DESIRE." By Philip C. Kolin. Cambridge, UK: Cambridge UP, 2000. xix + 229 pp. Hardbound, $54.95; paperback, $19.95.

Of the first eight titles in Cambridge's Plays in Production series, half are devoted to four indisputable classics of twentieth-century American theater, each written by one of America's major dramatists: Eugene O'Neill, Arthur Miller, Tennessee Williams, and Edward Albee. (For the record, the other four focus on Henrik Ibsen's *A Doll's House*, Molière's *Don Juan*, Oscar Wilde's *Salome*, and Bertolt Brecht's *Mother Courage*—which company, in itself, would seem to validate the claims of serious American drama as both literature and performance text.) Although the scholars who authored the volumes under review have exercised various degrees of latitude, each generally adheres to the format established by Brenda Murphy in the chronologically earliest of these books (*"Death of a Salesman"*) by providing information on the Broadway premiere; on other productions and revivals in English; on major productions in other languages; and on adaptations to other media—followed by such scholarly apparatus as a listing of productions, sometimes a discography and/or videography, and a selected bibliography. Taken together, these volumes implicitly suggest varying answers to the question of how objective a production history should attempt to be, of the desirable balance between historical record and critical interpretation. Linked inextricably to that issue is these authors' understanding of the purpose behind undertaking the writing of a production history, of the ways in which it can be of use to readers. True, passionate playgoers trying to recreate an evening's experience, along with theater researchers and even some cultural historians, may prefer something as close as possible to an unvarnished presentation of facts, but most students, scholar/teachers, and theater practitioners will more likely turn to the record of past performances mainly to help them imaginatively analyze and reinterpret the dramatic text for the present and the future. To read these books in tandem is to see how the apparent limitations and restrictions of production history as a form can be negotiated, so that the genre itself might become more expansive. Yet whether the expansion enriches the genre or not will depend largely upon the expectations of the reader.

In the earliest of these four books, Murphy—one of the preeminent theater historians and scholars of her generation—confirms the position of Miller's *Death of a Salesman* (1949) as a paradigmatic play, both in establishing the ascendancy of the director (in this instance, Elia Kazan) as a major creative partner in American drama and in developing a new stylistic conception of the stage setting for a realistic play. Already in the initial reviews of *Salesman*—which ran for 742 performances, won all the major prizes, remains the only play ever to be chosen as a main selection of the Book-of-the-Month Club, and is always being performed somewhere in the world—the question of whether a drama that works so brilliantly on the stage can be considered literature is raised and answered in the affirmative; within thirty years, the play's status as a classic seemed assured. For her discussion of the genesis of the playscript and its first production, Murphy artfully culls from the primary materials in several archival collections, as well as draws appropriately from Miller's autobiography, *Timebends: A Life* (1987), in order to discuss the collaborative process. She emphasizes the central role of the designer, Jo Mielziner, not only in achieving the distinctive, gauzy look of the play, but also in concretizing for audiences the spatial and temporal structure inherent in Miller's blend of realism and expressionism—a "subjective realism" that had been suggested to him, at least in part, from having seen Williams's *Streetcar*, also designed by Mielziner and directed by Kazan, two years earlier. Whereas Miller's draft sketchily designated only an empty playing space on various levels (presaging what would actually be the look of his *After the Fall* [1964] many years later), it was Mielziner's idea to put the Loman house itself on stage. In the theater, it became an oft-copied conception that pretty much held the stage up until the stripped-down, multileveled platforms of the 1963 production at the Guthrie Theatre in Minneapolis. The description of Mielziner's now-famous design was, in fact, an integral part of the printed version of the play, raising for literary scholars the interesting issue of how something not original with the author becomes accepted as part of the dramatic text, assuming textual authority.

In writing her stage history of *Salesman*, Murphy holds to her stated intent, admirably accomplished here in light of Miller's own agenda as a decidedly social dramatist, "to give as accurate an account as possible, and also to reflect the audience's view of the historical and cultural significance of [each] production and its aesthetic quality" (xvi). She accomplishes this in part by recurrently addressing certain issues: the physicality of Willy, and his Jewishness; the critique of the business ethic, and how this becomes relevant in other countries; and the playwright's own politics, and how that might affect audience reception here and abroad. When Miller began writing his play, he conceived of Willy as a little man; with the casting of Lee J. Cobb in the role, that conception was altered—with some critics coming to associate his imposing physical stature, in and of itself, with their sense of Loman as a tragic figure. When Hume Cronyn and Dustin Hoffman later starred in the part, "the actor's body as a signifier of the character's status" (83) afforded a different reading. Can discovery of one's smallness be considered a tragic recognition, or does that dilute, not only the size of the central character, but also the magnitude of the play itself? Miller himself seems oddly defensive of the universality of the role and overly suspicious of attaching any particular ethnicity to it. Despite a Yiddish production of *Salesman* in 1951, and even though the three actors—Cobb, Thomas Mitchell, and Hoffman—whose performances Miller has preferred above others, were all Jewish, he "has never accepted the idea that Willy is a 'Jewish role'" (94). Moreover, Miller's stated preference for an integrated rather than an all-black production because of a paucity of qualified acting talent, together with his suggestion that a black version at Center Stage in 1972 would allow the black actor "'to demonstrate to all his common humanity and his talent'" (85), seems unaccountably, if unintentionally, patronizing. Nonetheless, Miller's most valuable extratextual comments may well have to do with Willy's overdependency on his wife, Linda, to sustain him in his daydreams and illusions; his veiled resentment of her constant forgiveness of his flaws (which recalls the hatred of that other salesman Hickey for his wife, Evelyn, in O'Neill's *Iceman Cometh* [1946]); and an understanding that the women's enforced protectiveness to the point of complicity adds a "sinister side" and makes them "victims as well" (8).

In its thematic emphases on aggression and competition thwarting filial love, on the individualistic dream of unimpeded success as somehow appearing a birthright and proof of favor, and on the doctrine of getting ahead materially meaning that some will inevitably be left behind, *Salesman* has always seemed a peculiarly American drama, critiquing the ways in which the American Dream has been distorted and even perverted. The play has, however, proved extraordinarily popular worldwide, especially in "countries that do not fetishize business success" (107), as its critique of how the myth of success and the American Dream have been distorted and even perverted became easy fodder for Marxist and antibourgeois directors. Murphy surveys both these distortions and the perversions, as well as the sometimes altered foci of productions in languages other than English: although the Russian and Expressionistic German production still criticized the capitalist system, and the constructivist Italian one indicted consumerism, the abstract French version presented Willy more as a modern, existential Everyman. If the Japanese director found cultural similarities in Willy's madness and "'suicide and saving face'" (125), Miller in his own production in Beijing found common ground in emphasizing failed love between father and sons and its attendant guilt.

Miller's own liberal political stance, which raised questions about his loyalty to America during the cold war, and which led to his eventual summons to appear before the House Un-American Activities Committee and his being found in contempt—though never imprisoned—for refusing to name names, caused repercussions when *Salesman* was performed on stage and adapted to film in the early 1950s. At home the American Legion picketed the play while abroad the Dublin premiere was met with demonstrations against what was seen as the left-leaning agitation and subversiveness of the text. And even though Miller's social critique was somewhat muted in the original, 1951 film version (a movie that Miller claims to have "hated" [135]), Columbia Pictures still thought it advisable to have a short film shot at the Business School of City College in New York featuring interviews with apologist professors who claimed that the experience of Willy Loman was "entirely atypical" and reasserting that "nowadays selling was a fine profession with limitless spiritual compensations as well as financial ones" (137).

Of these four books, Murphy's volume on *Salesman* is certainly the one that will be most useful to high school and college teachers and students, and probably the one that will have the greatest appeal to interested theatergoers. The dozen illustrations, including some indispensable reproductions of Mielziner's drawings, are particularly well chosen; the notes to each chapter reflect meticulous scholarship; the chronology provides a record of fifty-two productions (though the book appeared too early to include Robert Falls's acclaimed 1999 revival starring Brian Dennehy as a clinically depressive Willy, which originated at Chicago's Goodman Theatre before moving on to Broadway); and the bibliographical listing of well over four hundred reviews is sensibly arranged chronologically by production rather than alphabetically by author.

Miller prohibited any production within one hundred miles of Broadway for twenty-five years after *Salesman*'s premiere. If O'Neill's explicit wishes had been adhered to, there would have been no publication of the text of *Long Day's Journey into Night* until twenty-five years after his death in 1953, and no performance ever of a play that has come to be considered "an endpoint in the development of realistic, humanistic, modern tragedy" (94). In her second contribution to the Cambridge series, Murphy retells with clarity and authority the fascinating story of the work's composition and of how O'Neill's widow, Carlotta Monterey O'Neill, circumvented the dramatist's stipulations, opening the way for five productions in 1956—first at the Royal Dramatic Theatre in Stockholm (which posthumously premiered four of the playwright's works); then in three other European cities; and finally in America under José Quintero's direction, produced by the Circle in the Square at the Helen Hayes Theatre on Broadway, where the play went on to run for 390 performances and won for O'Neill his fourth Pulitzer Prize. O'Neill began his deeply autobiographical *Journey* in 1939, though he discounted any connection between what he termed this "quiet" and personally best-liked of all his works and the "crisis-preoccupied time" of its writing. Quintero felt a particular kinship between himself and O'Neill, "almost as if he were an alter ego," sharing "'his anticlericalism; his mystical attitudes toward religion; his Dionysian inclinations' and 'the guilt that all men of the Western world, particularly those raised Catholic, have over the fact that their mothers had to have sex to have them'" (17).

Simply because Murphy tends to be the most objective among the three scholars in her presentation of factual and interpretive material, resisting any urge to insist emphatically upon a particular theoretical perspective, does not mean that either of her volumes lacks a unifying thesis or point of view. If Murphy's focus on the sociocultural milieu helps to shape and integrate her production history of *Salesman*, what provides structure for her examination of *Journey* on stage and screen is her emphasis on how different characters among the four leading ones, because of directorial decisions and the strengths of individual actors, come to dominate different productions. As she astutely argues, *Journey*'s "dynamics of conflict, and thus its thematic import, is by no means fixed. There is truly no protagonist in this play 'of old sorrow,' but four characters interacting in a form that is like a piece of classical music with a number of intricately interwoven motifs. . . . [T]he audience's understanding of the whole is quite different from performance to performance. . . . In the nearly fifty years of the play's stage life, it has become one of the excitements of each new production" (54). In a perhaps somewhat extreme variation on the play's musical architectonics, when Jonathan Miller directed it on Broadway in 1986, he considered the text so much a series of "competing discourses" that he had the characters' speeches overlap.

The roster of actors and actresses associated with the play is full of luminaries: Frederic March and Florence Eldredge; Laurence Olivier and Constance Cummings; Robert Ryan and Geraldine Fitzgerald, who would herself go on to direct a revival with an African American cast; Jason Robards and Colleen Dewhurst; William Hutt and Jessica Tandy; Jack Lemmon and Bethel Leslie; Ralph Richardson and Katharine Hepburn on film; as well as Mildred Dunnock, Zoe Caldwell, Michael Moriarity and Kevin Spacey. If the character of James Tyrone, the father, held center stage in the first New York opening and in the British television adaptation in the early 1970s, the focus in the Stockholm premiere, and later in London, Montreal, and for the New York, Quintero-directed revival in 1971, fell on Mary Tyrone, the mother, while in the 1975 revival, *Journey* seemed to be very much the authorial character Edmund's play—under the direction of Robards, perhaps the actor most associated with O'Neill, who previously had played both the role of the older brother Jamie in 1956 and of James in 1971, and now repeated his performance as James. Fitzgerald's 1981 black version brought to the fore the issue of how central to the work are questions of social class and ethnicity: the Irish-Catholic Tyrones are transient summer residents in New London among a largely WASP population, adding to Mary's sense of being an isolated outsider; and actors beginning with March have had to decide whether adopting an Irish brogue should be integral to James's characterization. Several actors, Fitzgerald and Hutt among them, have stressed what is surely one of the play's dominant thematic motifs, vocation, or the loss of vocation, in their interpretations. And two of the non–English language productions from the late 1980s, Ingmar Bergman's in Sweden and Sergei Yashin's in Russia, foregrounded "the modernist theme of the redemptive transformation of life by art" (103)—the former by adding pantomime scenes as a frame and by having Edmund, in somewhat Proustian fashion, begin writing the play the audience has just watched in a notebook at the end, and the latter by opening the curtain on Edmund writing the play that the audience is about to see.

Each of these directors also gave Edmund a stage property not designated by O'Neill: for Bergman, it was the black notebook; for Yashin, a teddy bear. Murphy is particularly adroit in singling out from the archival records elements of the visual codes (and not just the most obvious symbolism of the fog) that various directors and designers over the years have emphasized (or, in a few cases, interpolated) and that can help make scholar/teachers, students, and stage practitioners more attuned to the semiotics of theater and film. As he did for several of his plays, O'Neill drew sketches for the set of *Journey*, although David Hays generally ignored these drawings, as well as the actual relatively small, dark-paneled room in Monte Cristo Cottage, New London, Connecticut, when designing the first American production. If he had based his stage setting on the O'Neill's summer home—as the designer in London did—the effect would have been much more claustrophobic, emphasizing Mary's distress over being under the men's surveillance, and her "performing" for the others. For this is, as Quintero intuited, "a play about eyes" (41), of one character's constantly watching the other(s). Murphy's descriptions of Sidney Lumet's masterful 1962 film version, as well as of the 1973 British television adaptation in which the action is sometimes shot through windows, make clear how the aura of the panopticon is broadened to include the audience among the spies. And once again, as in her *Salesman* volume, Murphy's scholarly apparatus is user-friendly, providing details of over ninety major productions of *Journey* and listing nearly five hundred reviews.

As "another proof of the play's classic status," Murphy mentions briefly its deconstruction by the Wooster Group, who used O'Neill's *Journey* as the basis for part 2 of *Point Judith*, "an exploration of contemporary notions of masculinity" (74), complete with actor Willem Dafoe in drag as Mary Tyrone. In contrast, in his production history of Williams's *A Streetcar Named Desire*, Philip C. Kolin provides a full discussion (six pages in length) of a similar deconstruction from a gay perspective of Williams's classic play, the 1991 queer/camp *Belle Reprieve*, developed by members of London's Split Britches and Bloolips theater troupes. Kolin describes the evening as "a melange of cross-dressing, tap dancing, risque songs, farce, bathhouse humor, gay cabaret scenes, vaudeville, and British music hall skits" (143), resulting in "a distinct script under and through which lie many of *Streetcar*'s symbols, sets, and characters, transgressively rendered" (144–45) that made baldly explicit certain notions of gender identity that were only "latent and opaque" in the original. If *Belle Reprieve* had a salutary, if unintentional, effect, it was perhaps to demonstrate just how misguided any production of Williams's text that presented Blanche as a man in drag would be. Yet if it seems a questionable strategy on Kolin's part to elevate its status by giving it equal consideration along with other versions of the play, this reflects Kolin's own intention to situate *Streetcar* on stage, not only from a theatrical, but also from a literary theoretical point of view, bringing in Karl Marx and Michel Foucault, race and ethnicity, performativity and androgyny, and the female gaze. And Kolin, one of the most prolific writers on the work—the selected bibliography appended here lists a dozen of his own publications—and the editor of a substantial collection of scholarly approaches to the play subtitled "Essays in Cultural Pluralism," is superbly equipped to do this. In looking at the way *Streetcar*'s "sexual politics" have been "interrogated" and "destabilized," "radicalized" and "renegotiated" in over half a century of productions in various media (theater, film, ballet, television, opera), Kolin shares with Murphy the unerring ability to select just the right words from reviews to help readers "see" what was occurring on stage and screen—though here, too, the book's publication date precluded any mention of an important production (director Ivo van Hove's 1999 revisioning of the play when he stripped bare stage and actors alike and made a bathtub the focal point).

Beginning with the first, landmark production in 1947, designed by Jo Mielziner, which ran for 855 performances and staged interiority through a blend of realism and expressionism that, as was noted, would influence Miller's style in *Salesman* two years later, a central issue has always been achieving a proper balance between two such protean characters as Blanche (played over the years by Jessica Tandy, Uta Hagen, Vivien Leigh, Arletty, Tallulah Bankhead, Faye Dunaway, Claire Bloom, Blythe Danner, Jessica Lange, and Frances McDormand) and Stanley (played by Marlon Brando, Anthony Quinn, Jon Voight, Treat Williams, and Alec Baldwin, among others). In directing the premiere, Elia Kazan tipped the balance—unjustifiably, it could be argued—in favor of the proletarian Stanley in a swaggering and brutish if sensitive and even humorous performance by Brando that became iconic. A few years later, in a film version sanitized to remove any mention of homosexuality, yet still adult enough to be seen as helping to inaugurate an American art cinema (but that viewed today tends in places to border on camp), the T-shirted "male anatomy [is made] the object of desire" (156–57). Blanche's character has been even more ambiguous, making that role something of an American Hamlet, from the refined tragic victim of the double standard, the vulnerable, shimmering moth, performing and theatricalizing the self, to the hysteric, neurotic sexual predator, the sensualist who somehow achieves sanctification in madness.

If some of the American productions, particularly those with black or interracial casts, or those that foreground urban violence, have emphasized or even added a decidedly sociological dimension, it is in reporting on the international productions, which "incorporat[ed] their own cultural symbols, values, anxieties, and idioms" (41), that Kolin can discover instances of considerably more politicized *Streetcars* than the original one. In Rome, the 1949 staging by Luchino Visconti—which Williams preferred over all other European versions—emphasized America, and a morally decadent New Orleans, as the site of class struggle, with the worker Stanley, representative of primitivism, pitted against the elitist Blanche, who becomes the tragic victim enslaved by carnality. In Paris in 1949, Jean Cocteau scandalized some viewers by adding a "black presence" in the form of half-naked belly dancers to create an atmosphere of racial fear, equating Stanley's sexuality with that of the blacks. And in post-Occupation Japan in 1953, Blanche was simultaneously the intruder on the territory of others and the one violated, just as Japan had been violated by the imperialist Americans. Kolin cites reviews of these productions, as well as hundreds of critical notices of other stagings of *Streetcar*, in his endnotes, rather than in his bibliography, which he devotes to major scholarship by academics; he includes as well a production chronology of over forty stagings during the first half-century of the play's history.

As if to announce his intention of exploring the way in which production history might aid in theorizing about a dramatic text, Kolin devotes much of his preface to summarizing how awareness of issues of race, gender, and ethnicity encoded within the play have come to alter the ideological assumptions associated with more traditional readings of *Streetcar*. Stephen J. Bottoms, who rejects the idea that any production history can ever really be "neutral" or "impartial," veers even more radically from the series format that Murphy established in order to argue for Albee's *Who's Afraid of Virginia Woolf?* as a proto-postmodernist text, with all that implies about a contingent world in which truth and falsity are indeterminate. That he is consciously attempting to engage readers at a higher level of sophistication is supported by his announcement that many of his ideas were tried out with students in their final year of theater studies at the University of Glasgow. Arguing not only that *Virginia Woolf* became a cultural product because of viewer/reader response, but also that its popularity with audiences at the box office actually forced a re-evaluation by reviewers and critics, Bottoms posits that Albee's play is about performativity itself, about the need to (re)invent constantly what is essentially a fictional self where no true self exists and where manufacturing illusions creates the only reality. From a Derridian perspective, to shift one's focus to the ability or "force" of an utterance to initiate change "is to 'free the analysis of the performative from the value of truth, from the opposition of true/false'" (6). What is at issue, then, "is the *effect* of the characters' speech acts on each other" (182). The production that Bottoms singles out as best encapsulating this reading is the London production directed by Howard

Davies at the Almeida Theatre in 1996, which captured both the work's sociopolitical critique of America's flawed system of values and its emphasis on asserting power through manipulative language, as well as its "self-conscious theatricality" in presenting Nick and Honey "as the 'audience' for whose attention George and Martha compete in their verbal battle for domination" (75–76). Albee himself would apparently concur, acclaiming it as "among the very finest of the hundred or so productions" (76) he had experienced.

While admitting the historical significance of the play's 1962 Broadway premiere (which eventually ran for six hundred performances) for introducing "off-Broadway production principles into the Broadway arena" and inaugurating the concept of "preview performances" in place of an out-of-town tryout, Bottoms believes that it, like other early versions, seriously skewed and misrepresented the text by interpreting Martha as one who had deluded herself into believing in the literal existence of the imaginary child. The central point is not—and here Bottoms is right on target—the exorcism of an illusion of such long standing that it is mistaken for reality, but rather (in the playwright's own words) "the death of [a] metaphor that the couple was 'able to levitate [for] 21 years'" (67) and the subsequent imperative to rebuild "the very narrative structure on which [the] marriage . . . has been built" (183). If the play was subject to censorship of various sorts (the opening line in Boston was altered to "Mary H. Magdalene"; the Pulitzer Prize board denied it the prize the jurors had voted for; and Lord Olivier forbade Lady [Joan Plowright] Olivier from performing the role of Martha), Mike Nichols's hugely successful 1966 film version had, like the movie of *Streetcar*, something of a liberating effect in making American cinema more adult; and, in this case, it even helped bring about the demise of the stringent production code.

In attempting to establish the work's originality, however, Bottoms—perhaps in reaction against the analogy several critics drew between it and *Long Day's Journey*—seems to think it necessary to paint it as considerably more "unorthodox" than it really was. *Virginia Woolf*, of course, was never intended as the conventionally naturalistic play that some of its early critics made it out to be when they assailed the notion of the imaginary child; and Bottoms correctly valorizes Michael Smith's early review in the *Village Voice*, which presents the work's musical "structure [as] something like variations on a theme" (87). Yet to overestimate Albee's experimentalism in his first full-length drama, and to credit him with introducing the "new avant garde" to Broadway, is to ignore, among other things, the theatricalism of Thornton Wilder and the expressionism of Williams that had come before. Whether Albee here totally eschews "the liberal message-play model" (92) that many critics still insist on attributing to him remains open to debate; in any case, however, to imply that one somehow lessens Albee's masterwork as art by granting that it has "a 'proper' plot with an emotionally 'satisfying' resolution" (90)—as it most assuredly does—is to go overboard in an attempt to establish the play's claim to originality. This is not to discount the work's mystery and ambiguity but to reaffirm Albee's consummate abilities to make the dramatic form flexible and distinctively his. What Bottoms adamantly does reject is those critics who think that the only means of affirming Albee's "gay sensibility" is to refashion his two straight couples as homosexual, stating that Albee, "like Tennessee Williams, queers the heterosexist construction of conventional drama by presenting an Adonis-like male figure (Nick) . . . as the object of the play's erotic gaze" (108).

Although Bottoms does, like Murphy and Kolin, rehearse the essentials of all the major productions, unlike them he returns in the closing thirty or so pages of his volume to reconsider, character by character, all of the major performances in various media. This strategy brings the nuances of different handlings of the same role into sharp relief, providing the substantial bases for character analyses by students and teachers, as well as provocative (re)interpretations by actors and directors readying the play for the stage. If, in the hands of Arthur Hill, George came across as somewhat vicious and not "especially intelligent," he was less abrasive and "urbane, witty" as played by Ben Gazzara. Richard Burton's George exhibited "charm . . . alongside a controlled intensity which suggests all sorts of repressed inner demons" (159) while Paul Eddington limned a George fully aware that he never possessed "the inner emotional resources ever to have made more of himself" (160). Whereas Ray McAnally made George "drily hilarious" (162), David Suchet played him as vulnerable and inadequately masculine. Of all the actresses who have performed Martha (Uta Hagen, Kate Reid, Elizabeth Taylor, Colleen Dewhurst, Glenda Jackson, and Diana Rigg among them), both Bottoms and Albee himself seem to favor and consider definitive Elaine Stritch's dryly understated and subtle reading, first on stage in 1963 and then on radio in 1974. Hunting down comparative reviews of these performances is not as easy using Bottoms as it would be with Murphy or Kolin, however, since his bibliography lumps together all his references in alphabetical order—though he also provides production details in a chronological listing of forty stagings.

Bottoms, who for this type of scholarly publication probably makes too much of the fact that Stritch is herself a reformed alcoholic, closes his book rather peculiarly—given that he apparently wants to abjure the message play for something much more open and postmodern—by quoting her as saying: "I told Albee what I think George and Martha do when the play is over. I think they say, the next day: 'We won't have a drink until six in the evening.' That's a start" (186). But then, all of these volumes end rather abruptly (Murphy's on *Salesman* and *Journey*, with considerations, however thorough, of, respectively, the Hoffman and Hutt film versions; Kolin's on *Streetcar* with a discussion of Previn's opera), perhaps because of restrictions imposed by the series format that precludes much in the way of a considered conclusion. In each case, however, one yearns for a sharper concluding section that would situate production history as a hermeneutic for opening up these classic texts in new ways and that would reveal more of the stunning intellect-at-play of these three major scholars of American drama as literature and theater.

Book Reviews

THE HISTORY OF NORTH AMERICAN THEATER. THE UNITED STATES, CANADA, AND MEXICO: FROM PRE-COLUMBIAN TIMES TO THE PRESENT. By Felicia Hardison Londré and Daniel J. Watermeier. New York: Continuum, 2000. 541 pp. $39.95.

This amply illustrated, admirably inclusive history of ritual, theater, drama, and performance in general would be a valuable addition to the library of virtually anyone interested in the cultural history of North America. While formally concentrating on theater in a traditional sense, the volume generally identifies theater in a more liberal way to include rituals predating European discovery/influence, entertainments of every public sort throughout colonial times and up to the late twentieth century, plays and productions imported from Europe for North American consumption, and works and productions original to North American soil. Throughout all of the discussions, solid links are made to the related histories and cultures. The result is a book that tells a story of the public development of three separate but contiguous worlds (the Caribbean is also nominally included as a fourth) on stages variously religious, political, and aesthetic, high and low, legitimate and otherwise. And through the accident of contiguity, we also see cross-cultural influences even as efforts frequently persist to maintain some semblance of cultural purity.

Felicia Hardison Londré and Daniel J. Watermeier write with one voice in such a seamless and engaging fashion that reading this rather lengthy text in its entirety is a pleasurable experience. In order to concentrate the histories of three unique, dynamic worlds into one volume, the authors must have found their choices of inclusivity difficult. However, their decisions have resulted in an inclusive overview filled with a surprising amount of informative detail sufficient to make the text far more valuable than, say, a mere almanac of events. It can serve handily as a reference tool as well because, while this history is designed to be read from cover to cover, its two thorough indexes (Subject and Name) help provide quick access to points of relevance and facts of interest.

The book is divided into seven major chapters: "Pre-Columbian Performance"; "Theater in New Spain, the American Colonies, and New France"; "National Stages"; "Romantic Enactments, 1825–1870"; "Tradition and Transformation, 1870–1900"; "Entertainment and Art, 1900–1945"; and "Renewal and Experimentation, 1945 to the present." Each chapter is subdivided under the headings "The United States," "Mexico," and "Canada," with "The Caribbean" included when appropriate. Moving among native, Spanish, British, and French cultural influences; tapping into anthropology, history, cultural studies, theater, drama, and performance; and spanning up to one thousand years of human events (the four hundred years from the colonial to modern times being the most concentrated) are daunting tasks, to be sure. And though some sections of the volume are decidedly slim, each provides insights into periods separately familiar to many but collectively known to few. Bringing all of this together in one volume with one voice results in a work that digests the specialties of countless scholars and brings a sense of organic coherence not found elsewhere in a single volume.

The United States, of course, is the gravitational center of this world. Canada's history is one that concentrates on avoiding assimilation into the American sphere of influence, initially by a resistant French culture and later by a more general Canadian one. In Canada, there is also a more prolonged period of anti-theatrical sentiment, enforced by a well-entrenched Catholic Church, that results in a longer tradition of amateurism well outlined by this volume. The government itself does eventually become involved in a national theater movement, however, by encouraging a professional and nationalistic theater that breaks the grip of the Catholic Church's resistance and encourages both French- and English-speaking theaters to work together where they once operated separately. The United States sections present a history of theatrical resistance followed by widespread outbreaks of theatrical interest, becoming centralized in New York City and eventually working toward decentralization thanks to the regional theater movement beyond Broadway. From a Eurocentrically influenced theatrical regimen to a grassroots theater, the United States stage is clearly the most varied and dynamic on the continent. That is not to say, however, that it is always the most interesting. The theater of Mexico, drawing on pre-Columbian roots, created a dynamic native theatrical tradition still alive today. And its long tradition of popular entertainments vying with European imports has produced an activist theater only rarely seen in United States venues.

At first glance, the decision to divide all chapters into United States, Mexican, and Canadian sections seems rather arbitrarily to argue for discrete avenues of national development. However, the decision seems ultimately to be entirely appropriate, given the conscious tendency by Canada and Mexico to want to develop discretely. Furthermore, unique cultural and political influences led to unique evolutionary stages. Political turmoil and state and church influences restricted Mexican development; Catholic Church influences in Canada did the same. Despite these singularities, though, Canada was ultimately drawn into the United States sphere of influence, primarily the result of its population centers being so near the United States's northeastern population centers. In the final analysis, however, it appears that Canada has successfully maintained its unique identity. Mexico was less exposed to threats of absorption primarily because of its geographical distance from those same United States population centers, but also because of the inevitability of the language barrier. Furthermore, the quality of theater outside the United States was such that American efforts to co-opt its neighbors' theatrical products were minimized, and, because of the relatively underdeveloped theatrical infrastructures of Canada and Mexico, little exporting of American products occurred. The sense of separate national developments inherent in the text's structure is therefore a mere reflection of historical fact and not an arbitrary textual effect.

Points of convergence do occur within these historical chapters. Romanticism swept through all three nations, creating points of similarity, though in each case these broad movements took on nationally unique identities. In all three cases, the histories of women and generally underrepresented minorities are amply discussed in the volume, though, again, recognition, inclusion, and opportunity occurred at slightly different times and in slightly different ways. Attention is paid in particular to native, African American, Francophone, frontier, peasant, working class, feminist, ethnic, gay/lesbian, experimental, and many other traditions that grew and developed alongside and became parts of more mainstream stages.

While the inclusion and exclusion from the text inevitably involve editorial decisions that may ultimately reflect subjective tastes and preferences, it is difficult to see any overt bias in this work, except possibly for the laudable special attention given to theaters of underrepresented voices. Editorial comment is indeed rare, objective presentation being the goal. Londré and Watermeier do not shy away from making educated guesses: "The island of Santo Domingo (Hispaniola) can probably be signaled as having the earliest European play performed in North America" (63). Critiques by way of summarizing historical assessments are included: "Personality actresses, as they were called, were frequently accused of playing themselves no matter the role" (204); and when describing postmodern stage director Peter Sellars: "While Sellars has been criticized for self-indulgence, aesthetic foolishness, his interpretations are invariably inventive and thought-provoking" (435). Occasionally, a well-placed lament does surface: "As the 1990s wane, however, the future of the American musical, one of the cornerstones of modern Broadway theater, looks bleak" (431). Or, "[Tennessee] Williams continued to write but his later plays—over twenty in total—have not yet been granted the recognition due to them" (404). The overall result is a fact-packed volume humanized by intelligent assessment and appropriately positioned, occasional commentary.

In sum, Londré and Watermeier have produced an impressive work, having digested a massive amount of theater/performance information. They have incorporated that information into social, historical, and aesthetic contexts, providing an entirely readable, encyclopedic work that its readers and possessors will find invaluable for reference, general background, and contextualization into the worlds beyond the theater, influencing and influenced by them as theater inevitably is.

William W. Demastes
Louisiana State University

NOTHING ABSTRACT: INVESTIGATIONS IN THE AMERICAN LITERARY IMAGINATION. By Tom Quirk. Columbia: U of Missouri P, 2001. viii + 234 pp. $39.95.

These essays, written over the course of two decades, offer a rationale and a defense of what the author calls the "genetic method" of literary inquiry. Rather than the self-conscious methodologies of contemporary theory, Tom Quirk offers spirited support for the values and practical benefits of source and influence study, evidenced-based research that draws upon the biographical backgrounds of authors, their position in cultural and literary history, and their textual practices. As befits a volume titled *Nothing Abstract*, Quirk does not engage in a point-by-point refutation of theoretical principles and assumptions. Rather, he asserts that source and influence study, supplanted in some circles by attention to intertextuality, is not as narrow, reductive, and positivistic as some theorists have claimed. The tone in this highly readable and engaging volume is neither polemical nor confrontational. Quirk prefers to make his case by recourse to demonstration and by a range of relevant and colorful instances from a remarkably diverse group of nineteenth- and twentieth-century authors. Among the writers discussed in detail are Nathaniel Hawthorne, Edgar Allan Poe, Herman Melville, Mark Twain, Ambrose Bierce, Willa Cather, F. Scott Fitzgerald, Wallace Stevens, Joyce Carol Oates, and Tony Hillerman. Additionally, authors who receive more than brief mention are Jack London, Stephen Crane, Flannery O'Connor, Henry James, Robert Frost, Richard Wright, and William Faulkner.

The essays that introduce the volume are the most recently composed, and as Quirk notes, "provide a lens through which to view the subsequent essays" (3). In "Sources, Influences, and Intertexts," he produces a fairly comprehensive bibliography of intertextuality (from which one notes with some bemusement that his work is omitted) before proceeding to a series of carefully chosen examples. His aim is to show that one can indeed study "focal texts in relation to other texts" (19) without lapsing into interpretive confusion or drift. A source and an influence do not form a relationship of sameness or recurrence, but the former may complement, mediate, or supplement the text that is affected. In "Authors, Intentions, and Texts," Quirk likewise resists the tendency of some theorists and cultural critics to simplify or even to caricature the notion of authorial intention. Once again marshaling a series of apt examples, Quirk shows that what lies behind most discussions of authorial intention is an implicit debate about a literary work's coherence or comprehensibility. Both essays show that issues of influence and intention are varied, complicated, and even vexing. The two introductory position statements, one of which is here revised from its first appearance in *Resources for American Literary Study* in 1995, offer a foreground and rationale for the subsequent pieces that focus more sharply on individual authors and the genesis of specific works.

Of the subsequent essays, three touch on writers of the American Renaissance. In "What if Poe's Humorous Tales Were Funny?" Quirk juxtaposes Poe's "X-ing a Paragrab" and Twain's "Journalism in Tennessee," comic treatments of competing newspaper editors. He concludes that frontier humor did not appeal to Poe's sensibility and that his antisocial stance precluded the vulnerability and exposure experienced by Twain's comic personae. In "Hawthorne's Last Tales and 'The Custom-House,'" Quirk examines "Main-Street," "Feathertop," "The Snow-Image," and "The Great Stone Face." These four tales, all written after *Mosses from an Old Manse*, address problems of artistic creation and thus look forward to the concerns of Hawthorne's "Custom-House" sketch. The topic of "The Judge Dragged to the Bar" is Melville's knowledge of Judge Lemuel Shaw's (his father-in-law's) presiding role in the sensational trial following the November 1849 murder of Dr. George Parkman by Professor John White Webster. Melville, Quirk convincingly demonstrates, drew upon aspects of the famous "Murder at Harvard" and its attendant legal proceedings for passages in *Moby-Dick*. Quirk is even more persuasive when he claims that issues raised by the case—innocence vs. guilt, malice of intent, the fate of murderers, human vs. divine judgment—occupied Melville throughout the later stages of his career.

Quirk reprints two essays that actually had their origin as introductions to Penguin paperbacks designed for classroom use. As an instructor who has used Quirk's paperback edition of Twain's short works in my classes, I can vouch for the value of his insightful essay "Mark Twain in His Short Works," as well as for the aptness of the selections discussed. Quirk devotes significant attention to early journalistic experiments, such as "Letter from Carson City" (1863), which anticipate techniques in later works by Twain. The overview of Twain's career runs the gamut of the generic categories within which he practiced and performed: tale, essay, speech, and sketch. Quirk's essay on *Tales of Soldiers and Civilians and Other Stories* is likewise sensitive to the variety of output in Bierce's career and the resistance of the author's works to pat categories. Bierce's experiments with different tonalities and points of view, moreover, receive intelligent discussion.

A common thread among the remaining essays in *Nothing Abstract* is the continuity from the realistic tradition to literary modernism. In the first of two essays on Cather, Quirk draws upon her 1925 preface to Sarah Orne Jewett's *The Country of the Pointed Firs*, in which Hawthorne and Twain are cited as significant literary models. Quirk is led to a detailed examination of the southwestern landscape of *Death Comes for the Archbishop*, or more properly, what he calls the novel's "moral geography." The dilemma for Cather's central character Father Latour is the human "capacity to confront change with serenity" (174). In "Fitzgerald and Cather: *The Great Gatsby*," Quirk builds on the work of previous critics who have detected formal and stylistic influence. By detecting provincial and romantic tendencies in Jay Gatsby and the central character of Cather's *Alexander's Bridge*, Quirk finds thematic affinity between the two authors. The last section of this essay is devoted primarily to Fitzgerald, but the theme of the divided self (what Quirk calls "doubleness of personality") may be central to Cather's fiction. Perhaps the most surprising and original essay in this section of *Nothing Abstract*, because it applies a knowledge of realism to a modern poet difficult to pigeonhole, is subtitled "Some Reflections on American Realism and the Poetry of Wallace Stevens." Employing a subtle and supple understanding of American Realism, Quirk establishes a bridge between the Jameses, both William and Henry, and Stevens, a self-described "poet of reality."

Two short essays on contemporary fiction round off the essays on individual authors. Quirk uncovers a real-life criminal as a source for Arnold Friend in Oates's "Where Are You Going, Where Have You Been?" His murderous exploits publicized in *Time*, *Life*, and *Newsweek* in 1965 and 1966, the so-called "Pied Piper of Tucson" emerges in Oates's imaginative characterization as a figure that undermines elements of the American Dream. In "Justice on the Reservation," Quirk returns to a discussion of legal issues, in this case, the way in which complex matters of jurisdiction inform the crime fiction of the popular author Tony Hillerman. The collision between the primitive, traditional claims of Native Americans and the demands of an intrusive modern legal bureaucracy are profitably explored in Hillerman's *The Dance Hall of the Dead* (1975).

If these essays offer convincing evidence that source study and textual history are as important for an understanding of a literary work as its social, political, and linguistic background, Quirk turns to the practical consequences of the genetic method for teachers in his final postscript. He reminds us that widely used anthologies have the potential for introducing students to the genetic method. The editors of *The Norton Anthology of American Literature* juxtapose the 1855 and 1881 editions of Walt Whitman's *Leaves of Grass* for purposes of comparison and contrast, or they present Henry David Thoreau's journal entries that were eventually transformed into the more polished prose of *Walden*. In this final essay Quirk is at his most provocative by reminding scholar-teachers that they ignore the mountains of accumulated textual evidence in scholarly editions at their own peril, that attention to textual changes and compositional history can assist instructors in problem solving and in reducing questionable interpretations.

Quirk makes his strongest case for his preferred methods when citing provocative or pertinent examples from his wide reading or when wittily recounting anecdotes from his own scholarly investigations. He is less persuasive when his tone becomes defensive or beleaguered. Perhaps the least effective essay is the one on Poe: the claim that raw frontier humor did not appeal to Poe may overlook that author's appreciative review of Augustus Baldwin Longstreet's *Georgia Scenes*. Quirk might have acknowledged that the editorial drudgery outlined in "X-ing a Paragrab" may reflect Poe's self-described status as a "poor devil author," living a hand-to-mouth existence by working in the antebellum magazine trade. The essays on Twain, however, reflect the work of an experienced scholar-critic in full command of his subject, and the work here on Fitzgerald and Cather offers compelling evidence of the value of genetic inquiry. Although more examples might have been drawn from the scholarly editions of the authors studied, Quirk's postscript should motivate graduate students and practicing scholars to a greater understanding of the vocabulary and concepts that lie behind the creation, revision, and transmission of some of our most celebrated texts. This volume merits wide attention, not only for its cogent defense of genetic inquiry, but also for its thoughtful application of that methodology to the study of individual authors.

Kent P. Ljungquist
Worcester Polytechnic Institute

FINDING COLONIAL AMERICAS: ESSAYS HONORING J. A. LEO LEMAY. Edited by Carla Mulford and David S. Shields. Newark: U of Delaware P; London: Associated UP, 2001. 481 pp. $59.50.

"Finding colonial Americas" aptly describes the career of honored literary scholar J. A. Leo Lemay, and it also marks a broader impetus in early American studies toward scholarship more richly reflective of the fascinating multiplicity, hybrid originality, regional spontaneity, and generic variety of North American colonial cultures. The potential of this belletristic and humanistic approach is demonstrated in twenty-six essays contributed to this *festschrift* by former teachers and students and current colleagues and admirers of Lemay in the fields of English and American literature, history, art history, and material culture. According to volume editors Carla Mulford and David S. Shields, the project of "finding colonial Americas," which is exemplified by Lemay, means unsettling the Puritan New England narrative of American origins and establishing "the importance of alternative views of early American literary history in delineating the different versions of 'America'" (17). This volume is a fitting tribute to that project and to a scholar deeply influential in its success.

The essays that comprise the first section of *Finding Colonial Americas*, "Comparative Colonialisms," shift geographical perspectives in order to decenter New England as a site of early American study. Ralph Bauer demonstrates the clarifying value of a comparative view of colonial Americas with his analysis of how contrasting missionary rhetorics and "comparative ethnologies" enable the imperial writers of Puritan New England and Franciscan New Spain to frame their imperial projects as competing for the souls of native peoples. Similarly, in his essay "Communion in Captivity," Gordon Sayre compares representations of torture as sites of potential symbolic exchange and imperial self-definition in Puritan New English and Jesuit French Indian captivity narratives. While native peoples of the Northeast viewed torture as producing "opportunities for heroism," "not simply the degradation of the victim" (52), Sayre argues, English accounts such as Mary Rowlandson's resolutely resist representations of torture so as to deny "Indians as conscious creators of meaning" (54), and French Jesuits hagiographically celebrate captive sufferings as an opportunity for extended engagement with native peoples and thus martyrdom for the missionary cause. Three subsequent essays examine exchanges between English and Anglo-American literary correspondents as sites of colonial self-definition. Armin Paul Frank unravels the complex "intercultural" satire of Ebenezer Cook's poem *The Sot-Weed Factor* (1708) within a transatlantic Restoration context. Anglo-American colonial elites also engaged in a sophisticated transatlantic scientific exchange, Carla Mulford writes, using new naturalistic knowledge about North American and Caribbean environments to construct a particularly American literary identity and authority. Finally, Leonard Tennenhouse investigates how Charles Brockden Brown's fictional accounts of the West Indies comparatively construct British and American readers, colonial identities, and masculinities.

Literary configurations of region provide a unifying theme for section 2, "Southern Dreaming," a tribute to Lemay's archival reconstruction of the belletristic tradition of the planter colonies, especially Maryland. Jim Egan discovers the colonial politics of bodies, boundaries, and identities in George Alsop's promotional poem *A Character of the Province of Mary-land* (1666), while Nanette Tamer reads Richard Lewis's Horatian ode *Carmen Seculare* (1732) as an Americanized panegyric advocating the interests of Marylanders to colonial proprietors. Essays by Susan Clair Imbarrato and Robert Micklus focus on works by an esteemed Maryland man of letters, Alexander Hamilton: his *Itinerarium* (1744), according to Imbarrato, is an important document of changing social and economic class hierarchies, while the editorial history of Hamilton's *History of the Tuesday Club* (1756) causes Micklus to reflect thoughtfully on how eighteenth-century writings sometimes fail to connect with contemporary readers. This section closes with an essay by A. Owen Aldridge on *The Religious Impostor Unmasked* (1795), an anonymous epic mockery of Methodism in the American South, and with an effort by Robert Arner to win notice for southern poet Joseph Dumbleton's "The Paper Mill" (1744) as a uniquely rich reflection on colonial print culture.

Lemay's engagement with material culture and the fine arts through the Winterthur program at the University of Delaware is celebrated in section 3, "Manor Culture, Cultural Authority, and the Domestic and Fine Arts." Susan Stabile offers a richly evocative comparative reading of the "vernacular architecture" (229) of Philadelphian Sarah Wister's commonplace book (1777–85) and the design of her home and gardens, thus modeling a "materialist approach" to understanding "topological, metaphorical, and authorial space for eighteenth-century women" (246). Similarly, Bernard Herman explores the architecture of Benjamin Franklin's residences in London and Philadelphia as emblematic of Franklin's self-positioning as "a cosmopolitan arbiter of transatlantic taste and letters" (250). Painting rather than architecture is the subject of Wayne Craven's study of American artist Washington Allston as an exponent of a conjointly visual and poetic romanticism emergent at the turn of the nineteenth century.

Section 4, "Benjamin Franklin and His Friends," honors Lemay's career in Franklin studies, including his anticipated multivolume critical biography of the American icon. Frank Shuffleton locates Franklin within a network of early American science writers and publishers, including Andrew Bradford, Cadwallader Colden, John Bartram, and David Rittenhouse, who socially and intellectually constituted a new national or "continental" consciousness. Franklin's transatlantic friendship with David Hume and its shaping effect on the *Autobiography* (1793) is the subject of Thomas Haslam's essay. Daniel Royot elucidates Franklin's "humorous vision of sexual mores" (307) in his writings about women, while Pattie Cowell reconstructs his mentoring relationship with a young Londoner named Mary Stevenson Hewson as evidence of the "many kinds of learning" beyond the classroom available to women in the eighteenth century (317). This section closes with three editorial and bibliographical contributions to Franklin studies: Barbara Oberg's introduction of a newly discovered essay by Franklin, "Observations on the Means of Extinguishing a Fire" (1787); James Green's description of Franklin's personal library; and a bibliography of visual and material cultural Franklin artifacts compiled by American Philosophical Society librarian Roy Goodman.

The final section in the volume examines individuals and places that have exerted a shaping influence in American history and culture. "The Creations of History, American Selves, and American Cultural Memory" opens with an essay by Kevin Hayes on how eighteenth-century New England historian Thomas Prince carefully studied John Smith's *Generall Histories of Virginia* (1627) and adopted from Smith key elements of his own historical vision. Paul Zall contributes a brief essay on Thomas Jefferson's conflicted attempt to set straight his own historical record in a manuscript autobiography. David S. Shields measures the weight of Plymouth Rock against that of William Bradford's gubernatorial chair as competing symbols of American origins during the late eighteenth century. Two final essays examine the nineteenth-century legacies of colonial histories. Karen Schramm reviews Henry David Thoreau's "subversion" (413) of the representation of wilderness as diabolical in Puritan histories by Cotton Mather and others while John Seelye defends the honor of Sir Walter Scott and *Ivanhoe* (1819) against literary critics from Mark Twain to Amy Kaplan who have charged his chivalric fantasies with inspiring dishonorable episodes in American war and imperialism. Unfortunately, the essays by Schramm and Seelye are so historically and thematically removed from the framing concerns of the volume as to make for a most unsatisfying conclusion, even if we sympathize with the editors' decision to conclude the volume with an essay by an important name or recognize the larger editorial problem of cultivating cohesion in an essay collection.

Perhaps a *festschrift* volume such as *Finding Colonial Americas* is most valuable as a document of how the careers of individual scholars intersect with and contribute to larger patterns of scholarship. Just as we learn from Lemay's brand of scholarship how regionally and imperially contiguous networks of intellectual and cultural exchange shape early American literature and culture, we gain from these essays a sense of how institutional and social networks of scholarly exchange produce new knowledge and new schools of thought. As it appears in this volume, the vision of early America(s) espoused by the Lemay-Mulford-Shields school is graciously receptive to odd ephemera and minor elite personalities, modest in its theoretical propositions, polite in its secularism, belletristic in its tastes, peripatetic in its interests, and scientific in its habits; it is more witty than passionate, more cultivated than evangelical, more cooked than raw, and in its undertones more patriotic than apocalyptic. Those who were trained as I was in the Miller-Heimert-Bercovitch school may find this vision too free from the throes of sin, perdition, and redemption; or, as my mentor Michael Colacurcio once put it, "the big medicine of Jesus." We may never like Annapolis or Charleston as well as the Connecticut River Valley. We may never really love the story of America the transatlantic and hybrid—except perhaps as told from the perspective of the slaves (which is not at all represented in this volume). Still, it is good to understand that there are indeed other colonial Americas, interesting places to visit, where the weather is milder, the sights are pleasant, and the scholarship is flourishing.

Joanna Brooks
University of Texas at Austin

THE CORRESPONDENCE OF JOHN COTTON. Edited by Sargent Bush Jr. Chapel Hill: U of North Carolina P for the Omohundro Institute of Early American History and Culture, 2001. xxvii + 548 pp. $79.95.

MAKING HERETICS: MILITANT PROTESTANTISM AND FREE GRACE IN MASSACHUSETTS, 1636–1641. By Michael P. Winship. Princeton: Princeton UP, 2002. xviii + 322 pp. $31.95.

In the introduction to *Making Heretics*, an elegant and deeply researched new account of the Antinomian Controversy, Michael P. Winship at once regrets and accepts—as he must—"the dizzying gulfs of archival blankness" (10) that threaten any and all interpretive histories of the matter. At the same time, it is the business of Sargent Bush Jr., in his definitive edition of *The Correspondence of John Cotton*, to fill in a measure of that blankness and give a firmer foundation to our understanding. Since these books were simultaneously in the making, each had the advantage of the other's new light.

In rather different yet immensely interesting ways, both books foreground the problem of the archive. The greater part of Cotton's correspondence is lost beyond hope of recovery, leaving fragments or complete texts of seventy-three letters composed by him and fifty-two letters that he received. Most of the few extant manuscripts, moreover, are seriously damaged, leaving innumerable "frustrating holes" (83) that often make a hash of the text. Reading what is left is frankly difficult, nor is the job eased by the plethora of brackets, braces, carets, italics, and other marks signifying aspects of the manuscript or effects of the editorial hand—including, it must be said, a deployment of quotation marks that has no precedent in any other book. Typographically the work might conceivably have been made more reader-friendly, but the unavoidable lacunae and the sometimes avoidable assertion of the editorial presence result in a text that manages never to feel like ordinary competent prose, even of that artificial period, while at the same time hinting in an almost satisfactory way at the kind of problems that Cotton's contemporaries had in construing his meanings, or, indeed, that he had in construing theirs.

The question of how well or poorly Cotton was being understood was at the center of what has heretofore been called the Antinomian Controversy, so that if we struggle to grasp Cotton's meanings, we do no more now than his friends and enemies did then. In a 1641 letter to Cotton, the minister's old friend John Coddington wrote from his sad Rhode Island exile to say that "it hath bene reported to us that Mr Cotton Now houlds forth things so darkely that if we had not knowne what he had houlden forth before we knew not how to understand him" (347). That is to say, as Anne Hutchinson had said to the Court, his expression alters, but not his judgment. Then, too, the controversy began when Thomas Shepard, hoping to get Cotton to declare himself and finding his sermons too full of doubtful flourishes, required him to "giue vs satisfaction by way of wrighting rather then speech for this on time" (226). The maneuver scarcely differed from Anne Hutchinson's requirement at trial that the accusing ministers testify on oath: both were shifts to eliminate an increasingly intolerable margin of denotative looseness that had come to typify ordinary formal discourse.

How little people understood the effects of their own rhetoric is stunningly illustrated in John Wheelwright's letter to Cotton in 1640, in which he wonders that his notorious Fast Day sermon had been so strenuously objected to. One suspects that this foreswearing of responsibility for the upshot of one's speaking might be likewise in play when Cotton refused to acknowledge that Antinomian or Familist conclusions could have been drawn from his own doctrines, choosing to believe instead that the heretics were independent in their errors and—slow as he was to admit it—that they had been conscious liars in claiming to hold forth "noething, but according to the Doctrine publickly taught be me" (367).

Cotton's early letters show him as a man resorted to by younger clergy to resolve knotty problems in ethics or theology. Significantly, there are no examples of his asking advice from anyone else. His success as a learned casuistical thinker and the deference he was shown in this role may have contributed to a finally dangerous confidence in his ability to understand things. On the whole, the letters provide an experience rather like looking at a landscape through a picket fence: what we see in the intervals of textual clarity is a man who was a good deal better at opening scripture than he was at opening himself.

The single most interesting and profitable maneuver in Winship's *Making Heretics* is the ground-clearing decision to draw attention away from the accumulated stereotypes of "Antinomianism," to insist on conceptually centering the issue of free grace, and to assert more frankly than has hitherto been done that Familism was at the bottom of it all: "Had it simply been an 'antinomian' and not a 'familist' controversy, it never would have reached such a level of intensity" (229). In some respects the proposition could be still more aggressively pursued so as to sustain yet more weight. If Cotton had his left-wing acolyte in Hutchinson, she had hers in the mysterious Jane Hawkins of St. Ives, a town surely not in Cornwall as is always said (e.g., Richard S. Dunn, James Savage, and Letitia Yaendle, eds., *The Journal of John Winthrop, 1630–1649* [Cambridge, MA: Belknap P of Harvard UP, 1996] 253n), but squarely and famously in the Stour Valley of Cambridgeshire, near Ely, the very seat and center of English Familism. There is an obscure reference in Shepard's testimony to his having spoken to Hutchinson "at St. Ives" (David D. Hall, ed., *The Antinomian Controversy, 1636–1638: A Documentary History* 2nd ed. [Durham: Duke UP, 1990], 303, cf. 352–53), which makes sense only on the supposition that her Boston residence (where Hawkins boarded) was widely known by that characteristic appellation. The emphasis on Familism illuminates Winthrop's role, for while he is portrayed here as more of a pragmatist than an all-out ideologue, his position seems in fact to have hardened in proportion as the Familism became evident to him. The influence on the Winthrop family of the old anti-Familist John Knewstub is probably underasserted in the one sentence devoted to it (92): his 1579 *Confutation of Monstrous and Horrible Heresies* indeed makes very interesting background reading.

But the productively novel assessment enabled by Winship's conceptual demotion of Antinomianism inevitably has its downside: the controversy as here defined is dominated not by Anne Hutchinson at all, but by such figures as Cotton (centrally) and Shepard (agonistically), together with Wheelwright and Henry Vane. It may be that as a matter of the archive these are the figures about whom there is simply more to be newly known, and certainly the reinterpretation of Shepard's role will strike everyone as thoroughly brilliant. But Winship cannot quite finesse the detail that these figures emerge not contemporaneously with the damage, but after it was done, so that we engage them always in the act merely (yet significantly and contentiously) of talking about it. The point is usefully established that the making of heretics is always, of course, an act of retrospection and always in the hands of the orthodox. And yet the book slightly disappoints historical curiosity by being vague about where and how "the first disobedience" arose; and, to the extent that heresy is a problem of the learned Brethren rather than of the "simple Weomen" (who have, relatively, no archive), the study deals less assuredly than it might with the great glaring issue of gender. If Cotton's *Correspondence* spends its force a little into a tangle of typography, *Making Heretics* spends its a bit into that tangle of doctrinal niceties and sectarian categories according to which, after the fact, the scandal was rehearsed by Cambridge graduates. It is certainly true that there is no hope of understanding the issues without a firm grasp of the soteriological options, but there is some price to pay on the other side in multiplying distinctions: even the distinction between Familism and Antinomianism (which Winship defines, I think, rather too restrictively) tends to disguise their shared connection with permanent and historically recurrent forms of spirituality. But, in the end, all the niceties and categories seem hardly to matter, even to the principals, since resolution lay not so much in a consolidated orthodoxy as in a kind of gentlemen's agreement that, the human casualties at last removed from the colony, the clergy of New England would stop trying to eat each other for breakfast.

Albert J. von Frank
Washington State University

THE SPY. A TALE OF THE NEUTRAL GROUND. By James Fenimore Cooper. THE WRITINGS OF JAMES FENIMORE COOPER. Historical Introduction by James P. Elliott; Explanatory Notes by James H. Pickering; Text Established by James P. Elliott, Lance Schachterle, and Jeffrey Walker. New York: AMS Press, 2002. xxxv + 551 pp. $115.

The publication of this volume, the eighteenth to appear in the now-revived Cooper edition that was begun in 1980 under the imprint of the State University of New York Press but was suspended by SUNY in 1991, is doubly auspicious. It is good to see that important editorial venture revived at its new home at AMS Press, which promises more volumes soon. It also is good to have this particular novel available for the first time in an important new version that supersedes all previous texts, most of which were seriously flawed.

When James Fenimore Cooper began his career as a writer in 1820, it was on an impulse usually ascribed to a humorous challenge delivered by his then-ailing wife, Susan. The often-repeated story claims that James was reading aloud to Susan from an unnamed, recently imported British novel as she reclined on a sofa in their home, "Angevine," in rural Westchester County. Taking a particular dislike to the volume in hand, Cooper threw it aside, exclaiming that he could write a better book than that himself. His wife revived at this outburst and demanded that he do just that. After trying his hand at what he called a "moral tale," traces of which may survive in his *Tales for Fifteen* (1823), Cooper soon settled down and, within a month, finished what was to become *Precaution* (1820). The novel was set in the English countryside, where Sir Edward and Lady Anne Moseley, like their counterparts in the novels of Jane Austen, fret about how to arrange suitable marriages for their children.

Some of the friends with whom Cooper shared *Precaution* in manuscript joined his wife in urging him to publish it. They apparently tempered their praise, however, with a caveat: any subsequent venture, should there be one, ought to have an American setting and American themes. The same advice emerged in a brief notice of *Precaution* that appeared in the *Literary and Scientific Repository*, a New York journal recently established by Charles K. Gardner, Cooper's messmate during his navy days. Even before Cooper conveyed the manuscript of *Precaution* to his printer in June 1820, he launched into another tale partly intended to compensate for the postcolonial mimicry of the first one. For his new setting, he chose the landscape immediately outside the windows of his study at "Angevine." And for the action of the new book, he turned to the historical and moral complexities of that landscape (the "Neutral Ground" of his subtitle) during the American Revolution. In the process, he invented the American historical romance and the espionage novel.

Cooper's attraction to the subject was enormous, but after a fast start on *The Spy*, his energies flagged. Having begun the book in June 1820, while still writing *Precaution*, Cooper quickly finished about sixty pages of the new manuscript—representing perhaps the first eight chapters of the novel as it eventually was published. Initially, Cooper thought he would finish the new book as early as that October. By July, however, he was putting off the completion date until later in the fall. And, in fact, he was able to complete only the first volume by then. In January 1821, that volume was in press. But Cooper did not even start work on the second volume, the editors of the present edition infer, until the following July (xxii). His progress on it was so slow (as Cooper recalled for Rufus Griswold in 1843) that his agent, Charles Wiley, became concerned that the work would grow to an unacceptable length. Cooper therefore wrote the final chapter and let Wiley set it in type and produce page proofs for it—meaning, of course, that the book thereafter had an established ending point toward which the author would be obliged to aim both his plot and his accumulating manuscript pages. Small wonder that in the first edition, which at last was ready for sale late in December 1821, the penultimate chapter of the second volume ran to only about half the length of those chapters leading up to it.

As this story indicates, the composition of *The Spy* was quite irregular. It also suffered from the usual accidents plaguing many of Cooper's earliest books. As is true for the bulk of Cooper's personal and professional papers from the period prior to his European sojourn (1826–33), none of the original manuscript leaves of *The Spy* survive. If they did, they doubtless would reveal many instances in which Cooper's ambiguous handwriting and inconsistent punctuation misled typesetters, as was certainly the case with regard to *Precaution* (for which the bulk of the manuscript, preserved by its printer, in fact does survive). Cooper and the typesetters were both responsible for the problems in *Precaution*, but, aside from insisting on some changes in proofs and the addition of errata sheets, the author managed to correct only a few of them. Not until almost two decades later, when he revised *Precaution* for a new edition, was he able to go through the book and make major improvements. In the case of *The Spy*, he could introduce analogous changes much sooner. Due to its enormous popularity and brisk sales, two new editions were soon called for. Appearing in March and May 1822, they contained not only new prefatory material but also hundreds of corrections, revisions, and stylistic and syntactical alterations. By detailed study of these changes, the editors of the present text have been able to offer close commentary on Cooper's emergent habits as a professional writer.

Their sense of Cooper's multiple agendas in carrying out the 1822 changes in the novel is impressively applied in their own construction of the text that the AMS version itself establishes. Of even more use to them in their work was a hybrid version of *The Spy* that survives from 1831. In that year, Cooper reached an agreement with British publishers Colburn and Bentley to revise his earlier works of fiction for inclusion in their new "Standard Novels" series. His preferred method of revising those books was to work with a copy of an existing printed text, rebound with blank sheets interleaved. For the AMS version of *The Spy*, the changes written by Cooper on the interleaved sheets bound in a copy of the Carey, Lea & Carey fifth edition of 1827, which of itself had had no independent authorial input, provide the great majority of readings, some of which Colburn and Bentley themselves missed.

That interleaved *Spy* is one of only two such hand-altered copies surviving for the seven novels that were issued by Colburn and Bentley and included to date in the Cooper edition. The editors of the present volume note that the revisions introduced via the interleaved copy are more extensive than those made by Cooper for any of the other works he revised by the same means (443). In the case of the single other work for which the interleaved copy survives, *The Prairie* (1827), the more limited nature of the changes on the interleaved sheets, as well as the survival of much of the original manuscript and parts of an amanuensis copy of it, made the interleaved copy of considerably less importance for the editors of that novel in the SUNY text (1985). In the case of *The Spy*, as a consequence of these differences, we have a thoroughly new edition of the book that established Cooper's reputation. The editors point out that, due to the "extraordinary proliferation of editions of *Spy* throughout and beyond Cooper's lifetime, copies derived from different stages of revision were often in circulation simultaneously" (437). In their own "eclectic, unmodernized text" (452), the editors' copy-text is the first edition (New York: Wiley & Halsted, 1821), emended by reference to the interleaved copy and several other texts over which Cooper exercised authorial control—including, for instance, those two revised editions also issued by Wiley & Halsted in March and May 1822.

The editors have done a splendid job of finally making available the novel Cooper envisioned in a particularly creative month in 1820—a novel that suffered more than its share of accidents as it made its way to what proved an enthusiastic audience. Some things are downplayed in this version, to be sure. The "bitch doctor" of 1821 (to cite a famous instance of the earliest editions' sometimes rougher language, in this case a description applied to both Katy Haynes and Betty Flanagan) is gone from the AMS edition (which, following the interleaved copy, prefers "petticoat doctor" [e.g., 154]). But the consequent loss in saltiness is more than made up for by the rich revelations of the new text. It is a masterpiece of modern editing that makes a substantial contribution to the ongoing revaluation of America's first professional novelist.

Wayne Franklin
Northeastern University

BOOK REVIEWS 357

THE HUMOR OF THE OLD SOUTH. Edited by M. Thomas Inge and Edward J. Piacentino. Lexington: UP of Kentucky, 2001. x + 321 pp. $29.95.

AUGUSTUS BALDWIN LONGSTREET'S "GEORGIA SCENES" COMPLETED: A SCHOLARLY TEXT. Edited by David Rachels. Athens: U of Georgia P, 1998. lxvii + 351 pp. $19.95.

M. Thomas Inge and Edward J. Piacentino's *The Humor of the Old South* is a strong essay collection that not enough people will read. Well-balanced between reprints of seminal articles and new essays, the volume usefully develops and complicates the reader's understanding of "Southwestern humor," its practitioners, and its legacy. Not enough people will read it because, as readers and scholars, we believe we already know how to use this material in the sophomore survey. Obviously, we should mention Southwestern humor on the day we introduce Mark Twain.

Yet *The Humor of the Old South* clearly demonstrates that the genre of Southwestern humor can itself bear the weight of critical scrutiny, constituting important moments in narrative style and regional identity, as well as national self-consciousness. Thankfully, Inge and Piacentino are not interested in simply retracing a familiar trajectory (bawdy frontier humor → Mark Twain) or in rehashing arguments about the genre's realism versus its political import. They offer here a lively mix: eight previously published essays and ten (counting James H. Justus's provocative introduction) new essays that suggest fresh areas of interest. As Piacentino's indispensable and massive bibliography (listing both general studies and scholarship about individual authors) attests, the genre of Southwestern humor has inspired a steady critical response, not strictly confined to locating traces of it in the latter-day canon. Most importantly, there remains a great deal of room for further exploration.

Inge and Piacentino divide the book itself into three sections—"Origins and Influences," "Perspectives on Earlier Authors—1830–1860," and "The Literary Legacy"—and include both reprints and new material under each heading. The effect is to bring into dialogue selected scholarship from 1975 to the present (with a greater emphasis on scholarship from the last fifteen years), suggesting that little about the genre has been definitively resolved. Interestingly, the highest concentration of new essays is in the middle section, devoted to the discussion of individual writers. This fact suggests one of the editors' primary interests: promoting scholarship about writers less frequently studied, among them William Tappan Thompson, Joseph Glover Baldwin, and O. B. Mayer, here the subjects of full-length essays.

Justus's introduction sets an appropriate tone for a volume including articles such as these, as well as treatments of more easily recognizable figures, by first acknowledging the avenues by which critics have traditionally approached the genre and then striking off into new territory. His focus on the power of dialect in the tales leads to the important observation that Southwestern humor constitutes the "literary tradition of how regionalisms [are] produced" (5) and thus elevates the discussion to one about the power structures of nineteenth-century American life and the ways in which regional identities were even then constructed. Justus offers a new paradigm by which to classify the humorists themselves that displaces Kenneth Lynn's now-classic but much-contested political schemata; rather than seeing their Whiggish viewpoint as the common denominator, Justus prefers to call them "Moderns" (7), men who aligned themselves with the things of the future, namely, economic enterprise in lands successfully cleared by an inevitable tide of civilization. By that formula, says Justus, the Southern frontier was a thing of the past and the people populating it "Primitives" (10). Southwestern humor may celebrate their rough-and-tumble lives, but it does so on civilization's terms and in a lament for a time not yet gone but certainly doomed. Clearly labeling Southwestern humor "imaginative writing," Justus finds in the genre "a refracted image of the society that generated it" (10) and, so, wisely concedes what so many have inexplicably resisted. What this humorous writing finally shows us is not so much what life was literally like on the Southern frontier, but how, by the 1850s, the debate pitting "Primitives" against "Moderns" had become realigned along a North/South axis that linked the South with a damaging nostalgia in the American imagination and positioned it as outside of any mainstream national identity, marking it with a "foreignness" that may haunt it still.

Given the challenges that *The Humor of the Old South* finally mounts to conventional readings of Southwestern humor, the collection's two most valuable reprints are William Lenz's "The Function of Women in Old Southwestern Humor" and Ed Piacentino's "Contesting the Boundaries of Race and Gender in Old Southwestern Humor." Lenz's piece remains an invaluable re-seeing of the genre, offering incontrovertible evidence that women are not merely the targets of misogyny in this world traditionally conceived of as a masculine playground. Rather, Lenz finds female characters to be "an essential part" (48) of the genre, sometimes acting as trickster figures themselves, sometimes functioning as the subjects of satire, but consistently populating a parallel "world of backwoods domesticity" (40) that destabilizes both conventional gender roles and conventional readings of Southwestern humor as a genre immune to female power. Perhaps it is just that power, Lenz speculates, that makes masculine community necessary and possible on a frontier where everyone's roles are subject to redefinition. It is the slippery quality of the frontier that most intrigues Piacentino, who identifies in his essay actual narrative slips in the otherwise solid support that these tales offer for the racial and gender status quo. Humor periodically allows writers to question, consciously or subconsciously, the order of the world that they import to the frontier by way of their civilizing voices. Although the sketches ultimately reassert the boundaries that they tentatively question, we can gain from the cracks in their surface valuable insight into how the antebellum mind justified to itself the practices of its culture. Reading closely tales by John S. Robb, Hardin Taliaferro, and Francis James Robinson, Piacentino is particularly interested in moments when white narrators seem to glimpse the humanity of African American characters. When "Sam," the slave in Robb's sketch "The Pre-Emption Right" (1845), defends a woman from her abusive husband's wrath, his master confers a sort of honorary whiteness upon him in what Piacentino terms a "half-humorous" (53) gesture that alleviates through its comedy any potential discomfort in an audience to whom Huck Finn had not yet been introduced.

In "Darkness Visible: Race and Pollution in Southwestern Humor," the volume's most insightful new essay, Scott Romine reads some of the same material, but frames his argument differently. He is less interested in individual narrative slips and more concerned with the genre's cultural work as a whole, maintaining that it offers "a disturbing primer of racial codes elided by the plantation tradition" (81). Romine points to various textual moments in which Southwest humorists conflate blackness and pollution or contamination that requires communal purification. In these moments, blackness becomes a transferable stain, so that the whiteness awarded Sam in Robb's "The Pre-Emption Right" is matched by the blackness foisted onto the abusive squatter who is subsequently lynched because he represents a darkness that must be eradicated. In Robb's unmitigatedly racist "Letters from a Baby" (1845), Romine finds racial pollution "enabled by women who fail in their domestic roles" (77), a disturbing formula he develops convincingly here and in readings of other stories. Thus, the threats that antebellum Southern fiction elsewhere struggles to contain— the power of blackness and the chaos attendant upon racial or gender disorder— crashes through the frames of Southwestern humor, despite our traditional reading of the genre as one in which white men easily control such forces.

Certainly one of the most important of those men was Augustus Baldwin Longstreet, whose 1835 collection of sketches, *Georgia Scenes*, usually receives credit as the first book-length example of Southwestern humor. Inge and Piacentino include two essays exclusively devoted to Longstreet, and he works his way into discussions throughout the volume. Kurt Albert Mayer and David Rachels both challenge the often-recited image of Longstreet as an upper-class gentleman bemused by frontier spectacles that he felt ought to be recorded before they were refined out of existence. Reminding us that "Longstreet was a planter patrician only by marriage" (103), Mayer argues for a reading of *Georgia Scenes* that allows the individual sketches to reflect Longstreet's evolving political conservatism as he grappled with a dawning certainty of nullification's impracticalities. Rachels is even more direct, characterizing *Georgia Scenes* as a book about Longstreet himself and his "attempt to negotiate a social position in keeping with his ambitions while not forgetting his origins" (114), rooted as they were in the rough neighborhood of Edgefield, South Carolina, where the Yale graduate, college president, and minister had quite a reputation as a fighter. Like his narrators Hall and Baldwin, then, Longstreet may have known what it was to be a man astraddle two worlds.

Although Rachels's scholarly edition of *Georgia Scenes* predates *The Humor of the Old South* by three years, the collection will have the desired effect of sending readers in search of primary material. Rachels includes, in addition to a lengthy introduction and the nineteen pieces readers know as *Georgia Scenes*, eight uncollected sketches, likely evidence that Longstreet contemplated releasing a second volume of sketches that would have widened his study of social classes to include those above the stations occupied by most characters in the published *Georgia Scenes*. In a section called "Attributed Items," Rachels reproduces a number of short, unsigned pieces from the newspaper that Longstreet edited, the *Augusta State Rights' Sentinel*. Although Longstreet may not be the author in every case, he certainly wrote many of these pieces and selected all of them. As a result, the modern reader gains a fuller sense of what reading the *State Rights' Sentinel* might have been like and acquires a more developed picture of Longstreet as a humorist. Rachels provides, in addition to various appendices, a list of "Lost Georgia Scenes," a catalogue of references in periodicals, correspondence, or early critical treatments to tales that scholars have yet to recover. Meticulous "Textual Overview" and "Textual Apparatus" sections close out the volume and serve as final evidence of Rachels's careful editing.

Rachels takes issue in his introduction with several commonplace conclusions about Longstreet. He refutes the frequent assumption that, in his later life, Longstreet was ashamed of his humorous publications and actively suppressed them. Instead, Rachels finds in Longstreet's correspondence and in the correspondence of others a consistent affection on Longstreet's part for his literary creations and infrequent flirtations with reviving them. More curiously, Rachels quarrels with the academy's classification of Longstreet as a humorist, a designation he resists in favor of seeing Longstreet as a realist. He praises recent critical rediscoveries of the book's realism and encourages readers to accept Longstreet's own interpretation of his *Georgia Scenes* as history. From the time of the volume's earliest reviews, however, including a favorable notice from Edgar Allan Poe, critics have been as interested in the book's humor as in its realism. "This distressed Longstreet," Rachels reports, "who had hoped to do more than make people laugh" (xlviii). It clearly distresses Rachels as well, who maintains that Longstreet's designation as a Southwest humorist has given him a "one-dimensional literary reputation"; he agrees with James B. Meriwether that the label "humorist" is a "misclassification" of Longstreet's considerable skills (1). Thus, Rachels angles to secure Longstreet his rightful place in American literary history.

Longstreet himself worried over the reception of his book, not so much in the preface that accompanied it in 1835, as in a later and often-quoted piece of correspondence in which he laments that the "design of 'Georgia Scenes' has been wholly misapprehended"; the book has been "invariably received as a mere collection of fancy sketches, with no higher object than the entertainment of the reader, whereas the aim of the author was to supply a chasm in history which has always been overlooked" (qtd. in Rachels xlviii). But the reader of Longstreet's 1835 preface had good reason to be misled. In that short introduction's second sentence, Longstreet confesses to using "some little art"; in the next sentence, he describes his method as the "fanciful *combinations* of *real* incidents and characters" spiced up when necessary with "some personal incident or adventure of my own, real or imaginary" (3; emphasis in original). And then he promises this: "Some of the scenes are as literally true, as the frailities of memory would allow them to be" (3), a not-so-subtle way of excusing authorial invention. The formula that Longstreet offers for the production of his work, then, is as intriguing as Nathaniel Hawthorne's recipe for a romance or William Faulkner's indulgence of Quentin and Shreve's playing at history. What seems more enticing than firmly establishing him as a realist is considering this playful attitude that Longstreet himself introduces here and the function that humor ultimately serves in recording all things "Georgian." For, just as the work of the antebellum humorists clearly deserves critical consideration, not merely for its legacy, but also for its intrinsic interest, so critics have convincingly demonstrated that humor qualifies as a serious literary endeavor from which no one needs rescuing. A more interesting question than "What does *Georgia Scenes* show us about the antebellum South?" might be "What does the humor in Longstreet's account of the antebellum South make possible that a different sort of narration would prohibit?" The fact that we have no definitive answer to that question is yet more evidence that the genre of Southwestern humor remains fertile ground for scholarly inquiry.

Kathryn B. McKee
University of Mississippi

LILLIE DEVEREUX BLAKE: RETRACING A LIFE ERASED. By Grace Farrell. Amherst: U of Massachusetts P, 2002. 237 pp. $34.95.

Grace Farrell's *Lillie Devereux Blake: Retracing a Life Erased* has two equally compelling agendas: the first is to present the life of this writer, journalist, suffragist, and feminist thinker; the second is to explain why Blake (1833–1913) has remained so peripheral to nineteenth-century literary and social history. Farrell has woven these agendas into a sensitive and poetic biographical (and autobiographical) meditation on the politics of archival preservation and recovery, making the seldom-acknowledged adventures and investments of the researcher an integral theme of her biography.

Lillie Devereux Blake is divided into three sections: "Erasures" introduces the intertwined events of Blake's early life in New Haven with Yale University's demolition of her childhood home; "Recoveries" traces Blake's activities as a Civil War journalist, her nascent feminist sensibilities, and her involvement with the suffrage cause; and "Retracing" provides an extended commentary on the politics of preserving and recovering historical evidence. Each section is informed by Farrell's evident passion both for her subject and for the larger issues that consumed Blake's interest during her long life.

Farrell presents Blake's life with sympathy, verve, and precision, foregrounding literary texts in her analysis and explication. She structures her first chapter's consideration of literary detection and canon formation around excerpts from Wallace Stevens's "An Ordinary Evening in New Haven"; in later biographical chapters, passages excerpted from Blake's considerable oeuvre frame events of the writer's life and add dimension to contextual accounts of feminist, national, and political history. One of Farrell's challenges is to discuss and analyze little-known or wholly unfamiliar texts written by a woman who has not yet been recognized as part of the nineteenth-century literary tradition and who published much of her work in ephemeral periodicals. Farrell succeeds admirably at this challenge, foregoing lengthy summary for a more satisfying and significant analysis of these texts in which social history, geographical location, and the work of other figures—biographical, artistic, and fictional—are brought into conversation with Blake.

The great strength of the biography is that, within a relatively short compass, Farrell communicates the complexity of the life of a woman who was widely traveled and well connected and who wrote voluminously. Although one would wish for more details of Blake's final years, Farrell has sensitively traced the changes in outlook and philosophy that characterize any long life. Her discerning delineation is particularly apparent in the book's strongest chapter, "Of Loss and War." Rather than portray Blake as an uncomplicated partisan in the War between the States, Farrell probes the causes of Blake's southern sympathies and honors her ultimate decision to support the Union cause. Farrell helps the reader to recognize that the principals in this divisive event were embedded in a complex social web and continued to meet, socialize, and do business with one another even though they held conflicting views on the questions of sectionalism, secession, and slavery.

Through sensitive analysis of Blake's war writings, Farrell demonstrates that "the war's violence" cannot be separated from "the myth of inviolate domesticity" (91). In 1862, Blake complained in her journal: "Washington is a desert; the beaux are nearly all gone" (88). The public business of war quickly invaded private fortunes, as well. Blake wrote, "The financial pressure is awful. Hundreds of young men thrown out of employment, business stagnant.... My friends all gloomy, many of them with penury threatening them. And I can do nothing. I am only a woman. I cannot be a soldier, I can do nothing but keep quiet and suffer" (81). She quickly found a way to break silence, however, writing both journalism and fictions about the war. Her illustrated short fictions shared front-page space with war dispatches in such newspapers as the *War Press*; these stories made the participants of the war and its events central to their fictional plots.

Farrell continues her analysis by examining the discrepancies between the publicly acceptable opinions Blake expressed in her newspaper columns and those inscribed in her journals and letters. Such work has depended on the biographer's patient, painstaking, and exact(ing) archival research: locating print ephemera, as well as transcribing and then comparing multiple versions of handwritten letters, journals, autobiographies, and published texts (since Blake often wrote up to five versions of the same story for the multiple papers for which she served simultaneously as correspondent). Farrell combines thoroughness with a similarly expansive consideration of the scholarship and primary resources related to dozens of others of Blake's contemporaries, as well.

In her mature years, Lillie Devereux Blake came to consider herself an orator: following one of her earliest speeches before a suffrage convention in 1869, she wrote, "I uttered my appeal with passionate earnestness and sat down at its close glowing, intoxicated and triumphant with the knowledge that I had a portion of heaven's divinest gift, eloquence!" (123). Ironically, the book's treatment of the career that Blake considered to be her true calling is its least compelling one. The issue is, of course, how one writes with sympathy and analytical insight about nontextual events. Lacking transcripts of what others reported to be articulate and stirring speeches, Farrell must rely on summary, exposition, and narrative history that often cover the same ground as other scholarly studies of the nineteenth-century feminist/suffrage movements. Such exposition cannot capture the immediacy of Blake's connection with her audiences or the passionate intersubjectivity spawned in the heat of public interchange that sustained Blake through a long and divisive association with the nation's leading nineteenth-century feminist thinkers.

Similarly, the section(s) dealing with Blake's feminism, especially her conflicts with Susan B. Anthony and Anthony's supporters, are primarily expository because "we no longer have the handwritten diaries during a major portion of Blake's suffrage period, from 1870 to 1900" (188). Despite this lack, Farrell presents an alternate and more complete version of the account of record, Anthony's *History of Woman Suffrage* (1922), by tracing and analyzing the divisive and extended challenges raised by Blake and her supporters. Since Anthony and Blake became estranged in their later lives, Blake's significant contributions as a feminist theorist, legislative analyst, and leader of the suffrage movement were all but erased from Anthony's seamless and progressive *History*. Farrell restores to that history the infighting and damaging—but ultimately productive—disagreements about philosophy, strategy, and procedure that accompany any significant social revolution.

The story of Blake's life is framed and interpenetrated by a second narrative agenda, a literary detective story. This story has two chronological locations, one in the midst of nineteenth-century norms of domestic probity and the divisive politics of the suffrage movement, the other in present-day politics of canon formation, archiving, and university development. Here Farrell is at her best, tracing with anger and humor the instances of ideological formations thought long-since moribund. Scholars whose interests may not include nineteenth-century literature or feminism will surely be fascinated by the contemporary implications of Farrell's work. If one reads only the first chapter of this remarkable volume, which chronicles Yale University's willful and deceptively justified destruction of Maple Cottage, Blake's girlhood home and a nineteenth-century architectural landmark, one is compelled to recognize how issues central to nineteenth-century feminist politics can inform contemporary debates. Because Maple Cottage's occupant was a minor figure who had purportedly had a sexual dalliance with a Yale undergraduate during her youth, she was, therefore, a woman of loose repute, unworthy of having her memory preserved on the twenty-first-century Yale campus. The site of her home, razed in May 1999, "is now a parking lot" (23).

The University of Massachusetts Press is to be commended for giving Farrell the latitude to present in its fullest expansion the material of the last two chapters, titled "On Being Lost" and "Literary Detection: A Postscript on Process," as an integral portion of the book. These chapters might well be assigned as required reading for all graduate students working in nineteenth-century sources. Her meditation on the procedures, pleasures, and ethical entanglements of archival research is an exemplary text in an era when methodology courses have all but disappeared from curricula top-heavy with required theory courses. Farrell is a generous scholar. In these chapters, as well as in many footnotes, she acknowledges the substantive contribution of archivists and librarians, whose work, because "unpublished," too often goes uncited. As all feminist scholars know, the personal impinges upon the professional; as all archival researchers know, the rigors and emotional investments of the work is too often undervalued, both in tenure reviews and in the resulting publications. In this book, rather than occupying the periphery, these matters become central to the biography that Farrell traces. She has demonstrated both the importance of Lillie Devereux Blake's life as a writer and thinker and the long history of the politics of gender that she and Blake both combated.

Nicole Tonkovich
University of California, San Diego

THE LATER LECTURES OF RALPH WALDO EMERSON, 1843–1871. VOLUME 1: 1843–1854; VOLUME 2: 1855–1871. Edited by Ronald A. Bosco and Joel Myerson. Athens: U of Georgia P, 2001. lxii + 796 pp. $130. Electronic Textual Notes at <http://www.walden.org/emerson/Writings/Later_Lectures>.

The manuscripts for Emerson's lectures after 1842 are legendary: described as voluminous, confused, unorganizable, and fragmentary, they have long been considered impossible to edit.

But not by Ronald A. Bosco and Joel Myerson, who believe that, "to understand Emerson's writings," we must first see him "at work as a lecturer" (1: xx). The only way to do that is to read the lectures that brought him fame and fortune, in the context of what we can reconstruct about them as public performances. Moreover, Bosco and Myerson's careful inspection of the manuscripts led them to conclude that not all of this material was as incomplete and chaotic as had been assumed. Their survey of all available lecture sources (over 250 folders of materials from 1843 through 1879 in the "Lectures" section of the Emerson collection in Harvard's Houghton Library) yielded forty-eight lectures that met their criteria: the lectures should be complete, "on the whole unpublished," and "entirely in Emerson's hand" (1: xli). They also concluded that it would be "impossible" to publish anything from after 1871 "in any coherent and responsible fashion" (1: xl). The result of their labors is this splendid edition of a major writer's work, an edition that is already changing the landscape of Emerson scholarship.

"Responsible editorial judgment and common sense" (1: xxxvii) are the keystones of Bosco and Myerson's editorial policy, based on their recognition that, especially after 1842, Emerson's compositional practices changed, so that his lectures were "nearly always in the process of becoming" (1: xxviii) or "'work in progress'" (1: xli). Thus, their policy significantly modifies the practices used by the editors of Emerson's early lectures and sermons. As Bosco and Myerson explain, "[W]e have had to develop an editorial rationale that begins with theirs but is flexible enough to accommodate our printing of what is arguably the most textually complex (if not actually tortured) body of Emerson manuscript sources" (1: xxxv).

The editors' decision to present these lectures in clear text follows the usual treatment of "public" performances—Emerson's sermons, lectures, and essays—as opposed to "private" writing—journals and notebooks, where a "genetic" text preserves authorial changes on the reading page. A clear-text presentation requires the editors to decide on a copy-text—which version to print—relegating everything else to some form of textual apparatus. As their copy-text, Bosco and Myerson chose what they "assumed" to be "the latest version of Emerson's delivery of a lecture" (1: xli, xlii)—a useful but not entirely practicable rationale, given the condition of the manuscripts that not only Emerson but also his executor and editors revised and shuffled for repeated and various uses.

Readers interested in the genetic text can go to the Walden Organization Web site for the "Electronic Textual Notes," an interesting new feature of this edition, which report all authorial and editorial emendations to the texts. These textual notes also provide five complete lecture variants in genetic texts. These notes alone testify to the heroic task performed by the editors.

In the minor quibble department, one could point out that many of these lectures are not "complete": whole sections seem to be missing from lectures such as "Morals," "Art," and "Natural Religion," among others that were mined heavily by Emerson and his literary executors; others end abruptly, without the resounding conclusion that left Emerson's audiences feeling uplifted. Also, several cannot be considered "unpublished": the editors' decision to include four pieces in the same versions already printed in Len Gougeon and Myerson's edition of *Emerson's Antislavery Writings* (1995) is not explained—although having these, along with an 1843 temperance lecture and the 1855 "Address at the Woman's Rights Convention," gives a more complete picture of Emerson's many-faceted career. Several other lectures (including the Sleepy Hollow address, "Country Life," "Perpetual Forces," "Resources," and "The Fortune of the Republic") were also previously published, in the last five volumes of Emerson's *Complete Works* (1903, 1904), but in versions concocted by James Elliot Cabot and Edward W. Emerson, which differ vastly from the new versions.

Cabot and the younger Emerson attempted to create new essays from the salvageable manuscripts that had not been published; they followed what they believed to be Emerson's own practice of tightening and, at times, bringing together material from a variety of sources into a new whole. Bosco and Myerson, in contrast, want to restore the platform Emerson, whose lectures were always crafted with particular audiences in mind and typically reread (and revised accordingly) on multiple occasions. Their historical introduction provides the best discussion to date of Emerson as lecturer, since it focuses on his creation of a new public persona, his reasons for lecturing, his composing process, the public perception of his lecturing, his relationship to his audiences, and his "genius in creating a sense of spontaneity on the platform" (1: xxvii). Headnotes document each lecture's initial delivery, genealogy, subsequent history, fees received, and other pertinent information, along with providing a sampling of contemporary newspaper reportage and private, individual responses. This information greatly complicates the lectures, adding a time dimension erased from the inert clear text on the page. Reading these lectures within this context feels something like driving through a deep rock cut along a highway where many folded layers of the earth are exposed, telling the story of that spot over a long period of time.

In these volumes, as reporters of Emerson's lectures liked to say, readers will discover a "rich feast" or "rare intellectual banquet," far too much to digest in a quick reading. The breadth and variety of Emerson's topics is astonishing; the lectures are filled with deep thought and a sustained celebration of the "intellect" and are peppered with personal references, homely anecdotes, and sharp comments on contemporary events. For those who prefer to read for the "lustres," sparkling aphorisms appear on every page. A few of my favorites: "Wisdom may . . . be said to consist in keeping the soul liquid, or in resisting the tendency to too rapid petrifaction" (1: 146); "Like a fragment of ice in the sea, so man exists in the firmament of truth which made him. He is a thought embodied" (1: 148); "When we know not how to steer, and dare not hoist a sail, we can drift: The current knows the way, though we do not" (1: 176); "All our political disasters grow as logically out of our attempts in the past to do without justice, as the sinking of some part of your house comes of defect in the foundation" (2: 299); "Memory is the magnetism of the atom" (2: 114). Some of these may already be familiar to readers of the last five volumes of the 1903–4 *Complete Works*, and, indeed, part of the fun of reading these lectures is discovering the various uses Emerson can make of a single sentence, paragraph, or anecdote. As a Houghton cataloguer put it when describing Emerson's habit of "cannibalizing earlier lectures" for later ones, "The result, of course, is that many sections of manuscript rightly belong in two or more places" (*Lectures and Sermons of Ralph Waldo Emerson* [Finding aid; Cambridge, MA: Houghton Lib., 1966] 2). For good reasons, Bosco and Myerson have not attempted to identify parallel passages; they suggest that searchable databases will soon make this task easy for researchers who want to track the "labyrinthine" "genealogy of individual passages" (1: xlvii).

These two volumes roughly map a new "middle" for Emerson's career (in vol. 1; 1843–54) and a still-powerful later period (in vol. 2; 1855–71). The forty-eight lectures fill major gaps in our knowledge of Emerson's career, richly sampling important series not published in *Representative Men* (1850), *English Traits* (1856), *The Conduct of Life* (1860), and *Society and Solitude* (1870). Few of the lectures from which those volumes derive survive in manuscript, probably because Emerson's very different compositional practices after 1842 led to their use as copy-text for the printer. However, Bosco and Myerson do print lecture versions of three "Conduct of Life" lectures. Other lectures come from the series on "New England" (1843), "Topics of Modern Times" (1854), an untitled private series (1859), "Life and Literature" (1861), and "American Life" (1864). Four brilliant college addresses show Emerson continuing to champion the role of the scholar as priest of thought. A cluster of pieces read first between 1859 and 1862, for Theodore Parker's 28th Congregational Society meeting on Sunday mornings in Boston's huge Music Hall, might better be considered sermons; half of the Music Hall pieces were never delivered elsewhere. Three others were first read in the popular "Parker Fraternity" annual course of lectures, inaugurated in 1858.

The Parker-related lectures show Emerson's continued engagement with "natural religion." Another group reveals his long attempt to formulate a "natural method of mental philosophy"; indeed, these may be two sides of the same coin. Emerson's biographer Cabot, a lifelong student of philosophy himself, believed the "natural history of the intellect" project that Emerson worked on in five series of lectures between 1848 and 1871 was the "chief task of [Emerson's] life" (*A Memoir of Ralph Waldo Emerson* [New York: Houghton, 1887] 2: 633). The question that drove Emerson was, "[C]ould not a similar [to scientific observation and description] enumeration be made of the laws and powers of the Intellect?" (1: 137). As Bosco and Myerson point out, these notes toward a "new metaphysics" evidence "unchecked" idealism, not the pragmatism we have come to associate with the later Emerson, and represent a poetic rather than a scientific or philosophical "construction of the mind" (1: 132).

No longer can we assume that this project was a failure. Although the manuscripts for the courses read in 1866, 1870, and 1871 are far too fragmentary to warrant publication, Bosco and Myerson provide full texts (plus variants) of the three "philosophical" lectures from *Mind and Manners of the Nineteenth Century*, first read in London in 1848. They also print five of the lectures from the 1858 course, *The*

Natural Method of Mental Philosophy, first read at Boston. These—along with "The Spirit of the Times" (1848) and "Celebration of Intellect" (1861), among others—constitute a sustained and well-articulated investigation into the most elusive and mysterious of all subjects, the human mind, and lay bare the analogizing method that is central to Emerson's thought and expression. The "solar microscope of *Analogy*," Emerson claims in an 1858 lecture, is "the key that opens the Universe"—including "those sublimities which skulk and hide in the caverns of human consciousness" (2: 89). Grounded in Emerson's belief in the unity of nature and mind, these more philosophical lectures constitute an extended gloss on Emerson's claim in the 1837 "American Scholar" address: "[T]he ancient precept, 'Know thyself,' and the modern precept, 'Study nature,' become at last one maxim" (*Collected Works of Ralph Waldo Emerson, Volume 1* [Cambridge, MA: Belknap P of Harvard UP, 1971] 55). The difference is that in these lectures, Emerson grounds his metaphysical leaps in experience, demonstrating how thought, like everything in nature, is organic. The "source of power" is "the soul of God . . . poured into the world through the thoughts of men" (2: 129).

Throughout, these new texts force us to recognize that Emerson is even more complicated than we had realized; that his career cannot be neatly divided between an early, idealist, "transcendentalist" period and later years of skepticism, naturalism, pragmatism, and decline; and that his faith in the power of thought whose roots are ultimately spiritual continued unabated to the end of his long career.

Nancy Craig Simmons
Virginia Polytechnic and State University

THE COLLECTED FABLES OF AMBROSE BIERCE. Edited by S. T. Joshi. Columbus: Ohio State UP, 2000. xxiv + 389 pp. $65.

The Collected Fables of Ambrose Bierce brings together under a single cover Bierce's previously collected fables, with the understandable exception of his numerous dialect-heavy "Little Johnny" fables, and several hundred previously uncollected fables. Fresh from reading the fables collected in S. T. Joshi's book, I believe it is reasonable to think that Bierce's fables will eventually gain a degree of acclaim similar to that accorded his *Devil's Dictionary* (1911). Like the satiric definitions in that work, the fables that Joshi has collected are by and large darkly and richly satiric and fully deserve a much wider circulation. Calling the fables "unique of their kind," Joshi attributes their uniqueness to "their pungently satirical 'morals,' their skewering of a wide array of political, social, and even literary foibles, and their exemplification of Bierce's sharp skepticism in regard to human character and endeavor" (vii).

Speaking to the importance of the form to Bierce, Joshi collects 846 numbered fables produced over a period of more than thirty years. He has identified—in addition to Bierce's "Zambri, the Parsee"; fables collected in *Cobwebs from an Empty Skull*

(1874); and those in *Fantastic Fables*, first published in 1899 and revised and reissued by Bierce in the sixth volume of his *Collected Works* (1909–12)—seven fables embedded in *Devil's Dictionary* definitions, yielding a total of 447 previously collected fables. Included in this grouping, but counted separately, are fifteen variant "Zambri" fables revised by Bierce for his *Collected Works*. All but one of the remaining 399 fables have been recovered by Joshi from their original host publications; the exception was found in a typescript in the University of Virginia's Bierce holdings. Since both the collected and uncollected fables often exist in two or more variant authoritative forms, Joshi reprints the latest authoritative versions while citing "significant textual variants" (xxiii) in his "Commentary."

Assessed as a whole, the fables that Joshi has collected are logically ordered and attractively presented. The accompanying "Chronology of Bierce's Fables" and title and character indexes located at the back of the volume are particularly useful. The "Chronology" allows readers and researchers to see when and where particular fables were first published and to gain insight into Bierce's selection process for his collections—a process, as Joshi notes, that typically excluded the most sharply focused political fables (xix). Similarly, the "Commentary," which immediately follows the fables, makes a range of relevant textual, biographical, cultural, and historical information available. That said, the collection is not without serious shortcomings.

Joshi's introduction is not adequate for a scholarly edition that seeks to play a role in securing for Bierce's fables "a place in the canon of American Literature" (xxi). Beyond allotting fewer than two pages to an account of the fable's tradition in the English language from Roman times to the twentieth century, Joshi makes no attempt to locate Bierce's contribution to the fable form within the wider context of nineteenth-century satirical journalism. Against this oversimplified sketch, Joshi's opening assertion that "Bierce's fables are unique of their kind" (vii) rings somewhat hollow. More problematically, Joshi never carefully delineates the methodology used to search for and identify the 399 previously uncollected fables, which, with the previously collected fables, are put forward as a complete collection of Bierce's fables.

Instead, under the introductory subheading "Bierce and the Fable," Joshi outlines in five pages Bierce's decades-long engagement with the fable form. While the account is generally insightful, its brevity inevitably results in a series of unacceptable oversimplifications regarding the various serial publications for which Bierce wrote. Thus, Joshi has this to say about the *Wasp* milieu from which he has extracted fifty-two previously uncollected fables: "In December 1883 a column of fables entitled 'Anecdotes of Animals' appeared; and in September and October of 1884 five columns of fables, headed either 'Fables without Political Morals' or 'Fables without Political Meaning,' were published. All are unsigned. Are they by Bierce? There is clearly a great deal of unsigned material by Bierce in the *Wasp*; and he had used or would use two of the three titles of these fables in other work. . . . Given this, and given the thoroughly Biercian style and content of these fables, I believe their attribution to Bierce is sound" (xii). While Joshi's attribution is sound, in making it he has vastly oversimplified what lies within the pages of the *Wasp*, the weekly San Francisco paper that Bierce edited and contributed to between March 1881 and September 1886.

During Bierce's tenure, the *Wasp* reprinted fables lifted from the *Detroit Free Press* (four fables) and the satirical New York–based weeklies *Life* (six fables) and *Puck* (one fable). Joshi's introduction makes no mention of these fables even though most are similar in style to the fables that he attributes to Bierce. Moreover, a quick review of the *Wasp* numbers in my files reveals that the weekly intermittently published sharply satirical fables variously attributed to "Solomon Oldstone" (one fable, 9 Dec. 1882), "E. F. C." (eleven fables, 26 May and 9 June 1883), and "Outis" (five fables, 14 Mar. 1885). Again, none of these contributors or fables is cited by Joshi, but judging by their style and content, a reader may conclude that all of these fables may well be the work of Bierce. My review also revealed several dozen unsigned anecdotes that arguably could be called fables if judged against the 846 collected by Joshi, and it turned up two fables under the heading "Lempriere Revised" (16 June 1883), four under the heading "Fables of My Environment" (17 Oct. 1885), and four more under the heading "The New Arabian Nights" (12 Dec. 1885), all of which I believe are the work of Bierce's pen. If we add to these a large number of "Prattle"-based anecdotes with varying degrees of similarity to the traditional fable form, the number of fables possibly attributable to Bierce and not identified by Joshi is raised even higher. In short, "Prattle," Bierce's long-running signature column in a succession of weekly and daily newspapers, requires a more careful consideration. By way of illustration, the following obviously fable-like anecdote appears in Bierce's 5 May 1883 "Prattle" column:

> "See here, Doctor," said the father of a number of grown up daughters, to the venerable manager of the *Examiner*, "I've been taking your paper ever since your connection with it, but it is due to my own dignity to explain that I don't take it for its long editorials on how to bring up girls."
>
> "What's the matter with the editorials?" was the mild inquiry of the great journalist.
>
> "Nothing, only I think I know more about bringing up girls than you do. You'd think it impertinent if *I* were to instruct *you* in *your* business."
>
> "Strikes me that that's pretty nearly what you are doing," said the Doctor tranquilly.
>
> And he walked away to finish an elaborate leader on the best way to get the grease off the breakfast dishes, while his friend went thoughtfully home to bring up a girl.
>
> Moral—Every talent should have a fair field and no favor.

The situation at the *Examiner*, the original host of approximately 600 of the fables in this new collection, is somewhat less complicated, since the non-"Prattle"-based fables identified by Joshi always ran under descriptive headings and can be attributed to Bierce with a high degree of confidence. Thus, on 7 June 1887, eight entries appeared under the heading "Fables and Tales," including the following example, fable 508 in Joshi's volume:

> The Rev. Dr. Stebbins is a good and wise man, but he is not beautiful. Being in Hollister one day, he was invited to attend a hanging, the local parson having declined on the ground of prejudice: his wife had been the victim of the murder. Many strangers attended, and as the procession, headed by the

man of God, appeared at the jail door to cross the inclosure to the scaffold, it halted, leaving him just outside with a Deputy Sheriff visible behind him, "What a vicious countenance!" said a spectator. "Yes," said another, "his lawyer didn't have no fair show."

As it appears together with other fables under an appropriate descriptive heading, Joshi has a right to include this particular item in his collection; still, an explicit statement of his collecting principles would be helpful. This point is particularly relevant because Joshi collects four fables extracted from *Examiner*-based "Prattle" columns, thereby suggesting that he has exhaustively scoured many hundreds of "Prattle" columns for any and all fables. However, if fable 508 were used as a baseline, then searching several decades of "Prattle" columns for similar entries would yield hundreds of additional fables.

In other words, despite Joshi's assertion that the volume makes Bierce's fables "at last all available for consultation" (xxi), the collection does not achieve this goal. To his credit, Joshi belatedly concedes that his introduction's claim may be overstated in a "Note on Attribution" appended to the end of his "Commentary":

> There is always the possibility that other fables by Bierce remain undiscovered and uncollected. Although during the later years of his tenure with the *Examiner* Bierce maintained that he, being on a salary paid by Hearst, felt obligated not to write for any other periodicals, in his earlier years (1887 to at least 1892) he appeared to be under no such restriction, as his work appeared in the *Oakland Tribune*, *Town Topics*, the *Wave*, and perhaps other magazines and periodicals. Nevertheless, I am confident that this volume contains the overwhelming bulk of fables written by Ambrose Bierce. (369)

Unfortunately, confidence in the value of the collection's "overwhelming bulk" is not an acceptable substitute for forthright scholarly clarity on Joshi's part. Reading this passage with its listing of relevant publications, one might reasonably expect that Joshi has carefully searched each of these particular publications for fables, but neither is this explicitly stated nor does it appear to be the case: seven fables by Bierce appear in the 25 July 1891 number of the *Wave* under his name and the familiar heading "Fables and Anecdotes," and yet Joshi makes no mention of this fact. While earlier variants of five of the fables are collected by Joshi, two of the seven, including the following example, are uncollected:

> "Come," said a Lamb to a Lion whom she had met in the fields, "let us lie down together, as it has been predicted that we would."
>
> Instead of complying, the Lion started to run away in terror, greatly to the surprise of some peasants, who were even more astonished when they saw the Lamb in fierce pursuit. In a few moments the smaller beast had overtaken the larger, and, springing upon him, fastened her teeth in his throat and was soon eating the carcass at her leisure, This threw the peasants into the utmost consternation and they cried out that it was a miracle.
>
> "Miracle, your grandmother!" said an aged man who had thoughtfully ensued upon these events in order to expound their meaning; "the actors in this little tragedy are only our dear old friends, 'the Ass in a Lion's Skin' and 'the Wolf in Sheep's Clothing.'"

Although the omissions and faults addressed above are serious, I hope it is apparent that most of the collection's flaws could have been relatively easily corrected, and still could be corrected in a revised edition, by articulating the boundaries of the search conducted and the methodology employed in conducting that search. Even in its present imperfect form, Joshi's book will inevitably be of significance to scholars and general readers wishing to see more, but not all, of a master fabulist's work.

Donald T. Blume
Central Connecticut State University

BRET HARTE: PRINCE AND PAUPER. By Axel Nissen. Jackson: UP of Mississippi, 2000. xxiii + 326 pp. $28.

If Bret Harte's reputation really "has roughly the same resonance among literary critics that the administration of Millard Fillmore inspires among presidential historians," as Gary Scharnhorst suggested in *Bret Harte: Opening the American Literary West* ([Norman: U of Oklahoma P, 2000], 235), then the appearance within the last five years of two biographies, a collection of letters, a critical bibliography, and a handful of articles surely signals a reconsideration, if not a revival, of Harte and his work. In *Bret Harte: Prince and Pauper*, Axel Nissen argues that such attention is warranted, not only by Harte's significance as an influential writer who "reinvented the American short story and laid the foundation for the Western" (xv), but also by his status as "the first American author-celebrity in the age of mass newspapers" (xvi)—an author-celebrity who, according to Nissen, kept his share of secrets beneath the genial facade familiar to all who knew him.

Unlike previous biographers, Nissen avoids both straight chronological narration and the customary emphasis on the California years; his focus is on Bret Harte as cosmopolitan littérateur, a man equally at ease with the literary world of New York and the titled upper classes of London. The "Bret Harte Mystery," as W. D. Howells called him, was at once a celebrity and a man whom nobody knew. A persistent theme in Nissen's account is the way in which Harte ingeniously and, in Nissen's view, heroically protected his privacy and his art by eluding the claims of those who would pin him down: his creditors; literary giants such as James Russell Lowell, who sought but did not get the truth about Harte's Jewish ancestry in his eccentric quest to link artistic genius with Jewish heritage; his critics, who called the authenticity of his experiences into question; his publishers, who pressed him for manuscripts to pay off their advances to him; his superiors in the State Department, who sought to ensure that Harte performed his duties as consul in Crefeld, Germany, and Glasgow; and his family, from whom he was voluntarily separated for twenty years.

What Harte did choose to tell were the tales that helped to confirm his persona as a Westerner. By all accounts a brilliant conversationalist, Harte held his audiences spellbound, explaining, for example, that his hair had turned gray after riding beside the driver on stagecoaches beset by robbers—although, as Nissen scrupulously points out, the historical record shows that such robberies did not begin to occur until *after* Harte had given up "riding on the box seat" (36). Nissen excuses Harte for such tales, saying that the usually modest Harte "could not help but be implicated in the creation and re-creation of his own myth" (36), a seemingly paradoxical statement that sums up something of the ungovernable power of literary celebrity. Inadvertent or not, Harte's mythmaking caught up with him when, as Nissen explains, he was trapped by his own success into writing the Western stories that his public had come to expect. Nissen's sympathetic portrayal is an appealing feature of this book, one that offsets the well-known vitriolic attacks on Harte in Mark Twain's *Autobiography* (1924). And Nissen is quick both to counter Twain's claims and to highlight Harte's more attractive characteristics, such as his faithful support of his family even when separated from them and his pleas for tolerance of Jewish and Chinese immigrants in poems such as "That Ebrew Jew" (1877) and "Plain Language from Truthful James" (1870).

Nissen renders the scenes of Harte's life through a fictionalizing process described in his introduction, translating first-person letters and other primary source materials into a third-person "free indirect" (xxi) dramatized narrative. Although it occasionally devolves into a formulaic you-are-there device—"Had you been a resident in San Francisco in the mid-1860s you would probably have noticed . . ." (72) or "Had we been in the vicinity of Clay Street . . . " (87)—the technique is frequently effective, as when Nissen introduces Harte at the height of his fame rather than following a strict chronology. Born in Albany, New York, Harte moved to San Francisco in 1854, where, as a writer for the *Golden Era* and then for the higher-toned *Californian*, he made a name for himself with his satiric poetry and his "condensed novels." By the time he left San Francisco in 1871 with his wife, Anna, and their children, he was the successful editor of the *Overland Monthly* and had already published in it such classic stories as "Tennessee's Partner" (1869) and "The Luck of Roaring Camp" (1868). Newly anointed with literary prestige and a ten-thousand-dollar contract from the *Atlantic*, he had achieved a position that was the best the Eastern cultural establishment had to offer, and his social capital and literary prospects seemed limitless. But Harte rapidly squandered both social and monetary capital by living beyond his means, failing to "fulfill the role of a public poet" (120), and, in one case of disastrous misjudgment, dressing in "gaudy raiment and . . . green gloves" (117) to deliver a previously published poem as his speech at a Harvard commencement.

At this point in chronicling Harte's career, literary historians usually describe the rest of his life as a slow descent into debt and obscurity. As Nissen shows in his chapter "The Lord of Romance," previously published in *American Literary Realism* (Spring 1997), this characterization is not true: Harte's critical reputation may have dimmed, but Bret Harte, Western author, was still a marketable commodity. In 1871, in fact, Harte had nearly thirty years of a writing career left to him and "forty-six volumes yet to write" (115); works such as *Flip and Other Stories* (1882) and *A Waif of the Plains* (1890), virtually unknown today, sold thirteen thousand five hundred and seventeen thousand copies, respectively, in a day when most novels sold two thousand copies at best (201). Nissen demonstrates that, in contrast to the established picture of decline, Harte was in fact "earning more money in the 1880s and 1890s than he had ever earned before" (209), and his active social life among the members of the upper classes and his status as a permanent houseguest made these years "the happiest of Harte's life" (213). *Bret Harte: Prince and Pauper* is at its best in these sections on Harte's later writing career when Nissen draws on an impressive array of primary sources and weaves them skillfully into his narrative. Nissen also provides an interesting reading (previously published in *Studies in Short Fiction*, Summer 1997) of "The Luck of Roaring Camp" as Harte's revision of the cult of domesticity described in Catharine Beecher and Harriet Beecher Stowe's *The American Woman's Home* (1869).

Less successful is a chapter called "The Scent of Heliotrope," in which Nissen speculates about Harte's sexuality. The evidence he marshals is both tenuous and circumstantial; for example, Nissen emphasizes Harte's contemporaries' reactions to his dandified ways, such as the lavender spats and yellow gloves that Hamlin Garland noted during an 1899 visit (252). Other such evidence includes Harte's carrying a heliotrope plant with him when he traveled; Nissen includes an epigraph establishing that the scent of heliotrope was a homoerotic code in the 1893 novel *Teleny*. Oddly enough, although he states that "there is no way of knowing" (241) whether Harte had homosexual relationships, Nissen dismisses out of hand an affair between Harte and Madame Van de Velde, with whom Harte lived and traveled for many years. Richard O'Connor, in *Bret Harte: A Biography* (Boston: Little, 1966), suggested that this relationship was "ambiguous" (254) and Scharnhorst, in *Bret Harte: Opening the American Literary West*, describes Harte as "[b]eyond a doubt . . . smitten" (165) with "Madame," as Harte and his family called her, but Nissen rules out "the possibility of a romantic liaison" (232) because Harte's son and his wife visited him at Madame's house on occasion. Yet this flawed logic measures the evidence with a double standard: if there is "no way of knowing" about Harte's relationships with men, surely there is equally "no way of knowing" about Harte's relationship with Madame Van de Velde. Nissen also sees the well-known theme of male bonding in Harte's works as evidence of homoerotic attachments, calling "In the Tules" a "blatantly homoerotic" (237) story written in response to the Oscar Wilde trials of 1895. But yellow gloves, the scent of a heliotrope, and a story of male bonding do not constitute a sexual identity, even in Oscar Wilde's London, and Nissen's conclusions here are provocative but unproven.

Although it appeared in dissertation form in 1996 and won the King of Norway's Gold Medal the next year, *Bret Harte: Prince and Pauper* will inevitably be compared with the other biography appearing in 2000, *Bret Harte: Opening the American Literary West*, by Gary Scharnhorst, editor of two collections of Harte's letters and author of numerous works on Harte. Nissen's thesis is different from Scharnhorst's, however, and if Nissen's book provides less information about the works and their reception than does Scharnhorst's, it is because Nissen's primary purpose is different. With its wealth of original sources, *Bret Harte: Prince and Pauper* successfully and sympathetically dramatizes the puzzling, contradictory, and mystifyingly self-destructive events in the life of this enigmatic author.

Donna M. Campbell
Gonzaga University

PALACE-BURNER: THE SELECTED POETRY OF SARAH PIATT. By Sarah Piatt. Edited by Paula Bernat Bennett. Urbana: U of Illinois P, 2001. lx + 280 pp. $29.95.

The publication of this collection of Sarah Morgan Piatt's poetry may well be the most important event in nineteenth-century American poetry since Mabel Loomis Todd and Colonel Higginson manhandled Emily Dickinson's poetry into print. Fortunately, Paula Bernat Bennett's excellent editorial work reveals Piatt's work almost as much as Higginson's obscured Dickinson's. How good is Piatt? One of the cover blurbs for the book claims that "Piatt is a major figure who deserves a place in the nineteenth-century canon next to Emily Dickinson and Edgar Allan Poe." But this is probably too kind to Poe.

Those familiar with Paula Bernat Bennett's work over the past decade, and the ongoing effort to recover nineteenth-century American women's writings, will be familiar with Piatt. She figures prominently in two important anthologies: Karen L. Kilcup's *Nineteenth-Century American Women Writers* (1997) and Bennett's own *Nineteenth-Century American Women Poets* (1998). With this volume, however, Bennett gives us the first widely available collection of Piatt's poetry since her work first appeared. Further, Bennett gives us a startling new look at Piatt, who, until Bennett began her work on Piatt, had been seen as a very minor genteel poet of the late 1800s (if seen at all—Piatt to date has not merited entries in such basic reference sources as *The Oxford Companion to American Literature* or *The Dictionary of Literary Biography*). However, Bennett has recovered a collection of complex poems—blending sentimental, romantic, and realist aesthetics—which were never collected into book form, appearing only in the political and literary journals in which Piatt originally placed them. This discovery spurred Bennett to go back to Piatt's books, where she found many poems couched in the guise of the genteel tradition that repay closer reading with the same kind of realism and complexity found in the poems from the periodicals. The result is a multivocal poet of broad range and considerable power who bridges the apparent gap between the poetry of the high romantics and that of the high modernists. Bennett notes the poetry's "stylistic anticipations of modernism" (xix), and indeed the voice in Piatt's poems often sounds like T. S. Eliot's (or more likely, T. S. Eliot often sounds like a Victorian American).

With the publication of this collection, Sarah Piatt unambiguously jumps to the front-rank of nineteenth-century American poets. Only Walt Whitman and Dickinson clearly outstrip her in power and originality. Yet Piatt's poetry is quite different from that of other American "masters." Her mature work begins with a firm rejection of both escapist romanticism and high sentimentality in favor of a polyvocal, premodern aesthetic that confronts loss and isolation directly.

Like Emily Dickinson, Piatt often uses a childlike voice to clothe troublesome insights and questions in innocence. But where Dickinson's speaker is childlike, Piatt's speakers are more often staid middle-class women interrogated by children. The best example of this dynamic is the title poem of the book (already the most frequently anthologized of Piatt's poems), in which a mother and child discuss a *Harper's* illustration of a female Parisian Communard about to be executed (she is the palace-burner). The child's easy enthusiasm for the palace-burner causes the mother to question her own sense of self:

> You would have burned the palace? Just because
> You did not live in it yourself! Oh! why?
> Have I not taught you to respect the laws?
> *You* would have burned the palace. Would not *I*?
> Would I? Go to your play. Would I, indeed?
> *I*? Does the boy not know my soul to be
> Languid and worldly, with a dainty need
> For light and music? Yet he questions me.
> Can he have seen my soul more near than I?
> (39–40)

In other poems, however, such as the wickedly funny "Mock Diamonds" (1872), women speak with clear-eyed realism, in contrast to the romantic fantasies of men. In "Mock Diamonds," a woman tours a seaside resort after the war with her new husband, pointing out antebellum male acquaintances to him, much to his discomfort: "The handsome man there with the scar?— / (Who bow'd to me? Yes, slightly)—" (29). The husband is distressed to find out that his idealized wife has a history, but she brushes off his fears, gently scolding: "Leave your sweet jealousy unsaid: / Your bright child's fading mother / And that guerrilla from—the dead? / Are nothing to each other" (30). The delight and humor in poems like this one come from the contrast between the female speaker's complete comfort with reality and the male listener's adherence to romanticism and decorum (though, even here, there is an undertone of sorrow; the speaker, after all, is "fading").

Like other well-known women poets of the time, especially Phoebe Cary and Frances Osgood, Piatt continually toys with the reader; we are never quite sure whether she is being blithe or scathingly ironic. And as the husband in "Mock Diamonds" must have felt for the rest of his married life, we are always a little nervous that we have just missed something. The capacity for sharp but subtle irony is an important resource for a poet who produces mainly genteel poetry. It forces us to read all her work more closely, an effort that goes to the heart of the major critical issue that Bennett raises in her introduction. Claiming that Piatt's poetry "can never be recuperated as part of [the] formalist 'high art' tradition" that includes Whitman, Poe, Ralph Waldo Emerson, Herman Melville, and such, Bennett argues, "To read Sarah Piatt as she should be read will mean, therefore, not only grasping her irony. It will also mean becoming considerably more open in what we look for and value in poetry itself. It will mean, that is, learning to read for values beside the word" (li).

Piatt's poetry may not exhibit the verbal freshness of Whitman and Dickinson, but I think Bennett sells Piatt short when she claims that "her strongest poetry is too rooted in her own ground, her own time, her own set of desperate and particular concerns: child death, Civil War, bad-faith marriages and bad-faith politics, romanticism gone sour, poetry and art that gild over the truth or exploit it for their own ends, children who lose their innocence before they even know they have it in a society that from its origins was saturated in violence and blood" (li). Presumably, by "too rooted" Bennett means that it cannot be read out of context, in the way that, say, Emily Dickinson's "Because I could not stop for Death—" has been read without the context of mid-nineteenth-century Calvinist New England attitudes toward courtship, gender, and death. This may be true. Piatt's poetry is not hauntingly evocative like Dickinson's, or exuberantly suggestive like Whitman's. But if Piatt does not give us a poetry of verbal fireworks, she does give us a poetry of psychological and social insight that does not merely present viewpoints, but rather, as Kenneth Burke says of poetry, dances an attitude. In Piatt's poetry, we see the mind *talking* through situations, deciding how it will react to the world. Bennett is right that Piatt's poetry is difficult, and Bennett's notes help make the poetry more accessible. This difficulty, however, is not because Piatt's poetry model is based in "particular concerns" such as death, war, love, politics, and art, but because she is a complex poet writing about the complex world in which she lives.

Piatt's strongest work is marked by both an unflinching realism and a very deep emotional involvement in the world. This is best seen in the poems about her own dead children, in which, as Bennett says, "she sends up howls of pain . . . not to be matched again in women's poetry until Sylvia Plath" (xlvii). In "Her Blindness in Grief," published in 1873, three months after her newborn baby died (this loss was the first of three such losses), the grieving mother remains "blind" to the consoling clichés offered to mothers in such circumstances. Like Emerson, who says of the death of his son Waldo, "The only thing grief has taught me, is to know how shallow it is," Piatt refuses to make meaning out of her child's death:

> The grief is bitter. Let me be.
> He lies beneath that lonesome tree.
> I've heard the fierce rain beating there.
> Night covers it with cold moonshine.
> Despair can only be despair.
> God has his will. I have not mine.
>
> (51)

The lines—the quick, sharp diction; the short sentences; the directness—are to my mind some of the most authentically human lines of nineteenth-century American poetry. Unlike the unsentimental romantics—such as Melville or Henry David Thoreau—Piatt confronts human grief and experience directly, without intellectual mediation. And unlike sentimental writers such as Harriet Beecher Stowe, in whose writing no child is anything but stunningly beautiful, Piatt does not try to heighten the pathos by talking about the child's beauty. Further, she turns sentimental clichés on their head. The dead child's hands are not "white as snow"; they are "still as snows" (51).

As anyone familiar with her scholarship would expect, Bennett has done a superb job reintroducing Piatt in this volume. It opens with a thorough introduction to the author's life and poetics, which Bennett calls dramatic realism. And the poems themselves are rendered more accessible by ample footnotes containing both textual variants and background information. This text will serve as an excellent foundation for scholarship on Sarah Piatt, of which there should be a great deal in the future.

Andrew C. Higgins
Louisiana Tech University

BOOK REVIEWS

DEAR MUNIFICENT FRIENDS: HENRY JAMES'S LETTERS TO FOUR WOMEN.
Edited by Susan E. Gunter. Ann Arbor: U of Michigan P, 1999. xxiv + 288 pp. $45.

DEARLY BELOVED FRIENDS: HENRY JAMES'S LETTERS TO YOUNGER MEN.
Edited by Susan E. Gunter and Steven H. Jobe. Ann Arbor: U of Michigan P, 2001.
xxiii + 249 pp. $29.95.

Slowly but surely the vast reservoir of Henry James's epistolarium dribbles its way into print. For years scholars have complained about the difficulty of accessing James's letters, thousands of which remain secreted in disparate archives, at the same time that the faltering editorial practice of the Master's privileged biographer—the late Leon Edel—has led many to question the textual reliability of even that fraction of the correspondence sluggishly published under Harvard's imprint over the course of what seemed like an interminable decade (*Henry James Letters*, ed. Leon Edel, 4 vols. [1974–84]). The two companionate volumes under consideration here immediately nestle comfortably among a series of recent books that have helped to rectify this glaring inadequacy in James studies. The two volumes rightfully deserve a place on the serious student's shelf next to Philip Horne's *Henry James: A Life in Letters* (1999); Michael Anesko's *Letters, Fictions, Lives: Henry James and William Dean Howells* (1997); George Monteiro's *The Correspondence of Henry James and Henry Adams* (1992); and Lyall Powers's *Henry James and Edith Wharton Letters* (1990). Somewhat in contrast to these other volumes, however, *Dear Munificent Friends* and *Dearly Beloved Friends* reveal a distinctly *non*literary side of Henry James— if, in fact, he can be said to have had one. Instead of the Anglo-American *Überschriftsteller*, we find a surprisingly domesticated Master, dealing with the dynamics of family life, the rituals of social intercourse, and even—just possibly—the snares of romantic entanglement. This is Henry James at his gossipy best.

Each of these volumes contains a useful biographical register to identify and provide historical context for persons frequently mentioned in the course of the correspondence. The reader will also find chronologies of dates and events relevant to James generally and also to particular addressees. The editors devote their respective indexes largely to proper names, but under the listings for James and his various correspondents we find entries broken down according to what could be called subject headings, and these give us the best sense of what kinds of information the books disclose. In Susan E. Gunter's volume, the editor links James's name to "dental work," "dogs," "domestic arrangements," "food," "gardening," "health," "interior decorating," "marriage," and "shopping," besides the more expected topics of "drama," "travel," and "World War I." Specific references to titles of James's books—apart from those found in the editorial matter—number only thirteen. Because at least two of James's "younger men" were themselves writers, *Dearly Beloved Friends* has a somewhat more literary cast. But even here the compilers' preference favors the personal over the professional. The editorial ears prick up at James's suggestively erotic phrasing, even though, as Gunter and

Steven H. Jobe confess, "the reader who seeks herein the single sustained note of ardor will be disappointed" (xii).

In *Dear Munificent Friends*, Gunter proceeds on the assumption that the writer's letters to his intimates (as opposed to his professional colleagues) "hold the key to understanding Henry James the person because in them he wrote most freely" (x). Even if this were true, one would have to say that the documentary evidence contained in these volumes does not always support this conclusion. The lasting impression made by James's letters (whether "munificent" or "beloved") suggests that for him the epistolary gesture was always and inescapably performative. While the range of poses, attitudes, and impersonations one finds in James's correspondence helps immeasurably to humanize him, these same idiosyncrasies give the letters a theatrical—as opposed to confessional—air. The interest of these documents probably inheres less in *what* James says than in *how* he says it.

The four female recipients of James's postal attentions whom Gunter gathers together are his sister-in-law Alice Howe Gibbens James (1849–1922), the wife of William James; Mary Cadwalader Rawle Jones (1850–1935), with whom James traded notes about *her* sister-in-law, Edith Wharton; Margaret Frances Butcher Prothero (1854–1934), his occasional country neighbor in the village of Rye and wife of George Prothero, an English academic and man of letters; and Lady Louisa Erskine Wolseley (1843–1920), wife of the commander-in-chief of British forces in Ireland. *Dear Munificent Friends* does not pretend to be comprehensive; only a selection of James's letters to each of these women is included and none of theirs to him—presumably because James destroyed them. While the desire to print previously unpublished material is understandable, some of James's best letters are left out of the sequences—such as the extraordinary one of 20 August 1902 to Mary Cadwalader Jones (previously published in volume 4 of Edel's *Henry James Letters*), in which he insists that Edith Wharton should forsake historical romance in favor of the American world around her. "She *must* be tethered in native pastures," James implored, "even if it reduce her to a back-yard in New York" (237)—timely advice for a novelist who had yet to write *The House of Mirth* (1905). Still, one has to be grateful for the information that these epistolary unveilings bring forward. The letters to Alice H. G. James, especially, give new texture to the complicated relations among members of the James clan while those to female friends outside the family flash with wit, insight, and the anticipated flourishes of style. "We all have a lurking Vesuvius in the landscape of our lives," he writes consolingly to Mary Cadwalader Jones, "with our best Bays of Naples more or less at the mercy of it!" (147).

James's letters to his "younger" male correspondents are qualitatively different—less socially chatty and more trustingly intimate. Clearly, James felt that he could confide—and reveal—himself more to men than to women. As he tells one male correspondent after the death of his sister, Alice, in 1892, "It makes me wince—it makes me even surreptitiously shudder—to hear of 'kind women' talking of my affairs—& talking of them apparently with compassion—a sentiment that does a deep violence to the innermost parts of my being. But they mean well doubtless—& that is just when women are most deadly" (James to William Morton Fullerton, n.d. [1892], by permission of the Houghton Library, Harvard University [bMS Am 1094.1 (112)]). Gunter and Jobe unashamedly classify *Dear Munificent Friends* as a collection of love letters, but they also provide an extremely useful cautionary note on the first page of their concise—and psychologically shrewd—introduction:

The prevailing tenor of each group of letters is warmly adhesive, to resurrect by way of Whitman a phrenological term sufficiently broad to encompass the varieties of James's same-sex affections and attractions. But that is not to say that the letters are uniformly or unvaryingly passionate or erotic in tone or content. . . . James's language of attraction and desire, of commitment and convergence, is always contending with divergent forces that were anything but subtle or erotic: his final decades of alternating bouts of good and ill health, circumstances of proximity and distance, clashing tastes and wills and temperaments, and the inevitably disparate needs of relative youth and age. (xi–xii)

Not many of James's recent critics—so eager to expose his homoerotic leanings—share this kind of tact.

In the longest sequence of letters in *Dearly Beloved Friends*, James addresses Hendrik Andersen (1872–1940), a Norwegian-American sculptor of monumental (almost proto-Fascist) nudes, in whom the writer developed a rather improbable interest after their meeting at Rome in 1899 (though *Roderick Hudson* [1875] uncannily anticipates it). It is almost grotesque to see James cultivating a relationship with someone so curiously illiterate. Again and again he begs his young friend *not* to answer his letters; and, judging from the frequently pathetic extracts from Andersen's papers that the editors cite in footnotes, it is not hard to see why: whatever his physical or artistic gifts, the poor boy simply could not spell. When Andersen had the temerity to ask James for a copy of *The Wings of the Dove* (1902), the novelist wasted no time in warning him off: "I am forgetting to say that *now*—only now—my ponderous & long-winded book goes to you, since you so gallantly ask for it. I haven't thought it *fair* to send it sooner—fair, I mean, to the fact that you may possibly attempt, really, to read it. But *don't*, my dear Hendrik, do that—it will lay you low in the flower of your youth. Put it on your table, if you like, that the world may see I've sent it to you; but don't think [it] necessary to plough *through* it" (43). Not exactly a publisher's blurb, is it? But what an unexpected comfort to those who deplore James's later mandarin style!

Some of the other letters collected here—addressed to Jocelyn Persse (1873–1943), Howard Sturgis (1855–1920), and Hugh Walpole (1884–1941)—can rival this one in condescension. Especially notable are those directed at Sturgis, whose faults as a novelist James irrepressibly skewers. "I am a bad person, really," James admits, "to expose 'fictitious work' to—I, as a battered producer & 'technician' myself, have long since inevitably ceased to read with *naïveté*; I can only read critically, constructively, *re*-constructively, writing the thing over (if I can swallow it at all) *my* way, & looking at it, so to speak, from within. But even thus I 'pass' your book very—tenderly!" (131). The final em-dash might as well have been a stiletto. Sturgis decided to withdraw the book (*Belchamber* [1904])—only then to receive James's strongest words of encouragement! "Why should you have an inspiration so perverse & so criminal?" James wondered. "If it springs from anything I have said to you I must have expressed myself with strange & deplorable clumsiness" (136). The book appeared, but Sturgis published very little afterward.

The texts in both editions are generally reliable, although errors of transcription from James's notoriously difficult hand inevitably occur. Some might strike even a casual reader because of the uncharacteristic awkwardness that they occasion in

James's style. Writing to Howard Sturgis from his brother's country house at Chocorua, New Hampshire, James notes that he will stay with his family "till one of the last days of Sept., but Mrs. Wharton has held you out to me as a bait at Lenox and I have opened my month wide to the prospect of the same for 2 or 3 days" (138). Is "month" an uncorrected typo? Or is it, instead, a misreading of *mouth*, which James actually wrote? Quantitatively—and comparatively—speaking, I have discovered more errors in *Dear Munificent Friends*, and also some uninformed editorial guesswork. Writing to his sister-in-law in the midst of his American lecture tour in 1905, James was almost overwhelmed by the welcoming reception he found at Chicago, and he relayed his response to Alice with these words: "I have lectured twice here with brilliant success (unmistakably,) & the hospitality & importunity of the people touches me, really, brings tears to my eyes by its largeness, frankness &, as <c.r.u.?> would say, sweetness, even while it exhausts & prostrates me" (52). The Arnoldian criterion of "sweetness" can only be associated with Charles Eliot Norton—a longtime friend and neighbor of the James family in Cambridge—whose initials James has written in a downwardly sloping hand at the margin of his sheet.

Though modern editors sometimes seem wary of excessive annotation, there are many instances here where additional information would be helpful and others where misinformation has been given. A comparative tally of these would also be lopsided, as *Dear Munificent Friends* more frequently leaves the reader at a loss about the context of James's remarks. When James confides to Mary Cadwalader Jones that he has had "a lone, lorn, stranded & rather oppressive, though appreciative old friend" (154) with him at Christmastide 1909, the reader might very well like to know with whom he shared his turkey. The answer is not all that hard to find, either, since *The Complete Notebooks of Henry James* (1987) reveals James's visitor to be T. Bailey Saunders, a journalist who was having marital troubles. When James is on his way from the Riviera to Italy as a guest of the ever-ambulant Whartons, he writes to Sturgis that he still manages to make room for serious work, "which has not been all a matter of proofs, but a much tougher & as yet unfinished job" (147). The editors hypothesize, "The 'tougher & as yet unfinished job' might be pages he later added to his *Italian Hours* (1909) memorializing his journey" (171n77), but someone more familiar with James's work habits would know that he was then working his way through the voluminous proofs for The New York Edition and, at that moment, meticulously revising the text of *The Princess Casamassima* (cf. Hershel Parker, "Henry James 'In the Wood': Sequence and Significances of His Literary Labors, 1905–1907," *Nineteenth-Century Fiction* 38 [1984]: 505).

Editorial quibbles aside, most readers will find much to enjoy in these two handsome books, beautifully dust-jacketed and illustrated to boot. The editors are surely right when they assert that James ranks among the best letter writers in English; and their diligent labors have given us even more proof of that.

Michael Anesko
The Pennsylvania State University, University Park

THE CRUX: A NOVEL BY CHARLOTTE PERKINS GILMAN. Edited by Jennifer S. Tuttle. Newark, DE: University of Delaware P, 2002. 242 pp. $42.50.

If Charlotte Perkins Gilman (1860–1935) had never written another word after the publication of "The Yellow Wall-Paper" in 1892, her place in American literary history would still be secure. Gilman, did, however, publish prodigiously, and despite the fact that she fell into literary obscurity for nearly half a century, many of her works—short stories, poems, novels, diaries, and nonfiction books and essays—have been recovered and reprinted in recent decades, spawning scores of additional studies, articles, and conference papers. The revival of interest in Gilman, dating back to 1966, when Carl N. Degler published a reprint of Gilman's feminist treatise *Women and Economics* (1898), is still going strong and shows no signs of waning.

Gilman would likely be surprised—and pleased—by the renewed interest in her life and legacy. In her posthumously published autobiography, *The Living of Charlotte Perkins Gilman* (1935), she related a conversation that she exchanged with William Dean Howells when he asked her permission to include "The Yellow Wall-Paper" in his 1920 collection, *The Great Modern American Stories*. Gilman gave her consent but contended that the story was no different from her other works, since all of it was written with a specific purpose in mind.

An avowed social reformist who used her literature to advance various causes, Gilman infused her writing with what she deemed to be practical solutions to common problems. While her didacticism may not share the pulpit-pounding qualities of the sermons penned by her famous Beecher relatives, Gilman still managed to drive her point home. (Writer Mary Austin once complained that everything Gilman wrote was in the same key.) Indeed, with the exception of "The Yellow Wall-Paper" and a handful of other works, the majority of Gilman's writings are heavily formulaic and didactic. When she began having trouble placing her writing in the early part of the twentieth century—in large part because of her often heavy-handed moralizing—Theodore Dreiser suggested that Gilman tailor her writing to the demands of the contemporary marketplace. Rejecting Dreiser's advice, Gilman instead began her own magazine, *The Forerunner*, in print from 1909 to 1916. It was the venue in which much of her work first appeared, including *The Crux*, which was originally serialized in twelve installments in 1911 and published in a single volume later that year. An engaging novel that follows a group of women who escape the oppressive traditions of conservative New England by journeying west and beginning anew in a decidedly more progressive Colorado town, *The Crux* is among the latest of Gilman's works to be reprinted.

Meticulously edited by Jennifer S. Tuttle, this edition of *The Crux* features an eloquent and illuminating sixty-four-page critical introduction that offers various contexts for Gilman's novel, including Gilman's own biography and the genre of "The Western," long considered the province of the male writer. Tuttle persuasively argues that because the West played a critical role in allowing Gilman to regain her health when she traveled there in the late 1880s following a severe bout of neurasthenia, the setting is intricately connected to one of the major themes—the reclamation of selfhood—woven throughout the novel. Tuttle establishes clearly the gendered assumptions about the causes of neurasthenia and explores the dichotomy between the female "rest cure," which called for extended bed rest and the deprivation of intellectual activity, and the traditionally male "West cure," which encouraged male patients to travel west, to immerse themselves in the great outdoors, and to engage in physical activity. Using the example of writer Owen Wister, author of *The Virginian* (1902), who thrived on the curative powers of the West after seeking treatment for neurasthenia, Tuttle notes that through her Western setting, Gilman "calls the West Cure's gendered elements into question, and challenges by extension dominant cultural and medical views of healthy femininity" (45). Moreover, Tuttle does not shy away from addressing Gilman's darker side; rather, she exposes the racist, ethnocentric, and classist attitudes that often made Gilman insensitive to the plight of marginalized groups. The presence of those attitudes, Tuttle notes, has the potential to detract from an "otherwise compelling argument for women's sexual and medical self-determination" (56).

At the center of *The Crux* is the fictional heroine, Vivian Lane, a young product of conservative New England who, at the urging of a friend and mentor, Dr. Jane Bellair, relocates to Colorado. There she rekindles a romance with Morton Elder, with whom she had enjoyed a budding relationship some nine years earlier. Vivian is unaware, however, that since his departure from New England, Morton has contracted syphilis. When Dr. Bellair learns that Vivian plans to marry the syphilitic Morton, she confides Morton's medical status to Vivian. Brokenhearted by the disclosure, Vivian faces the classic struggle between the heart and the intellect. She is torn between her promise to marry Morton and the more rational action of breaking the engagement.

Not only does Gilman examine gendered assumptions about the West in *The Crux*, but also, more significantly—and consistent with her determination that her writing serve a useful purpose—she uses the novel to explore the impact of venereal disease on women in the early twentieth century. As Tuttle remarks, Gilman argued vehemently that the conventional mind-set, which placed female "innocence" about sexual diseases at a premium, was tragically misguided; and it "formed part of a sexual double standard that made [women] even more vulnerable to infection" (29) because they were uninformed about such matters as disease transmission. As she did in much of her fiction, Gilman used *The Crux* as a mouthpiece to trumpet a cause and to promote awareness of a critical medical condition about which she believed women needed to be educated.

The Crux was not alone in its early-twentieth-century treatment of venereal disease. Gilman herself would examine the issue again in such stories as "Wild Oats and Tame Wheat" (1913) and "The Vintage" (1916). Moreover, Tuttle notes, such works as James Oppenheim's novel *Wild Oats* (1910) and Eugene Brieux's play *Damaged Goods* (1913) were part of a growing literary tradition that examined the impact of sexually transmitted diseases. But, as Tuttle explains, Gilman used *The Crux* to explore not only "the social conditions leading to [the] perpetuation or eradication" of venereal diseases, but also "its symptoms and consequences" (35). Gilman was particularly incensed that there seemed to be a cultural imperative to keep women ignorant about STDs. Tuttle argues that "Gilman's critique of her culture's traditional handling of venereal disease" is in keeping with "her other attacks on the medical discourse of her time and the repressive gender ideology that underlay it. She criticizes not only the physical, psychological, and material damage such discourse does to women, but also the outdated belief system that justifies such treatment. Her novel presents itself as a practical manual offering her readers an alternative approach to the disease itself, as well as to social organization as a whole" (35–36).

Tuttle's superb editing of *The Crux* is a most welcome addition to the growing body of works by Gilman that have been recovered. Tuttle's well-researched critical introduction and her judicious use of explanatory notes makes this cautionary tale about the potential price of female innocence well worth reading during an age when much of the population continues to view venereal disease with either naiveté or denial. As a valuable commentary on gender issues, medical discourse, and American literary history, *The Crux* is highly recommended for all libraries.

Denise Knight
State University of New York, Cortland

PUBLISHING THE FAMILY. By June Howard. Durham: Duke UP, 2001. xiv + 336 pp. $18.95.

THE WHOLE FAMILY: A NOVEL BY TWELVE AUTHORS. By William Dean Howells, Mary E. Wilkins Freeman, Mary Heaton Vorse, Mary Stewart Cutting, Elizabeth Jordan, John Kendrick Bangs, Henry James, Elizabeth Stuart Phelps, Edith Wyatt, Mary Raymond Shipman Andrews, Alice Brown, and Henry Van Dyke. Introduction by Alfred Bendixen. Foreword by June Howard. Durham: Duke UP, 2001. li + 341 pp. $18.95.

Taken together, June Howard's *Publishing the Family* and Duke University Press's reprint of *The Whole Family* constitute a provocative case history for scholars and teachers. The latter book brings back into print the 1908 "composite novel" that Alfred Bendixen first contextualized for a contemporary audience in a 1986 reprint by Ungar Press. William Dean Howells proposed the collaborative project to Elizabeth Jordan, editor of *Harper's Bazaar*, suggesting a serial in which each participating author would examine a given story from the perspective of a different family member. He also suggested authors and proposed basic story elements such as the plot of a daughter's engagement, the issue of coeducation, and the composition of the family. The resulting production is notable for many reasons: the participants (Henry James accepted, but Mark Twain declined), the compositional wrangling over character and plot (including a "maiden aunt" who dramatically refuses the old maid stereotype), the behind-the-scenes authorial commentaries, and in general the modern commercial spectacle of it all. Situated clearly by

Bendixen's contextual materials, the project takes on the appearance of a postmodern "reality TV" gimmick in which performers' collaborations and conflicts are monitored from various angles. Indeed, Bendixen says that "[a]lmost all the reviewers compared the book to some kind of game" (xxxv), and one reviewer, Howard notes, called it "pure vaudeville" (*Publishing the Family* 104).

Bendixen's claim—echoed on the new back cover—that *The Whole Family* is "the result of one of the most fascinating literary experiments in the history of American writing" would seem to be an exaggeration, given the paucity of attention paid to it in the century since it was written. However, the novel certainly warrants easy availability for scholarly use and a more conspicuous place in literary history. If nothing else, it has the historical value (and perhaps even virtue) of making its own production explicit. As Howard states in her foreword to the novel, "*The Whole Family* dramatizes, almost literalizes, cultural critics' notion of the 'social text': narrative as a site on which struggles between historical positions are played out" (vi). The novel is always discussed first in terms of its performance and only secondarily in terms of its representations. Moreover, having multiple authors makes its representations uniquely contingent; they remain potential stories rather than necessary ones. And unlike other novels of the time, which passed from magazine serial to book form without a trace, *The Whole Family* embodies the fragmentation of its original commercial production and context. "To understand this novel," Howard insists, "we must give up any notion that the business of publishing is separate from the art of writing" (viii). By the same token, the text embodies and reveals a "heterosocial" literary marketplace that was "gender-inflected but not divided into separate spheres" (*Publishing the Family* 35). And certainly the authors—William Dean Howells, Mary E. Wilkins Freeman, Mary Heaton Vorse, Mary Stuart Cutting, Jordan, John Kendrick Bangs, James, Elizabeth Stuart Phelps, Edith Wyatt, Mary Raymond Shipman Andrews, Alice Brown, and Henry Van Dyke—represent other heterogeneities and homogeneities and historical entanglements worthy of examination and exploration.

This is not a new edition of *The Whole Family* in any substantial sense; it retains Bendixen's introduction and appendix (short biographical information on all twelve authors) from the Ungar edition and simply adds a brief foreword by Howard suggesting the novel's unique interest as social history. Duke also keeps the layout and pagination from the Ungar text, which was itself a reprinting of the original Harper & Brothers layout. The real scholarly significance of this latest reprint, of course, is as a ready accompaniment to Howard's thorough and engaging study of the novel in *Publishing the Family*. Actually, Howard treats the composite novel as a subject of "microhistorical" analysis—as "an extraordinary point of entry for an examination of print culture and social life in the early twentieth century" (2). Therefore, *Publishing the Family* "is not a book 'about' *The Whole Family*," but rather a book about "a historical process refracted through an episode" (3). Treating the novel as a prism reveals a spectrum of historical components that become discrete chapters of her book: the cultural situation of authors, the Harper & Brothers publishing house, the status and function of the family, the figure of the New Woman, and the nature and role of sentiment. Each chapter follows its chosen historical threads (the metaphor is Howard's) in considerable detail and yet with admirable clarity, in the process raising suggestive connections—and, occasionally, inspiring fruitful objections.

The major historical and cultural thread that Howard traces, as her title suggests, is the family, and this traverses and connects the other topics in various intriguing ways. She notes that the magazine marketplace fashioned reading into a family of choices, "soliciting the interest and purchasing power of men, women, and children separately, yet uniting them through their complementary participation in cultural consumption" (73). She gives examples of the widely varied professional advice by *Harper's Bazaar*, aimed at both "the up-to-date woman" and "countless women of less experience, less opportunity, [and] simpler ideas" (36–37), which helped to invent the modern family. In this context, "*The Whole Family* is revealed as a rather brilliant variation on the *Bazaar* formula of combining distinguished visitors with familiar voices to provide authoritative and vivid accounts of home life" (115). On a broader level, the novel and its contexts demonstrate that "the modern family form comes into being on social grounds partially constituted and ceaselessly traversed by print" (107). In addition to dramatizing a family, the participants in *The Whole Family* spoke of themselves as a kind of family, and each brought unique biographical and artistic concerns to the table. Similarly, pervasive family imagery was used to conceptualize the "House of Harper" (68). Howard examines the evolving ideal of the "companionate marriage" (112) and the concomitant realm of "masculine domesticity" (120), as well as the effects of new or "sometimes-new" (158) women on conceptions of family.

Publishing the Family pursues these basic subjects by engaging rich historical contexts, backgrounds, and connections. Howard's examination of Jordan as a professional woman is particularly useful historical material that brilliantly illuminates Howard's subtle explorations of gender. Similarly, the chapter on Harper & Brothers gathers material and cultural history in very suggestive ways. Chapter 5 combines a long examination of the concepts of sentiment and sentimentalism with contemporary scientific work in fields such as neurology and "the sociology of emotions" (219). Another strength is Howard's attention to material culture in such forms as Mansard roofs, Victorian sideboards, and the Arts and Crafts movement.

This constellation of interdisciplinary concerns connects in interesting ways to other work being done and should make her book of interest to scholars in many fields. It is notable that the cover of *Publishing the Family* features a painting by Ethel Pennewill Brown, "Girl with Red Fan," which appeared on the cover of the July 1908 issue of *Harper's Bazaar*. The painting shows a young woman with an enigmatic expression sitting in the foreground while three children play in the sun behind her. Howard considers it "the most striking cover of the period," admires how it captures the indistinct boundaries between private and public for this "possibly-new, sometimes-new woman," and calls it "the most evocative image of the necessary paradox I have called 'publishing the family'" (198). Howard knew only slight biographical information about the artist, however (see 297n23), and she therefore left this historical thread intuited rather than pursued. But art historian Jann Haynes Gilmore spent years researching Brown, whose married name was Leach, and Gilmore's biography (*Ethel Pennewill Brown Leach, Delaware Artist of Time, Place, and Season* [*Delaware History*, Fall-Winter 1998–99, Spring-Summer 1999]) reveals numerous provocative ways in which Ethel Pennewill Brown Leach's life resonates with Howard's conception of the "sometimes-new woman" (158). Gilmore's most recent work has expanded to include the art colony in Rehoboth Beach, Delaware, in which Ethel Leach was a central figure, and many other "almost forgotten" women artists in the region, all of whom constitute fascinating microhistorical subjects. ("Almost Forgotten" was the title of an art exhibition featuring the works of these artists.) Howard's study points toward such painstaking localized investigations, as well as the ways in which they connect to—indeed, constitute—the emergence of the national and international culture seen in and through the magazines.

Howard's treatment of these recursive subjects is admirably nuanced. In particular, she consistently emphasizes the "irregular complexity of historical process" (5) in which individuals (and even more so "families") are an amalgamation of "attitudes and practices thought of as following one another in a historical sequence" but that "in fact coexist" (96). However, this self-described "eclectic" analysis (7) does at times trigger questions and objections. Sometimes the issues are theoretical, as when she alternates between understanding the family as antisocial (following the socialist feminism of Michèle Barrett and Mary McIntosh) and as anti-individual, particularly toward women (following liberal feminist critiques). This would seem to be an important political knot to unravel, even if—especially if—the critical goal is "a marxism without guarantees" (4). At other times, the issues are questionable empirical observations. One of these observations would be the overly simple equation between the novel family and Howells's beliefs. Speaking of how the family's mother is critiqued by Freeman's portrayal of the single woman, Howard says that "Ada's world—which is Howells's—is not just superficial but delusory" (132). In fact, Howells's publications and letters amply demonstrate how intricately he observed middle-class life and how vehemently he judged his own class status.

However, the appearance of these and other issues is completely consistent with Howard's conviction that "the value of American studies is precisely that it is such a well-established site for relentlessly experimental and self-reflective dialogue" (3). Indeed, Howard's exemplary clarity, modesty, and self-consciousness about her interdisciplinary methods make *Publishing the Family* a particularly useful case history, and the fact that she sometimes presents her methodological concerns in broad strokes that beg theoretical questions only contributes to the work's usefulness. We may observe that she envisions her method of grouping analysis around a single text as "a more stubbornly empirical approach" than the now-familiar American studies method of "track[ing] one complex and consequential idea through many sites" (3). (Jackson Lears's latest book, *Something for Nothing: Luck in America* [2003], is evidence that the "complex and consequential idea" approach is still prominent.) It is not theoretically evident, however, how choosing a single site of study is more empirical than choosing a single idea—or, indeed, if the distinction is accurate, given (for example) Howard's recursive examination of the idea of "family" in different venues, or her reliance on intellectual history to contextualize the meanings of sentimentalism. Defining her work as microhistory is similarly puzzling, as historians who claim to practice microhistory typically point toward contemporary literary analysis as their inspiration—which would appear to make the label tautological for literary history. Howard makes clear that she is writing for an interdisciplinary audience, and no doubt this audience influences her choice of labels and explanations. Literary scholars, at any rate, will recognize her work to be the historical and interdisciplinary close reading characteristic of new historicism and cultural studies. Howard holds up her methodological practices and goals for clear scrutiny and thus makes them an integral part of her project.

Ultimately, then, Howard leaves the reader with complex patterns and connections rather than definitive conclusions. The result is a richly suggestive scholarly resource that can also serve well (together with the reprint of *The Whole Family*) as a teaching tool in the vein of case studies or Norton critical editions.

Gib Prettyman
The Pennsylvania State University, Fayette

LYRICS OF SUNSHINE AND SHADOW: THE TRAGIC COURTSHIP AND MARRIAGE OF PAUL LAURENCE DUNBAR AND ALICE RUTH MOORE, A HISTORY OF LOVE AND VIOLENCE AMONG THE AFRICAN AMERICAN ELITE. By Eleanor Alexander. New York: New York UP, 2001. 241 pp. $27.95.

> We wear the mask that grins and lies,
> It hides our cheeks and shades our eyes,—
> —Paul Laurence Dunbar

I am always delighted to see a new book about Paul Laurence Dunbar, and we have recently been given two books about him, both quite good and well worth the read. I am delighted with *In His Own Voice: The Dramatic and Other Uncollected Works by Paul Lawrence Dunbar* (2002), edited by Herbert Woodward Martin and Robert Primeau. The other is the volume by Eleanor Alexander presently under review.

Dunbar's wrestling with dialect poetry and standard English verse epitomize his relationship to the larger culture; he is truly the captive bird. It is not possible to think or write of Dunbar without acknowledging the complex dialectics of this son of former slaves who wrestled in such a complicated way with stereotypes of race and gender, in both his public and his private life. In both aspects, he was a man of his times.

As Alexander's book reveals for the first time, Dunbar was also invested in some aspects of turn-of-the-century patriarchal privilege that would make him virtually unmarriageable by today's standards. Alexander's book also gives the reader to understand that Dunbar violently raped his fiancée, possibly to force her into a position in which she could not break off an already somewhat-shaky engagement. This "one damned night of folly," Alexander argues, sowed the seeds for their future divorce.

When I wrote the introduction to the *Collected Poetry of Paul Laurence Dunbar* in 1993, I did not know that Dunbar could be a whining, manipulative, and sometimes violent man. I had chosen to focus on the poems themselves, the actual work written, with a goal of returning work long out of print to the reading public. I was satisfied to know that, though separated from Paul at the time, Alice Ruth Moore continued to write favorably of her former husband and to speak of him as a dear friend. I accepted Gloria Hull's assertion in *Give Us Each Day* (ed. Gloria T. Hull [New York: Norton, 1984]) that theirs was a "storytale" romance and courtship. And yet, I found things that hinted at another Dunbar. Every Dunbar critic knows the poem, "We Wear the Mask" (published in *Majors and Minors* [Toledo: Hadley & Hadley, 1895], 21), but I found a level of masking in Dunbar's life and work that, potentially, at least, went beyond the racial. And I kept it to myself. I shared the evidence, but withheld the analysis.

Meanwhile, despite the publication of Alice's diary and other volumes representing her work, we know considerably less about Alice Moore Dunbar Nelson than we do about Paul Laurence Dunbar, her first husband (of three husbands). That she was a beautiful Creole woman of mixed ancestry scholars agree. But though she published poetry, short stories, and essays of her own, "one notices," as Gloria Hull remarked, that, "during her entire career, she received attention for being Paul Lawrence Dunbar's wife and widow and not necessarily for her own achievement" (19).

Her diary, *Give Us Each Day*, edited by Hull and published in 1984, was only the second by a black woman to have appeared up to that time. "When he was alive," continued Hull, "she was thought of as the wife who incidentally 'wrote a little herself,' a secondary status she sometimes buttressed by her different poses and feminine role-playing." Why did she continue to carry his name, even after they were divorced, Hull asks. And she answers her own question: "[U]pon reflection it becomes clear that Dunbar-Nelson did this partly because of her awareness that, in a racist, sexist society, it could be helpful" (*Give Us Each Day* 19).

Add homophobic society. Because the real bombshell in Hull's edited volume was the revelation that Alice Dunbar-Nelson, teacher, club woman, and author, had, following her divorce from Dunbar, not only a secret marriage to a man twelve years her junior, but also at least two amorous relationships with women. This was virtually unknown before the publication of *Give Us Each Day*.

Hull struggled with her decision to leave the controversial material in the book, but decided, against the expressed wishes of Dunbar-Nelson's niece, to let the truth, as truth it was, stand. This revelation made many readers extremely uncomfortable, and while I praised Hull in *The Women's Review of Books* (July 1985) for advancing literary scholarship, I chided her, in our private correspondence, for "outing" the wife of my beloved Dunbar.

Now Eleanor Alexander has one-upped Hull, revealing the "tragic courtship and marriage" of Paul and Alice Dunbar. That Dunbar raped his fiancée, and that he told his friends and literary acquaintances that he had conjugal relations with Alice when she would have remained silent about the whole mess, I could not believe. And then I read from a letter quoted by Alexander in her *Lyrics of Sunshine and Shadow*: "[M]y heart cries out to you, Alice—Alice my darling. I wish I had died before it happened. . . . You will get better, dear. God will not let you suffer long for this sin of which I am the sole author. . . . Try to forgive me and believe in me again. I will never drink again, so help me God! . . . for God's sake rally and get well. Spare no expense. It will be my right to pay your bills. One thing dear be easy about, you are not with child. I was too drunk for *flow*. I might have told you before but I was ashamed even half-drunk as I was of my *own* bestiality" (130–31).

My Paul, my gentle Paul! Could it be that he was indeed a womanizer and a drunkard, not because of alcohol prescribed for tuberculosis, but because he loved drink? Could it be that Alice's mother opposed the marriage, not only because of Paul's dark skin, but also because of these real faults, and because he was always in debt?

There can be no arguing with Alexander's assertion that "Paul's broadcasting of his sexual conquest of Alice ruined her chances of making a suitable match elsewhere, for she was no longer a commodity in the marriage market" (131). I am still unprepared to think of noble Alice, who had a penchant for elegance and grace in all things, as a victim. But Paul, my *gentle* Mr. Dunbar! Can he be a myth—a figment of imagination and desire, a myth in a starched shirt and a tuxedo, peering out at me from inside a book cover? Alexander paints a portrait that I had not seen before, challenging accepted perceptions and raising new questions.

Despite my initial response, I must agree that Alexander's book is both fascinating and useful. Despite the fact that she seemingly "tells all," she argues that "the scope of *Lyrics of Sunshine and Shadow* is not limited to the Dunbars' romance." She writes, "The Dunbars did not live, love and eventually hate in a vacuum. The same external factors shaping their courtship and marriage enveloped the lives of other elite African Americans. . . . While I focus on the two poets, their complicated union is a means of analyzing the culture of middle-class African American courtship and marriage at the turn of the twentieth century. . . . Romantic love, courtship, and marriage are cultural products of specific eras" (5–6). In the course of these five chapters, we learn about the impact of race and racism on African American intimacy at the turn of the twentieth century.

Alexander generally writes from a psychological or psychosocial, rather than a literary, perspective. Do Paul's violent beatings by his father in childhood forecast his later physical brutality toward his wife, who received medical treatment from injuries that she may have sustained from him? What anxieties did the light-skinned Alice have about her attraction to the very dark-skinned Paul? Is it true that she generally disliked people of Paul's dark complexion, and does this book adequately explain why she married him anyway? Alexander uses letters, poems, and autobiographical data to examine what she calls "gender role dynamics" and the "etiquette of courtship" and to investigate "gendered responses" to sexual and spousal abuse. "The intimate history of elite African Americans is new territory," she argues. Nevertheless, when reading this book, I have the sense of being a voyeur. It is rather like looking into the bedroom of somebody's grandmother. Still, this is new territory, and worth the pain-filled and sometimes embarrassing view. The challenge is large.

In my earlier writing, while reviewing Hull's work on Alice, I argued that everything about a writer is important, whether we want to know or not, and that the perspective and/or prejudices of the critic are important, too. Still, I am saddened that as new books *about* Dunbar appear on the scene, sales of *The Collected Poetry of Paul Laurence Dunbar* (1993), which I edited, have declined. Sound like sour grapes? Maybe. But consider this: more people may be reading *about* Dunbar than reading work *by* him. And this, to my mind, would make for a most unfavorable situation indeed, for literary and other forms of scholarship.

Case in point: Why has no one in the ten years since the appearance of *The Collected Poetry* examined Dunbar's poem "Comrade," which I published from an undated manuscript source at the Ohio Historical Society? From all appearances, this is a homoerotic poem written from one man to another. Perhaps this poem and the questions raised by it are outside the scope of Alexander's study, but maybe not, especially when we know what we do about Alice's capacity to love across boundaries of color, class, and even gender. If Paul were similarly complicated, would it not add another level to our understanding of his marriage with Alice? And does such a question merit further inquiry, no matter what the conclusion? The poetry must be read, and that more carefully.

Joanne Braxton
College of William and Mary

AN EXEMPLARY CITIZEN: LETTERS OF CHARLES W. CHESNUTT, 1906–1932. Edited by Jesse S. Crisler, Robert C. Leitz III, and Joseph R. McElrath Jr. Stanford, CA: Stanford UP, 2002. xxxiv + 328 pp. $60.

CHARLES W. CHESNUTT AND THE FICTIONS OF RACE. By Dean McWilliams. Athens: U of Georgia P, 2002. xii + 261 pp. $39.95.

Since the early 1990s, interest in the work of African American writer Charles W. Chesnutt (1858–1932) has accelerated at a truly remarkable rate. A century ago, one could have readily described Chesnutt as a quintessential "race man." A friend to both W. E. B. Du Bois and Booker T. Washington, Chesnutt devoted much time and energy to championing the rights of African Americans. A century later, Chesnutt remains the quintessential race man, but now it is because his writings so thoroughly interrogate the idea of race. In writing about the "color line," Chesnutt demonstrates the permeability of this supposedly impermeable boundary and the ways in which a supposedly rigid linearity is repeatedly challenged by class, gender, national origins, and ideology. Chesnutt may not have suited then-modern tastes, but his writing resonates among postmodernists, and Chesnutt now matters more than ever.

It need also be said that Chesnutt looms larger because his corpus is now significantly larger than it was barely a decade ago. New scholarly resources began with the *Journals* (1993), edited by Richard Brodhead. In 1999, Jesse S. Crisler, Robert C. Leitz III, and Joseph R. McElrath Jr. collaborated on the edition of *Essays and Speeches*. That same team is responsible for one of the works under review, *An Exemplary Citizen: Letters of Charles W. Chesnutt, 1906–1932*. This latter volume marks the completion of the project on Chesnutt's letters that began with *"To Be an Author": Letters of Charles W. Chesnutt, 1889–1905* (1997), edited by McElrath and Leitz. The other work under review, Dean McWilliams's *Charles W. Chesnutt and the Fictions of Race*, makes ample use of these documentary and nonfiction writings, as well as the three Chesnutt novels published since 1997: *Mandy Oxendine*, edited by Charles Hackenberry (1997), and *Paul Marchand, F.M.C.* and *The Quarry*, both edited by Dean McWilliams (1999). In short, "Chesnutt" itself has become an expansive signifier, one that simultaneously registers shifting ideologies and an altered materiality.

An Exemplary Citizen: Letters of Charles W. Chesnutt, 1906–1932 takes us through the final third of Chesnutt's life. The year 1905 was a defining one in Chesnutt's career as a writer, for it marked the end of a major arc in that career. Chesnutt first gained a national audience in 1887 with the publication of "The Goophered Grapevine" in the *Atlantic Monthly*. Although he was already a successful businessman, Chesnutt longed for the writer's life and sufficient financial success as a writer to support himself and his family. He continued to publish stories in the *Atlantic* and elsewhere, and by 1899 his writing career seemed to have hit its stride. In that year, he published two collections of short stories and a book-length biography of Frederick Douglass, and he closed his legal stenography business. The following year, Chesnutt published his first novel, *The House Behind the Cedars*, which was greeted with critical approval and solid sales. After this success came *The Marrow of Tradition* (1901), a work that signaled Chesnutt's greater artistic maturity, even if it did not achieve the sales of his first novel. However, in 1905, Chesnutt experienced the full vagaries of the book business. His third published novel, *The Colonel's Dream*, was a critical and financial failure, and Chesnutt turned once more to court stenography as his chief means of income.

In theory, then, 1906 marks a turning away from authorship, a shift indicated by the different titles given to the two volumes of letters. However, *An Exemplary Citizen*, as one might now expect of Chesnutt, complicates and deepens this issue. Certainly, the post-1905 letters reveal an "exemplary citizen." Chesnutt is fairly immersed in the civic and national issues of his day, particularly as they relate to African Americans. The first letter in the volume, to Booker T. Washington (8 Jan. 1906), sets the tone (1). In it, Chesnutt congratulates Washington on the defeat of the Poe Amendment, a proposal to change the state constitution of Maryland in order to restrict African American suffrage. (From the first, one is grateful to the editors for their rigorous notes that provide invaluable historical, biographical, and cultural details on the myriad concerns addressed by Chesnutt and his peers.) Aside from family members, Washington ranks as the most frequent correspondent in the collection, and Chesnutt's letters fully illustrate the friendship and ideological differences between the two men. In terms of the number of letters, Du Bois is not far behind Washington, and it seems rather apropos that one of the longest letters in the collection is from Chesnutt to Du Bois *about* Washington (81–84).

Then, too, Chesnutt is also an exemplary father. Many of Chesnutt's letters to his children were first published by his daughter, Helen Chesnutt, in her biography, *Charles Waddell Chesnutt: Pioneer of the Color Line* (1952). Placed in the context of his quotidian dealings, they take on a fresh intensity. Chesnutt may offer pro forma responses to yet another charity appeal or request for literary advice, but he is keenly concerned about his family. These political, social, and familial letters offer a compelling portrait of a man happily enmeshed in multiple networks. In the last eighteen months of his life, when financial circumstances required Chesnutt to withdraw his support from several organizations, the narrowing of his social orbit seems to anticipate and even define his actual passing.

However, *An Exemplary Citizen* reminds us of the ways in which, after 1905, Chesnutt remained a writer and author. It includes but one instance of Chesnutt's correspondence related to his stenography business, and one might well wish for a few more letters in this vein. The letter to Walter C. Camp (4 June 1908) concerns a toast Camp gave at a Yale dinner (41). Camp (1859–1925), a former captain of the Yale football team and its coach for many years, was a prolific writer who also formulated many of the rules of modern football. Chesnutt's letter undercuts the notion that stenography was merely transcription, as Chesnutt asks Camp to collaborate in the reconstitution of his text. This process, in which two gentlemen thus coauthor a modest text, highlights the social enmeshment of Chesnutt; as a stenographer, he was far from anonymous. In addition, given the greater procedural complexity of this type of work, Chesnutt's frequent claims that business concerns delayed replies to other types of correspondence gains credibility. *An Exemplary Citizen* indicates how Chesnutt remained in the public eye, not only through his flourishing business, but also through his essays and speeches: the man was constantly writing. He was even writing novels, although he published no additional novels in his lifetime. In 1921, Chesnutt completed the manuscript of *Paul Marchand, F.M.C.*; *The Quarry* followed in 1928. *An Exemplary Citizen* is particularly useful in understanding how the latter novel, one imbued with the externalities of the Harlem Renaissance, ever came into being after the solid rejection of *Paul Marchand, F.M.C.* Chesnutt's letters to Du Bois and Carl Van Vechten from 1925 to 1928 make for fascinating reading. In all, this excellent volume affirms that Chesnutt was a man of letters in every sense.

Charles Chesnutt and the Fictions of Race, by Dean McWilliams, marks an important milestone in the critical analysis of Chesnutt's works. It is, according to McWilliams, "the first extended exploration of Chesnutt's fiction and nonfiction from the perspective of recent theories of language and the construction of racial identity" (5). It is also the first major overview of the expanded Chesnutt corpus. As McWilliams notes, the project began in 1995 when he was editing *Paul Marchand, F.M.C.* and *The Quarry* (xii). His close familiarity with these texts serves him well, not only in the specific readings of these texts, but also in the reformulation of Chesnutt's entire oeuvre. The twin agenda of the book is to explicate both Chesnutt's writing and the cultural codes or narrative upon which that writing is predicated. It is an ambitious project, but one that McWilliams ably accomplishes.

McWilliams's textual analyses begin with Chesnutt's short story "Baxter Procrustes" (1904). A story about an exquisitely bound book that is otherwise absent of text serves as an ideal test of theories on language, its meaning and commodification. However, as McWilliams reminds us, "Baxter Procrustes" is also a story about race. It turns on the old adage that one shouldn't judge a book by its cover, and the text grows in meaning "when we know that it was written by an African American who had been rejected by European Americans" (19). Chesnutt was initially denied admission to Cleveland's Rowfant Club, a group for bibliophiles founded in 1892, and an organization suspiciously similar to the Bodleian Club lampooned in "Baxter Procrustes." Here, as elsewhere in his work, McWilliams shows us how deeply imbricated issues of race are in the work of Chesnutt. It is not simply that Chesnutt is preoccupied with race, but that racism and racialism saturate his culture and ours. What Chesnutt's work does is make apparent the racial discourse that otherwise existed as background radiation in the lives of Americans a century ago. What McWilliams charts is the subtle methodology in Chesnutt's work of uncovering. To that end, he takes an approach to Chesnutt's nonfiction work that is especially welcome. For McWilliams, Chesnutt's diary and his essay "The Future American" (1900) are "texts, complete verbal enactments" in themselves (xi), rather than appendices to the fiction. When McWilliams notes that the nonfiction contains the same "contradictory tensions and pressures found in his stories and novels" (xii), he is offering part of a larger argument about Chesnutt's work, rather than an illustration or even indictment of the fiction.

Many of Chesnutt's most prominent characters are mixed race or mulatto. McWilliams argues that such characters represent more than just "autobiographical indulgence":

> Chesnutt returned again and again to the world of the Anglo-African because it was the ambiguous area where the arbitrary, socially conditioned nature of racist thinking could be most easily exposed. Racist ideology insists on rigidly exclusive categories: blacks and whites are fundamentally and immutably different, biologically and morally. . . . But the existence of people of mixed blood contradicted the assumption of absolute racial difference; mulattoes were living proof that desire and love had drawn whites and blacks together in ways that revealed their essential similarity. (101)

With the publication of the early novel *Mandy Oxendine*, Chesnutt challenged racist and racialist thinking. We can see how, in the succeeding novels, *The House Behind the Cedars* (1900) and *The Marrow of Tradition* (1901), Chesnutt deepened his interrogation of race and elevated his skills as a writer. *The Marrow of Tradition*, in particular, underscores the "essential similarity" through doubles and simulacra, tugging at the contested meanings of race and class in America. McWilliams cannot fully rehabilitate *The Colonel's Dream* (1905), but he does make a strong case for why the novel's failure matters. The colonel's focus was on economic and material gains for African Americans; however, the colonel's defeat "shows that economic progress would always be fragile and uncertain without effective political rights and legal protection for blacks" (181). As McWilliams notes, this argument is a rebuttal of the agenda set forth by Chesnutt's friend, Booker T. Washington (181). This analysis then explains Chesnutt's last two novels in which the protagonists, though European Americans, embrace African American identities: "[T]he logic of Chesnutt's assimilationism requires that whites must first become blacks before blacks can become white. Whites must be persuaded to enter the black world, morally and spiritually, to see the black condition from the inside" (224). Over a forty-year period of writing, Chesnutt sought to illuminate that condition. McWilliams has respected that journey and produced an illuminating document of his own.

Keith Williams
Southern Methodist University

SUSAN GLASPELL: A CRITICAL BIOGRAPHY. By Barbara Ozieblo. Chapel Hill: U of North Carolina P, 2000. xiii + 345 pp. Hardbound, $55; paperback, $22.50.

Although scholarly interest in playwright and novelist Susan Glaspell (1876–1948) has grown steadily in the past several decades, Barbara Ozieblo's study is the first book-length critical biography since Marcia Noe's *Voice from the Heartland* in 1983. Ozieblo, who teaches American literature and women's studies at the University of Málaga, Spain, has produced the most comprehensive overview to date of Glaspell's life and work, documenting both in considerable detail and exploring interrelationships between the two. In addition to providing close readings of all available works by Glaspell, the author has drawn on an abundance of other primary sources, citing special collections in more than twenty research libraries, interviews with descendants of Glaspell's colleagues and intimate associates, and published memoirs of Glaspell's contemporaries.

Ozieblo is interested in illuminating both the life and the work of her subject, and especially in unlocking the key to Glaspell's elusive personality—"trying to understand why the rebel in her chose so often to acquiesce to convention" (1). Attempting to reconcile the revolutionary impulses expressed in Glaspell's work and the sublimation and self-effacement in Glaspell's personal relations, Ozieblo considers sociohistorical as well as psychological factors. Ultimately, the picture of Glaspell that emerges is that of a woman very much a product of her time—born in Davenport, Iowa, in 1876, reaching full adulthood as the twentieth century dawned, and perpetually torn between "duty and desire, Victorian submission and modern self-assertion" (5).

Ozieblo provides, in the first two chapters of her chronological survey, the most richly detailed account to date of Glaspell's biological and cultural roots, her youth, education, and early writing career. Apparently drawing from an adventurous pioneer heritage as well as modern stirrings of New Womanhood, young Glaspell escaped her conventional upbringing, winning prestige as a writer and orator at Drake University before embarking on a writing career. After a dozen or so years as a reporter and writer of short fiction, Glaspell published her first novel, *The Glory of the Conquered*, in 1909. This novel features a protagonist common to almost all of Glaspell's major works, the strong and gifted woman struggling to live and love independently, and a frequently recurring theme, sacrifice inspired by love. Ozieblo highlights the autobiographical nature of these works and offers details of Glaspell's personal life as proof.

In keeping with her primary interest, Ozieblo devotes six of her ten chapters to Glaspell's relationship with George Cram "Jig" Cook, the "exalted husband" most detrimental to Glaspell's personal autonomy. A number of scholars have faulted Cook as a womanizer and drinker, haunted by failure and prone to self-pity. Glaspell has always seemed a bit saintly by contrast, and Ozieblo offers one of the more extreme versions of this commonly held perception. For Ozieblo, Cook was an "obstreperous megalomaniac" (225) who badgered and bullied Glaspell into acquiescence to his dreams and schemes. Glaspell's years with Cook (1913–24) are dominated by their association with the Provincetown Players, the experimental theater company founded in Provincetown, Massachusetts, in 1915; transplanted to Greenwich Village during 1916–22; and most noted for first producing the works of Eugene O'Neill. Ozieblo has sifted through various conflicting reports of these events to reveal Glaspell's role in accepting and mentoring the younger playwright, as well as to establish Glaspell's own wide-ranging contributions to the company. Ozieblo provides plot summaries and brief critical analyses of Glaspell's Provincetown plays, identifying recurring themes such as the "dilemmas of womanhood" (142) and the "right of the individual to self-development" (138) and formal innovations such as the unseen protagonist, introduced in *Trifles* and repeated in *Bernice* (1919), and the linguistic experiments of *The Verge* (1921). Ozieblo perceives special significance in Glaspell's *Chains of Dew* (produced by the Players in 1922), in which a woman married to a childishly dependent man "succumbs to domesticity" (164), suggesting that Glaspell may have written the play as a means of "reconciling her qualms" about her own personal choices (166).

Despite Glaspell's significant contributions to the Provincetown Players, and therefore American theater and drama in general, Ozieblo sees the impetus for these contributions as wifely submission to Cook's dreams. In seeking Glaspell's perspective on these years, Ozieblo, like most Provincetown historians, is in the paradoxical position of relying on Glaspell's biography of Cook, *Road to the Temple* (1927), for emotional truths while simultaneously discrediting it as "mythmaking" and "hagiography" (224–25, 230). Although the image of Glaspell as a reluctant participant in the Provincetown experiment is one that Glaspell herself helped create, both in her self-effacing *Road to the Temple* and in several published interviews, it is not entirely convincing. As Ozieblo observes, Glaspell "refashioned herself to fit the myth she created" (230). The couple's two-year sojourn in Greece (1922–24), however, does seem a sacrifice on Glaspell's part, and Ozieblo's depiction of these years as lonely and frustrating ones for Glaspell is convincing. Letters from Cook to Glaspell support Ozieblo's characterization of Cook as self-obsessed and needy, but most of Glaspell's personal correspondence, as Ozieblo reports, was destroyed, and the portrait of this intriguing and troubled relationship that emerges is fragmented.

If Glaspell's marriage to Cook was, indeed, eleven years of unrelieved misery, she embarked on a similarly disastrous relationship, shortly after Cook's death in 1924, with writer Norman Matson. Glaspell spent considerable effort promoting her younger and less-talented lover, even cowriting a play with him, *The Comic Artist* (1928), which she later disclaimed. Despite the time and effort Glaspell expended on Matson's career, however, she produced a number of notable novels and several plays during her years with him, including the Pulitzer Prize–winning *Alison's House* (1930). In 1932, Glaspell's professional reputation was at its height when Matson left her to marry the nineteen-year-old daughter of one of Glaspell's best friends. Ozieblo chronicles their personal and professional relationship in a chapter suitably titled "Betrayal of Trust."

Ozieblo examines in her final chapter Glaspell's two-year stint in Chicago as Director of the Midwest Play Bureau of the Federal Theatre Project and her last years of solitary living and writing in Provincetown. Ozieblo's discussion of Glaspell's work with the Federal Theatre, which has been given minimal attention, is of special interest. Ozieblo also offers brief analyses of Glaspell's later works, giving special attention to her final novel, *Judd Rankin's Daughter* (1945), which features Glaspell's most atypical depictions of men ("for the first time, she has created male characters we can admire" [273]) and women ("Glaspell acknowledges that, in a patriarchy, it is up to the men to act—she limits women to the role of passive inspirer or muse" [273]). Noting the singular characterizations in this novel, Ozieblo concludes that Glaspell's voice was silenced in the 1950s because her characters generally "did not conform to postwar consumer society role models. Glaspell [typically] created forceful women who dare to risk all for love while maintaining more than a measure of independence; her men are ineffective, weak, and entirely dependent on women" (279).

As this study persuasively demonstrates, Glaspell's "plays and novels do bring us closer to the dilemmas of the people of her time," as well as our own (278). This extensively researched and sensitive interpretation of Glaspell's life and work is essential reading for Glaspell scholars and will be welcomed by anyone interested in this significant era in America's cultural and intellectual life.

Cheryl Black
University of Missouri–Columbia

REMEMBER ME TO HARLEM: THE LETTERS OF LANGSTON HUGHES AND CARL VAN VECHTEN. Edited by Emily Bernard. New York: Vintage, 2001. xxxix + 356 pp. $15.

THE POLITICAL PLAYS OF LANGSTON HUGHES. By Langston Hughes. With introductions and analyses by Susan Duffy. Carbondale: Southern Illinois UP, 2000. xi + 221 pp. $19.95.

In 2002, scholars, lay readers, students, actors, and musicians gathered in cities throughout the United States to celebrate the centennial of the birth of Langston Hughes. The centennial issue of the *Langston Hughes Review* highlighted a few of the speeches that commemorated the occasion, and a short-lived stamp marked the event in philatelic circles. One of the clarion calls from major scholars during the centennial celebrations was to venture away from the overworked territory of "Theme for English B" (1949) and "The Negro Mother" (1931) and to cultivate new ground in the second century of Hughes. With the University of Missouri's fifteen-volume *Collected Works of Langston Hughes* now available, readers who thought they knew Hughes must acknowledge that they knew only a portion of the man and a fraction of the works. Editions such as *Remember Me to Harlem* and *The Political Plays of Langston Hughes* preceded the centennial rush to offer major contributions to this new look at the man and his works.

Susan Duffy has published several volumes on political theater, and her presentation of texts and analyses of four of Hughes's political plays from the 1930s sheds light on items that had previously been mostly passing references in biographical outlines. Many people have read *The Big Sea* (1940) and *I Wonder As I Wander* (1956). Thus, many readers are aware of Hughes's blue-collar jobs and his involvement with the Scottsboro case. However, few of us have read "Scottsboro, Limited: A One-Act Play" (1932). Duffy's introduction to the play provides a useful description of agit-prop techniques, thereby illuminating the use and placement of the "voices in the audience" that Hughes lists among the characters in the play. "Harvest" (better known as "Blood on the Fields") and "Angelo Herndon Jones" were far more obscure, never having been published or produced on stage. Duffy has done an admirable job of establishing a version of the scripts to present in this volume. She has offered a useful introduction to "Angelo Herndon Jones," by far the longest play in the volume. It evidently won the competition sponsored by *New Theater* for which Hughes submitted the one-act play, but the script was neither published nor staged. Thus, Duffy's presentation of it certainly accomplishes her desire to "open doors for further investigations" (x).

"De Organizer" (1940), one of two plays in the book to have been produced, recently enjoyed another brief moment in the spotlight, thanks to the discovery of a partial score recently included in the papers of the late musical director Dr. Eva Jessye. University of Michigan music professor James Dapogny recognized the significance of this score and used it to restore the one-act opera, a collaboration between Hughes and jazz pianist and composer James P. Johnson. When National Public Radio, on "Morning Edition" (3 Dec. 2002), reported on the restored opera, Susan Duffy was among the voices included in its coverage. With Duffy focusing upon the text and with Dapogny evaluating the music, scholars and audiences in this second century of Hughes have a wonderful new field to cultivate.

While Duffy makes extremely valuable contributions to the Hughes canon, she does not reflect in her work adequate research and representation of those who preceded her in their own groundbreaking scholarship on the texts and productions of Hughes's theatrical writings. As a result, Duffy states more than once that these works have "gone unnoticed and unexamined" (2). Her bibliography offers many useful sources, but she misses a few significant ones. VeVe Clark's interview with Amiri Baraka in *Black Scholar* in 1979 examines the prospects of "Restaging Langston Hughes's *Scottsboro Limited.*" Joseph McLaren's 1997 book, *Langston Hughes: Folk Dramatist in the Protest Tradition, 1921–1943*, actually discusses all four of the plays included in Duffy's work. Granted, McLaren's illustrated and detailed study had not been published in 1993 when Duffy began her work, but it had been in print for a few years before *The Political Plays* was actually published. The two most conspicuous omissions involve Leslie Sanders and Faith Berry. Duffy's bibliography never mentions Sanders, a widely recognized scholar who has published numerous works on Hughes's plays. Among those that would have been available to Duffy are a 1991 article from *Black American Literature Forum* (reprinted in Gates and Appiah, eds., *Langston Hughes: Critical Perspectives Past and Present* [1993]) and her book *The Development of Black Theater in America: From Shadows to Selves* (1988). While Duffy includes in her bibliography Faith Berry's 1983 biography of Hughes, she neglects the more pertinent anthology edited by Berry, *Good Morning Revolution* (1973). Without question, Berry is the literary archeologist who excavated Hughes's political works in poetry and prose. Duffy need not have bravely claimed that "bringing to light the leftist plays of Langston Hughes will not cause a fall from literary grace"

(35) because Berry had already safely established the social protest works of Hughes as part of his canon. Overall, then, while Duffy's work makes available important new primary texts and offers useful analyses of these four plays, the second century of Hughes scholarship must include other references to keep an accurate and comprehensive view of the scholarship.

By contrast, Emily Bernard has selected a very specific little corner of Hughes's world, and she unpretentiously highlights only a segment of that corner. Her work is intoxicating, fresh, rich, and enduring. Anyone who knows anything about the extensive collection of Hughes's manuscripts and letters housed in the James Weldon Johnson Collection at the Beinecke Library at Yale University knows that Carl Van Vechten established that collection and encouraged Hughes and other notable Black Americans to donate to it. Anyone who has seen Rudolph Byrd's magnificent selection of Van Vechten's photographs, *Generations in Black and White* (1993), recognizes the degree to which Van Vechten celebrated and cherished the icons of African American arts and letters. Until Bernard offered her carefully selected "mere fraction of the nearly one thousand five hundred letters exchanged by Langston Hughes and Carl Van Vechten between 1925 and 1964" (xxix), however, few of us had been able to observe the delightful friendship and literary symbiosis they shared.

Bruce Kellner, author of the 1968 biography of Van Vechten and literary trustee of the Van Vechten estate, has already taken Bernard's collection to the next dimension, with a lively staged reading of a selection of the letters. Kellner read Van Vechten's letters and Irvin Scott read Hughes's letters in an unforgettable presentation at Hughes's alma mater, Lincoln University in Pennsylvania, on 19 October 2002. Read aloud in the respective voices of Hughes and Van Vechten, the customized and creative closings of the letters became indelibly etched in the minds of those who attended this reading. In one of her careful yet unobtrusive endnotes, Bernard observes that Van Vechten had a penchant for such sign-offs as "chrysanthemums and moss-roses to you!" (30), "Turkeys and Cranberries to you!" (31), and "Pine needles and snow to you" (33). Hughes adopted such signatures, too, and the Bernard collection might very well lead a few more of us to abandon the boring "Yours truly."

Bernard's edition is introduced with a compelling overview of the forty years during which these two men exchanged their correspondence. She also weaves into her prose well-chosen illustrations, including drawings and photographs, to help the reader feel even more familiar with the material. Her editorial wisdom is impeccable in that she carefully omits letters that would have been repetitive or might have been too painstakingly linked to book projects in which the two were engaged. She occasionally rescues a striking sentence from an otherwise-omitted letter. Her work reflects an invaluable familiarity with the letters, as well as a greatly appreciated sensitivity to the needs and tastes of her readers.

Bernard's contribution to the Hughes canon has accomplished her goal to present "two people, one famous, one formerly famous but now mostly unknown, who lived during an extraordinary period in American history" (xxvi). Anyone who begins reading these letters—with or without pausing to examine the well-documented endnotes—will not want to stop until the conclusion of the book. More important, anyone who reads these letters will come away with a wonderful new appreciation for Hughes's friendship and collaborations with Van Vechten.

Taken together, these two works expand the Hughes canon even farther than *The Collected Works of Langston Hughes* because Bernard and Duffy bring to the public otherwise unpublished words by the Dean of African American literature. The second century of Hughes is off to a roaring start.

Donna Akiba Harper
Spelman College

ZORA NEALE HURSTON: A LIFE IN LETTERS. Edited by Carla Kaplan. New York: Doubleday, 2002. 880 pp. $40.

DOUBLE-TAKE: A REVISIONIST HARLEM RENAISSANCE ANTHOLOGY. Edited by Venetria K. Patton and Maureen Honey. New Brunswick: Rutgers UP, 2001. xliv + 619 pp. Hardbound, $60; paperback, $28.

In a 1971 essay, "When We Dead Awaken: Writing as Revision," collected in her *On Lies, Secrets, and Silence* (1979), Adrienne Rich offers an insightful definition of the revisionist project. She writes, "Re-vision—the act of looking back, of seeing with fresh eyes, of entering an old text from a new critical direction" (35). The two edited volumes under review offer us the chance to re-vision, not just revise, but really re-see, the literature of the Harlem Renaissance and the life of a key Harlem Renaissance writer, Zora Neale Hurston. Carla Kaplan's meticulously edited and carefully annotated collection of Hurston's letters offers a complicated view of this enigmatic woman that does not blindly celebrate her contributions but instead pays tribute to her contradictions. Venetria K. Patton and Maureen Honey's anthology of Harlem Renaissance writings and drawings offers a more nuanced view of the Harlem Renaissance as an interdisciplinary and multigenre revolution in artistic expression. Together, these two works allow us to move beyond our comfortable "additive" model of canon revision to reconsider instead the artists in new contexts.

Kaplan's weighty volume (at 880 pages, it is best to avoid carrying this book on vacation) presents a revealing collection of letters by a woman who longed for self-revelation but never felt safe to express it. Kaplan, a leading Hurston scholar, has gathered more than six hundred letters—and an occasional postcard or telegram, as well as photographs—from more than three-dozen locations. Compiled with the support of the Hurston family, this inclusive volume spans four decades, from the 1920s to the 1950s, until just before Hurston's death in January 1960.

A superb source for any Hurston scholar and enthusiast, *A Life in Letters* represents one of the most significant contributions in the flood of Hurston scholarship since her work was rediscovered in the 1970s. The letters are organized chronologically by decade, and each includes its salutation and closing, which are themselves very revealing. Kaplan has refrained from modifying these letters in deference to Hurston's complaints about the liberties that editors took with her writing. Throughout, Kaplan provides superb footnotes that clarify without overpowering and provide information for those interested in further research. The volume includes a comprehensive introduction, written colloquially enough for a general audience but without sacrificing complexity, and intervening introductions to each of the four decades covered in the volume. When these decade overviews focus on what new insight the letters provide into the many debates and contradictory assumptions about Hurston, they are especially helpful, although the metacommentary sometimes gets lost in the biographical summary of Hurston's life and the period, material already available in the two thorough Hurston biographies by Robert Hemenway (1977) and Valerie Boyd (2002).

Other supporting material includes a chronology of Hurston's life and an index of recipients, particularly useful for those who wish to trace Hurston's letters by correspondent rather than chronologically. Kaplan has also provided a wonderfully informative glossary of people, organizations, and publications mentioned in the letters. Worth reading for its own sake, this glossary provides a sense of the wide network of contacts and circle of friends that this flamboyant woman developed, from the literary to the anthropological to the academic and personal. The volume also includes an extensive bibliography of published and unpublished works by Hurston, although many of the short stories listed in "unpublished works" do not include posthumous publication information.

Highlighting Hurston's storytelling abilities, her uncompromising quest for self-fulfillment, her genius as a writer, and her expressive personality, Hurston's correspondence modulates from obsequious letters that reveal Hurston's masking to blunt letters that are painfully honest, as Kaplan notes. At times, Hurston theorizes about racial difference and "Anglo-Saxon supremacy" (475) (as she wrote to Claude Barnett, founder and director of the Associated Negro Press) while at others she gossips about well-known Harlem Renaissance figures or makes derogatory quips about her white benefactors and leading figures of the period. In the first letter of the volume, written in 1917 or 1918 to William Pickens, Hurston asserts her desire to "know," "really know" (54) the president of Morgan State Academy, where Hurston finished high school, and then she acknowledges how "impertinent" this demand is. The collection of letters allows us to "know" Hurston in a new context and reveals how impertinent we are for having this desire, for these letters also reveal that we cannot ever really "know" Hurston.

Yet the letters do reveal new insight into some of the unanswered questions about her life. They provide proof of what Kaplan calls Hurston's "political savvy" (14), despite criticisms that her work is apolitical and naive; examples of her anger about American racism; insight into her contradictory views about race; confirmation of her profound commitment to the value of black culture; evidence of how prolific she was in the 1940s, even though publishers turned down her projects repeatedly; her reaction to the false charges in 1948 of child molestation and their devastating effect on her; insight into her strong anticommunism and her turn to the conservative right in the 1950s; and details of her continual struggle for economic security, a recurring theme throughout the four decades of letters. Contradicting generally accepted views, the letters clarify the nature of her friendship with Langston Hughes, which did not end with their falling out over their shared project, *Mule*

Bone (1931). Although the letters mention little of her personal life, we do learn that she was married three times, not twice, as previous Hurston scholarship has maintained. Perhaps what is most exciting about this portable archive is the scholarship it will enable and inspire in the future. Easy access to these letters will allow researchers virtually anywhere to consider Hurston in all of her complexity without completely violating the privacy Hurston herself sought.

While *A Life in Letters* gathers Hurston's unpublished letters from a wide range of sources, the multigenre collection *Double-Take* brings together important writings and drawings from a wide range of Harlem Renaissance periodicals and anthologies, many of them never before reprinted. Patton and Honey have produced the first Harlem Renaissance anthology to include equal numbers of men and women artists. They have worked, as part of their revisionist project, to restore the role of drama to the Harlem Renaissance canon, as well as that of drawings and song lyrics, in addition to that of the more frequently anthologized genres of prose and poetry. Their selections include texts by men and women, canonized and less-known authors, and works with homoerotic themes and subtexts often left out of Harlem Renaissance anthologies.

Designed to accompany a selection of novels, this anthology (unlike many anthologies) largely avoids novel excerpts and instead focuses on essays, poetry, short stories, and plays, most of which are included in their entirety. The first section includes twenty-three essays, which are arranged by subject matter (e.g., the African American artist, the role of art, gender, Africa), although those themes are not noted. While a few key essays are missing (e.g., Carter G. Woodson's "The Migration of the Talented Tenth" [1918] and Arthur A. Schomburg's "The Negro Digs Up His Past" [1925]), of note is the inclusion of several rarely anthologized and fascinating essays on womanhood, including Marita O. Bonner's "On Being Young—a Woman—and Colored" (1925), Alice Dunbar-Nelson's "Woman's Most Serious Problem" (1927), and Marion Vera Cuthbert's "Problems Facing Negro Young Women" (1936).

The second section, creative writing, which makes up the bulk of the anthology, is arranged by author's date of birth rather than by theme. For each author, a useful one-to-two-page biography precedes creative works, which are grouped by genre, with poetry first, followed by short stories and drama. One of the richest features of this anthology, the inclusion of multiple genres by a single author, allows readers to see each writer, not just as a prose or poetry writer or a playwright or a novelist, as many single-genre anthologies do, but rather as a multidisciplinary artist who used different forms to explore central questions and themes of the period. This section includes thirty-three authors in all, from the frequently anthologized Hurston, Hughes, Nella Larsen, Jean Toomer, to the more recently recovered Alice Dunbar-Nelson, Angelina Weld Grimké, Jessie Redmon Fauset, Marita O. Bonner, and Mae V. Cowdery, to the rarely reprinted Effie Lee Newsome, John F. Matheus, Fenton Johnson, Anita Scott Coleman, and Gladys May Casely Hayford. Additionally, this anthology includes lesser-known and seldom-anthologized works by some of the key figures of the Harlem Renaissance alongside their most frequently anthologized pieces. Examples include Hughes's often-ignored poem "Lullaby" (1926) and a love poem by Hurston—this latter work a fascinating opportunity to read verse by an artist better known for her fiction and folklore. Because excerpts of long works are not included, neither creative writing by W. E. B. Du Bois or George Schulyer nor prose by Countee Cullen appears.

Furthering their multidisciplinary focus, the editors have scattered through the volume some thirty black-and-white illustrations from key African American periodicals of the period, as well as song lyrics performed by African American artists of the period. The song lyrics often seem to be an afterthought and include no information beyond the name of the performer and the year of recording. But the captivating illustrations that are reprinted make up for this lack; never-before-reprinted artwork and wonderful drawings by both men and women yield a more vivid portrait of the context in which the creative writing appeared.

One might wonder why yet another Harlem Renaissance anthology is needed, particularly with the publication of several single-genre (fiction, poetry, or drama) compilations of the Harlem Renaissance and several excellent collections of writings by African American women. This volume, however, fulfills a critical need for a single text that includes male alongside female writers, familiar alongside less familiar authors, and works in many genres. Most significantly, this anthology includes drama alongside other genres, something that David Levering Lewis's superb (and less expensive) anthology, *The Portable Harlem Renaissance Reader* (1994), with its focus on essays and poetry and fiction, does not include. In *Double-Take*, Grimké's groundbreaking play *Rachel* (1916), Georgia Douglas Johnson's highly acclaimed drama *Plumes: A Folk Tragedy* (1927), and Hughes's play *Mulattoes* (1935) appear alongside the authors' poetry and fiction (although *Mule Bone*, the failed collaboration between Hurston and Hughes, is a notable omission from this volume). This breadth does mean a sacrifice in depth: only a handful of works by each author is included and only works written or published from 1916 to 1937 are included, even though many of the artists kept writing beyond the Harlem Renaissance. James Weldon Johnson's "O Black and Unknown Bards" (1922) and Hughes's "I, Too" (1925), "Harlem" (1951), and "Good Morning" (1951) are missing. But the inclusion of varied artists and genres allows for cross-gender, multidisciplinary dialogues that highlight the commonalities and divergences among the diverse voices of the Harlem Renaissance.

The editors' attention to restoring suppressed works of the period is commendable. To correct biases of earlier anthologies that ignored many women artists and texts with homoerotic themes, the editors have reprinted works from nearly a dozen periodicals and anthologies of the era representing a range of views. While some will argue that this anthology suffers from bouts of political correctness, the editors make a strong and convincing case for the need to address the gender imbalance and omissions of past collections. Despite the fact that many of the women featured in this volume were lauded by African American critics at the time, most have subsequently been left out of anthologies. Unearthing their texts restores them to the influential roles they occupied during the period. Additionally, by recovering suppressed texts with homoerotic themes by both known and less-known authors, this anthology reveals that gay and lesbian issues played a significant role in the Harlem Renaissance.

Alain Locke's *The New Negro* (1925; rpt. 1999) is still a must-have for Harlem Renaissance enthusiasts and Lewis's *The Portable Harlem Renaissance Reader* (1999) is still a strong competitor, but this revisionist anthology fills in some crucial gaps—

particularly in the recovery of female-authored texts, the inclusion of drama and artwork alongside other genres, and the restoration of sexuality as a thematic concern of the period. *Double-Take* is a rich text for teaching, and at the relatively inexpensive price of $28 (paperback), this anthology would be a superb addition, not only to the library of Harlem Renaissance enthusiasts, but also to multigenre courses on the Harlem Renaissance, from undergraduate African American literature surveys to specialized graduate courses on the Harlem Renaissance.

Alicia Kent
University of Michigan–Flint

MINNESOTA DIARY 1942–46. By Sinclair Lewis. Edited by George Killough. Moscow: U of Idaho P, 2000. xi + 293 pp. $39.95.

Sinclair Lewis was one of the most perceptive critics of the American character in the first half of the twentieth century. In such novels as *Main Street* (1920), *Babbitt* (1922), *Arrowsmith* (1925), *Elmer Gantry* (1927), *It Can't Happen Here* (1935), and *Kingsblood Royal* (1947), he presents many aspects of American society—some good, some bad, and most needing improvement. He looks at ordinary middle-class Americans, including businessmen, doctors, social reformers, and ministers, in such an insightful way that his fiction still resonates with readers today.

Lewis focuses in his writing on the details that make up his characters—what they read, what they eat for breakfast, what they wear—as a way to represent their inner lives. Lewis's characters do not speak very much about their emotions; the reader has to intuit how they feel. The silence about emotions reflects both Lewis the person and the culture in which he grew up. He was born in 1885 in Sauk Centre, Minnesota. His mother died when he was six, and his father did not encourage displays of emotion. His stoicism was reinforced by "the village atmosphere among middle-class Protestants with a Calvinist heritage" (19) and the traditionally laconic Scandinavians whom he knew. It becomes clear that as a writer he chose a sort of shorthand that readers need to appreciate in order to understand the interior lives of his characters.

There is very little outside of his fiction that marks what Lewis the man was like. Although he wrote many letters over the course of his life, there is only one collection, the too-long-out-of-print *From Main Street to Stockholm* (1952), that contains a significant number of letters, and these are all from his fabulously successful decade of the 1920s. Although there have been two notable biographies, Mark Schorer's *Sinclair Lewis: An American Life* (1961) and Richard Lingeman's *Sinclair Lewis: Rebel from Main Street* (2002), *Minnesota Diary 1942–46* fills a gap in Lewis scholarship, for it lets him speak for himself about his own life.

The *Minnesota Diary* was written during a turbulent time in both Lewis's life and his professional career. He was just divorced from his second wife, the influential political columnist Dorothy Thompson, in 1942, and was in the middle of a long-term affair with the actress Marcella Powers, thirty-six years his junior. Although he won the Nobel Prize in 1930, his novels of the 1930s were a mixed lot, with only *Ann Vickers* (1933) and *It Can't Happen Here* receiving much critical praise. He decided that he needed to return to the state in which he was born in order to reflect on his life and to gather material for what became a trilogy of novels set in Minnesota—*Cass Timberlane* (1945), *Kingsblood Royal*, and *The God-Seeker* (1949).

George Killough, the editor of the diary, has done a splendid job of setting out the circumstances in which Lewis wrote and pointing out the more thoughtful, reflective Lewis that the diary reveals. He notes the early influence of Henry David Thoreau on Lewis and sees it borne out through the details that Lewis provides of the changing nature of the landscape, including the weather, the birds, and the animals that he sees ("a sheep madonna and child" [90]), and even the variations of prairie life. Killough also provides painstaking critical apparatus to complement the diary itself. He discusses the physical makeup of the notebooks, provides an appendix explaining Lewis's abbreviations (e.g., "p.d." for "perfect day"), and perhaps most impressively, identifies the people with whom Lewis socialized. Killough spent a number of years interviewing Minnesotans who remembered Lewis when he was living in Minneapolis and Duluth, and the knowledge garnered from the interviews makes the book even more valuable.

A diary can be a problematic kind of literary text. Since the primary audience for the diary is the writer himself, it is usually fragmented, with a kind of shorthand that makes sense only to the author. Killough notes, "[T]he value of diaries often lies in their lack of polished coherence, their lack of spin and controlled suggestion. One sometimes finds the diarist unmasked. This peculiar combination of fact, feeling, and silence in 'Minnesota Diary' reveals a private Sinclair Lewis of remarkable sensitivity and restraint" (15).

Lewis's diary can be read for a number of reasons. It gives readers insight into Lewis as man and author, as well as into his relationships with Marcella Powers, his family, and his friends. Sometimes he is the great writer, either enjoying or bemoaning his celebrity. He sees people who remind him of the Babbitts and the Dodsworths, even jots down possible ideas for novels. Sometimes, he is the social critic, noting when he has met anti-Semites or racists. He is also fascinated by travel itself. He comments on Burma Shave signs, religious slogans on billboards, women wearing trousers, the variations in the hotels he stays in and the places where he eats. Sometimes he is a father who realizes his shortcomings ("I am badly trained as a parent" [140]), even as he takes his younger son camping and visits his older son at an army camp. On D-day he writes, "Glad Wells [his son who was later killed in October 1944] is in Italy, not this big invasion" (188). Sometimes he is the lover, writing of the glories of Minnesota so that Marcella will come and visit.

The diary provides glimpses of Lewis as he recalls incidents that happened in the late nineteenth-century prairie town of Sauk Centre: "Remember how as a boy, viewing Sauk Centre from the cemetery, admired how it stretched out surely a full mile—a very considerable city!" (69). He remembers how farmhouses used to bank dirt or manure around the lower part of the house in winter (38–39), the "dusty but exciting smell in dark wheat elevator, above bins, and feeling of danger of falling down into that quicksand" (42), duck hunting (60), and "poison ivy on Sunday School picnics" (107). During a camping trip with his twelve-year-old son Michael, he writes to Marcella, "There are no bathrooms; my mind goes back to Sauk Centre and that questionable period known as youth as I wash with a tin pitcher and bowl, and attend the country backhouse" (141). There are glimpses of the man who wanted to travel and experience new things: "Remember as a boy: eagerness for anything out of Sauk Centre usual, or special in town: the derrick, a stranger in town, house with small tower, odd-shaped window in neighboring town" (102).

He can be melancholic as well. He visits the graves of his paternal grandparents in Elysian and remembers that his father later paid the mortgage on their farm: "Is all transition, spiritual and political as well as architectural, always harsh, usually hideous?" (99). His most revealing notation may be the following: "Grownup, returning, may care much more to learn all about a district than did as child. Often he also has a much more affectionate attitude. Is this more normal—or more beaten?" (113). And as he thinks about how prairie villages have changed over time, he wonders, "Did the complaining Carol Kennicott [the heroine of *Main Street*] help?" (89).

Lewis's writing also provides a window into life in the Midwest during World War II. The war is not mentioned with any regularity, but there are frequent references to how life has changed, such as the coming of gas rationing (and Lewis's plans to try and obtain more gas when Marcella visits so that he can show her more of his state), and War Saving Time ("and by God's time it's 5:15 AM" [38]). On 4 July 1942, he writes, "Perhaps first eve of July 4th, and 4th itself, in life, while in America, that didn't hear one firecracker explode, one toy pistol. Forbidden, re war. Many people on roads in another putative last fling before threatened gas rationing. Egypt now menaced by Rommel—we talk mostly of that, if mention the war at all" (123). He even wonders, "Will this war finally end the notorious American waste of resources—and end it too late?" (120).

And finally the diary provides an appreciation of nature, with descriptions so beautiful that it seems that Lewis most shows real feeling when describing things outside of himself. On 20 May 1942, he writes, "The dark clouds in sky, apricot to silver, are solid seeming and unmoving / There is a new moon in sky that behind it still seems blue, and bats flit against clear spaces of sky seen behind silhouetted trees on the shore. There is a peace like a dream" (84–85). Later he writes, "The effect of moving leaves seen through the slats of the sleeping porch blinds is magic—like a living moving picture" (149).

Sinclair Lewis's *Minnesota Diary 1942–46* is a revealing portrait of a brilliant and troubled author during a tumultuous time in our nation's history. It should be savored on many levels as one reads through the fragmented writing to get to the beauty of the feelings underneath.

Sally E. Parry
Illinois State University

BLOOD OF MY BLOOD. By Marjorie Kinnan Rawlings. Edited by Anne Blythe Meriwether. Gainesville: UP of Florida, 2002. vii + 170 pp. $24.95.

MAX AND MARJORIE: THE CORRESPONDENCE BETWEEN MAXWELL E. PERKINS AND MARJORIE KINNAN RAWLINGS. Edited by Rodger L. Tarr. Gainesville: UP of Florida, 1999. xi + 628 pp. $34.95.

There is a certain pleasure in reading the early, not-great works of successful writers, and reading someone else's mail can even be a bit of a thrill. Two recently published books on Marjorie Kinnan Rawlings, best known as the author of *The Yearling* (1938) and *Cross Creek* (1942), add significantly to Rawlings scholarship, as well as hold forth these little pleasures.

The never-before-published *Blood of My Blood* (2002) was written before any of Rawlings's other novels and is a thinly disguised story of her early years. Revealing, in particular, Rawlings's troubled perception of her mother, it is more personal than any of her later works and considerably less polished. However, though significantly flawed, the book has great value for Rawlings scholars, as well as for readers interested in early twentieth-century women's writing and autobiography. In contrast, *Max and Marjorie: The Correspondence between Maxwell E. Perkins and Marjorie Kinnan Rawlings*, which details the seventeen-year correspondence between Rawlings and her Scribner's editor, illuminates her successful later years. And, as is almost always the case with letters, they reveal much about the person behind the writing—in this case, a very different character from the young "Marjorie" of *Blood of My Blood*.

Together these books give us a more personal look at Rawlings than any of her other works (including the seemingly autobiographical *Cross Creek*). They create a sort of narrative about the kind of person she began as (or perceives herself to have been) and the kind of person she ended up being. It is an interesting and surprising journey.

Rawlings submitted the manuscript of her first novel, *Blood of My Blood*, to a writing contest in 1928. She kept both the novel and the rejection slip, but, perhaps recognizing the flaws of the book, she never again attempted to get it published. (Indeed, editor Meriwether faced a court battle to get the book published nearly seventy-five years later.) However, for both scholars and Rawlings fans, it is rich precisely because of its flaws—the unclear line between autobiography and fiction (not as self-conscious or controlled as contemporary blurrings), the anger that seeps through the narrative, and the self-loathing. Although she calls the book a novel, Rawlings does not change the names of her own family members. Thus, the overbearing mother of "the girl" is, like her own mother, named Ida Traphagen; the loving father, Arthur Kinnan; and the "self-satisfied" and "insufferable" (102) daughter, "Marjorie."

The first half of *Blood of My Blood* introduces the extremely flawed mother and terribly spoiled daughter. The second half sees the real growth of the daughter, all a result of her various failures: rejection by "the best" sororities for false-name-dropping, overreaching, and lack of sophistication; harsh criticism by writing professors;

rebuff by editors. The daughter's eventual, hard-won success seems to be the result of rejecting everything she learned from her mother—particularly about her own glorified place in the world.

Rawlings attempts to posit a kind of growth in the mother as well, but, perhaps because she tries to fit it into the last eleven pages of the book, it has a false, tacked-on feel. Up until these pages, Ida remains the same small-minded, interfering mother that she has been throughout. At the end, Rawlings tries to imply some sort of inner change in Ida, but the plot moves away from specifics into cloying abstractions. Even the page layout looks fragmented and rushed, and the book concludes unconvincingly.

Blood of My Blood does not stand up to Rawlings's later writing. The heavy-handed narrative style reveals the writer's own judgments and bitterness a bit too clearly, her attempts to be fair to the mother often fall short, and the shallow Ida seems one-dimensional. Nonetheless, even readers unfamiliar with Rawlings may find her sociological observations of interest (especially for the 1920s), including her discussion of her parents' doomed-from-the-start marriage, and her analysis of social climbing and Washington circles. Most revealing, however, is her view of motherhood, with her mother as the prime example. Rawlings writes, "Maternity, with the rarest of exceptions, is always sheer egotism. . . . In the case of Ida, we see the phenomenon of a deliberate extension of her own life for a deliberate purpose; a deliberate intent to live the new life. A peculiarly ruthless mother love is at work" (46–47). Rawlings's twin beliefs that her mother's vicarious living through her was wrong and that it inevitably created a selfish child are the threads that bind the book together. However, the very portrayal of the pettish young Marjorie, as well as the narrator's acid commentary on her behavior, shows the adult Rawlings's distance from that early self.

Blood of My Blood reveals Rawlings's childhood, but *Max and Marjorie* shows us who she became as an adult. Indeed, reading *Max and Marjorie* along with *Blood of My Blood*, one cannot help but wonder how the bratty Marjorie Kinnan grew up to be the wonderfully self-deprecating Rawlings who mocks her own "foot-stampings" and "vicious" moods. The girl whose mother would not allow her to be criticized grows up to be a woman who takes criticism very well indeed.

If (as almost every existing review points out) every writer deserves an editor like Maxwell Perkins, then it is equally true that every editor probably longs for a writer as straightforward and low-maintenance as Marjorie Kinnan Rawlings, perhaps especially Perkins, who had to deal with both the various problems of F. Scott Fitzgerald and Ernest Hemingway and the gargantuan job of editing the oh-so-verbose Thomas Wolfe during this period. As the letters add up and the writer and editor move from "Mr. Perkins" and "Mrs. Rawlings" to "Max" and "Marjorie," we see the development of trust in each other and the subtle relationship of encouraging, directing, and compromising. Literary scholars will be interested in the letters' insightful and sometimes gossipy discussions of Hemingway, Fitzgerald, and Wolfe; teachers and writers will be envious of Perkins's analytical and diplomatic skills; and just about everyone will enjoy Rawlings's funny, incisive narratives and occasional snippy outbursts. Perkins is a respectful editor; Rawlings is a gracious and willing listener.

While Perkins repeatedly tells her in various ways, "But you are the only one to decide,—you are the only judge of (my criticism's) validity, and you must not be beguiled into anything that you do not think is right" (171), he nonetheless comments extensively on everything. Rather than bristling, as one might expect from the "self-satisfied" (78) Marjorie in *Blood*, Rawlings thrives on criticism. Certainly her trust in Perkins has as much to do with his criticism as with his deference. At one point, rather early in their relationship, she says of his comments on *South Moon Under* (1933): "I am so much stirred by your letter of criticism . . . I agree with you almost entirely, with the most enormous feeling of relief. . . . It is odd, but I am much happier to have had you find this particular fault with a portion of the manuscript, than if you had accepted it more or less in toto . . . I felt so acutely that much was wrong, that if you found it acceptable I should always have had a more blurred feeling in judging what I was doing" (175–76).

Rawlings's implicit point seems to be that if Perkins had simply approved the manuscript, she might have doubted his editorial skills. This comment sets the tone for their correspondence. Indeed, about a later work, she writes, "I don't blame anyone but myself for 'Golden Apples' being interesting trash rather than literature. But you should have bullied me and shamed me further" (225). It is hard not to wonder—even in these days of post- "genetic" criticism—if Rawlings's stringent self-criticism has its roots in a mother who tells her, "I wanted you to be perfect" (*Blood* 68).

An obvious value of *Max and Marjorie* is the opportunity to see the editor-writer relationship at work. Another is to learn more about Rawlings. She confides much about her personal life to Perkins as time goes on. Even in the phase during which she still refers to him as "Mr. Perkins," she is more forthcoming on her personal life than she ever really is in *Cross Creek*. She states, "I was granted a divorce yesterday from my husband. The end, simply—I hope—of fourteen years of Hell" (131). Furthermore, Rawlings's own rigorous standards and personal discipline become clear, as does her saving sense of humor. Indeed, her writing on other writers, her anecdotes, and even her disagreements with Perkins are all infused with humor—interestingly enough, the very ingredient that *Blood of My Blood* is entirely lacking. This wit, combined with Rawlings's insight, makes the letters wonderful reading.

Along these lines, most readers will enjoy her insightful and intimate comments on other writers, particularly fellow Perkins-dependents. While Rawlings can be quite generous to other writers, she is rarely without a strong opinion. She writes of Wolfe's "gorgeous bedlam" (143), of Hemingway's *Death in the Afternoon* ("I find it insane and entirely stirring" [59]), and of Fitzgerald's *Tender is the Night* ("a book disturbing, bitter and beautiful . . . about quite trivial people and dealing with trivial situations" [140]). And on one book Perkins sends her, she writes, "I found his broken sentences annoying, and an occasional prissy quaintsy-waintsy style as well." But even then she adds, "the first part was good reading" (489).

The same humor that informs her comments on writers manifests itself in the entertaining mini-anecdotes that pepper her letters. The world around her amuses her, and she has a keen ear for dialogue. In a later letter, she writes of her visiting eighty-four-year-old "adopted aunt": "It is impossible to work with the old lady in the house. . . . She is a very amusing old lady in many ways, especially because of her Malaprop-isms. She informed me that a certain old man had finally died, after lying for a week in a semi-comma. Having often lain myself for a week in a semi-comma, I was all sympathy" (572).

Even in the midst of a minor skirmish with Perkins about a Scribner's publishing error, she uses humor to lighten the situation. When she blames Scribner's,

Perkins insists on taking responsibility, claiming it "was wholly my fault" (98). Rawlings responds good-naturedly, saying, "If you've decided to back up Mr. Scribner (when he wouldn't back you up) . . . I shan't quarrel about it ever again. . . . In all seriousness, all is forgiven and forgotten about the Brandt mix-up—I understand your viewpoint and quite harmlessly disagree. . . . PS Use your engraved stationery some time when you're not solemnly taking me to task! It's not fair to use your dressiest stuff for purposes of chastisement!" (99, 101).

Here, as throughout, it is almost impossible not to like these two forthright writers, Perkins for being willing to take all blame upon himself and Rawlings for being willing to refer wryly to her own "foot stampings" and to make her opinion clear while keeping her sense of humor intact. By the end, one feels privileged to have entered into such witty and intelligent discourse.

These two books appear as bookends of Rawlings's career. *Blood of My Blood* shows Rawlings the inexperienced writer as well as young Rawlings the flawed character. In the correspondence, we see that Rawlings grew beyond the bitter, nearly humorless narrator of *Blood of My Blood* into the compassionate woman able to see the heroism in the poor whites of Florida and the humor in her own shortcomings. Tarr and Meriwether have extended our knowledge of a perhaps-still-underresearched writer and opened a window onto what it took for one writer to move from her clumsy first work to the surefooted mastery that would earn her the coveted Pulitzer Prize for *The Yearling*.

Jill C. Jones
Rollins College

THE SELECTED LETTERS OF TENNESSEE WILLIAMS: VOLUME 1, 1920–1945. Edited by Albert J. Devlin and Nancy M. Tischler. New York: New Directions, 2000. xxv + 608 pp. $35.

Albert J. Devlin and Nancy M. Tischler, both veteran Tennessee Williams scholars, have given us what is best termed an excellent partial epistolary biography—carefully selecting and adding explanatory notes for 330 of Williams's letters to illuminate the early life of what Lyle Leverich aptly called, in his 1995 biography, the years of "the unknown Tennessee Williams." This volume and the one that will follow are the fruits of dedicated and thorough research, as Devlin and Tischler tracked down 2800 "letters, notes, telegrams, and other pertinent documents" (xi) written by Williams and held in private collections or in institutions housing not only Williams papers but also papers of his contemporaries. Moreover, the editors consulted existing Williams scholarship and interviewed family, friends, and associates in the places that the peripatetic playwright made ports in his restless voyage: St. Louis, New Orleans, New York, Taos, Provincetown, Hollywood, Key West, Mexico, and more. Almost all the letters in this volume are published for the first time.

The result is a highly readable and occasionally fascinating compilation that can serve not only Williams scholars, who can use it for their own research or to read as a companion to Leverich's volume (*Tom: The Unknown Tennessee Williams*) and Williams's own journal (forthcoming from Yale University Press), but also more casual readers who want to learn more about the successor to Eugene O'Neill as America's most important playwright. Devlin and Tischler know their subject and thus their selection offers, in Williams's own words, dramatic glimpses into important moments in his life, from the precocious boy taunted as a "sissy," not only by his male contemporaries in St. Louis, but also by his own father, to the restless, struggling vagabond writer whose *The Glass Menagerie* (1945), the combination memory play and homage to Rose, his lobotomized sister, went to Broadway to launch his extraordinary fame.

These letters show Williams's inner complexity, for example, in his dutifully writing to his mother, Edwina Dakin Williams, and other family members in ways both reassuring and concealing, and then writing to homosexual friends such as Joseph Hazan and Paul Bigelow in ways both frankly intimate and humorous. Letters to his tenaciously wise and protective agent Audrey Wood show his vulnerability, as well as his conviction that he was meant to write, regardless of consequence. Letters to producers and publishers, such as Lawrence Langner of the Theatre Guild and James ("Jay") Laughlin, New Directions founder and publisher, show his awareness of his need for them to bring his work before the public. He knew his audiences, even when they were simply the individuals to whom he wrote, and he knew how long the odds were against his success, especially in the ego- and market-driven world of Broadway.

These letters make it clear that Williams knew what he was meant to do. He betrayed his ambitions amusingly in a 1935 "fan" letter to recent Pulitzer Prize–winning author Josephine Winslow Johnson when, referring to a recent visit he had made to Oxford, Mississippi, where residents held a low opinion of William Faulkner as being "stuck-up," Williams defended the eventual Nobel Prize winner by writing, "I think he's just absent-minded, like me and most other great writers" (76). After his struggles for a first New York production ended in the failure of *Battle of Angels* in Boston, Williams wrote to Theatre Guild producer Lawrence Langner, "Now I'm just a bubble that burst in Boston! You all know that I'm something more than that. But nobody else knows it" (306). More than two years after his letter to Langner, his muse suffocated by a frustrating Hollywood screenwriting job, he poignantly wrote to Wood: "Let's face it!—I can only write for love. Even then, not yet well-enough to set the world on fire. But all this effort, all this longing to create something of value—it will be thrown away, gone up the spout, nothing finally gained—If I don't adhere very strictly to the most honest writing, that I am capable of" (476). Indeed, these letters offer a compelling reminder that the road to success is difficult, requiring belief, good fortune, and the will to endure.

Williams was particularly eloquent on the subject of endurance. From Mexico City on 3 September 1940, he wrote to his friend Hazan: "We are clutching at hard, firm things that will hold us up, the few eternal values which we are able to grasp in this welter of broken pieces, wreckage, that floats on the surface of life. Yes, it is possible, I think, to surround one's self with stone pillars that hold the roof off your head. It takes time to build them, time and careful selection of materials, infinite patience, endurance. We must make a religion of that last thing—endurance" (274).

Given what we already know about the denouement of Williams's life after fame came to him, and the rich material that we can anticipate in succeeding biographical volumes and letters collections, we can see here in Devlin and Tischler's work that the endurance of his belief in his writing destiny may be the most remarkable thing of all about this two-time Pulitzer Prize winner.

These letters bear ample evidence of Williams's great dramatic subject matter— the complexity of family relations, the elusiveness of love, and the peregrinations of a restless heart. There are more letters in this collection to Edwina than to anyone else, and there are also letters to his beloved maternal grandparents; his tragic sister, Rose (more on whom below); his father, Cornelius; and his younger brother Dakin. It is ironic but also appropriate that when he finally wrote and shaped *The Glass Menagerie* at nearly a fever pitch, it was at the family home in suburban St. Louis—a place he constantly sought to escape (441). Williams's gay ontogeny now seems classic viewed from an informed psychological perspective outside his family, but the great difference comes in his creations, now among the most famous in the world, of members of the Wingfield, DuBois, Winemiller, Pollitt, Venable, and other stage families, almost all of whom can be discerned in varying degrees in Williams himself and within his own family circle, to which he was always both inextricably bound and yet from which he was paradoxically a fugitive. Literally and creatively, Williams could never escape his family. He may have tried to write "social drama" in the Odets/Group Theatre vein in the 1930s (*Candles to the Sun* [1937], *Not About Nightingales* [1938]), but his truest and best drama was always far more personal, and it was to come in torrents after *The Glass Menagerie*.

The Glass Menagerie so closely mirrors Edwina, Rose, and Tennessee Williams that its sources and conflicts cannot be mistaken. Tom Wingfield, the protagonist-narrator, claims to have escaped not only his domineeringly protective mother, Amanda, but also his retiring and dependent sister, Laura. In retrospect, the escape was mostly wish fulfillment via drama, and many interpreters have discovered incestuous as well as gay escapist themes in the play, especially in regard to Tom and Laura. Knowing his devotion to his sister and his lifelong support of her after their parents agreed to her being institutionalized in 1937 and lobotomized in 1943, we read, in a 1942 letter to Wood: "The great psychological trauma of my life was my sister's tragedy, who had the same precarious balance of nerves that I have to live with and who found it too much and escaped" (401–2). And, even more tellingly, we read in a letter to Edwina written just a few months after Rose's lobotomy, "I did not at all understand the news about Rose. What kind of operation was it, and what for?" (429). Plays like *The Glass Menagerie, The Purification* (1944), and especially *The Two-Character Play* (1967) are the issue of the family love relationship between Tennessee and Rose Williams, in all likelihood chaste but undeniably fertile, and these collected letters add poignancy to that dynamic.

Consequent to his family background and the formation of his homosexuality, Williams found love to be elusive, and it, too, became one of his most important dramatic subjects. His romantic temperament made him want to believe in the possibility of lasting love with another human being; Devlin and Tischler quote a passage from his journal after his love affair with the dancer Kip Kiernan broke up in 1940: "Somewhere there is another rare and beautiful stranger waiting for me" (264). But his lifelong inability to find and hold a lasting companion is foreshadowed in a letter to James Laughlin five years later: "The evils of promiscuity are exageratted [the editors did not change all instances of Williams's 'erratic spelling' or punctuation (xviii)]. Somebody said it has at least the advantage of making you take more baths. But I think one picks a rose from each person, each of a somewhat different scent and color. Each affair can make some new disclosure, and whether it builds or reduces your range of feeling and understanding depends pretty much on yourself. Of course you pay for it with something—perhaps a cumulative distrust of what is called 'real love'" (553).

Finally, there is the restless, searching, homeless spirit. From the "Hotel Costa Verde" (a name he used years later in *The Night of the Iguana* [1961]), Williams wrote to Hazan in 1940: "I am sure, now, that I will never find one particular place where I feel altogether at home, will just have to keep moving about and absorbing as I go" (284). It is revealing that the context for this statement is Williams's effort to put the broken love affair with Kiernan behind him, cultivating the role of the fugitive, the sensitive vagabond, the creative nomad, the ultimate loner who absorbs experience and the occasional "kindness of strangers" as he moves about—like Valentine Xavier, Tom Wingfield, Blanche DuBois, Alma Winemiller, Kilroy on the *Camino Real* (1953), and legions more—and who finally writes about it from rented rooms and houses domestic and foreign.

Not surprisingly, these letters also show us an intelligent, perceptive person who uses imaginative literary allusions and memorable metaphors (referring to New York as a place where "lies come as naturally as flies at a church-picnic" [283]), and who shows sharp awareness of the tensions between commerce and art (e.g., Letter #227 to Wood [379–80] and Letter #290 to Frederic McConnell [490–91]). He predicted a revitalized American theater after World War II, for example, when writing to Horton Foote on 24 April 1943: "We must remember that a new theatre is coming after the war with a completely new criticism, thank God" (443). He could not have known then what a great part he would play in that "new theatre."

We see here, too, his great admiration of other writers and theater figures (D.H. Lawrence and the Taos colony he established; favored poets like Hart Crane); his "fan" letters to writers as diverse as Robert P. Tristram Coffin, William Saroyan, Katherine Anne Porter, and Carson McCullers; his first use of the pseudonym "Tennessee," and the "En Avant!" and "10" signature letter closings (440) that would become so familiar; his first use of the memorable "colored lights" (516) phrase from *Streetcar* (to refer to his creativity in full tide, not sex); his identification of his creative doubts and fears as "blue devils" (307); his colorful description of his futile attempt to write a screenplay for Lana Turner as trying to fashion a "celluloid brassiere" (455) for her.

Devlin and Tischler have brilliantly advanced Tennessee Williams scholarship with this volume, in which they offer a brief but illuminating introduction; a helpful editorial note that makes it easy to identify, locate, and use individual letters; a general index; an index of recipients; and an index of Williams's works. Several photographs enhance the collection that, fittingly, is published by New Directions, the publisher Williams always used after contractual obligations required Random House to publish *The Glass Menagerie*.

Ralph F. Voss
University of Alabama

BOOK REVIEWS   413

DAVE SMITH: A LITERARY ARCHIVE. By Robert J. DeMott. Athens: Ohio U Lib., 2000. xvi + 134 pp.

Robert J. DeMott's book, distributed—in a limited hardcover edition of 50 copies, as well as in a paperbound version—free of charge by the Ohio University Libraries, describes his personal archive of materials associated with the contemporary poet Dave Smith (b. 1942), an assemblage of books, manuscripts, letters, and other items now a part of the Ohio University Libraries' foundational Dave Smith Collection. But this volume's real purpose is to tell the story of how the archive was built as a product of DeMott's professional involvement and close friendship with Smith, dating from the poet's graduate student days. That narrative, told via six pages of anecdotal acknowledgments and a thirty-one-page introduction, presents a useful historical and critical introduction to Smith's work. The archive itself was originally intended to support a full-fledged analysis. But as DeMott himself went through some life changes, he discovered that the materials themselves and his act of collecting them provided a better statement about Smith's literary career than would a conventionally interpretive volume.

Consequently, DeMott, author of three important books on John Steinbeck, emerges here as "Bob" to his readers and as "Big Mott" to his friend the poet, whose two-year-old daughter coined the nickname. He makes occasional critical judgments and chronicles most important literary history, all the while involved with Smith in various editorial and academic endeavors. More important, he reads Smith's work and collects it. Here is where DeMott makes his real contribution: not just presenting an analysis of this writer's art, but recreating the whole experience of learning about the material and investing three decades of his life in working with it.

Dave Smith: A Literary Archive thus gives testimony to how deeply appreciative reading takes place. More honestly than a conventional work of literary criticism could manage, it replicates the act of relating to literature; and much more so than a traditional bibliography, it is invested with the spirit behind acquiring, organizing, and describing the work of a genuinely important writer. Through his involvement with Smith, DeMott came to understand the process—how when readers encounter literary art that appeals to them, they seek out more of it, *collecting* it in the most basic sense of that word. Soon the collection not only represents the writer's canon, but also takes on a life of its own, a life of literature that the collector can share. If the reader happens to know the writer, all the better. But personal acquaintance is not necessary, for it is a larger sense of the writer's work that now speaks to the reader. There is a proof for this, as it is not unusual when writer and reader do know each other that the latter gets praised for knowing the former's work even better than the writer himself or herself does.

The body of DeMott's book presents his evidence for this knowledge. Books, magazines, and manuscripts add up to nearly three hundred items. Each is given a full bibliographic description, and some of the more important are graced with DeMott's brief commentary. The book's largest section describes one hundred thirty-five letters that Smith sent to the author between 1973 and 1999, a remarkable record of a person's growth from graduate student to major literary figure. Although friends, Smith and DeMott are ever focused on their profession of English, and these letters are rich with shoptalk and the academic business with which everyone in this field must deal. How comforting to know that even a brilliant poet with an emerging national reputation still suffers from an English Department's administrative uncooperativeness, and how rewarding to learn that he can use part of a National Endowment for the Arts grant "to buy a used Porsche if a decent one can be found" (88). Summer writing conferences are a lot of work and a lot of fun, running the gamut from all-day workshops to evening readings and all-night parties, one of which ends with a wee-hours search for Ted Roethke's former house in Bennington.

Other sections include dust-jacket encomia and various association items. Blurb writing is hardly a high art, and in itself promises no real critical insight. Does Russell Banks expect tough analysis when his publisher asks Smith to endorse the novel *Continental Drift* (1985)? But it does serve literary history to know that for this, Banks's breakthrough work, Harper & Row thought to solicit comments from a still-young poet whose reputation was anything but secure. Then there is the range of authors for whom Smith provided comments—revealing, as DeMott notes in his introduction, a breadth of taste much wider than that of his critics. From DeMott's point of view, all this is part of the collection and creates a larger understanding of the poet and his work. In a critical study, he could have summarized the comments and made an analytical point. Here he lets readers find the connections themselves, which will be connections better made.

Concluding the volume is a thumbnail sketch of what else resides in the Dave Smith Collection at Ohio: forty-one Hollinger boxes (fourteen cubic feet) comprising a rare book purchase and the full collection of Smith's papers, and a container list that is available online (http://www.library.ohiou.edu/libinfo/depts/archives/archives.htm). To readers who might object that such information should be printed here, *Dave Smith: A Literary Archive* answers with its embodiment of the collection's spirit, for that is what DeMott's efforts have achieved. Without his personal archive as a start, there might well be no larger foundational collection. There would still be Smith's poetry, of course. But without a reader to respond, one fears the effect of it would be like the proverbial tree falling in a forest with no one there to hear it.

Jerome Klinkowitz
University of Northern Iowa

Index to Volumes 28 and 29 of
Resources for American Literary Study

HEATHER McHALE
University of Maryland

This index is divided into three parts: an author index, a subject index, and an index of books reviewed. The author index lists the articles and reviews by the name of the author. The subject index references articles and books reviewed, by topic. The index of books reviewed lists the books that have been reviewed, by the name of the book's author, and gives the name of the reviewer in parentheses.

Works of literature are listed by the name of the author; books of letters and journals are listed by the name of the editor. Each article, then, is listed by author and subject, and each review by the author of the book, the author of the review, and the subject(s). All entries give volume and page numbers. Unless otherwise noted, cross-references are to the same section of the index as the entry containing the cross-reference.

Author Index

Adler, Thomas P., "Classics of Twentieth-Century American Theater" (review-essay), 29: 331–42

Anesko, Michael, Review: Susan E. Gunter, ed., *Dear Munificent Friends: Henry James's Letters to Four Women*, and Susan E. Gunter and Steven H. Jobe, eds., *Dearly Beloved Friends: Henry James's Letters to Younger Men*, 29: 377–80

Austenfeld, Thomas, Review: Susan J. Rosowski, *Birthing a Nation: Gender, Creativity, and the West in American Literature*, 28: 189–91

Axelrod, Stephen Gould, "Jeffers Redux" (review-essay), 29: 317–30

Balakian, Jan, Review: Don B. Wilmeth and Christopher Bigsby, eds., *The Cambridge History of American Theatre: Volume II, 1870–1945*, 28: 197–203

Bassett, John, Review: Emmanuel S. Nelson, ed., *African American Authors, 1745–1945: A Bio-Bibliographical Sourcebook*, 28: 170–71

Black, Cheryl, Review: Barbara Ozieblo, *Susan Glaspell: A Critical Biography*, 29: 394–96

Blume, Donald T., Review: S. T. Joshi, ed., *The Collected Fables of Ambrose Bierce*, 29: 367–71

Brada-Williams, Noelle, "Asian American Literary Studies at Maturity" (review-essay), 29: 285–300

Braxton, Joanne, Review: Eleanor Alexander, *Lyrics of Sunshine and Shadow: The Tragic Courtship and Marriage of Paul Laurence Dunbar and Alice Ruth Moore, a History of Love and Violence among the African American Elite*, 29: 387–90

Brooks, Joanna, Review: Carla Mulford and David S. Shields, eds., *Finding Colonial Americas: Essays Honoring J. A. Leo Lemay*, 29: 348–51

Burt, John, Review: Paul Mariani, *The Broken Tower: A Life of Hart Crane*, 28: 211–17

Campbell, Donna M., Review: Axel Nissen, *Bret Harte: Prince and Pauper*, 29: 371–73

Cantalupo, Barbara, "The Letters of Israel Zangwill to Emma Wolf: Transatlantic Mentoring in the 1890s," 28: 121–38

Clinton, Craig, "Transformative Stages: Williams's *Vieux Carré* in New York and London," 29: 235–51

Cook, Jonathan A., Review: Kevin J. Hayes, *Melville's Folk Roots*, 28: 192–94

Crisler, Jesse S., "Frank Norris, College Man," 28: 111–20

Daugherty, Sarah B., "Prospects for the Study of William Dean Howells," 29: 9–24

Demastes, William W., Review: Felicia Hardison Londré and Daniel J. Watermeier, *The History of North American Theater. The United States, Canada, and Mexico: From Pre-Columbian Times to the Present*, 29: 343–45

Erben, Patrick M., "Promoting Pennsylvania: Penn, Pastorius, and the Creation of a Transnational Community," 29: 25–65

Franklin, Wayne, Review: James Fenimore Cooper, *The Spy: A Tale of the Neutral Ground*, James P. Elliott (introduction); James H. Pickering (notes); and James P. Elliott, Lance Schachterle, and Jeffrey Walker (textual editing), 29: 354–56

Giles, Paul, Review: Maria Diedrich, *Love Across Color Lines: Ottilie Assing and Frederick Douglass*, and Christopher Lohmann, ed., *Radical Passion: Ottilie Assing's Reports from America and Letters to Frederick Douglass*, 28: 186–89

Hanley, Brian, "Andre Dubus: A Survey of Research and Criticism," 28: 1–16

Harper, Donna Akiba, Review: Emily Bernard, ed., *Remember Me To Harlem: The Letters of Langston Hughes and Carl Van Vechten*, and Susan Duffy, ed., *The Political Plays of Langston Hughes*, 29: 396–99

Higgins, Andrew C., Review: Paula Bernat Bennett, ed., *Palace-Burner: The Selected Poetry of Sarah Piatt*, 29: 374–76

Homestead, Melissa J., Review: Ezra Greenspan, *George Palmer Putnam: Representative American Publisher*, and Ezra Greenspan, ed., *The House of Putnam, 1837–1872: A Documentary Volume*, 28: 180–83

Inge, M. Thomas, "Founding a Journal: *Resources for American Literary Study*," 29: 1–8

Jones, Jill C., Review: Marjorie Kinnan Rawlings, *Blood of My Blood*, ed. Anne Blythe Meriwether, and Rodger L. Tarr, ed., *Max and Marjorie: The Correspondence between Maxwell E. Perkins and Marjorie Kinnan Rawlings*, 29: 406–9

Justice, Hilary K., "Tragic Stasis: Love, War, and the Composition of Hemingway's 'Big Two-Hearted River,'" 29: 199–215

Keil, James C., Review: Steven Fink and Susan S. Williams, eds., *Reciprocal Influences: Literary Production, Distribution, and Consumption in America*, 28: 163–66

Kent, Alicia, Review: Carla Kaplan, ed., *Zora Neale Hurston: A Life in Letters*, and Venetria K. Patton and Maureen Honey, eds., *Double-Take: A Revisionist Harlem Renaissance Anthology*, 29: 399–403

Klinkowitz, Jerome, Review: Robert J. DeMott, *Dave Smith: A Literary Archive*, 29: 413–14

Knight, Denise, Review: Jennifer S. Tuttle, ed., *The Crux: A Novel by Charlotte Perkins Gilman*, 29: 381–83

Kolin, Philip C., "An Unpublished Tennessee Williams Letter to William Carlos Williams," 28: 159–62

Ljungquist, Kent P., "'Fellowship with Other Poets': Lowell, Longfellow, and Poe Correspond with A. M. Ide Jr.," 28: 27–52; Review: John Conron, *American Picturesque*, 28: 171–73; Review: Tom Quirk, *Nothing Abstract: Investigations in the American Literary Imagination*, 29: 345–48

Lott, Deshae E., "On the Margins and in the Margins: Margaret Fuller and the Testaments," 28: 83–110

MacLeod, Glen, "The James Family and the Boston Athenaeum: A Bibliography," 29: 89–140

Marovitz, Sanford E., "Parker's *Melville*: The Life Complete" (review-essay), 29: 275–83

McKee, Kathryn B., Review: M. Thomas Inge and Edward J. Piacentino, eds., *The Humor of the Old South*, and David Rachels, ed., *Augustus Baldwin Longstreet's "Georgia Scenes" Completed: A Scholarly Text*, 29: 357–61

Mignon, Charles W., "Willa Cather's Process of Composing," 29: 165–84

Moore, Rayburn S., Review: Philip Horne, ed., *Henry James: A Life in Letters*, 28: 195–97

Parry, Sally E., Review: Sinclair Lewis, *Minnesota Diary 1943–46*, ed. George Killough, 29: 403–5

Patton, Venetria K., Review: Pamela Bordelon, ed., *Go Gator and Muddy the Water: Writings by Zora Neale Hurston from the Federal Writers' Project*, 28: 217–19

Petrulionis, Sandra Harbert, "Fugitive Slave-Running on the *Moby-Dick*: Captain Austin Bearse and the Abolitionist Crusade," 28: 53–82

Petry, Alice Hall, Review: Karen L. Kilcup, ed., *Soft Canons: American Women Writers and Masculine Tradition*, 28: 174–76

Piacentino, Ed, Review: Hugh T. Keenan, *The Library of Joel Chandler Harris: An Annotated Book List*, 28: 203–5

Post, Constance J., "Making the A-List: Reformation and Revolution in Crocker's *Observations on the real rights of women*," 29: 67–88

Prettyman, Gib, Review: June Howard, *Publishing the Family*, and William Dean Howells, Mary E. Wilkins Freeman, Mary Heaton Vorse, Mary Stewart Cutting, Elizabeth Jordan, John Kendrick Bangs, Henry James, Elizabeth Stuart Phelps, Edith Wyatt, Mary Raymond Shipman Andrews, Alice Brown, and Henry Van Dyke, *The Whole Family: A Novel by Twelve Authors*, 29: 383–87

Rachels, David, "The First Southern Story: Oliver Hillhouse Prince's 'Dear Fugey,'" 28: 17–25

Richardson, Betty, Review: Catherine Ross Nickerson, *The Web of Iniquity: Early Detective Fiction by American Women*, 28: 183–86

Rosowski, Susan J., "What Are We Doing in the Humanities Today? Cather as Case Study" (review-essay), 29: 301–15

Sanders, David, "Fostering the Poet: An Unpublished Robert Frost Letter," 29: 185–98

Scharnhorst, Gary F., "Kate Field: A Primary Bibliography," 29: 141–63

Schneider, Richard J., Review: Bradley P. Dean, ed., *"Wild Fruits": Thoreau's Rediscovered Last Manuscripts*, 28: 176–79

Simmons, Nancy Craig, Review: Ronald A. Bosco and Joel Myerson, eds., *The Later Lectures of Ralph Waldo Emerson, 1843–1871. Volume 1: 1843–1854; Volume 2: 1855–1871*, 29: 364–67

Singer, Marc, "Two Unpublished Letters from F. Scott and Zelda Fitzgerald to Thornton Wilder," 28: 153–57

Taylor, Corey M., "'Wish I Were There': Ten Letters from William S. Burroughs to Paul Bowles, 1972–79," 29: 253–74

Thompson, Roger, "Two Unpublished Longfellow Letters from the Agassiz/Shaw Family Autograph Book," 28: 149–52

Tonkovich, Nicole, Review: Grace Farrell, *Lillie Devereux Blake: Retracing a Life Erased*, 29: 361–63

Travisano, Thomas, "'Precipitation into Poetry': The Bishop-Lowell Letters and the Boundaries of the Canon," 29: 217–33

Tucker, Edward L., "Five Letters from William Cullen Bryant to William Ware," 28: 139–48

Van Egmond, Peter, Review: Jay Parini, *Robert Frost: A Life*, 28: 206–7

von Frank, Albert J., Review: Sargent Bush Jr., ed., *The Correspondence of John Cotton*, and Michael P. Winship, *Making Heretics: Militant Protestantism and Free Grace in Massachusetts, 1636–1641*, 29: 351–54

Voss, Ralph F., Review: Albert J. Devlin and Nancy M. Tischler, eds., *The Selected Letters of Tennessee Williams: Volume 1, 1920–1945*, 29: 409–12

Walden, Daniel, Review: Joel Shatzky and Michael Taub, eds., *Contemporary Jewish-American Dramatists and Poets: A Bio-Critical Sourcebook*, 28: 220–21

Williams, Keith, Review: Jesse S. Crisler, Robert C. Leitz III, and Joseph R. McElrath Jr., eds., *An Exemplary Citizen: Letters of Charles W. Chesnutt, 1906–1932*, and Dean McWilliams, *Charles W. Chesnutt and the Fictions of Race*, 29: 390–93

Winans, Amy, Review: Thomas W. Krise, ed., *Caribbeana: An Anthology of English Literature of the West Indies, 1657–1777*, 28: 167–70

Witemeyer, Hugh, Review: Omar Pound and Robert Spoo, eds., *Ezra and Dorothy Pound: Letters in Captivity, 1945–1946*, and Demetres P. Tryphonopoulos and Leon Surette, eds., *"I Cease Not to Yowl": Ezra Pound's Letters to Olivia Rossetti Agresti*, 28: 207–11

Subject Index

Abolitionists: Sandra Harbert Petrulionis, "Fugitive Slave-Running on the *Moby-Dick*: Captain Austin Bearse and the Abolitionist Crusade," 28: 53–82

African American literature: Review: Emmanuel S. Nelson, ed., *African American Authors, 1745–1945: A Bio-Bibliographical Sourcebook* (John Bassett), 28: 170–71

Albee, Edward: Thomas P. Adler, "Classics of Twentieth-Century American Theater" (review-essay), 29: 331–42

Andrews, Mary Raymond Shipman: Review: June Howard, *Publishing the Family*, and William Dean Howells, Mary E. Wilkins Freeman, Mary Heaton Vorse, Mary Stewart Cutting, Elizabeth Jordan, John Kendrick Bangs, Henry James, Elizabeth Stuart Phelps, Edith Wyatt, Mary Raymond Shipman Andrews, Alice Brown, and Henry Van Dyke, *The Whole Family: A Novel by Twelve Authors* (Gib Prettyman), 29: 383–87

archival studies: Review: Sargent Bush Jr., ed., *The Correspondence of John Cotton*, and Michael P. Winship, *Making Heretics: Militant Protestantism and Free Grace in Massachusetts, 1636–1641* (Albert J. von Frank), 29: 351–54

Asian American literature: Noelle Brada-Williams, "Asian American Literary Studies at Maturity" (review-essay), 29: 285–300

Assing, Ottilie: Review: Maria Diedrich, *Love Across Color Lines: Ottilie Assing and Frederick Douglass*, and Christopher Lohmann, ed., *Radical Passion: Ottilie Assing's Reports from America and Letters to Frederick Douglass* (Paul Giles), 28: 186–89

Bangs, John Kendrick: Review: June Howard, *Publishing the Family*, and William Dean Howells, Mary E. Wilkins Freeman, Mary Heaton Vorse, Mary Stewart Cutting, Elizabeth Jordan, John Kendrick Bangs, Henry James, Elizabeth Stuart Phelps, Edith Wyatt, Mary Raymond Shipman Andrews, Alice Brown, and Henry Van Dyke, *The Whole Family: A Novel by Twelve Authors* (Gib Prettyman), 29: 383–87

Bearse, Austin: Sandra Harbert Petrulionis, "Fugitive Slave-Running on the *Moby-Dick*: Captain Austin Bearse and the Abolitionist Crusade," 28: 53–82

Bierce, Ambrose: Review: S. T. Joshi, ed., *The Collected Fables of Ambrose Bierce* (Donald T. Blume), 29: 367–71

Bishop, Elizabeth: Thomas Travisano, "'Precipitation into Poetry': The Bishop-Lowell Letters and the Boundaries of the Canon," 29: 217–33

Blake, Lillie Devereux: Review: Grace Farrell, *Lillie Devereux Blake: Retracing a Life Erased* (Nicole Tonkovich), 29: 361–63

INDEX

Bowles, Paul: Corey M. Taylor, "'Wish I Were There': Ten Letters from William S. Burroughs to Paul Bowles, 1972–79," 29: 253–74
Brown, Alice: Review: June Howard, *Publishing the Family*, and William Dean Howells, Mary E. Wilkins Freeman, Mary Heaton Vorse, Mary Stewart Cutting, Elizabeth Jordan, John Kendrick Bangs, Henry James, Elizabeth Stuart Phelps, Edith Wyatt, Mary Raymond Shipman Andrews, Alice Brown, and Henry Van Dyke, *The Whole Family: A Novel by Twelve Authors* (Gib Prettyman), 29: 383–87
Bryant, William Cullen: Edward L. Tucker, "Five Letters from William Cullen Bryant to William Ware," 28: 139–48
Burroughs, William S.: Corey M. Taylor, "'Wish I Were There': Ten Letters from William S. Burroughs to Paul Bowles, 1972–79," 29: 253–74

canonicity: Review: Karen L. Kilcup, ed., *Soft Canons: American Women Writers and Masculine Tradition* (Alice Hall Petry), 28: 174–76; Thomas Travisano, "'Precipitation into Poetry': The Bishop-Lowell Letters and the Boundaries of the Canon," 29: 217–33
Caribbean literature: Review: Thomas W. Krise, ed., *Caribbeana: An Anthology of English Literature of the West Indies, 1657–1777* (Amy Winans), 28: 167–70
Cather, Willa: Charles W. Mignon, "Willa Cather's Process of Composing," 29: 165–84; Susan J. Rosowski, "What Are We Doing in the Humanities Today? Cather as Case Study" (review-essay), 29: 301–15
Chesnutt, Charles: Review: Jesse S. Crisler, Robert C. Leitz III, and Joseph R. McElrath Jr., eds., *An Exemplary Citizen: Letters of Charles W. Chesnutt, 1906–1932*, and Dean McWilliams, *Charles W. Chesnutt and the Fictions of Race* (Keith Williams), 29: 390–93
colonial studies: Review: Carla Mulford and David S. Shields, eds., *Finding Colonial Americas: Essays Honoring J. A. Leo Lemay* (Joanna Brooks), 29: 348–51

Cooper, James Fenimore: Review: James Fenimore Cooper, *The Spy: A Tale of the Neutral Ground*, James P. Elliott (introduction); James H. Pickering (notes); and James P. Elliott, Lance Schachterle, and Jeffrey Walker (textual editing) (Wayne Franklin), 29: 354–56
Cotton, John: Review: Sargent Bush Jr., ed., *The Correspondence of John Cotton* (Albert J. von Frank), 29: 351–54
Crane, Hart: Review: Paul Mariani, *The Broken Tower: A Life of Hart Crane* (John Burt), 28: 211–17
Crocker, Hannah Mather: Constance J. Post, "Making the A-List: Reformation and Revolution in Crocker's *Observations on the real rights of women*," 29: 67–88
Cutting, Mary Stewart: Review: June Howard, *Publishing the Family*, and William Dean Howells, Mary E. Wilkins Freeman, Mary Heaton Vorse, Mary Stewart Cutting, Elizabeth Jordan, John Kendrick Bangs, Henry James, Elizabeth Stuart Phelps, Edith Wyatt, Mary Raymond Shipman Andrews, Alice Brown, and Henry Van Dyke, *The Whole Family: A Novel by Twelve Authors* (Gib Prettyman), 29: 383–87

detective fiction: Review: Catherine Ross Nickerson, *The Web of Iniquity: Early Detective Fiction by American Women* (Betty Richardson), 28: 183–86
Douglass, Frederick: Review: Maria Diedrich, *Love Across Color Lines: Ottilie Assing and Frederick Douglass*, and Christopher Lohmann, ed., *Radical Passion: Ottilie Assing's Reports from America and Letters to Frederick Douglass* (Paul Giles), 28: 186–89
Dubus, Andre: Brian Hanley, "Andre Dubus: A Survey of Research and Criticism," 28: 1–16
Dunbar, Paul Laurence: Review: Eleanor Alexander, *Lyrics of Sunshine and Shadow: The Tragic Courtship and Marriage of Paul Laurence Dunbar and Alice Ruth Moore, a History of Love and Violence among the African American Elite* (Joanne Braxton), 29: 387–90

Emerson, Ralph Waldo: Review: Ronald A. Bosco and Joel Myerson, eds., *The Later Lectures of Ralph Waldo Emerson, 1843–1871. Volume 1: 1843–1854; Volume 2: 1855–1871* (Nancy Craig Simmons), 29: 364–67

Federal Writers' Project: Review: Pamela Bordelon, ed., *Go Gator and Muddy the Water: Writings by Zora Neale Hurston from the Federal Writers' Project* (Venetria K. Patton), 28: 217–19
Field, Kate: Gary F. Scharnhorst, "Kate Field: A Primary Bibliography," 29: 141–63
Fitzgerald, F. Scott: Marc Singer, "Two Unpublished Letters from F. Scott and Zelda Fitzgerald to Thornton Wilder," 28: 153–57
Fitzgerald, Zelda: Marc Singer, "Two Unpublished Letters from F. Scott and Zelda Fitzgerald to Thornton Wilder," 28: 153–57
Freeman, Mary E. Wilkins: Review: June Howard, *Publishing the Family*, and William Dean Howells, Mary E. Wilkins Freeman, Mary Heaton Vorse, Mary Stewart Cutting, Elizabeth Jordan, John Kendrick Bangs, Henry James, Elizabeth Stuart Phelps, Edith Wyatt, Mary Raymond Shipman Andrews, Alice Brown, and Henry Van Dyke, *The Whole Family: A Novel by Twelve Authors* (Gib Prettyman), 29: 383–87
Frost, Robert: Review: Jay Parini, *Robert Frost: A Life* (Peter Van Egmond), 28: 206–7; David Sanders, "Fostering the Poet: An Unpublished Robert Frost Letter," 29: 185–98
Fuller, Margaret: Deshae E. Lott, "On the Margins and in the Margins: Margaret Fuller and the Testaments," 28: 83–110

Gay-Tifft, Eugene: David Sanders, "Fostering the Poet: An Unpublished Robert Frost Letter," 29: 185–98
gender: Review: Susan J. Rosowski, *Birthing a Nation: Gender, Creativity, and the West in American Literature* (Thomas Austenfeld), 28: 189–91; Constance J. Post, "Making the A-List: Reformation and Revolution in Crocker's *Observations on the real rights of women*," 29: 67–88. See also women's writing

Gilman, Charlotte Perkins: Review: Jennifer S. Tuttle, ed. *The Crux: A Novel by Charlotte Perkins Gilman* (Denise Knight), 29: 381–83
Glaspell, Susan: Review: Barbara Ozieblo, *Susan Glaspell: A Critical Biography* (Cheryl Black), 29: 394–96

Harlem Renaissance: Review: Emily Bernard, ed., *Remember Me To Harlem: The Letters of Langston Hughes and Carl Van Vechten*, and Susan Duffy, ed., *The Political Plays of Langston Hughes* (Donna Akiba Harper), 29: 396–99; Review: Venetria K. Patton and Maureen Honey, eds., *Double-Take: A Revisionist Harlem Renaissance Anthology* (Alicia Kent), 29: 399–403
Harris, Joel Chandler: Review: Hugh T. Keenan, *The Library of Joel Chandler Harris: An Annotated Book List* (Ed Piacentino), 28: 203–5
Harte, Bret: Review: Axel Nissen, *Bret Harte: Prince and Pauper* (Donna M. Campbell), 29: 371–73
Hemingway, Ernest: Hilary K. Justice, "Tragic Stasis: Love, War, and the Composition of Hemingway's 'Big Two-Hearted River,'" 29: 199–215
Howells, William Dean: Sarah B. Daugherty, "Prospects for the Study of William Dean Howells," 29: 9–24; Review: June Howard, *Publishing the Family*, and William Dean Howells, Mary E. Wilkins Freeman, Mary Heaton Vorse, Mary Stewart Cutting, Elizabeth Jordan, John Kendrick Bangs, Henry James, Elizabeth Stuart Phelps, Edith Wyatt, Mary Raymond Shipman Andrews, Alice Brown, and Henry Van Dyke, *The Whole Family: A Novel by Twelve Authors* (Gib Prettyman), 29: 383–87
Hughes, Langston: Review: Emily Bernard, ed., *Remember Me To Harlem: The Letters of Langston Hughes and Carl Van Vechten*, and Susan Duffy, ed., *The Political Plays of Langston Hughes* (Donna Akiba Harper), 29: 396–99
humor: Review: M. Thomas Inge and Edward J. Piacentino, eds., *The Humor of the Old South* (Kathryn B. McKee), 29: 357–61

INDEX

Hurston, Zora Neale: Review: Pamela Bordelon, ed., *Go Gator and Muddy the Water: Writings by Zora Neale Hurston from the Federal Writers' Project* (Venetria K. Patton), 28: 217–19; Review: Carla Kaplan, ed., *Zora Neale Hurston: A Life in Letters* (Alicia Kent), 29: 399–403

Ide, A. M., Jr.: Kent P. Ljungquist, "'Fellowship with Other Poets': Lowell, Longfellow, and Poe Correspond with A. M. Ide Jr.," 28: 27–52

James, Henry: Review: Philip Horne, ed., *Henry James: A Life in Letters* (Rayburn S. Moore), 28: 195–97; Glen MacLeod, "The James Family and the Boston Athenaeum: A Bibliography," 29: 89–140; Review: Susan E. Gunter, ed., *Dear Munificent Friends: Henry James's Letters to Four Women*, and Susan E. Gunter and Steven H. Jobe, eds., *Dearly Beloved Friends: Henry James's Letters to Younger Men* (Michael Anesko), 29: 377–80; Review: June Howard, *Publishing the Family*, and William Dean Howells, Mary E. Wilkins Freeman, Mary Heaton Vorse, Mary Stewart Cutting, Elizabeth Jordan, John Kendrick Bangs, Henry James, Elizabeth Stuart Phelps, Edith Wyatt, Mary Raymond Shipman Andrews, Alice Brown, and Henry Van Dyke, *The Whole Family: A Novel by Twelve Authors* (Gib Prettyman), 29: 383–87

Jeffers, Robinson: Stephen Gould Axelrod, "Jeffers Redux" (review-essay), 29: 317–30

Jewish-American literature: Review: Joel Shatzky and Michael Taub, eds., *Contemporary Jewish-American Dramatists and Poets: A Bio-Critical Sourcebook* (Daniel Walden), 28: 220–21

Jordan, Elizabeth: Review: June Howard, *Publishing the Family*, and William Dean Howells, Mary E. Wilkins Freeman, Mary Heaton Vorse, Mary Stewart Cutting, Elizabeth Jordan, John Kendrick Bangs, Henry James, Elizabeth Stuart Phelps, Edith Wyatt, Mary Raymond Shipman Andrews, Alice Brown, and Henry Van Dyke, *The Whole Family: A Novel by Twelve Authors* (Gib Prettyman), 29: 383–87

Lewis, Sinclair: Review: Sinclair Lewis, *Minnesota Diary 1943–46*, ed. George Killough (Sally E. Parry), 29: 403–5

Longfellow, Henry Wadsworth: Kent P. Ljungquist, "'Fellowship with Other Poets': Lowell, Longfellow, and Poe Correspond with A. M. Ide Jr.," 28: 27–52; Roger Thompson, "Two Unpublished Longfellow Letters from the Agassiz/Shaw Family Autograph Book," 28: 149–52

Longstreet, Augustus Baldwin: Review: David Rachels, ed., *Augustus Baldwin Longstreet's "Georgia Scenes" Completed: A Scholarly Text* (Kathryn B. McKee), 29: 357–61

Lowell, James Russell: Kent P. Ljungquist, "'Fellowship with Other Poets': Lowell, Longfellow, and Poe Correspond with A. M. Ide Jr.," 28: 27–52

Lowell, Robert: Thomas Travisano, "'Precipitation into Poetry': The Bishop-Lowell Letters and the Boundaries of the Canon," 29: 217–33

Melville, Herman: Sandra Harbert Petrulionis, "Fugitive Slave-Running on the *Moby-Dick*: Captain Austin Bearse and the Abolitionist Crusade," 28: 53–82; Review: Kevin J. Hayes, *Melville's Folk Roots* (Jonathan A. Cook), 28: 192–94; Sanford E. Marovitz, "Parker's *Melville*: A Life Complete" (review-essay), 29: 275–83

Miller, Arthur: Thomas P. Adler, "Classics of Twentieth-Century American Theater" (review-essay), 29: 331–42

Norris, Frank: Jesse S. Crisler, "Frank Norris, College Man," 28: 111–20

O'Neill, Eugene: Thomas P. Adler, "Classics of Twentieth-Century American Theater" (review-essay), 29: 331–42

Pastorius, Francis Daniel: Patrick Erben, "Promoting Pennsylvania: Penn, Pastorius, and the Creation of a Transnational Community," 29: 25–65

Penn, William: Patrick Erben, "Promoting Pennsylvania: Penn, Pastorius, and the Creation of a Transnational Community," 29: 25–65

Pennsylvania: Patrick Erben, "Promoting Pennsylvania: Penn, Pastorius, and the Creation of a Transnational Community," 29: 25–65

Perkins, Maxwell: Review: Rodger L. Tarr, ed., *Max and Marjorie: The Correspondence between Maxwell E. Perkins and Marjorie Kinnan Rawlings* (Jill C. Jones), 29: 406–9

Phelps, Elizabeth Stuart: Review: June Howard, *Publishing the Family,* and William Dean Howells, Mary E. Wilkins Freeman, Mary Heaton Vorse, Mary Stewart Cutting, Elizabeth Jordan, John Kendrick Bangs, Henry James, Elizabeth Stuart Phelps, Edith Wyatt, Mary Raymond Shipman Andrews, Alice Brown, and Henry Van Dyke, *The Whole Family: A Novel by Twelve Authors* (Gib Prettyman), 29: 383–87

Piatt, Sarah: Review: Paula Bernat Bennett, ed., *Palace-Burner: The Selected Poetry of Sarah Piatt* (Andrew C. Higgins), 29: 374–76

Poe, Edgar Allan: Kent P. Ljungquist, "'Fellowship with Other Poets': Lowell, Longfellow, and Poe Correspond with A. M. Ide Jr.," 28: 27–52

poetry: Kent P. Ljungquist, "'Fellowship with Other Poets': Lowell, Longfellow, and Poe Correspond with A. M. Ide Jr.," 28: 27–52; Review: Joel Shatzky and Michael Taub, eds., *Contemporary Jewish-American Dramatists and Poets: A Bio-Critical Sourcebook* (Daniel Walden), 28: 220–21

Pound, Dorothy: Review: Omar Pound and Robert Spoo, eds., *Ezra and Dorothy Pound: Letters in Captivity, 1945–1946,* and Demetres P. Tryphonopoulos and Leon Surette, eds., *"I Cease Not to Yowl": Ezra Pound's Letters to Olivia Rossetti Agresti* (Hugh Witemeyer), 28: 207–11

Pound, Ezra: Review: Omar Pound and Robert Spoo, eds., *Ezra and Dorothy Pound: Letters in Captivity, 1945–1946,* and Demetres P. Tryphonopoulos and Leon Surette, eds., *"I Cease Not to Yowl": Ezra Pound's Letters to Olivia Rossetti Agresti* (Hugh Witemeyer), 28: 207–11

Prince, Oliver Hillhouse: David Rachels, "The First Southern Story: Oliver Hillhouse Prince's 'Dear Fugey,'" 28: 17–25

publishing: Review: Steven Fink and Susan S. Williams, eds., *Reciprocal Influences: Literary Production, Distribution, and Consumption in America* (James C. Keil), 28: 163–66; Review: Ezra Greenspan, *George Palmer Putnam: Representative American Publisher,* and Ezra Greenspan, ed., *The House of Putnam, 1837–1872: A Documentary Volume* (Melissa J. Homestead), 28: 180–83

Putnam, George Palmer: Review: Ezra Greenspan, *George Palmer Putnam: Representative American Publisher,* and Ezra Greenspan, ed., *The House of Putnam, 1837–1872: A Documentary Volume* (Melissa J. Homestead), 28: 180–83

Rawlings, Marjorie Kinnan: Review: Marjorie Kinnan Rawlings, *Blood of My Blood,* ed. Anne Blythe Meriwether, and Rodger L. Tarr, ed., *Max and Marjorie: The Correspondence between Maxwell E. Perkins and Marjorie Kinnan Rawlings,* 29: 406–9

Resources for American Literary Study: M. Thomas Inge, "Founding a Journal: *Resources for American Literary Study*," 29: 1–8

Smith, Dave: Review: Robert J. DeMott, *Dave Smith: A Literary Archive* (Jerome Klinkowitz), 29: 413–14

South (American): Review: M. Thomas Inge and Edward J. Piacentino, eds., *The Humor of the Old South* (Kathryn B. McKee), 29: 357–61

theater (American): Review: Don B. Wilmeth and Christopher Bigsby, eds., *The Cambridge History of American Theatre: Volume II, 1870–1945* (Jan Balakian), 28: 197–203; Review: Joel Shatzky and Michael Taub, eds., *Contemporary Jewish-American Dramatists and Poets: A Bio-Critical Sourcebook* (Daniel Walden), 28: 220–21; Craig Clinton, "Transformative Stages: Williams's *Vieux Carré* in New York and London," 29: 235–51; Thomas P. Adler, "Classics of Twentieth-Century American Theater" (review-essay), 29:

331–42; Review: Felicia Hardison Londré and Daniel J. Watermeier, *The History of North American Theater: The United States, Canada, and Mexico: From Pre-Columbian Times to the Present* (William W. Demastes), 29: 343–45
Thoreau, Henry David: Review: Bradley P. Dean, ed., *"Wild Fruits": Thoreau's Rediscovered Last Manuscripts* (Richard J. Schneider), 28: 176–79

Van Dyke, Henry: Review: June Howard, *Publishing the Family*, and William Dean Howells, Mary E. Wilkins Freeman, Mary Heaton Vorse, Mary Stewart Cutting, Elizabeth Jordan, John Kendrick Bangs, Henry James, Elizabeth Stuart Phelps, Edith Wyatt, Mary Raymond Shipman Andrews, Alice Brown, and Henry Van Dyke, *The Whole Family: A Novel by Twelve Authors* (Gib Prettyman), 29: 383–87
Van Vechten, Carl: Review: Emily Bernard, ed., *Remember Me To Harlem: The Letters of Langston Hughes and Carl Van Vechten*, and Susan Duffy, ed., *The Political Plays of Langston Hughes* (Donna Akiba Harper), 29: 396–99
Vorse, Mary Heaton: Review: June Howard, *Publishing the Family*, and William Dean Howells, Mary E. Wilkins Freeman, Mary Heaton Vorse, Mary Stewart Cutting, Elizabeth Jordan, John Kendrick Bangs, Henry James, Elizabeth Stuart Phelps, Edith Wyatt, Mary Raymond Shipman Andrews, Alice Brown, and Henry Van Dyke, *The Whole Family: A Novel by Twelve Authors* (Gib Prettyman), 29: 383–87

Ware, William: Edward L. Tucker, "Five Letters from William Cullen Bryant to William Ware," 28: 139–48
West (American): Review: Susan J. Rosowski, *Birthing a Nation: Gender, Creativity, and the West in American Literature* (Thomas Austenfeld), 28: 189–91

Wilder, Thornton: Marc Singer, "Two Unpublished Letters from F. Scott and Zelda Fitzgerald to Thornton Wilder," 28: 153–57
Williams, Tennessee: Philip C. Kolin, "An Unpublished Tennessee Williams Letter to William Carlos Williams," 28: 159–62; Craig Clinton, "Transformative Stages: Williams's *Vieux Carré* in New York and London," 29: 235–51; Thomas P. Adler, "Classics of Twentieth-Century American Theater" (review-essay), 29: 331–42; Review: Albert J. Devlin and Nancy M. Tischler, eds., *The Selected Letters of Tennessee Williams: Volume 1, 1920–1945* (Ralph F. Voss), 29: 409–12
Williams, William Carlos: Philip C. Kolin, "An Unpublished Tennessee Williams Letter to William Carlos Williams," 28: 159–62
Wolf, Emma: Barbara Cantalupo, "The Letters of Israel Zangwill to Emma Wolf: Transatlantic Mentoring in the 1890s," 28: 121–38
women's writing: Review: Karen L. Kilcup, ed., *Soft Canons: American Women Writers and Masculine Tradition* (Alice Hall Petry), 28: 174–76; Review: Catherine Ross Nickerson, *The Web of Iniquity: Early Detective Fiction by American Women* (Betty Richardson), 28: 183–86
Wyatt, Edith: Review: June Howard, *Publishing the Family*, and William Dean Howells, Mary E. Wilkins Freeman, Mary Heaton Vorse, Mary Stewart Cutting, Elizabeth Jordan, John Kendrick Bangs, Henry James, Elizabeth Stuart Phelps, Edith Wyatt, Mary Raymond Shipman Andrews, Alice Brown, and Henry Van Dyke, *The Whole Family: A Novel by Twelve Authors* (Gib Prettyman), 29: 383–87

Zangwill, Israel: Barbara Cantalupo, "The Letters of Israel Zangwill to Emma Wolf: Transatlantic Mentoring in the 1890s," 28: 121–38

Index of Books Reviewed

Acocella, Joan, *Willa Cather and the Politics of Criticism* (Susan J. Rosowski, review-essay, "What Are We Doing in the Humanities Today? Cather as Case Study"), 29: 301–15

Alexander, Eleanor, *Lyrics of Sunshine and Shadow: The Tragic Courtship and Marriage of Paul Laurence Dunbar and Alice Ruth Moore, a History of Love and Violence among the African American Elite* (Joanne Braxton), 29: 387–90

Anders, John P., *Willa Cather's Sexual Aesthetics and the Male Homosexual Literary Tradition* (Susan J. Rosowski, review-essay, "What Are We Doing in the Humanities Today? Cather as Case Study"), 29: 301–15

Andrews, Mary Raymond Shipman. *See* Howells, William Dean, et al.

Bangs, John Kendrick. *See* Howells, William Dean, et al.

Bennett, Paula Bernat, ed., *Palace-Burner: The Selected Poetry of Sarah Piatt* (Andrew C. Higgins), 29: 374–76

Bernard, Emily, ed., *Remember Me To Harlem: The Letters of Langston Hughes and Carl Van Vechten* (Donna Akiba Harper), 29: 396–99

Bigsby, Christopher. *See* Wilmeth, Don B., and Christopher Bigsby

Bohlke, L. Brent, and Sharon Hoover, eds., *Willa Cather Remembered* (Susan J. Rosowski, review-essay, "What Are We Doing in the Humanities Today? Cather as Case Study"), 29: 301–15

Bordelon, Pamela, ed., *Go Gator and Muddy the Water: Writings by Zora Neale Hurston from the Federal Writers' Project* (Venetria K. Patton), 28: 217–19

Bosco, Ronald A., and Joel Myerson, eds., *The Later Lectures of Ralph Waldo Emerson, 1843–1871. Volume 1: 1843–1854; Volume 2: 1855–1871* (Nancy Craig Simmons), 29: 364–67

Bottoms, Stephen J., ed., *Albee: "Who's Afraid of Virginia Woolf"* (Thomas P. Adler, review-essay, "Classics of Twentieth-Century American Theater"), 29: 331–42

Brown, Alice. *See* Howells, William Dean, et al.

Bush, Sargent, Jr., ed., *The Correspondence of John Cotton* (Albert J. von Frank), 29: 351–54

Cheung, King-Kok, ed., *Words Matter: Conversations with Asian American Writers* (Noelle Brada-Williams, review-essay, "Asian American Literary Studies at Maturity"), 29: 285–300

Conron, John, *American Picturesque* (Kent P. Ljungquist), 28: 171–73

Cooper, James Fenimore, *The Spy: A Tale of the Neutral Ground*, James P. Elliott (introduction); James H. Pickering (notes); and James P. Elliott, Lance Schachterle, and Jeffrey Walker (textual editing) (Wayne Franklin), 29: 354–56

Crisler, Jesse S., Robert C. Leitz III, and Joseph R. McElrath Jr., eds., *An Exemplary Citizen: Letters of Charles W. Chesnutt, 1906–1932* (Keith Williams), 29: 390–93

Cutting, Mary Stewart. *See* Howells, William Dean, et al.

Dean, Bradley P., ed., *"Wild Fruits": Thoreau's Rediscovered Last Manuscripts* (Richard J. Schneider), 28: 176–79

DeMott, Robert J., *Dave Smith: A Literary Archive* (Jerome Klinkowitz), 29: 413–14

Devlin, Albert J., and Nancy M. Tischler, eds., *The Selected Letters of Tennessee Williams: Volume 1, 1920–1945* (Ralph F. Voss), 29: 409–12

Diedrich, Maria, *Love Across Color Lines: Ottilie Assing and Frederick Douglass* (Paul Giles), 28: 186–89

Duffy, Susan, ed., *The Political Plays of Langston Hughes* (Donna Akiba Harper), 29: 396–99

Elliott, James P. *See* Cooper, James Fenimore

Farrell, Grace, *Lillie Devereux Blake: Retracing a Life Erased* (Nicole Tonkovich), 29: 361–63

INDEX

Fink, Steven, and Susan S. Williams, eds., *Reciprocal Influences: Literary Production, Distribution, and Consumption in America* (James C. Keil), 28: 163–66
Freeman, Mary E. Wilkins. *See* Howells, William Dean, et al.

Goldberg, Jonathan, *Willa Cather and Others* (Susan J. Rosowski, review-essay, "What Are We Doing in the Humanities Today? Cather as Case Study"), 29: 301–15
Greenspan, Ezra, *George Palmer Putnam: Representative American Publisher* (Melissa J. Homestead), 28: 180–83; ed., *The House of Putnam, 1837–1872: A Documentary Volume* (Melissa J. Homestead), 28: 180–83
Gunter, Susan E., ed., *Dear Munificent Friends: Henry James's Letters to Four Women* (Michael Anesko), 29: 377–80. *See also* Gunter, Susan E., and Steven H. Jobe
Gunter, Susan E., and Steven H. Jobe, eds., *Dearly Beloved Friends: Henry James's Letters to Younger Men* (Michael Anesko), 29; 377–80

Hayes, Kevin J., *Melville's Folk Roots* (Jonathan A. Cook), 28: 192–94
Hoover, Sharon. *See* Bohlke, L. Brent, and Sharon Hoover
Honey, Maureen. *See* Patton, Venetria K., and Maureen Honey
Horne, Philip, ed., *Henry James: A Life in Letters* (Rayburn S. Moore), 28: 195–97
Howard, June, *Publishing the Family* (Gib Prettyman), 29: 383–87
Howells, William Dean, Mary E. Wilkins Freeman, Mary Heaton Vorse, Mary Stewart Cutting, Elizabeth Jordan, John Kendrick Bangs, Henry James, Elizabeth Stuart Phelps, Edith Wyatt, Mary Raymond Shipman Andrews, Alice Brown, and Henry Van Dyke, *The Whole Family: A Novel by Twelve Authors* (Gib Prettyman), 29: 383–87
Hunt, Tim, ed., *The Collected Poetry of Robinson Jeffers, Volume 1: 1920–1928* (Stephen Gould Axelrod, review-essay, "Jeffers Redux"), 29: 317–30; ed., *The Collected Poetry of Robinson Jeffers, Volume 2: 1928–1938* (Stephen Gould Axelrod, review-essay, "Jeffers Redux"), 29: 317–30; ed., *The Collected Poetry of Robinson Jeffers, Volume 3: 1939–1962* (Stephen Gould Axelrod, review-essay, "Jeffers Redux"), 29: 317–30; ed., *The Collected Poetry of Robinson Jeffers, Volume 4: Poetry 1903–1920, Prose, and Unpublished Writings* (Stephen Gould Axelrod, review-essay, "Jeffers Redux"), 29: 317–30; ed., *The Collected Poetry of Robinson Jeffers, Volume 5: Textual Evidence and Commentary* (Stephen Gould Axelrod, review-essay, "Jeffers Redux"), 29: 317–30; ed., *The Selected Poetry of Robinson Jeffers* (Stephen Gould Axelrod, review-essay, "Jeffers Redux"), 29: 317–30

Inge, M. Thomas, and Edward J. Piacentino, eds., *The Humor of the Old South* (Kathryn B. McKee), 29: 357–61
Iwanaga, Esther. *See* Srikanth, Rajini, and Esther Iwanaga

James, Henry. *See* Howells, William Dean, et al.
Jobe, Steven H. *See* Gunter, Susan E., and Steven H. Jobe
Jordan, Elizabeth. *See* Howells, William Dean, et al.
Joshi, S. T., ed., *The Collected Fables of Ambrose Bierce* (Donald T. Blume), 29: 367–71

Kaplan, Carla, ed., *Zora Neale Hurston: A Life in Letters* (Alicia Kent), 29: 399–403
Karman, James, ed., *Stones of the Sur: Poetry by Robinson Jeffers* (Stephen Gould Axelrod, review-essay, "Jeffers Redux"), 29: 317–30
Keenan, Hugh T., *The Library of Joel Chandler Harris: An Annotated Book List* (Ed Piacentino), 28: 203–5
Kilcup, Karen L., ed., *Soft Canons: American Women Writers and Masculine Tradition* (Alice Hall Petry), 28: 174–76
Killough, George. *See* Lewis, Sinclair
Kolin, Philip C., *Williams: "A Streetcar Named Desire"* (Thomas P. Adler, review-essay, "Classics of Twentieth-Century American Theater"), 29: 331–42
Krise, Thomas W., ed., *Caribbeana: An Anthology of English Literature of the West Indies, 1657–1777* (Amy Winans), 28: 167–70

Leitz, Robert C., III. *See* Crisler, Jesse S., Robert C. Leitz III, and Joseph R. McElrath Jr.

Lewis, Sinclair, *Minnesota Diary 1943–46*, ed. George Killough (Sally E. Parry), 29: 403–5

Lindemann, Marilee, *Willa Cather: Queering America* (Susan J. Rosowski, review-essay, "What Are We Doing in the Humanities Today? Cather as Case Study"), 29: 301–15

Lohmann, Christopher, ed., *Radical Passion: Ottilie Assing's Reports from America and Letters to Frederick Douglass* (Paul Giles), 28: 186–89

Londré, Felicia Hardison, and Daniel J. Watermeier, *The History of North American Theater. The United States, Canada, and Mexico: From Pre-Columbian Times to the Present* (William W. Demastes), 29: 343–45

Mariani, Paul, *The Broken Tower: A Life of Hart Crane* (John Burt), 28: 211–17

McElrath, Joseph R., Jr. *See* Crisler, Jesse S., Robert C. Leitz III, and Joseph R. McElrath Jr.

McWilliams, Dean, *Charles W. Chesnutt and the Fictions of Race* (Keith Williams), 29: 390–93

Meriwether, Anne Blythe. *See* Rawlings, Marjorie Kinnan

Mulford, Carla, and David S. Shields, eds., *Finding Colonial Americas: Essays Honoring J. A. Leo Lemay* (Joanna Brooks), 29: 348–51

Murphy, Brenda, *Miller: "Death of a Salesman"* (Thomas P. Adler, review-essay, "Classics of Twentieth-Century American Theater"), 29: 331–42; *O'Neill: "Long Day's Journey Into Night"* (Thomas P. Adler, review-essay, "Classics of Twentieth-Century American Theater"), 29: 331–42

Myerson, Joel. *See* Bosco, Ronald A., and Joel Myerson

Nelson, Emmanuel S., ed., *African American Authors, 1745–1945: A Bio-Bibliographical Sourcebook* (John Bassett), 28: 170–71; ed., *Asian American Novelists: A Bio-Bibliographical Critical Sourcebook* (Noelle Brada-Williams, review-essay, "Asian American Literary Studies at Maturity"), 29: 285–300

Nickerson, Catherine Ross, *The Web of Iniquity: Early Detective Fiction by American Women* (Betty Richardson), 28: 183–86

Nissen, Axel, *Bret Harte: Prince and Pauper* (Donna M. Campbell), 29: 371–73

O'Connor, Margaret Anne, ed., *Willa Cather: The Contemporary Reviews* (Susan J. Rosowski, review-essay, "What Are We Doing in the Humanities Today? Cather as Case Study"), 29: 301–15

Ozieblo, Barbara, *Susan Glaspell: A Critical Biography* (Cheryl Black), 29: 394–96

Parini, Jay, *Robert Frost: A Life* (Peter Van Egmond), 28: 206–7

Parker, Hershel, *Herman Melville: A Biography. Volume 2, 1851–1891* (Sanford E. Marovitz, review-essay, "Parker's *Melville*: A Life Complete"), 29: 275–83

Patton, Venetria K., and Maureen Honey, eds., *Double-Take: A Revisionist Harlem Renaissance Anthology* (Alicia Kent), 29: 399–403

Phelps, Elizabeth Stuart. *See* Howells, William Dean, et al.

Piacentino, Edward J. *See* Inge, M. Thomas, and Edward J. Piacentino

Pickering, James H. *See* Cooper, James Fenimore

Pound, Omar, and Robert Spoo, eds., *Ezra and Dorothy Pound: Letters in Captivity, 1945–1946* (Hugh Witemeyer), 28: 207–11

Quirk, Tom, *Nothing Abstract: Investigations in the American Literary Imagination* (Kent P. Ljungquist), 29: 345–48

Rachels, David, ed., *Augustus Baldwin Longstreet's "Georgia Scenes" Completed: A Scholarly Text* (Kathryn B. McKee), 29: 357–61

Rawlings, Marjorie Kinnan, *Blood of My Blood*, ed. Anne Blythe Meriwether (Jill C. Jones), 29: 406–9

Rosowski, Susan J., *Birthing a Nation: Gender, Creativity, and the West in American Literature* (Thomas Austenfeld), 28: 189–91

Schachterle, Lance. *See* Cooper, James Fenimore
Shatzky, Joel, and Michael Taub, eds., *Contemporary Jewish-American Dramatists and Poets: A Bio-Critical Sourcebook* (Daniel Walden), 28: 220–21
Shields, David S. *See* Mulford, Carla, and David S. Shields
Spoo, Robert. *See* Pound, Omar, and Robert Spoo
Srikanth, Rajini, and Esther Iwanaga, eds., *Bold Words: A Century of Asian American Writing* (Noelle Brada-Williams, review-essay, "Asian American Literary Studies at Maturity"), 29: 285–300
Stout, Janis P., ed., *A Calendar of the Letters of Willa Cather* (Susan J. Rosowski, review-essay, "What Are We Doing in the Humanities Today? Cather as Case Study"), 29: 301–15
Sumida, Stephen H. *See* Wong, Sau-ling Cynthia, and Stephen H. Sumida
Surette, Leon. *See* Tryphonopoulos, Demetres P., and Leon Surette

Tarr, Rodger L., ed., *Max and Marjorie: The Correspondence between Maxwell E. Perkins and Marjorie Kinnan Rawlings* (Jill C. Jones), 29: 406–9
Taub, Michael. *See* Shatzky, Joel, and Michael Taub
Tischler, Nancy M. *See* Devlin, Albert J., and Nancy M. Tischler
Trout, Steven, *Memorial Fictions: Willa Cather and the First World War* (Susan J. Rosowski, review-essay, "What Are We Doing in the Humanities Today? Cather as Case Study"), 29: 301–15
Tryphonopoulos, Demetres P., and Leon Surette, eds., *"I Cease Not to Yowl": Ezra Pound's Letters to Olivia Rossetti Agresti* (Hugh Witemeyer), 28: 207–11
Tuttle, Jennifer S., ed., *The Crux: A Novel by Charlotte Perkins Gilman* (Denise Knight), 29: 381–83

Van Dyke, Henry. *See* Howells, William Dean, et al.
Vorse, Mary Heaton. *See* Howells, William Dean, et al.

Walker, Jeffrey. *See* Cooper, James Fenimore
Watermeier, Daniel J. *See* Londré, Felicia Hardison, and Daniel J. Watermeier
Williams, Susan S. *See* Fink, Steven, and Susan S. Williams
Wilmeth, Don B., and Christopher Bigsby, eds., *The Cambridge History of American Theatre: Volume II, 1870–1945* (Jan Balakian), 28: 197–203
Winship, Michael P., *Making Heretics: Militant Protestantism and Free Grace in Massachusetts, 1636–1641* (Albert J. von Frank), 29: 351–54
Wong, Sau-ling Cynthia, and Stephen H. Sumida, eds., *A Resource Guide to Asian American Literature* (Noelle Brada-Williams, review-essay, "Asian American Literary Studies at Maturity"), 29: 285–300
Wyatt, Edith. *See* Howells, William Dean, et al.